1987

STRATEGIC MANAGEMENT OF MULTINATIONAL CORPORATIONS: THE ESSENTIALS

WILEY SERIES IN INTERNATIONAL BUSINESS

STRATEGIC MANAGEMENT OF MULTINATIONAL CORPORATIONS: THE ESSENTIALS

Heidi Vernon Wortzel
Northeastern University

Lawrence H. Wortzel
Boston University

JOHN WILEY & SONS
New York / Chichester / Brisbane / Toronto / Singapore

Library of Congress Cataloging in Publication Data:

Wortzel, Heidi Vernon.
  Strategic management of multinational corporations.

  (Wiley series in international business, ISSN 0277-271X)
  Includes index.
  1. International business enterprises—Management.
2. International business enterprises—Planning.
3. International economic relations.   4. Competition,
International.   I. Wortzel, Lawrence H.   II. Title.
III. Series.

HD62.4.W68   1985   658'.049   84-15180
ISBN 0-471-80741-9 (pbk.)

Printed in the United States of America

10 9 8 7 6 5 4 3 2 1

To Joshua and Jennifer who
provided the incentive

Preface

As more and more U.S. managers are discovering, the world of business does not begin in Boston or New York and end in San Francisco or Los Angeles. Increasingly, both opportunities and threats have their origin outside the United States. Faced with limited growth opportunities and rising costs at home, U.S. firms look outside their home countries for new markets, new products, and new production sites from which to supply their existing markets. The U.S. manager must know how to search for, identify, and capitalize on overseas opportunities. Increasingly, because of a large existing network of foreign subsidiaries already in place, many U.S. managers find themselves managing ongoing multinational businesses.

The U.S. managers in a firm that produces and markets only domestically still cannot escape contact with the international environment. Foreign firms seeking new ways in which to expand their businesses look to the United States as the land of opportunity. In virtually every product line, the set of competitors includes foreign as well as domestic firms. Thus, the domestic manager must know how to anticipate and cope with foreign competitors at home as well as abroad.

The existence of threats from foreign firms and opportunity in foreign markets is the result of an international environment in which international trade and investment has not only been possible, but has been, in many cases, encouraged. To be sure, there have been protectionist efforts restricting foreign investment or placing quotas on imports that have in specific circumstances limited the growth of international trade or investment. And there is an inkling that some governments may take future actions that are trade and investment limiting. This does not mean that international businesses or the multinational corporations are creatures of the past; it means simply that the rules of production, marketing, and finance, may change once more.

In any event, today's managers and aspiring managers must understand international as well as domestic business. Strategic planning must take place in recognition of foreign as well as domestic opportunity competitors. Plans must be made in light of different and changing political environments with different degrees and kinds of risks. A wider range of planning tools is required. The business functions—marketing, production, finance and control, and research and development—are more complex to manage because they take place in a wider and more diverse range of environments, and organizations must be managed in different country cultures with people from different cultural backgrounds. All this must often be accomplished against the backdrop of different legal systems.

Perhaps the world of business we have just described seems terribly complex. It may be, but it is also exciting and challenging. Moreover, the experience of many U.S. firms indicates that the international business world can be conquered. The continuing international success of such firms as IBM, Caterpillar, General Motors, Coca-Cola, and Colgate-Palmolive demonstrates that. The international success of firms such as Philips (from The Netherlands), Hoffman-LaRoche (Switzerland), and Matsushita (Japan), and the burgeoning international position of Samsung & Daewoo (Korea) tell us that the international competitive environment includes firms from many countries.

In this book, we have tried to put together the "essentials," the ideas, concepts, techniques, and knowledge that will provide the best possible base for strategic management in a multinational environment. In selecting readings, we have tried to pay close attention to the 3 Rs: readability, recency, and relevance. Mastery of the material in this book means that you have learned the fundamentals, that you have extended your knowledge in the business functions and have built a solid base for further international business study.

This book is designed to give the undergraduate and the M.B.A. student a firm grasp of issues central to the management of multinational corporations. Instructors will find that these readings, in combination with internationally focused cases can be used in lieu of a textbook. The volume can be integrated with a text if a more environmental approach is desired. We are grateful to those who reviewed the introductory essays and suggested additions and deletions of articles: William Davidson, *University of Virginia*, Robert Holloway, *University of Minnesota*, Richard Moxon, *University of Washington*, and Arnold Weinstein, *Arthur D Little School of Management Education*.

HEIDI VERNON WORTZEL
LAWRENCE H. WORTZEL

Contents

SECTION 1
The Strategic Planning Environment

Someone once described executives in international business as falling into two categories: those who look for similarities across countries and cultures and those who look for differences. A thorough analysis of the international environment would prove that both categories of executives do exist. Countries are becoming more similar in their industrial structure and in their consumption patterns. Interdependencies among countries have increased. But political environments are still diverse. Countries at different styles of economic development may be similar to other countries at the same stage but markedly different from countries at other stages of development. We must operate in a world in which there are increasing similarities, but in which persistent differences still exist across countries. And we must learn to look for both the similarities and the differences.

Strategic planning has become a key activity for virtually every successful firm, whether domestic or multinational. One of the keys to successful strategic planning is identifying and then correctly interpreting those elements of the environment that are most crucial to the success of the firm. The "basics" of strategic planning are the same for multinationals as for domestic firms. The multinational planner is still concerned with analyzing factors such as economic and consumer environments, competitors' strengths and weaknesses, and the firm's own capabilities to identify strategic opportunities and threats. But there are more environments and competitors with which to contend.

The need for understanding the international environment extends beyond the multinational corporation (MNC). Managers who do strategic planning in firms that are purely domestic must be concerned about the activities of firms based outside their domestic market, for such firms are often strong potential competitors that all too soon become real competitors. Events in the Italian pasta industry, the Korean steel industry, and the Hong Kong electronics industry increasingly have an impact on their counterpart domestic industries in other countries.

READING SELECTIONS

Magaziner and Reich argue that U.S. firms have not participated as strongly in the international marketplace as they should have. They point out and describe specific types of opportunities that they believe U.S firms have not seized or that they have wrongly seized. These include a failure to manage the business ''globally,'' a reluctance to enter and remain in competitors' home markets, a failure to be responsive to marketing opportunities in developing countries (the Third World), an overly heavy reliance on low labor costs in developing countries as a way of remaining competitive, and poor strategies in licensing technology.

Although one could point to any number of firms as being less than completely successful multinationally, there is also a long list of firms that have been outstandingly successful in international markets. A study of the highly successful U.S. multinationals would certainly reveal that each had taken advantage of one or more of the opportunities they describe. Magaziner and Reich's discussion of each of these opportunity types, therefore, should not be read as a broad indictment of the U.S. firm's failure to capitalize on opportunities. Rather, it should be viewed as an illuminating discussion of some strategic considerations that can lead to success in the international environment.

Gluck illuminates some of the points made by Magaziner and Reich. Gluck focuses on the globalization of markets, not just for products but for energy, currency, labor, and business skills. He argues that international competition is going to be more rational in the 1980s than it has been in the past because firms have free access to these resources in and from many countries. Both oil and currencies (in many, but not all countries, Gluck is careful to point out) are freely traded. The firm's choice of production sites is greatly broadened. The net result is both opportunity and threat. The opportunity is to gain a competitive edge or to neutralize a foreign competitor's threat by recognizing early when an industry is likely to become global and quickly taking appropriate action.

According to some, ecological problems, population pressures, and raw materials shortages are going to limit growth severely over the next two decades, especially in the developing countries. If true, this would severely constrain the opportunities available to firms.

Vernon focuses on the corporate environment. He identifies some significant changes in the behavior of multinational firms that have occurred over the last decade and shows how changes in the international corporate environment have led to these changes in behavior. He organizes his analysis around the diminishing ability of the product life-cycle hypothesis to explain the trade and investment behavior of multinational corporations. Markets have grown and become increasingly similar; this means that the number of country markets that can provide stimuli for innovation has increased substantially. Moreover, the spread of multinational firms' subsidiaries around the world provides an "infrastructure" within which an innovation can be quickly introduced around the world.

Vernon identifies three multinational firm types that may coexist in this new environment, even within the same product line. The global scanner, which he points out is still hypothetical, might innovate in response to a stimulus in any one of many markets. It would produce in whatever country seemed best and would diffuse the innovation through its system of subsidiaries as demand indicated. His second firm type is already in existence in the production of globally standardized products. Here, innovation activity is likely to be centralized and production is likely to be carried out in a network of integrated plants. The third firm type is one whose innovation and production site choices are focused on its home market. In this type of firm, each subsidiary decides which of the parent's products it will sell in its own market. It is well worth trying to think through the ramifications of these different structures in terms of their implications for strategic planning.

Doz introduces a complicated, but very important, constraint into the multinational environment. He notes a basic conflict between the desires of multinational firms and the demands of governments. He describes this as a tug-of-war among corporate, economic, and political imperatives, but it could be just as accurately described as a tug-of-war between rival economic interests. Multinational firms, especially those striving for global standardization, would like to deploy their production resources so as to maximize their efficiency worldwide. However, the pursuit of this strategy would inevitably result in some nations being importers. Governments of those nations supplied through offshore production are likely to consider the MNCs' action as damaging to their economic position. They will feel that they are being discriminated against and will attempt either to regulate imports or to develop their own national champions.

The conflict is most acute in the new high-technology industries. Governments have come to believe that a strong indigenous base of high-technology industries is important to their countries' continued growth. As a result, they take actions that they perceive will help to achieve that end. The problem that this creates for multinationals, of course, is that they cannot always pursue global integration strategies in the face of government action. Consequently, an alternative strategy based on national responsiveness might be required. This strategy, however, is much more difficult to administer because it is significantly more ambiguous.

1

International Strategies

Ira C. Magaziner
Robert B. Reich

• • •

The large U.S. domestic market is the envy of every company in Europe. Without venturing beyond U.S. borders, most U.S. companies can gain a huge market base over which to amortize fixed costs and the costs of research and development. They can build world-scale plants, and gain considerable experience in a business, without having to challenge export markets. This large market has been a mixed blessing, however, for it has made U.S. companies less aggressive abroad. As the U.S. market has matured in many industries, and high-growth markets have simultaneously arisen abroad, foreign competitors (often with U.S. licensed technology) have used their rapidly growing home markets to gain experience and improve their cost positions.

Many U.S. companies sought unsuccessfully to become more international in the late 1950s and 1960s. They found some European markets to be partially protected and European governments sometimes hostile to their initiatives. In general, these international ventures were less profitable than opportunities in the U.S. At the same time, Japan was well protected. The only way to gain entrance to the Japanese market was through technology licenses or somewhat unequal joint ventures. Licenses were preferred, since they provided short-term profits with little short-term risk, while joint ventures were relatively unprofitable. Finally, developing countries were unpredictable and highly risky markets.

As a result of these problems, by the early

Source: Ira C. Magaziner and Robert B. Reich, "International Strategies," Ch. 11 in *Minding America's Business* (New York: Harcourt Brace Jovanovich, 1982), pp. 135–142. Copyright © 1982, Law and Business, Inc. Reprinted by permission.

1970s, international divisions of U.S companies were often viewed as "Siberia" by corporate managers. Horror stories abounded about the failure of international ventures.

Because of this legacy, many U.S. companies today are not particularly adept at competing internationally. This chapter explores some of the reasons why this ineptness continues.

THE MEANING OF INTERNATIONAL BUSINESSES

Companies often mean very different things when they talk about "international businesses." U.S. companies in sheltered businesses may expand to become international by buying similar sheltered businesses in other countries. This has been the case for some wholesale and retail businesses, such as food companies and department stores. In these circumstances, there is little potential synergy among the different international operations of the company.

Alternatively, U.S. companies may export products when high-profit opportunities arise abroad. This has been the case, for example, with exports of large appliances or automobiles to the Middle East. These exports usually require little product modification or other investment, and are viewed as "icing on the cake" rather than as intrinsic parts of a U.S. business.

In still other cases, U.S. companies in sheltered or highly specialized businesses may sell technology licenses or enter short-lived joint ventures abroad, in order to better amortize their research and development activities and add to their cash flow without significant investment.

In none of these cases are the businesses

truly "international" in the sense of requiring a worldwide integrated strategy. Truly international businesses are those in which there is a considerable flow of products and investments across borders, and competitive interactions in one part of the world have a direct effect on the business in other parts of the world.

Although U.S. companies that have developed international activities in sheltered businesses or on an opportunistic basis have often been successful, U.S. companies have generally faltered in truly international businesses. This faltering stems from the failure of U.S. companies to manage the business as one international entity, their reluctance to enter and remain in competitors' home markets, their lack of responsiveness to Third World sales, their over reliance on the low labor costs of developing countries, and their lack of sophistication in licensing of technology.

FAILURE TO MANAGE THE BUSINESS AS ONE INTERNATIONAL ENTITY

U.S. companies often view overseas markets as providing only incremental volume to support the home operation. While the U.S. market is often the largest market for many products, it is now generally among the slower-growing markets. In many businesses, scale in component manufacture, R&D, or application engineering may be significantly boosted through foreign sales. Many U.S. companies do not recognize this opportunity.

By contrast, Japanese companies with a smaller home market follow an aggressive export strategy. They often begin by exporting to Third World markets, which are growing quickly but are still small relative to the U.S. market. These markets collectively add significant sales volume, which allows the Japanese company to overcome its smaller home market disadvantage. This penetration is often spearheaded by price reductions.

Typically, managers of U.S. companies in these markets are concerned about their current profitability, and do not look beyond a two- or three-year period, after which they will return to the home office. Accordingly, they are willing to sacrifice market share to the Japanese competitor rather than experience a decline in current profits. Moreover, since the Japanese market share is often taken from market growth, it does not affect the current sales level of the U.S. company. Such short-sighted strategies usually go unnoticed by management in the U.S.; market-share data, especially in Third World countries, are difficult to track. Subsequently, when the Japanese come to dominate a foreign market and growth turns negative for the U.S. company, these developments are viewed as just another sign that overseas businesses are "losers."

The most crucial problem with this strategy for U.S. companies is not the loss of opportunity in the foreign market or even the current loss in component volume, R&D, and amortization, though these are also serious. Most importantly, this strategy strengthens the Japanese competitor; by virtue of added scale and experience it is then in a better position to challenge the U.S. company in its domestic market.

U.S. companies must view international businesses as one integrated chessboard on which every move is planned for its strategic effect on the whole game. Seen in this light, it might be appropriate for certain foreign profit centers to lose money for a number of years while they fight a foreign challenge—in order to better protect the base business in the U.S. over the long term. In other cases, individual markets may need to be sacrificed in order to marshall resources for battles in other markets. Volume, profit, and price targets for each market must be seen in relation to the business as a whole, worldwide.

Just as market strategies must be coordinated, so too must product strategies be integrated. It is crucial for U.S. companies to determine which elements of a product are to be internationally uniform and traded, and which are to be tailored to local markets. In some businesses whose end product is too big and bulky to ship, Japanese or European companies have internationalized the supply of key components or capital equipment for automating product manufacture. This helps them achieve competitive cost advantages in key areas of the business and also improves productivity at home.

An international product strategy requires knowledge of which aspects of the cost structure are crucial and where leverage can be gained from broader amortization. The goal is to identify specific components that comprise a significant enough part of total product cost and for which savings from international scale will outweigh transport and customization costs. For example, motors for table saws can be an international business even though the saws themselves may not be. Significant international manufacturing-scale economies can be gained in the motors that more than offset the costs of transportation and of modifying the voltage from one country to another. U.S. companies have been slower than their Japanese and European counterparts to identify these sorts of opportunities. When their final product is not significantly traded in international markets, they do not regard themselves as being in potentially international businesses.

Companies that fail to integrate their domestic and international markets and product strategies will be at an increasing disadvantage relative to those that do.

RELUCTANCE TO ENTER AND REMAIN IN COMPETITORS' HOME MARKETS

Another serious mistake of U.S. companies is their reluctance to enter their competitors' home markets, particularly in France, West Germany, and Japan. To be sure, all three of these markets have been extremely difficult to enter in many product areas. Unfamiliar standards and other nontariff barriers, complex distribution, and nationalistic consumer preferences have made life difficult for would-be U.S. exporters. Despite these obstacles, it is essential that U.S. companies confront their international competitors in the competitors' home

markets. Even if these operations do not show a profit, they can have significant competitive value.

A competitor that is challenged in its home market is prevented from using that market as a source of capital with which to make large penetration investments in other markets. The competitor is also prevented from "matrix pricing" in the U.S. market—that is, cutting its price in the U.S., where it has small volume relative to its total world volume, thereby jeopardizing the larger volume of the U.S. company, which will suffer greater proportional losses by meeting the price cut. Finally, by participating in a competitors' home market, the U.S. company can gain valuable information about a competitors' strengths, weaknesses, and plans.

Although U.S. companies have invested in Japan, France, and Germany, they have not often been willing to sustain the necessary losses for a long enough time to reap the full competitive benefits of the investment. There have been notable exceptions—such as IBM, Polaroid, Texas Instruments, Caterpillar, and Omark—who have endured hardships to become significant competitors in the Japanese market. In general, however, the French, German, and Japanese marketplaces are littered with U.S. firms that came, stayed a few years, and left after a few setbacks. By contrast, Japanese firms often expect to lose money for five or more years when entering U.S. or European markets, and will sustain losses for even longer periods if necessary.

LACK OF RESPONSIVENESS TO THIRD WORLD MARKETING

Many U.S. firms have lost ground to European and Japanese companies by failing to be sufficiently flexible and farsighted in their dealings with developing countries. Flexibility involves willingness to do many things: to give up control of significant parts of the business, to reinvest profits within the host country, to accept local content requirements, to negotiate with government officials, to accept export requirements, and to provide liberal financing. The governments of developing countries with large or growing home markets often insist on technical assistance, local content, and/or export requirements for local investment. Local companies based in these countries often insist on majority or parity share in joint ventures. In addition, the foreign company often must invest considerable time and energy in negotiations and in developing projects. U.S. companies often are unwilling to take these steps.

As governments and companies in the newly industrializing countries become more sophisticated, many U.S. companies, accustomed to being dominant in such relationships and to taking high profits at will from their foreign operations, find themselves displaced by French, German, Japanese, and Italian firms that are willing to be more flexible.

Two recent examples illustrate this shortsightedness. The first involves a bid to build a plant for a commodity plastic in a Latin American country. A German firm agreed to buy part of the output of the plant to sell in Germany and in other countries. The firm also agreed to a very liberal financing plan that was assisted by the German government and to liberal ownership provisions. In return, it negotiated guaranteed contracts for export to the Latin American country of related specialty chemicals and for use of German equipment in the commodity resin operation and certain downstream plants. The German company received the benefits of a guaranteed fast-growth market, thus allowing increased scale potential at its new specialty chemical plant in Germany. The company also gained the ability to sell and further amortize the development of its process technology in the mature commodity chemical process, plus a lucrative engineering and construction contract for the Latin American plant.

Through its liberal financing assistance, the German government helped support the competitive development of one of its companies and considerably increased exports. The government also helped support the increasing sophistication of its work force by trading some jobs and exports in a mature commodity chemical business for an expansion of the more sophisticated specialty chemical business. Two U.S. competitors, leaders in the field, reviewed the requirements for local content, equity structure for the venture, and financing, and decided not to bid.

The other example involves two U.S. and one French company in a vehicle business competing for a series of orders in developing countries. Local assembly, financing, and, to a lesser extent, purchase price were the keys to a foreign government's decisions to approve a vendor. The French company made offers that would not have returned any profit whatsoever from the equipment orders and that involved the French government in a very liberal financing package. The justification for this decision rested on two basic competitive factors. First, sales of spare parts make up 30 percent of total sales in the business and 50 percent of total profits in any given year. Second, a relatively small number of these pieces of equipment are sold in each product generation. Securing volume in order to amortize the expensive development costs of each generation is crucial to long-term profitability and to the ability of a company to fund the next generation.

The French company had a small base for its previous generation and had difficulty contemplating its next development generation. The two U.S. companies were both much larger. To them, the extra volume and future cash generation from sales of spare parts seemed too long term an issue to be concerned with. As a result, the French company picked up orders in Third World countries for 15 percent of the world market, allowing it to become a significant force in the business worldwide. Its next generation of the product, developed with the underpinnings of revenues from spare parts gained from these orders years later, has made significant inroads into the U.S. market.

Developing countries offer important growing markets for many products. The larger volume of sales can be critical to the international competitive position of many companies. In becoming more flexible, U.S. companies would not only be enhancing the development of these countries but would also be defending their own competitive positions.

OVERRELIANCE ON LOW LABOR COSTS IN DEVELOPING COUNTRIES

U.S. firms have been among the most aggressive in moving their factories offshore to take advantage of cheap labor in less developed countries. This is particularly true of the clothing, consumer electronics, metal-working, and electrical equipment industries. Although this strategy is often an appropriate means of encouraging development in a country and of improving the cost position of the U.S. company, it can result in inefficiences that offset any such advantages.

A low-labor-cost offshore manufacturing base increases a company's transport and tariff costs. It may also generate hidden costs, such as increased problems in quality control, a long pipeline of costly in-process inventory, and slow response time for coordination between designers and the factory or the factory and the field. Japanese and German companies have sought low-cost labor to a much more limited extent than have U.S. firms. Their offshore moves tend to be designed for market penetration rather than strictly for low-cost labor. Moreover, when Japanese or German companies move offshore, they tend to keep a factory in the home country. They automate this factory so they can compare its production costs to those in the low-cost, labor-intensive factory abroad. Eventually, they often automate the factory in the low-labor-cost country as well.

Many U.S. companies, particularly those in the electronics industry, are being challenged by Japanese competitors that have found ways to automate the same processes that the U.S. companies are undertaking with low-wage labor in Mexico, Singapore, and Malaysia. U.S. firms may fail to recognize the hidden costs associated with their dependence on low-wage labor, particularly when they use it as a substitute for new investment in process engineering.

TECHNOLOGY LICENSING

Japan and West Germany, the countries with the most rapid growth in living standard, have maintained negative trade balances in technology for many years. Furthermore, they grant licenses for their technologies more slowly and to a lesser extent than do their U.S. counterparts.

Licensing of technology can be an easy method of amortizing development costs and making quick profits without additional capital investment, which raises ROIs. But licensees can become competitors. Licenses in nonsheltered businesses should only be provided to foreign companies in cases where technology is changing quickly and the U.S. company is confident of its ability to stay in the lead of technological change, or where the U.S. company can maintain significant manufacturing or marketing leadership in the product area.

In short, U.S. companies must become more aware of international competition and the international marketplace. If the U.S. and its companies are to prosper, they can no longer view international businesses as an adjunct to domestic business or as a source of quick profits. Rather, international business must be integrated into a worldwide competitive strategy.

2

Global Competition in the 1980s
Frederick Gluck

• • •

Many people have come to believe that there is a good case for pessimisim about the future of international business. It seems only reasonable for managements to focus their efforts on safe and familiar domestic markets.

If one looks beyond the immediate problems, however, a case can be made for the bullish side. While the dislocations of the 1970s were severe and are still having a significant impact, they do not mean continuing and escalating chaos on the international economic scene. The 1970s can be viewed as the period of transition that paved the way for the emergence of new global markets for products and services. The changes that took place were abrupt and painful, but they were necessary.

Before, there had been an elaborate international network of regulations and cartels. Now, there are global free markets for energy, currency, labor, and other vital business skills.

BETTER CLIMATE IN BUSINESS AHEAD

The climate for international business in the 1980s is going to be much more favorable and rational than it has been in recent years. Indeed, it is going to be quite possible for American companies to be more aggressive on the international scene. In fact, in some industries, it is going to be very hard to maintain a competitive edge by staying close to home.

While managers may need some new skills to compete successfully in the 1980s, what they'll need even more will be strategies and manage-

Source: Frederick Gluck, ''Global Competition in the 1980s,'' pp. 22–27. Reprinted by permission from the *Journal of Business Strategy*. Spring, 1983, Volume 3, Number 4, © 1983, Warren, Gorham & Lamont, Inc., 210 South Street, Boston, Mass. All rights reserved.

ment approaches that reflect the realities of global competition in the particular industries in which they compete.

Let's examine why international competition in the 1980s is going to be more rational than one might expect.

CHANGES IN THE OIL MARKET

The oil business was once a pretty comfortable business to be in. In the 1950s and 1960s, oil prices were low and stable. And production was regulated by the Railroad Commission in Texas and by agreements between the seven sisters in the Middle East. By the 1970s, because of heavy regulation, the energy supply had shifted from abundance to shortage without any noticeable change in the price of oil.

When OPEC tripled the price of oil in 1974, the old regulatory mechanisms were destroyed. For a while, everyone thought they had been replaced by another, more tightly disciplined cartel. However, that was not a good description of OPEC. Both prices and production in the 1970s actually reflected shortages of oil, the continued regulation of market forces in the Western world, and varying economic condictions and motives in individual OPEC countries.

Today, OPEC is still around, and many U.S. government energy regulations are still in place. But, on the whole, energy pricing is now subject to the independent actions of the various market participants. OPEC now produces less than half the world's oil. As exploration and production proliferate throughout the world, individual players have less and less influence. Oil is truly becoming a world commodity, and prices are coming down.

What are the implications of a free—or nearly free—market in energy? The price of oil will continue to fluctuate, but probably no more than that of sugar or any other commodity traded on the Chicago Board of Trade. The impact of these fluctuations will be cushioned by the same type of hedging mechanisms now used in the copper industry, for example. Barring world-shaking events, there shouldn't be any surprises. The Rotterdam spot market has become a fairly sensitive early warning device on prices.

If one is in an industry that depends on petroleum as a raw material, a free market for oil means greater freedom for the company strategists, who no longer have to concentrate so much time on assuring sources of supply. For example, the chemical industry can now focus on making chemicals. They don't have to integrate backward into oil production. As a strategic move, DuPont's acquisition of Conoco probably makes less sense now than it would have five years ago.

For oil producers, the implications are more complex. On one hand, since oil is becoming a freely traded commodity, low-cost producers should prevail. On the other hand, the cheapest resources may not be found in the world's safest locations. So, an oil producer has to weigh the costs against the risks.

The evidence, however, would seem to suggest that the oil industry may be opting too strongly for security over costs.

Last year, 40 percent of the free world's exploration and development took place on American soil at a cost of about $40 billion. Yet, the United States has only 5 percent of the free world's reserve. And, it costs almost ten times more to find a barrel of oil here than it costs in other parts of the world.

These huge investments in domestic exploration may explain in part why the market values of oil companies have fallen even more sharply than the stock market as a whole. Investors may be saying that $40 billion a year is too much to spend on domestic exploration and that

they don't agree with the strategic choice of safety over costs. They may have a point.

For example, the governments of the oil-rich nations can probably be expected to behave more reasonably than they have in the past for several reasons.

First, those governments haven't been successful in doing the jobs private firms used to handle. They're ready to admit, grudgingly, that there's real economic value in the extracting, refining, and marketing of raw resources.

Second, local populations are more demanding than ever before. So, governments will feel more pressure to put foreign exchange earnings ahead of nationalistic sentiment.

And third, deals are more likely to stick now that they are being made in the atmosphere of mutual respect. When the Thai Government decided to develop the reserves in the Gulf of Siam, the bidding was wide open. The final contract will be pretty much the result of what economists call a "voluntary exchange" between two parties.

In addition, resource companies may be able to pass along the risk that remains. Today, U.S. government units like OPIC (Overseas Private Investment Corporation), international development institutions like the World Bank, and even commercial banks are willing to assume most of the political risks of project development abroad. The fees they charge are much less than the 10-to-1 premium one pays to explore in the United States.

There's always the possibility of simply selling expertise outright, instead of owning resources overseas. American resource companies have technology, skills, and experience that are in critically short supply in the nations that have the low-cost resources. As Mr. Yamani says, "Aramco doesn't make a profit. It is paid a fee."

The U.S. energy companies are now in a situation that resource-short Japanese and European firms have lived with for decades. It requires a different perspective and some different skills. American companies too must learn to negotiate to transfer risks to financial institutions and to spread their activities across the globe.

THE IMPACT OF FLOATING RATES ON THE CURRENCY MARKETS

The world currency market exhibits a similar pattern. A cartel of central bankers fixed prices for two decades. Then, the cartel collapsed after Nixon devalued the dollar in August 1971. Gradually, a market mechanism of floating exchange rates emerged and created a whole new set of problems for financial officers. But, in the long run, these floating rates will be a boon to international competition.

Floating rates, in fact, moderate the risks of operations internationally. Even the troubled U.S. auto industry would be in substantially worse shape if floating rates had not made the dollar cheaper relative to the yen in the late 1970s, and provided some needed relief from Japanese competition.

In free-float countries like Germany, Japan, and Britain, capital controls have also been relaxed. So a multinational manager there can focus on making a profit without worrying about the accounting complications and dubious legality of remitting funds back home. Since he has free access to the local debt market, he can make long-term investments without being forced into a simultaneous gamble on the local currency.

Floating rates have also led to the development of forward markets and currency futures contracts. All these changes have, in fact, made it easier to make sound business decisions. Consider the relative situations of two managers working for an American multinational, one in Germany and one in Brazil, trying to make some investment decisions.

Both managers have reason to worry that inflationary government policies will lead to a depreciating currency. But the German manager can look at floating exchange rates and an active forward market for clues about the deutsche mark's future value. He also knows there will be no overnight devaluation.

Since the currency rate in Brazil is fixed by the government, the Brazilian manager has to rely on rumor to find out when and how much the cruzeiro will fall.

The German manager can hedge his exposure simply by short selling deutsche mark contracts. The Brazilian can only reduce his exposure by deferring capital expenditures, stretching out payables, or reducing receivables. However, all these defensive moves may hurt his long-term business interests.

Many companies will probably have to develop new skills to take full advantage of these developments as they increase the scope of their international operations. They will need to become more familiar with the capital markets of Europe and Asia and adept at trading currency futures. Companies with large fixed investments abroad will need experience with long-term debt in the countries where they operate.

There are pitfalls, of course, as in the case of Laker Airways. According to the London *Economist,* Laker borrowed $240 million from U.S. banks two years ago to finance its growing fleet of jets. That seemed to be a good deal at the time, since British interest rates were way above the U.S. levels. But because Laker sold advance tickets to British travelers with fares fixed in pounds, the borrowing took Sir Freddie far from his primary business of providing low-cost transatlantic travel. In fact, he was speculating in currencies.

The speculation turned sour when U.S. interest rates rose and the U.S. dollar began to skyrocket. Two-thirds of Laker's receipts in the summer of 1981 were in sterling. The fares had been fixed in late 1980 when the pound was at $2.40. But Laker's U.S. bank loans had to be repaid in dollars in August 1981, when the pound was worth only $1.93. The loss represented more than a quarter of the company's net worth. By February 1982, Laker Airways was bankrupt.

The payoff and the need for developing international money management skills is there. A strong internationally minded corporate financial officer can moderate the risks of currency fluctuations and free up the business managers to spend their energy and time on the problems of business strategy and execution which should be their primary concern.

SHIFTS IN THE LABOR MARKET

Now, let's take a look at the world labor market. In the years since World War II, labor markets have slowly but steadily become more international as more and more countries have welcomed foreign capital.

East Asian countries became market leaders in labor-intensive industries. Then Ireland, Spain, Greece, and eventually even larger developing nations like Mexico and Brazil began to shift toward export-led, foreign-capital-based economies. It seems like a sound projection that, with lower projected growth rates for the world economy, more developing countries will welcome foreign capital in the near future.

Japan took the first step, but now, with manufacturing islands like Hong Kong, Taiwan, Korea, Ireland, and the Mexican-American border region, access to a low-wage labor pool is open to anyone.

The other day, a colleague at McKinsey opened up a personal computer and, without looking too hard, found parts in it from thirteen different countries. A good example is found in Hewlett-Packard's manufacturing chain which reaches halfway around the globe, from well-paid, skilled engineers in California to low-wage assembly workers in Malaysia.

General Electric has survived as a manufacturer of inexpensive audio products by centralizing its world production in Singapore. Matsushita has a mind-boggling array of production facilities covering a multitude of product lines in over twenty-five countries.

Obviously, these companies figured out long ago that worldwide sourcing was a skill that would make a big difference to competitors in their industries. They saw the international labor market opening up and used that change to gain a competitive advantage.

Two other developments in recent years may leave some companies with very little choice about becoming more international.

AGGRESSIVE COMPETITION

The first is that more and more countries around the world are developing the capacity and the will to compete aggressively in world markets. People are very aware of world market trends, and very confident that they can reach new markets. They're eager to improve economic conditions and the standard of living. They're willing to learn, adapt, and innovate.

American companies may have to run harder just to stay in place. Thirty years ago, American companies assumed they could beat foreign competitors with relative ease. This country had the best technology, the best management skills, and that famous American "can do" attitude. Today there are many competitive new technologies in Europe, Japan, and elsewhere. This country may not have the lead in management skills all the time either. Too many U.S. managers have been thinking of strategy as the buying and selling of businesses and have been neglecting the fundamental questions of how their industries are changing, especially with respect to global competition and what they will have to do to adapt or, even better, to seize the initiative.

The Japanese, on the other hand, seldom forget that providing superior value to one's customers or achieving superior cost performance are the only ways to guarantee long-term competitive success.

PROLIFERATION OF GLOBAL MARKETS

The second development that makes competing internationally almost a must in many industries is the proliferation of global product markets.

While there used to be major barriers to the growth of world product markets, all those barriers have weakened in the last decade. Tariffs have been reduced by GATT agreements. Transportation costs have declined with the use of containerization and larger-capacity ships. Many products have emerged that pack very high value added in very small packages. Consumer needs in the industrialized nations have grown more similar. In certain Third World and OPEC countries, purchasing power has increased dramatically. As a result of these developments, a true world market is emerging from a multitude of distinct national markets. This, too, can be a source of competitive advantage for companies that plan their strategies accordingly.

A few examples suggest how extensive the phenomenon of global products has already become. Kids everywhere are playing Pac-Man and bouncing along the streets to the sounds of a Sony Walkman. The video tape recorder market took off simultaneously in Japan, Europe, and the United States, but the most extensive use of VTRs today is probably in places like Riad and Caracas. Shopping centers from Dusseldorf to Rio sell Gucci shoes, Yves St. Laurent suits, and Gloria Vanderbilt jeans. Siemens and ITT telephones can be found somewhere in almost every country in the world. Mercedes Benz and the Toyota Corolla are as much objects of passion in Manila as they are in California.

Just about every gas turbine sold in the world has some General Electric technology or component in it, and which country doesn't need a few? How many airlines could survive if they didn't consider buying Boeing or McDonnell Douglas equipment? Markets for high-voltage transmission equipment and diesel-electric locomotives are bigger in the developing countries than in the developed. And new industries seem to be born global; robotics, videodiscs, fiber optics, satellite networks, high-technology plastics, artificial diamonds.

Obviously, each of these industries became global for a different reason. Convergence of income levels and standardization of tastes is what made Gucci bags or designer clothing universal products. Aircraft became global because of the massive R&D investments required to stay ahead and the need to amortize these investments over many markets. Consumer electronics became global because producers discovered that they could drive themselves further and faster down the learning curve if they went after the faster-growing overseas markets. But while the reasons may have been different, the implications of globalization have been the same in all industries.

The main implication is simple: Companies in global industries have had to reshape their strategies in very fundamental ways. They have had to recognize that the most profitable competitor will be the one who takes advantage of the fact of global markets and designs his whole system of doing business accordingly.

Thus, when they choose a technology, they look around the world for the best technology, whatever its source, and pick one that seems to have promise for the largest number of markets (as the Japanese did in plain paper copiers, for example).

When they design a product, they design it to be marketable in the maximum number of countries (as Caterpillar has done with its heavy equipment), to serve an identifiable world market segment (as Toyota did with the Corolla), or to be easily adaptable to slightly differing markets (as Ericssen has done in tele-communications equipment).

When they manufacture, they pick the lowest-cost source which may be Malaysia for simple electronics, Sri Lanka for textiles, Tokyo for advanced semiconductors, the United States for personal computers, and Europe for precision machinery and they design a manufacturing system geared to the scale requirements of the world market.

If scale is important to product economics, they design a marketing system that gives them the broadest coverage of world markets and the most rapid penetration of these markets, even if this involves signing cross-marketing agreements with their competitors, selling under other people's brand names, or marketing through distributors and dealers over whom they can exercise relatively little control.

The point is that they have had to think about what being in a global business means to the economics of their business; where the economic leverage points in the business will be; and how they must shape their own business systems to take advantage of these leverage points.

Some experts describe the role of GATT as being to get government out of the trade business so entrepreneurs can make decisions on the basis of economic considerations unfettered by government interference. If so, then entrepreneurs had better make sure that they've made the changes and adjustments necessary to compete effectively as globalization of business takes place.

RESPONDING TO GLOBALIZATION

This process of adjustment can be illustrated by looking at what is happening in the automobile industry today. As usual, the Japanese have been the first to sense and respond to globalization. They have recognized that since components make up most of the cost of a car, the key to being competitive is to minimize the number of components, standardize the components used in different models, design models that will sell in many countries, and push for maximum scale. In doing so, they have established phenomenal cost advantages over European and U.S. competitors (estimated at between $1,000 and $2,000 for a typical small car). These competitors are now being forced to respond in kind.

Those who have the resources to become truly global themselves are doing so, witness General Motors' world car concepts, its massive investments in integrated production systems that include Japan, Australia, Austria,

Spain, Brazil, and Mexico, as well as the United States, and its sourcing of technology and product from Japan through tie-ups with Isuzu and Suzuki. Smaller competitors are globalizing through cooperation with other companies—British Leyland in joint design with Honda, Alfa in joint production with Nissan, the French through growing cooperation with U.S. producers. Hardly anyone can doubt, however, that competitors who fail to respond adequately to globalization will be out of existence within a few years.

This example drives home two other points about global industries: Those who take the initiative in taking advantage of globalization reap very great rewards and put their competitors on the defensive; those whose response is late or slow often fall by the wayside. It is no exaggeration that in an industry that is, or is rapidly becoming, global, the riskiest possible posture is to remain a domestic competitor. The domestic competitor will not participate in the world's fastest-growth market areas. He will watch as more aggressive companies use this growth to capture economies of scale and learning. And he will then be faced with an attack on domestic markets using different (and possibly superior) technology, product design, manufacturing, and marketing approaches.

Therefore, it is absolutely critical to fully understand where one's industry is in this process of globalization and how rapidly it is likely to evolve toward global status. Because of the diffusion of technologies, management capability, and willingness to compete, the process of globalization is accelerating; failure to recognize this may lead to being shocked out of complacency by a foreign competitor not even heard of five years ago.

If one finds oneself in an industry that is not global or will not become so, one can breathe a little easier. Defense of domestic markets will not require internalization. A Heinz, Nabisco Brands, or Unilever, for example, can be more selective in the extent and pace at which they internationalize. However, even such companies should remember that being in a number of different national markets lowers risk of simultaneous decline or low growth, or of substitution by other technologies, products, or competitors. In addition, technologies, products, and marketing approaches that arise in particular markets may turn out to be applicable to others. Even though internationalization may not be critical for a specific company, the company could still certainly benefit from developing the necessary skills to compete internationally—the financial skills to match the new monetary order, production and logistical skills to take advantage of a freer labor market, and information systems to monitor new technologies and marketing approaches.

Finally, if one is in a global, or soon-to-be global, industry, one must evaluate carefully where the company is in the evolution of its international skills and recognize the magnitude of the challenge that faces the company. If one is an AT&T or Western Electric, one faces a momentous challenge because it is a domestic competitor in a global industry and must transform quickly into a global competitor. This will unquestionably require a major upgrading of skills, a revamping of management organization and systems, and a big change in strategy.

If one is one of the venerable multinationals such as Philips, Siemens, Olivetti, Rhone Poulenac, General Electric, and Westinghouse, the challenge is in distinguishing the global businesses from the more local ones and then developing unique worldwide strategies for each

global business and designing organization structures and management systems that provide the necessary coordination of worldwide technology, product, and manufacturing decisions without losing the ability to adapt marketing and distribution approaches to each country. This will be quite a challenge because traditional values, structures, and systems are more suited to an earlier competitive environment in which each national or regional market could be treated as being different and one did not have to worry about the interconnections among them.

A company like IBM, which is already quite global in orientation, must face up to the need to compete against determined competitors who have explicitly designed their business systems to become leaders in global competition.

Japanese multinationals, which have been on the forefront of globalization, need to ask how long they can sustain this by exporting from Japan and how quickly they should be taking on the more difficult task of building a manufacturing and direct marketing presence in major markets.

Despite occasional setbacks, the world is moving rapidly toward global markets. The number of industries that are globalizing and the pace at which they're doing so is accelerating. This can only mean a continuing series of strategic and organizational readjustments for corporations who compete in these businesses. In the future, the reward for each success will be the opportunity to make more changes.

3

The Product Cycle Hypothesis in a New International Environment
Raymond Vernon

• • •

The last decade has produced a flowering of hypotheses that purport to explain the international trade and direct investment activities of firms in terms of the so-called product cycle. My purpose in this paper is to suggest that the power of such hypotheses has been changing. Two reasons account for that change: one, an increase in the geographical reach of many of the enterprises that are involved in the introduction of new products, a consequence of their having established many overseas subsidiaries; the other, a change in the national markets of the advanced industrialized countries, which has reduced some of the differences that had previously existed between such markets.

A WORD ON THEORY

The fact that new products constantly appear, then mature, and eventually die has always fitted awkwardly into the mainstream theories of international trade and international investment. Hume, Ricardo, Marshall, Ohlin, Williams, and others have observed the phenomenon in passing, without attempting any rigorous formulation of its implications for international trade and investment theory. In the past decade or two, however, numerous efforts have been made to fill the gap. Some have dealt mainly with the trade aspects of the phenomenon.[1] But some have pushed beyond the immediate trade

effects, tracing out a pattern that eventually culminated in foreign direct investments on the part of the innovating firm.[2]

According to the product cycle hypothesis, firms that set up foreign producing facilities characteristically do so in reliance on some real or imagined monopolistic advantage. In the absence of such a perceived advantage, firms are loath to take on the special costs and uncertainties of operating a subsidiary in a foreign environment.[3] One such special strength is an innovational lead.

The product cycle hypothesis begins with the assumption that the stimulus to innovation is typically provided by some threat or promise in the market.[4] But according to the hypothesis, firms are acutely myopic; their managers tend to be stimulated by the needs and opportunities of the market closest at hand, the home market.

The home market in fact plays a dual role in the hypothesis. Not only is it the source of stimulus for the innovating firm; it is also the preferred location for the actual development of the innovation. The first factor that has pushed innovating firms to do their development work in the home market has been simply the need for engineers and scientists with the requisite skills. That requirement, when gauged through the eyes of the typical innovating firm, has tended to rule out sites in most developing countries and has narrowed the choice to some site in the advanced industrialized world. As between such advanced country sites, the home market has generally prevailed.[5] Locating in the home market, engineers and scientists can interact easily with the prospective customers whose needs they hope to satisfy, and can check constantly with (or be checked by) the

Source: Raymond Vernon, "The Product Cycle Hypothesis in a New International Environment," pp. 255–267 (*OBES* 41:4 November 1979). Copyright © 1979. Reprinted by permission.

specialists at headquarters who are concerned with financial and production planning.

The propensity to cluster in the home market is fortified by the fact that there are some well-recognized economies to be captured by an innovating team that is brought together at a common location.[6] These include the usual advantages that go with subdividing any task among a number of specialists, and the added advantages of maintaining efficiency of communication among the research specialists.[7]

The upshot is that the innovations of firms headquartered in some given market tend to reflect the characteristics of that market. Historically, therefore, U.S. firms have developed and produced products that were labour-saving or responded to high-income wants; continental European firms, products and processes that were material-saving and capital-saving; and Japanese firms, products that conserved not only material and capital but also space.[8]

If innovating firms tend to scan their home markets with special intensity, the chances are greatly increased that their first production facilities will also be located in the home market. In many cases, the transitions from development work to pilot plant operation to first commercial production take place in imperceptible steps. But other factors also figure in the choice. One is the fact that if the firm perceives its principal market as being at home, it may prefer a home location to minimize transport costs. The second factor is that the specifications for new products and the optimal methods for manufacturing such products are typically in flux for some time; hence, fixing the optimal location of the first production site is bound to be an exercise based on guesswork. A final factor that may explain the tendency to produce at home is the characteristic inelasticity in the demand of the earliest users of many new products. That inelasticity is thought to make the innovator relatively indifferent to questions of production cost at the time of introduction of a new product.

Once the innovator has set up its first produc-

tion unit in the home market, any demand that may develop in a foreign market would ordinarily be served from the existing production unit. Eventually, however, the firm may consider other alternatives, such as that of licensing a foreign producer or of setting up its own producing subsidiary abroad. For new products, the licensing alternative may prove an inferior choice because of inefficiences in the international market for technology.[9] If licensing is not the preferred choice, then the firm makes the usual familiar comparison between the delivered cost of exports and the cost of overseas production. That is, the marginal costs of producing for export in the home unit plus international transport costs and duties are compared with the full cost of producing the required amount in a foreign subsidiary.

Although not essential to the product cycle hypothesis, it is commonly assumed that a triggering event is likely to be required before the producer will seriously make the calculations that could lead to the creation of a foreign producing facility. The triggering event ordinarily occurs when the innovator is threatened with losing its monopoly position. In the usual case, rival producers appear, prepared to manufacture the product from locations that could undersell the original innovator.

The obvious question is why the original innovator was not already aware that the costs of production might be lower abroad. Part of the answer may lie in the indeterminateness of the threat before it has actually materialized: the difficulty of deciding what is at stake in failing to find the least-cost location, what alternative sites need to be investigated, and what the costs of investigation are likely to be.

These conditions change, however, as the threat begins to crystallize. Eventually, it may be clear that the innovator is threatened with the loss of its business in a given foreign market. At that point, the areas to be investigated as possible production sites have been narrowed while the size of the risk has been more explicitly defined. Accordingly, the decision whether to invest in added information is more readily made. Once having felt compelled to focus on the issue, the innovator will decide in some cases to set up a local producing unit in order to prolong some of the advantages that were created by its original monopoly.

TWO CRITICAL CHANGES

The Networks' Spread

For the past three decades or so, the process of innovation, export, and investment has been progressing full tilt. One result has been a transformation in the industries in which innovations tend to be especially prominent, such as chemicals, electronics, machinery, and transportation equipment. In industries such as these, innovating firms that are limited to their own home markets no longer are very common. Instead, enterprises with highly developed multinational networks of producing units typically account for more than half the global output in their respective product lines.

In spreading their networks of subsidiaries around the world, multinational companies have followed some reasonably well-defined patterns. These patterns offer some strong clues regarding the changing perceptions of the enterprises and their likely lines of future behaviour.

First, a word on the extent of the spread itself. Table 1 compares the scope of the overseas subsidiary networks of a group of the world's largest firms in 1950 with the networks of those same firms in the 1970s. The dramatic increase in the overseas networks of such firms is apparent.

Detailed data have been developed for the 180 U.S. firms in the group, indicating more exactly how the overseas spread took place.[10] According to these data, the overseas spread of the firms in our sample was consistent and stable throughout the three decades following World War II. Firms typically set up their subsidiaries, product lines, and new products in a sequence that began with the geographical areas with which they were most familiar, such as Canada and the United Kingdom, and eventually spread to those that had originally been least familiar, such as Asia and Africa. As time went on, however, the unfamiliar became less so, and the disposition to move first into the traditional areas visibly declined. To illustrate: For product lines introduced abroad by the 180 firms before 1946, the probability that a Canadian location would come earlier than an Asian location was 79 percent; but for product lines that were introduced abroad after 1960, the probability that Canada would take precedence over Asia had dropped to only 59 percent.

The consequences of this steady shift in preferences could be seen in a corresponding shift in the geographical distribution of the foreign subsidiaries of the 180 firms. Before 1946, about 23 percent of the subsidiaries had been located in Canada; but by 1975, the proportion was about 13 percent, with the offsetting gains being

Table 1   Networks of Foreign Manufacturing Subsidiaries of 315 Multinational Companies, 1950 and 1970s

Number of Enterprises with Networks Including	180 US-Based MNCs		135 MNCs Based in UK and Europe	
	1950	**1975**	**1950**	**1970**
Fewer than 6 countries	138	9	116	31
6 to 20 countries	43	128	16	75
More than 20 countries	0	44	3	29

Source: Harvard Multinational Enterprise Project.

Table 2 Spread of Production of 954 New Products by 57 U.S.-Based MNCs to their Foreign Manufacturing Subsidiaries, Classified by Period when initially introduced in the United States, 1945–1975

Period When Introduced in U.S.	Number of Products	Percentage Transferred Abroad, by Number of Years between U.S. Introduction and Initial Transfer	
		Within 1 Year After	Within 2–3 Years After
1945	56	10.7%	8.9%
1946–1950	149	8.1	10.1
1951–1955	147	7.5	10.2
1956–1960	180	13.3	17.8
1961–1965	165	22.4	17.0
1966–1970	158	29.7	15.8
1971–1975	99	35.4	16.2
Total	954	18.0	14.0

Source: Vernon and Davidson, cited in text.

recorded principally in Asia, Africa, and the Middle East.[11]

With numerous indications that U.S. firms were feeling at ease over a wider portion of the earth's surface, it comes as no surprise that the interval of time between the introduction of any new product in the United States and its first production in a foreign location has been rapidly shrinking. Table 2 portrays the time lapse between the introduction of 954 products in the United States and their first overseas production via the manufacturing subsidiaries of the introducing firm.

The data also suggest in various ways that the trends just discussed have been strongly self-reinforcing. For instance, firms that had experienced a considerable number of prior transfers to their foreign producing subsidiaries were quite consistently quicker off the mark with any new product that were firms with fewer prior transfers. Besides, as firms introduced one product after another into a given country, the lapse of time between the introduction of successive products in that country steadily declined.

All told, therefore, the picture is one of an organic change in the overseas networks of large U.S.-based firms. The rate of spread of these networks, whether measured by subsidiaries or by product lines, is slightly lower in the first half of the 1970's than in the latter half of the 1960's; but the spread persists at rates that are rapid by historical standards. Besides, the changes in the rate of spread, according to various econometric tests, seem quite impervious to changes in exchange rates or in price-adjusted exchange rates;[12] so it seems reasonable to assume that we confront a basic change in the institutional structure of the MNCs concerned.[13]

The Environmental Changes

In the period after World War II, the descriptive power of the product cycle hypothesis, at least as it applied to U.S.-based enterprises, had been enhanced by some special factors. In the early part of the postwar period, the U.S. economy was the repository of a storehouse of innovations not yet exploited abroad, innovations that responded to the labour-scarce high-income conditions of the U.S. market. As the years went on, other countries eventually achieved the income levels and acquired the relative labour costs that had prevailed earlier in the United States. As these countries tracked the terrain already traversed by the U.S. economy, they developed an increasing demand for the products that had previously been generated in response to U.S. needs. That circumstance provided the consequences characteristically associated with the product cycle sequence: exports from the United States in mounting volume, followed eventually by the establishment of foreign producing subsidiaries on the part of the erstwhile U.S. exporters.

But many of the advanced industrialized countries that were tracking over the U.S. terrain were doing something more: They were closing in on the United States, narrowing or obliterating the income gap that had existed in the immediate postwar period. In 1949, for instance, the per capita income of Germany and of France was less than one-third that of the United States; but by the latter 1970s, the per capita income of all three countries was practically equal. In the same interval, Japan increased its per capita income from 6 percent of the U.S. level to nearly 70 percent of that level. That shrinkage, of course, weakened a critical assumption of the product cycle hypothesis, namely, that the entrepreneurs of large enterprises confronted markedly different conditions in their respective home markets. As European and Japanese incomes approached those of the United States, these differences were reduced. And as the United States came to rely increasingly on imported raw materials, the differences in the factor costs of the various markets declined further still.

Not only have the differences in income levels among these major markets been shrinking; the differences in their overall dimensions also have declined. This has been due partly to the convergence of such income levels, but partly also to the development of the European Economic Community. As a result, entrepreneurs with their home base in these different markets confront conditions that are much more similar than they had been in the past.

Some of the starting assumptions of the product cycle hypothesis therefore are clearly in

question. It is no longer easy to assume that innovating firms are uninformed about conditions in foreign markets, whether in other advanced countries or in the developing world. Nor can it be assumed that U.S. firms are exposed to a very different home environment from European and Japanese firms; although the gap between most of the developing countries and the advanced industrialized countries palpably remains, the differences among the advanced industrialized countries are reduced to trivial dimensions. With some key assumptions of the product cycle hypothesis in doubt, what organizing concepts are still available by which one can observe and assess the role of innovation in the operations of the multinational enterprises of different countries?

THE GLOBAL NETWORK IN OPERATION

To try to answer the question, I have classified multinational companies crudely into three ideal types, and have sought to explore their likely behaviour.

The first type is purely hypothetical, a result of armchair speculation. Picture an MNC with an innovating capability that has developed a powerful capacity for global scanning. Communication is virtually costless between any two points of the globe; information, once received, is digested and interpreted at little or no cost. Ignorance or uncertainty, therefore, is no longer a function of distance; markets, wherever located, have an equal opportunity to stimulate the firm to innovation and production; and factory sites, wherever located, have an equal chance to be weighed for their costs and risks. But some significant economies of scale continue to exist in the development activities as well as in the production activities of the firm.

An enterprise of this sort, we can presume, will from time to time develop an innovation in response to the promise or threat of one of the many markets to which it was exposed. The firm might launch the innovative process in the market that had produced the stimulus; or, if economies of scale were important and an appropriate facility existed elsewhere in the system, in a location well removed from the prospective market. In either case, once the innovation was developed, the global scanner would be in a position to serve any market in which it was aware that demand existed; and would be in a position to detect and serve new demands in other markets as they subsequently arose. Presumably such demands would grow in other countries as they attained the income levels or the factor cost configurations of the country whose needs had first stimulated the invention. For some products, such as consumer goods, the demand in different national markets could be expected to appear in a predictable pecking order, based largely on income levels and labour costs.

The global scanner, therefore, would be in an advantageous position as compared with those firms without such a scanning capability. Firms that were confined to a country which was down the ladder in the pecking order, including most firms headquartered in the developing countries, would be at a disadvantage in relation to the global scanner. As the incomes of their home countries grew, the nonglobal producers might well perceive the opportunity to fill a growing demand; but they would be handicapped by comparison with the enterprises that were already producing in the higher income countries, including the global scanners.

In a world composed of such firms, the product cycle hypothesis would play only a very little role. Although innovating firms might prefer locations in one of the advanced industrialized countries due to the supply of engineers and scientists, the preference for a location in the home market would be weaker. The exports generated by the innovations might come from the country in which the product had initially been introduced; but then again they might not. Whatever the original source of the exports might be, the hold of the exporting country would be tenuous, as the global scanner continuously recalculated the parameters that determined the optimal production location.

The hypothetical global scanner, of course, is not to be found in the real world. The acquisition of information is seldom altogether costless; and the digestion and interpretation of information always entails cost. The typical patterns of behaviour that one observes in the real world reflect that fact.

One typical pattern, which provides the basis for a second model, consists of firms that develop and produce a line of standardized products which they think responds to a homogeneous world demand rather than to the distinctive needs of individual markets. Some firms have been able to take this approach from the very first, because of the nature of their products; the oil, chemical, and crude metals industries, for instance, were always in a position to develop and purvey a standardized line of products to world markets. But the trend has been moving beyond such products to well-elaborated manufactures: to aircraft, computers, pharmaceuticals, and automobiles, for instance. The trends of the automobile industry in that direction are particularly striking.[14]

By standardizing their product on a world basis, firms can hope for two kinds of benefit: they can reduce or avoid the costs of processing and interpreting the information that bears on the distinctive needs of individual markets; and they can capture the scale economies of production and marketing on a global scale. Whether those advantages outweigh the disadvantages of being unresponsive to the needs of individual markets is an empirical question the answer to which may well vary by product lines and other factors; those firms that decide in the affirmative for some or all of their product lines cannot be said to be engaged in an irrational response.

Firms in this category, innovating for a global market, are obliged to play their innovational gambles for relatively heavy stakes. Accordingly, they can be expected to maintain the central core of their innovational activities close to headquarters, where complex face-to-face consultation among key personnel will be possible; in this respect, such firms are likely to perform consistently with the product cycle pattern. To be sure, with increased ease of communication and transportation, various routine aspects of the development work, not involving the most critical choices in the development process, can be spun off to more distant locations. To reduce their development costs and to respond to the pressures of various governments in whose territories they hope to do business, firms in this category are commonly prepared to establish some carefully selected development activities at distant points; but integration at the centre is still needed.[15]

Firms in this category also have a strong need to integrate their global production facilities. Seeking to exploit scale economies, they are likely to establish various component plants in both advanced industrialized countries and developing countries, and to crosshaul between plants for the assembly of final products. That pattern will be at variance with product cycle expectations.

It need not be anticipated, however, that all firms with a capacity for global scanning will commit themselves unequivocally to the development of standard global products such as the IBM 370, the Boeing 757, or the GM world car. General Motors, after all, continues to respond to certain distinctive national characteristics in some of its product lines, in spite of its commitment to a world sourcing strategy. Other automobile firms, including Renault and Chrysler, seem prepared to respond to national factors for even a larger proportion of their output, forgoing the advantages of a world product and long production runs. In computers, a number of IBM's rivals survive by their willingness and ability to adapt to the requirements of local markets, including the requirements of national governments, to a degree that would be incompatible with the standardization of their products and the global rationalization of their facilities.[16] Many European and Japanese firms still find it useful to treat the U.S. market as a dis-

tinctive entity, justifying distinctive products and strategies.[17]

Accordingly, we can picture firms that make different decisions on the benefits of global optimization, according to the characteristics of each product line. And we can picture markets in which different firms have settled on somewhat different strategies for closely competing products. If past history is any guide, such differences can persist in a given product market over extended periods of time.[18]

A third type of innovating MNC that merits some speculative consideration is the firm whose choices of innovations and production sites remain myopically oriented to the home market while leaving all analysis of foreign markets to its individual foreign producing subsidiaries. Firms in this category simply put out their home-based innovations for production by their foreign subsidiaries; or, perhaps even more commonly, such firms allow the initiative for such decisions to come from the subsidiaries themselves.[19] Drawing from a shopping list of products generated by the headquarters unit, subsidiaries choose those that seem appropriate for intensive exploitation in their local markets. As long as the proposed production in the subsidiary seems to have no considerable impact on the facilities of the firm located in other countries, the managers at headquarters are disposed to give the local managers their head.

Firms that pursue a policy of this sort can justify their approach readily enough: One possibility is that the firm perceives the cost of interpreting the information needed for pursuing a more centralized policy in production and marketing as exceeding the likely benefits. Another possibility is that the firm has found it impossible to fashion an organization that has the capability for absorbing and being influenced by signals that originate in the subsidiaries.[20]

Where this pattern of operation exists, the hypothesized behaviour of the product cycle may still be visible. But the phase of the product cycle in which the parent is responsible for serving foreign markets will be foreshortened and the oligopolistic strength of the innovating firm will be relatively weak, given the existence of firms in other markets that face similar demands and factor cost conditions.

Cases in this category will of course deviate from the pattern that a global scanner would generate. First, as long as the subsidiary is the initiator, the geographical spread of products will be affected by the risk-taking propensities and drives of individual subsidiary managers and by the resource slack of individual subsidiaries rather than by a consistent set of decision rules and allocations from the centre.[21] Second, in cases in which the initiative for transfer comes from the subsidiary rather than the parent, the possibility of producing in some third country where neither the parent nor the subsidiary is located is unlikely to be considered.

All this leads to a simple conclusion. As we search for a hypothesis that would replace the product cycle concept as an explicator of the trading and investing behaviour of the innovating multinational company, a simple variant such as that of the global scanner will not take us very far. Global scanning is not costless, even when a network of foreign subsidiaries is already in place; costs of collecting and interpreting the information, as the firm perceives those costs, may not be commensurate with its expected benefits. In assessing the benefits, flexibility may be a problem: either the flexibility that firms have lost from decisions in the past, or the flexibility they are fearful of losing in an uncertain future.

So the day of the global scanner as I defined it a few pages back is not yet here. Nevertheless, even if the global scanner is not yet the dominant model, nor perhaps ever will be, the power of the product cycle hypothesis is certainly weakened.

THE PRODUCT CYCLE RECONSIDERED

The evidence is fairly persuasive that the product cycle hypothesis had strong predictive power in the first two or three decades after World War II, especially in explaining the composition of U.S. trade and in projecting the likely patterns of foreign direct investment by U.S. firms. But certain conditions of that period are gone. For one thing, the leading MNCs have now developed global networks of subsidiaries; for another, the U.S. market is no longer unique among national markets either in size or factor cost configuration. It seems plausible to assume that the product cycle will be less useful in explaining the relationship of the U.S. economy to other advanced industrialized countries, and will lose some of its power in explaining the relationship of advanced industrialized countries to developing countries. But strong traces of the sequence are likely to remain.[22]

One such trace is likely to be provided by the innovating activities of smaller firms, firms that have not yet acquired a capacity for global scanning through a network of foreign manufacturing subsidiaries already in place. The assumptions of the product cycle hypothesis may still apply to such firms, as they move from home-based innovation to the possibility of exports and ultimately of overseas investment.

Moreover, even firms with a well-developed scanning capability and a willingness to use it may be found behaving according to the expectations of the product cycle hypothesis. As noted earlier, the specifications of new products are usually in such a state of flux that it is infeasible for a time to fix on a least-cost location. Some firms therefore are unlikely to make intensive use of their scanning capability when siting their first production facility. To be sure, such innovators cannot expect to retain their innovational lead for very long, in view of the fact that the innovators of many countries now confront such similar home conditions. But a shadow of the hypothesized behaviour may well remain.

Moreover, the product cycle may gain some support as a predictive device from other developments.

One such development is the improved position of European and Japanese firms as innovators. As noted earlier, the innovations of these firms, when compared with those of U.S.

firms, have tended to place greater emphasis on material-saving and capital-saving objectives, while placing lesser relative emphasis on labour-saving measures and on new mass consumer wants. The costs of materials and capital have risen rapidly over the past few years, both in relative and absolute terms. Accordingly, it may be that the long-time emphasis of the Europeans and Japanese firms will generate an increasing demand for their innovations. The world's increased use of European and Japanese small-car technology and of Japanese steel technology are cases in point, fitting nicely within the structure of the product cycle hypothesis.

However, the product cycle hypothesis would also predict that the European-Japanese advantage on this front will only be temporary. As U.S. firms confront factor-cost conditions in their home market that are similar to those of Europe and Japan, one would expect a stream of innovations from the Americans similar to those of their overseas competitors; General Motors, for instance, is now seen as a potential threat to European and Japanese car makers for the 1980s.

A less equivocal case for the continued usefulness of the product cycle concept is found in analysing the situation of the less-developed countries. Although income, market size, and factor cost patterns have converged among the more advanced industrialized countries, a wide gap still separates such countries from many developing areas. Accordingly, despite the fact that so many MNCs have created producing networks all over the globe, the subsidiaries of such firms located in the developing countries have yet to acquire all of the products that their parents and affiliates produce in richer and larger markets. Most of the developing countries, therefore, are still in process of absorbing the innovations of other countries introduced earlier, according to patterns that remain reasonably consistent with product cycle expectations.

The performance of firms in some developing countries, moreover, follows the expectations of the product cycle in a very different sense. Firms operating in the more rapidly industrializing group—in countries such as Mexico, Brazil, India, and Korea—are demonstrating a considerable capability for producing innovations that respond to the special conditions of their own economies.[23] Once having responded to those special conditions with a new product or process or with a significant adaptation of an existing product or process, firms of that sort are in a position to initiate their own cycle of exportation and eventual direct investment; their target, according to the hypothesis, would be the markets of the other developing countries that were lagging a bit behind them in the industrialized pecking order.

Indications that some such process was going on in a limited way in the developing countries were already being reported in the 1960s in occasional illustrations and anecdotal materials; but those early cases for the most part involved the subsidiaries of multinational enterprises, which were making modest adaptations of products and processes originally received from the foreign parents.[24] Innovations such as these sometimes gave the subsidiaries a basis for exporting more effectively to neighbouring countries that were lower on the development scale.

In the 1970s, however, the anecdotal materials began to involve firms that were headquartered in developing countries.[25] Firms were reported developing products and processes of special importance to other developing countries, to be followed eventually by the creation of producing subsidiaries in those countries.[26] Of course, the direct investments of the firms of developing countries in other developing countries have not all been of the product cycle variety. The foreign subsidiaries of firms headquartered in developing countries often maintain their position through oligopolistic strengths other than a technological lead.[27]

Accordingly, the product cycle concept continues to explain and predict a certain category of foreign direct investments. Although it no longer can be relied on to provide as powerful an explanation of the behaviour of U.S. firms as in decades past, it is likely to continue to provide a guide to the motivations and response of some enterprises in all countries of the world.

NOTES

1. For instance, M. V. Posner, "International Trade and Technical Change," *Oxford Economic Papers,* October 1961, pp. 323–341; Gary Hufbauer, *Synthetic Materials and the Theory of International Trade* (Cambridge, Mass.: Harvard University Press, 1966); Seev Hirsch, "The Product Cycle Model of International Trade—A Multi-Country Cross Section Analysis," *Oxford Bulletin of Economics and Statistics,* Vol. 37, no. 4, November 1975, pp. 305–317; W. B. Walker, "Industrial Innovation and International Trading Performance," mimeo. Science Policy Research Unit, Sussex University, October 30, 1975; and M. P. Claudon, *International Trade and Technology: Models of Dynamic Comparative Advantages* (Washington, D.C.: University Press of America, 1977).

2. S. H. Hymer, *The International Operations of National Firms* (Cambridge, Mass.: MIT Press, 1976), based on the author's 1960 Ph.D. thesis; Raymond Vernon, "International Investment and International Trade in the Product Cycle," *Quarterly Journal of Economics,* May 1966, pp. 190–207; W. H. Gruber and others, "The R & D Factor in International Investment of US Industries," *Journal of Political Economy,* February 1967, pp. 20–37; Thomas Horst, "The Firm and Industry Determinants of the Decision to Invest Abroad: An Empirical Study," *Review of Economics and Statistics,* Vol. 54, August 1972, pp. 258–266; S. P. Magee, "Multinational Corporations, The Industry Technology Cycle and Development," *Journal of World Trade Law,* Vol. 11, no. 4, July–August 1977, pp. 297–321; P. J. Buckley and Mark Casson, *The Future of the Multinational Enterprise* (New York: Holmes and Meier, 1976); Paul Krugman, "A Model of Innovation, Technology Transfer, and The World Distribution of Income," *Journal of Political Economy,* April 1979, pp. 253–266.

3. That is a central proposition of the S. H. Hymer work, cited earlier. See also my "The Location of Economic Activity," in J. H. Dunning, *Economic Analysis and the Multinational Enterprise* (London: George Allen and Unwin, 1970), pp. 83–114.

4. Various empirical studies demonstrate that innovations which do not arise out of a market stimulus—innovations, for instance, that are dreamed up by the laboratory as a clever application of some new scientific capability—have a relatively low chance of industrial success. See for instance Sumner Myers and Donald Marquis, *Successful Industrial Innovations,* National Science Foundation Report No. 69-

17 (Washington, D.C.: Government Printing Office, 1969), p. 31.

5. For econometric evidence of the tie between the choice of a production location, skills and innovation, see Sanjaya Lall, "Monopolistic Advantages and Foreign Involvement by U.S. Manufacturing Industry," *Oxford Economic Papers,* forthcoming, March 1980.

6. For evidence of such clustering, see D. B. Creamer, *Overseas Research and Development by United States Multinationals, 1966–1975* (New York: The Conference Board, 1976); Robert Ronstadt, *Research and Developmental Abroad by U.S.Multinationals* (New York: Praeger Publishers, 1977); and Vernon, *Storm Over the Multinationals,* pp. 43–45.

7. See especially T. J. Allen, *Managing the Flow of Technology* (Cambridge, Mass.: MIT Press, 1978). An important exception is pharmaceuticals, a case in which U.S. regulation has driven the innovation process abroad. See, e.g., H. G. Grabowski and J. M. Vernon, "Innovation and Invention: Consumer Protection Regulation in Ethical Drugs," *American Economic Review,* Vol. 67, no. 1, 1977, pp. 359–364.

8. For evidence, see W. H. Davidson, "Paterns of Factor-Saving Innovation in the Industrialized World," *European Economic Review,* no. 8, 1976, pp. 207–217.

9. See Buckley and Casson, pp. 36, 45, 68–69. Their observations are strengthened by data presented in Raymond Vernon and W. H. Davidson, "Foreign Production of Technology-Intensive Products by U.S.-Based Multinational Enterprises," Working Paper 79-5, Harvard Business School, 1979, xeroxed, p. 66. These data show that in establishing a source of foreign production for 221 innovations, 32 large U.S.-based multinational enterprises elected the subsidiary route far more frequently than licensing, but the degree of preference declined as the innovation aged. For similar conclusions relating to petrochemicals, see R. B. Stobaugh, "The Product Life Cycle, U.S. Exports, and International Investment," unpublished D.B.A. thesis, Harvard Business School, 1968.

10. The data on which the next few paragraphs are based are presented in detail in Raymond Vernon and W. H. Davidson, "Foreign Production of Technology-Intensive Products by U.S.-Based Multinational Enterprises," cited earlier.

11. Some measures employed in the Vernon Davidson study—counts based on 954 individual products rather than on subsidiaries or product lines—show Latin America also increasing its relative share. See Table 17, p. 52 of the report.

12. Vernon and Davidson, pp. 19–20.

13. Although the data for testing the assumption are not at hand, I have assumed that parallel changes are occurring in European and Japanese firms.

14. See A. J. Harman, "Innovations, Technology, and the Pure Theory of International Trade," unpublished Ph.D. thesis, MIT, September 1968, pp. 131–134; J. M. Callahan, "GM Adopting Worldwide Purchasing Coordination,"

Chilton's Automotive Industries, July 1978, pp. 47–49; "Ford's Fiesta Makes a Big Splash," *Business Week,* August 22, 1977, pp. 38–39; and "SKF Reintegrates Internationally," *Mulitnational Business,* The Economist Intelligence Unit, No. 4, 1976, pp. 1–7.

15. Compare the observations of Sanjaya Lall, "The International Allocation of Research Activity by U.S. Multinationals," in this issue.

16. This point is being developed in detail by Yves Doz at the Harvard Business School.

17. For evidence on Japanese firms in this category, see Terutomo Ozawa, *Japan's Technological Challenge to the West, 1950–1974* (Cambridge, Mass.: MIT Press, 1974), pp. 97–98.

18. This proposition is of course consistent with the theory of strategic groups; see R. E. Caves and M. E. Porter, "From Entry Bariers to Mobility Barriers: Conjectural Decisions and Contrived Deterrence to New Competition," *Quarterly Journal of Economics,* Vol. XCI, no. 2, 1977, pp. 241–261 It is consistent also with the long-established observation that different geographical locations offer different combinations of benefits and costs such that widely separated locations applying different production techniques may be competitive for sustained periods. See Max Hall, *Made in New York* (Cambridge, Mass.: Harvard University Press, 1959).

19. For illustrations, see "IBM World Trade Corporation" and "YKK (Yoshida Kogyo KK)," both in Stanley M. Davis, *Managing and Organizing Multinational Corporations* (New York: Pergamon Press, 1979). Also, from Intercollegiate Case Clearing House, see *Corning Glass Works (A), (B), and (C)* (numbers 9–477–024, 9–477–073, and 9–477–074); *International Calculators (Australia) Pty. Limited* (9–572–641); *Veedol France* (ICH 10 M 31); *The International Harvester Company (B)* (9–512–009); *Princess Housewares Gmb H (A)* (ICH 13 M 117); *General Foods Corporation—International Division (D2)* (ICH 13 G 214); *AB Thorsten (A)* (9–414–035); and *Sanpix Industries* (9–278–673).

20. For indications of the formidable difficulties associated with developing such an organizational capability, see Allen, *Managing the Flow of Technology,* op. cit.

21. This, of course, is a familiar phenomenon, long observed by business historians and organizational behaviourists. More recently the concept has been elevated to the status of theory in Harvey Leibenstein's formulation of his X-inefficiency concept; see his *Beyond Economic Man: A New Foundation for Microeconomics* (Cambridge, Mass.: Harvard University Press, 1976).

22. But see I. H. Giddy, "The Demise of the Product Cycle Model in International Business Theory," *Columbia Journal of World Business,* Vol. xiii, no. 1, Spring 1978, pp. 90–97.

23. See, e.g., Julio Fidel et al., "The Argentine Cigarette Industry: Technological Profile and Behavior," IDB/ECLA Research Programme in Science and Technology, Buenos Aires, September 1978, pp. 92–94; C.J. Dahlman, "From Technological Dependence to Technological Development: The Case of the USIMINAS Steel Plant in Brazil," IDB/ECLA Research Programme in Science and Technology, Buenos Aires, October 1978; and Jorge Katz et al., "Productivity, Technology and Domestic Efforts in Research and Development," IDB/ECLA Research Programme in Science and Technology, Buenos Aires, July 1978. For evidence of the increasing capacity of some developing countries to sell plants and engineering services, see Sanjaya Lall, "Developing Countries as Exporters of Industrial Technology," *Research Policy,* forthcoming, Vol. 9, no. 1, January 1980.

24. W. A. Yeoman, "Selection of Production Processes for the Manufacturing Subsidiaries of U.S.-Based Multinational Corporations," D.B.A. thesis, Harvard University, April 1968, Chap. 5; Jorge Katz and Eduardo Ablin, "Technology and Industrial Exports: A Micro-Economic Analysis of Argentina's Recent Experience," IDB/ECLA Research Programme in Science and Technology, Buenos Aires, August 1978; and by the same authors, "From Infant Industry to Technology Exports: The Argentine Experience in the International Sale of Industrial Plants and Engineering Works," IDB/ECLA Research Programme in Science and Technology, Buenos Aires, October 1978.

25. See for instance L. T. Wells, Jr., "The Internationalization of Firms from Developing Countries," in Tamir Agmon and C. P. Kindleberger, *Multinationals from Small Countries* (Cambridge, Mass.: MIT Press, 1977), pp. 133–166; by the same author, "Foreign Investment from the Third World: The Experience of Chinese Firms from Hong Kong," *Columbia Journal of World Business,* Spring 1978, pp. 39–49; and A. J. Prasad, "Export of Technology from India," unpublished Ph.D. thesis, Columbia University, 1978, pp. 123–156.

26. Extensive data on this tendency are being developed by L. T. Wells, Jr., for eventual publication.

27. Such firms also have been known, for instance, to develop special skills in the maintenance and repair of second hand machinery, and a supply of scarce spare parts for such machinery. See Wells, "Hong Kong," and Prasad, "India," p. 147.

4

Strategic Management in Multinational Companies
Yves L. Doz

• • •

The evolution of multinational companies (MNCs) over the last decade has been characterized by a growing conflict between the requirements for economic survival and success (the economic imperative) and the adjustments made necessary by the demands of host governments (the political imperative). The lowering of trade barriers and the substantial economies of scale still available in many industries combined with vigorous competition from low cost exporters push the MNCs toward the integration and rationalization of their activities among various countries.[1] Yet, the very international interdependence created by freer trade and MNC rationalization make individual countries more vulnerable to external factors and their traditional domestic economic policies less effective.[2] As a result, most governments turn more and more to specific sectorial policies implemented through direct negotiations with the companies involved and through incentives tailored to them.[3] Both the economic and political imperatives thus take on increasing importance in the management of the multinationals.

This article, based on intensive field research of the management processes in about a dozen MNCs, analyzes *strategies and administrative processes* used by MNCs to reconcile the conflicting economic and political imperatives. Findings are presented in four sections. First, MNC strategies to respond to the dual imperatives are described and contrasted. Second, conditions under which MNCs are likely to find

one or another strategy most suitable for individual businesses are reviewed. Third, the interaction between strategies and the nature of internal management processes is analyzed. Fourth, implications for the management of interdependencies between businesses in diversified multinationals are outlined. In the conclusion, means to increase the overall managerial capability of the company are explored.

MULTINATIONAL STRATEGIES

Faced with the conflict between the economic and political imperatives within a business, MNCs can respond in several ways. Some companies clearly respond first to the economic imperatives, and follow a worldwide (or regional)[4] business strategy where the activities in various countries are integrated and centrally managed. Other companies forgo the economic benefits of integration and let their subsidiaries adjust to the demands of their host government (as if they were national companies), thus clearly giving the upper hand to the political imperative. Finally, some companies try to leave their strategy unclear and reap benefits from economic integration and political responsiveness, in turn, or find compromises between the two. These three strategies are described in this section.

Worldwide Integration Strategy

Some companies choose to respond to the economic imperative and improve their international competitiveness. For companies that already have extensive manufacturing operations in several countries, the most attractive solu-

Source: Yves L. Doz, "Strategic Management in Multinational Companies," *Sloan Management Review,* Vol. 21, No. 2, pp. 27–46. Reprinted by permission of the publisher. Copyright © 1980 by the Sloan Management Review Association. All rights reserved.

tion is to integrate and rationalize their activities among these countries. Individual plants are to provide only part of the product range (but for sales in all subsidiaries), thereby achieving greater economies of scale.[5] Plants can also be specialized by stages in the production process, and can be located in various countries according to the cost and availability of production factors for each stage (energy, labor, raw materials, skills).[6] Texas Instrument's location of labor-intensive semiconductor finishing activities in Southwest Asia, or Ford's and GM's Europe-wide manufacturing rationalization, as well as their investments in Spain, illustrate this integration strategy.

Extensive transshipments of components and finished products between subsidiaries located in different countries result from such a strategy. Integration also involves the development of products acceptable on a worldwide basis. The "world car" concept pushed by GM, Ford, and Japanese exporters is an example of this approach. The driving principle of this integration strategy is the reduction of unit costs and the capture of large sales volumes; in industries where economies of scale are significant and not fully exploited within the size of national markets, it can bring sizable productivity advantages. For instance, Ford's unit direct manufacturing costs in Europe were estimated to be well below those of national competitors supplying a comparable car range. In industries where dynamic economies of scale are very strong (such as semiconductors), the cost level differences between such leaders as Texas Instruments and smaller national firms were significant. Similarly, IBM was believed to have costs significantly lower than its competitors.[7]

Where integration brought substantial cost advantages over competitors, the integrated firms could allocate part of the benefits from their higher internal efficiency to incur "good citizenship" costs in the host countries, and still remain competitive with nonintegrated firms. Some companies had a policy of full employment, balanced internal trade among countries, and performance of R&D in various countries. Such a policy may lead to less than optimal decisions, in a short-term financial sense, as it has some opportunity costs (for instance, the location of new plants and research centers in countries where a company sells more than it buys, instead of in low wage or low manufacturing cost countries). However, such a policy may also be the key to host countries' long-term acceptance of companies as leading worldwide corporations.

The benefits of integration not only enable the MNC to be better tolerated thanks to its ability to incur higher good citizenship costs, but integration itself can be seen as making expropriation less likely in developing countries.[8] Integration provides more bargaining power to MNCs for ongoing operations and also makes extreme solutions to conflicts with host governments (such as expropriation) into outcomes where both the host country and the MNC stand to lose.

A well-articulated, worldwide integration strategy also simplifies the management of international operations by providing a point of view on the environment, a framework to identify key sources of uncertainties, and a purpose in dealing with them. The worldwide integration strategy can guide managers in adopting a *proactive* stance. The simplicity of the driving principle of the integration strategy also makes a consistent, detailed strategic planning process possible, as it provides a unifying focus to the various parts of the organization. This process both guides the implementation of strategy and provides for its refinement and evolution over time.

National Responsiveness Strategy

Some companies forgo the potential benefits of integration and give much more leeway to their subsidiaries to respond to the political imperative by having them behave almost as if they were national companies. Yet, the affiliation of subsidiaries to a multinational company can bring them four distinct advantages over purely national competitors. These advantages are

1. The pooling of financial risks;
2. The spreading of research and development costs over a larger sales volume (than that of local competitors) without the difficulties involved in licensing transactions;
3. The coordination of export marketing to increase overall success in export markets;
4. The transfer of specific skills between subsidiaries (e.g., process technology or merchandising methods).

In this approach, each subsidiary remains free to pursue an autonomous economic or political strategy nationally as its management sees fit, given the situation of the national industry. In industries where the government plays a key role (nuclear engineering and electrical power, for instance), national strategies are primarily political; in industries where other local factors are important sources of differentiation (e.g., food processing), but where government plays a less prominent role, strategies are economic.[9]

In a nationally responsive MNC, the resources, know-how, or services of the headquarters (or of other subsidiaries) are called upon only when the subsidiary management finds them helpful. Little central influence is exercised on the subsidiaries. The nationally responsive MNC, as a whole, has no strategy, except in a limited sense (Brown Boveri's technical excellence, for instance), and the strategy is usually not binding: subsidiaries follow it only when they see it in their own interest. Manufacturing is usually done on a local-for-local basis, with few intersubsidiary transfers. Coordination of R&D and avoidance of duplications are often difficult, particularly when host governments insist upon R&D being carried on locally on specific projects for which government support is available (new telecommunica-

tion technologies or microelectronics, for instance).

Administrative Coordination Strategy

Rejecting both clear-cut strategic solutions to the conflict between the economic and political imperatives offered by worldwide integration and national responsiveness, MNCs can choose to live with the conflict and look for structural and administrative adjustments instead of strategic solutions. Such adjustments are aimed at providing some of the benefits of both worldwide (or regional) integration and national responsiveness.

The strategy (literally) is to have no set strategy, but to let each strategic decision be made on its own merits and to challenge prior commitments. Individual decisions thus do not fit into the logic of clear goals, the reasonableness of which is tested against a comprehensive analysis of the environment and an assessment of the organization's capabilities. Strategy is not the search for an overall optimal fit, but a series of limited adjustments made in response to specific developments, without an attempt to integrate these adjustments into a consistent comprehensive strategy.[10]

The need for such adjustments emerges when new uncertainties are identified. These uncertainties can offer opportunities (e.g., the possibility to invest in a new country) or threats (e.g., the development of new technologies by competitors), or lend themselves to conflicting interpretation (the willingness of a government to grant R&D subsidies, but with some local production requirements). Instead of taking a stable proactive stance vis-à-vis the environment and relying on the chosen strategy to provide a framework within which to deal with sources of uncertainties and to make specific decisions as the need arises, companies using administrative coordination absorb uncertainties and try to resolve conflicts internally each time new uncertainties question prior allocations of strategic resources. In short, strategy becomes unclear, shifting with the perceived importance of changes in the economic or political environment, and it may become dissolved into a set of incremental decisions with a pattern which may make sense only *ex post*. Administrative coordination does not allow strategic planning: we are farther from the "timed sequence of conditional moves" representing the usual goal of strategic planning and much closer to public administration where issues get shaped, defined, attended to, and resolved one at a time in a "muddling through" process that never gives analytical consideration to the full implications of a step.[11]

By adopting such an internally flexible and negotiable posture, administratively coordinated companies make themselves more accessible to government influence, and become Janus-faced. On certain issues and at certain points in time, a view consistent with worldwide rationalization will prevail; in other cases national responsiveness will prevail, and in many cases some uneasy blend of the two will result. Some of the central control of the subsidiaries so critical in multinational integration is abandoned, making it easier for subsidiaries to cooperate with powerful partners such as government agencies or national companies or specific projects. Because commitments of resources are not all made consistently over time, and as the company is not likely to be very rationalized (given the role accorded to host governments' demands), excess resources are not likely to allow for large costs of good citizenship. In short, compared with multinational integration, *administrative coordination trades off internal efficiency for external flexibility*. Whereas multinational integration seeks to provide the organization with enough economic power for success, administrative coordination seeks to provide the flexibility needed for a constantly adjusted coalignment of the firm with the more powerful factors in the environment and with the most critical sources of

uncertainty.[12] Acceptability to host governments derives from flexibility.

The Three Strategies Compared

Both the worldwide (or regional) integration strategy and the national responsiveness strategy correspond to clear tradeoffs between the economic and the political imperatives. Integration demonstrates a clear preference for the economic imperative; the MNC attempts to fully exploit integration's potential for economic performance and shows willingness to incur large citizenship costs in exchange for being allowed to be very different from national companies. Conversely, national responsiveness minimizes the difference between the MNC and national companies, and thus minimizes the acceptability problems. It expresses a clear sensitivity to the political imperative, at the expense of economic performance. The economic advantages of multinationality are confined to a few domains: financial risks, amortization of R&D costs, export marketing, and skill transfers among the subsidiaries.

Administrative coordination, because it aims at a constantly fluctuating balance between the imperatives, is an ambiguous form of management. There is a constant tension within the organization between the drive for economic success based on clear economic strategy, and the need to consider major uncertainties springing from the political imperative. The following comment, made by a senior manager in an administratively coordinated MNC, illustrates the tension:

In the long run we risk becoming a collection of inefficient, government-subsidized national companies unable to compete on the world market. Yet, if we rationalize our operations, we lose our preferential access to government R&D contracts and subsidies. So we try to develop an overall strategic plan that makes some competitive sense, and then bargain for each part of it with individual governments, trying to sell them on particular programs that contribute to the plan as a whole. Often we have to revise or abandon parts of our plan for lack of government support.

MARKETS, COMPETITION, TECHNOLOGY, AND STRATEGY

In thinking about which type of strategy may suit a particular MNC or an individual business within a diversified MNC, it is important to consider the markets being served, the competition being faced, and the technology being used by the firm. The argument will focus on products and industries for which multinational integration pressures are significant, leaving aside products for which national taste differences (food), high bulk to value added ratio (furniture), dependence on perishable products (food), small optimal size (garments and leather goods), or other such factors usually make rationalization unattractive or unfeasible.

Market Structure and Competition

The range of possible multinational strategies depends upon the structure of the world market in terms of customers and barriers to trade. First, for some products (such as electrical power systems or telecommunications equipment), the technology and economies of production would very strongly suggest global rationalization, but political imperatives are so strong as to prevent it. The international trade volumes, either captive within MNCs or in toto, for telecommunications equipment or power systems are extremely low.[13] In developed countries theoretically committed to free trade, restrictions come through monopoly market power of government-controlled entities—Post, Telegraph, Telephone (PTT), for instance—or through complex legislation and regulation that create artificial market differentiation. EEC regulations on trucks, officially designed for safety and road degradation reasons, effectively create barriers to entry for importers. In a similar way, inspection regulations

for equipment (including the parts and components) purchased by state agencies in many European countries, effectively make it difficult to incorporate imported components into end products sold to the state.

In developing countries, market access restrictions are more straightforward. Under such conditions of restricted trade and controlled market access, worldwide strategic integration is obviously difficult. Often, the very nature of the goods, their strategic importance, as well as characteristics such as bulky, massive equipment produced in small volumes for a few large customers, reinforce the desire on the part of governments to control suppliers closely.[14]

Second, at another extreme, there are some goods that are traded quite freely, whose sales do not depend on location of manufacture or nationality of the manufacturer, and for which economies of scale beyond the size of national markets are significant. In such industries the only viable strategy is worldwide (or regional) integration. This is the strategy followed by all volume car manufacturers in Europe, led by Ford and General Motors but also including such national champions as Fiat, Renault, or Volkswagen. Smaller companies are adopting a specialization strategy by moving out of the price-sensitive volume market and serving the world market from a single location (BMW, Daimler Benz).

Third, and most interesting, are businesses (such as computers or semiconductors) whose markets are partly government-controlled and partly internationally competitive. In such businesses the market is split between customers who select their suppliers on economic grounds and customers that are state-owned or state-influenced and evidence strong preference for some control over their suppliers. Products, such as computers or integrated circuits, are of sufficient strategic and economic importance for host governments to try to have some control over their technology and their production.[15] In such industries governments try to restrict the strategic freedom of all multinationals and show great willingness to reward flexibility. Honeywell, for instance, was liberally rewarded for agreeing to create a joint venture between its French subsidiary and Compagnie Internationale pour l'Informatique, the ailing leader of the French computer industry. In addition to favored access to the French state-controlled markets, the joint venture received substantial grants and research contracts.

In these industries where both the economic and political imperatives are critical, multinationals face the most difficult choice between various possible strategies. Some companies may choose to integrate their operations multinationally, and some may choose to decentralize their operations to better match the demands of individual governments and benefit from their support and assistance. Still others may not make a clear strategic commitment and may instead resort to administrative coordination.

Yet, this choice is likely to look significantly different to various MNCs according to their competitive posture within their industry. In broad terms, *firms with the largest overall shares of the world market are likely to find integration more desirable.* There are several reasons for this choice.

Benefits of Integration. First, still assuming that there are unexploited economies of scale, large firms can achieve lower costs through integration than can smaller firms. The company with the largest overall share of the world market can become the low cost producer in an industry by integrating its operations, thus making life difficult for smaller competitors. Conversely, smaller firms (with significant market shares in only a few countries) can remain cost competitive so long as larger competitors do not move to regional or worldwide integration. Firms that integrate across boundaries in a market that is partly price competitive and partly government-controlled, can expect to gain a larger share of the price competitive market and confine smaller competitors to segments protected by governments that value flexibility and control more than lower prices.[16]

Influence. Second, one can hypothesize that larger firms can have more influence on their environment than smaller ones, and thus find it more suitable to centralize strategic decision making and ignore some of the uncertainty and variety in the environment.[17] In particular, larger firms can take a tougher stance vis-à-vis individual governments when needed, and woo them with higher costs of good citizenship. How much integrated firms may be willing to give to host governments as costs of citizenship to maintain strategic integration may vary substantially. One can argue that a leading integrated firm in a partly government-controlled market with no comparable direct competitor (IBM, for instance), may be willing to provide a lot to host countries in order to maintain its integration. Conversely, when keen worldwide competition takes place among integrated-companies of comparable strength (e.g., Texas Instruments, Motorola, and Fairchild), the economic imperative becomes much more demanding for each of them, and none may be willing to be accommodating for fear that the others would not match such behavior. In short, the following proposition can be made: *the more one integrated firm is submitted to direct competition from other integrated companies, the less it will be willing to provide host governments, except in exchange for profitable non-matchable moves.*

The implications of this proposition in terms of public policy toward industry structure are significant. At the regional or worldwide level it raises the issue of whether to encourage competition, or to favor the emergence of a single integrated leading MNC and then bargain with that company on the sharing of revenues. Similarly, a significant industrial policy issue at the national level is whether to encourage competition, or to provide a single multinational with the opportunity for a profitable nonmatchable move.[18]

Conversely, smaller firms (such as Honeywell in comparison with IBM) could draw only lesser benefits from rationalization and had to be extremely flexible in dealing with the uncertainties represented by host governments. Thus, *smaller firms are likely to find administrative coordination more suitable and will enlist host governments' support and subsidies to compete against leading MNCs.* Market access protection, financial assistance, or both can be the only way for these smaller firms—multinational or not—to keep a semblance of competitiveness. In the same way that firms in competitive markets can differentiate their products (or even their strategy) to avoid competing head on against larger firms, firms in these markets under partial government control differentiate their strategy by trading off central control over their strategy for government protection. The willingness of governments to trade off economic efficiency for some amount of political control, as well as the importance of short-term social issues (chiefly employment protection) make such strategic differentiation possible.[19]

For smaller MNCs such differentiation usually involves forgoing integration and letting host governments gain a say in strategic decisions affecting the various subsidiaries. Yet, because the MNC still attempts to maintain some competitiveness in market segments not protected by governments, it is likely to find administrative coordination—despite the ambiguity and managerial difficulty it involves—the least evil.

Finally, national companies can attempt to achieve some economies of scale through interfirm agreements for the joint manufacture of particular components (car engines) or product lines (Airbus A300). Over time, national companies can move to develop a globally integrated system. A case in point is Volkswagen, whose U.S.-assembled "Rabbits" incorporate parts from Brazil, Germany, and Mexico. Where free trade prevails among developed countries, as in the automobile industry, this may be the only suitable strategy for national companies.

In summary, one can hypothesize a relationship between the extent of government control over (and limits to) international trade in an industry, the relative international market share of a firm active in that industry, and the type of strategy it adopts. In industries where free trade prevails, all competitors are expected to have to follow a worldwide (or regional) integration strategy. In industries in which governments take a keen interest, but where they control the markets only partly, and where formal free trade prevails (computers, for instance), all three strategies are likely to coexist within an industry. Finally, in industries where the political imperatives prevail and whose markets are mostly state-controlled, all competitors can be expected to adopt a national responsiveness strategy.

Data supporting the relationship summarized above are presented graphically in Figure 1. It shows the results of the in-depth study of six industries where the economic and the political imperatives strongly conflict. However, one word of caution is necessary here: the patterns shown can only represent the *preferred* strategy of a company. Most companies will have deviant subsidiaries, because within a given industry trade restrictions vary among countries. The figure was built from data in Western Europe, and assumes that in a given industry, trade restrictions are about the same for all countries. That may be approximately true within Western Europe, but is obviously false in other regions. For instance, Ford's European operations achieve integration at the regional level; Ford's other international subsidiaries are much more nationally responsive and often isolated by tough local content restrictions (for instance, in Latin America). In passing, it may

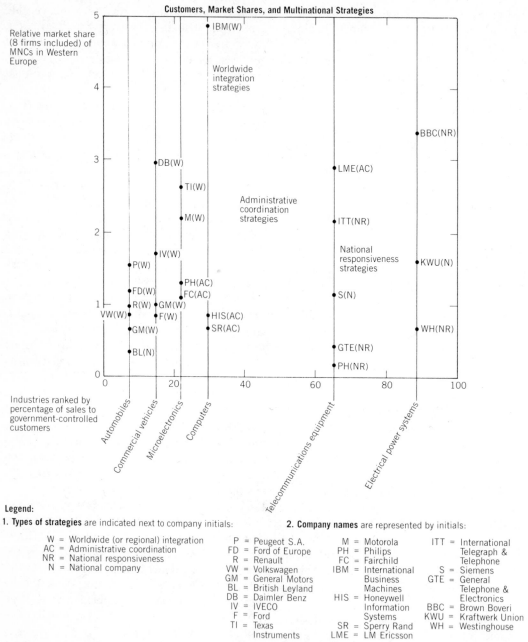

Figure 1 Customers, market shares, and multinational strategies.

be hypothesized that companies with substantial operations in numerous countries (within the same industry) break them up into regional management units when they face wide differences in the conditions of trade among the regions. Obviously, the value added of products with respect to their weight or bulk also plays a role in limiting worldwide integration in a few industries where the value added per unit of weight is very high, and economies of scale and/or factor cost differences among regions are substantial (e.g., microelectronics).

Technology

Technology is usually seen as an important variable in the interface between MNCs and host governments. The introduction by MNCs of many innovative high technology products and the high market shares they still enjoy in their sales create much tension with host governments. Major industries, such as computers, microelectronics, or aerospace, remain dominated by U.S. multinationals. In tensions between economic and political imperatives within an industry, technology then plays a key role. MNCs that control the technology of specific industries have more power in bargaining with governments and also create technology barriers to competition from national firms. Often the minimal scale requirements increase so rapidly in high technology industries as to make it almost impossible for national firms to catch up.[20]

Technology, Trade, and Strategic Integration. Higher technology products are likely to correspond to freer trade. First, there is ample evidence that MNCs most often introduce their innovations in their home markets first.[21] So long as the new technology is not adopted by many countries, freer trade is likely to prevail for newer products than for older ones. Second, during the technology diffusion process within the MNC, the need to transfer the new technology quickly to subsidiaries creates pressures to increase coordination among them. Companies thus find it more desirable and easier to integrate regionally or to tilt their administrative coordination toward more integration. In terms of the graphics of Figure 1, a new higher technology can be represented by a move to the left. The move can affect a given industry as a whole if the technology is available to all MNCs but not to any national company, or more likely the move can be firm-specific.

In the study of the telecommunications industry, both moves were found. First, the shift to electronic switching and digital coding led the industry as a whole to be characterized by freer trade and by the opening of markets to new suppliers, as the various national PTTs were deciding upon their first orders for new equipmen in the 1970s. Second, within the industry, L. M. Ericsson has always tried to be "one step ahead" of its competitors in technology, and to run its operations in a more integrated way than its competition. Conversely, ITT has most often been a technology follower, but let its subsidiaries be quite responsive to the demands of their host governments. It can be hypothesized that, *within an industry where the political imperatives are significant, higher technology firms (relative to their competitors) strive for integration, and can achieve some measure of it, and lower technology firms (relative to their competitors) strive for national responsiveness.*

Technology, Scale, and Government Intervention. It is also important to recognize that technological evolution can increase the minimal efficient scale of an industry and call to question the viability of national responsiveness. Even where restricted trade prevails, as the efficient scale increases in a high technology industry, pressures grow for domestic mergers and rationalization. Where multinational and national firms compete, the multinationals are unlikely to be the winners in a merger drive. Government interest is likely to prompt mergers into the "national champion" rather than to let the national industry be entirely controlled from outside. A national responsiveness strategy, i.e., a rather autonomous national subsidiary, makes such mergers into a national champion easier for the government to implement.

The examples of the French electrical power industry and telecommunications equipment in France and Great Britain tend to confirm the above analysis. In the case of electrical power systems, the transition from fossil fuel boilers to nuclear steam supply not only led to higher minimal efficient scale in the manufacture of turbogenerators, but also increased the interests of host governments in the industry. Two distinct effects were thus combined: minimal size increase and governments' greater interest in the technology itself.[22]

The Influence of Technology. This leaves us with less than a full understanding of the role of technology in the interface between MNCs and host governments in developed countries. On the one hand, for a given industry, a move to higher technology and new products can permit a firm (or all firms in an industry if they have access to the new technology) to be more multinationally integrated and centrally managed than it would otherwise be. There is some unclear causal relationship here, as integration is made possible by higher technology but is also required to facilitate technology transfer within the MNC.[23] On the other hand, it seems that very high technologies become extremely important in developed countries and prompt governments to try to narrowly control their development and use. Also, the move to higher technology often results in larger minimal efficient scale. This scale can be used by integrated multinationals to defend their market shares and attack smaller or less integrated firms, e.g., in microelectronics. In industries where trade is restricted, the government's usual responses are mergers into an emerging "national champion" first, and development of multinational government-sponsored programs second.

In both cases multinationals do not stand to benefit. This was clearly the case in electrical power systems. Telecommunications equipment was more ambiguous. Some countries were moving toward national consolidation (Brazil, France, the U.K.), and in others new electronic technology resulted in more open markets (Australia, South Africa, Spain, and several small European countries). Electronic technologies obviously increased the importance of the industry, yet provided opportunities to more integrated firms (e.g., L. M. Ericsson) or national firms with a distinctive technology (e.g., C.I.T. Alcatel). When technology increases both the pressures to integrate within the industry and the interest governments take in the industry, either integration within MNCs across boundaries or integration within a country through a government-directed merger can prevail.

Managerial Implications

In practice, it is important to an MNC, or to executives running individual businesses in diversified multinationals, to recognize those changes in market openness, industry structure, and technology of an industry that foreshadow a need to change the overall strategy. Two simple examples are illuminating. Until the mid-1970s, General Motors ran its international operations as a collection of nationally responsive autonomous subsidiaries. With the globalization of the industry and the rationalization and integration of key competitors (mainly Ford), this posture became untenable. The strongest of the subsidiaries, Adam Opel in Germany was able to hold its own in Europe, competing as a national company. But other subsidiaries, particularly Vauxhall in the U.K., were severely hurt. In 1975, General Motors started to bring the various subsidiaries together more closely through a series of administrative changes. By 1978, these moves resulted in an administrative coordination approach where numerous contradictions and ambiguities emerged. GM Overseas Operations' top management considered such administrative coordination as a transitional stage toward global integration. Many GMOO managers, however, felt that contradictions between the lingering desire for national subsidiaries' responsiveness and the emerging worldwide integration needs would not be easily resolved. In any case, the company had missed several precious years and had to struggle hard to remain competitive in Europe.

Conversely, in the late 1960s, Westinghouse was looking for acquisitions in the European electrical power system industry. It hoped to expand its business in Europe quickly, thanks to its light water nuclear reactor technology that was emerging as a clear technological winner over indigenous European technologies. To ''better'' manage its European operations, Westinghouse moved to a worldwide product group structure, aiming at multinational integration. At the same time, as we have seen, the increased minimal scale of the industry, the strategic importance of nuclear-related technologies, and the failure of Europe's own efforts in commercial reactors all combined to increase government sensitiveness about the industry. The discrepancy between the national responsiveness demanded by governments and what Westinghouse appeared willing to provide resulted in tensions in Belgium, France, and Germany, a substantial scale-down of Westinghouse's European expansion plans, and a shift in its strategy. In 1975, a former president of Westinghouse's Power Group commented to the author: ''Our basic policy (for nuclear engineering and power plants sales) is to do it in whatever way a country would require.'' Yet, Westinghouse had probably lost the one opportunity to become a lasting factor in the European power system industry.

CHOICE OF STRATEGY AND MANAGEMENT PROCESS

We have seen that both worldwide (or regional) integration and national responsiveness lead to relatively straightforward management processes that are grounded in a clear strategy and a clear-cut delineation of headquarters,' and subsidiaries' roles and responsibilities. Yet, the relative managerial simplicity both these strategies offer has an opportunity cost: it makes specific adjustment to the varying demands of governments difficult, and may prevent the company from entering certain businesses or certain countries. Such limitations make administrative coordination attractive as a way to increase the MNC's flexibility in finding balances between the economic and the political imperatives that match more closely the specific conditions of a given business in a given country. It is important to recognize that both worldwide integration and national responsiveness almost represent ideal polar opposites. Some MNCs are likely not to wish (or be able) to exercise a clear choice, and thus find themselves improvising compromises through some process of administrative coordination.

In particular, when the political imperative is significant, its very nature makes clear-cut analytical choices impossible. Contrary to the economic imperative, information on the political imperative is most often indirect and not controllable centrally. When a subsidiary manager claims that his plans rest on the word of local intermediaries or on his relationships with national government officials, it is difficult, at best, for managers at headquarters to determine the soundness of his assumptions. The fact that the government's public logic is often quite different from the reality of the situation and from actual policy-making processes, makes it even more difficult for corporate or regional managers to understand the situation. As a result, top management's inability to reach an analytical choice on decisions involving the political imperative leads to adaptive coalitional decision making in which the firm internalizes tensions and uncertainties and tries to incorporate them into its decision-making process.

Decision Processes and Administrative Coordination

On any particular strategic decision, the company is trying to reach a satisfactory compromise given past decisions and past commitments of resources. Decisions cannot be left to either the subsidiary or the regional (or global) headquarters levels. They have to be reached by some group that collectively captures contradictions in the environment, internalizes them, and resolves them through contention, coalition, and consensus. Individual managers, representing different interests within the company and approaching questions from different points of view, are left to take sides on decisions according to how they perceive problems and how they prefer to deal with sources of uncertainty. In short, the question of deciding "what is right" becomes linked to that of "who is right" and "whose views are favored." Top management, instead of providing the inspiration for a strategic design and managing its implementation, shifts to a new role of deciding how to make decisions; who should be represented, with which voice, on which decisions. Top management can also provide some limits: would such decisions represent too wide a departure from the usual to be accepted? Choices on how to reach decisions can still be guided by a sense of which decisions, or which classes of decisions, should be made with integration as a priority, and which should be made with responsiveness as a priority. The way to convey such sense of priority is not to decide in substance on specific decisions (except when irreconcilable conflicts occur) but to act on the way in which decisions are made, to influence the making and undoing of specific coalitions or to help the shift of coalitions among decisions.

Managing Dependencies. How can top management achieve such influence? Primarily by keeping control of dependencies between subunits competing for power and by regulating the game they pursue. Strategic and operational dependencies can be used to determine who, in the long run, has power over which class of decisions or what functions. For instance, the subsidiaries can be made dependent on the corporate headquarters or on domestic product divisions for key components or for process technology. Conversely, the domestic divisions can be dependent on subsidiaries for export sales. A central difficulty of this approach is the divisiveness introduced within the company by managing dependencies through arm's-length power relationships. Top management also has to develop some integrative forces (for instance, through training, career paths, and compensation) to balance these divisive forces and preserve some sense of corporate identity and loyalty.

Over the long run, successful administrative coordination thus hinges on the maintenance of a balance between divisive and integrative forces that reflects a structure of dependencies among subunits. Careful control of the dependencies between national subsidiary managers, and product unit managers through the use of functional managers and administrative managers, was found to provide top management tools for maintaining such a balance.

Functional Managers. The substantive expertise of functional managers is needed by supporters of multinational integration as well as by supporters of national responsiveness. Managers preferring multinational integration still depend upon functional managers and "the field" (in various countries) to achieve such integration. Conversely, national managers depend on support from functional and administrative headquarters staff and product divisions even though they try to pursue national responsiveness strategies. Because the power of functional managers is based on needed expertise, they may preserve a relatively uncommitted posture between multinational integration and national responsiveness.

Yet functional managers, over time, can develop a functional logic that is aligned to either national responsiveness or worldwide integration. Manufacturing staffs, for instance, can develop a logic that calls for integration and rationalization or for flexible local plants serving separate national markets. Within each function, of course, further distinctions can develop. For instance, rationalized component plants and local-for-local end-product plants can be favored, or distribution channels can be perceived as very different, whereas similar advertising can be used. By influencing corporate functional managers directly in the development of their preference for integration or responsiveness, and by then bringing them to throw their weight to particular issues and not to others, top management can develop a repertoire of intervention methods on the making of particular decisions.

Administrative Managers. Administrative procedures and the managers in charge of them can also be used by top management to maintain the tension between integration and responsiveness. To begin with, the formal structure usually provides a dominant orientation. Even when this structure is a matrix, it is usually complemented by fairly elaborate administrative procedures and guidelines that provide a dominant orientation by defining who is responsible for what and whether it is a primary or a secondary responsibility. Various devices, such as committees and task forces that cut across the formal structure, can be used to bring about changes in perception or to reach actual decisions. Planning processes can also be designed so that integration and responsiveness are considered. For instance, a contention process can exist between subsidiaries and product divisions (e.g., L. M. Ericsson). Interestingly, IBM had such a system very formalized and well developed among its regions and product groups, and between them and corporate functional staffs. Measurement systems can be set so that managers will see it as their duty to call to top management's attention ''excessive'' integration, autonomy, or responsiveness (e.g., GTE[24] or GM). Personal reward and punishment systems may be designed to reinforce tensions or ease them according to the measurement criteria and yardsticks used. Management of career paths can also be used to provide multiple views and facilitate coordination.

Administrative staff managers, and the way they design and run their administrative sys-

tems, provide top management with the same type of leverage as functional managers. One can expect the controller to strive for uniformity of accounting practices and comparability of results worldwide, opposing differentiation between subsidiaries. Personnel management, on the other hand, can either favor uniformity of pay scales and benefits worldwide, or leave this decision to subsidiaries. The way in which the administrative function develops its own operating paradigm[25] can be managed so that its specific procedures support responsiveness or integration.

Dangers of Administrative Coordination

Even with the potential offered by functional and administrative managers for managing administrative coordination effectively, certain drawbacks are inescapable. In particular, administrative coordination may lead to strategic paralysis, fragmentation, or bureaucratization.

Strategic Paralysis. The willingness to respond to environmental changes when the environment is intrinsically ambiguous and contradictory is likely to lead to strategic paralysis. Students of ambiguous situations where several environments are relevant to decisions have stressed the danger of paralysis created by giving relatively equal power to managers most sensitive to different aspects of the environment.[26] Not using a stable pattern of resource commitment over time, according to spelled out goals, may lead to considerable waste and overall failure. It is fascinating to see that, in an environment where IBM is a strong leader, the agreements on the merger between C2I and Honeywell Bull in France spelled out a substantive strategy to avoid the risk of strategic paralysis. On the other hand, one could draw numerous examples of strategic paralysis from very refined, stable administrative coordination processes.[27]

Strategic Fragmentation. Administrative coordination involves the use of dependencies and the management of power, which create divisive forces. In the absence of a strategic design, the management groups' loyalty must be maintained lest managers' frustrations lead to increasingly disjointed and partial decisions and to fragmentation. Cultural identity is often a means to circumvent these divisive forces. For instance, all top managers at L. M. Ericsson come from the same Stockholm telecommunications engineering school; the whole top management of Philips remains Dutch and has gone through the same formative experiences. Similarly, strong cultural identity facilitates the foreign expansion of Japanese companies.

Bureaucratization. Managers faced with very uncertain situations and power relationships may be tempted to reduce their perceived uncertainties. By developing bureaucratic procedure to cope with uncertainties, managers will gain power for themselves. Bureaucratic procedure also creates uncertainties for other members of the organization.[28] This leads to bureaucratization and lack of sensitivity to the outside environment. More time is spent on infighting than on external action.

Even assuming that administrative coordination does not lead to strategic paralysis, fragmentation, or bureaucracy, it remains an expensive way to run a business. The internal management process, with its multiple negotiations and complex coalitional processes, consumes much managerial energy and time, and can slow down decision processes considerably. It can also lead to "horse trading" and more suboptimal decisions than would be warranted by the situation at hand.

Should administrative coordination be avoided wherever possible, then? The answer is probably yes, but with the qualifications developed in the first part of this article. When free trade prevails and competitors follow a worldwide integration strategy, a clear choice should be made between committing enough resources to a business and divestment. In industries where governments evince interest, administrative coordination seems, at best, to be a way for the weaker, smaller international com-

panies to stay in certain industries (Honeywell in data processing, Philips in integrated circuits). In industries where trade is restricted, the alternative is between national responsiveness and administrative coordination. For technology leaders within their industry, administrative coordination makes sense, as it can possibly provide for easier technology transfer, and host governments can accept such coordination as a price for receiving the technology.

STRATEGY IN THE DIVERSIFIED MULTINATIONAL[29]

So long as the several businesses of the multinational rely on the same strategy, the overall corporate management task is not greatly complicated by business diversity. Texas Instruments uses one extreme posture which applies the same semiconductor business logic and global integration framework across the board to all of its businesses.

Another extreme would be a multinational conglomerate adopting a purely financial approach and letting each business develop its own business logic independently. Yet, in most cases, such simple solutions as that of Texas Instruments or the multinational conglomerate are not applicable: the various businesses of the diversified multinational straddle several adaptation patterns and are interdependent. This raises the issues of strategic and administrative differentiation among the businesses, and of managing the interdependencies among differentiated businesses.

Differentiation and Interdependencies

Difficulties develop when the various businesses of a multinational straddle several adaptation patterns; some are most suitably managed through global strategic integration, others through administrative coordination, and still others through national responsiveness. It usually happens that, because of a history of dominance in one business, one pattern is preferred and applied across the board. For instance, Brown Boveri was slow to recognize that its industrial businesses, particularly small motors and breakers, would be faced with worldwide competition following the EEC trade liberalization. When competition came, Brown Boveri was even slower to react, because the logic of the whole organization and the energy of top management were geared to success in the government-controlled, restricted trade power system and heavy electrical equipment businesses.

In a similar vein, after World War II, Philips had strong national organizations and weak worldwide product groups coordinating its activities. With freer trade (following the development of the EEC), moves were made to increase the power of product divisions and to foster integration in similar businesses between national organizations. This led to a balanced product-geography-function matrix that faced great difficulties in businesses where administrative coordination did not fit well. Businesses, such as TV picture tubes or standard semiconductors, did not achieve full integration at a regional (color TV) or global (semiconductors) level, and telecommunications equipment did not enjoy sufficient national autonomy to achieve responsiveness comparable to that of competitors.

An obvious response to the difficulties faced by Brown Boveri or Philips is to differentiate the management among product lines, letting each find the appropriate balance between the economic and the political imperatives.

Yet, extensive interdependencies among businesses would usually make this management differentiation difficult. Interdependencies are of several types. They can involve common technologies among several businesses. For instance, magnetic tape technology at Philips served several product groups: data systems, instrumentation, medical products, professional recording, and audio consumer products. Interdependencies can also derive from vertical integration. The bulk of Philips's electronic component production was transferred internally to be incorporated into Philips's end products; still Philips also wanted to compete on the open market for semiconductors. Interdependencies are also market related, with different products sold to the same customers. IBM's Data Processing Complex's and General Business Group's system offerings overlap at the lower end of medium systems and compete against each other for the same orders. Finally, when products are sold to government-controlled customers, interdependencies may become political. Brown Boveri was commonly told: "We are willing to import your power stations, but what about you creating an export-oriented motor plant in one of our depressed areas to generate employment and offset the trade deficit that importing your power stations would create?"

It is important to recognize the difference in nature between internal interdependencies (common technology, joint production, vertical integration) and external ones (same customers, host governments, and so forth). When interdependencies are internal, the choice of how to relate businesses (from pure arm's length to joint administration) can be made by management. When interdependencies are external, such choice is usually imposed by external agents. The terms under which to coordinate component and TV set production could be decided internally in Philips. However, the Belgian Government's orders for Philips's computers were conditional upon the maintenance of Philips's employment levels in Belgium. The consumer product groups, whose internal interdependencies with the computer group were negligible, but who had high cost factories they wanted to close down in Belgium, suffered from the deal. Allegedly, this problem played some role in Philips's decision to withdraw from the mainframe computer business entirely.

Managing Interdependencies

The central tradeoff in the examples presented above is that between strategic and administrative clarity for individual businesses (i.e., enabling clear choices to be made between worldwide integration and national responsiveness), and the complexity of managing interdependencies.

Developing some clarity usually involves selectivity in the management of interdependencies. It is important to recognize that, within a diversified multinational, the relative importance of various interdependencies may change over time as the "critical factors"[30] in the strategy of a business evolve. ITT was able to revise frequently the formal structure of its European operations to respond to changes in the relative importance of interdependencies. The basic method used by ITT was to organize itself into several product groups worldwide. Each of these was managed somewhat differently: the Automotive Group (auto parts and accessories) and the Microelectronics Group, for instance, were pursuing worldwide integration strongly, whereas the Telecommunications Equipment Group stuck to its national responsiveness strategy. The Business Systems Group pursued regional integration in Europe. Individual businesses could be moved among these groups as warranted by competitive, technological, and government intervention changes. In the mid-1970s, ITT moved the private telephone exchange switching product line from the Telecommunications Equipment Group to the Business Systems Group, where it joined other office equipment. The successful adaptation of electronic switching technology to private exchange and the penetration of the private exchange market by such aggressive, integrated firms as IBM had shifted the key dependency from technology (Telecommunications Equipment Group) to marketing (Business Systems Group). In a similar vein, when ITT adopted worldwide strategic integration for its microelectronics business, it spun off the telecommunication-related components to the Telecommunications Equipment Group. Also ITT decreased the interdependencies between microelectronics and telecommunications in order to achieve a clear strategy for each business.

The development of clarity for Brown Boveri and Philips was more difficult than for ITT. Because they were less widely diversified (most of their products were related), they could not reduce any interdependencies easily. Yet some of their businesses were subject to worldwide product standardization and price competition (for instance, radios at Philips and motors at BBC), and others were more affected by regional or national differences (power systems at BBC, hi-fi at Philips). These different competitive conditions led to divergent strategic directions among businesses.

An approach to interbusiness coordination, under such circumstances, that is being tried by several companies, is the use of corporate functional staff in conjunction with planning committees. At Brown Boveri, corporate marketing staffs coordinated the activities of the various national subsidiaries product line by product line. It was between various members of the corporate marketing staffs that tradeoffs between businesses could be made and the interdependencies could be managed. Assisting the corporate marketing staff in the strategic coordination of each business were several levels of committees. Some of these committees were functional and others were product-oriented. Functional committees could coordinate certain types of interdependencies among technologies and markets of several product groups. Other committees regrouped product division managers of the different subsidiaries and were in charge of managing the regional integration/national responsiveness tradeoffs. Unfortunately, the committees often lacked the consensus necessary for action, as each member adopted a parochial view.

Faced with similar problems, IBM gave operating units the right to formally take issue with the plans of other operating units ("nonconcurrence" in IBM's internal language) that would impact their activities adversely. Through this approach IBM was able to force subunits to consider interdependencies in their planning and budgeting process and to reach a joint solution before their plans could be approved. Top management could also take the initiative of presenting key strategic issues that would require coordination between subunits as "focus issues" to be dealt with explicitly in the planning process.[31] Other companies also sometimes pulled key interdependencies of great strategic importance out of the regular structure: Brown Boveri, for instance, established a separate nuclear policy committee with the task of managing all interdependencies relating to nuclear energy.

Despite the efforts described above, the management of interdependencies raises difficult issues. Because costs and benefits of interdependencies lend themselves to ambiguous conflicting interpretations, interdependencies provide a rich arena for power plays and coalition bargaining. While particular coalition configurations seem endless in their variety, they add to the task of strategic management. Furthermore, coalitions often involve external agents. For instance, individual managers can rely on their government to establish linkages among product groups. It is not uncommon for alliances to develop, at least tacitly, between host governments and subsidiaries to decrease the dependence of the subsidiary on headquarters and to develop "binding" commitments with the government.

Faced with such difficulties, the MNC corporate management level is likely to strive for administrative uniformity across businesses. Yet, unless all businesses can be successful with the same strategic logic, some degree of differentiation between businesses remains necessary. In short, uniformity is impossible when businesses straddle several adaptation patterns. Uniformity is possible on some aspects (financial reporting and measurement at ITT, for instance), provided that great leeway for differentiation is left to other aspects. Yet, to avoid cognitive overload at the corporate management level, there are strong pressures toward administrative uniformity, thus making the substance of decisions at the business unit level accessible to the corporate level in a common

format. Such administrative pressure for uniformity may prevent the appropriate strategic differentiation among businesses and the development of strategic clarity. These necessary strategic and administrative differentiations suggest that it is usually not possible to maintain unitary corporate office dealing with the substance of decisions. Similarly, a diversified multinational needs (beyond the divisionalized form) a corporate office that only manages selected aspects of the operations and influences decision processes while leaving room for differentiation among businesses—unless all follow the same worldwide integration strategy.

As a concluding note for this section, it may be hypothesized that the complex multinational structures, usually called matrix (or grid) and mixed types, represent an attempt by diversified MNCs to respond to the problems of combining the development of a strategy for each business with the need to manage interdependencies between businesses. Thus, they are not aberrant or transitory structural stages only. Matrix structures correspond to the corporate desire to manage interdependencies among businesses while allowing strategic integration to develop. Mixed structures correspond to a clear differentiation and separation between businesses that follow different adaptation patterns.

CONCLUSION—COMBINING STRATEGIC CLARITY AND ADMINISTRATIVE COORDINATION?

The most difficult tradeoff for the diversified MNC is the one between clarity at the business level (multicountry integration or national responsiveness) and the benefits derived from operating and strategic interdependencies between businesses. The added complexity, compared to domestic diversified companies, of coping with broader environmental variety, makes the management of interdependencies less straightforward and more difficult.

Some simplification can be obtained by limiting and buffering interdependencies. For instance, at L. M. Ericsson, the national subsidiaries were dependent upon the center for components and technology, but the center could be severed from any subsidiary without great difficulty. Interdependencies between subsidiaries were negligible. Japanese companies usually adopted similar approaches to manage their joint ventures abroad. Philips was treating its semiconductor acquisition in the U.S., Signetics, differently from its European operations, leaving much strategic freedom to the company. So both operating and strategic interdependencies can be structured in such a way as to minimize the need for managing them. There is a tradeoff between the complexity of managing many interdependencies and the joint benefits they bring.

One way companies have tried to order the above tradeoff is to manage simultaneously along several dimensions. For instance, as the Dow Chemical matrix was becoming unbalanced, the operating responsibilities moved toward area executives, thus providing regional integration across vertically interdependent businesses at the area level (Europe, Far East, etc.). Yet, a Corporate Product Department was created with veto power over strategic resource allocation and control over interdependencies between areas.[32] Administrative systems were used by Dow to provide autonomy for regional strategic integration, except for the planning and resource allocation process that was used to check strategic integration and keep the autonomy of areas within bounds.

In an even more discriminating way, IBM's strategic planning process provided for functions, product lines, and areas (or countries) to be managed jointly in a cohesive process. At various stages during the process, inputs and control points were set up so that both the need for integration in relevant units (that differed between functions, businesses, and areas of the world) and the administrative coordination needed between interdependent businesses

were recognized, in turn, and conflicts were resolved through a contention process.

ITT was not only letting different businesses develop their own strategies, but also used the various management levels differently. Regional headquarters controlled product and business strategies, but their weight, compared to that of national subsidiary managers, varied considerably from one business to another. The overall planning process was managed from worldwide product group headquarters in New York. Finally, measurement control, and evaluation were corporate level responsibilities.

More research is needed to conceptualize adequately the responses of these companies. However, these companies illustrate very sophisticated methods for providing both strategic integration and administrative coordination according to the needs for strategic focus and operating or strategic interdependencies between subunits.

NOTES

1. See, for instance, L. G. Franko, *The European Multinationals* (Stamford, Conn.: Greylock, 1976).
2. See, for instance, J. Dunning and M. Gilman, "Alternative Policy Prescriptions," in *The Multinational Enterprise in a Hostile World,* ed. Curzon and Curzon (London: Macmillan & Co., 1977); also see R. Vernon, *Storm over the Multinationals* (Cambridge, Mass.: Harvard University Press, 1977); and R. Vernon, *Sovereignty at Bay* (New York: Basic Books, 1971).
3. See, for instance, C. Stoffaes, *La Grande Menace Industrielle* (Paris: Calmann-Levy, 1977).
4. Some authors have opposed worldwide and regional management within MNCs. See J. M. Stopford and L. T. Wells, Jr., *Managing the Multinational Enterprise* (New York: Basic Books, 1972). The evidence in the companies studied suggests that in either case a business strategy responding to the economic imperative underlies regional or worldwide management. Which strategy is preferred in a particular company depends upon cost analysis based primarily on difference in factor costs, freight rates, and barriers to trade between various countries and regions of the world. In terms of responsiveness to individual country policies, there is little difference between regional and worldwide management. See L. G. Franko, *Joint Venture Survival in Multinational Corporations* (New York: Praeger, Publishers, 1972).

5. See Y. Doz, "Managing Manufacturing Rationalization within Multinational Companies," *Columbia Journal of World Business,* Fall 1978.

6. See R. Vernon, "The Location of Economic Activity," in *Economic Analysis and the Multinational Corporation,* ed. Dunning (London: Allen and Unwin, 1974).

7. Ford's costs are estimated by the author from various industry interviews. For many product families, experience curve models suggested unit cost levels in smaller European firms equal to several times the costs in such firms as Texas Instruments for integrated circuits or Motorola for discrete semiconductors. Exact figures are not public, but their significance can be deducted from the Boston Consulting Group and Mackintosh publications. Large losses among European national semiconductor companies and private communications about losses in Philips's or Siemens's semiconductor businesses support the same point. See P. Gadonneix, "Le Plan Calcul," DBA diss., Harvard Business School, 1974.

8. See D. G. Bradley, "Managing against Expropriation," *Harvard Business Review,* July–August 1977, pp. 75–83; and B. D. Wilson, "The Disinvestment of Foreign Subsidiaries by U.S. Multinational Companies," DBA diss., Harvard Business School, 1979.

9. For political strategies, see J. Zysman, *Political Strategies for Industrial Order* (Berkeley: University of California Press, 1976); Y. Doz, *Government Control and Multinational Strategic Management* (New York: Praeger Publishers, 1979). For economic strategies, see U. Wiechmann, "Integrating Multinational Marketing Activities," *Columbia Journal of World Business,* Winter 1974. Wiechmann studied intensively the food and beverage industries.

10. For a comprehensive treatment of strategy as an optimal fit between environmental opportunities and threats and the organizational strengths and weaknesses (consistent with the personal values of top management and the social responsibilities of the corporation), see K. R. Andrews, *The Concept of Corporate Strategy* (Homewood, Ill.: Dow Jones–Irwin, 1971); and D. Braybrooke and C. E. Lindblom, *A Strategy of Decision* (New York: The Free Press, 1963).

11. On strategic planning, see, for example, G. A. Steiner, *Top Management Planning* (New York: Macmillan, 1966); H. I. Ansoff, *Corporate Strategy* (New York: McGraw-Hill, 1965); and P. Lorange and R. F. Vancil, eds., *Strategic Planning Systems* (Englewood Cliffs, N.J.: Prentice-Hall, 1977). On "muddling through," see Braybrooke and Lindblom (1963); R. Cyert and J. March, *A Behaviorial Theory of the Firm* (Englewood Cliffs, N.J., Prentice-Hall, 1963); and J. D. Steinbruner, *The Cybernetic Theory of Decision* (Princeton, N.J.: Princeton University Press, 1974).

12. For instance, see S. M. Davis and P. R. Lawrence, *Matrix* (Reading, Mass.: Addison-Wesley, 1977).

13. See N. Jéquier, *Les Télécommunications et l'Europe* (Geneva: Centre d'Etudes Industrielles, 1976); and J. Surrey, *World Market for Electric Power Equipment* (Brighton, England: SPRI, University of Sussex, 1972).

14. See O. Williamson, *Markets and Hierarchies: Analysis and Antitrust Implications* (New York: The Free Press, 1975).

15. See Y. S. Hu, *The Impact of U.S. Investment in Europe* (New York: Praeger Publishers, 1973); and N. Jéquier, "Computers," in *Big Business and the State,* ed. R. Vernon (Cambridge, Mass.: Harvard University Press, 1974).

16. There is ample evidence of this phenomenon in the computer and microelectronics industries. See E. Sciberras, *Multinational Electronic Companies and National Economic Policies* (Greenwich, Conn.: JAI Press, 1977); and "International Business Machines: Can the Europeans Ever Compete?" *Multinational Business,* 1973, pp. 37–46.

17. For a discussion of strategic decision making and environmental uncertainty, see E. Rhenman, *Organization Theory for Long-Range Planning* (New York: John Wiley & Sons, 1973).

18. See F. T. Knickerbocker, *Oligopolistic Reaction and Mulitnational Enterprise* (Boston: Harvard Business School Division of Research, 1973).

19. For a discussion of strategic differentiation and competition in a domestic oligopoly, see R. Caves and M. Porter, "From Barrier to Entry to Barrier to Mobility," *Quarterly Journal of Economics,* May 1977.

20. For instance, see Vernon (1977), Chap. 3. The evolution of industries such as nuclear power or aerospace is revealing. As the technology for a given product (e.g., light water nuclear reactors or bypass turbofan jet engines) becomes more widespread, the bargaining power of MNCs is eroded. See H. R. Nau, *National Politics and International Technology* (Baltimore, Md.: Johns Hopkins University Press, 1974); for lesser developed countries, see N. Fagre and L. T. Wells, "Bargaining Power of Multinationals and Host Governments" (Mimeo, 14 July 1978); on increasing economies of scale, for instance, see M. S. Hochmuth, "Aerospace," in *Big Business and the State,* ed. R. Vernon (Cambridge, Mass.: Harvard University Press, 1974).

21. Innovations in mature products are an occasional exception. They are sometimes introduced in the most competitive market. For instance, Sony introduced several innovations in the U.S. before introducing them in Japan. Yet many other Sony innovations were first introduced in Japan. For a summary, see Vernon (1977), Chap. 3.

22. See Doz (1979). For recent evidence, see "ITT Fights U.K. Bid for Plessey Control of STC," *Electronic News,* Vol. 23, October 1978, p. 4. On electrical power, see B. Epstein, *The Politics of Trade in Power Plants* (London: The Atlantic Trade Center, 1972); Central Policy Review Staff, *The Future of the United Kingdom Power Plant Manufacturing Industry* (London: Her Majesty's Station-

ery Office, 1976); and Commission des Communautés Européenes, *Situation et Perspective des Industries des Gros Equipements Electromécaniques et Nucléaires liés à la Production d'Energie de la Communauté* (Brussels: CEE, 1976). For related data on the U.S., see I. Bupp, Jr. and J. C. Derian, *Light Water: How the Nuclear Dream Dissolved* (New York: Basic Books, 1978).

23. See J. Behrman and H. Wallender, *Transfers of Manufacturing Technology Within Multinational Enterprises* (Cambridge, Mass.: Ballinger, 1976).

24. For a detailed analysis of GTE and L. M. Ericsson's administrative mechanisms, see Doz (1979).

25. Used here in the sense given by Steinbruner (1974), as the simplifying logic used by a particular function to reduce complexity in its environment by focusing on a few key parameters and taking cybernetic decisions based on them.

26. See Davis and Lawrence (1977); and C.K. Prahalad, "The Strategic Process in a Multinational Company," D.B.A. diss., Harvard Business School, 1975.

27. See C. K. Prahalad and Y. Doz, "Strategic Change in the Multidimensional Organization," Harvard Business School–University of Michigan Working Paper, October 1979.

28. See M. Crozier, *The Bureaucratic Phenomenon* (Chicago: University of Chicago Press, 1964); and D. J. Hickson et al., "A Strategic Contingencies' Theory of Intraorganizational Power," *Administrative Science Quarterly,* Vol. 2, 1971, pp. 216–229.

29. This section draws upon Y. Doz and C. K. Prahalad. "Strategic Management in Diversified Multinationals," in *Functioning of the Multinational Corporation in the Global Context,* ed. A. Negandhi (New York: Pergamon Press, forthcoming).

30. Taken here in the sense of Barnard's "strategic factors" or Selznick's "critical factor." See C. L. Barnard, *The Functions of the Executive* (Cambridge, Mass.: Harvard University Press, 1938); and P. Selznick, *Leadership in Administration* (New York: Harper & Row, 1957).

31. See A. Katz, "Planning in the IBM Corporation," Paper submitted to the TIMS-ORSA Strategic Planning Conference, New Orleans, February 16–17, 1977.

32. See S. M. Davis, "Trends in the Organization of Multinational Corporations," *Columbia Journal of World Business,* Summer 1976, pp. 59–71. Information on Dow Chemical came from the 1976 *Annual Report* and the author's interviews.

SECTION 2
Tools and Techniques for Strategic Planning

Strategic planning provides a framework into which each operating plan of the corporation can be integrated so that the entire multinational corporation (MNC) operates as efficiently as possible everywhere in the world. Major business decisions have to be made about the allocation of limited resources so that firms can take the greatest advantage of opportunities and gain a competitive edge over opponents. Those firms that adopt a comprehensive or global strategy seem to enjoy economic and strategic advantages over locally oriented firms.[1]

As companies grow from domestic firms into MNCs, globally oriented executives shift their primary focus from domestic planning to the management of world opportunities, markets, and world resources. As part of this endeavor, managers must continuously consider and assess both the international and national environments in which their activities are to be carried out as they work within the culture and structure of the firm. There are areas basic to all MNCs from which planning should be formulated, namely (1) methods of entering foreign markets, (2) growth—internal development, (3) geographical diversification, (4) product diversification, (5) product portfolio optimization, (6) foreign exchange risk management, (7) human resources development, and (8) organization structure.[2]

Usually, strategic planning begins with an assessment of the external environment. Based on an analysis of host country economic and social policy, planners try to determine the degree of risk that they are likely to encounter on both the macro and micro levels. In addition to risk, they look at such factors as

[1] William H. Davidson, *Global Strategic Management* (New York: John Wiley & Sons, 1982), p. 11.
[2] Arvin D. V. Phatak, *International Dimensions of Management* (Boston: Kent Publishing Company, 1983), pp. 60–62.

long-term trends in GNP and worldwide levels of technological development. They consider what may happen in the long and short run in industries in which they already operate or may operate in the future. Yet another external environmental issue appropriate for managerial analysis is the behavior of domestic and foreign currencies in world money markets and the opportunities for international financial investment. At all times, competition will have a significant impact on the planning process. The better the sources of information are, the greater will be the ability of the firm to anticipate the actions of others and the impact of world events on local markets.[3]

The second stage of strategic planning is the undertaking of an examination and assessment of the firm's internal strengths and weaknesses. In the financial area, planners have to know the state of their resources, cash flow, long- and short-term availability of capital, their profits, and transferability of funds. In the management of human resources, MNC planners have to take an inventory of the specific functional skills required to assure that the firm uses its capabilities to capacity. Just as the company assesses the likelihood of being able to attract and use capital, it must analyze the potential work force that will fit its requirements. Superior marketing expertise and technological superiority also represent significant advantages for the globally oriented firm.

Once top managers have assessed the external and internal environment of their firm, they begin to set its objectives. Goals are determined for the corporation's products and sales; for geographic expansion or contraction, acquisitions, and divestitures; and for the order in which each should be addressed. As part of the objective-setting process, managers should develop alternative plans of action so that they retain the greatest flexibility. For example, a company might target several countries in which it might expand operations or develop alternative sources to ensure a steady supply of parts or raw materials.

Implementation of corporate objectives should come only after the objectives have been defined and a course of action planned. This strategy determines and defines the design of the company's operations everywhere in the world. The value and accuracy of strategic planning depends upon the collection of reliable data, its careful interpretation, and the development of plans to carry out the carefully designed objectives. The articles in this section deal with critical aspects of the strategic planning process from data collection to implementation.

READING SELECTIONS

Alvin J. Karchere looks at one essential part of the environmental analysis, that is, the state of economic growth worldwide and the ability of the company to forecast what that economy will be in the future. Karchere examines the rele-

---

[3] Davidson, *Global Strategic Management*, p. 15.

vance of economic forecasting in general, and specifically its role in IBM's strategic planning process. IBM, like many other highly divisionalized corporations, centralizes its policymaking at headquarters but decentralizes operations. Forecasting is done by economists at headquarters, regional, and country levels. This iterative process is used to resolve differences of opinion about the results and methodology of the economic forecast and to inform the appropriate management levels if resolution is impossible. Karchere discusses the use of the forecast in microrisk planning and the problems that the company would encounter if the forecast were faulty. He concludes that errors will occur despite the use of the best econometric models and that management will have to plan to deal with these errors.

In "Scanning the International Environment," O'Connell and Zimmerman look at how and why businesses scan for trends and events that shape the strategic decision-making process. In a survey of American and European executives, the authors found that the respondents focused on economic and technological aspects of the environment as those particular ones that shaped their decisions. They tended to reject data based on social, political, and ecological findings. In companies with the best scanning practices, the chief executive officer tied the strategy of the firm to the comprehensive scanning process and then generated questions for the firm's managers based on an analysis of collected data.

Once options are clarified through the collection of internal and external environmental information, managers try to identify "strategic options most relevant to the corporation and to 'narrow down' these options into one best plan."[4] Peter Lorange observes that for MNCs to identify their most relevant strategic options, they must adapt to their environments and must integrate their activities so that they can arrive at the best plan. He identifies four types of MNCs that he places on an organizational continuum from highly product oriented to highly area oriented. The adaptation and integration needs of each type are analyzed for planning purposes. Lorange notes that the two needs shift from one end of the continuum to the other. Costs of planning should be a major consideration in determining the balance between adaptation and integration.

The formulation and implementation of strategy must always be done with the competition in mind. Competitors' actions affect decisions about what markets to enter and the degree of strategic importance to be placed on each kind of product, pricing decision, distribution channel choice and promotion technique. The degree to which MNCs incorporate the impact of the activities of competitors into the strategic planning process may be a major determinant of success.

William Rapp takes the position that companies that want to be internationally competitive must develop an explicit international strategy. The strategy must incorporate, among other factors, a scheme for product market segmenta-

[4] Peter Lorange, A Framework for Strategic Planning in Multinational Corporations," *Long Range Planning,* June, 1976, p. 30.

tion. To be competitive, firms need to dominate a selected group of segments in the world. At any time, the segments may change according to customer grouping and production economics. To appreciate the competitive importance of world market share, companies can examine cost-volume relationships that, when combined with segmentation analysis, demonstrate many reasons for competitive success and failure. Critical to successful performance is the firm's view of the world as a single market made up of discrete market segments.

Bettis and Hall discuss the popularity of the portfolio or SBU (strategic business unit) concept approach to strategic planning. They point out that some managers think of the portfolio concept as a tool to be used in specific situations. Other managers have a broader perception that stresses its use as a complete system for strategic management. Firms turn to the concept to deal with three types of problems: poor financial performance, too rapid growth, and the absence of strategic issues surfacing. The portfolio concept, when applied most effectively, supports the planning skills of the company by giving the firm a common language and set of administrative systems.

5

Economic Forecasting in International Business
Alvin J. Karchere

• • •

Why forecast? A business must forecast because decisions it makes in the present have an impact on the company in the future. For example, a decision to raise prices will affect future demand and future revenue; a decision regarding hiring or plant expansion will affect future supply and future costs. Indeed almost any decision becomes significant because of its future consequences.

Why should a business be concerned with forecasts of the economy? When the economy is expanding, demand is increasing and the demand for a given company's products will, gen-

erally, increase. In the same way, in recession the demand for the average company's products will decrease. A company whose sales are increasing much more rapidly than the average for the economy, because it has a new and desirable product, may find that its sales continue to increase in a recession but it will find that the rate of growth is slower than would be the case in a period of economic expansion. A company that acquires the resources that would be needed to satisfy demand in a period of expansion, and then finds that the economy suffers a recession, will experience costs that could have been avoided. A company that expects recession and therefore reduces its resources and ability to produce, and then finds that the economy expands, will miss sales opportunities or else will have to scurry to acquire additional resources, probably at higher cost. In either

Source: Alfred J. Karchere, "Economic Forecasting in International Business," *The Columbia Journal of World Business,* Winter 1976, pp. 62–69. Copyright © 1976 by the Trustees of Columbia University in the City of New York. Reprinted by permission.

case, it will make less profit than it would have, had it forecast economic activity correctly. A company that makes a generous settlement with the union representing its workers on the expectation that prices generally will be rising rapidly, and that it will be able to recoup the higher wages with higher prices, may find that it is unable to do so if the increase in prices begins to slow down. A company that bids on a contract on the expectation that its raw material prices will remain constant over the life of the contract may suffer serious losses if its raw materials rise rapidly in price.

I have not exhausted the various ways in which forecasts of the economy are important for business decision making but, perhaps, the examples given are sufficient to make the point that good business planning requires forecasts of the economy.

No one disputes the proposition that economists, because of their training, are better prepared than others to make economic forecasts, but why should economists forecast other matters of importance to company planning, such as sales or shipments?

Training in econometrics, which combines economic theory and statistics, gives the economist skills needed to make business forecasts. There is, however, another reason. Economics has given much of its attention to the effect of prices on demand and supply. The term elasticity of demand, for example, is a standard tool of the economist. Defined as the percent change in quantity demanded for a given percent change in price, it is deceptively simple.

In industries where companies produce products that are close substitutes for products of other companies, businessmen are aware that there may be a fairly rapid and large-drop in their sales if they raise the price of their products, while the price of their competitors' similar products are unchanged. The effect may be difficult to forecast with accuracy but, in the circumstances I have described, it is easily perceived. The response of demand for the products of an *industry* is frequently less obvious. A

reduction in the price of an industry's products will result in a substitution of the products of that industry for other industries' products. However, the products of one industry are not usually good substitutes for the products of other industries; therefore the immediate effect may be relatively small and difficult to observe because it may be obscured by other developments such as business cycle movements. In the long run, when the market adjusts fully to the change in price, the effects may be large, but, if the adjustment is stretched over a period of years, measurement of the effect by ordinary rule of thumb methods may be difficult or impossible.

The problem of understanding and measuring the elasticity of demand to a change in price is even harder when the industry's product is not a consumer good which is desired for itself, but is a major item of equipment for making the consumer good that it is ultimately used to produce equipment is derived from the demand for the consumer good that is ultimately used to produce. A reduction in the price of the equipment has as one of its effects a reduction in the price of the consumer good; and therefore an increase in the demand for the consumer good and hence, indirectly, an increase in the demand for the capital equipment. This is not the end of the effects of a reduction in the price of the capital equipment. If the price of that equipment is reduced, the demand for it may be increased because its lower price may encourage its substitution for other more expensive equipment or for labor. This of course is not a complete analysis, but is intended only to suggest some of the complexities.

In circumstances in which the effects of a price reduction are complex and take place over a long period, it is not surprising that businessmen frequently under-estimate the elasticity of demand with respect to price changes. Since circumstances for different companies and industries vary greatly, economic analysis can be helpful in understanding particular situations, and econometrics helpful in obtaining estimates of the elasticity of demand with respect to price changes.

ECONOMICS, FORECASTS AND PLANNING IN IBM

IBM is characterized by centralized control of policy but decentralized management of operations. There are a large number of operating units in IBM, because of the many countries in which IBM operates, and also because of the varied IBM businesses. Each operating unit, where possible, has profit and loss responsibility, and is expected to make its production and sales decisions as independently as possible. The operating unit management is responsible for the development and implementation of its own plan. Prior to implementation, operating plans are reviewed and approved by corporate management.

These characteristics of planning in IBM are not unique. In his study of business planning, which was based on interviews with sixty large U.S. and foreign firms, Gunnar Eliasson concludes that planning is primarily a device for controlling the business ". . . without unduly inhibiting initiative and reducing flexibility. Hence planning is very much a vehicle for delegating routine management out of the Corporate Headquarters." And further ". . . the planning system was often characterized (mostly in U.S. firms) as a means of decentralizing decision making, keeping only the most essential reins for CHQ . . ."[1]

Given these principles of organization and planning how should the work of the economists be organized? The experience of IBM illustrates one way of dealing with this problem. Each IBM affiliate in each of the countries in which IBM operates is responsible for the development and implementation of its own plan. The economic forecast for the country is a critical characteristic of the environment that the affiliate's plan must take into consideration. To prepare the economic forecast each affiliate has one or more full time economists or, in the smaller countries, a part-time economist who also functions in planning or finance. The economist is of the nationality of the country in which the affiliate operates and is responsible to the management of his own company.

The responsibility for the forecast does not end in the IBM affiliate. There is, for example, an IBM headquarters staff for operations in Europe, the Middle East and Africa, located in Paris. There is an economist on that staff. He is responsible to the management in the Paris headquarters for the economic forecasts of the countries in that headquarter's territory. In addition, there is an economics staff in the corporate headquarters of IBM, in the United States, responsible to the corporate management for the same economic forecasts.

With these arrangements, the possibility of three different forecasts for the same country is readily apparent, but the plan reviews in the Paris and corporate headquarters would be nightmares for the managements involved unless, generally, there was prior agreement on the economic forecasts. How could the Paris management for instance review a given affiliate's plan if that plan were predicated on a recession in the plan period and the Paris management was advised by its economist that the economic outlook for that country was expansion?

The purpose of the plan reviews at the various headquarters levels is to have the staffs subject the plans to critical examination to determine whether genuine differences of opinion exist that should be brought to senior management's attention for arbitration and decision. Following this principle, the economists at the country and staff levels have an obligation to inform management whenever they have significant differences of opinion. It is clear, however, that these differences should not arise out of misunderstandings or poor communications. How can these be avoided?

It is important to avoid disagreements on the data when trying to resolve differences about an economic forecast, and for this reason the use of a common data base is of critical importance. When the data base is constructed, differences regarding the appropriate series to monitor for various purposes can be worked out without the tensions associated with disagreements about an economic forecast. At that time responsibility for maintaining and updating the data base should be assigned.

The use of an econometric model also facilitates analysis and discussion of forecast differences. The model is an expression of systematic relationships in the economy. There will of course be factors not included in the model that will affect a particular forecast. In addition, the forecast calculated with a model is conditional on assumptions of economic policy. This provides scope for differences of opinion regarding a forecast. However, if there is prior agreement on the model, the scope for disagreement is a good deal smaller than it would be without a model and the prospects for coming to a common understanding on the forecast are much greater.

Even if there is a common data base and an agreed econometric model, differences can arise because of poor communications. A constant flow of letters, telexes, and telephone conversations, together with periodic meetings, are required to avoid misunderstandings.

With all this, genuine differences of opinion can arise among economists in various positions in IBM. In that case they are required to inform the appropriate managements of their differences and where necessary ask the management to resolve them.

When a business desires to use a common economic forecast for a given country in its plans for various operating units in that country, there is another issue that must be addressed. How does management know that the economic forecast is being well used, or even whether it is being used at all by the various operating units? The most effective way to accomplish this is to ask the economist to examine the plan of the operating unit to determine whether the plan is consistent with the eco-

nomic forecast, and to make that review part of the formal plan review process. This procedure not only will insure that the operating unit does its best to take account of the economic forecast in its plans, but it also will encourage the operating unit to make good consultive use of the economist's interest and ability to make forecasts of the company's business in a way that takes the effects of the economy into account.

There is the possibility of duplication of effort in this review process but this can generally be avoided. The operating unit is generally required to make detailed product forecasts for its supply planning; its plan will be built from a bottom-up approach. The economist, when reviewing the plan, should use an aggregate approach and thus avoid duplicate effort. For this purpose econometrics is a powerful tool. Moreover, it generally will be easier to obtain reliable estimates of the effect of the economy on demand for the products of the operating unit at the aggregative level. In addition, since the demand for the operating unit's products depends on their prices, as well as on economic activity, the economist will develop estimates of the price elasticity of demand for the company's products. In this way, the economist's obligation to review the plan for consistency with the economic outlook will develop into a valuable aggregate cross-check on the operating unit's bottom-up forecast; it will provide estimates of the effect if the economy on the company's sales and shipments; and it also will provide estimates of the price elasticity of demand that will be valuable for other planning purposes.

FORECAST ERROR AND PLANNING

Anyone involved with the practical aspects of business planning knows from hard-won experience that forecasts usually are wrong and frequently wrong by a significant amount. How can the costs of forecast errors be minimized in business planning?

This problem is a difficult one because of its

business planning aspects. The plan is, in part, a commitment made by the operating unit to its corporate headquarters. Within the operating unit, its various subunits have plans that represent their commitments to their own management. The organization responsible for achieving a plan must have conviction in the plan's viability. This can best be achieved if the organization responsible for achieving the plan is also responsible for creating it. The plan, therefore, will be built from the bottom up and not imposed from the top down. This requirement makes the preparation of the plan a lengthy process. If it were imposed from the top it would be possible to use models and computers to make the plan, and this could be done very quickly. The length of the process is such that, in IBM, the operating plan for the two years following the current year is begun in the late spring of the current year and not finished until late November of the current year.

Since the economic forecast must lead the plan process, the forecast for the following year must be made early in the current year. This increases the span of the forecast and tends to increase the error in the forecast for the following year. This lengthy process of plan development makes it desirable to develop a risk plan at the same time the base plan is developed. For example, in the spring of 1974 our base plan for the United States, to which we assigned a 60% subjective probability, called for a continuation of mild recession into 1975. Our risk case, with a subjective probability of 40%, called for the development of a serious recession in 1975. The assignment of the probability told the management and the planning staffs that the economists were uncertain about the economic forecast and this was taken as an indication to take the risk case seriously. As we moved into the fall of 1974 it became apparent that the economy was on the track of the risk case and that the risk case was now the most probable forecast. The management was informed and decided to adopt the risk plan in place of the base plan, and the operating units were informed.

With very short notice, in some cases within two weeks, the operating units were able to switch from the base plan to the risk plan. This could not have been done in such a short time if the risk plan had not been developed in advance.

IBM also has used risk planning in the strategic or long-term plan. In the last strategic plan, for example, for the period that started in 1976, we concluded that there was a 30% probability of a recession in the United States in 1978. Management's concern was that a recession in 1978 would bring IBM's full employment practice under pressure. The operating units were asked to determine the strain on the full employment practice if a recession, of the character described in the risk case, were to take place.

There is another procedure that can be employed to reduce the cost of forecast error. It is early recognition of error and plan revision. It can be considered from two perspectives; from the point of view of forecasting and from the broader aspect of planning. From the forecasting point of view, the counsel of perfection is to identify the variables where accuracy of forecast is most important in terms of minimizing the cost of forecast error. Then apply enough forecasting resources to reduce the cost of error to an "acceptable" minimum. This course of action may be impractical in the sense that it may be impossible to reduce forecast error to the "acceptable" minimum, and even in those cases where it is possible to do so, the costs of a more accurate forecast may exceed the benefits. The alternative is to install tracking procedures in order to recognize error early and revise the forecast when the error is recognized. The advantage of this procedure is that tracking models that lead to forecast error recognition are simple and economical to produce; and, while circumstances vary, it could easily be that early recognition of error and forecast revision will reduce a substantial part of the cost of the initial forecast error.

The planning system can make early recognition of error part of the calendar of events in the plan cycle. This can be accomplished by requiring a formal examination of the need for a plan revision in the spring of the plan year. By that time, six months or more may have passed since the forecasts for the plan year were made and the prospects for increasing the forecast accuracy for the plan year and the year following will be much improved.

The principal argument against the procedure of plan revision is that it weakens the commitment of the operating unit to plan attainment. It is true that any possibility of plan revision has that tendency and it can be argued that anything that relieves the operating unit of the need to live up to its initial commitment has the result that some plans that might have been accomplished by extra effort are not attained. This is a serious objection, but the danger in holding to a plan with unrealistic objectives is that even with extra effort the plan may not be achieved, and, in the process of attempting to attain the plan, resources will be wasted. In other words stubborn adherence to a plan that cannot be made, will result in costs that could have been avoided. The resolution of this dilemma requires a management decision based on the costs and benefits of plan revision in the given specific case.

ECONOMETRICS AND FORECASTING

We make extensive use of econometric models in making general economic forecasts and forecasts of IBM's sales and shipments. We are committed to their use for a variety of reasons that I will describe later, but our experience with econometric models suggests that forecasting with econometric models is not just a matter of turning the model's handle to produce a forecast. Rather, there is a complex interaction between the model and forecaster.

The interaction between model and forecaster is required because the model is not a perfect forecasting instrument. That models are less than perfect forecasters is not arguable; the

record speaks for itself. Why models are less than perfect is a matter of opinion. There are two broad alternative explanations. One is that the relationships that are used in forecasting, such as the influence of income on consumption, even if they could be estimated correctly, are not stable, so one can have no confidence that a parameter computed from data of a particular period will provide a good forecast for another period. The alternative explanation is more complex. It could be called the missing variable, multicollinearity argument. This argument suggests that the magnitude of any dependent variable is a function of many independent variables, some with greater, others with lesser importance. Unfortunately, for econometrics, many economic variables move through time in the same direction, more or less parallel to one another. This parallel movement sometimes makes it impossible to estimate the true individual relationship between a particular independent and dependent variable.

In addition, it sometimes happens that a variable that theoretically should have an effect on a given dependent variable does not appear in an econometric model. This happens because that variable moves so much in parallel with another independent variable that it is not possible to obtain estimates of parameters for both variables that pass the usual statistical tests. In cases of this kind, the parameter for the variable that is in the model represents the influence of both variables. This causes no difficulty in forecasting, so long as both variables move together in the forecast period, just as they did in the period that was used to calculate the estimate of the parameter. Should this not be the case, the forecast will not be accurate.

The econometrician therefore is confronted with a dilemma. If he includes the independent variables that theory suggests, his statistical tests will tell him that the parameters in his function are not reliable. Moreover in some cases, even when his parameters pass the usual tests, the values of the parameters he has estimated may be influenced so much by the correlation between two or more of his independent variables, in the period of fit, that his forecast will prove to be inaccurate if that correlation of the independent variables is disturbed in the forecast period. In that case, when the data for the forecast period become available, and the model is re-estimated to include that data, it will be found that the parameters are different from those originally estimated.

The practicing econometrician's experience is filled with examples of parameters whose values change as more data become available. In my judgment, this results mainly from the problems of changing correlations among the independent variables, or because the correlations change between independent variables in the model and an omitted variable—an omitted variable that, according to economic theory, should have been included. It is possible that the underlying true relationships among variables shift from time to time, but, I believe, most of what econometricians observe as shifts in parameters is the result of changing multicollinearity between independent variables in the model and between omitted variables and independent variables in the model.

This discussion so far has concerned the variables in an econometric model. There also is the problem of the data from which model parameters are estimated. There are cases where just one or a few data points can have an extraordinarily large influence on the parameters in the model. The model builder may conclude that this is appropriate in some cases but not in others. With present procedures, the model builder may be unaware of this kind of influence on his estimates.

It is unfortunate but true that the usual statistical tests frequently do not discover the defects in a model that will cause it to make inaccurate forecasts. Edwin Kuh and Roy E. Welsch recently have proposed pioneering research to deal with this problem. The model builder ". . . will need to look for places where the fit (model and parameters) may break down by actively intervening and altering in a reasonably controlled and systematic way the assumptions and data upon which the fit is based. In a sense he needs to test his structure much as an engineer would test a design for a new bridge . . ."[2]

Kuh and Welsch and others in the community of scholars are pressing forward to invent a new set of tools for applied econometricians. This work will improve the forecast accuracy of econometric models by giving econometricians reasons to reject models that they otherwise would accept, and by making it possible to improve the estimation of parameters. How great the improvement will be only time will tell. In the meantime forecasting with econometric models remains a procedure in which the model is a tool, a sophisticated tool that requires a well trained user to produce the desired results.

If this is the state of econometrics, why use models at all? The first reason is forecast accuracy. At the present time, when almost all forecasters have access to model forecasts of United States economic activity, comparisons between model and non-model forecasts are all but meaningless. This was not so some years ago. Victor Zarnowitz collected forecasts made by a selected group of forecasters for the period 1966 to 1969 and compared them with forecasts produced using econometric models. It was quite evident that the econometric forecasts had a superior record.

The second reason is continuity of performance in an organization. The use of a model provides continuity of forecasting methods that is reasonably independent of the individual making the forecast. This is important in an organization where people move from one job to another.

The third reason is communication of forecast results in an organization. This point has been discussed earlier.

The fourth reason is econometrics as a scientific discipline is not static. Research improving the characteristics of econometric models is always going on. Scholars now are concentrating on research that may be of particular use to applied econometricians.

Finally econometrics makes progressive improvement possible. A forecast fundamentally is a claim that the forecaster understands the phenomenon he is forecasting. In other words, the forecast is a hypothesis that can be tested. The test is the accuracy of the forecast. If the forecast is accurate the forecaster can maintain that he understands the process. If the forecast is not accurate, and its errors cannot be traced to the assumptions on which the forecast is based, then the forecaster must confess that he does not understand the phenomenon. The model proves an essential record of what has been tried and found wanting. It is, therefore, the foundation for building an alternative hypothesis about the phenomenon that can be tested against the future. Econometrics prevents us from repeating the same errors and makes it possible to learn from mistakes.

CONCLUSION

Economic forecasts are required for business planning. The work of the economist can be made more effective if he is given a review responsibility for the plan. This will make it necessary for the economist to develop aggregative forecast models to determine whether the plan is consistent with the economic forecast. Econometric models improve forecast accuracy and have other significant advantages, particularly in a large complex organization. Nevertheless, errors must be expected in economic forecasts and in business forecasts, as well, therefore planning must be organized to deal with forecast errors.

NOTES

1. Gunnar Eliasson, *Business Economic Planning* (New York: John Wiley & Sons; Stockholm: Federation of Swedish Industries, 1976), pp. 13 and 37.
2. *Measures of Robustness and Reliability for the Validation of Econometric Models,* mimeograph Edwin Kuh and Roy E. Welsch, Computer Research Center for Economics and Management Science, National Bureau of Economic Reseach, Inc.
3. Victor Zarnowitz, *Forecasting Economic Conditions: The Record and the Prospect,* in *The Business Cycle Today, Fiftieth Anniversary Colloquium I* (National Bureau of Economic Research, 1972).

6

Scanning the International Environment

Jeremiah J. O'Connell
John W. Zimmerman

• • •

On the battlefield of Waterloo not far from Brussels, one often sees the curious tourist or the sage history buff surveying the scene from the Duke of Wellington's vantage point

Source: Jeremiah J. O'Connell and John W. Zimmerman, "Scanning the International Environment." Copyright © 1979 by the Regents of the University of California. Reprinted from *California Management Review,* Volume XXII, Number 2, pp. 15–23 by permission of the Regents.

where the elm tree once stood on that fateful Sunday in June 1815. Others trek over to Napoleon's command post a mile away beyond La Belle Alliance and peer through imaginary telescopes over the rough terrain. What could the adversaries see? As they planned and adjusted the strategies that pitted 170,000 men in bloody competition, what did they know, what intelligence did they have? Why the doubt and confusion over the movement of Blücker and the Prussians' advance to Wellington's aid? Why the indecisiveness in ordering Marshall Grouchy to reinforce Napoleon's flank?

What Wellington and Napoleon perceived that Sunday was only marginally the product of personal observation. Like the duke and emperor, today's business strategists rely heavily on the organization's perception of the environment—a social process of incredible complexity and sensitivity. Historians will go on disagreeing on how well each leader was served by his organization's perception of the environment and what weight the quality of the military strategists' view of the environment had on the battle's outcome. Napoleon and Wellington behaved differently, played different roles in environmental scanning. We will return to those differences for lessons for chief executives after we have:

- examined more closely what's going on in environmental scanning in multinationals on both sides of the Atlantic;
- identified the trouble spots in scanning practices especially from the headquarters, or chief executive's viewpoint;
- explained why there is dissatisfaction with the ways many organizations perceive their external environment; and
- explored ways of improving the scanning system.

There may be many reasons why a firm scans its international environment. This article narrowly focuses on scanning the environment for trends, events, and expectations influencing those decisions which shape the nature and direction of the business, that is, strategic decisions. Admittedly, executives must and do search the external environment for information relevant to administrative and operational decisions. The narrow focus here is justified because strategic decisions are more dependent on external data than are other decisions.

Data on corporate capability and management values play a part as well in shaping strategic decisions, yet it's in the external environment we find customers and suppliers. If such Drucker-like logic isn't sufficiently cogent, research does show a very positive correlation between profit performance and the gathering and dissemination of environmental data.[1]

Involvement in executive education, management consultancy, and formal research has given the authors the conviction that—while we are far from science—prescriptions can be drawn from our survey findings and work with companies.[2] The vast literature on the subject, though strong on systems and tools, has a gaping hole on the process or human side of scanning.[3] Before becoming normative, it will be useful to describe via survey results what's going on and to analyze the need for different executive behavior in the environmental scanning process.

SURVEY OF TWO SIDES OF THE ATLANTIC

Focus on Current Scanning Activities

In the classroom or consultancy setting it has been necessary to restrain executives from roaming the external environment with enthusiastic indiscipline. As executives scan the environment, they most often do so without explicit criteria for aiming or focusing their antennae. Yet, in our questionnaire survey of U.S. and European executives, the respondents unambiguously focused on the economic and technological domains of the external environment as those which most affect today's strategic decisions.[4]

Even though both samples see the economic and technological domains as prepotent in both present and future impact on strategic decisions, differences among Americans and Europeans show up in how each sample sees the social environment. For the Europeans, the social domain ranked fourth in actual impact and the third in potential impact. In the U.S. sample, the social domain stayed fifth even though its potential impact was perceived as increasing more than any other domain.[5]

Table 1   Relative Impact of Information from Environmental Domains on Today's Strategic Decisions*

Domains	U.S. Sample		European Sample	
	Mean	Rank	Mean	Rank
Social	2.58†	5	2.88	4
Political	2.98	3	3.18	3
Ecological	2.82	4	2.78	5
Economic	4.39	1	4.44	1
Technological	3.98	2	3.92	2

*Not trusting the tendency to report conventional wisdom on such surveys, we inquired further about the potential impact of information from the five domains on future strategic decisions (see Table 2).
†From 5 point scale; 5 is high, 1 is low.

Resource Allocation Pattern

As a check on the executives' expressed beliefs concerning the relative impact of the various environmental domains, respondents on both sides of the Atlantic were asked about the pattern of resource commitment to monitoring the different domains external to the firm. Shouldn't this increasing awareness (even among U.S. executives) of the potential impact of social determinants of strategy begin to show up in how firms invest in environment surveillance? (See Table 3.) As expected, both samples of executives named the economic and technological domains as the primary focuses of

Table 3   Relative Degree of Involvement of Firm's Resources in Data Gathering in the Five Domains

Domains	U.S. Sample		European Sample	
	Mean	Rank	Mean	Rank
Social	2.88*	5	2.96	4
Political	3.33	3	3.14	3
Ecological	3.04	4	2.84	5
Economic	4.41	1	4.39	1
Technological	3.90	2	3.49	2

*From 5 point scale; 5 is high, 1 is low.

resource involvement for environmental data gathering. In fact, the U.S. sample remained fully consistent in resource allocation and belief in the relative impact (same rank at present and in the future) of information from the five domains. The Europeans describe a resource allocation pattern which more closely matches their beliefs about potential future impact from the five domains.

Would this perfectly reasonable relationship between believed impact and investment pattern in environmental data gathering hold up as we look at the second phase (impact assessment) of the environmental surveillance process? The two samples of executives identified investment patterns virtually identical to those in data gathering when asked about the activities of interpreting and evaluating the data

Table 2   Relative Potential Impact of Information from Environmental Domains on Future Strategic Decisions

Domains	U.S. Sample		European Sample	
	Mean	Rank	Mean	Rank
Social	3.16*	5	3.60	3
Political	3.41	3	3.40	4
Ecological	3.35	4	3.02	5
Economic	4.67	1	4.68	1
Technological	4.34	2	4.32	2

*From 5 point scale; 5 is high, 1 is low.

Table 4   Degree of Formality in Interpreting and Evaluating Data From the Five Domains

Domains	% "Highly Formal" Response	
	U.S. Sample	European Sample
Social	22%	36%
Political	17	22
Ecological	36	42
Economic	82	82
Technological	60	66

Table 5 Relative Importance of Data Sources for the Five Environmental Domains (Combined U.S. and European Samples)

Domains	Outside Services	Outside Experts	Home Office Staff	Home Office Top Management	Business Unit Top Management
Social	1.84*	1.11	2.41	2.80	2.27
Political	1.80	1.32	2.31	2.82	1.96
Ecological	1.77	1.51	2.49	2.06	2.27
Economic	1.67	1.65	2.86	2.60	2.07
Technological	1.47	1.58	2.79	2.30	2.46

*From 5 point scale; 5 is "most important" in terms of frequency of use by headquarters and 1 is "least important" source.

gathered in search of threats or opportunities relevant to the business. Even though, when asked about their major frustrations with environmental scanning, several reported inability to interpret sociopolitical trends, the relative difficulty in dealing with different kinds of data did not change the investment pattern in impact assessment.

The original logic holds: high perceived and expected impact on strategy leads to high investment in data gathering and interpretation/ evaluation. Or, is the causality reversed? Because companies invest so heavily in gathering and interpreting economic and technological data, are strategic decisions *per force* largely determined by economic and technological variables? Is the causal chain environment-strategy-structure-process, so much part of management thought since Chandler's work, causing us to ignore the very real possibility that what we are organizationally today will shape what we will become via strategic choice tomorrow?[6,7]

To further explore resource allocation and use in the surveillance process the two samples of executives were asked to characterize their manner of interpreting and evaluating data from each of the five domains as "highly formal" (structured, planned, with guidelines, procedures, forms) or "informal" (intuitive, unscheduled, ad hoc, unstructured).

Once economic and technological data have been gathered, they are "suctioned," as it

were, into a ready and waiting processing "machine" which is evidently missing in the other domains.[8] In the absence of such a machine, will data gatherers tend to ignore data from the "softer" environmental domains?

To complete the picture of resource allocation and use, the two samples of executives were asked to classify the relative importance of several sources of environmental data. (See Table 5.) The survey respondents (with only insignificant differences between the U.S. and European samples) identified men in their own positions as the chief sources of external environmental data. In the social and political domains "Home Office Top Management" came out as the most important source. In the other three domains, "Home Office Staff" came out as the most important source. It would appear that these results, which depreciate human and nonhuman external sources, contradict Walter Keegan's findings.[9] Not necessarily so! Keegan traced sources for a wider range of decision uses than our narrow strategic decision focus. Also, in finding that about two-thirds of the sources were outside the organization, Keegan traced not just the final or direct source of information used in a decision but also the earlier and indirect sources. Our respondents clearly concentrated on the final link in the transmission chain. In our survey—more so than Keegan's—is there a warning against the selectivity and distortion of environmental data fed to the decision process by "organization men" who are intimately involved in the internal power structure? With so much reliance by the decision makers on internal sources—men shaped by the organization, rewarded by the organization, living with the organization policies—will the organization's ability to perceive the external environment be "biased" by the perhaps conscious workings of their values and needs?

THE HUMAN SIDE OF SCANNING

Several questions have been posed in the report of the survey of executives on both sides of the Atlantic. Strategy formulators themselves ask similar questions and frequently voice doubts that they are well-served by their strategic intelligence systems. European executives report these frustrations:

- inability to organize for environmental scanning;
- difficulty of matching individual beliefs with detectable trends;
- delay between external developments and our interpretation;
- difficulty in applying a systematic approach; and
- problems with finding relevance.

From the other side of the Atlantic we receive similar complaints:

- inability to move faster;
- inhibitions concerning pessimistic discussions;
- conflict between the desire for stability and the reality of constant change;
- missed opportunities because of poor timing; and
- motivation of the management team to discuss the issues.

Observation convinces us that it is neither the system of techniques nor the amount or quality of resources which explain the misgivings about scanning. It is the management of the scanning process itself and particularly the roles played in it by strategy formulators. Exploring scanning as an exercise in organizational perception

analogous to individual perception will reveal why difficulties arise and will suggest remedial action.

SCANNING ANALOGOUS TO PERCEPTION

Examined in light of what we know about perception, the issues raised in our survey report become less puzzling. In purposeful economic organizations, there is a great need for data relevant to the fulfillment of what is an essentially economic mission in society. "We see what we need" is the cornerstone principle of perception.[10] Confirming this conclusion is the tendency in Europe to expand the enterprise's mission to the socioeconomic sphere which is reflected in the survey results showing the Europeans' need for data from the social domain is greater than that of the Americans.

Another principle of perception is that the perceiver tends to ignore that which is mildly threatening. Time and time again we have seen executives reject or rationalize data from social, political, and ecological domains. Opportunities lie in the economic and technological domains; threats emanate from the other three. Few careers are made by Jeremiahs who constantly prophesy doom. Unless a threat persists and grows more intense, it will be ignored. Long-term threats or opportunities will have difficulty breaking into the perceptual field of those conditioned to short-run planning horizons. Long-term trends may persist but without sufficient intensity to be noticed.

Completeness and accuracy of perception lie not only in the head of the perceiver. The character, volume, and presentation of the data, modify the process of perception. Economic data (and frequently technological data as well) have the easy-to-communicate character of measurable quantity. It takes a cynic like H. L. Mencken to remind us of the perceptual trap of such data: "For every problem economists have an answer. Simple, neat, and wrong." How much more credible and welcome are capital investment forecasts in the *Wall Street Journal* or the *Economist* than the graffiti on a university construction site or the obscure message of a counterculture poet on leftist Dutch TV! Not only are the social, political, and ecological domains relatively unstructured and complex but executives see them as more uncertain than the economic and technological domains.

Selectivity and distortion can enter into the environmental surveillance process via the data-gathering behavior of the "field observer" or the "boundary person" in the organization.[11] Perceptual bias can also enter the process at the stage of interpreting or evaluating the data, often performed by someone other than the data gatherer.[12] Not to be forgotten is the likelihood of perceptual bias at the data transmission linkage between the data gatherers and the interpreters and between the interpreters and users. It is in these activity "boxes" and along these transmission "arrows"—so uncomplicated in Ansovian process flow charts—that the serious problems occur.[13]

The analogy to perception may help explain the recent growth of International Advisory Councils.[14] Top executives, users of external data in strategic decisions, want environmental data without all the selectivity and distortion introduced by staff or line colleagues whose world view may be conditioned to perpetuate comfortable illusions. We see the same effort to get personally involved in the complexities of the international environment in attendance at and behavior in senior executive seminars or conferences.

MANAGING THE SCANNING PROCESS

Distinguishing the Strategic from the Operational

In recognition of the power of needs in the organizational process of perception, the first matter to be checked is whether appropriate resources are committed to strategic thinking versus short-run, operational preoccupations. If all scanning efforts are tied to the planning calendar, today's stable needs will tend to predominate and tomorrow's changing needs will not be served. Bundling strategic intelligence efforts around an annual strategic review serves some companies well, depending on their need for change and the uncertainty of their environments.[15] But one annual review could foster the erroneous view that strategic management is an annual episode rather than a day-to-day process requiring ongoing monitoring of the environment. In certain cases it is wise to not only uncouple the strategic from the operational process but to formally recognize that the normal organization structure does not serve well for the strategic intelligence system.[16]

Phasic, Not Sequential, Process

The hazards of organizational perception are heightened when the scanning process is seen as a sequence of three steps—data gathering, interpretation/evaluation, and use. In picturing the scanning process psychologically we must recognize that the three phases are inextricably intertwined (see Figure 1).

Without some anticipation of how environmental data will be used in strategy management, there will be no criteria to interpret or evaluate the impact of the data on strategy. Also, without selection criteria from the "use" and "interpretation" phases, data gathering will be selective on some unspecified basis. Montaigne cautioned, "A wise man sees as much as he ought, not as much as he can." The focus of the scanning apparatus comes via the interplay among the phases and the iteration

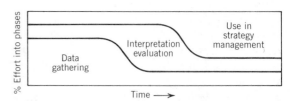

Figure 1 The phasic scanning process.

from one to the other. Such an appreciation is obvious in those companies wherein the number of environmental premises in a strategic review are five or six not fifteen or twenty.[17] It's possible to really test and be specific about the impact of a few critical issues on the nature and direction of the business. A large number of issues normally is symptomatic of undigested data or mere "assumptions on which this plan is based," the rationale behind the expansiveness or conservatism of forecasts or projections. Experience shows (and the concept of bounded rationality argues) that a top management team can give in-depth treatment to only a half dozen issues at a time.

If the scanning phases are so intertwined, can one phase really be delegated? Not if delegation implies that the strategy formulators are uninvolved in the phase once delegated! The greatest temptation has been to delegate the data-gathering phase—"Tell us what's going on out there and then we'll formulate strategy." There is no surer formula for waste and frustration on all sides.

Chief Executive Officers' Role in the Scanning Process

In those companies with best scanning practices the chief executive officers (CEOs—individuals or a team) are directly involved in all phases of the process. A CEO will play different roles in each phase. Informally and day-to-day, scanning becomes part of his ongoing strategy management function. In the more formal and periodic process of scanning, the CEO launches the effort with a set statement, "We have to know more about. . . ." The inspiration for his short list is the current strategy of the business which becomes the touchstone for relevant environmental data.[18] If this solid base is laid for the "data-gathering" phase, it will be relatively easy to institute a free-wheeling, thinking-the-unthinkable session for top management to insure against a too conservative and history-bound approach. Initially, then, the

chief executive officer gives direction and energizes the process. It has proved useful for the CEO to be known to have multiple personal sources for his intelligence or to gather data first hand. He may even displace his board to another continent to give it direct access to data.[19] Some companies have used international advisory councils as a way of adding believability to data shared among peers, foreign accents and all.

In the "interpretation" phase the chief executive officers may have to protect the bearers of bad news from executive colleagues whose kingdoms are identified as having some environmental exposure. He may also have to reward the questioners not just the answerers. The CEO may have to invoke a whole range of analytic techniques, from group dynamics and "force field analysis" to computer-based dynamic simulations to insure both a proper balance of analytic rigor and executive judgment and of "mechanical" versus social process.

In the "use" phase, the chief executive officer should control or check that the organization is satisfied it has learned more about and acted on the half dozen critical issues announced at the beginning of the process. If every business unit, country company, or operating subsidiary knows it will have to defend its strategic proposals against the critical issues, the difficulty of getting environmental data to penetrate the organization and be actually used will be largely solved. The officer's role in this phase is as a questioner: "How are you going to anticipate this or that critical issue? Can you tell me how your strategic proposals help us to cope with such and such critical issue?" When there has been adequate strategic response to an issue, it can be bumped from the list. Operating units will vie to add the next critical issue because the short list of critical issues will expand or contract their strategic field of maneuver.

Direct involvement of strategic decision makers in the scanning process is the surest way to avoid the hazards of organizational perception. Too often we accept flow chart presentations of such complex social processes without sufficient challenge. In the Ansoff chart cited above, the first box in the northwest corner reads, "Planning staff: environmental surveillance, opportunity/vulnerability profile."[20] If the process truly starts there, the staff will generate expertise in answering the unasked question. Bottom drawers will become even more clogged with unused reports and top management will complain louder about blind guides. Strategic decision makers have to kick off the process and stay with the process, changing roles at each phase and adjusting roles depending on the domain being scanned. Such behavior will focus the scanning antennae on the organization's real needs and will support the penetration of useful if unpleasant data to strategic decision makers.

CONCLUSION

Our survey, classroom, and consulting experience, and the literature raise questions about how well the environmental surveillance process is managed, given the hazards discussed above. True, not all firms have the same need for information from the external environment. Also, some managements are convinced that in their particular circumstances they can wait until the threats and opportunities are thrust upon them. Given lean and flexible organizations, some companies may indeed be able to use a catch-up, responding style. However, for the majority of companies, either offensive or defensive logic makes it increasingly necessary to have dependable environmental scanning.

Like Napoleon and Wellington, top management has to decide their own involvement in the scanning process. Except for the very beginning and end of the battle of Waterloo, Napoleon stayed back without line-of-sight command of the front. By so doing, he avoided the distraction of horse, cannon, and cries from the dying. Also, he left his officers and staff with the responsibility of deciding what information to provide and when to provide it. The Duke of

Wellington, on the other hand, patrolled the ridge overlooking the battlefield that whole long afternoon. He risked not only the random rifle or cannon shot but also risked losing his perspective on the whole by the distraction of a cavalry charge here or a cannonade there. Also before midafternoon, smoke obscured much of the rolling terrain so he couldn't maintain personal touch with all units. What did the Duke gain by involving himself so much in the scanning of the battle? His officers and staff knew directly what information he needed. Intelligence gatherers and interpreters performed in the knowledge that the leader had his own personal perspective on the battle. Wellington had shortened the communication lines and prevented the filtering process from "blinding" him. The French author Victor Hugo might tartly insist: "Waterloo was a battle of the first order won by a captain of the second," but Wellington at least managed the environmental scanning part of his job better than the man whose final view of Waterloo was over his stooped shoulder.

NOTES

1. Phillipe de Woot, Hubert Heyvaert, and Francois Martou, "Strategic Management: An Empirical Study of 168 Belgian Firms," *International Studies of Management and Organization,* Fall–Winter, 1977–1978, p. 50.
2. The authors' two organizations (Center for Education in International Management in Geneva, Switzerland, and Kepner-Tregoe, Inc., in Princeton, New Jersey), cosponsored a research project on environmental surveillance which has provided material for this article. The authors acknowledge and express appreciation for the work of Mr. Norman B. Solomon who carried out the research under their joint supervision.
3. In the generally technique-oriented literature some recent pieces stand out as having some sensitivity to the character of the human process: P. T. Terry, "Mechanisms for Environmental Scanning," *Long Range Planning,* June 1977; Ralph H. Kilmann and Kyung-Ll Ghymn, "The MAPS Design Technology: Designing Strategic Intelligence Systems for MNC's," *Columbia Journal of World Business,* Summer 1976; R. J. Rummel and David A. Heenan, "How Multinationals Analyze Political Risk," *Harvard Business Review,* January–February 1978; Eli Segev,

"Triggering the Strategic Decision Making Process," *Management Decisions,* Vol. 14, no. 5 (1976).

4. A mail survey of a convenience sample of large multidivision companies, yielding fifty U.S. respondents (25 percent return rate) and fifty European respondents (18 percent return rate), 70 percent of whom were policy-level executives. The rest were headquarters-planning or similar staff managers. Questions focused on environmental scanning practices of the headquarters or group-company level.

5. Similar low ranking for the social domain was uncovered in the U.S. in a study by Liam Fahey and William R. King, "Environmental Scanning for Corporate Planning," *Business Horizons,* August 1977; see also "Capitalizing on Social Change," *Business Week,* October 29, 1979.

6. Alfred D. Chandler, *Strategy and Structure* (Cambridge, Mass.: MIT Press, 1962), pp. 17, 299–300, 315–315.

7. This point has been made in experimental work by George P. Huber, Michael J. O'Connell, and Larry L. Cummings, "Perceived Environmental Uncertainty: Effects of Information and Structure," *Academy of Management Journal,* December 1975, p. 738.

8. For a convincing example of the formality of the process for utilizing economic data in a company (IBM), see Alvin J. Karchere, "Economic Forecasting in International Business," *Columbia Journal of World Business,* Winter 1976.

9. Warren J. Keegan, "Multinational Scanning: A Study of Information Sources Utilized by Headquarters Executives in Multinational Companies," *Administrative Science Quarterly,* September 1974, p. 420.

10. Harold J. Leavitt, *Managerial Psychology* (Chicago: University of Chicago Press, 1972), pp. 25ff.

11. "Boundary spanning" has received much attention lately. See, for example, Richard Leifer and Geroge P. Huber, "Relations Among Perceived Environmental Uncertainty, Organization Structure and Boundary Spanning," *Administrative Science Quarterly,* June 1977; Michael L. Tuchman, "Special Boundary Roles in the Innovation Process," *Administrative Science Quarterly,* December 1977; Howard Aldrich and Dianne Herker, "Boundary Scanning Roles and Organization Structure," *Academy of Management Review,* April 1977.

12. Carl R. Anderson and Frank T. Paine, "Managerial Perceptions and Strategic Behavior," *Academy of Management Journal,* December 1975, p. 812.

13. See, for instance, Igor Ansoff, "Managing Strategic Surprise by Response to Weak Signals," *California Management Review,* Winter 1975, p. 31, Figure 6.

14. Roy Hill, "The Benefits of an International Advisory Board," *International Management,* June 1976, pp. 28–31; Roger M. Kenny, "Helpful Guidance from International Advisory Boards," *Harvard Business Review,* March–April 1976, pp. 14–19, 156.

15. See Fahey and King, op. cit.; Maurice Marks, "Organizational Adjustment to Uncertainty," *Journal of Management Studies,* no. 1 (1977); Carl R. Anderson and Frank T. Paine, op. cit.

16. On the debilitating effect of long-range planning on strategic thinking, see B. B. Tregoe and J. W. Zimmerman, "Strategic Thinking," *Management Review,* February 1979. The impact of structure is traced by Kilmann and Ghymn, op. cit.

17. See Rummel and Heenan, op. cit. p. 72, for the story of a major petrochemical company which "daily assesses its overseas markets by examining almost 400 separate variables." The authors do not report whether this company forecast the oil boycott and price increase in 1973.

18. For examples of how mission and strategy can be used as both starting point and screen, see F. Friedrich Neubauer and Norman B. Solomon, "A Managerial Approach to Environmental Assessment," *Long Range Planning,* April 1977; Terry, op. cit.

19. Sir Leslie Smith, chairman of BOC International Ltd., brought his board from London to Washington in the midst of a challenge to the BOC acquisition of AIRCO. He also brought the board to South Africa during the debate about doing business in that part of Africa.

20. Ansoff, op. cit.

7

A Framework for Strategic Planning in Multinational Corporations

Peter Lorange

• • •

INTRODUCTION

Strategic planning in a multinational corporation has a two-fold task: to identify the strategic options most relevant to the corporation and to 'narrow down' these options into the one best plan. Stated this way there is of course nothing fundamentally different between the strategic planning task of a multinational corporation and that of any other large corporation. However, since multinationals offer several complex and distinctively different approaches to organizational design and planning, it is useful to examine some of the problems of strategic planning in the context of the multinationals.

The broad definition of the strategic planning tasks given above has several implications. In order to be able to identify the most relevant strategic options, the corporation needs to *adapt* continuously to the environment. Also, in order to narrow down the strategic options into the one best plan, the corporation must be able to *integrate* its many diverse activities. In this article we shall attempt to clarify the major purposes of planning in the multinationals in terms of adaptation and integration needs.

Given the diversity of settings in which multinationals operate, the adaptation and integration tasks will not be the same for all multinationals. Indeed, the opposite is true; each multinational will be faced with unique adapta-

tion and integration tasks. However, in order for us to develop some generalizations about the adaptation and integration tasks of planning in multinationals, we shall start out by identifying a few multinational corporate archetypes, followed by a discussion of their planning purposes in terms of adaptation and integration. We shall then present some normative propositions about adaptation/integration and the costs of striking a reasonable balance between the two in planning systems.

Empirical findings on long range planning in multinationals reported by others indicate that (a) it is hard to find actual examples of multinationals that in all respects fit into any of the archetypes to be suggested[1] and (b) the formal planning systems of multinationals seem to be much less developed than those we recommend here.[2] However, we do not see this as limiting the value of the arguments to be presented. We intend to propose some fundamental dimensions of planning for multinationals that might be useful to improve the understanding of the planning phenomenon. Obviously the proposed normative framework is not intended for uncritical adaptation in specific cases.

A TAXONOMY OF MULTINATIONAL CORPORATIONS

We shall distinguish between types of multinational corporations according to the dimensions along which the organization has been structured.[3] There seem to be two dimensions that

Source: Peter Lorange, "A Framework for Strategic Planning in Multinational Corporations," *Long Range Planning,* June 1976, pp. 30–36. Pergamon Press. Reprinted by permission.

might dominate the organizational structure: the product dimension, which occurs in companies which have adopted a so-called divisionalized structure, with each division responsible for one class of products; and the geographical area dimension, wherein each division is responsible for carrying out all the corporation's business within a given geographical area.

Complete domination of corporate structure by one dimension can prove to be inefficient. For instance, there might be considerable duplication of effort by having the product divisions operate their own separate organizations in one country. When evolving from such a product structure, the matrix structure might be described as consisting of a *leading* product dimension and a *grown* area dimension.[4]

Alternatively, when evolving out of an area-dominated structure the matrix structure would have a leading area dimension and a grown product dimension.[5]

So we perceive four types of multinationals, depending on the degree of emphasis they put on the product dimension and/or the area dimension. This continuum of multinationals is shown in Figure 1.

It should be stressed that typologizing into four categories is an oversimplification, since we are really dealing with a continuum. Further, dimensions other than product versus area orientation are likely to be considered in a realistic taxonomy of multinational corporations. In an integrated oil company, for instance, the *functional* dimension will typically be prominent, together with the area dimension. Also, the taxonomy adopted does not apply to the early evolutionary stages of corporate inter-

nationalization. Thus, much richer and probably also more realistic classifications may conceivably be developed.[6] However, keeping the purpose of this article in mind, little seems to be gained by adopting a more detailed taxonomy of multinationals.

PLANNING PURPOSES: ADAPTATION AND INTEGRATION NEEDS

Let us analyze the nature of the requirements for adaptation and integration in each of the four multinational archetypes we are considering.

The Product-Organized Corporation

This corporation will conduct its worldwide activities by means of several divisions, each responsible for carrying out the business strategy for one class of products on a worldwide basis. In terms of *adaptation,* then, each *division* will be responsible for scanning its own business environment. This implies a heavy pressure on each division to adapt to changes in each national market. How should the marketing promotion campaign be laid out for the promotion of a division's products in a particular country? Which models seem particularly worthwhile emphasizing in a given country? The pressures for scanning and adaptation within each worldwide product division will be on monitoring changes in area trends and taking advantage of the resulting opportunities. The major responsibility for carrying out this scanning rests on functional managers within each division. Among the advantages of this form of adaptation will be a basis for the development of strong international plans for each business, which may enjoy the benefits of economies of scales in worldwide product strategies. Among the disadvantages may be the lack of adaptation to diverse geographical area inputs. Potential duplication of efforts by several divisions in interpreting the need for adaptation to the same geographical area may also be a problem.

Figure 1 The taxonomy of multinational corporations according to relative emphasis on product orientation versus area orientation.

At the *corporate* level of the product-division type of corporation *adaptation* tasks will center on the "mix" of the portfolio of divisions. Multinational strategy questions will not be addressed at headquarters, except when reviewing division plans to probe their soundness. Important issues for corporate management are how to adapt to changing patterns of inflation/deflation and/or devaluation/revaluation, and which divisions should receive added/diminished emphasis, given differences in the nature of products, capital intensity, and relative strength in an area that is becoming more/less attractive. At the extreme, these resulting corporate adaptation needs may lead to the triggering of acquisitions, i.e., involvement in new business lines on a worldwide basis, or divestitures, i.e., pull-out of a business on a worldwide basis.

The *integrating* task of the worldwide product *division* will be primarily to make sure that the overall activities of the division are consistent. There will be a need to integrate the strategic programs within each product division as well as the various functional activities. On the other hand there will probably be relatively less need for area integration, since that each program and/or function is slated to work independently within the worldwide area. Thus, the main coordination focus will be on each worldwide business line activity.

At the *corporate* level there will be a need to integrate and coordinate the portfolio of worldwide business divisions, emphasizing financial funds flow interrelations among the divisions. Again, any portfolio adjustments resulting from a need for stronger integration will be in modification of the plans of one or more of the product divisions, and not in area coordination directly.

It can be deduced that the formal organization structure itself plays a major role in facilitating the integration task. A major reason for the particular choice of the worldwide product division structure is in fact the need to integrate this type of company's worldwide activities along the product dimension. Thus, the formal organizational chart will typically be a reflection of the integration needs of an organization.[7]

The Geographically Area-Organized Corporation

In order to dichotomize the adaptation needs among the various multinational archetypes and clearly as possible we shall consider the opposite of the product-organized in a number of geographical divisions, each undertaking a relatively broad spectrum of businesses within its own area of the world. We shall first discuss the adaptation needs within each area division, and then consider adaptation challenges at the corporate level.

A primary task for each area *division* will be adapting its product portfolio to the area conditions and determining which products or businesses to emphasize. This will be the main responsibility of the general manager of the division, who will rely to a large extent on his business managers within the area. Thus, each area division will have considerable autonomy in providing environmental scanning data from its part of the world. Headquarters for the area divisions will probably be staffed with executives mostly from the host country and have broader local expertise than the product-oriented divisions. The latter divisions will probably have general worldwide rather than local geographical expertise and will most likely be staffed with executives from several nations. Divisions of the area-dominated multinational will have the potential for strong geographical area strategies and plans. The biggest disadvantage is probably the lack of adaptation of product strategies to several geographical areas. The adaptive efforts might lead to too much duplication of efforts in production, new product development, etc. among the areas and the risk of too much fragmentation, particularly if the geographical areas are small.

At the *corporate* level the *adaptation* requirements will be related to balancing the portfolio of area divisions. The task will be to assess the long-term health of each area given the composition of products of each division. Given devaluation/revaluation and/or inflation/deflation opportunities and/or threats, corporate will evaluate which products seem to have the best future in various areas and which should be deemphasized; this may lead to changes in the portfolio. The central question will be whether the firm is emphasizing a set of products which result in the best worldwide geographical balance. We shall expect to find a much higher need for international staffing and broad worldwide expertise at the corporate level in the area-dominated multinational than in that which is product-oriented.

There seem to be diametrical differences between the two multinational archetypes in their needs for international competence and staff skills to carry out the adaptation tasks of planning at corporate as well as at divisional levels.[8] This is not surprising since the adaptation needs for the geographical area-organized multinational generally are so different from the adaptation needs of the world-wide product-oriented multinational. The product division will focus on adapting to changing geographical area patterns, the geographical area division to changing business or product opportunities. At the corporate level, too, the adaptation challenges will be fundamentally different, although in both instances the task will be to monitor the balance of the portfolio of divisions according to devaluation/revaluation and/or inflation/deflation patterns. Thus, the adaptation needs for the divisional and corporate levels of the two types of multinationals will be structured along the *opposite* dimension to the one on which the corporation is organized.

The *divisional* level needs for *integration* will focus on pulling together the diverse business activities within the given area. This implies that product policies within the area should be integrated, and that the program and/or functional activities within the area will be coordinated. There will probably be less pressure to integrate the businesses worldwide, though, since each division is responsible for adapting a business or product exclusively to its given area. The *corporate* level will coordinate the several area divisions so that the portfolio may become integrated; portfolio adjustments will probably be in terms of areas, not products. Again, the choice of organizational structure, which in this case is primarily along the area dimension directly reflects the integrative needs of the corporation.

Let us now leave the two extreme positions and consider the matrix structures, which will be faced with adaptation and integration tasks along *both* the product *and* area dimension. Before discussing the adaptation and integration tasks of our two matrix-based archetypes, however, let us review some relevant facts about coordination between the dimensions of a matrix structure. Effective coordination between the matrix dimensions must involve people; managers representing each dimension must get together to share information and work out decisions that take into account the considerations of each dimension. In order to facilitate coordination, then, it seems reasonable to form committees.[9] Staffing of these committees should reflect the matrix dimensions involved, and also be manned with executives from appropriate organizational levels. A major implication of the decentralized organizational structures considered here is that the responsibility for business strategy formulation and implementation as well as the bulk of the action program decisions will be made at the division level. Consequently, it will be at this level that integration of the inputs from the various diemensions will have to take place, as each dimension should influence the way that business strategy decisions are made and carried out. It should be noted that a matrix structure does not imply that representatives from each dimension will have to cooperate in detail to reach decisions at each level of the organization. Rather, the multidimensional cooperative will take place at *one* level, namely through the business coordination committees at the division level. Below this, there will generally be unidimensional reporting to cope with the functional strategy tasks. At the corporate level only the leading dimension will be represented to formulate and implement a portfolio strategy.

Product Leading/Area Grown Matrix Structure

This type of multinational will have a product-dominated organizational structure. However, going all the way along the product dimension with parallel business divisions operating worldwide would mean forfeiture of many of the benefits of being a large multinational and not merely a collection of business division. Thus, the rationale for the matrix structure is the acknowledgment that more than one dimension might be beneficial and a willingness to capitalize on potential economies of scale.

What requirements for *adaptation* face the product leading/area grown matrix structure? The answer is a combination of the adaptation requirements facing the worldwide product division organizations and the geographical area division organizations, but with relatively more emphasis of the factors discussed for the product division organization. Thus, at the divisional level the adaptation requirement will be dominated by changes in the area conditions. However, some emphasis will also be put on assessing changes in the business product dimension within each area. At the corporate level, similarly, adaptation of the portfolio should be primarily a response to area reconsiderations but also for business line reconsiderations.

In this type of corporation, which typically has evolved from a very strong dominance of the product dimension to the present balance, the *integrating* needs will probably not be too different from those of the worldwide product-organized corporation. At the division level the primary integrative concern will be to get the

product lines together. However, a secondary concern will be to ensure the product integration in such a way that the areas also are integrated to the largest possible extent. At the corporate level the product dimension will again be the one receiving the most attention for integration, so that the portfolio of worldwide product activities will be coordinated. However, this portfolio will need to be modified to take into account area coordination.

Area Leading/Product Line Grown Matrix Structures

For this last type of matrix structure the opposite of what was the case in the previous section will be the pattern. The *adaptation* requirements of the product dimension will be the most important, both at divisional and corporate levels. However, the area adaptation dimension will also play a role.

The *integrative* needs are likely to be similar to those of the corporation which is geographical area divisionalized. At the divisional as well as the corporate level the area dimension will probably be the one requiring the most integrative attention. This should be modified by the need to integrate the product dimension as well.

Summary Pattern of Adaptation and Integration Requirements

A summary of the adaptation and integration requirements of each of our four multinational archetypes is presented in Table 1. As we see there is a continuing shift in adaptation and integration requirements as we go from one organizational extreme to the other. It is important to recognize that the adaptation needs fall into a pattern along a continuum which goes *contrary* to the product/area organizational structure continuum of multinationals, while the integration needs fall along a continuum that goes in the *same* direction as the organization structure. This leads us to our first normative statement, namely that while the *integration task* of planning should be undertaken in such a way

Table 1 Summary of the Integration and Adaptation Planning Tasks of the Multinational Corporations in our Taxonomy.

Taxonomy of Corporations	Adaptation	Integration
Worldwide product divisions	Along area dimension	Along product dimension
Product leading/area grown matrix	Primarily along area dimension; some along product dimension	Primarily along product dimension; some along area dimension
Area leading/product grown matrix	Primarily along product dimension; some along area dimension	Primary along area dimension; some along product dimension
Geographical Area Divisions	Along product dimension	Along area dimension

that it *follows the organizational structure,* the *adaptation task* should be carried out in a direction *contrary to organizational structure.*

COSTS OF PLANNING IN MULTINATIONALS

In this section we shall consider some of the costs of undertaking planning in each multinational archetype. One might ask whether it would not have been more natural to discuss first the issues of design and implementation of planning systems so that they might fulfill the requirements outlined in the previous section, then to consider the costs associated with the systems design alternatives. It shall turn out, however, that cost considerations may have a major influence on the choice of the planning systems design approach. Thus, by discussing costs of planning at this point, we shall be able to advance a more cost-effective planning systems design approach.

The relative proportion of overall planning costs attributed to the area dimension versus the business dimension of course changes as one moves from the one extreme to the other, as illustrated in Figure 2.[10]

We see that the relative importance of each dimension's planning cost segment will be dependent on the multinational archetype at hand. This, however does not imply that the *absolute*

costs of planning remain the same for each archetype. For instance, evolving from a structure with geographic area divisions to a matrix with the area dimension dominated and product dimensions grown, the purpose will be to maintain a planning strength along *both* dimensions. The planning costs of the area dimension will remain more or less the same, and the planning costs of the product dimension will be added. Thus, the nature of the absolute costs of planning implies that Figure 2 will have to be modified, as illustrated in Figure 3.

From Figure 3 one will see that the choice of organizational structure is not a free one, since the planning costs associated with a matrix structure may be substantially higher than for

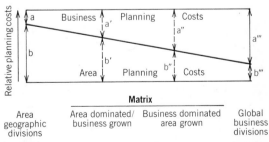

Figure 2 The relative proportion of planning costs attributable to the product dimension versus the area dimension. The "a's" indicate product dimension cost functions. The "b's" indicate area dimension cost functions.

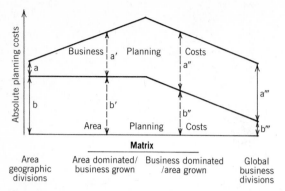

Figure 3 The absolute proportion of planning costs attributable to the product dimension versus the area dimension. The "a's" indicate product dimension cost functions. The "b's" indicate area dimension cost functions.

'extreme' structures dominated by one dimension. Thus, one may conclude that only in instances in which the added benefits accrued by carrying two dimensions outweigh the added costs will the adoption of a matrix structure be justified. Also, the instances in which a matrix planning structure will be justified cost benefit-wise will probably be fewer than commonly anticipated, given the significantly higher than expected planning costs associated with such systems.

Diminishing the Costs of Planning in Matrix Archetypes

Given the obvious potential payoffs of adapting and integrating along more than one dimension, and disregarding the added planning costs, we should discuss the two ways of changing the cost/benefit tradeoff point: increasing the benefits from planning in the matrix archetypes, and decreasing the planning costs of these archetypes. We shall propose a way of decreasing the planning costs which turns out also to increase the benefits of planning.

Keeping in mind that the planning process implies a narrowing down of strategic options

which may come about through a series of stages, say objectives-setting, planning, and budgeting, we may ask the following question: Are the adaptation and integration requirements equally important at each stage of progressive narrowing down?

First we should consider which is the more important purpose of the objectives-setting stage, to ensure adaptation or integration. At this stage the major planning task should be to reexamine the fundamental assumptions for being in business, evaluate opportunities and threats, and consider whether the rationale for the firm's policies is still valid; in other words, where the firm stands relative to the environment. A realistic and effective adaptation to the current environmental conditions is the major concern. Integration, on the other hand, plays a lesser role at the objectives-setting stage.

At the next narrowing down stage, the planning stage, we still have to cater to the need for adaptation. More detailed plans will be developed in order to follow up on the major issues for adaptation to the environment identified in the objectives-setting stage. Typically, there will be the calculation and evaluation of a number of "what ifs" to assess the effects of various environmental changes. There will, however, be an increasing need for integration at this stage to ensure that the various parts of the plans are consistent, that they are exhaustive when taken together, based on common assumptions, and that all relevant people have had a chance to contribute to the plans.

At the third and final stage of narrowing down the task will be to prepare more detailed budgets within the framework set out in the plans. Here the major thrust will be on integration, with little concern for adaptation at this stage.[11]

We have shown that in each of the matrix archetypes there will be different roles for the business and the area dimensions with respect to performing the adaptive and integrative tasks, and that the relative importance of these tasks shifts over the stages of narrowing down.

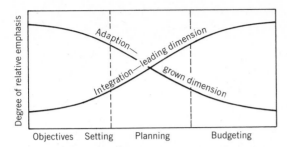

Figure 4 The relative importance of the adaptation function of the grown dimension versus the integration function of the leading dimension at each of the "narrowing down" stages.

We can now suggest a division of labor between the dimensions, as indicated in Figure 4.

We see that the adaptation task, to be performed primarily by the grown dimension (in accordance with the argument summarized in Table 1), will play a *relatively* more important role in the early part of the narrowing down process than the integration task to be performed by the leading dimension. Later in the narrowing down process, however, the roles will be reversed and the leading dimension will be relatively more dominating.

Before dicussing the specific implications of this opportunity for division of labor in the planning function of the matrix archetypes, let us emphasize that we are talking about *relative* importance of the tasks of the two dimensions. For instance, in a matrix structure with a mature and strong worldwide product dimension and a recent and weak area dimension the *absolute* importance of the leading dimension may prevail at all stages, although the relative emphasis will nevertheless follow the pattern indicated in Figure 4.

Let us also consider how the planning tasks of our two extreme organizational structures, the worldwide product organization and the area organization, can be interpreted in terms of Figure 4. If neither of these organizational forms has a grown dimension, will the adaptation task be taken care of? Yes, to some extent, since the leading dimension will adapt to environmental changes within relatively narrow limits. However, a lesser need for environmental adaptation will be perceived in a structure organized along one of the two extreme archetype forms. Also, the capacity for environmental adaptation will be much greater in a matrix organization. In fact the environmental adaptation need is probably the major reason for organizing along a matrix structure.

What are some of the implications that the pattern outlined in Figure 4 will have on the division of labor in the execution of the planning function? We see that extensive interaction among executives of the two dimensions of the matrix structure does not have to take place all through the narrowing down process, but only during the middle stage, i.e., the planning stage. An added sense of direction can probably be achieved in that it will be clearer which group of people will be primarily responsible at each stage of the narrowing down. The communication flows of the planning system can be simplified and be more explicit in terms of indicating who is responsible for what.

In addition to improving planning by instilling an added sense of task direction there will probably also be considerable cost savings. The cost of planning in a matrix should be considerably less through division of labor than if the conventional approach were followed, namely full-blown interaction between the dimensions at each stage of the narrowing down process.

This brings us to our second general normative statement, that *costs of planning* should be a major consideration in establishing an *appropriate balance* between adaptation and integration. The relative balance will be skewed towards more integration emphasis and less adaptation emphasis because of the costs associated with planning. However, emphasizing adaptation during the early stages of planning and integration during the later stages will tend to counteract this relative imbalance and allow for a strengthening of the system's adaptation ability.

CONCLUSION

We have analyzed the adaptation and integration requirements of several corporations within a taxonomy of multinationals and have come up with a pattern of planning tasks for the multinationals. It turned out that to carry out this planning would be exceedingly expensive for several of the corporations. However, we were able to suggest a way to simplify planning and utilize task specialization. We suggest that this approach might lead to an operational, simplified, more effective, and less expensive planning activity in multinational corporations.

NOTES

1. See Derek F. Channon, "Prediction and Practice in Multinational Strategic Planning," Paper presented at the *2nd Annual European Seminar on International Business,* European Institute for Advanced Studies in Management, 1974.

2. See John S. Schwendiman, "International Strategic Planning: Still in Its Infancy," *Worldwide P & I Planning,* September–October 1971.

3. This section is based heavily on Peter Lorange, "Formal Planning in Multinational Corporations," *Columbia Journal of World Business,* Summer 1973. See also Lorange, "La procedure de planification dans les entreprises multinationals," *Revue Economique et Sociale,* March 1973. Other classifications have been proposed in David P. Rutenberg, "Organizational Archetypes of a Multinational Company," *Management Science,* Vol. 16, no. 6 (1970);

Howard V. Perlmutter, "L'entreprise internationale—Trois conceptions," *Revue Economique et Sociale,* May 1965; and Richard D. Robinson, *International Business Management,* New York: Holt, Rinehart & Winston, 1973, Chap. 8.

4. Davis has developed the concepts of "leading" and "grown" dimensions of matrix structures. See Stanley M. Davis, "Two Models of Organization: Unity of Command versus Balance of Power," *Sloan Management Review,* Fall 1974.

5. We shall, however, not imply that the evolution of matrix structures will have to be towards an ultimate equal balance between the two dimensions.

6. See Robinson, op. cit.

7. See Alfred D. Chandler, *Strategy and Structure* (Cambridge, Mass.: MIT Press, 1962); and Jay Galbraith, *Designing Complex Organizations,* Reading, Mass.: Addison–Wesley, 1973.

8. Some of the differences in staffing patterns for nationals vs. non-nationals of four large European-based multinationals found by Davis, Edstrom, and Galbraith support this. See Harry Davis, Anders Edstrom, and Jay Galbraith, "Transfer of Managers in Multinational Organizations," European Institute for Advanced Studies in Management, Working Paper 74–19, Brussels 1974.

9. See William Goggin, "How the Multi-Dimensional Structure Works at Dow–Corning," *Harvard Business Review,* January–February 1974. See also Davis, op. cit.

10. Galbraith has suggested this exhibit. See Jay R. Galbraith, "Matrix Organization Design: How to Combine Functional and Project Forms," *Business Horizons,* Summer 1971, Exhibit 3, p. 70.

11. See Richard F. Vancil and Peter Lorange, "Strategic Planning in Diversified Corporations," *Harvard Business Review,* January–Feruary 1975, for an approach to a three-step narrowing down of strategic options.

8

Strategy Formulation and International Competition
William V. Rapp

• • •

Nationally oriented business strategies are usually unsuccessful for commodities that are or can be traded internationally.[1] Corporations today compete on an international basis, but merely being multinational is insufficient. One must also have an appropriate international business strategy which can give telling advantages over competitors.

The increased number of firms doing business abroad attests that many managers appreciate the need to be international. Most businessmen recognize that as domestic markets mature, demand in other countries is rising. They recognize that as their own facilities become high cost, foreign locations are more economic. Yet managers rarely have an integrated or systematic approach to their international business operations. "International" operations are usually separated from "domestic," and "international" decisions are often on a country-by-country basis. These international companies are really loose federations, each unit having its own nationally oriented strategy. Such firms as well as domestically restricted firms cannot compete with more sophisticated rivals. These international competitors will serve large multinational markets and will take advantage of international production specialization. Volume and cost advantage will be translated into aggressive penetration pricing on a worldwide basis. The insular company is confronted with the equally unattractive options of losing market share to low-priced imports or of reducing prices, hence margins. To

deal with this dilemma requires a conceptual framework to analyze and predict patterns of international competition and subsequently develop an integrated system of investment, marketing, pricing, and financial programs.[2] The main elements of this analytical framework for strategy formulation are market segmentation, cost-volume relationships, and portfolio management.

INTERNATIONAL PRODUCT LIFE CYCLES

One can observe for most products, industries, and economies a definite industrial development pattern. A developing country begins by simple primary-product processing, then develops simple manufacturing industries that produce products with high domestic demand, such as textiles or handicrafts. Subsequently, vertical integration stimulates demand for machinery, steel, and so on. As industrialization progresses, so do capital accumulation and labor force skills, which facilitate production of more technically complex and capital-intensive goods. At the same time, rising domestic incomes create demand for such products. Demand-and-supply conditions are therefore mutually re-enforcing with respect to the development process. The net result is a shifting comparative and absolute advantage toward the follower countries.

Inter-industry product-cycle development is both well-documented historically and an accepted part of current thinking on economic development. But in addition to the more notable inter-industry evolutions, intra-industry shifts take place. One observes the importance of synthetic relative to cotton textiles; of specialty relative to carbon steels; or of integrated cir-

Source: William K. Rapp, "Strategy Formulation and International Competition," *The Columbia Journal of World Business,* Summer 1973, pp. 98–112. Copyright © 1973 by the Trustees of Columbia University in the City of New York. Reprinted by permission.

cuits and large-scale integrated circuits relative to transistors and diodes. But both inter- and intra-industry shifts are part of the same product life cycle phenomenon.

A nation's industrial character and competitiveness is therefore constantly changing. Advanced countries generally have a greater demand for sophisticated products and are better able to produce them. However, less developed countries have a greater need for basic commodities and can often produce these at lower cost than highly developed countries. The scientific and material resources needed for the invention and commercialization of a new product are concentrated in a few advanced countries. A wide range of innovations are stimulated by these countries' domestic demand-and-supply conditions: high wage rates promote labor-saving innovations; high personal incomes stimulate demand for new products; large military and space programs support technical innovations, ultimately having consumer applications; large capital and skilled labor availability permits development to occur.

These demand-and-supply conditions do not occur in the less developed countries until income levels rise. Less developed countries therefore lag behind the advanced countries in a product's development. On the other hand, they usually attain the required demand levels and being production when the advanced countries' demand is slowing down. This process results in the intra- and inter-industry shifts noted above. Industrial emphasis moves toward industries which require more capital, more labor skill, and greater technological sophistication.

COMPETITIVE CONDITIONS

The interaction of demand and production costs leading to international product-cycle evolution is fairly straight-forward. However, the competitive conditions and assumptions underlying the observed shifts in comparative advantage that are coupled with industry failures in particular countries are rarely discussed. An indus-

try's decline is in fact due to the decline of the firms composing the industry. The United States has experienced several such situations relative to Japan, e.g., textiles, steel, automobiles, and ball bearings. Many firms in these industries have declined or disappeared given a shift in comparative advantage overseas. But some firms have not failed and continue to be successful. The reason for this discrepancy is that traditional product-cycle development assumes certain competitive conditions that need not hold, namely that:

- a firm, its production, and its markets are inextricably intertwined with a particular country

- a product whose comparative advantage is being shifted offshore cannot be replaced by newer, more technically advanced products

- no new defendable market segment is emerging which can replace the older product's importance to the firm

- the declining product is of such significance that failure to produce and sell it threatens the firm's existence

- a firm is not strategically responsive to changes in its worldwide competitive position

In all industries which follower countries have successfully developed, the conditions above have always held. Whether one examines cotton textiles, shoes, carbon steel, automobiles, television, or ships, at some time the United States was the world's low-cost and major producer. Yet when production economics and world demand growth moved offshore, U.S. producers did not generally respond in terms of overseas investment or exports. In those cases where they did invest abroad, it was to supply the local market only and not to develop a low-cost production source for the United States and third-country markets. This was true even though an offshore production strategy might have enabled these companies to continue U.S. production of their high-technology products and to continue employment of their highly skilled, high-value-added personnel such as engineers, designers, staff specialists, and managers.

Ball bearings is a case in point. American companies were pressed by Japanese competition because American producers' high-profit items were the high-volume, low-technology products which represented the bulk of their sales. However, their comparative production economics only justified production of the limited-run, high-technology bearings in the United States. Absolute advantage in the low-technology end of the product line had shifted offshore. Failure in turn to source the volume product abroad thus resulted in an uncompetitive position relative to Japanese producers, penetration of the U.S. market, and loss of major end-users. Under the resulting cash flow conditions, American ball bearing manufacturers could no longer sustain their R and D efforts, employ their highly skilled U.S. personnel, or produce the high-technology items in the United States. Many went out of business, and the industry is no longer a viable and competitive part of the U.S. economy.

But shoe companies such as Thom McAn that source certain items overseas, or textile companies such as Kayser-Roth and Indian Head Mills that specialize in and dominate growth segments within the U.S. textile market (e.g., panty hose or fashion fabrics), demonstrate that pursuing strategies appropriate to growth, market change, and worldwide competition can be good business in a declining market. A firm should not be confined by the geographical boundaries of its home-country market or by the type of goods it first produced.

PRODUCT-MARKET SEGMENTATION

However, many U.S. and European firms have not been responsive to emerging markets at home and abroad nor to the changing economics of a given production location. It has been this unresponsive attitude in combination with the competitive behavior of new firms and/or more sophisticated rivals which has allowed successful followers to grow and compete. But this lack of response may be partly due to inadequate analytical tools.

One way of analyzing the competitive implications of new demand-supply developments for strategic purposes is in terms of product-market segmentation. [A product-market segment is determined by the economics of supplying (production and distribution) a customer group with a common purchasing attribute.] Many companies have difficulty competing with internationally oriented competitors despite an understanding of world trade patterns because they lack basic insights about changes in market segments. They do not understand the competitive interaction created by changes in production economics and customer groupings. Since competitive survival demands domination of a selected group of segments in the world as a whole, successful participation in world markets requires an explicit concept of segmentation. Major successes in world markets, despite overall industry declines, are attributable to an extension of a clear segmentation concept. For example, the success of General Motors vis-à-vis Ford in the U.S. market is directly attributable to Alfred P. Sloan's perception of several emerging passenger-car market segments (according to income levels) which made production of "a car for every purse and purpose" appropriate.

A product-market segment exists if there is a sharp differential in the cost of or ability to supply a given product to an end-user group (e.g., customers needing after-sales service, customers subject to import competition, or customers who are price sensitive). A product-market segment therefore defines a particular relationship between revenues (sales to customers) and expenditures. Any large change in this relationship indicates a strategic problem. For example, Japanese and European manufacturers dominate their small-car markets. This market segment represents the bulk of their sales, production, and profits. On the other hand, the U.S. producers' strength is in the medium-car market. Yet it is the U.S. small-car market segment that is growing rapidly, and vehicle production economics are such that it is easier to move horizontally than vertically. Small-car production is different enough in terms of parts, tooling, and so on to represent a significant additional cost to U.S. producers, but of course no additional cost to foreign small-car producers. Since ocean logistics costs are falling dramatically and U.S. tariff rates are low, no barrier exists between European or Japanese sourcing points and the United States. The logical response for U.S. auto producers would seem to be to completely source abroad for the small-car segment. This strategy would benefit the U.S. economy as well as U.S. auto producers since producers could continue to support their distributors, designers, engineers, staff, and managers even if a few assembly jobs appeared to be exported. (In fact these jobs are not exported since foreign cars would be sold into this market segment.)

Growth and technical change imply the emergence of new market segments even if an industry is declining relative to other sectors. Failure to dominate each new segment opens an opportunity for competitors who may grow quite large. The innovator's advantage is not that he will inevitably maintain his position but that he has an initial advantage in pursuing new segments while holding on to old ones. But he must have a strategy to continue dominance over his competitors.

One type of emerging market segment is the development of markets in follower countries. Other new segments may be the large price-sensitive user who requires little service or the affluent, style-conscious consumer in a world market. Geography is only one possible segmentation scheme, and it is appropriate only when protection or other barriers exist. It is not appropriate when large reductions in ocean logistics costs and tariff barriers between industrial countries create world markets. U.S. steel and automobile producers made a major strategic mistake when they failed to recognize what volume could do to ocean freight costs and the competitiveness of foreign products in the U.S. market. More generally, there is a new relationship between revenues and expenditures every time a segment emerges, the parameters defining an existing segment shift, or the supply cost to a segment change. These new situations represent strategic problems.

Traditional product-cycle theory states that the cost of supplying a given segment shifts from country to country and that this cost shift parallels the emergence of a corresponding geographical market segment. The net result of these two conditions in the past has been the emergence of new competitors overseas.

COMPETITIVE DEVELOPMENT

The migration of competitive advantage from original producers to follower firms, either domestically or internationally, is not just a function of changing factor costs and demand patterns. It is also the result of the innovator's failure to control this competitive evolution by pursuing an international business strategy aimed at dominating a set of product-market segments.

Dominating a market segment means controlling market share. Loss of dominance means loss of world market share. A convenient way of appreciating the competitive importance of world market share is in terms of cost-volume relationships (experience curves). When combined with segmentation analysis, this approach clearly demonstrates many of the reasons for competitive success and failure.

COST-VOLUME RELATIONSHIPS

A critical aspect of many industries' competitive development has been their demonstrated ability to lower rapidly a product's supply costs (especially in high-growth follower economies such as Japan). Japanese firms have usually begun as internationally high-cost producers in most products, but in a few years they have

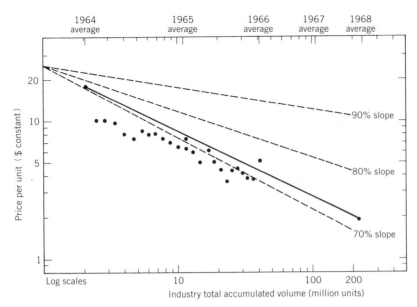

Figure 1 Integrated circuits in the United States (monthly price).

become very competitive. This phenomenon will be illustrated shortly for Japanese television producers, but it applies to a wide range of commodities and countries. Traditional product-cycle analysis explains this increased competitiveness as the result of market growth and changing factor supplies. But this explanation has an unwarranted ring of historical inevitability, and on further examination it is analytically unsatisfying. A firm's ability to lower a product's cost and price in fact depends on the volume it produces. The key determinant of volume is world market share.

The Boston Consulting Group and other researchers have demonstrated for a variety of products that total cost per unit in constant dollars or other currency will decline by a characteristic amount (usually 20% to 30%) each time accumulated production experience (total amount ever produced) doubles.[3] This statistical phenomenon is observed in many localities, including the United States, Europe, and Japan, and is an accepted part of cost projection formulations in the aircraft and semiconductor industries.[4] Though the precise reasons for the relationship are not well documented, it appears to be a combination of learning-by-doing, management experience, cost-reduction investments, and economies of scale. Because the concept relates the rate of cost decline with the rate of accumulation, a company's cost-experience relationship is plotted on log-log paper and is usually a straight line. (Figures 1 and 2.)

The cost-experience effect over time is more noticeable in new products. New products have a small experience base and a high demand growth; accumulated production experience can double rapidly, and costs will fall accordingly. In mature industries, the effects of inflation will obscure the decline in real dollar (yen, marks, or francs) costs.[5] To obtain an accurate picture, one must factor out inflation.

The distorting effect of inflation is eliminated by deflating the current dollar (or other currency) unit costs by the GNP deflator. Given a product's historical experience curve, one can predict future real costs at various levels of accumulated experience. To estimate actual future costs, though, one must reinflate by multi-

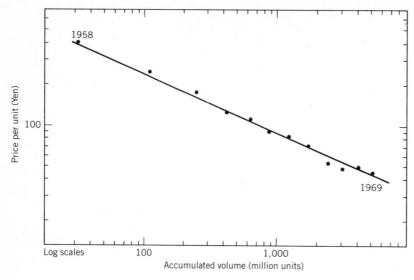

Figure 2 Transistors in Japan, 1958–1969.

plying the constant cost projections by the expected rate of inflation.

THE IMPORTANCE OF MARKET SHARE

Given the relationship between cost and volume, an individual firm's cost position within an industry depends on its growth relative to the entire industry, that is, on its market share. Conversely, an industry's ability to lower prices for a given amount of production experience depends on the market shares of the individual producers, i.e., on the industry's concentration. (With greater concentration, industry experience is spread among fewer producers.)

The implication of the cost-experience effect for international competition is that growth directly determines a competitor's ability to accumulate experience and lower costs, and market share determines his ability to lower costs relative to competitors, domestic and foreign. The successful follower is therefore the firm who captures a dominant share of the world demand represented by its home-market growth and subsequently by export demand.

INNOVATORS AND FOLLOWERS

For example, if a follower firm accumulates experience at 30% per year, it will double experience in less than three years and will lower real costs 20% to 30%. If inflation in his country is 5% a year, the firm's current costs will decline between 5% and 15% over the three-year period. If industry demand is growing at 15% per annum, and the industry growth rate has approached industry demand growth, the firm is capturing more than its share of incremental experience. It is gaining market share relative to competitors and is improving cost position.

At a fixed exchange rate, our follower firm also lowers current dollar costs. If a mature U.S. market is growing at 5% with the same 5% inflation rate as the follower, the follower is rapidly gaining absolute cost advantage relative to U.S. producers (innovators), assuming relatively stable U.S. market shares (a reasonable assumption in a mature market). By definition, however, the follower's production serves to satisfy growing domestic demand for products first produced elsewhere, frequently in the United States. Therefore, U.S. innovators have begun or gone through the product's development or growth phase. They have substantial cost-experience advantage relative to the follower. The follower's ability to serve his country's emerging world market segment has thus depended on transportation cost differentials, local government protection (tariffs, quotas, and subsidies), and/or no foreign marketing effort. Once it is producing, though, the firm's ability to become internationally competitive is a function of its initial real production costs, the slope of the experience curve, its country's inflation rate, exchange rates, and the firm's accumulation rate.

Conversely, an innovator's ability to maintain price competitiveness and dominance in a product it has introduced depends on an appropriate combination of the following:

- lower real start-up and initial production costs than the follower
- steeper experience curve slope
- lower inflation rate
- continuous devaluation
- faster accumulation rate

In reality, few of these conditions can be met. The innovator usually has higher initial production and development costs than the follower. Given a product's existence and the availability of production equipment and know-how, the cost of transferring a given technology decreases over time. The follower need not accumulate equivalent experience to become competitive.

Actual international comparisons by The Boston Consulting Group have yet to show any appreciable slope differentials for the same product between leading industrial countries. Technological factors and industrial organiza-tion at a given stage of development for the same product would seem similar, and cost management by successful firms producing the product are roughly equivalent.

Inflation and exchange rates are macroeconomic variables over which firms have little control. Nevertheless, it must be recognized that U.S. inflation rates, for example, which have been approaching Japanese levels since 1967, have seriously affected U.S. companies competitiveness. Until that time, the 2% inflation differential between the United States and Japan offset the relative real-cost reduction of Japan's higher manufacturing growth rate. The recent revaluations compensated for the absence of this inflation differential during the last five or six years.

However, despite the above factors, innovators do have some control over follower firms' ability to capture world market share, to accumulate experience, and to become cost competitive. This is true even if they have not generally done so. Innovators usually have lower current costs when the follower begins production (even though start-up costs in real terms are higher). There is thus a minimum accumulation rate that a follower requires over some time period to become cost competitive. The innovator can remain the dominant and low-cost producer if the follower fails to grow at this rate.

During the follower's initial production phase, the innovator can rarely accumulate experience as rapidly as the follower. The innovator is the initial producer and has a larger accumulated production base; consequently, he takes longer to double experience. As the follower's smaller market is saturated and as its experience base gets larger, though, further doublings and cost reductions become more difficult. The innovator must use his initial cost advantage, therefore, to participate in the follower's home market and/or shut off export development. (This strategy may still require moving offshore later, but then production

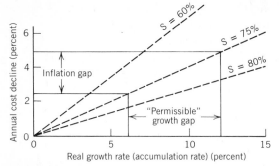

Figure 3   Real growth and annual cost decline. The annual rate of cost decline is equal to the mathematical slope of the experience curve times the accumulation rate. The mathematical slope equals log S/log 2, where S is the slope of the experience curve. For a 75% curve, $S = .75$ and the mathematical slope = .42.

should be concentrated at the new location.) Only in this way can the innovator deny the follower the growth necessary for fully competitive cost reduction. But his time horizon is limited.

An easy way of assessing a follower's competitive requirement is to calculate the "permissible" growth (accumulation rate) gap allowed by differences in the follower's rate of inflation or by exchange rate revaluations. (This gap equals the inflation or exchange rate differential divided by the mathematical slope of the experience curve.) Given current costs and prices, if a follower's relative growth exceeds this "permissible" gap, the innovator's cost position is improving. A smaller inflation differential and/ or a steeper product experience curve narrows the "permissible" growth gap for a particular product (Figure 3).

The object of a successful international business strategy is to capture enough world market growth so that no foreign (or domestic[6]) competitor can exceed the "permissible" growth gap long enough to become cost competitive.

But many U.S. and European innovators have not captured this required market growth. Thus, for many years, follower firms in Japan and other countries have exceeded the "per-

missible" gap in many products. At fixed exchange rates, this normally leads to large and persistent foreign exchange surpluses for the high-growth economy due to improved relative and absolute cost position. These surpluses can then be offset by tariff reductions, exchange rate adjustments, or other measures. But even though total trade may become balanced, specific products and industries will continue to lose competitive position. Not all products have the same experience curve slopes or are growing at the same rates.

Further, a currency appreciation or tariff reduction raises a competitor's relative prices only once. If comparative government and business policies do not change, relative long-term growth rates will not change and relative annual cost changes should continue as before. That is, devaluation represents an expensive investment by a country in buying world market share. Failure to support this expenditure by new marketing and investment policies domestically and overseas implies that the country's producers will not permanently improve their accumulation rate, their world market share, or their relative cost position. Another devaluation then becomes inevitable (e.g., the pound or dollar vis-à-vis the yen or mark).

THE CASE OF COLOR TELEVISION

Japanese television producers offer a pointed illustration of competitive development along the lines described above. It is a pattern systematically repeated in international competition. Television is especially interesting, however, because U.S. companies' strategic errors were exemplified not once but twice[7] and because the rapidly growing Japanese market was unprotected compared to computers, steel, or autos. The government never considered consumer electronics a strategic or an important industry. Its development did not depend on special quotas, marketing restrictions, high tariff barriers, or other protections. There was little to prevent U.S. exports and Japanese mar-

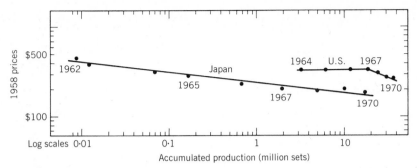

Figure 4 Color television: Real wholesale prices and accumulated production.

ket penetration when the United States was the world's low-cost producer. But no real effort was made. The eventual size and competitiveness of Japanese producers testifies to U.S. firms' strategic misperception. (Color production in 1970 was $1.9 billion.)

A brief comparison of the U.S. and Japanese price-experience curves for color television in Figure 4 indicates that the U.S. maintained a large cost-price advantage before 1965. In 1962, Japanese average wholesale prices compared with U.S. prices were $500 a set versus $350. Still, there were no exports to the Japanese market despite its rapid growth. Just how rapidly production grew compared to the United States is documented in Table 1. Japanese producers between 1962 and 1970 accumulated experience at 170% per year versus 56% in the United States. The result of this large differential accumulation rate was inevitable. A differential accumulation rate of 114% more than exceeded what could be permitted by a 1% to 2% inflation differential, and absolute cost advantage at a fixed exchange rate was gained quickly. Yet this was based on domestic market growth. Exports did not begin until Japanese domestic prices were below U.S. prices, and penetration of the U.S. market did not occur until the price differential was substantial and third country export experience and distribu-

Table 1 Color Television*

	United States (%)		Japan (%)	
	1962–1970	1965–1970	1962–1970	1965–1970
Real accumulation rate	56.0	41.0	170.0	196.0
Real growth rate	35.0	12.0	167.0	182.0
Annual decline in constant dollars or Yen (85% curve)	13.0	9.6	39.6	45.6
Inflation rate	3.1	4.0	4.9	4.7
Annual change in costs in current dollars	−9.9	−5.6	−34.7	−40.9
Competitor's cost advantage	—	—	24.8	35.3

*Exchange rate fixed at Y360 = $1.00

Table 2 Japanese Production and Exports (Monochrome Television, 1,000 units)

	1955	1960	1963	1965	1967	1969	1970
Production	137	3,552	4,878	4,060	5,681	7,284	6,089
Exports	—	45	686	1,414	1,922	3,286	3,715
Percent to U.S.	—	18%	66%	75%	68%	70%	66%
Export/Production	—	1%	14%	35%	34%	45%	61%

Source: Ministry of Finance and Ministry of International Trade and Industry.

tion had already been developed in monochrome (Table 2).

This was a typical "follower" scenario of competitive development. But as the economics of monochrome and color production have shifted in turn from Japan to countries such as Taiwan and Korea, the response of Japanese managers has differed from U.S. experience. Their response to the emergence of competitors in the LDCs, the belated move of American companies offshore, and their own changing production economics, has been to establish monochrome and now color television plants in Taiwan or Korea. Again unlike U.S. producers, they are not supplying just their own domestic market in Japan but are using or are planning to use these sources to supply markets worldwide (the United States, Japan, Europe, the LDCs, etc.). In this approach they remain one step ahead of U.S. manufacturers who produce offshore only for the U.S. market; U.S. manufacturers will lose relative cost position owing to their smaller volume and experience growth at the new location. Competitive initiative in the television industry would seen to have passed from the U.S. innovators to the Japanese followers.

We have now described and illustrated the underlying competitive dynamics responsible for traditional product-cycle development. However, this analysis also indicates an effective strategy alternative.

TRADITIONAL PRODUCT-CYCLE SCENARIO

After successful domestic development, a follower generally exports first to less developed countries, where there is little domestic competition, where demand is growing, and where the innovator has no innate advantage. These exports serve multiple competitive functions. They impair the innovator's ability to grow and lower costs relative to the follower. They also enhance the follower's ability to grow and to lower costs. Competitively, it is a zero-sum-game with a double relative-cost effect. These overseas markets are very important when the follower's home market is relatively small and quickly saturated, or when costs need to be lowered to stimulate additional domestic demand. Finally, these exports develop overseas marketing experience.

All these factors are necessary to gain enough competitive strength to penetrate the innovator's market. This task is always difficult because the innovator's domestic market is growing slowly, there is in-place capacity, and domestic competition exists.

However, the follower often benefits from economic conditions present in the innovator's mature market. The innovator has higher wage rates and slower productivity increases. The innovator also frequently decides to forgo continued growth (requiring investment and aggressive pricing) and attempts to earn a higher return on past investment by maintaining a constant real price level (price umbrella). Quotas and high tariffs are seldom applied until the home industry is in trouble. Further, a mature market usually has large, price-sensitive users that are easily segmented (e.g., U.S. ball bearings market). Moreover, the innovator often feels that foreign markets and competitors are not large enough to justify fighting protective policies or aggressively pursuing export markets.

These policies in the long run are self-defeating. As a market matures, it becomes increasingly price sensitive and vulnerable to low-priced products. Ignoring foreign competitors and holding a domestic price umbrella results in eventual market penetration by low-priced imports and hence competitive decline. These competitive forces have constantly pushed innovators into the development of newer and more sophisticated products or of new domestic market segments. If no new products or markets are found, the firm declines or disappears. This competitive process is repeated by a second follower (e.g., LDC), as appears to be happening in textiles and other simple manufactured products.

However, this traditional product-cycle view is simplistic if it argues the required concommitant demise of major companies making these products in the innovator or first follower country. This view fails to uncouple a firm's future production economics from its country of origin, its current production costs, and its domestic market—all invalid assumptions. The multinational or international firm has a wider strategy and more successful future open to it because it can utilize segmentation principles and cost-volume interaction on a worldwide basis.

Traditional product cycles have evolved because of the almost universally common managerial behavior described above. However, the fact that wider options are open is apparent. Past managerial behavior need not be continued. There are in fact sensitive points within the product cycle for each country and firm: initial production, initial export development, and initial penetration of the innovator's market. At these stages, key variables such as margins can be influenced by external pressures. The ability to apply or resist such pressures depends on a firm's relative competitive position in the product cycle and its integrated system of investment, marketing, pricing, and financial strategies.

IMPLICATIONS FOR INDIVIDUAL CORPORATIONS

It is now clear that business success depends on the development of an integrated set of investment, marketing, pricing, and financial strategies designed to ensure worldwide dominance of selected product-market segments. The conceptual basis for this overall strategy formulation is experience analysis and market segmentation. These two insights into international business strategy can help a manager turn traditional product-cycle development into an asset rather than a problem.

More specifically, an innovator firm should use aggressive or offensive strategies in growth markets to capture market share and to lower costs. But defensive strategies should be employed in mature markets to maintain market dominance and generate cash flows.

A follower firm, on the other hand, should pursue the same strategy as the innovator in its domestic and in second follower markets. Later, the follower will want to penetrate aggressively the innovator's mature or declining market. Such a strategy will continually provide the firm with a spectrum of growth and mature business, reducing long-run business risk.

But successful implementation of this strategy requires that the firm view the world as a single market composed of discrete market segments. This view reveals the importance of changes in world market share for both international and domestic competition. Yet it does not obscure the need for different implementation strategies in different market segments.

The value of market share (domestic or world) depends on one's ability to make this analysis and implement the appropriate strategy. Thus, an Italian or French firm must realize that a competitor's export sales reduce his costs and improve his overall competitiveness just as much as his domestic sales do.

Similarly, Japanese exports to the United States or to Southeast Asia improve Japan's competitiveness vis-à-vis European firms in Europe. Japanese sales in Europe have an analogous competitive effect. Thus, it is naive for U.S. auto producers to see Europe as an alternative or safety valve for Japanese exports. Those exports will merely make Japan relatively more competitive in both markets and worldwide (e.g., automobiles).[8]

STRATEGIES FOR MULTINATIONAL FIRMS

At present, U.S. companies usually have the advantage of being innovators for many products. Competitive relations between Japan and Europe, however, are more direct as both are followers at similar stages of development. That is, they compete within the same phase of the product cycle in many commodities. Their relative long-term success depends therefore on their ability to succeed as followers. The ability of the United States to defend its innovator position, on the other hand, represents the opposite side of the competitive equation.

The strategic issues confronting a large multinational firm compound in complexity according to the diversity of products it produces. It must pursue a different strategy for each product in each market segment, depending on its market share, the market segment's growth rate, and the nature of the product.

That is, LDCs lack the demand for and the ability to produce technically advanced products. However, they are able to produce mature and technically unsophisticated products at lower cost than advanced countries. In the case of sophisticated products, therefore, the multinational corporation should try to dominate its domestic market. (Presumably this is the market in the innovating country.) It should then try to preempt growth in follower countries to maintain domestic and international competitiveness. Failing this, it must confine follower firms to their home markets and prevent competitive export development.

This strategy should enable the firm to enjoy market leadership and high profit margins as growth slows in each geographical market segment. If this is done for all product lines in im-

portant market segments, the firm will have a mix of high and low growth businesses in which it has good market position. As growth requires cash to finance investment and aggressive pricing, this means that low-growth businesses will be cash generators and high-growth businesses will be cash users. Thus, the above strategy should produce a kind of balanced and secure portfolio of low- and high-growth businesses dominating a spectrum of market segments.

If the multinational firm cannot dominate its domestic market or if it is located in a follower country, its strategy should be somewhat different. Its objective should be to capture the growth emerging abroad or in a new domestic market segment. (This strategy may require moving production facilities overseas to gain lower costs.) After establishing a dominant position in this new segment, the company should then use this competitive-experience base to capture export markets from the dominant producer, first probably in the LDCs but later in that producer's home market. At the same time, the challenger must defend against development of the next round of followers.

If the challenger is headquartered in the innovating country, this strategy sequence is probably the only way to convert an unfavorable situation into success. Failure to pursue this strategy on the other hand will result in a permanent cost disadvantage in the innovating country's low-growth market.

The programs that a multinational firm can independently (of government) employ to achieve its strategic goals are roughly as follows:

Investment Strategies

The dominant producer should continually develop new products to supply the high growth and sophisticated product-market segments emerging in the advanced countries. At the same time, he should combine this new product investment with international sourcing investments in established products to preempt growth emerging in other countries or to serve mature domestic market segments.

On the other hand, follower or nondominant producers should expand aggressively in their own or emerging markets, building an experience base. They should invest abroad only to gain access to technology, raw materials, export markets, or a lower-cost production facility. They should not dilute experience. Once they have built their strength on the new market segment, they should fight for world market position, playing on the dominant producer's weaknesses in other markets. Having achieved this, they will be the new world leader and should pursue a dominant producer's strategy.

Marketing Strategies

Though many firms see the importance of domestic market dominance, few perceive the importance of world market share. Exports are often considered a fringe area or an incremental production market. However, production experience effects are independent of where the product is sold. Overseas markets are thus as important as domestic markets. An established international marketing policy and system can result in lower overseas distribution costs and lower production costs, permanently increasing exports, and worldwide cost competitiveness.

Pricing Strategies

Companies should vary their prices depending on the location and characteristics of a market segment. Low export prices enable a firm to penetrate rapidly foreign markets and to keep foreign competitors from gaining a foothold outside their domestic markets. At the same time, a dominant producer can reap profits from his large but slow-growing domesic market by maintaining profit margins at a level that stabilizes current market shares.

This strategy preserves his dominant domestic position for a longer period by frustrating potential foreign and domestic competition and by enabling him to fund overseas growth from domestic sales. An export pricing policy of "domestic price plus freight and insurance" is inappropriate and dangerous in this contest, even if dumping issues must be watched.

On the other hand, if a foreign competitor does penetrate a firm's domestic market, that firm should lower its domestic prices. This can be a problem for a dominant U.S. producer if such a price cut threatens smaller U.S. producers and invites possible antitrust action. But this consideration only makes an aggressive export pricing policy an even more important competitive element for large U.S. multinational companies. It is the only way to keep a foreign competitor from getting large enough to enter the U.S. market.

Financial Strategies

As growth uses cash, a low dividend payout and aggressive use of debt facilitates high financial and thus high business growth. In meeting foreign competition and in developing high-growth (foreign or domestic) markets, differential financial policies are thus required. When growth slows, a higher net cash flow is expected from a given product-market segment. If the same net cash flow were required from a high-growth foreign subsidiary or high-growth export market, the business would be starved for cash and could not preempt growth. Foreign competitors would then gain world market share and would increase their relative competitiveness. An appropriate financial strategy therefore leverages its high-growth businesses while funding from its lower-growth businesses.

IMPLEMENTATION IN SEMI-CONDUCTORS

An excellent example of an integrated use of these strategies on a multinational basis is the U.S. semi-conductor industry, where experience-curve analysis is well understood and widely applied. This industry now produces fourth- and fifth-generation semiconductors, integrated circuits, and large-scale integrated circuits in the United States, but it produces older established products abroad (e.g., in Korea, Hong Kong, Taiwan, and Mexico). These products are then exported to the United States and other countries where the parent company markets them. Production costs in these foreign subsidiaries are about 30% below Japan's for the same products.

The American producers have successfully encircled potential Japanese competition. They have been accidentally helped in this process by the fragmentation of Japan's semiconductor industry,[9] but the basic strategy remains their own. Moreover, the industry is pressing for freer access to the Japanese market using Japan's favorable trade balances with Taiwan and Korea as a lever. The U.S. firms have simultaneously preempted any future local competitive development in sourcing countries such as Taiwan and Korea. In sum, the industry as a whole has pursued an extremely intelligent international competitive strategy.

Many industries, such as aircraft assembly, shipbuilding, and steel production, are composed of what may be called single-product, single-plant firms. Their strategic problems are somewhat different than those of multinational firms. These problems are more restricted, and the industries have fewer strategic options. They must rely heavily on pricing and export marketing to capture world market share and to contain potential competitors. Overseas investment is limited as a strategic tool for capturing incremental world market growth and for reducing costs.

STRATEGIES FOR SINGLE PLANT FIRMS

The strategic objective of these industries, however, remains the same as those of multinational firms.[10] The single-plant company must still dominate a spectrum of product-market segments in the world as a whole. It should thus attempt to prevent competitive development in follower countries. Failing to do this, it should shut off their potential export development,

even if this tactic means lower profits on exports to certain growth markets. For such companies, trade liberalization and antitrust are therefore critical issues. Export market access is necessary for continued world dominance, and a large domestic market provides a secure experience and cash flow base.

The strategic program for the single-product, single-plan firm is indicated as follows:

Investment Strategies

The dominant producer must invest in process as well as in product improvement. Maintaining world market dominance from a single sourcing point requires not only developing and dominating new segments but keeping cost competitive in old ones. Investment for both high-quality products and lower costs is necessary. The ability to shift to other production sites is restricted.

Follower firms, on the other hand, should try to build and maintain a domestic experience base from which an aggressive export strategy can be launched. Some specialized investment with respect to a world market segment is probably advisable.

Marketing Strategies

Exports are absolutely critical to the single-plant firm's continued competitiveness. Though domestic market dominance is necessary as an experience and cash base, once domestic demands level off, future growth and cost reduction ultimately depend on exports. The single-plant firm thus needs an overseas marketing system and strategy. It must seek to reduce overseas marketing costs through integrated handling systems, specialized transports, cooperative marketing organizations, trading companies, etc. (Aircraft and shipbuilding have lent themselves to this kind of world strategy owing to their "built-in" transportation and large unit size.)

The firm's objective is to dominate a spectrum of world market segments by creating technological, cost, price, service, legal, or other barriers. This program will discourage entry by potential competitors in either follower countries or related industries. Worldwide competitive surveillance of potential competitors is an important element.

Pricing Strategies

Differential pricing strategies at home and abroad are the single-plant, single-product company's most important strategic tool. Differential pricing can keep foreign competitors from getting a foothold outside their own countries. It may even prevent them from developing their own domestic industries. At the same time, differential pricing allows the firm to earn large enough profits in mature markets, particularly in its domestic market, to fund penetration of new growth areas. By capturing world market growth in this manner, the firm will lower its costs further and will enhance its profitability in all markets. A "domestic price plus freight and insurance" export pricing policy can be disastrous when a firm lacks the overseas investment options open to the multinational, multiproduct corporation.

Domestic pricing policies should be designed to maintain market dominance and to discourage imports. Higher margins and profitability can probably be anticipated more in the domestic market than in the export market. But the firm must guard against holding a real price umbrella, trying to recoup past investment too quickly.

Financial Strategies

Heavy use of debt and low dividend payout are important in the early stages of domestic market growth and development. However, they are less necessary for the successful producer in later stages of development. (They may be appropriate for a follower or nondominant producer as a way of compensating for a low market share and high-cost position.) Still, some sacrifice of returns on previous investment will be required to pursue appropriate differential pricing strategies.

IMPLEMENTATION IN SHIPBUILDING

An outstanding example of a successful follower and consolidation strategy for essentially single-product, single-plant companies is found in the Japanese shipbuilding[11] industry. Japan's shipbuilding capability was essentially destroyed during World War II, and previous production experience was largely related to warships. However, with government support the industry developed rapidly in response to raw material shortages and large postwar replacement demand. Based on this large and rapidly expanding domestic demand, the Japanese achieved dramatic cost reductions (Figure 5). This was especially noticeable for the bulk carriers and tankers needed to supply raw materials and oil to Japan's growing economy. These large cost declines for bulk carriers and tankers in turn revolutionized the economics of shipping and transportation while stimulating Japanese ship exports.

Japanese shipbuilders' export success was, however, the result of a conscious business strategy:

- continued reductions in cost per ton (experience effect) supported by technological improvement and rapid capacity expansions

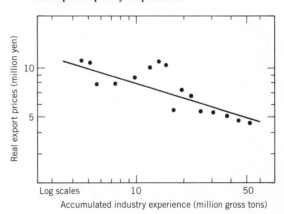

Figure 5 Japanese shipbuilding, 1958–1968.

- world market segmentation, initial penetration being in the free-ship markets (Liberia, Greece, Panama, and Norway), combined with aggressive international marketing and differential pricing policies
- highly leveraged operations substantially financed by the Industrial Bank of Japan and the Japanese Export-Import Bank

Maintenance of these strategic policies has resulted in Japan's continued dominance of the world shipbuilding industry for several years, especially for bulk carriers and tankers. Given cost-experience effects, this world market dominance is self-reinforcing as long as basic business policies continue.[12] The only option for other shipbuilders is to find a new segment that can be expanded and defended.

TAKING THE WORLD VIEW

In meeting modern international competition, merely appreciating traditional product-cycle development or having "international" business operations is inadequate for long-term success. A company must have an explicit international strategy that incorporates a definite segmentation scheme and is based on an understanding of cost-volume relationships. Only a world view of products and markets can offer long-term solutions to strategy problems for internationally traded commodities. Companies that fail to take such a view are taking a large business risk since they will become subject to increased competitive pressures from truly internationally oriented rivals, both domestic and foreign. Recognizing this fact is the first step in international strategy formulation and in meeting international competition. However, ultimately the firm must become an integrated international company with a system of investment, marketing, pricing, and financial strategies with which it can dominate a spectrum of worldwide market segments. Otherwise, it will find future survival difficult in an increasingly competitive world environment.

NOTES

1. The author would like to express his appreciation to his former colleagues of The Boston Consulting Group for their comments and advice, especially Dr. Seymour Tilles. However, he takes full responsibility for the views and errors contained in this article.
2. This historical and on-going process of the competitive migration of products and industries from country to country was first identified formally by Professor Akamatsu in the 1930s. Professor R. Vernon in his 1966 *Quarterly Journal* article has given it a more precise and elegant statement. The author has made a thorough documentation of its applicability to Japan in "Theory of Changing Trade Patterns," *Yale Economic Essays,* Fall 1967.
3. The Boston Consulting Group, *Perspectives on Experience.*
4. Since cost data are not always available, one can derive curves from price data on the assumption that prices follow costs over time and market shares change slowly. The phenomenon is basically a country-firm-cost relationship and a country-industry-price relationship. Price curves are displayed in this paper for two electronic components and for television. Cost is total cost to the end-user, including direct overhead and marketing.
5. If industry growth is g_0, and the growth in accumulated experience at time t is gn(t), then

$$1/[\Sigma(1 + g_0)t] + g_0 = gn(t).$$

Thus, the accumulation rate substantially exceeds the market growth rate in the early production stages, but approaches it as the market matures.
6. In the case of a domestic competitor, the "permissible" gap is zero as there is no inflation or exchange rate differential, although one should make allowance for possible regional cost differentials.
7. Although this discussion is restricted to color television, monochrome followed a similar competitive development. (This is discussed in J. C. Abegglen and W. V. Rapp, "Competitive Impact of Japanese Growth," in J. Cohen, ed., *Pacific Partnership: U.S.-Japan Trade, Prospects and Recommendations for the 1970's,* New York:. D. C. Heath & Co., 1972.) With the examples of transistor radios, tape recorders, stereo equipment, not to mention monochrome television, as guides, there seems little reason for U.S. misperception. Yet it did occur again. It is for this reason that the effectiveness of revaluation is open to question. A price advantage is effective only if it is used for market penetration. But U.S. television producers twice did not use a price advantage when they had it, and the price differential was systematically eroded.
8. T. Hout and W. V. Rapp, "Competitive Development of the Japanese Automobile Industry," ibid.
9. This fragmentation results from the Japanese government's insistence on the diffusion of technological informa-

tion and the encouragement of multiple producers. This policy diluted the experience base available to any one firm to become internationally cost competitive.

10. Some international companies will have divisions which are essentially single-plant firms. They should be run differently from those in which more flexibility is possible. Indeed, it is a strategic error to treat a single-plant operation as if a multisourcing strategy were appropriate.

11. A similar argument could be made for the Japanese steel industry. J. Dresser, T. Hout, and W. Rapp, "Competitive Development of the Japanese Steel Industry," ibid.

12. Shipping economies have reduced raw material costs for steelmaking to such an extent that economically efficient steel mills can only be built at harbor sites. This in turn has made Japanese steel and thus ships less expensive, creating a greater demand for both steel and ships.

9

Strategic Portfolio Management in the Multibusiness Firm

Richard A. Bettis
William K. Hall

• • •

During the past decade the concept of corporate strategy has enjoyed widespread and increased popularity in large firms througout the Western world as these firms try to grapple with complexity, uncertainty, and a more hostile external environment. This popularity has resulted in several new approaches to long-range planning, including the portfolio or strategic-business-unit (SBU) concept, which has become especially popular within large, diversified firms in the United States and Europe. Indeed, the authors' research suggests that at least 200 of the *Fortune* 500 companies (and probably substantially more) are using the portfolio planning concept in some manner, and informal discussions suggest a similar rate of adoption in Western Europe.

Despite this popularity, there has been surprisingly little research on the processes by which firms are implementing the portfolio concept and the implications of these processes for effective strategic management. In numerous

Source: Richard A. Bettis and William K. Hall, "Strategic Portfolio Management in the Multibusiness Firm." Copyright © 1981 by the Regents of the University of California. Reprinted from *California Management Review,* Volume XXIV, Number 1, pp. 23–38 by permission of the Regents.

conversations with senior executives, the authors found that implementation problems are vital and pressing. It seems logical to pause at this point and give a status report on implementation progress and problems. This report should provide an essential foundation for progress in the effective application of the portfolio concept during the decade of the 1980s.

THE PORTFOLIO CONCEPT

Although there are numerous slight variations of the portfolio concept, they all rely on a matrix or grid similar to the one shown in Figure 1. Within such a matrix, each business in the multibusiness firm is categorized along two dimensions: measuring product/market attractiveness along one axis and competitive position along the other. In current practice, there are two basic approaches to measurement along these scales. One approach relies on a single numerical criterion along each axis, while an alternative approach uses multiple measures (including subjective ones) along each axis (see Figure 2). Typically, the matrices or grids are divided into either four or nine boxes, although the authors

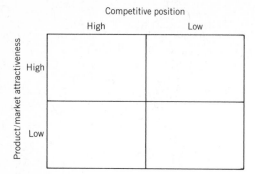

Figure 1   The portfolio concept: Conceptual matrix.

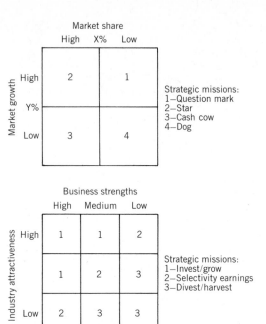

Figure 2   Two popular matrices.

have observed some corporations using significantly more units of analysis in their matrix categorizations. Figure 2 illustrates two of the most commonly encountered matrices.

Regardless of the particular layout chosen for the matrix, the basic idea behind the portfolio concept remains the same: the position (or box) that a business unit occupies within the matrix should determine the strategic mission and the general characteristics of the strategy for the business. Although these missions vary somewhat depending on which matrix approach is chosen, Figure 2 provides a typical illustration. Here the mission of the "cash cows" is to generate cash flow that can be redeployed to promising "question marks," while the mission of the question marks is to aggressively gain competitive position with the needed investment funds coming from the cash cows. (Obviously the number of question marks in the corporate portfolio must be balanced with the cash-generation capabilities of the cash cows.) Simultaneously, the mission of the "stars" is to ensure their own long-term competitive position, while the mission of the "dogs" is to generate positive cash flow while they are harvested or until they can be opportunistically divested. (The reader who is unfamiliar with the theory behind the concept or who desires a deeper understanding can refer to several references.)[1]

THE RESEARCH

The research on which this status report is based consisted of clinical studies conducted within a sample of twelve large, diversified firms during 1977, 1978, and 1979. In developing this sample, the authors contacted approximately thirty-five firms which were using the portfolio concept. A significant level of access was obtained in ten of these, and two other firms permitted limited but useful access. Table 1 summarizes some general financial characteristics of the final sample, and Table 2 describes the diversification posture of each firm in terms of a diversification typology developed by Leonard Wrigley and Richard Rumelt, which is summarized in Table 3.[2]

Table 4 summarizes the number and organizational level of interviews that were eventually conducted within each of the twelve firms. The actual interviews lasted from half an hour to a full day each. (In some cases multiple interviews were conducted with a single manager.

Table 1 Financial Data on Sample of Firms

Company	1977 Sales Net	Percent of 1973*	1977 Income Net	Percent of 1973*	1977 Assets Net	Percent of 1973*
ABC	$ 1– 5 billion	140%	$ 50–100 million	198%	$ 1– 5 billion	145%
DEF	> 15 billion	147	> 1 billion	164	10–15 billion	168
GHI	0.5– 1 billion	157	50–100 million	144	0.5– 1 billion	167
JKL	1– 5 billion	134	50–100 million	102	1– 5 billion	115
MNO	5–10 billion	120	100–500 million	155	5–10 billion	125
PQR	1– 5 billion	148	100–500 million	113	1– 5 billion	130
UVW	1– 5 billion	178	50–100 million	190	1– 5 billion	200
XYZ	1– 1 billion	144	100–500 million	147	1– 5 billion	154
S	1– 5 billion	155	50–100 million	140	1– 5 billion	143
T	1– 5 billion	131	100–500 million	146	1– 5 billion	124

*(1977 figure ÷ 1973) × 1—%.

These instances were only counted as single interviews in compiling Table 4.) Each interview typically had a structured and an unstructured portion. In all interviews, relevant documents, such as planning manuals and actual plans, were requested. After each interview, the researchers requested, and were usually granted, the right to call back to clarify specific points. This privilege was exercised on several occasions. In addition to the in-company interviews, all relevant public domain information was examined, and several consultants familiar with various firms in the sample were interviewed.

The data were subjected to intensive analysis

Table 2 Diversification Categories of Sample Firms

Firm	Category
ABC	Related constrained
DEF	Related linked
GHI*	Related constrained
JKL	Dominant vertical
MNO	Related linked
PQR	Dominant vertical
UVW*	Related linked
XYZ*	Related linked
S	Related constrained
T	Related linked

*Not included in Rumelt's original study.

by the authors in order to develop managerially meaningful insights and academically useful frameworks to facilitate further research. The resulting status report was organized around several important questions, each addressed separately, though not independently. A conclusive answer for every question is not possible at this time (hence the term *status report*).

FIRM USE OF THE PORTFOLIO CONCEPT

The research showed that large, multibusiness firms are using the portfolio concept in one of two different ways. The difference was captured by the responses of corporate-level managers in two firms to the question, "What does the term portfolio or SBU concept mean in your company?" According to the first manager:

It can mean just about anything in business today, and that's the problem, but not around here—at least not as far as I'm concerned. You see, we don't get too hung up on the latest trends. We take what we think is useful and use it, but we never have and we never will get involved in some new religion of management that comes complete with high priests. So, yes, we use portfolio grids around here but they're just another tool. They haven't replaced anything, but they have helped us on a few occasions. We don't have anything we call SBUs but we do suggest

Table 3 Summary of Rumelt's Diversification Categories

Single business: a firm deriving greater than 95 percent of annual revenues from the base business.

Dominant business: a firm deriving 70–95 percent of annual revenues from the base business. A firm is dominant vertical if the base business is vertically integrated.

Related business: a firm deriving less than 70 percent of revenues from the base business, and in which diversification has been accomplished by "relating" new activities to old. This relatedness is defined in terms of markets served, distribution systems, production technologies, or exploitation of science-based research. A firm is considered to be related constrained (as opposed to related linked) when all component businesses are related to each other.

Conglomerate business: a firm that is committed to the conglomeration and operation of totally unrelated businesses.

to our division managers that grid analysis is useful. We use it and we expect some of them to use it when it might be useful. That's the key—to do it when it makes sense.

The second manager stated:

To me personally it means corporate strategy for a big company like this one. When I first came to work here sixteen or seventeen years ago, we operated without a strategy. Sure, we had a strategy in the division I first worked in. It was simple. We used technology—we weren't allowed to say automation—to lower costs and we priced 3% below the industry leader . . . Now the whole game has changed. We've split the whole company into SBUs, got them all plotted in terms of growth and market share . . . Now if a guy is running a cash cow, you had better be able to recognize that in his five-year plan. We're dealing in this game and he better not be asking for more chips every year. Occasionally it's all right . . . Our stars and question marks or whatever better perform the way they are expected to, also. We're running this company by strategic thinking and everything better be tied to strategy. Now don't misunderstand me. There is a lot of day-to-day stuff that has to be looked after and it's important stuff too. We've always done a good job on that, and we get better every year. The thing that is important is that there is a reason behind everything and that is what strategic thinking is about.

These two responses embody substantially different views of the portfolio concept. Though some features of both responses reflect the individual more than the organization, further interviews showed that these responses generally captured the major differences in the two firm's understanding of the term *portfolio concept*. There was a substantially different paradigm operating in each firm. The first manager's comments were conditioned by a view of the portfolio concept as a tool useful in the analysis of certain situations. The second manager's response indicated a broader view stressing a complete system for strategic management. This difference seemed to characterize all of the organizations studied, where the portfolio concept was used either as a tool of analysis or in a portfolio management system (PMS). To fur-

Table 4 Number of Managers Interviewed

Firm	Corporate/Group Level		Division/Business Level	
	Line	Staff	Line	Staff
ABC	1	2	1	
DEF	1	2		1
GHI	3	1	1	
JKL	1	1	1	
MNO	4	6	4	3
PQR	1	1	1	
UVW	1	1		
XYZ	1	1	1	
S	1	2		
T		1		
Total	14	18	9	4

ther delineate the differences in these two approaches, we will discuss Firm ABC, a PMS example, and Firm XYZ, a tool example.

FIRM ABC AND THE PMS

The ABC Corporation is a large, diversified manufacturing firm that earned about $100 million in 1977 on sales and assets, which were each substantially above $1 billion. Sales have increased 40 percent, earnings 98 percent, and net assets 45 percent in the last five years.

For many years, the firm was involved mainly in the manufacture of a group of commodity items that were related on the basis of a common production technology. In 1977 this core business accounted for about 75 percent of earnings and over 50 percent of sales. In the mid-1960s the firm diversified into areas unrelated to the base business. This diversification included consumer, commodity, and industrial products, gained primarily through acquisition. In 1977 the total scope of activities outside of the base business (including forward integration and unrelated diversification) was about 25 percent of sales and slightly less than 50 percent of operating earnings. Both of these figures were down significantly from earlier peaks in the 1970s. The company has continued to acquire businesses in areas unrelated to the core business during recent years, and public statements indicate that this policy will continue. In addition, in the 1970s ABC had sold off or closed some parts of the base business, but these divestures have been diminishing during the last few years.

The ABC Corporation began implementing the portfolio concept in 1969. By early 1977 the ABC Corporation was organized into twenty-four strategic business units. It was corporate policy that each one of these SBUs be directed toward and defined in terms of a particular market segment. SBU managers were initially titled "market managers," and in most cases the position corresponded to that of the traditional division manager. However, this ideal was

difficult to realize, and the company frequently found it necessary to redefine SBUs because of a changing view of the market. This frequently led to a new strategic mission (such as cash cow or dog). These SBUs generally fell at what would be called the product division level. A few divisions were composed of more than one SBU, generally when the SBUs were small and closely related. Although company policy stated that SBUs should coincide with profit centers, this was not always the case.

The corporate-level planning staff was composed of only five professionals and reported to the vice-chairman of the board, who was considered to be the chief strategic officer. This planning staff had been in existence for only a couple of years; the intent was that nobody remain on this staff or as one of the SBU planners for more than four years before being transferred into a line job. This policy was aimed at ensuring that planning remain primarily a line manager's job. Staff planning positions were filled by high potential employees, and the assignment was intended to give future line executives a strategic perspective. The role of the corporate planning staff was seen as one of managing the planning process, helping SBU managers, and conducting selected inhouse studies.

The ABC Company used the single-objective-criterion approach to evaluate SBUs on the master strategy matrix. Product/market attractiveness were measured in terms of market growth relative to growth in the gross national product, and competitive position was measured in terms of market share relative to the largest competitor. A four-block matrix was used with the break point for product/market attractiveness being a growth rate 10 percent, and the break point for competitive position being a market share 1.5 times that of the next largest competitor. Businesses were reevaluated every year to determine if the strategic mission was correct.

The planning horizon for the SBUs was five years and these plans were rolled over every year. The planning cycle started in April and ended in November with several reviews and iterations at the SBU and group level. Strategic and operational planning were closely intertwined, but some differences were tolerated. The corporate planning staff and the vice-chairman supervised the planning process, and attempted to assure that the plan and corporate objectives were synchronized when the aggregated companywide plan was reviewed annually by the board of directors. These corporate objectives were set and reviewed by a committee of the board of directors that was composed entirely of outside directors. The format of the five-year SBU plans included a combination of a few rigid requirements imposed by the planning staff and some less structured sections. There was enough freedom within this format for managers with different strategic missions to submit the necessary variety of strategies.

The matching of managers to the appropriate strategic missions (such as cash cow and star) was considered important by every corporate-level manager interviewed. Within a span of about three years, nineteen SBU managers had been reassigned to achieve a better match of management to each SBU strategic mission.

The capital-budgeting system was also tied to the planning process. Capital budgets were part of the annual plan and hence tied to the strategic mission for each SBU. At the corporate level, the capital-budgeting process was viewed as a primary tool for assuring that the appropriate strategic mission was being pursued. The capital budgeting system used different criteria to evaluate projects in different types of SBUs (those with different strategic missions). Furthermore, this system of differential criteria was tied closely to the five-year planning system and vice versa, forcing capital budgeting proposals to pass both a strategy review and a financial review that was differentiated by strategic mission.

The incentive compensation system for SBU managers at ABC varied somewhat by strategic mission. This compensation was split in half, with 50 percent being determined on the basis of a formula using corporate profits as the base, and 50 percent being discretionary and intended to reflect performance against the plan (this portion was tied generally to the plan and not to any specific measures within the plan). It was possible for an SBU manager to generate no profits (if his or her strategic mission emphasized other aspects) and still receive a bonus comparable to an SBU manager who generated substantial profits. However, the connection between strategy and incentive compensation was not explicit, and it seems reasonable to suspect that other factors besides strategy could be important. For example, it would seem difficult to penalize a manager whose SBU generated substantial profits but who had done so in a manner different than the plan had indicated.

The incentive compensation system included one other mechanism for tying strategies to compensation. Beginning with the given strategic mission, an SBU manager developed each year a comprehensive five-year plan that represented the complete strategy (including financial objectives) for his or her SBU. These strategies were ranked by the corporate planning staff on a scale of degree of difficulty from one to five. A lower degree of difficulty was explicitly stated to result in a lower potential bonus unless the financial objectives were substantially exceeded. SBU plans were often revised during the planning process by the SBU manager to achieve a higher level of difficulty. This level-of-difficulty rating scheme was considered a good working tool at the corporate level for matching SBU plans to corporate objectives and for defeating the tendency to set conservative financial objectives.

FIRM XYZ: PORTFOLIO PLANNING AS A TOOL OF ANALYSIS

XYZ was roughly comparable in size and diversity to ABC, although it had grown somewhat

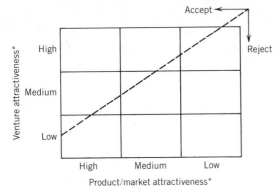

*Measured along multiple proprietary criteria
which are scaled numerically.

Figure 3 Portfolio analysis as an acquisition screen in XYZ corporation.

slower than ABC in recent years. In the XYZ Corporation the use of the portfolio concept as a tool of analysis occurred at the corporate staff level. Specifically, it was used as a primary technique to analyze potential acquisitions. Acquisitions were evaluated on a grid as is shown in Figure 3. If an acquisition candidate fell into the indicated area, it was given further consideration; those not falling into this zone were dropped from consideration. It was implicit company policy that the portfolio concept not be applied to existing divisions as a basis for planning. As a corporate-level planning executive put it, "We don't want people putting their businesses into a straightjacket, like by thinking of themselves as cash cows when they could really grow if they found the right strategy." There was absolutely no intention of adopting anything like the system construct used in ABC in the foreseeable future.

WHO'S USING THE PORTFOLIO CONCEPT?

The rest of this article is concerned with the PMS approach. A quick examination of Table 2 shows that it is composed entirely of dominant vertical and related diversified firms (both constrained and linked). No single business or con-

glomerate firms were found in the authors' investigation. One can tentatively conclude that the firms' choice of diversification posture would seem to be a primal determinant in the decision to use the portfolio concept.

In the case of the two dominant vertical firms in this sample, the portfolio concept was being adopted as a result of attempts to diversify away from core businesses with little growth potential and generally low profit potential (see Figure 4). The portfolio concept was seen as a means of managing this diversification and for identifying appropriate strategic missions for various segments of the vertically integrated core business.

If the management of diversification is a rationale for using the portfolio concept in firms with low levels of diversification (that is, dominant verticals), the logic would seem to be even more forceful for related firms and conglomerates. Why then were only related firms found to be using the portfolio concept and no conglomerates found? The answer revolves around the administrative problems of using the portfolio concept as a system for strategic planning and administration. Conglomerates are not finding the portfolio concept useful as a system for strategic planning and administration because the unrelatedness and extent of diversification causes the number of SBUs that are necessary to be "unmanageably large."

As an example of the problems caused by the extent of diversification consider the Eaton Corporation. Eaton, which had sales of $2.11 billion in 1977, is definitely not considered to be a conglomerate. However, in the Eaton 1977 annual report, reference is made to over four hundred product/market segments that are said to consist of "a single product or family of related products which go into a well defined and unified market." Examples given include economy truck transmissions, narrow-aisle lift trucks, agricultural scales, and gas-control valves. If each of these product/market segments is defined as an SBU, a meaningful strategy and performance review certainly cannot

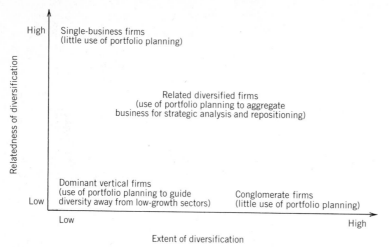

Figure 4   Use of the portfolio concept by types of diversity.

be conducted by corporate management. Furthermore, a huge staff would be needed merely to develop and maintain the information necessary for positioning these segments on the matrix. The scope of such efforts at the corporate level would certainly need to be heroic, if not foolish. What do related firms possess that allows them to overcome these problems that conglomerate firms do not possess? The answer seems to be that the relatedness of businesses in these firms allows them to meaningfully aggregate businesses for planning and review, while no such aggregation is possible in conglomerate firms.

In a related diversified firm, groups of related businesses can be aggregated together to form aggregated SBUs (see Figure 4). Consider a firm that, among other things, manufactures and markets appliances. An appliance SBU can be formed around dishwashers, trash compacters, washers and dryers, and microwave ovens. In this situation, *industry attractiveness* and *competitive position* are still meaningful for the aggregation. Contrast this situation with that of a conglomerate, whose various businesses are unrelated. How can a sheet steel business be aggregated with a perfume company, or a car rental agency with an insurance

company? What possible meaning could be ascribed to *industry attractiveness* and *competitive position* for such aggregations? Because of the way they assemble their portfolio, strategically meaningful aggregation is difficult if not impossible for most large conglomerates. Conglomerates find the portfolio concept unattractive because the number of necessary SBUs overwhelms corporate management. Related diversified firms are able to aggregate businesses up to a level where the number of SBUs becomes manageable. (This does not preclude the application of the portfolio concept at a lower level, such as a division within a conglomerate.)

WHY DO THEY USE IT?

The authors found that, with few exceptions, firms appear to be using the portfolio concept in response to perceived problems. The authors identified three types of problems that seem to be triggering usage. Poor financial performance, frequently observed as a trigger to adoption, was often characterized as a "crisis" by managers within the firm and the financial community. In three of the firms studied (ABC, DEF, and MND in Table 5), management presenta-

Table 5   Factors in Adoption

Firm	Poor Financial Performance	Too Much Growth	Strategic Issues Not Surfacing
ABC	×	×	×
DEF	×	×	×
GHI	×	×	×
JKL	×	×	×
MNO	×		×
PQR	×		×

tions introducing the portfolio concept specifically referred to a financial crisis as the reason for adoption.

Interestingly, adoption also seemed to result from a very different circumstance, too much growth. As a result of rapid growth, capital rationing was encountered and exacerbated the need for a managerially meaningful approach to resource allocation. The portfolio concept was seen as providing this. Adoption was also triggered by the perception that strategic issues were not surfacing. As one manager put it, "We need a way to separate out the cream." Table 5 summarizes the presence of these three factors in the adoption decisions of the firms studied.

In addition to the problems that triggered adoption, there appeared to be two other factors that were ultimately important in implementation: an internal advocate and a consulting firm. In describing the scenario leading to adoption, managers often referred to the internal advocate as the "sponsor" or "father" of the system, and to adoption as the advocate's "baby." This individual was in all cases a corporate-level executive, but not always the chief executive. The role of the internal advocate was characterized as one of initiating consideration of the portfolio concept and then pushing hard for adoption. He or she was seen as an organizational force around which a coalition formed that eventually succeeded in securing adoption.

In addition to an internal advocate, consulting firms were involved in adoption. Typically, the involvement started before formal consideration of adoption began and proceeded through the adoption process. In all firms, the consultant was seen as supplying the technical skills necessary to facilitate implementation.

WHAT'S CHANGED?

The use of PMS for ongoing administration represents a substantial departure from administration in the traditional, diversified, divisionalized, decentralized firm. The traditional approach assumes that the role of each division is to increase or maximize earnings or return on investment, while under the portfolio concept, each SBU may have a different strategic mission. With PMS, managerial systems must be adjusted for each different strategic mission. Administrative processes must vary among SBUs as directed by differences in strategic mission. The problem is to clarify and reinforce the differences in strategic mission among SBUs while maintaining the overall unity of the firm.

The transition from the traditional approach to the PMS approach must logically begin with the definition of SBUs. We refer now to aggregated SBUs. SBUs must be the basic planning entities, but should they be the basic organizational entities? Superimposed on this consideration is the necessity to make an SBU meaningful as a competitive entity, in terms of the dimensions of the matrix (product/market attractiveness and competitive position). Consideration needs also to be given to the alignment of the accounting system with the SBU. To develop meaningful plans for an SBU, the

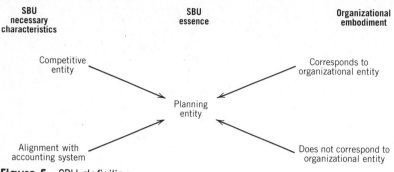

Figure 5 SBU definition

accounting system must collect information relevant to it. Figure 5 summarizes the nature of the problem of defining an SBU. Here, the necessity of having a business unit which is aligned with the accounting system is assumed. Given these preconditions, the options are to utilize organizational entities as the SBUs or to keep the organizational entities separate from the SBUs as planning entities.

Unfortunately, none of the firms studied were able to utilize the logic portrayed in Figure 5. The general nature of the problem was that when the PMS approach was adopted the current organizational entities (such as divisions) did not always correspond to competitive entities, and the current accounting system was aligned with the current organizational structure. If the more reasonable business units were defined as SBUs, then either the accounting system or the accounting system and the organizational structure both had to be realigned. By contrast, the use of the current accounting system and organizational structure sacrificed the competitive nature of an SBU.

In all firms studied, there was a general consensus that organizational structure and the accounting system should eventually be aligned with the SBUs. However, the achievement of this goal called for massive changes, and it was felt that such changes could and should only be achieved over considerable time. Generally, the emphasis was on getting the proper alignment of the accounting system first. If the accounting

could be properly aligned, planning could proceed on a logical basis, with organizational alignment following later. The researchers generally observed this to be happening. Firms would often start by merely redefining the current divisions (with their aligned accounting systems) as SBUs and then gradually move the accounting system and the organizational structure to correspond more closely to a true competitive entity. The more experience a firm had with PMS, the more closely SBU definition approximated Figure 5. With this discussion of organizational structure in mind, we now proceed to the variation of several managerial parameters across strategic missions (SBUs), in particular, managerial selection and promotion, incentive compensation, and capital budgeting.

SELECTION AND PROMOTION

Selection and promotion of managers appropriate to each strategic mission was viewed as important in all six firms fully adopting the PMS approach. Several corporate and group-level executives were unhesitant in pointing out that this was the most important means for implementing the strategic missions. Typical of these comments is the following by a group vice-president:

You always have to match the players to the game if you want to get the job done. There just isn't any other way that is practical. Selecting the right people for the right job and promoting them for successful efforts is the best way I have to get a strategy implemented. Certain people do better with cash cows, while others are great with wildcats. I make some mistakes, but eventually I hope to be able to tell what kinds of businesses each of our managers is suited for and what kinds they are not.

Of course, such comments are not new or revolutionary to the portfolio concept. Selection and promotion have always been viewed as primary tools of management. However, the strategic missions provide a new and more specific template for measuring the manager against the job. Certain people tend to be superior managers of rapidly growing, dynamic businesses but would be lost in a mature or declining business.

Incentive Compensation

The researchers originally expected that the method of allocating incentive compensation would be differentiated for SBU managers by strategic mission. For example, bonuses would be closely tied to some measure of cash generation in cash cow SBUs and to a measure of improvement in competitive position (such as increase in market share) in question mark SBUs.

In the three firms with the longest experience operating under the SBU concept (ABC, DEF, GHI), incentive compensation was found to be differentiated by generic strategy, although the manner of achieving this differentiation varied. The system in GHI was the most highly differentiated. For each SBU manager (and in some cases lower-level managers), a specific plan was developed and tailored to the SBU's strategy (not just generic strategy) as reflected in the approved long-range plan. This resulted in about four dozen custom-tailored incentive plans. For each of these plans, an attempt was made to agree on specific, measurable criteria, but in some cases where accurate measurement was not possible, subjective criteria were introduced.

In DEF Corporation, the three generic strate-

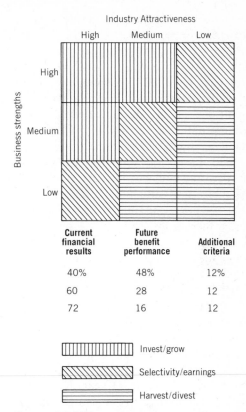

Figure 6 DEF master strategy matrix.

gies shown on the nine-block master strategy matrix in Figure 6 provided the basis for differentiation of incentive compensation. For managers following an invest/grow generic strategy, 40 percent of incentive compensation was based on current financial results, as measured by residual income. Forty-eight percent was based on what was called "future benefit performance," which represented performance against negotiated goals in areas such as new product development, market penetration, and cost reduction, which were supposed to embody key elements of the SBU strategy. For a manager following a selectivity/earnings generic strategy, the percentages were 60 percent for current financial results and 28 percent for future benefit criteria. For a manager following a harvest/divest strategy, the percentages were

72 percent for current financial results and 16 percent for future benefit performance.

Within ABC Corporation the incentive compensation of SBU managers was divided into two parts, each intended to constitute about 50 percent of the total figure. The first part was based entirely on a formula tied to corporatewide profits; the second, on a subjective assessment of overall performance against plan. The second part was intended to reward strategic performance, but because of the admittedly subjective nature of the assessment, was under review at the time of the research.

The other three firms (JKL, MNO, and PQR) had less experience operating under the portfolio concept, and displayed little differentiation of the incentive compensation system. In MNO Corporation, the system had changed in each of the previous two years and was expected to change again in the current year. Its system had always been informally based on meeting short-term financial objectives, and most executives interviewed felt this tendency would continue in the current year. However, most of these same executives also felt that a few managers, especially on the division and SBU level, were starting to see strategy considerations reflected in their annual bonuses. One division manager, who was considered to be an outstanding performer on both strategic and operating matters, felt the potential role of incentive compensation in strategy implementation was small:

A bonus is just icing on the cake, and no good manager should ever count on it. You develop a good strategy and you pursue it. Whether you get a bonus as a direct result is irrelevant. Your career is going to benefit because strategic thinking is good management, and over the long run results will reflect this.

In JKL Corporation, the intent was to allocate incentive compensation based on performance against plan (annual budget) during the year. In PQR Corporation, there was no attempt to tie incentive compensation to generic strategy in any manner. One corporate-level executive stated simply that "we are just not

ready to start measuring people against an annual budget, let alone a complete strategy."

CAPITAL BUDGETING

The researchers originally expected that the capital budgeting system would be differentiated by setting acceptance criteria that varied depending on the SBU's location on the master strategy matrix. The capital-budgeting system in ABC Corporation, described earlier, was found to mirror this expectation. Different explicit hurdle rates were used for each specific strategic mission.

The system within DEF Corporation was interesting because it avoided the use of explicitly different hurdle rates, and yet achieved an implicit differentiation in acceptance criteria through the capital budget's review process. The hurdle rate for acceptance was set at a very low (proprietary) level and was not varied across SBUs. The philosophy behind this was summarized by a corporate-level executive:

No matter how high the hurdle rate is set, any good manager will be able to get the numbers to come out right. There is nothing wrong with this. It shows commitment to projects instead of numbers. We don't want managers to concentrate on rigging the numbers. We want them to concentrate on whether a specific project makes strategic sense. If it does, then the numbers are meaningless. If it doesn't then no artificially concocted rate of return is high enough. We want managers to run the numbers, but we don't want the numbers to drive out the strategy.

The result of this low hurdle rate was that capital-appropriation requests concentrated on justifying an appropriation in terms of strategy. Hence, a request had to make sense in terms of the generic strategy. Furthermore, capital appropriations were always reviewed by individuals familiar with the unit's strategy. In many cases, the individual who had primary responsibility for reviewing a unit's strategy also had primary responsibility for reviewing the capital appropriation requests. The coupling of strategic considerations to capital expenditures led naturally to an implicit differentiation of acceptance criteria. For example, to make good sense strategically, a major capacity expansion in a dog SBU would have to have an extremely high return, while such an expansion in a question mark SBU could have a contrastingly low return. In this manner, the process implicitly forced each capital project to pass a strategy review. Capital appropriations were evaluated against the appropriate strategic mission; that is, the process implicitly differentiated acceptance criteria across the generic strategies.

The system in GHI was almost identical in terms of major features to the one in DEF, with implicit differentiation of acceptance criteria achieved by emphasizing strategy considerations in the capital-budgeting process instead of relying on purely financial criteria.

The approach within the other three firms (JKL, MNO, PQR) also emphasized implicit differentiation of acceptance criteria based on strategic considerations, but, possibly because of less experience operating under the portfolio concept, the process was not as well developed. Specifically, the expectations were not as well understood at the SBU level. SBU-level managers expressed substantially more uncertainty about what was expected of capital-budget requests than in the other three firms. The words of one SBU manager typify the uncertainty:

I know that I'm expected to return more on investment than some units with different strategies, but I don't know what the differences are supposed to be. When we know a project would be good, we have to be sure the return is plenty high, or the request bounces right back to us before a formal review. I'm slowly finding out what headquarters expects of me, but in the meantime I have to play it safe on the numbers . . . I'm learning how to tie projects into the strategy in a meaningful and persuasive manner. I guess they are learning at headquarters, too. It should all be easier once they know exactly what they want.

It would seem reasonable that as JKL, MNO, and PQR accumulated experience with the portfolio concept, the uncertainty associated with implicitly differentiating the capital-budgeting system would decrease.

IMPROVED PERFORMANCE?

At the present time, given the limited experience that firms have had with the portfolio concept, it is impossible to definitively determine if the portfolio concept (PMS) has resulted in improved financial performance when utilized in large, diversified firms. As knowledge and data continue to accrue, a definitive determination will be possible and should form an important agenda item for future research in business policy. There are some limited data available which indicate that firms do perform better when operating under the portfolio concept.

As we have observed, three of the firms studied, ABC, DEF, and GHI, had substantial experience operating under the portfolio concept. DEF had adopted the portfolio concept in 1970, while ABC and GHI had adopted it in 1971. Has performance subsequently improved for these firms? A reasonable standard for comparison would seem to be the major competitors of these firms.

The base business of ABC is common to several large competitors, and several of these competitors are diversified in a manner similar to ABC's. A group of fifteen firms including ABC is usually referred to in the business press as constituting a particular industry. None of these firms except ABC adopted the portfolio concept before 1976. Table 6 compares the performance of ABC to the other fourteen firms in this industry in terms of return on total capital for the years 1968, 1973, and 1978.[3] In 1968, before adoption of the portfolio concept, ABC ranked thirteenth in this industry. By 1973, shortly after adoption, ABC had risen to tenth place, and by 1978, ABC ranked third. During this same period (1968–1978), ABC's return on total assets went from 1.7 percent below the industry average to 2 percent above it and more than doubled in absolute magnitude. Such results show a dramatic improvement during the period since adoption of the portfolio concept.

Table 6   Return on Total Capital* for Fifteen Largest Firms Participating in Same Base Business as ABC

Rank	1978	1973	1968
1	12.9%	19.2%	12.2%
2	12.7	12.4	9.3
3	12.4 (ABC)	11.8	9.0
4	12.1	11.6	8.6
5	11.6	11.2	8.5
6	11.3	10.4	8.0
7	10.5	10.1	7.7
8	10.4	9.7	7.3
9	9.9	9.2	7.1
10	9.5	8.1 (ABC)	7.0
11	9.0	8.1	6.6
12	8.8	8.0	6.2
13	8.7	7.6	6.0 (ABC)
14	8.5	7.3	6.0
15	7.2	7.0	5.6
Average	10.4	10.1	7.7

*Return on total capital = profits after taxes but before interest/(owner's equity + long-term debt).
Source: Value Line and published financial reports.

For both DEF and GHI, a comparison against several firms considered to be in the same industry is not possible. Although each of these firms competes with numerous others in small to medium-size market segments, they each have only one domestic broad-line competitor. This broad line competition with a single competitor is recognized both by the business press and by DEF and GHI. A paired comparison of DEF and GHI with their respective broad-line competitors is appropriate. Table 7 shows these comparisons in terms of return on total capital from 1968 through 1978. DEF definitely improved its competitive position since adoption of the portfolio concept.[4] The situation in GHI is less clear. To help

Table 7   Return on Total Capital for DEF and GHI versus Competitors

Year	DEF	DEF Competitor	GHI	GHI Competitor
78	16.7%	11.6%	13.7%	*
77	15.7	10.7	10.5	*
76	14.9	9.2	8.8	10.3%
75	12.1	7.2	7.3	8.9
74	13.1	1.9	9.4	10.8
73	14.3	6.9	8.5	9.0
72	13.8	8.5	6.2	7.9
71	13.7	8.1	5.2	6.6
70	10.5	6.9	5.1	7.5
69	9.2	9.0	7.2	7.7
68	11.6	8.6	6.8	7.8

*Firm was acquired in 1977.
Source: Value Line and published financial reports.

Table 8 Return on Total Assets* for DEF and GHI versus Competitors

Year	DEF		DEF Competitor		GHI		GHI Competitor	
77	7.94%		4.53%		6.72%		†	
76	13.51		4.20		6.08		6.16%	
75	10.93	11.70 (avg.)	3.40	3.28	5.76	6.38	6.41	5.90
74	12.57		0.58		5.91		5.79	
73	13.57		3.67		7.77		5.23	
68	6.28		5.94		5.45		5.52	
67	6.85		5.90		4.51		5.09	
66	7.08	7.25	6.19	5.81	6.93	6.6	7.68	6.73
65	8.34		6.25		7.85		8.07	
64	7.68		4.77		8.29		7.27	

*Return on total assets equals net income/total assets.
†Firm was acquired in 1977.
Source: Value Line and published financial reports.

clarify this situation and to further delineate the competitive improvement of DEF, Table 8 compares the firms on the basis of return on total assets for the five years before adoption (1964–1968) and for the five years after adoption (1973–1977). The years 1969 through 1972 are omitted since they constitute a period of transition (or disequilibrium), when DEF and GHI were contemplating adoption and starting the implementation process. As the table shows, DEF's competitive performance improved on the average by 7 percent (11.70 − 3.28 − (7.25 − 5.81)). GHI's competitive performance also improved on the average but only by 0.6 percent—a marginally measurable amount. GHI's competitive performance was certainly no worse after adoption of the portfolio concept, but neither was it substantially better.

In ABC and DEF, there is evidence that competitive performance improved substantially after adoption of the portfolio concept; in GHI, there is no such evidence. A more definitive study of the relationship between portfolio planning and subsequent performance will have to wait for a longer time frame and a larger statistical sample.

FACTORS THAT FRUSTRATE CHANGE

If a firm could be unambiguously divided into a "reasonable" number of independent "single businesses," then these businesses could be defined as SBUs and each assigned a strategic mission independent of the others. Here the term *reasonable* means that the number of businesses (constituted as SBUs) is small enough that a matrix position for each can be developed at the corporate level, and corporate executives have adequate time and knowledge of each SBU to conduct a meaningful strategy review.

Given that these conditions are fulfilled, management can be purposefully and extensively varied among different strategic missions. However, the earlier discussion of administrative practices showed only limited variation. There are several reasons why further changes have been deterred:

- SBUs cannot be unambiguously constituted as single businesses;
- the extent of diversification precludes the reasonable-number criterion;
- the relatedness of diversification can preclude the independence of the SBUs; and

- the history of the organization can be a constraint on change.

The concept of what constitutes a single business is difficult to define in operational terms. In the process of defining SBUs, this difficulty must be resolved. The nature of the problem stems from the fact that a product/market segment can be defined in a variety of ways. In fact, there is generally a whole hierarchy of product/market segments. Consider a firm that, among other things, manufacturers and markets appliances. A logical breakdown might be into specific products (washers, ranges, microwave ovens). Alternative breakdowns (from among many possibilities) could be into commercial and home appliances, into different price or quality segments, or into different geographic segments. These breakdowns could be combined to yield increasingly finer segments, such as the commercial, microwave-oven business, or the European, high-quality home-dishwasher business. In sum, SBUs could be defined in a myriad of different ways, ranging from the entire appliance business to much smaller segments. Regardless of which segments are eventually chosen to define these businesses, arguments could be advanced for other segments. Since segments finer than those finally selected will generally exist, arguments could be advanced that the definition aggregates several single businesses. It is easy to see that the position of the business on the matrix may depend on the definition chosen for the SBU. If the entire appliance business is defined as an SBU, then a cash-cow mission may be appropriate. However, in a finer breakdown, by product, the microwave-oven business could quite conceivably be defined as an SBU with a question mark mission.

Closely related to the problems caused by the ambiguous nature of a single business are the problems inherent in the extent of diversification present in large, diversified firms. The number of product/market segments in which these firms participate is so large that it completely swamps the reasonable-number criterion.

Intimately interwoven with the ambiguous nature of a single business is the related manner in which most large firms tend to diversify into areas related to their core business, the notable exceptions being the conglomerates. This relatedness of diversification exacerbates the already ambiguous nature of a single business and simultaneously prevents the achievement of independent SBUs. The residual dependency among SBUs frustrates the assignment of missions independently to each SBU because the SBUs themselves are no longer strategically independent entities.

Consider the previous example of appliances, but assume the firm initially only manufactures and markets home washers and dryers. Diversification could logically take this firm into the manufacture and sale of home microwave ovens and trash compacters. This move itself will exacerbate the problems associated with business definition, as previously discussed. Assume also that the washers and dryers are defined as a "home-laundry" SBU and that the microwave ovens and trash compacters are defined as a "home-kitchen" SBU. These two SBUs are obviously not strategically independent since, among other things, they may share distribution channels, may often be bought in combination (say, by housing contractors), share a common assembly facility, and mutually benefit from brand-name advertising efforts. Inevitably, there must be some coordination of strategy among the two, and this will be extremely difficult if different strategic missions are assigned (such as cash cow for the laundry SBU and question mark for the kitchen SBU). Grouping them all together into an appliance SBU will probably result in the assignment of an inappropriate mission for the trash compacters, and breaking them down further (washers, dryers, microwave ovens, and trash compacters) will only increase the interdependency. As this example illustrates, the related nature of much diversification prevents the achievement of independent SBUs.

The organizational history also influenced the extent of change in administrative practice. The general nature of this phenomenon resulted from the persistence of the original formal organizational structure after adoption of the portfolio concept—a reorganization in terms of "rationally" defined SBUs only partially supplanted the organizational structure. The extreme version of this phenomenon was typified by JKL Corporation, which adopted the portfolio concept by simply redefining the six product divisions as SBUs even though all managers interviewed agreed that within each division there existed a wide diversity of businesses and strategic missions. However, in the three firms with the most experience operating under the portfolio concept, managers indicated that some of these "historical" SBUs had been redefined over the years in a more rational manner. Although limited data are available, it would seem reasonable to assume that the influence of organizational history will decay over time.

TRENDS IN PMS IMPLEMENTATION

The researchers investigated two potential trends in implementation: the movement from analytical tool to PMS approach; and the recentralization of strategic planning at the corporate level. Available evidence indicated that the first was not occurring, and regarding the second possibility, the amount of recentralization was found to be severely limited.

A reasonable adoption scenario would be to start by adopting the analytical-tool concept and then to move gradually toward the PMS approach. In fact, the researchers found that this was not occuring nor is it likely to occur. There are two related reasons for the absence of this approach. First, the tool and PMS approach are vastly different. The PMS approach

is a different way of managing, requiring major management changes, while the tool approach requires almost no changes and is merely an incremental management technique. There is a clearly different philosophy behind each, and the use of an analytical tool does not lead logically to the major restructuring of management required by the PMS approach.

Second, the PMS approach requires enormous commitment to implementation. The basic conduct of administration in the firm must be changed by substantially altering managerial processes. Such changes are fundamental and cannot occur incrementally, nor do they evolve naturally. At some point, SBUs must be defined and assigned strategic missions. The presence of the tool concept cannot logically ease such a large change. Rather, an ongoing commitment must be present. Such a commitment must start with the chief executive officer and extend throughout the management team. When such commitment is present, the utility of starting with the tool concept is marginal, and immediate adoption of the system concept is called for.

The researchers also attempted to determine if the portfolio concept was resulting in a recentralization of the substantive aspects of strategy. The answer was mixed. Because definition and evaluation of the SBUs takes place at the corporate level, some recentralization is certainly possible, but the aggregated nature of SBUs puts a limit on recentralization. The view that the portfolio concept places strategic planning back "at the top" is oversimplified and naive. Instead, the concept requires increased planning skills at all levels—corporate, group, and business—if it is to succeed. In its best application, the concept gives a common language and set of administrative systems to support and promote these planning skills. The authors' research suggests that sophisticated firms recognize this early in implementation and accordingly promote the portfolio concept either as a useful tool or a useful system at all levels.

NOTES

1. See, for example, William K. Hall, "SBU's: Hot New Topic in the Management of Diversification," *Business Horizon,* Vol. 21 (February 1978); and Charles W. Hofer and Dan Schendel, *Strategy Formulation: Analytical Concepts* (St. Louis: West Publishing, 1978).

2. Leonard Wrigley, *Divisional Autonomy and Diversification,* unpublished doctoral dissertation, Harvard Business School (1970); Richard P. Rumelt, *Strategy, Structure and Economic Performance* (Cambridge, Mass.: Harvard University Press, 1974).

3. Return on total capital measures the returns available to both debt and equity investors. Hence, the financial leverage question of long-term debt to equity is eliminated from consideration.

4. Interestingly, DEF's competitor adopted the portfolio concept in 1975, and, at the time of research, was busy implementing it.

SECTION 3
Political Risk and the Political Environment

Political risk and the ways in which it can be anticipated have been a growing concern of managers in recent years. A company is at risk, to some degree, whenever there are unexpected changes in its political environment that interfere with managerial autonomy or the ability of the firm to carry out its objectives. For firms that have a global strategy, the cost of uncertainty or interference may become unacceptably high.

Threats of war, large-scale nationalization of industry, politically inspired executive kidnappings, and full-scale revolution, while dramatic and attention getting, are relatively rare. These substantial risks, often called "macro" risks, include events such as the Iranian revolution, the Latin American snatching of foreign executives, and the Chilean seizure of ITT's operations. The repercussions from macrorisk may not be the same for all firms, but every foreign and many domestic firms located in a nation in which they are present are affected to some degree. The likelihood of any or all of these events taking place could constitute sufficient reasons for the foreign company to decide not to invest or to withdraw established enterprises. On the other hand, the benefits, present and potential, might be great enough to outweigh the risk.

In April 1982, for example, the Mobil Corporation began negotiations with the Libyan government to follow Exxon's example in pulling its operations out of Libya. To be sure, the increasing unprofitability of Libyan operations and the oil glut had a great deal to do with the two oil giants' decision. Nevertheless, a number of analysts said that the Mobil and Exxon moves were a direct response to the escalating political tension between the U.S. and Libya.[1] Smaller oil companies used different variables to assess the risk of staying, and some decided that the benefits outweighed costs.

Most companies do not face cataclysmic political events when they assess

[1] *The Wall Street Journal,* April 13, 1982.

risk in an environment. The international manager is much more likely to deal with the sudden policy changes directed toward a specific firm, industry, or project. This "micro" risk, or impact on an individual firm depends upon the kind of industry, level of technology, managerial style, or structure of the organization. The factors that encourage a host nation to promote its own interests through political means may not actually jeopardize the continuation of a project in a foreign country or result in the seizure of its assets. Nevertheless, the enterprise may find that its operations and global strategy are compromised. Host country insistence upon such factors as a greater number of locals in the work force, host country ownership control, higher proportion of locally made components in the finished product, or a limit or the repatriation of profits may or may not be acceptable to the firm. Mexico's insistence in 1973 that new foreign investment be 51 percent local ownership is an example of microrisk. Established firms were not affected by the new law, and new Mexican partners were often entirely passive participants.

On September 1, 1982, political risk became a much greater problem for foreign-held and even domestic firms in Mexico. Overnight, the Mexican government nationalized its banks and made it nearly impossible for foreign firms legally to send money out of the country or to buy foreign components for dollars. Companies such as Goodyear International Corporation cut shipments to these Mexican plants to the essentials.[2] Anderson Clayton's Mexican affiliate had anticipated the government's action and had stockpiled foreign ingredients for its pancake mix and other food products. Its operations were not nearly as dramatically affected as were those of U.S. automakers whose Mexican production depended on large quantities of imported raw materials and parts. Still other companies benefited from the policies. Seven Oaks International, Inc., paid Mexican women $1.72 an hour to sort grocery coupons in the beginning of August. By the end of October, the company had dropped its wages to $0.82 an hour, thereby reducing labor costs, which constituted 50 percent of total operating expenses, to half of what they had been.[3] Some firms considered the actions of the Mexican government to constitute a major business crisis. Others were relatively unaffected, while still others were able to use it to their advantage.

What can a company do to protect itself against dislocations and political risk? In the case of macrorisk, it may simply decide to buy protection. In 1969, Congress created the Overseas Private Investment Corporation (OPIC). This company provides political risk insurance and financial services to American companies in less developed countries (LDCs). In 1981, OPIC had record earnings of over $76 million through insurance sales that covered risk from expropriations, currency inconvertibility, wars, revolutions, and insurrections.[4] Insurance, however, cannot cover a firm for the discontinuities that it is much more likely to encounter with microrisk. Companies with foreign holdings or those that are planning to make foreign investments may find the alter-

---

[2] *Business Week,* October 4, 1982.
[3] *The Wall Street Journal,* October 26, 1982.
[4] *The New York Times,* April 25, 1982

native of simply staying out of potentially unstable environments an unacceptable alternative to dealing with risk. They may try to hedge their investment position by undertaking political risk analysis.

The four articles in this section look at the nature of political risk, the responses of organizations to it, and ways in which risk analysis can be integrated into the routine strategic management of the firm.

READING SELECTIONS

Vernon's "Organizational and Institutional Responses to International Risk" looks at risk-reducing strategies undertaken by firms that invest abroad. While political risk is a central concern of foreign investors, there are other risks that will have an impact on their decision making. Risk of competition, risk of diminution of cash flow, and risk of losing a technological lead are also important considerations for the firm. The primary risk-reducing arrangement for the foreign firm is the establishment of a joint venture. The joint venture may take several forms. It may be as part of a consortium of foreigners, a partnership with a host country, or an agreement with a state-owned enterprise. There are times when the risk of expropriation can be minimized but another risk, that of preemption by a competitor, is substituted. In this case, other arrangements such as long-term contracts or licensing agreements are undertaken to reduce risk. Vernon asserts that individual firms have only limited power to affect the prices and actions of rival, yet interdependent, firms. Nor can the firm, with any degree of certainty, eliminate the likelihood of expropriation even though a joint venture. Although investors respond both organizationally and institutionally to risk, it has not yet been incorporated or formalized within the discipline of economics.

Stephen J. Kobrin examines the literature to determine what constitutes political risk. Events, however upsetting they may appear, are not political risks for the firm unless they can or do affect operations. A usable definition of political risk is the "distribution of probable returns which is . . . a function of the probable impacts of political events on operations." As he points out, for business risk to exist, there has to be uncertainty. Political events that do not subject the firm to that uncertainty do not constitute risk; they simply entail an assessment and evaluation of events on the well-being of the company. Kobrin finds that most managers do not rigorously and systematically evaluate the impact of politics on operations. Instead, they rely on rather superficial and subjective perceptions of the degree to which they are likely to encounter risk. He recommends that much more work remains to be done to give managers a better definition of risk, a conceptual structure that will relate politics to the firm, and information about the impact of the political environment on the firm.

Warnock Davies warns managers that a country-specific analysis is an inadequate predictor of political risk vulnerability. He advises firms to use the information that they have gathered from home and host country sources at all levels. Once information is collected and a decision has been made to make an investment, corporations should continue to monitor for sociopolitical risk. The environment and the very nature of the investment changes over time and so does risk. Some issues that the assessment process identifies as carrying risk may be unmanageable. These issues, such as the nature of host country political regimes and currency stability, should be left alone since interference by the corporation may raise, rather than lower, its vulnerability. Other issues may be unmanageable before investment but manageable thereafter. The firm, Davies says, should presume that there is a continuum between country-specific and corporate-specific factors and that risk should be assessed along that continuum.

The final article, "Globescan: A Way to Better International Risk Assessment," provides a specific technique for domestic businesses and multinationals that have, or are planning to have, investments abroad. Hofer and Haller review some of the established models with which firms have tried to assess risk. They find that all of them have some serious limiting flaws. They propose, as an alternative, GLOBESCAN, an approach that they assert provides a "systematic framework for integrating international business risk assessment processes with international strategic decision making . . .". Unlike some other models of risk assessment that can be used by the firm itself, this one depends upon the services of outside consultants who gather and process the information. They undertake a number of checks and cross-checks on the information and use established models to build a picture for the firm of the types and sources of risk that they are likely to encounter. The management of risk is undertaken as part of an overall international decision-making process. The authors predict that their approach, which is derivative of the others but is far more comprehensive and analytical, will help the corporation formulate its strategy on a global scale with a clearer idea of potential risks and opportunities than it would have otherwise.

10

Organizational and Institutional Responses to International Risk

Raymond Vernon

• • •

My mandate is to deal with the organizational and institutional responses that foreign direct investors have developed in their efforts to deal with international risk. The boundaries of that mandate are not very sharp.

One problem in drawing the boundaries is to define an institutional response. By implication, some responses to risk exist that are thought to be separable from institutions; I have had some difficulty in picturing what those responses may be. I hope I shall be forgiven therefore if, from time to time, this discussion wanders beyond the organizational and institutional dimensions

Source: Raymond Vernon, "Organizational and Institutional Responses to International Risk," Reprinted from *Managing International Risk.* Essays commissioned in honor of the centenary of the Wharton School, University of Pennsylvania, ed. Richard J. Herring © Cambridge University Press. Reprinted by permission.

into areas that some would regard as economics.

A second problem in drawing the boundaries of this chapter has been to decide which of the many different types of international risk could usefully be addressed. In one respect, the decision on boundaries is easy. This chapter is concerned both with the risks that arise from the investor's ignorance and with the risks that arise from random error. In other respects, however, the boundaries are less easily drawn. Direct investment internalizes a set of international transactions that otherwise would be conducted at arm's length with independent buyers or sellers, and one major purpose of this internalization is to avoid some of the risks that exist when dealing with such independent parties. Accordingly, a direct investment commonly represents a response to certain kinds of international risk. An exploration of this phenomenon seems almost indispensable as a preliminary for exploring the responses to the risks associated with the direct investment itself.

DIRECT INVESTMENT AS A RESPONSE TO RISK

The desire of managers to internalize certain transactions as a way of avoiding risk is a phenomenon that is encountered in domestic as well as international settings, occurring most commonly when the number of firms in the market is small, when the surrounding environment is uncertain, and when the representations or commitments of the parties concerned are difficult to verify or enforce.[1] Nevertheless, numerous writers have observed that the internalization of certain transactions is likely to be especially important as a risk-reducing measure when the transactions straddle national boundaries (Caves 1973, p. 117; Buckley and Casson 1976, pp. 33–59; Casson 1979, pp. 45–62).

Establishing the Foreign Subsidiary

The drive for internalization, it is generally agreed, stems from the firm's view that there is some marked imperfection in the market for the product or service concerned, a view that stimulates the firm to create its own internal market and to accept the narrowing of choice that is commonly involved in that decision. Two types of industry in which such internalization is particularly common are the exploitation and processing of oil and minerals and the development and application of advanced technologies. Not surprisingly, therefore, these industries prove to be heavily overrepresented among foreign direct investors (Vernon 1971, pp. 4–17; United Nations 1978, pp. 45–46).

In the case of raw materials, large indivisible costs and high barriers to entry keep the numbers small. The entry barriers are created in part by the difficulties of achieving agreements with host countries on the terms of entry and in part by the size of the capital commitment needed to finance the extensive developmental work and infrastructure that go with the launching of large raw material projects.[2] Meanwhile, the dispersed location of overseas operations and the tenuous links among the participating parties create uncertainties and hamper fact finding to a degree that is especially acute.[3]

The entry barriers that are typical in the technologically advanced industries are of a different kind, but are commonly no less formidable. They are created by the fact that a considerable expenditure of money and time is commonly required while firms accumulate the necessary knowledge, skills, and reputation that may be necessary for the effective marketing of the product. Like the raw material industries, too, the high-technology firms typically incur developmental costs in the launching of new businesses that are relatively high when compared with the actual costs of production (Freeman 1974, p. 126; Hochmuth 1974, pp. 145–69; Brock 1975, pp. 27–41, 57; Measday 1977, pp. 266–8; Parker 1978, pp. 112–19). After beginning production, individual firms characteristically experience a persistent decline in production costs that appears to be a function of their accumulated production, a fact that represents an added deterrent for newcomers (Hartley 1965, pp. 122–8; Abernathy and Wayne, 1974, pp. 74–141; Conley 1981).

Both the firms in the raw materials industries and those in the high technology industries, then, begin with large sunk costs on which they hope for a return. The importance of reducing uncertainties in industries that have such a cost structure has been sufficiently explored. Firms in such industries place more than the usual stress on avoiding variations in output, inasmuch as small variations in output can generate disproportionate swings in their return on investment. But there are some differences in the two types of industry as well.

In the raw materials industries, the firm's problem of securing a stable return on its sunk commitments is exacerbated by the fact that a relatively high proportion of its operating costs is also fixed. Variations in output generate disproportionate fluctuations in net profits. Accordingly, a persistent objective in the strategy of firms in these industries has been to find ways of stabilizing the demand for their output and to safeguard themselves against interruptions in the supply of needed materials.

On the demand side, of course, the price elasticities of aggregate demand for an industrial raw material such as iron ore or crude oil are typically fairly low, especially in the short run. Individual firms, however, face a demand curve that is considerably more elastic than that of the industry as a whole, so that the risk of losing customers in a declining market can be fairly substantial. Insurance, in this case, takes the form of acquiring tied customers who do not have the option to shift their sources of supply.

On the supply side, the integrating imperative is just as obvious. Because of high barriers to entry, the suppliers are usually limited in number. For the processor that does not control its own source of supply, any large increase in price or outright interruption in supply, whatever its cause, can be dangerous. But a particularly disastrous type of price increase or supply interruption is one initiated by a supplier that also controls processing facilities downstream,

that is, a supplier that is also a competitor in the processor's market.[4] In that case, the supplier may be found taking over the customers of its unintegrated rival.

Events in the oil industry over the past decade have provided occasional illustrations of such a risk turned into reality. At various times during the 1970s, as multinational sellers were faced with reduced supplies of crude oil, they cut off practically all of the unintegrated processors that they had previously supplied, while continuing to supply their own downstream processing facilities and distributors (Commission of the European Communities 1975, pp. 144–5; OECD 1977a, pp. 23, 25; Levy 1982).

Nevertheless, the fact that such risks exist in the oligopolistic industries that process raw materials does not mean the risks always lead to vertical integration. Such integration has a cost. It requires an investment of capital, which has to be justified in terms of expected yield or an equivalent reduction in risk. Moreover, the capital investment entails risks of its own, which may outweigh the risk-reducing aspects of the investment. Besides, the flexibility of the integrated units is reduced as compared with unintegrated competitors; in times of easy supply, the integrated entity is inhibited from turning to cheaper sources of supply and in times of tight supply is restrained from abandoning its captive markets for markets in which profit margins are higher.

Why then is vertical integration so pervasive in the raw material industries? The strong tendency toward vertical integration seems to derive from the fact that, in an industry that is only partially integrated, there are always some participants who see themselves especially exposed by that fact; as long as partial state of integration exists in the industry, a new move toward vertical integration on the part of any firm withdraws a source of supply or a potential customer from the market and thereby increases the perceived risks of those that remain unintegrated. Acccordingly, any movement toward integration seems likely to snowball, until all the actors have rendered themselves equally invulnerable by integration.[5] If the markets concerned are global in scope—a situation that clearly exists for oil and aluminum and exists in part for copper and steel—the interactions between the firms will also be global in their reach.

The high-technology industries, as I have already suggested, face a set of risks that differs somewhat from the raw material industries. The challenge to the raw materials industries is to secure a firm link to supplies and markets, a challenge to which it commonly responds with vertical integration. The challenge to the high-technology firm is to secure a reliable return on its unique skills or knowledge. Unlike firms in the raw materials industries, however, those in the high-technology industries rarely exhaust the static and dynamic scale economies that can be exploited at any given production site, so that the costs of setting up another production point can sometimes be fairly high; besides, the relative unimportance of freight costs usually reduces the advantages of creating multiple production sites (Vernon 1977, p. 51). In addition, some high-technology firms such as those in the aircraft industry have been influenced in part by a desire to stay close to the military authorities in their own country, in order to avoid questions of divided loyalty or of security.

Nevertheless, risk-reducing considerations have pushed the firms in high-technology industries to set up overseas subsidiaries for a portion of their foreign business. The most obvious risk leading to direct investment has been that, as the technological edge of the firm is eaten away, foreign countries may begin to bar their products in favor of producers on their own soil.[6] Faced with that risk, firms in high-technology industries have commonly chosen the subsidiary alternative.[7]

But that response, as a rule, has not put an end to the risks to which the firms in high-technology industries have been exposed. The first move of such firms into foreign production sites has usually been limited, consisting of a facility designed to serve the local market. Countries with bargaining power, however, have sometimes obliged foreign firms to develop a more substantive response. In such cases, some firms have responded by establishing a world-scale plant in an important foreign market and shipping some of the output to other countries. That response has been particularly strong in the automobile industry, generating a shift in the location of production facilities, including a shift from the facilities at home; this development is very likely increasing the international flow of components and automobiles (Jenkins 1977, pp. 213–16; Bennett and Sharpe 1979, pp. 177–82; Frank 1980, pp. 102–5).

Once again, therefore, the avoidance of risk has contributed to the growth of foreign direct investment, as enterprises have shuffled their production facilities among countries in an effort to protect their access to the markets that otherwise might be denied to them.

Follow the Leader

What the discussion suggests so far is that the foreign direct investment of any firm may represent a response to threats of various kinds. One such risk is that competitors may imperil the foreigner's access to a raw material or a market by making investments of their own. That response, as it turns out, follows some predictable patterns.

Consider a world market, such as the market for nickel or aluminum, dominated by half a dozen leading firms, each capable of observing the main moves of the others. The price elasticity of aggregate demand for the final product, the processed metal, is low; the marginal cost of production in relation to full cost is also low. The challenge for the industry, therefore, is to ensure that no participating producer upsets the existing equilibrium by cutting its prices and enlarging its market share. If that should happen, there is a risk that other producers will also be obliged to cut their prices, thereby reducing the rent for the industry as a whole.

Now assume that in those circumstances, one of the participants, troubled by the risk of being cut off from its existing sources, nevertheless undertakes the development of some new mining properties in a remote corner of the world where no such mining had previously taken place. In circumstances of that sort, history suggests that the other members of the oligopoly are unlikely to be totally ignorant of the geological characteristics of the new areas. In the typical case, they will have some information based on local folklore, observation of outcroppings, or even systematic borings. But the information will be grossly incomplete, thus placing a heavy discount on the value of the most likely estimate. What is the optimum response of the other members of the oligopoly?

Consider the nature of the risk that the others face. The quality of the initiating firm's information is not clear; it may be good or bad. If bad, it may burden the firm with a cost that will have to be absorbed in the rent generated by its other operations. But if good, it may eventually arm the leader with a source of ore whose low cost or strategic geographical location poses a threat to the stability of the oligopoly. If other members of the oligopoly are risk avoiders, they will want to learn about the new location as rapidly as possible. If the acquisition and processing of information take time, the firm that is slow to respond faces the risk of being preempted by the hastier action of a rival firm. Accordingly, the risk avoiders are likely to turn their limited facilities for information-gathering to an examination of the new location, even if that means curtailing their search in other directions.[8] Indeed, some firms may want to commit themselves to the new territories even without all the requisite information. The propensity to move will be enhanced by the expectation that if a sufficient number of members of the oligopoly make a similar move and if all of them eventually prove mistaken, the oligopoly will pass on part of the cost of the error to buyers in the form of higher prices. Hence, the follow-the-leader pattern.

On similar lines, risk-avoiding members of an oligopolistically structured industry will be expected to pursue one another into any substantial foreign market in which one of them has set up a producing subsidiary. In this case, the risk of preemption will be particularly great, inasmuch as the first entrant can be expected to urge the government to impose restrictions on any further imports and to limit the number of foreign producers allowed to set up production facilities in the country. The followers may possess little knowledge about the market's potential; projections about future demand may be inescapably subject to large error, but if the number of possible entrants is limited and if the aggregate demand for the product is thought to be inelastic, the followers can contemplate the possibility of cutting their collective losses by raising the prices.[9]

The urge of members in a tight oligopoly to maintain their relative positions in the industry, even if it entails some risky investments, stems in part from their desire to avoid what they perceive as an even greater risk. There is a common conviction among enterprises in oligopolistic industries that the enterprise is in special danger when its cash flow is diminishing in relation to that of its rivals. Behind that fear lie some strong assumptions about the efficiency of the capital markets. Internal capital is usually thought to be much cheaper than external capital; indeed, external capital is commonly viewed as a scarce, rationed commodity. (See Stigler 1967, pp. 287–92; Eiteman and Stonehill 1979, pp. 346–75. See also the various essays in Heslop 1977.) If oligopolists must match the moves of their rivals in order to maintain equilibrium, those with a reduced cash flow may therefore find themselves out of the competitive running. Worries such as these led a Ford executive to say:

If we don't spend the money, our products will not be competitive. We will not get 25 percent. We will get 20 percent. And if you fall back and take two or three years to recover, soon it will be 20 percent, then 18 percent. Then you can't spend money fast enough to catch up again. (*The New York Times,* December 4, 1975, pp. 1, 9.)

Although the quotation goes back to 1975, it suggests a certain prescience regarding the conditions that would prevail in the automobile industry six years later.

The recognition that enterprises tend to move in unison in their foreign direct investments is hardly new, having been advanced as a behavioral proposition at least a quarter of a century ago (e.g., Barlow and Wender 1955, pp. 146, 149). In manufacturing, the evidence is quite extensive and systematic.[10] Now and then, the pattern is so pronounced that it pervades an industry. Outstanding examples have been the wave of investment in semiconductor and microcircuit production in Southeast Asia during the 1960s and the leapfrog patterns of investment among the soap companies and the soft drink companies in Latin America during the same period.

In the raw materials industry, the available data are only impressionistic, but cumulatively they carry some weight. In oil, a surge of investment in the years before the 1930s carried the leading British and American oil companies to the lands surrounding the Gulf of Mexico, from Venezuela to Texas. In the two decades after World War II, another surge of investment greatly expanded oil investments in the countries surrounding the Persian Gulf. Similar waves of investment were to be seen in metallic ores: bauxite investments in the Caribbean area from 1950 to 1965; copper investments in Chile from 1947 to 1958, and in Peru from 1955 to 1960; and iron ore in Venezuela from 1946 to 1960, and in Liberia from 1960 to 1965.

The fact that rival members of an oligopoly tend to move together into a new geographical area, of course, does not conclusively demonstrate that a follow-the-leader pattern exists. A rival possibility, not to be dismissed, is that all of them have been stirred to action by a common stimulus: by the pacification of a hitherto unsafe area, by the appearance of a new consumer market, or by some other such factor. But the empirical evidence is fairly strong for concluding that the follow-the-leader factor is important.

Some of the most obvious illustrations of linked behavior are found in the occasional agreements in the raw material industries under which rivals have explicitly given up the right to act independently. The red-line agreement of 1928 among the world's leading oil companies was one such case. This agreement covered a large portion of the Middle East and remained in force for a decade or two; under its terms, each enterprise undertook not to develop any new fields in the indicated territories except in partnership with the others (see U.S. Federal Trade Commission 1952, pp. 65–7; Jacoby 1974, pp. 29–30, 34–6).

In a very different time and place, other strong illustrations appear of the importance of linkage among members of an oligopoly, albeit not in the form of agreements or consortia. In many markets of the developing world during the 1960s, the leading automobile companies scrambled with one another to set up producing facilities. In at least two cases, that of Argentina and South Africa, the number of firms prepared to enter the scramble and the amount of capacity they were prepared to put in place were so far in excess of prospective market demand as to suggest strongly that some of the investors were reacting to the decisions of the others (Baranson 1969, pp. 46–7, 53; Sundelson 1970, pp. 243, 246–9; Jenkins 1977, pp. 39–42, 56–8). The seemingly nonrational behavior of the firms could be explained in a number of ways. The explanation I find most plausible, however, is that they were driven by a desire to hold down risk, defining that risk in the terms suggested earlier.

More systematic evidence that the follow-the-leader phenomenon reflects a risk-reducing reaction on the part of the participants in an oligopolistic industry is found in the Knickerbocker study mentioned earlier (1973, pp. 111–

44). Knickerbocker found that the degree of the parallel behavior of U.S. firms in any industry was positively correlated with the degree of concentration in that industry—but only up to a point. The strongest patterns of parallel behavior were found in industries in which three or four near-equal firms were the leaders; in industries with an even higher concentration—say, one or two dominant firms, surrounded by a fringe of lesser enterprises—parallel behavior was not as strong. Knickerbocker also found that parallel behavior was a little less pronounced in firms with a relatively high level of technological inputs, where product differentiation was important, than in those with lower technological content. These added bits of information contribute marginally to the credibility of the follow-the-leader hypothesis as a factor in explaining foreign direct investment patterns.

The Exchange of Threats

Researchers also claim to see risk-reducing objectives in other seemingly imitative investments of the multinational enterprises. It has repeatedly been observed, for instance, that the U.S.-based industries that were generating the highest rates of foreign direct investments in Europe were much the same as the European industries that more or less simultaneously were investing in the United States (Hymer and Rowthorn 1970, pp. 80–2). One explanation for this behavior is provided by the so-called exchange-of-threat hypothesis. Threatened by the establishment of a foreign-owned subsidiary in their home market, the response of the leading firms in that market is to set up subsidiaries in the invader's home market. This cross-investment conveys a warning to the invading firm that any excessively energetic efforts to compete in the foreign market may be countered by similar efforts in the home market of the invader.[11]

The two-way flows of foreign direct investment in the same set of industries, moreover,

may serve to reduce a somewhat different kind of risk, namely, the risk of lagging behind in the global technological race. In many oligopolistic industries, a limited number of multinational enterprises encounter each other in competition in many different national markets. In the computer mainframe industry, IBM, Fujitsu, and Siemens are world competitors; in chemicals, ICI, Dupont, and Rhone-Poulenc cross paths in international markets; and so on. Most multinational enterprises, however, do the bulk of their research and development within their home market (Samuelsson 1974; Ronstadt 1977, pp. xiii–xiv, 2; Lall 1980, pp. 102, 119–20); and, most of these enterprises are greatly influenced by the conditions of the home market as they develop the niche that differentiates their products and processes (Davidson 1976, pp. 207, 216; Franko 1976, pp. 27–44). The U.S. stress on labor-saving, mass-produced products, for instance, was traditionally based on the high cost of labor and the absolute scarcity of artisan skills (see Habakkuk 1962, Ch. 3 and 4; Rosenberg 1976, Ch. 1 and 3; also Rosenberg 1969, pp. 17–18).

One risk for multinational enterprises in industries with rapid innovational change is that their rivals in other countries, exposed to different conditions in their home markets, may develop a technological lead that will eventually prove threatening elsewhere. American automobile manufacturers, for instance, were eventually threatened by the Japanese mastery of small fuel-saving automobiles, a capability that the Japanese originally developed largely in response to the special needs of their own market. Aware of the risk of falling behind, some multinational enterprises have maintained a constant surveillance over their rivals in other countries and have sought licenses for foreign technology whenever they felt the need (Abegglen 1970, pp. 117–28; Ozawa 1974, pp. 52–6, 67–80). But some have preferred to acquire subsidiaries as a technological listening post in the territory of their rivals (Franko 1971, pp. 8, 14–15, 23; Michalet and Delapierre 1975; see also Vernon

1980, pp. 150, 153–4, and *Business Week* 1980, pp. 55, 59, 121). When that has occurred, the multinationalizing process has been the firm's response to a risk generated by the action of its competitors.

JOINT VENTURES AS RISK REDUCERS

Once a firm has determined that an international investment may be desirable as a means of reducing risk, it is still faced at times with the possibility of going it alone or investing in partnership with others. The choice among the various alternatives is commonly affected by questions of risk. But once again, the risks to be avoided are of various kinds.

Consortia of Foreigners

For reasons already discussed, firms in the raw material industries typically place a high premium on reducing the risks of the unforeseen, such as wars, strikes, and earthquakes. But in operations in which scale economies are large, such diversification can be costly, especially on the part of the smaller firms in the oligopoly. The solution is for such firms to multiply their sources by joining others in a number of consortia. (For aluminum, the subject is fully explored in Stuckey 1981.) That response has had the effect of producing various consortia composed of firms engaged in the common exploitation of a raw material in a country that is foreign to all of them.

Consortia of this sort in raw materials industries, however, also respond to another risk that has already been noted: the risk that a rival firm might be in a position to upset the stability of an oligopoly by securing its materials at an especially advantageous cost. This second motive is, of course, difficult to distinguish from the first.

Some consortia in the raw materials industries, however, are formed with still a third group of risks in mind, namely, the category that is usually described as political risk. In practice, political risk can be of many different types. It can arise because of a host country's hostility to some specific foreign country and its nationals; or because of a host country's hostility to foreigners in general, irrespective of nationality; or because of a host country's efforts, without hostility to any foreigners in particular or in general, to improve an existing bargain.[12]

Whatever the variety of political risk may be, a consortium composed of foreigners of different nationalities is ordinarily seen as reducing the risk. If the risk to be reduced is a host country's hostility to one country, the consortium can be seen as diluting the exposure of any firm that is based in that country. If the risk is a deterioration in the position of foreigners in general, without regard to any particular country, the consortium can be seen as a counterforce that may be able to enlist the support of a number of different governments.

Although consortia among foreigners also are to be found in the manufacturing industries, especially those that require large-scale and heavy investment, such consortia are relatively uncommon. Occasionally, consortia of this type are imposed on the manufacturing firms by host governments. Foreign automobile producers in Peru and Mexico, for instance, have been compelled to merge their production activities in order to reduce the number of automobile types in the country and to achieve some obvious economies of scale.[13] But the reduction of risk is also a factor in such consortia.

One reason why consortia among foreign firms are less common in manufacturing than in mining or oil production is that manufacturing firms generally have better ways of diversifying their portfolios of direct investment. Although some foreign-owned manufacturing subsidiaries produce goods for export from the countries in which they are located, most market the bulk of their production within the host country (Vaupel and Curhan 1973, pp. 376–7; Curhan, Davidson, and Suri 1977, pp. 392–3, 398–9, Tables 7.2.1 and 7.2.6; U.S. Department of Commerce 1977, pp. 318–19, Tables III.H.1

and III.H.2). Firms in manufacturing, therefore, can often diversify their market risks by setting up subsidiaries in a number of different countries, relying on transportation costs or protective devices in each market to buffer them from outside competitors. Firms engaged in extractive activities, however, typically sell their products in world markets, so that high-cost production sites represent a real handicap. With fewer locations from which to choose, the raw materials firms find themselves obliged to turn more often to the consortium possibility in achieving adequate diversification.[14]

Finally, if the factors specified thus far were not enough to explain the lesser use of consortia by manufacturing firms, the nature of their strategies would provide a sufficient explanation. Unlike the raw materials producers, manufacturers commonly build such strategies on product differentiation, building up distinctive trade names and unique services to customers as their route to success. The consortium approach in any market, combining the offerings of rival producers, would be incompatible with a product-differentiating strategy.

Joint Ventures with Local Firms

When manufacturing firms take local partners with an eye to reducing risk, the risk they generally have in mind is political risk. To be sure, multinational enterprises have a number of other reasons for setting up joint ventures with local stockholders. In some cases, they have no choice; host governments lay down and enforce a joint venture requirement (Turner 1973; United Nations 1973, pp. 83–4; Robinson 1976, United Nations Economic and Social Council 1978, pp. 22–3). In other instances, the decision to take a local partner may free the subsidiary of various discriminatory restrictions, such as disqualification from selling to government enterprises or borrowing from local banks. In still other cases, the joint venture may represent the right decision on the part of both partners simply on the basis of the classic choice of a profit-maximizing firm. It may allow both partners to

put slack resources to work in a single entity; it may allow each of the partners to earn returns on their investments that were higher than their respective opportunity costs; and it may reduce the risks to the multinational enterprise of securing local distribution channels, while reducing the risks to the local distributor of securing assured supplies (Dubin 1976, pp. 27–43; Radetzki and Zorn 1979, pp. 57–61). The objective of reducing political risk, however, is ordinarily of some importance in such arrangements (see especially Franko 1977, p. 29; Pfeffer and Nowek 1976, p. 332; Caves 1970, pp. 283–302; Hogberg 1977, pp. 6–25; Tomlinson 1970, p. 5).

Apart from the direct testimony of business-people, the sense that risk reduction must be playing some significant role in the decision to set up joint ventures is supported by a number of studies of the behavioral patterns of the multinational enterprises. Two analyses, when interpreted in tandem, point in that direction. One of these studies offers strong evidence for the view that, as manufacturing firms gain experience in manufacturing in any market, they tend to assign a lower level of risk to that market. The second study concludes that the less experienced the firm, the higher its propensity for entering into joint ventures with local partners.

The first study, linking experience to perceived risk, covered the introduction and subsequent dissemination of 406 new products by fifty-seven large U.S.-based multinational enterprises during the period from 1945–75 (Vernon and Davidson 1979). In the early decades of that period, the firms were slow to establish production units for these products abroad. But the products introduced in the latter decades were produced abroad with much greater alacrity and in many more locations. By breaking down the data by firms and products, the factors that contribute to this trend became more evident. For instance, firms with a high proportion of exports transferred more rapidly and more extensively than those with a low proportion; firms with several different product lines established production sites abroad more rapidly in their principal product lines than in less important lines; firms that had made many prior transfers responded more rapidly than those that had made only a few; and all firms responded more rapidly in countries to which they had made many previous transfers than in countries to which they had made a smaller number.

The study that links experience levels with the propensity to enter into joint ventures consists of an exhaustive analysis of the behavior of the 2,800 foreign manufacturing subsidiaries of 186 U.S.-based multinational enterprises over a fifty-year period. In various ways, the data linked increased foreign experience with a decline in the propensity of the firm to use joint ventures (Stopford and Wells 1973, p. 99).

More suggestive evidence on the connection between risk and joint ventures comes from another direction. It has been commonly observed that for any foreign-owned enterprise the risk of nationalization rises as the firm loses its capacity to offer a scarce resource to the host country, such as technology, capital, or access to foreign markets (Vernon 1971, pp. 46–52; Krasner 1978, pp. 138–42; Jodice 1980, pp. 204–5; Kobrin 1980, pp. 65–88). At the same time, several studies suggest that firms that appear to be in a relatively weak bargaining position in relation to host governments, that is, firms that have little to offer the country, tend to use joint ventures more than firms in a strong bargaining position (Stopford and Wells 1972, pp. 120, 150–6; Fagre and Wells in press).

Most of the studies cited here are less than conclusive, being dogged by difficult problems of multicollinearity and multiple causation. But cumulatively they lend a considerable degree of plausibility to the hypothesis that risk avoidance is a substantial factor in the decision of foreign-owned enterprises to take local partners.

Joint Ventures with State-Owned Enterprises

A special category of joint venture that has grown somewhat in recent years is partnerships between foreign firms and enterprises owned by the state. The oil-processing industries of the oil-exporting countries contain numerous examples of such enterprises (Ghadar 1977, pp. 17–46; Turner and Bedore 1979, pp. 13–36). But they are found in many other industries as well.

The reasons for such arrangements have been fairly well studied.[15] From the viewpoint of foreign partners, many of the reasons for entering into agreements with state-owned enterprises are the same as those that argue for local private partners: freedom from special restrictions, access to local resources, and protection from political risk. Foreign firms generally assume, however, that each of these factors gains a little strength when the partner is a state-owned enterprise. Whether the foreigner actually acquires greater immunity from political risks by entering into partnership with the state, however, seems quite uncertain; when enough experience develops for researchers to explore the question adequately, the likelihood is that a complex answer will emerge.

One difference between partnerships with private local firms and partnerships with the host state lies in the evolution of the local partner's interests over time. In a significant proportion of the joint ventures, the private partnership interest is held by a large number of local stockholders,[16] who commonly have even less power than public stockholders in the United States. In other cases, local stockholdings are more highly concentrated and fewer in number, but many of these stockholders, having received their equity interests as a gift, are content to play a passive role and to provide the protective coloration the foreigner has bargained for. Only a fraction of these joint ventures, therefore, represent active partnerships.

Managers of state-owned enterprises, on the other hand, generally find themselves much more actively involved in their partnerships with foreigners. Being exposed to the political process in the home country, state managers are often torn between buffering the foreign partner against political pressures in order to maintain the partnership, or swallowing up the foreign partner's interest in order to demonstrate their national commitment. In the Middle East oil industry, according to one study, those motivations have shifted over time in predictable patterns, ending characteristically in the nationalization of the foreigner's interest (Bradley 1977, pp. 75–83; Ghadar 1977, pp 25–7).

To be sure, oil may not prove to be a representative case, especially because of the period covered in existing studies. In other times and other industries, state-owned enterprises may see advantages in clinging to a foreign association, especially if technology or foreign market access is needed. But the recent history of the oil industry does suggest some of the difficult judgments that foreigners have been obliged to make when contemplating the use of joint ventures as insurance against risk.

OTHER ARRANGEMENTS FOR AVOIDING RISK

In an effort to reduce some of their various risks, firms have often been pushed to establish foreign subsidiaries, and, in an effort to reduce the risk to their subsidiaries, they have sometimes been compelled to enter into joint ventures. But there have been instances in which no subsidiary, whether joint venture or wholly owned, has seemed able to reduce their risks on balance. Such subsidiaries simply appeared to be substituting one set of risks for another—the risk of expropriation, for instance, for the risk of preemption by a competitor. Faced with such unpalatable alternatives, enterprises have sometimes groped toward some intermediate arrangement hoping to minimize both kinds of risks. These intermediate arrangements have commonly involved long-term contracts of various sorts.

Such contracts have taken a variety of forms. In both raw materials and high-technology industries, some long-term contracts have authorized and obligated foreign firms to exercise managerial functions over extended periods

(Bostock and Harvey 1972; Fabrikant 1973; Smith and Wells 1976, pp. 45–9; Zorn 1980, Ch. 12). Some of these arrangements have contemplated cash flows for the foreign firm whose discounted value was not very different from the expected stream generated by an analogous direct investment. In fixing the appropriate discount rate, of course, either stream would have to be recognized as subject to risks of various sorts. But in some of these cases, one would probably have been justified in discounting the anticipated income from fees paid under managerial contracts at lower rates than those applicable to the streams anticipated from foreign direct investments.[17]

Yet long-term contracts simply substitute one set of risks for another. In practice, long-term contracts for the sale of raw materials have often turned out to be nothing much more than a statement of intentions on the part of the parties. Critical elements of the contract, such as prices and quantities, have been subject to repeated renegotiations. In their efforts to reduce uncertainties of this kind, one party or another has sought to introduce various kinds of sanctions. Buyers of raw materials, for instance, have made loans to raw materials producers with provisions for immediate repayment whenever the producers failed to deliver specified quantities, and producers have insisted that buyers must forfeit their rights to interest on such loans whenever the buyers failed to accept specified quantities.

Despite such provisions, large elements of uncertainty have remained. Buyers have been accused of delaying the arrival of their vessels in order to avoid picking up shipments of bulk cargoes; sellers have been accused of stimulating their governments to impose export embargoes in order to avoid delivering their products. Moreover, businesspeople have had reservations about the enforceability of their contracts, especially when enforcement could only be achieved through the use of foreign courts.

For firms in the high-technology industries, long-term contracts have typically taken the form of a licensing agreement with independent producers in foreign countries. Such licenses have normally been written with various restraints. These restraints have sought to ensure that the licensee would not impart the information acquired under the license to an unauthorized third person; that the licensee would confine its use of the information to some specified geographical territory; and finally, especially when the licensee was authorized to use the licenser's trademark, that the licensee would produce the product in accordance with some specified standards. Each of these conditions, it is apparent, is aimed at reducing the licenser's risks: the risk of unauthorized appropriation, the risk of competition among license holders, and the risk of impairment of a valued trademark through inadequate quality control.

But long-term licenses, like long-term bulk purchase contracts in the raw materials industries, have had their limitations. Licensers have been aware that licensees can often disregard the contract because the sanctions for violation are notoriously limited. Information that has once been divulged cannot be retrieved; the licensee, therefore, may have little or nothing to fear from losing the licenser's goodwill. On top of that, if the foreign licenser is obliged to pursue its remedies in the home courts of the licensee, court orders directing the licensee to observe the terms of the contract and money damages for breach of contract may prove difficult to obtain.

Apart from the possibility that the courts may not be blind to the foreign nationality of the licenser, there is also the possibility that the underlying legal position of the licenser may be weak. A licenser that holds a strong patent position on an invention in its own home market will sometimes find that the patent protection on the same invention issued by foreign governments is much less secure (Maier 1969, pp. 207–31; Horowitz 1970, p. 539; Penrose 1973, p. 768; Scherer 1976). Moreover, in recent years, various developing countries have adopted laws outlawing the geographical restraints and other restraints that licensers have heretofore found useful to impose on their foreign licensees, further reducing the usefulness of that approach (OECD 1977b; UNCTAD 1979, pp. 24–39; Naryenya-Takirambudde 1977, pp. 71–3).

Perhaps the most tenuous arrangements for the avoidance of risks in host countries entail payments that in U.S. law and practice would be classified as bribes. The justification for condemning bribes can sometimes be couched in rational terms. In a country whose officials do not solicit bribes, for instance, the foreign offerer of a bribe contributes to the destruction of a public good—the competitive market—an act that could conceivably be costly to all those in the market, including the offerer. But arguments of that sort are not the real stuff of the debate. One side finds bribery prima facie offensive and refuses to use it, whatever the consequences; the other thinks it totally entrenched, presenting an inescapable hurdle for those who wish to operate in certain foreign markets.[18] Any "rational" discussion of the use of bribes as a risk-insuring device is therefore likely to be offensive to one side of the debate and unsatisfying to the other. It is almost inescapable, too, that such a discussion will be seen as an apologia for the practice.

There is perhaps one point worth making nevertheless. The problem of bribery is either a smaller one or a bigger one than is ordinarily described. In the interest of reducing their risk in various developing countries, foreign investors are often obliged to make various payments that are not labeled as bribes. Influential local figures are commonly offered blocks of stock in what is then dubbed a joint venture, at prices well below their reasonable value. Local government officials are appointed to directorships in the enterprise, with appropriate emoluments. Ironically, such measures are often applauded as a sign of the foreign investor's responsiveness to local sensibilities. In this shadowy area of risk avoidance, the line between international chicanery and local adaptation will never be clearly drawn.

THE ANALYTICAL CHALLENGE

The avoidance of risk is a quintessential element in the strategy of foreign investors. As a rule, the decision to invest is motivated by a desire to reduce risks of various sorts: the risk of government restrictions on foreign imports, the relative unenforceability of the investor's rights under law or contract, and above all, the risk of preemptive action on the part of a competitor. Risk avoidance also affects the form of the investment; some forms of joint venture help the investor with limited resources to diversify more widely, whereas other forms of joint venture are thought to reduce political risk. On the other hand, even as a direct investment reduces one set of risks, it exposes the investor to another set, including the risk of expropriation. Accordingly, firms often attempt to establish a firm link with foreign markets or foreign sources of materials by long-term arrangements short of investment, but these too produce uncertain results.

The firms involved in the making of these complex judgments come predominantly from industries that are oligopolistic in structure. Because their risks are those that arise in the never-never land of oligopoly, where individual firms can affect prices and the actions of rival firms are interdependent, the analytical power of our microeconomic concepts proves somewhat limited. Those risks are often more easily analyzed in game-theoretic terms than in the familiar paradigms of systematic and random variance. To add to the difficulties, foreign direct investors are not usually investors in the usual sense; a critical portion of their investments commonly takes an intangible form, entailing assets that have no ready market price. Even the cost of such assets offers little help; such assets as technology or access to markets are provided at near-zero marginal cost.

As a result, the role that risk plays in international direct investment cannot be captured by minor addenda to the principles of finance, such as calculating the appropriate risk adjustment for a target rate of return or computing the appropriate price to be paid for a hedge. Foreign direct investors will resort to a series of stratagems for reducing the uncertainty in their environment that do not fit easily into the mainstream discussions of risk. Faced with that fact, this chapter has discussed, for want of a better term, the "organizational and institutional" responses of such investors to risk. But it is only a matter of time before the economics profession will formalize those responses in ways that incorporate them within the discipline. Indeed, that process is already well under way.

NOTES

1. See Williamson (1975, pp. 82–131), Bernhardt (1977, pp. 213, 215), Porter (1980, pp. 306–7), and Scherer (1980, pp. 78, 89–91, 302–4). For a survey of recent literature on the incentives for vertical integration, see Kaserman (1978, pp. 483–510); also Jensen, Kehrberg, and Thomas (1962, pp. 378–9, 384).
2. On the economics of backward integration in the raw materials industries, see for instance, Gort (1962, Ch. 6) and Teece (1976, pp. 105, 115–18).
3. For descriptions of the international oil industry, especially in relation to the issue of vertical integration, see Adelman (1972, pp. 318–19), Cooper and Gaskel (1976, pp. 72–4, 188), Teece (1976, pp. 83–9, 116–17). Mansvelt Beck and Wiig (1977), and Levy (1982). For the nonferrous metals, Charles River Associates, Inc. (1970, pp. 51–7). Bosson and Varon (1977, pp. 46–7), Duke et al. (1977), Banks (1979, pp. 21, 27, 45), Mikesell (1979a, pp. 108–9), and Goohs (1980).
4. For a basic statement of this problem, see Caves (1977, pp. 43–5), Porter (1980, pp. 308, 317), and Scherer (1980, pp. 90–1).
5. For an effort to demonstrate in theoretical terms that equilibrium exists only at the extremes of full integration or full nonintegration, see Green (1974).
6. On "buy-at-home" policies as a nontariff barrier to international trade, see Curtis and Vastine (1971, pp. 202–4), and Cline, Kawarabe, Kronojo, and Williams (1978, pp. 189–94). On the attempts of European governments to set up and protect national champions in the aerospace and computer industries, see Hochmuth (1974, pp. 145–70) and Jéquier (1974, pp. 195–255). On the restrictions of developing countries, see Robinson (1976, pp. 169–238).
7. For a discussion of the factors in high-technology industries, such as computers, tending toward vertical integration, see Katz and Philipps (in press). An econometric demonstration that firms in high-technology industries favor

subsidiaries over independent licensees to a greater degree than in other industries is presented in Davidson and McFetridge (1981); the analysis is based on data presented in Vernon and Davidson (1979).

8. See, for instance, Cyert and March (1963, Ch. 6) and Cyert, Dill, and March (1970, pp. 87–8, 94–5, 107). The effort going into search can be considered a significant investment by the firm, as discussed generally in Arrow (1974, pp. 39–43).

9. The perceptions of prospective lenders in such oligopolistic situations are described in Stiglitz and Weiss (1981, pp. 393–411). These perceptions tend to favor follow-the-leader investors by increasing their ability to borrow.

10. The leading work on this point is Knickerbocker (1973). See also Aharoni (1966, pp. 55, 65–6) and Gray (1972, pp. 77, 96–8).

11. Koninklijke Nederlandsche Petroleum Maatschappij (1950, p. 18), *Forbes* (1964, pp. 40–1), Graham (1974, pp. 33–4, 75), Michalet and Delapierre (1975, p. 44). But rival explanations are also offered to explain the cross investment phenomenon; see, for instance, Franko (1976, pp. 166–72).

12. For illustrations, see Moran (1974, pp. 110–36), Thunell (1977, p. 99), Krasner (1978, p. 117), Radetzki and Zorn (1980, p. 186); also Zorn (1980, pp. 225–6).

13. Pressures of this sort are usually applied informally by administrative means and so are difficult to document. But see Turner (1973, p. 101). For data on the trend to greater concentration of automobile producers in Latin American countries, see Jenkins (1977, pp. 145–50).

14. Indicative of the more limited opportunities of the raw materials firms are data in Vernon (1971, pp. 39, 62).

15. The subject is dealt with in Vernon (1979, pp. 7–15) and Aharoni (1981, pp. 184–93).

16. For detailed data see Vaupel and Curhan (1973, pp. 309–19).

17. See, for example, Mikesell (1979b, pp. 52, 56–7). OPEC members' purchases of petroleum management services are generally at a price approaching the return on an equivalent direct foreign investment by the oil companies; see Eiteman and Stonehill (1979, p. 242).

18. For some of the more serious explorations of this subject see Kobrin (1976, pp. 105–11), U.S. Securities and Exchange Commission (1976), U.S. Senate (1976), Jacoby et al. (1977, pp. 125–45), Kugel and Gruenberg (1977, pp. 113–24), Kennedy and Simon (1978, pp. 1–5, 118–20).

REFERENCES

Abegglen, J. C. (ed.). *Business Strategies for Japan.* Tokyo: Sophia University, 1970.

Abernathy, W. J., and Kenneth Wayne. *The Bottom of the Learning Curve: The Dilemma of Innovation and Productivity.* Boston: Division of Research, Graduate School of Business Administration, Harvard University, 1974.

Adelman, M. A. *The World Petroleum Industry.* Baltimore, Md.: Johns Hopkins University Press, 1972.

Aharoni, Yair. *The Foreign Investment Decision Process.* Boston: Division of Research, Graduate School of Business Administration, Harvard University, 1966 and "Managerial Discretion." In Raymond Vernon and Yair Aharoni (eds.), *State-Owned Enterprise in the Western Economies.* London: Croom Helm, 1981.

Arrow, K. J. *The Limits of Organization.* New York: W. W. Norton, 1974.

Banks, F. E. *Bauxite and Aluminum: An Introduction to the Economics of Nonfuel Minerals.* Lexington, Mass.: Lexington Books, 1979.

Baranson, Jack. *Automotive Industries in Developing Countries.* Baltimore, Md.: Johns Hopkins University Press, 1969.

Barlow, E. R., and I. T. Wender, *Foreign Investment and Taxation.* Englewood Cliffs, N.J.: Prentice-Hall, 1955.

Bennett, David, and K. E. Sharpe. "Transnational Corporations and the Political Economy of Export Promotion: The Case of the Mexican Automobile Industry." *International Organization,* Vol. 33, no. 2, Spring 1979, pp. 177–201.

Bernhardt, I. "Vertical Integration and Demand Variability." *Journal of Industrial Economics,* Vol. 25, no. 3, March 1977, pp. 213–29.

Bosson, Rex, and Bension Varon. *The Mining Industry and the Developing Countries.* New York: Oxford University Press, 1977.

Bostock, Mark, and Charles Harvey (eds.). *Economic Independence and Zambian Copper: A Case Study of Foreign Investment.* New York: Praeger Publishers, 1972.

Bradley, David. "Managing Against Expropriation." *Harvard Business Review,* July–August 1977, pp. 75–83.

Brock, G. W. *The U.S. Computer Industry* (Cambridge, Mass.: Ballinger, 1975).

Buckley, P. J., and M. Casson. *The Future of Multinational Enterprise.* New York: Holmes and Meier Publishers, 1976.

Business Week. "The Reindustrialization of America," June 30, 1980, pp. 55–146.

Casson, M. *Alternatives to the Multinational Enterprise.* London: Macmillan, 1979.

Caves, R. E. "Uncertainty, Market Structure and Performance: Galbraith as Conventional Wisdom." In J. W. Markham and G. F. Papenek (eds.), *Industrial Organization and Economic Development*. Boston: Houghton Mifflin, 1970. Also see "Industrial Organization." In J. M. Dunning (ed.), *Economic Analysis and the Multinational Enterprise*. New York: Praeger Publishers, 1973 and *American Industry: Structure, Conduct, Performance*. Englewood Cliffs, N.J.: Prentice Hall, 1977.

Charles River Associates, Inc. "Economic Analysis of the Copper Industry." Prepared for the General Services Administration, March 1970.

Cline, W. R., Noboru Kawarabe, T. O. M. Kronojo, and Thomas Williams. *Trade Negotiations in the Tokyo Round: A Quantitative Assessment*. Washington, D.C.: The Brookings Institution, 1978.

Commission of the European Communities. *Report by the Commission on the Behavior of the Oil Companies in the Community during the Period from October 1973 to March 1974*. EEC Studies on Competition-Approximation of Legislation, no. 26. Brussels: European Economic Communities, December 1975.

Conley, Patrick. "Experience Curves as a Planning Tool." In R. R. Rothberg (ed.), *Corporate Strategy and Product Innovation*. New York: Free Press, 1981.

Cooper, B., and T. F. Gaskell. *The Adventure of North Sea Oil*. London: Heinemann, 1976.

Curhan, J. P., W. H. Davidson, and Rajan Suri. *Tracing the Multinationals: A Source Book on U.S.-Based Enterprises*. Cambridge, Mass.: Ballinger, 1977.

Curtis, T. B., and J. R. Vastine, Jr. *The Kennedy Round and the Future of American Trade*. New York: Praeger Publishers, 1971.

Cyert, R. M., W. R. Dill, and J. G. March. "The Role of Expectations in Business Decision Making." In L. A. Welsch and R. M. Cyert (eds.), *Management Decision Making*. London: Penguin Books, 1970.

Cyert, R. M., and J. G. March. *A Behavioral Theory of the Firm*. Englewood Cliffs, N.J.: Prentice-Hall, 1963.

Davidson, W. H. "Patterns of Factor-Saving Innovation in the Industrialized World." *European Economic Review*, Vol. 8, no. 3, October 1976, pp. 207–17.

Davidson, W. H., and D. G. McFetridge. "International Technology Transactions and The Theory of the Firm." Unpublished, Amos Tuck School, Dartmouth College, 1981.

Dubin, Michael. "Foreign Acquisitions and the Spread of the Multinational Firm." Unpublished DBA thesis, Harvard School of Business Administration, 1976.

Duke, R. M., R. L. Johnson, H. Mueller, P. D. Quaffs, C. T. Roush, Jr., and D. G. Tarr. *Staff Report on the United States Steel Industry and International Rivals*. Bureau of Economics, Federal Trade Commission, Washington, D.C., November 1977.

Eiteman, D. K., and A. I. Stonehill. *Multinational Business Finance*, 2nd ed. Reading, Mass.: Addison-Wesley, 1979.

Fabrikant, Robert. *Oil Discovery and Technical Change in Southeast Asia: Legal Aspects of Production-Sharing Contracts in the Indonesian Petroleum Industry*. Singapore: Institute of Southeast Asian Studies, 1973.

Fagre, Nathan, and L. T. Wells, Jr. "Bargaining Power of Multinationals and Host Governments." *Journal of International Business Studies*, in press.

Forbes. "The Game that Two Could Play." Vol. 94, no. 11, December 1, 1964, pp. 40–1.

Frank, Isaiah. *Foreign Enterprise in Developing Countries*. Baltimore, Md.: Johns Hopkins University Press, 1980.

Franko, L. G. *The European Multinationals, European Business Strategies in the United States*. Geneva: Business International, 1971. Also see *The European Multinationals*. Stamford, Conn.: Greylock Publishers, 1976; and *Joint Venture Survival in Multinational Corporation*. New York: Praeger Publishers, 1977.

Freeman, Christopher. *The Economics of Industrial Innovation*. London: Penguin Books, 1974.

Ghadar, Fariborz. *The Evolution of OPEC Strategy*. Lexington, Mass.: Lexington Books, 1977.

Goohs, C. A. "United States Taxation Policies and the Iron Ore Operations of the United States Steel Industry." Unpublished, J. F. Kennedy School, Cambridge, Mass., Spring 1980.

Gort, Michael. *Diversification and Integration in American Industry*. Princeton, N.J.: Princeton University Press, 1962.

Graham, E. M. "Oligopolistic Imitation and European Direct Investment in the United States.'' Unpublished DBA thesis, Harvard School of Business Administration, 1974.

Gray, H. P. *The Economics of Business Investment Abroad*. New York: Crane, Russak, 1972.

Green, J. R. ''Vertical Integration and the Assurance of Markets.'' Harvard Institute of Economic Research, Discussion Paper 383, October 1974.

Habakkuk, H. J. *American and British Technology in the Nineteenth Century*. Cambridge: Cambridge University Press, 1962.

Hartley, Keith. ''The Learning Curve and its Application to the Aircraft Industry.'' *Journal of Industrial Economics*. Vol. 13, no. 2, March 1965, pp. 122–8.

Heslop, Alan (ed.). *The World Capital Shortage*. Indianapolis: Bobbs-Merrill, 1977.

Hochmuth, M. S. ''Aerospace.'' In Raymond Vernon (ed.), *Big Business and the State*. Cambridge, Mass.: Harvard University Press, 1974.

Hogberg, Bengt. *Interfirm Cooperation and Strategic Development*. Ghoteborg: b BAS ek. fhoren, 1977.

Horowitz, Lester. ''Patents and World Trade.'' *Journal of World Trade Law*, Vol. 4, no. 4, July–August 1970, pp. 538–47.

Hymer, Stephen, and Robert Rowthorn. ''Multinational Corporations and International Oligopoly: The Non-American Challenge.'' In C. P. Kindleberger (ed.), *The International Corporation: A Symposium*. Cambridge, Mass.: MIT Press, 1970.

Jacoby, N. H. *Multinational Oil*. New York: Macmillan, 1974.

Jacoby, N. H., Peter Nehemkis, and Richard Eells. *Bribery and Extortion in World Business: A Study of Corporate Political Payments Abroad*. New York: Macmillan, 1977.

Jenkins, R. O. *Dependent Industrialization in Latin America: The Automobile Industry in Argentina, Chile, and Mexico*. New York: Praeger Publishers, 1977.

Jensen, H. R., E. W. Kehrberg, and D. W. Thomas. ''Integration as an Adjustment to Risk and Uncertainty.'' *Southern Economics Journal*, Vol. 28, no. 4 April 1962, pp. 378–84.

Jéquier, Nicolas. ''Computer.'' In Raymond Vernon (ed.), *Big Business and the State*. Cambridge, Mass.: Harvard University Press, 1974.

Jodice, D. A. ''Sources of Change in Third World Regimes for Foreign Direct Investment, 1968– 1976.'' *International Organization*, Vol. 34, no. 2, Spring 1980, pp. 177–206.

Kaserman, D. L. ''Theories of Vertical Integration: Implications for Antitrust Policy.'' *The Antitrust Bulletin*, Vol. 23, no. 3, Fall, 1978, pp. 483–510.

Katz, B. G., and Almarin Phillips. ''Government, Technological Opportunities, and the Emergence of the Computer Industry.'' In Herbert Giersch (ed.), *Emerging Technology*. Kiel: Institute of World Economics, in press.

Kennedy, Tom, and C. E. Simon, *An Examination of Questionable Payments and Practices*. New York: Praeger Publishers, 1978.

Knickerbocker, F. T. *Oligopolistic Reaction and Multinational Enterprise*. Boston: Division of Research, Graduate School of Business Administration, Harvard University, 1973.

Kobrin, S. J. ''Morality, Political Power and Illegal Payments.'' *Columbia Journal of World Business*, Vol. 11, no. 4, Winter 1976, pp. 105–10; and ''Foreign Enterprise and Forced Divestment in LDCs.'' *International Organization*, Vol. 34, no 1, Winter 1980, pp. 65–88.

Koninklijke Nederlandsche, Petroleum Maatschappij, N. W. *The Royal Dutch Petroleum Company 1890–1950*. The Hague, 1950.

Krasner, S. D. *Defending the National Interest*. Princeton, N.J.: Princeton University Press, 1978.

Kugel, Yerachmiel, and G. W. Gruenberg. ''Criteria and Guidelines for Decision Making: The Special Case of International Payoffs.'' *Columbia Journal of World Business*, Vol. 12, no. 3, Fall 1977, pp. 113–23.

Lall, Sanjaya. ''Monopolistic Advantages and Foreign Involvement by U.S. Manufacturing Industry.'' *Oxford Economic Papers*, Vol. 32, no. 1, March 1980, pp. 102–22.

Levy, Brian. ''World Oil Marketing in Transition.'' *International Organization*, Vol. 36, no. 1, Winter 1982, pp. 113–33.

Maier, H. G. ''International Patent Conventions and Access to Foreign Technology.'' *Journal of International Law and Economics*, Vol. 4, no. 2, Fall, 1969, pp. 207–31.

Mansvelt Beck, F. W., and K. M. Wiig. *The Economics of Offshore Oil and Gas Supplies*. Lexington, Mass.: Lexington Books, 1977.

Measday, W. S. ''The Pharmaceutical Industry.'' In Walter Adams (ed.), *The Structure of American Industry*. New York: Macmillan, 1977.

Michalet, C. A., and Michel Delapierre. *The Multinationalization of French Firms*. Chicago: Academy of International Business, 1975.

Mikesell, R. F. *The World Copper Industry: Structure and Economic Analysis*. Baltimore, Md.: Johns Hopkins University Press, 1979a; and *New Patterns of World Mineral Development*. New York: British-North American Committee, 1979b.

Moran, T. H. *Multinational Companies and the Politics of Dependence: Copper in Chile*. Princeton, N.J.: Princeton University Press, 1974.

Naryenya-Takirambudde, Peter. *Technology Transfer and International Law*. New York: Praeger Publishers, 1977.

The New York Times. "Ford Regroups for the Minicar Battle." December 4, 1975, pp. 1, 9.

Organization for Economic Cooperation and Development (OECD). *Restrictive Business Practices of Multinational Enterprises*, Report to the Committee of Experts on Restrictive Business Practices, Paris, 1977a; and *Transfer of Technology by Multinational Corporations*. Paris, 1977b.

Ozawa, Terutomo. *Japan's Technological Challenge to the West, 1950–1974: Motivation and Accomplishment*. Cambridge, Mass.: MIT Press, 1974.

Parker, J. E. S. *The Economics of Innovation*, 2nd ed. New York: Longman, 1978.

Penrose, E. T. "International Patenting and the Less-Developed Countries." *Economic Journal*, Vol. 83, no. 331, September 1973, pp. 768–86.

Pfeffer, Jeffrey, and Philip Nowek. "Patterns of Joint Venture Activity: Implications for Antitrust Policy." *The Antitrust Bulletin*, Vol. 21, no. 2, Summer 1976, pp. 315–39.

Porter, M. E. *Competitive Strategy: Techniques for Analyzing Industries and Competitors*. New York: Free Press, 1980.

Radetzki, Marion, and Stephen Zorn. *Financing Mining Projects in Developing Countries*. London: Mining Journal Books, 1979; "Foreign Finance for LDC Mining Projects." In Sandro Sideri and Sheridan Johns (eds.), *Mining for Development in the Third World: Multinational Corporations, State Enterprises and the International Economy*. New York: Pergamon Press, 1980.

Robinson, R. D. *National Control of Foreign Business Entry: A Survey of Fifteen Countries*. New York: Praeger Publishers, 1976.

Ronstadt, R. C. *Research and Development Abroad by U.S. Multinationals*. New York: Praeger Publishers, 1977.

Rosenberg, Nathan. "The Direction of Technological Change: Inducement Mechanisms and Focussing Devices." *Economic Development and Cultural Change*, Vol. 18, no. 1, pt. 1, October 1969, pp. 1–24; *Perspectives on Technology*. Cambridge: Cambridge University Press, 1976.

Samuelsson, H. F. "National Scientific and Technological Potential and the Activities of Multinational Corporations: The Case of Sweden." Mimeographed. Report to the OECD Committee for Scientific and Technological Policy, 1974.

Scherer, F.M. "Antitrust and Patent Policy." Mimeographed. Seminar on Technological Innovation, sponsored by U.S. National Science Foundation and the Government of the Federal Republic of Germany, Bonn, April 1976; and *Industrial Market Structure and Economic Performance*. Skokie, Ill.: Rand McNally, 1980.

Smith, D. M., and L. T. Wells, Jr. *Negotiating Third World Mineral Agreements: Promises as Prologue*. Cambridge, Mass.: Ballinger, 1976.

Stigler, G. J. "Imperfections in the Capital Market." *Journal of Political Economy*, Vol. 75, no. 3, June 1967, pp. 287–92.

Stiglitz, J. E., and Andrew Weiss. "Credit Rationing in Markets with Imperfect Information." *American Economic Review*, Vol. 71, no. 3, June 1981, pp. 393–109.

Stopford, J. M., and L. T. Wells, Jr. *Managing the Multinational*. New York: Basic Books, 1972.

Stuckey, J. A. "Vertical Integration and Joint Ventures in the International Aluminum Industry." Unpublished doctoral thesis, Harvard University, 1981.

Sundelson, J. W. "U.S. Automotive Investments Abroad," in C. P. Kindelberger (ed.), *The International Corporation*. Cambridge, Mass.: MIT Press, 1970.

Teece, D. J. "Vertical Integration in the U.S. Oil Industry," in E. J. Mitchell (ed.), *Vertical Integration in the Oil Industry*. Washington, D.C.: American Enterprise Institute, 1976.

Thunell, L. H. *Political Risks in International Business: Investment Behavior of Multinational Corporations*. New York: Praeger, 1977.

Tomlinson, J. W. C. *The Joint Venture in International Business*. Cambridge, Mass.: MIT Press, 1970.

Turner, Louis. *Multinational Companies and the Third World*. New York: Hill and Wang, 1973.

Turner, Louis, and J. M. Bedore. *Middle East Indus-*

trialization: A Study of Saudi and Iranian Down-stream Investments. Westnead, Farmborough, Hants, UK: Saxon House, 1979.

UNCTAD. *The Role of Trade Marks in Developing Countries*. New York: United Nations, 1979.

United Nations Economic and Social Council, Commission on Transnational Corporations. *Transnational Corporations in World Development: A Reexamination*. New York: United Nations, 1978.

United Nations, Department of Economic and Social Affairs. *Multinational Corporations in World Development*. New York, 1973.

U.S. Department of Commerce, Bureau of Economic Analysis. *U.S. Direct Investment Abroad, 1977*. Washington, D.C.: Government Printing Office, 1981.

U.S. Federal Trade Commission. *The International Petroleum Cartel*. Washington, D.C.: Government Printing Office, 1952.

U.S. Securities and Exchange Commission. *Report on Questionable and Illegal Corporate Payments and Practices*. Washington, D.C.: Government Printing Office, May 12, 1976.

U.S. Senate Committee on Banking, Housing and Urban Affairs. "Prohibiting Bribes to Foreign Officials." *Committee Hearings*. Washington, D.C.: Committee Print, May 18, 1976.

Vaupel, J. W., and J. P. Curhan. *The World's Multinational Enterprises: A Source Book of Tables*. Boston: Division of Research, Graduate School of Business Administration, Harvard University, 1973

Vernon, Raymond. *Sovereignty at Bay*. New York: Basic Books, 1971. *Storm Over the Multinationals*. Cambridge, Mass.: Harvard University Press, 1977; and "The International Aspects of State-Owned Enterprises." *Journal of International Business Studies,* Winter 1979, pp. 7–15; and "Gone are the Cash Cows of Yesteryear." *Harvard Business Review*. November–December 1980, pp. 150–5.

Vernon, Raymond, and W. H. Davidson, "Foreign Production of Technology-Intensive Products by U.S.-Based Multinational Enterprises." Report to the National Science Foundation, no. PB 80 148638, January 1979.

Williamson, O. E. *Markets and Hierarchies: Analysis and Antitrust Implications*. New York: Free Press, 1975.

Zorn, Stephen. "Recent Trends in LDC Mining Agreements," in Sandro Sideri and Sheridan Johns (eds.), *Mining for Development in the Third World: Multinational Corporations, State Enterprises and the International Economy*. Elmsford, N.Y.: Pergamon Press, 1980.

11

Political Risk: A Review and Reconsideration
Stephen J. Kobrin

• • •

When you enter an endeavor unsuccessfully then the planning was incorrect. The risk was above the gains and you stumble along the way . . . Sagacity, ingenuity, planning . . . it involves much weighing, odds against failure, odds against gain.

Source: Stephen J. Kobrin, "Political Risk: A Review and Reconsideration," *Journal of International Business Studies,* Spring/Summer, 1979, pp. 67–80. Copyright © 1979. Reprinted by permission.

INTRODUCTION

While there has been increasing academic interest in the intersection of politics and international business, it is still a relatively new and loosely defined field. It would appear worthwhile to review and summarize what has been accomplished thus far and to look toward future needs. This paper will attempt to serve that end by focusing upon one of the more salient issue areas: the political risk associated with foreign investment. It has three specific objectives: to review the existing literature, to build upon this literature by attempting to define more precisely the concept of political risk, and to suggest fruitful directions for future research.

POLITICAL RISK

Although the term "political risk" occurs frequently in the international business literature, agreement about its meaning is limited to an implication of unwanted consequences of political activity. It is most commonly conceived of in terms of (usually host) government interference with business operations. Weston and Sorge's (64) definition is representative: "[P]olitical risks arise from the actions of national governments which interfere with or prevent business transactions, or change the terms of agreements, or cause the confiscation of wholly or partially foreign owned business property" (p. 60). Similarly, Aliber (2), Baglini (4), Carlson (11), Eiteman and Stonehill (16), Greene (23), *The Journal of Commerce* (28), Lloyd (41), and Smith (56) all explicitly or implicitly define political risk as governmental or sovereign interference with business operations. This rather widespread conception of political risk in terms of government interference with private investment has important normative implications which will be discussed in the next section.

A second major cluster of authors defines political risk in terms of events—either political acts, constraints imposed upon the firm, or some combination of both. While there are differences among them, Greene (19, 20), Hershbarger and Noerager (27), Nehrt (44), Rodriguez and Carter (47), Van Agtmael (62), and Zink (66) all equate political risk with either environmental factors such as instability and direct violence or constraints on operations such as expropriation, discriminatory taxation, public sector competition, and the like. Others—such as, Daniels (13), Dymsza (14), and Brooke and Remmers (9)—do not explicitly

define the concept but rather note that the political environment (or the environment in general) is a source of business risk for the firm.

Robock, Root, and Haendel and West have considered the concept of political risk in considerable detail. Robock (46) suggests the following operational definition:

. . . political risk in international business exists (1) when discontinuities occur in the business environment, (2) when they are difficult to anticipate and (3) when they result from political change. To constitute a "risk" these changes in the business environment must have the potential for significantly affecting the profit or other goals of a particular enterprise. (p. 7)

The concepts of discontinuity and direct effects on the enterprise are central to Robock's definition. He notes that while all political environments are dynamic, changes which are gradual and progressive and are neither unexpected nor difficult to anticipate do not constitute political risk. He then clearly differentiates between political instability and political risk: ". . . political fluctuations which do not change the business environment significantly do not represent risk for international business. . . . Political instability, depending upon how it is defined, is a separate although related phenomenon from that of political risk" (p. 8). Robock also distinguishes between "macro risk" where political events result in constraints on all foreign enterprise (for example, Cuba in 1959–1960) and "micro risk" which affects only "selected fields of business activity or foreign enterprises with specific characteristics" (p. 9).

Root (50) defines political risk in terms of the:

. . . possible occurrence of a political event of any kind (such as war, revolution, coup d'etat, expropriation, taxation, devaluation, exchange controls and import restrictions) at home or abroad that can cause a loss of profit potential and/or assets in an international business operation. (p. 355)

Root emphasizes the difference between uncertainty and risk (drawing both normative and positive implications), attempts to separate political from other environmental risks, and develops several useful taxonomies. In a second paper (51) Root concludes that the distinction between political and economic risks breaks down at the experiential level as a result of the ". . . interdependence of economic and political phenomena: (p. 3). Still, an attempt at that distinction is made; [A]n uncertainty is political if it relates to (a) a potential government act . . . , or (b) general instability in the political/social system" (p. 4).

Root also categorizes political uncertainties in terms of the manner in which they affect the firm: (1) transfer—uncertainty about flows of capital, payments, technology, people, etc.; (2) operational—uncertainties about policies that directly constrain local operations; and (3) ownership/control—uncertainties about policies relating to ownership of managerial control (p. 357). He suggests that transfer and operations uncertainties flow primarily from political/ economic events and ownership/control from political/social.

Haendel and West (24) focus upon a distinction between risk and uncertainty: between "the probability of occurrence of an undesired political event[s] and the uncertainty generated by inadequate information concerning the occurrence of such an event[s]" (p. 44). Thus, political risk is defined as the "risk or probability of occurrence of some political event[s] that will change the prospects for the profitability of a given investment" (p. xi). (They later note explicitly that political risk is both investor and investment specific.)

The crux of their argument is that information—in this case information about the political environment—can help bridge the gap; it can enable investors to convert uncertainty to risk that is, at least potentially, "measurable, insurable and avoidable" (p. 46).

POLITICAL RISK: A RECONSIDERATION

One of the conclusions of this paper is that most managers' understanding of the concept of political risk, their assessment and evaluation of politics, and the manner in which they integrate political information into decision making

are all rather general, subjective, and superficial. We would argue that while the literature reflects substantial progress in a relatively short period of time, it still does not provide an analytic framework which can adequately contribute—in either a taxonomic or an operational sense—to improved practice.

As noted above, many authors simply view political risk in terms of an event occurring either in the environment (for example, instability) or at the junction of environment and enterprise (for example, a nationalization), typically associated with an act of government that has unfavorable consequences for the firm. Scholars who have explored the issue in more depth (24, 44, 46, 50) clearly distinguish between the political event[1] and the actual loss or gain to the firm. They note that the consequences of any given political event for the foreign investor depend upon its nature, the conditions under which it occurs, and the characteristics of the specific investment in question.

However, the existing state of the art limits operationalization in the context of the investment (or reinvestment) decision process. First, the phenomenon is not defined in a manner that allows for unambiguous classification of environmental events: that is, which are of concern and which are not. Second, while all of these authors deal with uncertainty in terms of both environmental processes (continuous versus discontinuous change) and decision makers' perceptions (uncertainty versus risk), the two processes are not explicitly linked in a manner that facilitates integration into investment decision making. Third, the concentration on discontinuous change or uncertainty limits unnecessarily the scope of political analysis. Last, the emphasis on the negative consequences of government intervention entails an implicit normative assumption that may not be universally valid.

The Political Environment

Root is correct when he claims that the analytical distinctions of the social scientist break down at the experiential level; society exists in the entirety. This most certainly applies to economics and politics. Gilpin (17), among others (8, 40), has argued that the relationship between the two is not at all distinct, but rather interactive and reciprocal. Lindblom (40) goes so far as to suggest that differences may be entirely perceptual.

It appears reasonable to ask whether there is any cause to consider the political environment separately—to distinguish between sources of business risk. There appear to be very pragmatic reasons for doing so. Economics and politics are sufficiently distinct, both as abstract phenomena and in terms of their impact upon the firm, to require separate analysis and managerial response. For example, it should be obvious that a Japanese producer's response to the U.S. imposition of steel trigger prices in 1977 would be quite different if analysis indicated that the primary motivation for trigger prices was the need to prevent the alienation of important domestic interest groups rather than strict balance of payments concerns.

Defining politics in terms of power or authority relationships exercised in the context of society at large (15, 39) can usefully distinguish it from economics. This paper is concerned with events, whether they appear to be political or economic (that is, directly concerned with the production and distribution of wealth), that are motivated by attempts to gain, maintain, or increase power at the state level, "to influence significantly the kind of authoritative policy adopted for society" (15, p. 127).

Although we can distinguish between economic and political determinants of events, they are obviously interrelated. First, at least in the short run, "politics largely determines the framework of economic activity" (17). A change in regime can result in a change from a market to a socialist economy (Cuba in 1959) or the reverse (Chile in 1973). Second, and following from the first, political or power concerns often influence economic policy. The converse is, of course, equally true. The production and

distribution of wealth directly affect the distribution of power; however, the distinction has heuristic value and can be applied in practice.

We would not, for example, consider a strike, or even a general strike, a political event if its motivation results from dissatisfaction over work-related issues. However, widescale strikes in Nicaragua in January 1978 protesting the Somoza regime were clearly political. Similarly, a general strike in Tunis at about the same time began as an economic event—a protest against wage restraints—and ended as a full challenge to the Bourguiba government.

The Environment and the Firm: Perceptions and Impact

The firm exists as a system within an environment. How do political events, which occur in the environment, affect the firm? The answer depends, to a large extent, on the nature of the world facing the firm. Three states of affairs—in terms of managerial perceptions of events and outcomes—are of interest.

If a single outcome can be unambiguously associated with a given event, certainty exists. The distinction between the second and third states, which Knight (34) called risk and uncertainty, depends upon whether probabilities can be associated with outcomes. In the former, one has perfect knowledge of both all possible outcomes associated with an event and the probability of their occurrence, either "through calculation a priori or from statistics of past experience" (34, p. 233). In the latter, neither knowledge of all possible outcomes nor "objective" probabilities (in the sense used earlier) exist. However, uncertainty is, following Shackle (54), bounded. Decision makers can make judgments about most of the important outcomes and their likelihood of occurrence. (Complete uncertainty is not of interest; it entails what Shackle calls a "powerless decision.")

To avoid semantic confusion (for example,

political risk, business risk, systematic risk) the first state may be called certainty; the second, objective uncertainty; and the third, subjective uncertainty. The distinction between objective and subjective uncertainty is quite important, particularly in international business. Uncertainty is subjective in the sense that opinions about the relative likelihood of events are based upon perceptions that are a function of the available information, previous experience, and individual cognitive processes which synthesize both into an imagined future.

It is clear that for virtually all business decisions of the type discussed here both certainty and objective uncertainty are ideal constructs. As the decisions can neither be repeated nor divided—that is, treated as one of a series of experiments and pooled (as can both deaths and auto accidents)—they are unique events. Perhaps, more importantly, the decisions are made by human beings in a very complex environment which makes it difficult to specify all possible, or even all important, alternatives. Since decisions are taken in the present, possible outcomes must be imagined outcomes, existing subjectively in the mind of the decision maker; however, both certainty and objective uncertainty can be approximated.

Certainty can be approximated by situations when one outcome dominates all others. Thus, the probability that the next President of the United States will be selected by a constitutional process and that he (or she) will not institute a program of broadscale nationalization of industry is so high as to be virtually certain. Certainty may also be approximated in situations that Robock (46) described as gradual change, which one can anticipate, based upon current trends. Objective uncertainty can be approximated by situations where, while one outcome does not dominate, all feasible outcomes are known, information is readily available, and all (or almost all) observers agree upon probabilities. Again, an example would be the outcome of most U.S. presidential elections.

We can now return to the question of the im-

pact of politics upon the firm. Several preliminary points are in order. First, one can say only that political events may affect the firm; whether they do so is a function of both environmental conditions and industry- and firm-specific factors. A coup, for example, may place a radical socialist government in power which expropriates all foreign-owned firms (as in Ethiopia); it may result in a conservative government which actually returns expropriated property (as in Chile in 1973), or it may simply replace governing elites without affecting foreign investors at all. Furthermore, as many authors have noted (for example, (46) and (50)), vulnerability is a function of enterprise-specific characteristics. Natural resource-based investment is generally more vulnerable, ceteris paribus, than are manufacturing firms producing essential products.

Second, one must clearly distinguish between the environment and the firm. Instability is a property of the environment and risk of the firm. It is the possible variation of a firm-specific variable (for example, returns) from its expected value that can be caused by environmental events. Last, risk may imply positive as well as negative variation about the mean; it can result in gains as well as losses. The distinction between pure risk, which involves only a chance of loss or no loss (for example, a fire or fraud), and speculative risk, which involves the possibility of both gain and loss (31), is useful.

Given certainty, the firm does not face business risk; both outcomes of events and their impact upon the firm are known; however, political events can still affect returns. As an example, assume it is absolutely certain that a new government will come to power in one month and that it will force a firm to divest 100 percent of equity in five years at present book value. Although the political event will reduce the value of future returns, it will not in any way contribute to their variation. There is no business risk associated with the change in government.

However, once uncertainty is introduced,

political events can both affect the expected value of returns and contribute to their variation. Political events are now a source of business risk. Whereas their impact upon the value of returns is not dependent upon whether the uncertainty is objective or subjective, the nature and extent of their contribution to risk clearly is. If uncertainty is objective, the contribution of political events to business risk is a function of only the events themselves. Risk, then, is the distribution of probable returns which is, ceteris paribus, a function of the probable impacts of political events on operations.

If uncertainty is subjective, the contribution of business risk is a function of both the events themselves and the fact that decision makers' perceptions of those events are inherently subjective—distorted by past experience, cognitive processes and the nature of the organization. This subjectivity factor is particularly important in international business operations where decisions are often taken in one sociopolitical environment based upon stimuli arising in another. As will be discussed later, the survey data indicate that managerial evaluations of political risk are typically subjective and ethnocentric.

A better understanding of the political process in general, the political environment in the country in question, and the potential impact of politics upon the firm's operations can thus obviously reduce risk by reducing the uncertainty about the actual probability distribution. However, the crucial point, one which forces us to take issue with the existing literature (for example, Haendel and West (24)), is that while better information can help eliminate misconceptions about both the political environment and its impact upon the firm, it can seldom convert uncertainty into risk or what we have called objective uncertainty. Opinions formed about future events (and particularly events which will take place in another culture) are inherently subjective. Hannah Arendt (3) put it well:

The world appears in the mode of it-seems-to-me, depending on particular perspectives determined by location in the world as well as by particular organs of perception. Not only does this produce error, which I can correct by changing my location, drawing closer to what appears, or by improving my imagination to take other perspectives into account; it also gives birth to true semblances—that is true deceptive appearances, which I cannot correct like an error. (pp. 108–109)

The term ''political risk'' thus appears overly constrained from both an analytical and operational viewpoint. What we are, or should be, concerned with is the impact of events which are political in the sense that they arise from power or authority relationships and which affect (or have the potential to affect) the firm's operations. Not the events, qua events, but their potential manifestation as constraints upon foreign investors should be of concern. Furthermore, although the same constraint (for example, restrictions on profit repatriations or a forced divestment of ownership) could be motivated by economic as well as political factors (or both) depending upon the circumstances, the two may be differentiated to facilitate analysis and response. Last, political events may affect only the value of returns, or they may also contribute to business risk depending upon whether outcomes are evaluated under conditions approximating certainty or uncertainty. If that uncertainty is subjective, as it is likely to be in an international business decision, the contribution to risk will be greater because one is uncertain about both outcomes and the probabilities associated wih them. Integration of the assessment of political risk into the investment decision process will be discussed next.

Integration Into Decision Making

The integration of political assessments into decision making is not a subject that has been widely discussed. The literature focuses typically upon deriving probabilistic estimates of political events and their impact upon the firm rather than how the estimates are utilized; this study conforms to that tradition.

Most authors who have considered the problem assume that decision makers will utilize political analysis to adjust either cash flows or the discount rate. Robock (46), for example, shows how risk analysis can be used to determine the political risks likely to arise during specific time periods and then suggests that "the present value of expected cash flows, or the internal rate of return from the investment project under consideration can be adjusted to reflect the timing and magnitude of risk probabilities" (p. 17). (In the example that follows, however, only cash flows are adjusted.)

After reviewing evidence showing how most firms analyze political and economic stability, Stobaugh (57) suggests two more "sophisticated techniques": range of estimates and risk analysis. However, while both provide probability distributions as well as expected values of cash flows, Stobaugh's examples entail only the adjustment of the level of cash flows.

Stonehill and Nathanson (58) object to simple discount rate adjustments to reflect political and foreign exchange uncertainties. They suggest that "A better way to allow for uncertainty in the multinational case would be to charge each period's incremental cash flows the cost of a program of uncertainty absorption for that period, whether or not the program was actually undertaken" (p. 46). The program of uncertainty absorption could entail the purchase of additional information, insurance (including investment guarantees), hedging, and the like. They, in essence, recommend using a market-determined approximation of a certainty equivalent.

Shapiro (55) deals with political and economic risk, and specifically with expropriation in the context of the capital budgeting process. He notes that neither of two methods (a higher discount rate or a shorter payback period) com-

monly used to account for political or economic risk "lends itself to a careful evaluation of a paticular risk's actual impact on investment returns. A thorough risk analysis requires an assessment of the magnitude of the risk's effect on cash flows as well as an estimate of the true pattern of the risk." (p. 6)

Shapiro then develops sophisticated techniques for adjusting cash flows given the probability of expropriation at a point in the future. However, he assumes that (1) the assumptions of the Capital Asset Pricing Model are relevant; and (2) the risks in question are nonsystematic in nature. Thus, the cash flow adjustments reflect only changes in expected values resulting from the impact of a given risk.

Although agreeing with Shapiro that, in evaluating the impact of the political environment on the firm, both the effect upon the magnitude of cash flows and on their distribution (that is, risk) must be taken into account, we would like to avoid entering the lists on the question of whether the firm should be viewed as a social organization reflecting managerial utilities (and risk preferences) or as a agent of the stockholders. Instead, we suggest that the potential effect of politics be evaluated in terms of the continuum discussed earlier. Under conditions giving rise to risk, whether one actually adjusts the discount rate or not will be determined by one's judgment as to (1) the applicability of the Capital Asset Pricing Model and (2) whether the risk is systematic or not.

Under conditions approximating certainty, decision makers should be concerned only with determining the effect of political events on the magnitude of cash flows. Risk, clearly is not a relevant concern; however, political assessment and evaluation is still necessary. Certain outcomes are not inherently obvious; they are certain, given sufficient information about the environment and the firm.

Under conditions approximating objective uncertainty, the decision maker must consider the impact of politics on both the expected value of cash flows and their distribution (or business risk). The estimate of the contribution to risk will flow solely from the distribution of the joint probability of a political event taking place and affecting cash flows. Last, under conditions of subjective uncertainty, the decision maker is again concerned with the effect of political events upon both expected values and risk. However, in this instance risk is increased because one is uncertain about the shape of the probability distribution. In fact one knows one's estimate is inherently distorted due to subjective factors and that the distortion can never be completely eliminated.

One additional point entails an implicit normative assumption which is counterproductive in terms of the very issue of concern:[2] The tendency to view political risk in terms of government interference with one's operations.

Much of the discussion of political risk appears to assume that governmental restrictions on FDI—such as, partial divestment or local content regulations—involve economically inefficient and perhaps even irrational tampering with flows of direct investment that provide net benefits to their recipients. It is obvious that this viewpoint is less than universally accepted and that what appears as economic nationalism[3] to an investor may be regarded as an attempt to implement a policy of indigenous industrialization by the host. In short, company and host country objectives differ and neither has a monopoly on goodness and light. A perception to the contrary, whether explicit or implicit, may well increase the risk one is attempting to evaluate.

POLITICAL EVENTS AND FOREIGN DIRECT INVESTMENT

A number of empirical studies have attempted to analyze the relationship between FDI and environmental factors—typically measures of political instability and market size and potential. With some relatively minor exceptions the results are consistent. The overwhelmingly im-

portant determinant of manufacturing investment is the size and potential of the market (20), (35), (61). A direct or simple relationship cannot be found between a general notion of instability and stocks or flows of FDI (7), (19), (20), (35). For example, in an early study Green (7) regressed stocks of U.S. FDI in manufacturing and trade on an index of political instability while controlling for gross national product per capita across 46 countries. He concluded that political instability did not affect the overall allocation of U.S. marketing FDI. In a 62-country cross-sectional study Kobrin (35) analyzed the relationship between flows of U.S. manufacturing FDI and seven indicators of economic, social, and political factors. While the environmental factors accounted for 64 percent of the variance of FDI, only market size, growth, and a measure of prior U.S. export involvement were significant.

There have been several exceptions to the overall pattern of results. Green and Smith (22) established a weak but statistically significant relationship between profitability of U.S. FDI and instability. However, methodological problems cloud interpretation of the results. Root and Ahmed (52) used discriminant analysis to attempt to account for differences between three groups of countries based upon per capita inflows of nonextractive FDI. While regular executive transfers was found to be a significant discriminator, it was the fifth variable selected by the stepwise procedure (the other five were market related), and its explanatory power, therefore, appears weak. Last, Knickerbocker (33), in his study of oligopolistic reaction, found a significant relationship between a measure of entry concentration and an index of stability across 21 countries. He concluded that "oligopolists were not inclined to make defensive investments in unstable markets" (p. 184).

At least two studies suggest a complex and indirect relationship between FDI and instability. Thunell (61), in a longitudinal study, attempted to analyze the relationship between major "trend" changes in the flow of FDI (the second derivative) and a number of indicators of elite and mass stability. An asymmetrical relationship was observed. A high level of mass violence precedes negative trend changes, whereas it takes both a low level of violence and a government transfer (which Thunell speculates implies a shift in policy) to generate a positive change. It should be noted that, although interesting, Thunell's results must be regarded as quite tentative due to problems of comparability and the absence (with one exception) of statistical analysis.

In a study of 48 countries, Kobrin (36) found a significant relationship between flows of FDI (controlling for market-related factors) and one dimension of intrastate conflict; focused antiregime violence. The relationship is intensified at higher levels of development and when host country administrative capacity is strong. That study concluded that political conflict has the highest probability of affecting foreign investors when it is of a nature and occurs under conditions which are likely to motivate relevant changes in government policy.

It would thus appear that political factors are not a major determinant of FDI. To the extent that a relationship does exist, it is rather complex and depends upon the probability that instability or conflict will result in changes in policy rather than in direct effects upon investors.

It should be obvious that all of the studies summarized have several glaring defects. First, they all focus upon instability when it is clear that political instability is neither a necessary nor a sufficient condition for changes in policy relevant to foreign investment. Second, they all utilize aggregate (typically cross-national) analysis when the risk posed by politics is markedly affected by industry, firm, and even project-specific factors. (This problem is somewhat alleviated by the focus of most of the studies on the manufacturing sector.) Last, all the studies entail major data and methodological problems ranging from the use of composite indices of instability to the almost universal use (with one exception) of cross-sectional techniques to in-

vestigate what is obviously a longitudinal phenomenon. In summary, while the results are useful and interesting, they must be taken as tentative.

THE POLITICAL ENVIRONMENT: ASSESSMENT AND RESPONSE

Surveys of managerial assessment and evaluation of the political environment consistently reveal an interesting paradox. With very few exceptions, managers rate political instability (or political risk) as one of the major influences on the foreign investment decision. Yet, again with very few exceptions, the same surveys report the absence of any formal or even rigorous and systematic assessment of political environments and their potential impact upon the firm.

Two early studies—those of Aharoni (1) and Basi (5)—found that political or economic stability was the first factor considered in the foreign investment decision. A second conclusion of Aharoni's described the assessment process: "Risk is not described in terms of the impact on a specific investment. It is, rather, described in general terms and stems from ignorance, generalizations, projection of U.S. culture and standards to other countries and on unqualified deduction from some general indicator to a specific investment" (p. 94). As we shall see, little can be found in reports of more recent surveys to support a challenge to Aharoni's conclusions.

Several other important studies were conducted (or reported) in the late 1960s. In two separate studies (48 and 49), Root surveyed executives in a large number of U.S. firms selected from the *Fortune 500* list. He reported that while executives indicated political risks and market opportunities are "the dominant factors in most (foreign) investment decisions . . . no executive offered any evidence of a systematic evaluation of political risks, involving their identification, their likely incidence, and their specific consequences for company operations" (49, p. 75). Furthermore, it is quite clear that executives' subjective perceptions of political instability were highly instrumental in shaping their attitudes toward the safety and profitability of investment climates.

A 1967–1968 Conference Board survey of investors in twelve countries (43) confirmed the earlier findings. First, estimates of political risk were typically based upon subjective perceptions: "The study makes it clear that obstacles to investment exist in the mind of the investor . . . certain countries are dismissed from consideration as investment sites on the basis of information that is incomplete, outdated or in some cases even erroneous" (p. 2). Second, politics is perceived as an important determinant of foreign investment, and a common response to perceived political risk is avoidance. Studies reported in the early 1970s—(45), (59), (66)—added little new information. While political or quasi-political factors continued to be of major concern to investors, few U.S. companies had as yet developed techniques for assessing the political environment or evaluating its impact upon operations.

The most recent studies reported are monotonously consistent with previous findings. In two Conference Board reports (37 and 38) LaPalombara and Blank conclude that while some sort of environmental analysis exists in most firms, it is typically rather loose and casual, developing and utilizing a subjective "feel for the political situation." During the course of the study, various planning materials and documents were reviewed. The conclusion drawn is to the point: "More often than not, the few paragraphs devoted to a host country's social and political dynamics is not better than one might find in leading parent country newspapers" (p. 65).

Drawing on his experience as a Vice President of a major bank, Van Agtmael (62) concluded that even large and active MNCs do not analyze political risk in a very sophisticated manner; and he agrees with other authors that the typical response to political risk is avoidance. "Even those corporations which have made commitments overseas, by and large, try to avoid political risk by investing in 'safe' countries" (p. 26). There remains one, somewhat specialized, area of the political environment assessment literature—that dealing with the sovereign (or country) risk inherent in private bank lending to LDCs. Rather than extend what is already a rather lengthy paper, the reader may be referred to the following: Goodman (18), Mueller (42), Van Agtmael (63), and Yassukouich (65).

Last, a brief review of the findings of the literature on managers' sources of information about politics shows that the earliest findings still stand. In a classic study, which while dealing primarily with trade certainly has broader implications, Bauer, de Sola Pool, and Dexter (6) concluded that, to businessmen, knowledge of the "outside world" came in a number of ways:

it came in part through the printed word, but what came that way was surprisingly general and unfocused. Our respondents read *Time, Business Week, The Wall Street Journal, The New York Times,* and other such journals. They read a great deal. They also read trade papers. But, in making specific business decisions, they did not do research in published sources. . . . Knowledge of foreign economic affairs came either from the most general news sources or, more vividly, from correspondence and personal experience. (p. 470)

Zink (66) found that managers' major sources of political information were reports from host country employees, general news sources, and financial institutions (in that order). Only 23 percent of respondents considered internal political staff as an important source, and only 9 percent so rated outside consultants on a continuous retainer. Keegan (30) concluded that his study of managers at MNC Headquarters emphasized "how little the systematic methods of information scanning have become a part of the way in which executives learn about their business environments" (p. 420). Executives stationed abroad (but not lower level employees), banks, and the public press were the most important sources of information for headquarters managers.

The findings reviewed here are impressively consistent. First, it is clear that managers consider political instability or political risk, typically quite loosely defined, to be an important factor in the foreign investment decision. Second, it is just as clear that rigorous and systematic assessment and evaluation of the political environment is exceptional. Most political analysis is superficial and subjective, not integrated formally into the decision-making process and assumes that instability and risk are one and the same. The response frequently is avoidance; firms simply do not get involved in countries, or even regions, that they perceive to be risky. Last, managers appear to rely for environmental information primarily on sources internal to the firm. When they look for outside data, they are most likely to go to their banks or the general and business media.

ENVIRONMENTAL ASSESSMENT METHODOLOGIES[4]

Existing screening models fit into two general categories: those aggregating subjective assessments (typically via a Delphi method) and those relying on quantified indicators of economic, social, and political factors. (A "soft/hard" distinction is not appropriate.) The best known examples of the former are Haner's "Business Environmental Risk Index" or BERI (25 and 26) and the Business International Index of Environmental Risk (10). Both attempt to assess the general investment climate in a number of countries by using the Delphi technique to poll a panel of experts. Haner (26) states that the objective of BERI is to assess the business environment in a country from the viewpoint of a foreign investor six months to one year in the future.

BERI's panel assesses fifteen environmental factors quarterly (for example, political stabil-

ity, attitude toward foreign investors, and economic growth). Each panelist scores each factor and the responses are then aggregated with the factors not equally weighted. The aggregate index and political, operations, and financial subindices are available. The BI system is quite similar.

While both indices attempt to screen the environment systematically, their usefulness is somewhat limited. First, they provide holistic rankings which are inherently independent of firm or industry factors. More importantly, they rely on a panel who may differ widely not only in terms of rankings, but in how they conceptualize the phenomena being evaluated. Last, while panel members are non-U.S. nationals, they also tend to be employees of industrial firms or financial institutions and their fundamental viewpoints are not likely to differ greatly from the users of the service. The net result, is, as Haner himself notes (25), that the index cannot forecast sudden changes in the political and economic environment. Again, however, both indices may be useful for general prescreening.

A second set of methodologies utilizes quantitative indices. Several authors (21) and (56) simply review existing indicators (or models) of political instability in terms of their managerial utility. There have also been attempts to develop more sophisticated quantitative indices of political risk. For example, Haendel and West (24) suggest what they call the Political System Stability Index (PSSI) which is composed of fifteen indicators of the system's stability/ adaptability grouped into three subindices: socioeconomic, governmental processes, and societal conflict. A score and an estimate of confidence in that score (1–5) are provided for the overall index and each of the three major subindices. Rummel and Heenan (53) suggest integrating qualitative assessments (such as, reliance on "old hands," or Delphi techniques) with quantitative assessments. As an example, they utilize multivariate analysis to predict two components of intrastate conflict—turmoil and rebellion—in Indonesia through 1980.

Juhl (29) compares a number of environmental indicators, including four measures of political instability and BERI. The results are of interest. First, while the relationships (rank order correlation) between the various indices are typically significant, they are rather weak. Second, none of them account for more than 25 percent of the variance of any of three indices of nationalization. Last, with one exception, the author could not establish a significant relationship between the BERI Nationalism subindex and flows of FDI.

Although there are inherent limits of aggregate quantitative, analysis—as with the Delphi techniques, it ignores industry and firm specific factors—it does offer a great deal of potential as a basis for systematic and rigorous assessment of the political environment. (However, that it can now, or at any point in the future, be utilized independently of qualitative judgments is not suggested.) In spite of the fact that most of the methodologies discussed were developed to aid in international firms' assessment of the political environment, they still measure political instability rather than the potential impact of politics upon the firm.

The problem transcends that of index development. While most authors reviewed agree that political instability and political risk are distinct phenomena, the fact of the matter is that enough is not known about how the former (and the political environment in general) affects the latter to construct reasonable predictive models.

CONCLUSIONS

Managers use a wide variety of techniques to reduce and cope with uncertainty in many areas of business operations. Most firms, for example, would not even consider basing a major new product introduction on a generalized feel for the market. Rather, they typically utilize a battery of relatively sophisticated research techniques to aid in reaching a judgment about both the product's potential and how to market it. Yet, judgments about the impact of politics upon operations appear, at least from the sources reviewed in this paper, to be rather superficial and typically based almost entirely on subjective perceptions.

To be absolutely clear, "sophisticated analysis" is not equated here with a complex mathematical model, but rather, what is suggested is a systematic and relatively rigorous approach to data gathering and problem solving. While stereotypes are admittedly unfair, the all too typical process, where political instability is equated with a poor investment climate and the market avoided, is a long way from that ideal. The literature reviewed in this paper reflects the substantial growth and development of a relatively new area; however, some fairly major gaps must be filled if it is to contribute to more systematic and rigorous assessment and evaluation of politics by managers of international firms and to the effective integration of the information into the decision-making process. The lacunae that exist are both conceptual and empirical. We need better definitions of the phenomena, a conceptual structure relating politics to the firm, and a great deal of information about the impact of the political environment. The three are, of course, related.

Although this paper represents a preliminary attempt to redefine the concept of political risk, much work obviously remains. In fact, the term "political risk" might well be dropped from usage. (This suggestion, however, is probably a futile one.) It is overly confining and confusing. Rather, the area of interest should be defined in terms of the current and potential impact(s) of the political environment upon the operations of the firm where:

1. The political environment is circumscribed in terms of events which, however they are manifest, are motivated by or have as their objective the maintenance or modification of power or authority relationships at the governmental level.
2. The impact of political events upon the firm is defined in terms of both effects upon the magnitude of cash flows or returns and upon the busi-

ness risk associated with them in the context of a specific project.

3. A significant impact on business operations cannot be assumed to be an inherent property of any political event.

In operational terms we are concerned with the probability that changes in the political environment will reduce returns to the point where the project would be no longer acceptable on the basis of ex ante criteria. Changes in the political environment can affect returns directly through damage to plant and equipment and degradation of the economy as a result of conflict. Returns can also be affected indirectly through changes in government policy such as expropriation, local content regulations, and restrictions on the remittance of dividends.

Last, research might be focused on the following areas:

1. *Empirical analyses of the conditions under which, and the process through which, political events affect the firm.* Further work (both theoretical and empirical) is needed to identify the types of environmental events likely to affect operations, the conditions under which they are most likely to do so, and the nature of the specific process through which effects are transmitted.

2. *More data on the effects themselves.* Aside from some limited data on nationalization, we really know very little about the relative importance of actual constraints imposed upon firms. Have, for example, pressures for local ownership, exchange controls, direct limits on operations, or restrictions on fees and royalties resulted from political change and how have they affected firms?

3. *Additional and more systematic studies of the assessment and evaluation of the political environment by multinational firms.* What factors affect the way the assessment and evaluation process is organized and executed? Where is it located in the organization? How is the resulting information integrated into decision making? Importantly, how does the process affect strategic decision making? Are there industrial or national differences? What affects managers' subjective

perceptions or political environments? How does information act upon them?

4. *In depth case studies.* Most of the research described in this paper is quantitative and cross-national. While it has been a valuable aid in mapping out the nature of relationships between variables, thorough case studies are needed to flesh out the skeleton. For example, a case study of the impact of a deteriorating political environment (Argentina in the late 1960s) on foreign investors could aid in understanding the exact nature of the impact of political events on foreign firms. Case studies could also help compensate for the lack of time-series data.

5. *Interdisciplinary research.* Work in this area, by definition, implies that one draw upon previous efforts in both management and political science; however, it is clear that efforts involving a number of the social sciences such as economics, organizational psychology, and anthropology are likely to bear fruit.

NOTES

1. As Baglini (4) notes, the political event is a cause of loss or a peril.

2. Bernard Mennis brought this point to my attention.

3. For a discussion of "economic nationalism" see Harry Johnson, "A Theoretical Model of Economic Nationalism in New and Developing States," *Political Science Quarterly,* June 1965, pp. 169–185.

4. While it could not be reviewed in this paper, the extensive literature on international business government relations is obviously relevant. For example see: Jack N. Behrman, J. J. Boddewyn, and Ashok Kapoor, *International Business—Government Relations* (Lexington, Mass.: Lexington Books, 1975) and Business International, *Corporate External Affairs* (New York: Business International, 1975).

REFERENCES

(1) Aharoni, Yair. *The Foreign Investment Decision Process.* Boston: Division of Research, Graduate School of Business Administration, Harvard University, 1966.

(2) Aliber, Robert Z. "Exchange Risk, Political Risk and Investor Demands for External Currency Deposits." *Journal of Money, Credit & Banking,* May 1975, pp. 161–179.

(3) Arendt, Hannah. "Reflections (Thinking—Part

1)." *The New Yorker,* 21 November 1977, pp. 65–140.

(4) Baglini, Norman A. *Risk Management in International Corporations.* New York: Risk Studies Foundation, 1976.

(5) Basi, R. S. *Determinants of United States Private Direct Investment in Foreign Countries.* Kent, Ohio: Kent State University, 1963.

(6) Bauer, Raymond A., Ithiel, de Sola Poor, and Lewis A. Dexter. *American Business and Public Policy,* 2nd ed. Chicago: Aldine-Atherton, 1972.

(7) Bennett, Peter D., and Robert T. Green. "Political Instability as a Determinant of Direct Foreign Investment in Marketing." *Journal of Marketing Research,* May 1972, pp. 182–186.

(8) Bergston, C. Fred, Robert O. Keohane, and Joseph S. Nye. "International Economics and International Politics: A Framework for Analysis." In *World Politics and International Economics,* edited by C. Fred Bergsten and Lawrence B. Krause. Washington, D.C.: Brookings Institute, 1975, pp. 3–36.

(9) Brooke, Michael, and H. Lee Remmers. *The Strategy of Multinational Enterprise.* London: Longman Group, 1970.

(10) Business International. New York: Business International Corporation, 1969.

(11) Carlson, Sunne. *International Financial Decisions.* Uppsala: The Institute of Business Studies, 1969.

(12) CitiBank. *The Multinational Corporation: An Environmental Analysis.* Investment Research Department, New York: unpublished, April 1976.

(13) Daniels, John D., Ernest W. Ogram, Jr., and Lee H. Radebaugh. *International Business: Environments and Operations.* Reading, Mass.: Addison-Wesley, 1976.

(14) Dymsza, William A. *Multinational Business Strategy.* New York: McGraw-Hill, 1972.

(15) Easton, David. *The Political System.* New York: Alfred A. Knopf, 1968 (1953).

(16) Eiteman, David K., and Stonehill, Arthur I. *Multinational Business Finance.* Reading, Mass.: Addison-Wesley, 1973.

(17) Gilpin, Robert. *U.S. Power and the Multinational Corporation.* New York: Basic Books, 1975.

(18) Goodman, Stephen. "How the Big Banks Really Evaluate Sovereign Risks." *Euromoney,* February 1977, pp. 105–110.

(19) Green, Robert T. *Political Instability as a De-*terminant *of U.S. Foreign Investment,* Austin: Bureau of Business Research, Graduate School of Business, University of Texas at Austin, 1972.

(20) ———., and William H. Cunningham. "The Determinants of U.S. Foreign Investments: An Empirical Examination." *Management International Review,* Vol. 3, February 1975, pp. 113–120.

(21) ———., and C. M. Korth. "Political Instability and The Foreign Investor." *California Management Revew,* Fall 1974, pp.23–31.

(22) ———., and Charles H. Smith. "Multinational Profitability as a Function of Political Instability." *Management International Review,* Vol. 6 (1972), pp. 23–29.

(23) Greene, Mark K. "The Management of Political Risk." *Best's Review (Property/Liability ed.),* July 1974, pp. 71–74.

(24) Haendel, Dan H., Gerald T. West, and Robert G. Meadow. *Overseas Investment and Political Risk.* Philadelphia: Foreign Policy Research Institute, 1975.

(25) Haner, F. T. "Business Environmental Risk Index." *Best's Review (Property/Liability ed.),* July 1975, pp. 47–50.

(26) ———. "General Assessments of the Foreign Environment." Unpublished, 1975.

(27) Hershbarger, Robert A., and John P. Noerager. "International Risk Management: Some Peculiar Constraints." *Risk Management,* April 1976, pp. 23–34.

(28) *Journal of Commerce.* "Risk Management." 14 December 1977.

(29) Juhl, Paulgeorg. "Prospects for Foreign Direct Investment in Developing Countries." In *Reshaping the World Economic Order,* edited by Herbert Giersch. Kiel: Tubingen, 1976.

(30) Keegan, Warren J. "Multinational Scanning: A Study of the Information Sources Utilized by Headquarters Executives in Multinational Companies." *Administrative Science Quarterly,* September 1974, pp. 411–421.

(31) Kelley, Margaret. "Evaluating the Risks of Expropriation." *Risk Management,* January 1974, pp. 23–43.

(32) Kissinger, Henry A. Speech before the Future of Business Project of the Center for Strategic and International Studies, Georgetown, Virginia, Washington, D.C.: 28 June 1977.

(33) Knickerbocker, Frederick T. *Oligopolistic Reaction and Multinational Enterprise.* Boston:

Division of Research, Graduate School of Business Administration, Harvard University, 1973.

(34) Knight, Frank H. *Risk Uncertainty and Profit* (1921). Chicago: University of Chicago Press, 1971.

(35) Kobrin, Stephen. "The Environmental Determinants of Foreign Direct Manufacturing Investment: An Ex-Post Empirical Analysis." *Journal of International Business Studies,* Fall–Winter 1976, pp. 29–42.

(36) ———. "When Does Political Instability Result in Increased Investment Risk." *The Columbia Journal of World Business,* October 1978.

(37) LaPalombara, Joseph, and Stephen Blank. *Multinational Corporations and National Elites: A Study in Tensions.* New York: The Conference Board, 1976.

(38) ———. *Multinational Corporations in Comparative Perspective.* New York: The Conference Board, 1977.

(39) Lasswell, Harold D., and Abraham Kaplan. *Power and Society.* New Haven, Conn.: Yale University Press, 1950.

(40) Lindblom, Charles E. *Politics and Markets.* New York: Basic Books, 1977.

(41) Lloyd, B. *Political Risk Management.* London: Keith Shipton Developments, 1976.

(42) Mueller, P. H., et al. "Assessing Country Exposure." *The Journal of Commercial Bank Lending,* December 1974, pp. 28–43.

(43) National Industrial Conference Board. *Obstacles and Incentives to Private Foreign Investment, 1967–68,* Volume 1: *Obstacles.* New York: National Industrial Conference Board, 1969.

(44) Nehrt, Lee Charles. *The Political Environment for Foreign Investment.* New York: Praeger Publishers, 1970.

(45) Piper, James R. "How U.S. Firms Evaluate Foreign Investment Opportunities." *MSU Business Topics,* Summer 1971, pp. 11–20.

(46) Robock, Stefan H. "Political Risk: Identification and Assessment." *Columbia Journal of World Business,* July–August 1971, pp. 6–20.

(47) Rodriguez, Rita M., and E. Eugene Carter. *International Financial Management.* Englewood Cliffs, N.J.: Prentice-Hall, 1976.

(48) Root, Franklin, R. "Attitudes of American Executives Towards Foreign Governmental Investment Opportunities." *Economics and Business Bulletin,* Temple University, January 1968, pp. 14–23.

(49) ———. "U.S. Business Abroad and Political Risks." *MSU Business Topics,* Winter, 1968, pp. 73–80.

(50) ———. "Analyzing Political Risks in International Business," in *The Multinational Enterprise in Transition,* edited by A. Kapoor and Philip D. Grub. Princeton, N.J.: Darwin Press, 1972, pp. 354–365.

(51) ———. "The Management by LDC Governments of the Political Risk Trade-off in Direct Foreign Investment." Paper presented to The International Studies Association, Toronto, February 1976.

(52) ———., and Ahmed A. Ahmed. "Empirical Determinants of Manufacturing Direct Foreign Investment in Developing Countries." Forthcoming, *Economic Development and Cultural Change.*

(53) Rummel, R. J., and David A. Heenan. "How Multinationals Analyze Political Risk." *Harvard Business Review,* January–February 1978, pp. 67–76.

(54) Shackle, G. L. S. *Decision, Order, and Time in Human Affairs,* 2nd ed. Cambridge, England: Cambridge University Press, 1969.

(55) Shapiro, Alan C. *Capital Budgeting for the Multinational Corporation. Financial Management,* Spring 1978.

(56) Smith, Clifford Neal. "Predicting the Political Environment of International Business." *Long Range Planning,* September 1971, pp. 7–14.

(57) Stobaugh, Robert B., Jr. "How to Analyze Foreign Investment Climates." *Harvard Business Review,* September–October 1969, pp. 100–107.

(58) Stonehill, Arthur, and Leonard Nathanson. "Capital Budgeting and the Multinational Corporation." *California Management Review,* Summer 1968, pp. 39–54.

(59) Swansborough, Robert H. "The American Investor's View of Latin American Economic Nationalism." *Inter-American Economic Affairs,* Winter 1972, pp. 61–82.

(60) Terkel, Studs. *Hard Times.* New York: Avon Books, 1971.

(61) Thunell, Lars H. *Political Risks in International Business.* New York: Praeger Publishers, 1977.

(62) Van Agtmael, Antoine. "How Business Has Dealt with Political Risk." *Financial Executive,* January 1976, pp. 26–30.

(63) ———. "Evaluating the Risks of Lending and Developing Countries." *Euromoney*, April 1976, pp. 16–30.

(64) Weston, V. Fred, and Bart W. Sorge. *International Managerial Finance*. Homewood, Ill.: Richard D. Irwin, 1972.

(65) Yassukovich, S. M. "The Growing Political Unrest and International Lending." *Euromoney*, April 1976, pp. 10–15.

(66) Zink, Dolph Warren. *The Political Risks for Multinational Enterprise in Developing Countries*. New York: Praeger Publishers, 1973.

12

Unsticking the State of the Art of Political Risk Management
Warnock Davies

• • •

The situation in Iran has resulted in unprecedented attention by corporate management to the sociopolitical exposure of foreign direct investment. But despite this increase in attention, the state of the art of political risk policy, strategy, and tactics has gotten stuck. This is due to a preoccupation with perfecting more country specific models, more elaborate risk assessment methods, and more finely tuned risk avoidance forecasts. In addition, country assessment techniques and systems have become ends in themselves.

All of these elements are necessary to the management of political risk vulnerability but, regardless of their sophistication, they are not sufficient. They are of limited value unless used as points of departure for continua that go beyond the conventional methodologies and preoccupations that are to blame for the present stalemate. To overcome this stalemate, management's focus must move from the country specific to the corporate specific, from risk assessment to vulnerability monitoring, and from risk avoidance to vulnerability management. (While the focus here is on the political risk

exposure of foreign direct investment, some of the principles, procedures, and concepts are applicable to foreign trade and foreign portfolio investment.)

FROM COUNTRY SPECIFIC TO CORPORATE SPECIFIC

Country specificity is the criterion for almost all sociopolitical deliberations by corporations, from in-depth political, social, and economic studies to casual questions that fall into the "What do you think is going to happen in country X?" category. Furthermore, it is responsible for producing the palace watchers, the coup predictors, and, as a legacy of Iran, a neurosis which can be called the Ayatollah Phobia. (The *bete noir* standing achieved by the Ayatollah Khomeini—which pales even that of Fidel Castro in his heyday—and the manner in which the Ayatollah materialized as if from nowhere, has preempted all other sociopolitical risk considerations. While this orientation has reduced the chance of being caught by an ayatollah clone, it has increased management's vulnerability to equally debilitating factors.)

The disproportionate emphasis given to country specific factors is due to the inherently country specific orientation of home country media and home country governments which,

Source: Warnock Davies, "Unsticking the State of the Art of Political Risk Management," *Sloan Management Review,* Summer, 1981, pp. 59–63. Reprinted by permission of the publisher. Copyright © 1981 by the Sloan Management Review Association. All rights reserved.

between the pervasiveness of one and the authority of the other, prescribe society's opinions and perceptions of foreign countries. These influences, together with the country specific base of country assessment services (and occasionally, the employment by corporations of former government personnel in political risk advisory positions) create an a posteriori bias to the evaluation and use of information and analysis.

Inappropriateness of Country Specificity

The operational consequence of country specificity is that it seriously impedes the perceptive objectivity of executives because it assumes that the sociopolitical environment of a host country is the key variable in determining the continuation of profitable operations of an investment. This orientation assumes that there is a direct correlation between the destiny of the host country and the destiny of all foreign investment in it.

During earlier stages of economic nationalism, this assumption may have been appropriate, but now it is not. The earthquake allegory (that managing political risk is comparable to attempting to manage earthquakes) no longer applies.[1] To the contrary, the issues that now determine the sociopolitical security of a foreign direct investment are specific to the private sector, to the investment's home country, and to the particular industry, subsector, corporation, and product or project. (This is due to a change in the actions of host governments, which are now exercising their sovereign prerogative through greater regulation of nonnational corporations, rather than through outright expropriation and nationalization. This shift from confiscation to constraints and control is accompanied by increasing corporate specific discrimination.) It is appropriate, therefore, to use all of these variables as criteria for deliberations and decisions concerning an existing foreign direct investment or an investment under consideration. It is these variables (country specific, private sector specific, industry specific, subsector specific, corporate specific, and product or project specific) that make up the country specific-corporate specific continuum.

Implementing Corporate Specific Criteria

In practice, we have found that the tendency to think in country specific terms can be compensated for by examining each variable on the continuum and by evaluating its possible significance over the life of the subject investment. This process also has been found useful because it provides a rational basis for weighting the subjects on which intelligence compilation and analysis should focus. Moreover, determining the relative significance of the variables and identifying the issues critical to progressive phases of an investment provide management with useful tools. They allow management to allocate priorities when monitoring and managing the sociopolitical vulnerability of ongoing operations and enable management to weight cognitively the sociopolitical variables relative to other factors in the investment decision-making process.

But traversing the variables of the continuum with a one-shot, albeit conscientious, analysis is not enough. Extreme changes occur in the relative significance of the variables throughout the life of an investment (especially during the early operational and maturation phases) as a result of changes in the personality of the investment, changes in the host sociopolitical environment, and a combination of the two. For this reason, it is necessary to check periodically that the focus is on those variables appropriate to the investment as it evolves and to reprioritize the issues being monitored.

FROM RISK ASSESSMENT TO VULNERABILITY MONITORING

Sociopolitical risk assessment also is necessary but, like country specificity, it is insufficient even when it employs the full range of country specific-corporate specific criteria. It is a tool appropriate only to the planning and entry phases of a foreign direct investment. When an investment is operationalized, the sociopolitical mode should be shifted from assessment to monitoring.

Monitoring the vulnerability of an investment certainly includes some elements of risk assessment, but the two are essentially different. The difference is that risk assessment is the static evaluation of a sociopolitical environment, whereas vulnerability monitoring is the process of identifying and prioritizing the issues which determine the sociopolitical vulnerability of a particular operationalized investment.

In practice, monitoring means dropping models and predictive scenarios and instead adopting the operationalized sociopolitical situation. This is a product of the operation of the investment and its actual sociopolitical environment. Elementary as this may appear, it is not normally done. Instead corporations continue to base their sociopolitical thinking on issues which were the subject prior to operationalization, and they continue to apply assessment methods, data, and criteria to the operationalized investment. Continuing to assess and reassess the preentry environment instead of monitoring the operationalized sociopolitical situation leads to watching the wrong issue. And focusing on the wrong issue, rather than inaccurate intelligence, is the cause of most poor political risk management.

Then why do they focus on assessment rather than on monitoring? Partly because a residual of planning thinking inevitably carries over into the operational phases (and rightly so), but mostly because technical assistance on political risk matters has been limited to insurance, to debates by academics over assessment methodologies, and to country assessment services. These services were first produced to aid chief financial officers with investment decisions and were used subsequently by banks to satisfy Federal Reserve requirements for rationalizing portfolio spread. In neither case were they meant as mechanisms for performing the issue identification and prioritizing functions of monitoring an operational investment.

Issue Identification and Prioritizing Methods

In practice, the best basis for vulnerability monitoring is information provided by individuals from within the subject company. Making use of accumulated information that exists within the corporation has the following advantages: it capitalizes on the accumulated knowledge within the organization; emphasizes the corporate specific issues; increases sociopolitical orientation and awareness within the organization; improves the understanding and acceptability of vulnerability management decisions (which result from the monitoring), and produces a higher degree of implementation efficacy. This procedure requires the soliciting of issues from a wide range of line and staff management at corporate and operating subsidiary or divisional level in both the home and the host countries, consolidating and editing the issues into a composite list, and subsequently circulating this list for prioritization. The result of this somewhat lengthy procedure is an exhaustive compilation of issues germane to the investment, with certain issues indicated as critical.

The prioritization phase of this process is essential. To try to monitor thirty or forty issues is impractical; to try to adjust behavior to mitigate the impact of twenty or thirty issues is impossible. The catch to relying too heavily on corporate sources for issue identification is that the list is likely to suffer omissions. Executives are frequently unaware of sociopolitical risk phenomena in other industries, or even within their own industry in parts of the world where they do not have current operating experience. These deficiencies can be compensated for by using one or more external sources during both the issue identification and prioritizing phases of the monitoring process.

Finally, by definition, monitoring must not be structured as a study. It must be designed and maintained as an ongoing, dynamic mechanism which identifies and automatically includes new issues and which regularly redefines the priority of the issues critical to the vulnerability of the investment. It is important that issues that initially received a low priority rating not be dropped from the list because changes occur in the operationalized sociopolitical situation.

FROM RISK AVOIDANCE TO VULNERABILITY MANAGEMENT

Risk avoidance, like risk assessment, is a function appropriate to the preentry phases of foreign direct investment decision making. Once the decision to invest has been made, however, the option to eliminate risk by avoidance either has been exercised or has been forfeited. Should the investment be proceeded with, it is necessary to shift from a risk avoidance mode to vulnerability management.

The basic mechanism of vulnerability management is the modification of behavior on the issues that the monitoring procedures have identified and prioritized as critical to the continuation of operations and return on the investment. For a particular investment, these may include issues such as the degree and form of local participation, the ratio of profits repatriation to reinvestment, the countries to which the subsidiary exports directly, the degree of import substitution or domestic displacement, and the compatibility of the product with the cultural values of the host country. For another investment in the same country, the issues may be: the indigenization of nontechnical administrative positions; the effects of local purchasing policy; the percentage of long-term debt drawn from local sources; the sophistication of the technology being transferred; the suitability of employee housing, education, and health facilities; the effect of the project on the physical environment; the operating subsidiary's relations with the authorities of the province in

which it operates; and the relations between the parent company's home and host governments.

Differentiation of Manageable and Nonmanageable Issues

Before beginning the development of policy, strategy, and tactics for reducing vulnerability on key issues, however, it is imperative to satisfy the antecedent—issues which are manageable must be differentiated from those which are not. It is the failure to make this preliminary distinction that is to blame for most of the past failures by corporations in managing their sociopolitical survival and for the notorious blunders which have given a bad name to the idea of managing political risk. These resulted from attempts by corporations to remove a risk by heavy handedly trying to alter history, rather than by managing their own affairs to reduce their vulnerability to the course of events. Moreover, the infamous cases were invariably single grand schemes, involving power plays between the public and private sectors. By contrast, sophisticated vulnerability management is designed to avoid the "whipping boy phenomenon" (where one company is singled out for punitive action by the host country government) by modifying behavior on several manageable issues.

An examination of the cases shows that, even in those situations where a single country specific factor was dominant, one or more other variables were responsible for raising the vulnerability threshold of the investment to an unmanageable level. Marginal issues frequently exacerbate otherwise innocuous country specific factors. The cases show that most poor sociopolitical vulnerability management is due to an attempt to manage issues which should have been designated unmanageable.

The degree to which an issue is manageable can be placed on a continuum. Issues such as the stability of the governing regime, the stability of the currency, the relations between the home and host countries, and the trends in international labor fall at one end; profits repatriation to reinvestment ratio, indigenization policy, and the sophistication of technology being transferred fall at the other. The relative manageability of most issues, however, places them at some point along the continuum rather than at either end. For example: local purchasing policy (which is discretionary only to the degree that the goods and services are locally available); the percentage of long-term debt drawn from local sources (again, limited by availability); and the effect of a project on the physical environment (which is often predetermined by the nature of the project). Generally, nonmanageable issues tend to fall at the country specific end of the country specific-corporate specific continuum, while those issues that are more corporate specific tend to be more manageable.

Because of this characteristic, the dictum of not trying to manage the unmanageable can, in some cases, be hedged by making the issue more corporate specific. This is done by distilling from the issue (such as indigenization legislation) its corporate specific and product or project specific elements. It is also characteristic that key issues tend to be nonmanageable at the preentry phase and become progressively more manageable with operationalization and investment maturation.

CHANGING MANAGEMENT'S MIND-SET

As an investment evolves further in its life cycle, the determining variables become more corporate specific. Conversely, the critical issues become less related to country specific factors, less susceptible to assessment, and less avoidable as the investment evolves. Because of the chronological diminution in the dependability of country specific factors, risk assess-

ment methods, and risk avoidance attempts, conventional wisdom holds that "political risk increases the further out you go."[2] Management adheres to conventional wisdom in that it attempts to predict coups, it is preoccupied with palaces, and it is paranoid of ayatollahs.

These processes and mechanisms all argue that management leave the palace alone and play the corporate end of the issue. They are premised on the fundamental that, in the current phase of economic nationalism, sociopolitical vulnerability reduction is largely dependent upon the ability of the subject corporation to depoliticize itself, while remaining socially active and responsible. The procedures and methods, therefore, act directly or indirectly as depoliticization mechanisms. They do not say that country factors are irrelevant to a corporation's foreign direct investment decisions, nor that risk assessment and risk avoidance are totally redundant. They argue that, to unstick the state of the art, management must work at moving its mind-set beyond the current preoccupation with these factors. To achieve this, they must activate the entire country specific-corporate specific continuum and shift to monitoring and managing the issues critical to the sociopolitical vulnerability of foreign direct investments.

NOTES

1. See W. Davies, "Beyond the Earthquake Allegory: Managing Political Risk Vulnerability," *Business Horizons*, July–August 1981.
2. Risk does increase when static tools are used to manage factors which are time sensitive and dynamic. Even the predictive scenarios used in both country assessment and strategic planning are not dynamic, as they are not designed to move with changes in the character of the investment and its environment. Rather, they are attempts to overcome the limitations of static mechanisms.

13

Globescan: A Way to Better International Risk Assessment
Charles W. Hofer
Terry P. Haller

• • •

The importance and allure of international ventures varies by country, by industry, and over time. Thus, until relatively recently, most U.S. firms did not have to seek overseas markets to survive or even to worry much about competition from overseas firms. By contrast, many large Japanese and South African firms had to expand overseas or die, while for major European firms, overseas markets were an important, though not absolutely essential, aspect of their operations.

Of course such generalizations vary across industries. Commercial aircraft production, shipbuilding, and oil, for example, have been world businesses for decades. On the other hand, most restaurants, tax services, and travel agents seem likely to remain far more limited in their scope for years. Most manufacturing businesses, however, seem to fall somewhere between these extremes. Furniture, book publishing, and housewares, for example, tend to be national, but not yet international in their orientation.

THE CHANGING INTERNATIONAL SCENE

Such patterns are changing over time, though. In the 1950s, when overseas labor was cheap and U.S. technology relatively more advanced, many U.S. companies pursued aggressive international expansion programs either to buy over-

Source: Charles W. Hofer and Terry P. Haller, "Globescan: A Way to Better International Risk Assessment," pp. 41–55. Reprinted by permission from the *Journal of Business Strategy*. Fall, 1980, Volume 1, Number 2, Copyright © 1980, Warren, Gorham & Lamont Inc., 210 South Street, Boston, Mass. All rights reserved.

seas, sell overseas, or both. This trend continued in the 1960s as an overvalued U.S. dollar made it highly profitable to import goods from overseas subsidiaries. In the 1970s, however, as the dollar declined and the U.S. labor climate became relatively less expensive and more congenial, international ventures lost some of the attractiveness they had had for U.S. firms in the 1950s and 1960s. This fact has been dramatically reflected in the ratio of U.S. foreign subsidiary formations to U.S. foreign subsidiary divestitures, which fell to a level of 1.4 in 1973 after being above 4.0 for most of the 1950s and 1960s, and still 3.3 as late as 1971. Just the opposite is true for most foreign manufacturers, though.

The results have been the entry and growth of a large number of well-managed and well-financed European and Japanese competitors on the international scene, with a concurrent internationalization of many industries, including automobiles, office equipment, computers, electronics, chemicals, motorcycles, bicycles, watches, and clothing. The changes in the automotive industry are both typical and illustrative of what may soon occur in other areas as well. From its start at the turn of the century through the early 1960s, this industry had been mostly national in its orientation, with the principal developments being increases in domestic demand and a corresponding reduction in the number of domestic competitors. Since the mid-1960s, though, the number of international competitors has increased from five to thirty-seven as just about every major firm in the industry has sought out new international markets. Many observers, however, expect this number to contract over the coming decades until the industry is dominated by five to ten major international firms.

In short, both the international environment and the nature of international risk have changed, which means that both the strategies and techniques of U.S. business must change as well. Many U.S. firms will find such changes especially difficult because of the "domestic" perspectives they have developed over the past half century—perspectives that are reinforced by the limited language and world history training offered in most of our public and private schools, and by the short-term financial orientation of most of our society's incentive structures. Such changes must occur, nonetheless, if we are to be successful in the increasingly international world of the future. Simple prescriptions to "go international" are clearly inadequate, however, as the failures of Chrysler in Europe and United Fruit/United Brands in Latin America show. What is needed, instead, is a systematic, comprehensive framework for analyzing international environments in order to identify the major opportunities and threats that will face international businesses during the foreseeable future and the development of strategies for effectively responding to these opportunities and threats. It is the purpose of this article to present one such framework, developed and used by the authors, called GLOBESCAN. Before discussing this approach, though, it will be useful to explore in a bit more detail the nature and sources of international risk, as well as to examine the current state of the art in industry practice and academic theory.

THE NATURE OF INTERNATIONAL RISK

International risk is seldom defined systematically, let alone precisely or well. Instead, such risk is usually referred to in terms of its most obvious manifestations such as "Country A is too risky because the government is on a nationalization binge," or "Country B is too risky because the odds are weighted in favor of domestic competitors." The emphasis is usually placed more on a few dramatic examples than on a composite, systematic assessment of the true opportunities and threats to successful business operations over either the short or the long term. Such risk arises because most nations, and many suppliers and customers as well, treat domestic and international competitors in the same industry differently. Generally, these differences are most pronounced in the legal, regulatory, and tax guidelines that such firms must follow. A second component of international risk involves the fact that most executives do not know foreign markets as well as they know their own. Thus, even though such uncertainty can be reduced over time through the use of local managerial personnel, as well as through the education of one's domestic executives, it must be factored into international strategic decision making. However, even if the latter risk were eliminated completely, international business would still remain more risky than domestic competition because of the former factors.[1]

Types of Risks

There are a variety of specific international risks that all companies face ranging from confiscation or expropriation of assets to unilateral breaches of contracts, discrimination, and operational restrictions. In general, these risks can be grouped into two categories: asset protection/investment recovery risks and operational profitability/cash flow risks. (See Exhibit 1.) This distinction is important because of the different causes and different probabilities of occurrence of these two types of risk. Yet it is a distinction seldom made in business practice or academic theory to date, where the major focus has been on asset protection/investment recovery risks. Such a focus is understandable given the dramatic and strategically significant nature of confiscation and expropriation threats. Nonetheless, as governments and businesses

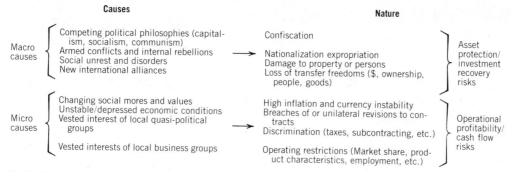

Exhibit 1 The nature and causes of international business risk. [*Source:* Adapted from Stefan H. Robuck's article, "Political Risk: Identification and Assessment," *Columbia Journal of World Business* (July/August 1971).]

both become more sophisticated, the latter threats are likely to become of equal, if not greater, importance than the former in many parts of the world. As long as major political changes such as those in Iran and Chile are possible, however, asset protection/investment recovery risks will remain. The major point to be made here is that any effective assessment of international risk must consider both types of risk rather than just one as in the past.

Sources of Risks

Just as there are a number of different types of international risks, so there are a number of different sources/causes from which such risks can spring, including competing political philosophies, social unrest and disorder, armed conflicts, and the vested interests of local businesses as indicated in Exhibit 1. Although generalizations across countries are difficult, it is clear that these different causes can affect international businesses in one of two ways; that is, they can either affect all international businesses in a particular country in the same or approximately the same ways, or they can affect some businesses/industries far more than others. Stefan Robuck of Columbia University has labeled the former "macrothreats" (risks) and the latter "microthreats" (risks). This dis-

tinction is important because of the different types of responses that are possible to these two different types of threats. Thus, once in a country, the only responses to macrothreats are to try to ameliorate the forces producing the threat or to reduce or eliminate one's presence in that country. An additional response is available in the case of microthreats, though—namely, to get into a different business within the same country as ITT did in Peru in the early 1970s. The distinction between macro- and microthreats is also important because of the different probabilities associated with these different types of threats. Macrothreats (such as the confiscations and expropriations of all foreign business in Eastern Europe and mainland China after World War II, in Cuba in 1959–1960, and in Chile in 1971, or the broad-based political boycotts by various Arab states of all foreign businesses that trade with Israel) are usually more dramatic and consequently often receive the greatest attention in the literature. Microthreats (such as the expropriation of public utilities and extractive industries, or the imposition of tariffs or other competitive restrictions in favor of domestic producers) are far more prevalent, though, and must therefore be built into any effective international risk assessment and strategic decision-making models.

RESPONDING TO INTERNATIONAL RISK

Because of the importance of international business, a variety of approaches have been taken to improve business responses to international risks. Such responses can be divided into three broad categories:

- Models and techniques for better assessing and forecasting of international business risks;
- Models and techniques for improving the utilization of such assessments and forecasts in the international strategic decision-making process, and
- The use of various specialized strategies and tactics to protect against or minimize the impact of such risks.

Unfortunately, few firms and no models that we know of do an outstanding job in each of these areas. To better illustrate the problems this causes, we shall review briefly the practices and theory in each of these areas.

Approaches to International Environmental Forecasting

In general, most firms use one or more of the following five methods to analyze the opportunities and threats to international business in the countries they are interested in.

The Grand Tour Approach "Grand tours" are what their name implies—tours of the country or region under consideration by an executive or team of executives from the domestic operations of the company involved. During such tours, contacts are usually made with local business, political, and social leaders, and tours are usually made of local markets, plants, etc. When the tour is completed, the team returns home, summarizes its findings, and presents them to senior management and/or the board.

The major strength of such tours in comparison with most of the other techniques used to analyze international risk is the detailed insights they provide of the micro, operating profitability risks facing a particular industry or business. Their two major weaknesses are their static nature and their selective perspective of macrorisks in the particular country. The former problem is especially important because it

limits the accuracy of future forecasts and, thus, limits a firm to reactive adjustments to events rather than proactive anticipation of them.

The Old Hands Approach "Old hands" refers to the use of analyses and forecasts prepared by businessmen, diplomats, journalists, educators, and others with years of firsthand experience in the area or country of interest. Such information can clearly add both perspective and judgment to the information gained from a grand tour and is, as a consequence, quite valuable. It can also suffer from two limitations, however. First, it usually tends to focus more on macro, asset protection/investment recovery opportunities and threats than on microrisks of either type. Such complementariness with the grand tour approach is useful. At the same time, it can lead to a false sense of security since little additional perspective is gained on the microthreats to the business, which as noted above, tend to be more likely to occur than most macrothreats. The second limitation of the old hands approach is that it is sometimes based on very selective information. Fortunately such selectivity is usually known to and explicitly noted by the "old hand" so that steps can be taken to fill in the gaps. Occasionally, however, such gaps are not noted or filled in. Should this happen in an area of potential instability, the results could be disastrous. Witness the problems in Iran after the fall of the Shah, an event that was seriously underestimated in the United States because our old hands had long before stopped taking the pulse of the Iranian man-in-the street.

Delphi Forecasts Delphi forecasts involve a more systematic approach to the analysis and forecasting of international business risks than the grand tours or old hands techniques. The usual procedure is to identify a broad range of factors that are felt to influence the nature and magnitude of international risk that a business will face, such as those listed in Exhibit 1. Sometimes these factors are then broken down into sets of subfactors that are easier to measure than the factors themselves. Next, each of these factors (or subfactors) is ranked on some predetermined scale (e.g., 0 to 10) by a panel of experts for the country or area in question, based on their knowledge of the area, and additional information on each of the factors (or subfactors) gathered by corporate staff. Depending on time and resources, the rationale for extreme rankings may be fed back to the panel for a second ranking and, occasionally, even a third. Once the final ranking is completed, these responses are then averaged for each factor (or subfactor), and a composite "risk score" is calculated based on a weighted average of these factors (or subfactors).

The two major benefits of Delphi forecasts are that they are systematic and provide a consistent "measure" of changes in the level of risk over time. Their major weaknesses are that they focus primarily on macro, asset protection/investment recovery risks, that their single measure is often an inadequate indicator of the level and types of risk involved (two different countries might each receive a score of "50" and yet represent entirely different kinds of risk to a particular firm), and that their "additive" approach to aggregating the various factors may in some situations seriously over- or underestimate the likelihood of particular risks because of synergy considerations.

Quantitative Models[2]   Quantitative models are similar to the Delphi approach in the sense that they also proceed by breaking down the causes of international risk into a series of factors or subfactors. Rather than using a panel of experts to rank these factors, however, the quantitative methods approach selects for each factor some easily quantifiable index as a measure of that factor. A weighing of the number of seats held by different political parties in the legislature might be used as a measure of the degree to which a particular country is capitalistic, socialistic, or communistic in its political orientation, for example. Historical data are then collected on each of these indices for a period of at least

ten years and, preferably, for as far back as the data are available and relevant. Once such data have been gathered, they can be analyzed using various multivariate statistical techniques to identify those factors that have been the best indicators of various types of international business risk in the past, and to project the likely trends of these factors in the future.

The major strengths of this approach are that it is systematic, that it can address both the macro- and microcomponents of international business risk,[3] that it empirically checks the significance of the different indices it uses for each country involved, and that it provides a relatively unbiased historical perspective. Its major limitations are the cost of initially building the model, the difficulty of obtaining the data needed, the fact that such data-gathering difficulties sometimes lead to the selection of less than optimal measures, the fact that it focuses more on asset protection/investment recovery risks (macro and micro) than on operating profitability risks, and the fact that such models are far better at predicting trends and slight changes in trends than they are at forecasting major turning points.

Systematic Causal Models   Systematic causal models usually involve attempts to corroborate the conclusions of other forecasting methods by constructing a systematic causal chain of actions and events leading from the present to the projected future. Such models almost always include an analysis of the key actors in the situation as well as of the political and economic processes of the country involved.

These models can be useful for verifying the conclusions of the other forecasting techniques, especially disaster sequences. They are also useful in dealing with the problems of time compression or elongation often found in the other models.[4]

Clearly the models and techniques described above have advanced the art of international environmental analysis and forecasting substantially beyond where it was even a decade

Exhibit 2 The Areas of Applicability of Current International Environmental Forecasting Techniques*

	Asset Protection and Investment Recovery Opportunities and Threats	Operating Profitability and Cash Flow Opportunities and Threats
Macrorisks	grand tours OLD HANDS DELPHI FORECASTS QUANTITATIVE MODELS Systems Analysis	grand tours Old Hands delphi forecasts Quantitative Models Systems Analysis
Microrisks	Grand Tours Old Hands Delphi Forecasts Quantitative Models SYSTEMS ANALYSIS	GRAND TOURS old hands — quantitative models systems analysis

*Note: ALL CAPS indicate areas of primary applicability; Initial Caps indicates areas of secondary applicability; no caps indicates areas of tertiary applicability.

ago. Still, there are limitations to each of these techniques, and some of these limitations remain even when all of these techniques are used together. Exhibit 2, which lists the primary and secondary applications of each of these techniques, highlights both the overall strengths and weaknesses of current practice. Three conclusions become immediately apparent from even a brief review of this table:

- First, it is quite clear that far more effort has gone into forecasting asset protection/investment recovery risks than into forecasting operating profitability/cash-flow risks.
- Second, we are also better at forecasting macrorisks than microrisks.
- Third, the most probable reason that firms still like grand tours, given the limitations of that technique, is that this is the only one of the major analysis and forecasting methods in use that focuses primarily on micro, operating profitability/cash-flow risks.

Approaches to International Strategic Decision Making

Once a firm has completed its analyses and forecasts of the international markets it is inter-

ested in, it must then decide whether it will invest in any or all of these markets, and, if so, how it will do so. According to Robert Stobaugh,[5] most firms tend to make these decisions in one of four ways:

- Go/no go choice
- Premium for risk approach
- Range of estimate approach
- Risk analysis model

The characteristics, strengths, and weaknesses of each of these approaches may be summarized as follows.

Go/No Go Choice Firms using this approach accept or reject proposals for investing in a particular country based on an examination of a small number (usually less than five) of risk parameters for that country. Typical of such choices is the statement of a manager of a major manufacturer of consumer durables who said: "We have not considered investing in South Africa since several members of our board would not want to have to respond to the questions concerning 'support of Apartheid' that would inevitably follow."

The major benefit of this approach is the limited information search and processing that it requires. Of course, this benefit is of dubious value if it leads to poor strategic choices. In some instances, however, it may be quite feasible to eliminate a country as a prospect for potential investment, save for the establishment of a sales office or two, based on the consideration of a limited number of criteria. For instance, businesses that require extremely high technological and labor inputs, and which can serve world markets from a few major plants, could very easily eliminate a large number of African, Southeast Asian, and Central American countries as prospects for a major new plant without exceptionally detailed analyses.

The major weaknesses of the go/no go approach are that some potentially attractive countries might be eliminated when a more thorough evaluation would have revealed their strengths, and the far more serious situation in which an otherwise unattractive country is selected for investment because it excelled on a few key parameters. Taken together, these strengths and weaknesses suggest that the go/no go approach should, with rare exceptions, not be used as the sole method for making strategic international investment choices. It may, however, be an excellent first step in a complex, multistage decision process.

Premium for Risk Approach In the premium for risk approach, companies assess the prospects of a particular foreign investment using the same tools and techniques they would in the United States. When it comes to actual decision making, though, these firms demand a higher ROI from projects in countries with high macro- and microrisks than in countries with low macro- and microrisks. Some of the firms using this approach charge a fixed premium for all high-risk situations. Others, especially those with Delphi forecasting techniques, use a sliding scale of premiums based on the level of risk involved.

The two major advantages of the premium for risk approach are that it does indeed charge a

premium for high-risk situations and yet is still relatively simple to use.

The premium for risk approach also has three major weaknesses:

- First, it does not differentiate among the types and timing of the risks involved. For instance, it would rank a project with a 30 percent chance of expropriation in year one in country *A* the same as a project in country *B* with a 50 percent chance of severe local content restrictions in year five, if the average ROIs of these projects were the same, despite the fact that their internal ROIs, net present value, and strategic significance would be far different.

- Second, it does not consider the interrelationships between the types of projects under consideration and the level of mirorisk involved. Thus, it would not differentiate between a low-technology, low-skill 25 percent ROI business that would compete with a variety of local competitors, and a high-technology, high-skill 25 percent ROI business in the same country that would compete primarily with foreign imports, even though the former business is far more likely than the latter to face a variety of operating restrictions in the near term.

- Finally, it does not consider the fit or lack of fit that a particular project has with the firm's overall strategy. Consequently, it might rank a 30 percent project in a high-risk country higher than a 20 percent project in a medium-risk country, even though the former might be tangential to the firm's overall activities while the latter is fundamental to its basic strategic character.

Despite these limitations, Stobaugh found that the vast majority of the U.S. firms he surveyed in 1969 used the premium for risk approach for international strategic decision making. The primary reason for this was the managers' "intuitive feelings that it is difficult to make accurate estimates about the future in foreign countries." Perhaps, so, but given the increasing challenge of the major, world-wide strategic investments being made by major European and Japanese firms, such a limited approach is unlikely to suffice in the coming struggle for success in the 1980s.

Range of Estimates Approach In this technique, a firm identifies the most critical variables influencing an international project's sales, profitability, ROI, etc., estimates what these variables will be at different times in the future, forecasts future sales, profits, ROI, etc., based on these estimates, and then performs a sensitivity analysis on these projections for the most critical of these factors. Usually this analysis is assisted by the fact that many of the key variables have been relatively stable in the past and can be projected to remain so in the future.

The major strengths of this approach are that it differentiates among the level and timing of risks and considers the interrelationships between project types and the microrisks that a business will face. Its major limitations are its computational complexity, the fact that the optimistic and pessimistic forecasts generated may not be statistically significant, and the fact that it does not consider the fit or lack of fit of a project with the firm's overall corporate strategy.

Risk Analysis Model This technique is similar to the range of estimates approach except that a probability distribution is now developed for each of the nonstable factors. These distributions are then put into a computer, which calculates probability distribution for profits, ROI, etc. This same computer program can then be used to determine the value of conducting various studies to improve the various input estimates.

The major strengths of this approach versus the range of estimates approach are that it eliminates the statistical weaknesses of the latter approach and permits far more powerful sensitivity analyses once it is set up. (It also differentiates among the level and timing of risks and considers the relationships between project types and microrisks faced, as does the range of estimates approach.) Its major limitations are its huge data requirements and the fact that it still does not consider the strategic aspects of different projects.

International Strategic Decision Making: A Summary

In many ways, the four different techniques for international strategic decision making described above correspond to the different types of financial techniques used for domestic capital budgeting, including payback period, average ROI, and NPV range of estimates, and risk analysis. And therein lies their greatest weakness, whether considered individually or as a group! This weakness is highlighted by Exhibit 3 which shows the principal and secondary

Exhibit 3 The Principal Character of Current International Strategic Decision-Making Techniques*

	Global Perspective	Country-by-Country Perspective
Investment strategy focus	range of estimates risk analysis	GO/NO GO ANALYSIS RISK PREMIUMS RANGE OF ESTIMATES RISK ANALYSIS
Competitive strategy focus		GO/NO GO ANALYSIS RANGE OF ESTIMATES RISK ANALYSIS

*Note: ALL CAPS indicates the primary nature of the technique; Initial Caps indicates the secondary nature of the technique; no caps indicates the tertiary nature of the technique.

areas of applicability of these techniques. The basic problem is that these approaches focus on short-term financial measures of performance rather than on long-term competitive strategies. They also tend to take a country-by-country perspective rather than an overall global perspective.

Of course, those schooled in traditional financial theory will tend to discount this point because they will point out that by maximizing the net present values of cash flows over the planning period, firms that follow these procedures should have more funds to invest later on than their competitors. The problem with this analysis is that it neglects several important "real world" phenomena that "turn the tide" the other way. These include experience curve effects which can enhance or retard the returns on existing projects more than normal financial forecasts would indicte; synergy among projects which raises the returns on future projects in the same area; and "strategic windows" which refers to the phenomenon that the height of the entry barriers to an industry rise exponentially after a window has passed, thus precluding late entry until the next window appears. In short, each of the techniques discussed above is based on an implicit and extremely limiting set of assumptions that could produce long-term strategic disasters in the international arena similar to those experienced by domestic competitors who have relied solely on financial rather than strategic considerations.

HOW GLOBESCAN WORKS

GLOBESCAN is the registered trade name given to the approach to international risk assessment and decision making that we have developed to overcome the problems and limitations discussed above. Overall, this approach provides a systematic framework for integrating international business risk assessment processes with international strategic decision making that is both comprehensive and flexible. The keys to this approach involve the consideration of all such projects from a strategic perspective and the sequencing of all analyses so as to maximize the value of the information they produce. In this process, we often use many of the techniques described above although usually in different ways than those mentioned so far. We also use several different techniques that we will describe as we proceed.

The first step is to briefly analyze the firm's existing corporate portfolio, as well as those of its major competitors, in order to identify the major strategic opportunities and challenges it will face domestically, the principal threats it will face over the planning period from international competitors, and the major contributions international ventures could make to the firm. Once this is completed, we develop a set of criteria based on this analysis that any international venture should satisfy. Using these criteria, a go/no go analysis is performed of all the major areas/countries in the world. The number of areas/countries eliminated by this analysis will vary depending on the firm's objectives, the discretionary strategic resources it has for such investments, the strengths and strategies of its major competitors, and the scope and nature of its existing international operations. Usually, however, the list is reduced by 50 percent or more so that more serious attention can be focused on those areas/countries offering the greatest prospects for success. In addition, we have generally found it is more effective to gain international experience in a series of gradual steps, each of which can serve as a base and learning experience for the next, unless competitive pressure or strategic windows preclude this option.[6] Consequently, we sometimes do a second, more sophisticated go/no go analysis to reduce the list even more, particularly if the firm has limited resources which it can expend on the search and analysis process. Once we get such a revised list, we usually turn to an assessment of the asset protection/investment recovery risks in the various areas/countries.

Assessing Protection/Investment Recovery Risks

Increasingly we are finding that the most important differences among the better countries and areas involve operating profitability/cash-flow risks. Nevertheless, we normally start our assessments of different countries and areas with a look at asset protection/investment recovery risks for two reasons. First, such risks do still exist as the recent events in Iran and Afghanistan clearly illustrate. Second, a good first cut can usually be made in this area which can then be used as an additional go/no go check, after which an operating profitability/cash-flow risk analysis can be performed before returning to a more detailed assessment of asset protection/investment recovery risks. Exhibit 4 indicates the types of analysis we normally perform, as well as the sequence of these analyses for our first and second round assessments of asset protection/investment recovery risks.

The first step is almost always to do a quick check of existing historical files on confiscations, nationalizations, expropriations, major damage to property or persons, and loss of transfer freedoms to see whether the various countries in question have a record of such actions. (See Exhibit 5 which lists selected expropriations of U.S. and British direct private

Exhibit 4 The Normal GLOBESCAN Approach for Assessing Asset Protection/Investment Recovery Rules

First Round: Go/No Go Analysis	Second Round: Final Section Analysis
1. Historical files on confiscations, expropriations, loss of transfer freedoms, etc.	1. Quantitative models (if needed)
2. Standard Delphi forecasts (sometimes)	2. Systems analysis (sometimes)
3. Limited old hands analysis	3. Old hands interpretations of models
	4. Grand tours

Exhibit 5 Selected Expropriations of U.S. and British Direct Private Foreign Investments

Expropriations of U.S. Investments	Expropriations of British Investments
Bolivia, 1952: tin and petroleum	Burma, 1948: agriculture, forestry, river transport and petroleum
Guatemala, 1953: land	
Argentina, 1958: utilities	
Brazil, 1959–60: utilities	Ceylon, 1948: rubber plantations and tea estates
Indonesia, 1960–65: petroleum and rubber plantations	
	Iran, 1951: petroleum
Ceylon, 1962: petroleum distribution	India, 1955: banking
	Egypt, 1956–64: Suez Canal Company, banking, agriculture, commerce, and manufacturing
Iraq, 1965: bank facilities	
Algeria, 1966–67: insurance and detergent manufacturer	Burma, 1963: banking and commerce
Chile, 1967: utilities	Tanzania, 1967: banking, manufacturing and trade

Source: J. F. Truitt, "Expropriation of Private Foreign Investment," unpublished dissertation, Indiana University, 1969.

investments for an example of such a file.) Usually we check such files in three different ways—by country being investigated, by industry involved, and by the country of the parent company—to see whether any particular tendencies exist. Typically, the questions asked include:

- Does the country involved have a history of confiscation, nationalization, expropriation, etc.?
- Does it tend to focus its attention on particular industries?
- Does it focus on firms of particular countries?
- Does it lag behind the pattern of country A by x years?

Once we have completed this process, we will sometimes turn to a standard Delphi forecast on the country if the historical files were not definitive one way or the other. The major criterion we have here is that the Delphi have some track record for purposes of comparison. One such Delphi that can be used in this context is that produced by F. T. Haner, Professor of International Business at the University of Delaware and President of Business Environment Risk Index Ltd. the private consulting firm established to market his index.[7] Our final step of the first round of assessments is to check the assessments derived above with a few "old hands" for the countries involved.

During the second round of such analysis, quantitative models and/or systems analyses will be developed if needed. In almost all instances, however, a second "old hands" analysis will be conducted to review all the work/ analyses to date and make recommendations for the "grand tour" which can then be conducted in a far more informed fashion than it would normally be.

The keys to this process are:

- Maintaining a strategic perspective throughout (never losing sight of what the purpose of the investment is or how it is to fit into the firm's corporate portfolio);

- Gathering in the broad sweep of history in each area/country to the maximum degree possible;

- Using the information in each step as building blocks for the next step (in this context, the most sensitive and/or most expensive steps come toward the end), and

- Providing checks throughout, such as the old hands' analysis of the historical files and Delphi or a Key Actor Systems analysis check if there seems to be time compression or elongation problems.

Evaluating Operating Profitability and Cash-Flow Risk

After an initial asset protection/investment recovery risk assessment is made, it is usually time to assess the operating profitability/cash-flow risks associated with investments in the various countries. This assessment will rest on two factors. First, an analysis of the sales, profitability, ROI, etc., prospects for the partic-

ular project, and second, a projection of how these prospects will be affected by factors such as inflation rates, currency instability, discrimination, operational requirements on market share, and local sourcing.

The traditional ways to perform the first step are to develop a set of pro forma financial statements for the project or to develop a simulation model of it. The second step can then be performed either by attaching some general percentage risk penalty to the project to compensate for the level of macrorisk in the country, or by identifying the specific macro- and microrisks facing the project that will affect is operating profitability and cash flows and then calculating the impact they will have either via a range of estimates or by risk analyses.

We utilize these tools too, but in a somewhat different way. First, we develop a "rough cut" cash-flow model of the project that can be used as a simulation model. Then we project an initial set of pro forma financial statements from it. Next, however, we do a Limited Information Model (LIM) or Profit Impact of Market Strategy (PIMS) analysis of the business using the Strategic Planning Institute's LIM or PIMS models, depending on the data that is available. This gives a preliminary check of whether the "rough cut" simulation model has any validity at all. Next we analyze the various macro- and micro-factors that could affect operating profitability and make the indicated changes in these factors in both the simulation and LIM (or PIMS) models, again to get a consistency check between them. When this is done, we develop a strategic analysis of the business, with particular focus on its competitive position which is then compared to the recommended strategy moves of the LIM (or PIMS) model. On occasion, this may be supplemented by a detailed market analysis if uncertainties remain. Also, the sophistication of the simulation model can be improved if that appears necessary. Finally, if there are any major differences among any of these analyses, the specific assumptions on which they differ can be identified explicitly so that the appropriate managerial personnel can be forewarned regarding the specific conditions they should be checking for on their grand tour.

The major differences in and keys to our process are:

- The reality check provided by the LIM (PIMS) model;
- The detailed analysis of specific macro- and micro-factors affecting profitability (which we often do with a special "old hands" analysis), and
- The strategic perspective from which the investment is viewed from the earliest stages.

Assessing Global Sector Attractiveness

In addition to assessing the investment prospects for any particular country, firms also often seek to determine the prospects for investments in particular areas of the world. Sometimes the focus is on the international risk exposure of the corporation from participating in the area, while at other times it is on the opportunities afforded. In either case, there are two components to such analysis. The first is to determine the average prospects/risks for the region. The second is to determine whether there are any positive or negative synergies that would increase or decrease the total.

The first assessment can be made in one of two ways. One is to do a separate macro- and micro-analysis of the asset protection/investment recovery risks for each country in the region, using the techniques described above, and then to average these assessments using the relative GNPs of the countries as weights. The second is to construct a portfolio of pro forma projects for the area using the Strategic Planning Institute's LIM program to project sales, profits, ROIs, etc., for each such business. A range of estimate adjustments can then be made to this portfolio using data from historical files and selected "old hands" to project the overall sensitivity of the portfolio to probable events in the region. Whichever approach is used, the result is an average prospect/risk profile for the region that can be used to rank different regions on a first-act basis.

In most instances such analyses will be sufficient for the purposes at hand. In a few cases, however, it will be necessary to go farther to determine the synergies that one may derive from being in a particular region. This type of analysis requires a detailed knowledge of the trading relationships among countries in the region, a detailed assessment of the linkages between environmental events in the region, and the construction of a simulation model of the firm's actual or planned operations in the region. With all of this in hand, a number of simulation runs can be made to determine the net prospects/risks for the region.

MAKING INTERNATIONAL STRATEGIC DECISIONS WITH GLOBESCAN

In order to complete the strategic decision-making task, it is necessary to gather all of the individual assessments made above and weave the results into a coherent global strategy that will maximize the firm's prospects for achieving its objectives while parrying the threats of multinational competition and risk. There are many ways this can be done. One would be to develop a separate corporate portfolio for each of the major international ventures being contemplated, and then compare each of these portfolios to the firm's objectives and the portfolios of its competitors under a variety of possible environmental scenarios. There are two major weaknesses to such an approach apart from the computational and information processing complexities involved. The first is that for firms just starting international expansion, the proposed international ventures would usually be swamped by their domestic counterparts for the first several years. The second is that such an approach does not permit the effective comparison of various different types of international ventures from a global perspective.

We have found four types of analysis useful in dealing with these issues. The first is to construct a risk/reward matrix of the various proposed international ventures such as that shown in Exhibit 6. This is usually supplemented by

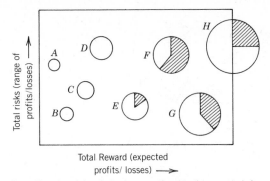

Note: The size of the circles is proportional to the expected size of the venture. The pie slices are proportional to the size of the local market obtained.

Exhibit 6   A risk/reward comparison of various international ventures.

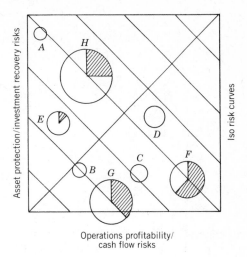

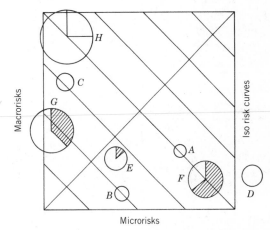

Exhibit 7   International risk profile matrices.

two international risk profile matrices such as those shown in Exhibit 7. One of these normally depicts the venture's asset protection/investment recovery risks versus its operating profitability/cash-flow risks, while the other indicates the primary source of the risks (i.e., macro- vs. microthreats). Based on all of these factors, some judgments can begin to be made. For instance, it is quite clear that with no changes in the projects, venture G would be the most attractive from a risk/reward perspective. It has the second largest reward and the lowest overall risk, and most of the latter is of an operational nature involving factors such as local content restrictions that affect all the international businesses in the country about equally. Business H, by contrast, is the least attractive. It has the lowest return and the second highest risk, most of which involves a possible loss of assets or restrictions that preclude the recovery of this investment which pertains primarily to the business involved (for that country). The second most attractive businesses appear to be E and H which seem to dominate B and C, and D and F, respectively. Business H, however, faces high asset protection/investment recovery risks that are macro in character, while business F primarily faces operating profitability/cash-flow risks that are micro in character, which might well stem from the high share of

market it is projected to obtain. If so, it might be possible to substantially decrease these risks by changing the nature of this venture; for example, by increasing its size so it would also serve export markets, or by structuring it as a joint venture with local investors. In that case, business F would become the second most attractive venture. Morever, similar analyses could be done for each of the other ventures. For example, often noting the low asset protection/investment recovery and low macrorisks associated with venture B, one might ask whether other projects with greater potential might be possible in that country. And so on.

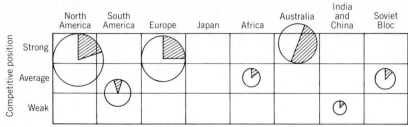

Note: The areas of the circles represent the relative size of the markets and the pie shaped wedges indicate Competitor X's relative shares of each of these markets.

Exhibit 8 A geographic scope/competitor strength profile for competitor X.

In general, the key benefits of Exhibits 6 and 7 are that when used together they highlight the most salient risk characteristics of such international ventures, and also point to directions in which these ventures might be modified to improve their risk/return characteristics. They do this by separating a venture's total international risk into its various components so that a more accurate perspective can be gained on the various opportunities and threats that exist in a particular situation.

The second type of analysis we have found useful in such situations is the construction of geographic scope/competitive strength and geographic scope/resource deployment matrices, such as those shown in Exhibits 8 and 9 for each

Exhibit 9 A Geographic Scope/Resource Deployment Matrix for Competitor X

	North America	South America	Europe	Japan	Africa	Australia	India and China	Soviet Bloc
R&D laboratories								
Raw materials sourcing								
Component sourcing and manufacture								
Assembly operations								
Distribution facilities								
Source of financing								
Marketing and sales								
Management								

of the major competitors in the industry in question. Whenever possible, such matrices should be developed not only for the present, but also for several different points in the past (e.g., for five, ten, fifteen, and twenty years ago). Their purpose is twofold: first, to profile the present strategic postures of the various key competitors in the industry; second, to reveal the long-term global strategies of these competitors verify operating profitabilities and cash flows. through a comparison of the changes in their scope, focus, and resource deployments over time. When combined, these analyses usually give a clear indication of the types of competitive opportunities and threats a firm will face in the future.

THE USE OF PIMS IN GLOBESCAN

Part of the GLOBESCAN technique for international risk assessment and decision making involves the use of the Strategic Planning Institute's LIM and PIMS models to project and verify operating profitabilities and cash flows. The use of these models in this way requires at least a brief explanation for a reason any PIMS user knows well: namely, the fact that less than 10 percent of the over 1,500 businesses in the data base compete primarily in foreign markets, and almost all of these are based in Europe. That is, the PIMS data base does not include any data on businesses based in Central or South America, Africa, or Asia, and very little on businesses in Australia.

PIMS is, above all else, a data base. It is also a multiple regression program that attempts to explain the economic performance of the various businesses in the data base in terms of various characteristics of their environment and of their strategy for competing in that environment. Specifically, the main PIMS program is an equation of the sort:

$$\text{Performance} = \text{Constant} + f_1(x_1) + f_2(x_2) + \cdots + f_n(x_n) + \text{error term}$$

Performance is measured in terms of ROI, cash flow, or net income, while the various Xs represent factors such as absolute and relative market share, short- and long-term market growth rates, capital intensity, price, quality, vertical integration, degree of automation, inflation, etc. Using this equation, PIMS has explained about 80 percent of the variation in performance in the firms in the data base using thirty-eight different factors, while the shorter LIM model has explained about 60 percent of the variation in profitability with just eighteen factors. None of these factors, however, is the name of the industry involved. This according to PIMS is irrelevant.

Stated differently, to predict the performance of firms in the steel industry it is not necessary to know that they are in the steel industry. It is necessary, however, to know that the industry is highly capital intensive, that it is vertically integrated, that there are a few differences among firms in price or quality of product, that the industry serves a large number of customers, but that a few of them (such as automobiles) take a relatively large percentage of its output. What PIMS has done is to break industries down into their constituent elements. Once this has been done, though, one can reverse the process and build up "new" industries just the way a chemist could build new compounds. There is only one constraint to this process. One cannot build industries which have characteristics not represented in the data base, just as a chemist could not build a new compound that required elements not in the original compound that he broke down.

The basic question of whether the PIMS and LIM models can be used in the way we describe in GLOBESCAN revolves around two questions:

- Does this build-up process work for industries not previously represented in the data base, provided that all their key characteristics fall within the prescribed ranges?
- Are the PIMS findings invariant across countries?

With respect to the first question, the answer is a clear yes. New businesses and industries have been added to the data base constantly over the past eight years with only modest variations in the equation. And almost all of these variations have involved questions of level or degree rather than of kind or direction. Moreover, the PIMS findings since 1972 essentially replicate the earlier results that were developed while the project was part of GE's intensive business research efforts.

What evidence is there that these findings are invariant across countries? There are three sets of data that support this conclusion. First, the PIMS findings have now been corroborated in several other countries, including the U.K., France, Germany, Switzerland, and Belgium. The corroboration was not 100 percent, as there were a few minor differences in level between the U.S. and European equations. With one or two exceptions, however, these involved questions of level or degree. The U.S. equations could be used to project results for European businesses, and in almost all cases the differences between the projections of the U.S. and European equations would be less than 5 percent. Moreover, since the number of European businesses in the data base now totals nearly 150, it is unlikely that there will be any major changes in the future. Furthermore, the early experiences in Australia suggest that the U.S. equations will work well there too. One might, therefore, conclude that the PIMS/LIM equations will be valid for most of the developed countries in the western world.

What about the developing countries? Business conditions there are somewhat different from those in the developed countries. One might, therefore, expect some greater differences between the equations for the developing countries and those of the developed countries, or perhaps even that no such equations could be constructed for developing countries. But again, the data that bear on this question favor the use of the PIMS/LIM equations, though they are not so strong as the data above.

The first such evidence is the experiences of a few firms that have tried such projections for subsidiaries in developing countries. In all cases, the projected performance was quite close to actual performance. While positive, this corroboration is still quite tenuous, however, since the number of cases involved of which we are aware is quite small.

Much stronger evidence, though of a different sort, is provided by the comparisons that economists have done of concentration ratios across both developed and developing economies. In both developed and developing economies certain industries are always the most concentrated, and they are the same industries. Since each of these countries had literally hundreds of industries in their economies, the probability that essentially the same twenty would always end up as the most concentrated if such rankings were determined by random chance is quite literally thousands to one. The inescapable conclusion is that there are certain economic laws of the marketplace at work that produce these results. Moreover, the consistency of the rankings between developed and developing countries clearly indicates that these laws are invariant across countries. Consequently, it is almost certain that when the PIMS data base is extended to developing countries, the results will be the same. There may be a few differences in level as there are between the U.S. and Europe and, perhaps, even one or two in direction. Overall, however, the broad patterns should stand up. What this means, of course, is that while it would be desirable to have separate PIMS/LIM equations for developing countries, we can still use the U.S. equations with reasonably accurate results until we do.

The third analysis we normally perform is to construct a corporate portfolio matrix such as that shown in Exhibit 10 for each of the major competitors in the industry. Such matrices complement the analysis above by indicating the degree to which the competitor is likely to invest strategic discretionary resources in building his position in the industry in question. They can also be compared with one's own corporate portfolio to identify other areas where

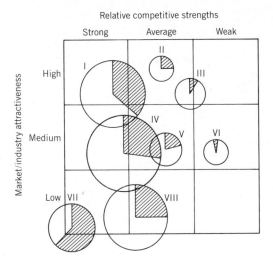

Exhibit 10 A corporate portfolio matrix for competitor X.

the firms compete. These additional interfaces can then be studied to see whether there is a general pattern to the strategic behavior of the competitor or whether each of its businesses is managed in a relatively independent fashion. During such an analysis, it is as important, if not more important, to examine the responses various competitors make to strategic thrusts by their competitors as it is to study the strategic actions they initiate, since these response patterns may reveal opportunities to use the competitor's own actions against it. Thus, if a particular firm counterattacks strongly to any attack, it might on occasion be useful to attack it in area *A* in order to gain time in area *B*.

The final type of analysis we have found it useful to perform in international strategic decision making is a compilation of the various social and political strategies used by the various competitors in each geographic area. This is especially important both because of the increasing political dimensions of international business and because U.S. businesses have traditionally been far less skilled in these areas than their European and Japanese counterparts. As a consequence, such analyses often reveal a variety of new weapons that can be used by U.S. firms, as well as indicating a variety of previously unnoticed competitive threats.

Once all these analyses are completed, the process of strategic decision making can begin. During it, all the creative insights identified above will be utilized and a number of new ones generated. Out of this cauldron of ideas and insights will eventually come a strategy for competing on a global scale. And it is this strategy, as well as existing tactical realities, that should then dictate the various specific international investments that the firm will make, and not just the results of a particular set of financial calculations. Perhaps the best illustration of this point is the game of chess. In that game, there are various tactical rules that must usually be obeyed, as well as a few general strategic precepts that have been laid down. All of these have been programmed into computers and such programs regularly defeat amateurs who are prone to a variety of mistakes. These same programs, however, have been hopelessly outclassed every time they have been matched against international masters and grand masters. And the reason is quite obvious. No set of quasi-random tactics, no matter how perfectly executed, can ever beat a soundly conceived strategy over the long run. Moreover, even when such perfect tactics are combined with a few rudimentary strategic concepts, they will almost always lose to a superior strategist unless there was a great disparity in resources to begin with. Thus, while the various calculations and analysis we have suggested may "rule out" specific international investments as bad moves, the ultimate choices should be based on broad strategic considerations. Furthermore, there may even be times when such strategic considerations dictate an investment with marginal or perhaps even negative short-term payoffs, just as in chess where short-term sacrifices are sometimes required in order to achieve long-term gains.

CONCLUSIONS

Today as in the past, the world of business continues to change. On a global basis, the growth of old markets is beginning to slow, while that of new markets is taking off. Concurrently, the barriers between all markets are beginning to erode and large, well-managed, well-financed, non-U.S. multinational competitors are starting to appear in all corners of the globe. In short, in most industries business is becoming truly multinational. Given these developments, the strategies and tactics we adopt for 1980s must be different from those of the 1960s and 1970s, or all of our industries may go the way of watches, TVs, motorcycles, and cameras. Among other things, this will require new techniques for international environmental analysis and strategic decision making. GLOBESCAN is one such technique. In comparison to most existing techniques, it focuses (1) more on strategy than on tactics; (2) on a global rather than a country-by-country perspective; (3) more on opportunities than on risks; (4) on operating profitability and cash flow as much as on asset protection and investment recovery, and (5) on the entirety of the international strategic decision-making process rather than parts of it. Techniques alone, however, cannot do the job; only more effective strategies can. And these require insight, judgment, creativity, and a willingness to take risks as well as improved management techniques.

NOTES

1. A further complication in this equation is the fact that most U.S. executives tend to think along tactical, competitive lines, while foreign executives tend to think more along strategic and political lines.
2. See R. J. Rummel and David A. Heenan, "How Multi-Nationals Analyze Political Risk," *Harvard Business Review*, January–February 1978, for a fuller description of these techniques.
3. While quantitative models can be used to forecast microrisks, the limited data reporting practices of foreign governments and countries often make it difficult to get the data necessary to do so.
4. This observation refers to the fact that many forecasting models, especially Delphi techniques, may correctly predict the occurrence of a particular event, but seriously err in over- or underestimating the date when the event will occur.
5. See Robert B. Stobaugh, Jr., "How to Analyze Foreign Investment Climates," *Harvard Business Review*, September–October 1969.
6. Deere and Company made major investments in European farm equipment during the mid-1960s despite more profitable options elsewhere because it felt that the European industry was rapidly "shaking out," and that if it did not establish a strong position by the mid-1970s, the major opportunity for it to do so would have passed, perhaps forever.
7. See F. T. Haner, "Rating Investment Risks Abroad." *Business Horizons*, April 1979, for a description of Haner's approach.

SECTION 4
Finance & Control

Finance and control are, of course, concerned respectively with allocating and investing funds, and with measuring and evaluating performance. These activities are much more complex in the multinational corporation than in the firm which operates only in its home country. The increased complexity is the result of having to work with more than one currency. National currencies do not maintain a fixed relationship to each other; they fluctuate. Thus, an investment or a holding in a foreign currency may appreciate or depreciate against the domestic currency in which the firm keeps its accounts and reports its results.

There are a variety of activities that may involve foreign currencies. Borrowing money is one such activity, and there are several alternative ways to borrow. For example a foreign subsidiary might borrow in its local currency creating an obligation in that foreign currency rather than in the currency of the parent. Or, a parent might borrow in its home country and relend to a foreign subsidiary. In this case, the subsidiary would probably convert the proceeds of the loan into its local currency, but the obligation would be in the currency of the parent. Alternatively, a loan for a subsidiary might be arranged in a third country, denominated in that country's currency. In choosing a borrowing alternative, the firm must balance several factors including currency convertibility, relative interest rates and expected future currency relationships.

Valuing earnings is also more difficult. The multinational corporation has a portfolio of foreign subsidiaries which earn money in various foreign countries. These earnings are of course denominated in the foreign currencies in which they are earned. Managers of multinationals have some freedom to choose the makeup of their portfolio of foreign subsidiaries. They must recognize that "a dollar earned" may not appear to investors to be "a dollar earned" if it is earned in a foreign currency, especially if these foreign earnings are not repatriated. They must consider the relationship between their portfolio of investments in foreign subsidiaries and how their firms are valued by the market.

Capital budgeting presents a similarly complicated set of problems. The number of variables that must be considered in a foreign capital investment decision is considerably greater than in a purely domestic decision. Managers must estimate and then balance the risks and expected returns from making investments in different countries. Questions of future currency relationships, repatriation of profits, and even of possible expropriation of assets must be raised. Cash management is also more difficult because the multinational firm generates cash denominated in a variety of currencies. In a world of free-floating currencies, relationships among them can change very quickly; therefore, there may be a constant need to convert currencies from one denomination to another in order to maintain a balanced portfolio. Obviously, then, there is also a need to decide on the desired makeup of the cash portfolio. Unfortunately, though, the desired portfolio does not remain constant because of changing currency relationships. The effective portfolio manager must be able to anticipate currency changes, modify the desired cash portfolio accordingly, and then take action to see that the actual portfolio matches the desired portfolio.

Asset management is still another area of complexity. Currency depreciation can drive the book value of a fixed asset such as a production plant down to almost nothing, while the economic value of the asset may remain completely unimpaired. The problem of valuing inventory is similar. Valuing inventory at market may seriously misstate its economic value when currency relationships change. The manager must understand both the accounting valuation and the economic value of assets, and be able to distinguish between the two.

Changing currency relationships make the problem of control and performance measurement more difficult also. Balance sheet and income statement data are commonly used to evaluate the performance of a business unit and of its management. In order to assess the performance of a foreign subsidiary, it is necessary to separate out those dimensions which really reflect management performance from those which reflect only changed currency relationships, should there be such changes. It is especially important to net out currency effects if the task is to compare performance across subsidiaries.

READING SELECTIONS

Stanley addresses two key areas of concern to financial managers, capital structure and cost of capital. Her article is an analytical review of concepts and models that have been proposed to deal with the special problems in these two areas which are brought about by multinationalization. The focus is on financing, rather than on investment decisions; however, the material she presents should be most useful in predicting the likely effects of an investment decision on the valuation of the firm. She organizes her review around two of the most widely cited frameworks in corporate finance, the Modigliani-Miller and the capital asset pricing model. She first reviews and analyzes separately the work that has been done using each framework, and then points out conflicts and knowledge gaps in the two frameworks.

Stanley's discussion of the Modigliani-Miller model and its various extensions illuminates the manifold problems with which the multinational financial manager must contend. One of the most important of these is that the multinational firm's cost of capital, when it borrows in two or more countries, is affected not only by interest rates but by foreign exchange gains or losses over the life of the borrowing. These gains or losses cannot be known at the time the loan is initiated. Her following discussion of problems in forecasting the behavior of foreign exchange markets underlines questions as to the applicability of the Modigliani-Miller model when extended to the multinational firm.

The subsequent discussion of the capital asset pricing model raises some problems with it also. For example, this model assumes perfect markets, but there are good reasons to suspect imperfect markets. In this regard, Stanley raises a most interesting point, whether the MNC itself may be an investment of market integration. If so, the capital asset pricing model might be more useful. In any event, these two models might provide some guidelines for the financial managers.

Bavashi compares theory and practice among U.S. MNCs in handling the investment side of multinational finance. His study further illuminates some of the complications of multinational finance. He notes, for example, that the literature describes alternative possible means for evaluating the cash flows expected to result from an investment. His study shows that, in practice, different firms use different methods. Similarly, he observes that there is no agreement in either theory or practice in firms' choice of discounted cash flow methods or in establishing a discount rate. Bavashi discusses the ramifications of alternative choices and makes recommendations as to which appear to be most useful.

Dunfey & Giddy add additional perspective to financing and investment decisions by focusing on the forecasting required for financial planning in the MNC. They identify as the major financial planning decisions those affecting the choice of timing, maturity, and currency of denomination. Making these decisions requires forecasts of the relevant interest rates and exchange rates.

Dunfey & Giddy believe that such forecasts are implicitly provided by financial and currency markets and can be understood by studying the proper indicators. This is not a matter, however, of simply using the present price of futures as a prediction of the active future value of, for example, a currency. In order to make the most accurate forecast, some careful adjustments must be made. The adjustment techniques suggested can be useful in even a wider range of forecasting situations than those connected with investment decisions. The author's discussion of the use of market based forecasts should make this clear, as they suggest applications in such areas as budgeting and performance evaluation.

Eaker covers another aspect of multinational financial management, denominating transactions. As goods are bought and sold in the normal course of its business, the MNC is involved in a large number of both inter- and intra-firm financial transactions. His work focuses on intra–firm transactions. The currency denomination in which an intra–firm transaction is executed can affect the firm's cash flows, its taxes, and then its profits. His article presents a model for calculating the value of making the correct choice of denomination and discusses strategies for making the options clear.

The potential value of the model, though, might extend beyond intra-firm transfers. Sometimes a firm can choose the currency denomination in which it will buy from or sell to others. Moreover, the firm may be able to increase the chance of being able to choose its currency denomination by raising the price at which it will buy (or lowering the price at which it will sell) in that currency. Perhaps the Eaker model can provide some insight into tradeoffs. Although the Eaker and the Dunfey & Giddy articles deal with ostensibly different managerial problems, it is interesting to compare the two approaches. What are the similarities and differences in their approaches?

Calderon-Russell concentrates on a specific situation, guarding against the foreign exchange risks of a single transaction. Where only one transaction is involved, it is sometimes possible to hedge. Thee are, though, several alternative hedging strategies which may be available. Each may have a different cost and may provide somewhat different coverage. He offers a procedure by which the manager can evaluate alternative hedging strategies. Although the procedure is designed for single transactions, it may be applicable to a wider range of situations. For example, a firm may forecast that a particular currency will be over represented in its portfolios for a length of time. Hedging can be an alternative to converting. It is also worth considering whether Calderon-Russell's procedure can be used for multiple transactions if their size and timing are known.

Virtually every corporation, domestic or MNC, wants to evaluate and control the sub units making up the corporation. Shapiro tells us that designing proper evaluation and control systems for MNC units is extremely difficult because of the many additional factors which must be considered. He describes the evaluation task as an art rather than a science and as judgment rather than theory based. Nevertheless, Shapiro is able to propose a workable set of guidelines for developing such a system.

He proposes a four stage system, beginning with the all-important task of specifying the purposes of the system. The second stage requires specifying both the particular decisions to be made and the information required to make each of the decisions. The third and fourth stages are concerned with systems design and cost/benefit analysis. Shapiro then describes the design of a measurement and evaluation system using as an example the allocation of capital across subsidiaries. Following the example through illustrates the difference between domestic and international capital budgeting decisions. Following the example through also points out another kind of difference: that changes in currency relationships can affect the measured performance of a subsidiary and can thus distort one's assessment of that subsidiary's management.

Dietmann proposes that the management of a subsidiary should be held at least partly accountable for earnings deviations resulting from changes in currency relationships, and he describes and illustrates some alternative methods of evaluating subsidiaries' performance. Each alternative has some problems, so Dietmann then proposes some ways of making adjustments to the figures in order to prevent financial results most accurately. His method starts with FAS No. 8, which requires currency gains and loses to be entered into the determination of current income.

A study of Dietmann's proposal points up the difference between financial accounting to prepare reports for stockholders and control accounting to evaluate managers' performance. It might be said that the purpose of financial accounting reports is to place a value on the firm, while the purpose of control accounting reports is to place a value on its management. It's worth noting the extent to which dealing in multiple currencies widens the breadth of potential valuations of each, making an exact determination extremely difficult.

14

Capital Structure and Cost-of-Capital for the Multinational Firm
Marjorie Thines Stanley

• • •

INTRODUCTION

The objective of this paper is to review recent developments in models dealing with capital structure and cost of capital as these have been extended to the multinational case. The models address a number of issues which bear upon the financing decisions of the multinational firm. The questions relating to capital structure include: Is there an optimal capital structure for the multinational firm? How does multinationality affect this question? Does subsidiary capital structure "matter"? The questions relating to cost of capital include: What is the effect, if any, of multinationality upon parent cost of equity? Is the multinational firm's cost of capital affected by its debt financing decisions?

Source: Marjorie Thines Stanley, "Capital Structure and Cost-of-Capital for the Multinational Firm," *Journal of International Business Studies,* Spring/Summer 1981. pp. 103–120. Copyright © 1981. Reprinted by permission.

Does currency of denomination exert an influence of its own which is relevant to debt financing decisions? If so, what is the nature of this influence? Is it possible for the multinational firm to benefit from international differentials in nominal interest rates? Do firms attempt to do so? Underlying these specific issues is the basic theoretical and empirical question of the degree of segmentation or integration of international money and capital markets and a related question with regard to the efficiency of the foreign exchange market.

The models employed in research dealing with cost of capital and capital structure for the multinational firm are themselves a subject of controversy. Partially for this reason, the review of the literature has been organized on the basis of the models employed, in each case attempting to point out the specific problems addressed in individual studies, subsequent critiques of the studies, and the nature of the evolution of the theoretical and empirical research. The paper will be concerned not only with the contribution which the individual research studies may make to a resolution of the earlier enumerated questions related to the financial policy of the multinational firm, but will seek to comment also upon the realism and relevance of the models' theoretical assumptions and the practicability of empirical testing of the theoretical constructs.

The scope of the paper has been limited, perhaps somewhat arbitrarily, so as to exclude detailed examination of the issue of the separation/integration of the financing decision and the investment decision, and only tangential consideration will be given to the foreign investment decision itself. Reference to the comprehensive literature on foreign exchange market efficiency and to the extensive literature on international integration of financial markets which has a primarily macro thrust will be limited to conclusions drawn from selected studies which have direct relevance to issues of capital structure or cost of capital for the multinational firm. In short, the articles reviewed will be selected and evaluated primarily on the basis of their relevance to the financing decisions of the multinational firm, with occasional reference to closely related capital budgeting and international investment decisions.

Because the extension of domestic models to the multinational case has been done within or disputing the Modigliani-Miller framework and within the capital asset pricing model framework, the next section of the paper will examine models within or disputing the Modigliani-Miller framework (3; 34; 44; 45; 59; 66; 85; 98). This will be followed by a section addressing research conducted within or disputing the capital asset pricing model framework (1; 6; 11; 14; 28; 32; 37; 40; 52; 57; 86; 87–91). The paper will conclude with two sections summarizing the current state of knowledge—the first will emphasize current areas of conflict, data problems which hamper resolution of these conflicts, and areas for future research; the final

summary will emphasize the financial policy prescribed or suggested for the firm by the current state of knowledge.

MODELS WITHIN OR DISPUTING THE MODIGLIANI-MILLER FRAMEWORK

Within the Modigliani-Miller framework, Krainer presented an extension analyzing the question of the capital structure and valuation of the multinational firm (44). Abstracting from corporate income taxes and beginning with "a world where firms make physical investments and finance within a single capital market but portfolio investors are free to make investments in different national capital markets," Krainer explored the question of whether a firm can be in the same risk class in two different national capital markets. He concluded that, in a world where currencies are convertible into one another at varying rates and in varying degrees, the claimants to the uncertain earnings stream of foreign firms face currency risks that cause the risk/return relationship to differ as between a firm's foreign and domestic claimants, so "there is no reason to expect the level or structure of capitalization rates appropriate to (a firm's) securities to be the same in two different countries;" that is, arbitrage, though operative, will not completely eliminate a difference in capitalization rates associated with currency rate and repatriation risks. Krainer then argued that this result may enable a firm that invests and finances in several national capital markets to influence the cutoff rate at which it accepts new capital projects by altering its capital structure, given the condition that domestic portfolio investors are not "preferred borrowers" in foreign capital markets; that is, for the M-M results to hold for the multinational firm, portfolio investors must be able to issue personal debt in national capital markets open to the firm. Krainer concluded that financial planners for MNCs should study capital market conditions in "the larger national capital markets in order to take advantage of possible opportunities to reduce the average cost of capital'' (44, p. 563).

Dropping the no-tax assumptions, Krainer concluded that the tax deductibility of interest payments and the associated ''rebate'' to the shareholders of the levered firm, when capitalized at a favorable foreign rate, provide an incentive for the multinational firm to issue debt up to its maximum debt limit (44, p. 564), imposed by either the firm itself or its creditors. Presumably, the self-imposed limit would be ''prudential'' in nature or, perhaps, be influenced by finance managers' perceptions of the effect of leverage upon expectations (54, pp. 40–42).

A critique of Krainer by Adler (3) raised several theoretical issues. Basically, these amounted to a criticism of the choice of the M-M model as opposed to a portfolio diversification approach and an emphasis upon default risk rather than foreign exchange risk as the relevant question to ask in extending the M-M model (3, pp. 850–851). Adler reached this conclusion by assuming riskless and costless forward exchange transactions and uniform investor expectations with regard to security returns and exchange rate changes. Krainer found the first assumption unacceptable: ''Where there is a real risk, it will not do . . . to ignore the cost of insuring against that risk'' (45, p. 861). In part, then, the issue between Krainer and Adler is one of choice of models and realism and relevance of assumptions. [Note that recent foreign exchange market research models have explicitly introduced transaction costs and diverse expectations on the part of market participants (25; 21).]

Krainer stressed (45, pp. 859, 861) that Adler's comment did not note that Krainer had mentioned degrees of currency convertibility, as well as changing exchange rates, as a reason for a possible breakdown of international arbitrage or for a redefining of risk classes (44, p. 555). In later literature inconvertibility seems to have been relegated to the category of political risk and thus often excluded from financial models. Potential currency inconvertibility is nevertheless a factor likely to influence financial decisions of the firm and the security investor in ways relevant to the financial structure issue; it enters the literature at the financial management textbook level as a factor influencing planning (18, pp. 413-424). Further empirical study of this issue is needed.

Another point mentioned but not pursued by Adler is that exchange risk affects expected returns on equities differently from the way it affects fixed-income bonds (3, p. 850). This point, assumed away by Krainer (44, p. 556; 45, p. 862), relates to the economic effects of exchange rate risk. The distinction among translation, transactions, and economic effects of exchange risk has been receiving increased attention from financial managers since the advent of floating exchange rates and the adoption in the U.S. of Financial Accounting Standard No. 8 (95). The economic effects of exchange rate fluctuations upon the corporation and its security holders are an area for future research.

Clearly, several issues raised or assumed away by Krainer's pioneering extension of the M-M model to the international case remain to be resolved.

Naumann-Etienne has dismissed ''Krainer's findings that exchange rate and repatriation risk are sufficient to invalidate the Modigliani-Miller theorem in an otherwise perfect world capital market,'' because ''the world-wide existence of corporate income taxes . . . achieves the same result'' (61, p. 860); however, the many reasons for international validity of the M-M theorem may be of practical importance to the financial policy of the multinational firm.

A critique of Krainer by Severn (81) raised questions relevant to Krainer's original empirical testing of his theoretical constructs. Krainer had attempted to test whether U.S.-based multinational firms had altered the magnitude of their foreign debt financing in response to changes in relative borrowing costs. Three tests were conducted: the results of these tests tended to support Krainer's hypothesis that multinational firms alter the country source of their debt financing in response to what Krainer perceived to be changes in relative borrowing costs. Severn's criticism was primarily centered on the influence of OFDI regulations on financing decisions during the 1965–1970 period; regressing the ratio of international bond issues of U.S. firms to domestic and international bond issues on the rates of European to U.S. interest rates, he obtained a positive, not negative, relationship over the 1968–1972 period. In response, Krainer took the ratio of foreign currency bond issues of U.S. firms (rather than the formerly employed total international bond issues of U.S. firms) to domestic offerings as it related to the ratio of European interest rates to U.S. Aa corporate bond yields and concluded that cost minimization was an important consideration in the formation of financial policy of U.S.-based multinational firms (45).

It should be noted that if U.S. multinationals were indeed changing the source and currency mix of their financing in response to what Krainer perceived as changes in borrowing costs, the "fact" that they were doing so does not necessarily make such behavior normative. Apropos of this and of Severn's point with regard to the influence on financing decisions of the U.S. OFDI regulations, a study of U.S. firms that issued international and foreign bonds in the first half of 1968, following the imposition of compulsory regulations, indicated that 60 percent of the issuing firms found cost to be higher than U.S. borrowing would have been (96, p. 58). Of those who found it to be lower, one noted it to be so, "providing foreign exchange risk is contained." With the benefit of hindsight we now know that, for those firms whose financing was denominated in the deutschmark or Swiss franc, relative nominal interest rates prevailing at the time of issue were an inadequate measure of ultimate cost of matured debt in dollar terms. A major data problem, then, for empirical studies relative to multinational cost of capital and financing behavior of the multinational firm is the inability to measure directly expectations with regard to foreign exchange rate changes for relevant currencies over the time periods involved in long-term financing, and the rarity of a spectrum of market conditions which might allow one to infer such expectations from interest rate differentials on differently denominated long-term issues (15, pp. 77–106; 92; 63, pp. 169–171).

Other weaknesses of Krainer's data certainly included such items as: (1) the use of an "average European" nominal interest rate (even if weighted, does it have economic content and significance?—it is easy to imagine funds flowing from the U.S. to a particular European country, and to the U.S. from another European country.); (2) the use of a U.S. vs. Europe dichotomy in the debt categories employed [is lira-denominated debt equivalent to deutschmark-denominated debt?—data presented by Rugman reveal a correlation of Italian with West German long-term interest rates of .5903 for quarterly data, 1954–1973 (77, p. 40)]; (3) the use of heterogeneous debt measures, for example, inclusive of trade credit (adjusted for intracompany debt?); (4) the inclusion of convertible debt with straight debt [perhaps necessitated by the fact that, at a certain time under OFDI, convertible debt was "about the only thing that could be sold" (96, p. 60)]. In short, the use of such data leads to conclusions which fail to convince and satisfy.

An inevitable result of data problems is that researchers are likely to shun a topic. Stevens is one who did otherwise and attempted to develop and test a theoretical model, consistent with maximization of the market value of the firm, with the goal of explaining capital flows associated with the financing of foreign asset accumulations by international firms (98). Relying on the M-M thesis, he stated that "it does not matter how the firm divides the financing of its foreign assets between capital flows from the United States and foreign sources" (98, p. 327),[1] but postulated a secondary goal for the firm in the form of minimization of risk of losses due to exchange rate fluctuations. Stevens' goal in developing the model was to examine the impact of voluntary and mandatory controls on foreign direct investment; his efforts received faint praise from Robbins and Stobaugh, who referred to his "imaginative use of the statistics that are available" and expressed their reservations with regard to the relevance of M-M for the international firm: "in the very real world of the multinational firm, the distribution of the subsidiaries' capital structure has a very real influence on the level of after-tax earnings" (66, p. 356).

Hirshleifer has also challenged the relevance of M-M to the international firm and has provided an analysis which underscores the importance of complete markets (34), as opposed to the market imperfections stressed by other writers. Thus, Hirshleifer noted that the M-M equation depends upon an assumption of complete markets, as well as the absence of taxes, bankruptcy, and transactions costs, so that individuals and firms together form a "closed system, with no losses to the outside" (34, p. 264). With incomplete markets, he argues, the arbitrage opportunities necessary to equate the sum of the market value of the securities issues with the present certainty equivalent value of the income stream are not present, leaving open possibilities at the margin for profitable financing decisions (34, pp. 271–272). Inasmuch as capital markets are not highly developed in many countries which host subsidiaries of MNCs, a major proportion of foreign debt financing is in the form of private placements or bank loans (93), and Hirshleifer's position is particularly relevant.

An examination of financing decisions and the cost of capital to be used in appraising the profitability of foreign investments was the goal of Shapiro in a recent paper (85). He began by extending the weighted cost of capital concept to the multinational firm. While noting the M-M position that leverage is irrelevant in the absence of taxes, Shapiro assumed the marginal cost of capital to be constant and thus equal to

the cost of new funds, minimized by choosing an appropriate capital structure and, following Adler (1, p. 120), assumed that suppliers of capital to the MNC would associate the risk of default with the MNC's consolidated worldwide debt ratio. In his conclusions, however, he noted that investor perceptions of the riskiness of MNCs are likely to be affected by the location as well as the percentage of foreign source earnings (85, p. 224). Such a conclusion would appear to be consistent with the possibility that perceived risk of default may be affected by the location of sources as well as uses of funds, in addition to being affected by the ratio of total debt to assets.

Given his assumption to the contrary, Shapiro proceeded with the costing of various sources of funds and provided a formula for the incremental weighted cost of capital. This employs: (1) the parent's marginal cost of capital ("provided that the foreign investments undertaken do not change the overall riskiness of the MNC's operations"); (2) the cost of retained earnings abroad, using the cost of parent equity here unless tax and transfer costs are significant [which they may be (78, p. 671), but potential for misspecification of cost of subsidiary retained earnings also exists (62)]; (3) the cost of depreciation-generated funds, equal to the firm's incremental average cost of capital, and (4) the after-tax dollar cost of borrowing locally, equal to "the sum of interest expense and the exchange gain or loss" (85, p. 214). The incremental weighted cost of capital can then be calculated including a term for over- or under-leveraging abroad which is associated with the opportunity cost of additional equity needed to restore the consolidated target debt ratio. If the foreign investment changes the parent risk characteristics, then the parent's cost of equity must be adjusted.

A major problem in making the formula operational is of course the determination of the after-tax dollar cost of borrowing locally, which, as noted, Shapiro defined as being equal to "the sum of interest expense and the exchange gain or loss'' (85, p. 214). Because the exchange gain or loss cannot be known in advance, expectations must be introduced into the cost of capital formulation. These expectations are not necessarily adequately observable in market-determined prices and/or rates. Thus, excluding such considerations as those associated with inflation-adjusted accounting and legally required indexing—for example, of bond principal and interest payments—the introduction of such expectations represents a fundamental change in the nature of the concept of cost of capital generally associated with single-currency financing.

When foreign-currency financing is employed, exchange rate expectations not only enter into the calculation of the cost of capital, but they do so in a much more complex way than in Shapiro's cost of capital formula, because the direction, amount, and timing of foreign exchange changes are all relevant. Shapiro employed the expected rate at the end of one year. This has the major advantage of being objectively observable in the form of forward market quotations for currencies for which uncontrolled forward markets exist. In fact, for a one-year period forward cover could be purchased and cost of capital could include this actual known cost, rather than the expected one as revealed by the forward rate. Unfortunately, forward markets for many currencies are nonexistent, thin, or subject to intervention or control, and the corporation is thrown back upon its own internally generated forecasts or those of an advisory service. Furthermore, a cost of capital formula which employs expectations of future exchange rates only one year forward is inadequate, while one that employs expectations of future exchange rates and their time path from date of debt issue to date of debt maturity is highly dependent upon forecasting and probability analysis. Unless international financial markets are perfectly integrated, and the expectations theory of the term structure, international interest rate parity, and purchasing power parity, or the international Fisher ef-

fect prevail, the extension to the multinational firm of the concept of weighted average cost of capital entails this difficulty of forecasting and quantifying expected changes in the exchange rate over the maturity of long-term debt.

On the other hand, to the extent that the forward premium and, thus, the short-term interest rate differential provide unbiased estimates of the expected rate of change of the exchange rate, the currency of denomination of short-term debt is a matter of indifference to borrowers. To the extent that the international Fisher effect holds, expected changes in exchange rates are reflected in international interest rate differentials, and changes in exchange rates offset differential inflation rates, thereby tending to keep relative purchasing power costs of debt denominated in different currencies constant. Then, the currency of denomination per se is a matter of indifference, and such factors as availability and tax effects become predominant in the debt financing decision; that is, the firm's cost of local-currency borrowing will be equivalent in an expected value sense to the cost of dollar borrowing, provided that the tax system does not discriminate in its treatment of interest costs on the basis of currency of denomination; such as, by virtue of its treatment of foreign exchange gain or loss. [Shapiro explicitly noted the importance of the latter factor (85, p. 214)].

The work of a number of researchers is relevant to the question of foreign exchange rate behavior and forecasting. First, about the international Fisher effect, Dufey and Giddy note that ''by comparing the term structure of interest rates in two Eurocurrency markets, one may readily derive the term structure of exchange-rate expectations'' (15, p. 79). However, a number of studies show poor correlations between exchange rate changes and relative interest rates in the short run (26; 48). Giddy found that the relationship held better over a three-year period than over three-month periods (26, p. 28). He also observed that there were persistent small deviations from the international Fisher effect in long as well as short periods but noted that deviations might stem from errors in expectations rather than from interest rates incorrectly reflecting the expectations (26, p. 30).

In a test of forecasting models, Levich (48) found that Fisher external outperformed other forecasting models, judging "performance" on the basis of the mean squared error of forecasts for one-month, three-month, and six-month forecasting horizons for nine currencies in the period 1967–1975. For 27 country-horizon episodes, the Fisher external model had the lowest mean squared error on 13 episodes, followed closely by a lagged-spot model which was lowest on 12 episodes (48, pp. 134–137). Forecast errors tended to be smaller during pegged rate periods, except when there was a discrete change in the rate; forecast errors became larger and more volatile during the manager-float period, with some evidence that they are becoming smaller as the managed float continues (48, pp. 146–147). As in Levich's study, most empirical tests of foreign exchange rate forecasting models have stressed relatively short forecasting horizons.

Solnik and Grall have suggested that market-implied expectations of exchange rate fluctuations are revealed by the currency structure of yield differentials in the new-issue Eurobound market (92, p. 225). From end-of-quarter variables from October 1967 to March 1973, the data implied an average annual rate of devaluation of .7 percent for the dollar vis-à-vis the Deutschmark (92, pp. 219, 227); in the period March 1973 through December 1978, the actual average annual rate of devaluation was in excess of 5.5 percent (38). Thus, the actual rate of change far exceeded the expected rate of change implied by Eurobond yield differentials.

Similarly, Quinn has cited the segmented secondary-market price behavior of Deutschmark- and dollar-denominated Eurobond issues as indicators of expectations of devaluation, although emphasizing a relatively short time horizon (63, pp. 169–172); expected dollar devaluation was imminent; large differentials in

yield to maturity in dollar versus Deutschmark bonds appeared: "In terms of the immediate exchange rate changes that transpired the market overreacted" (63, p. 171). The practical import of this particular market overreaction for cost of capital expectations was probably small, however, because, given the market conditions studied, new-issue activity by foreign borrowers tended to dry up.

Note that these researchers focused upon the Euromarkets, not the domestic markets, as being likely to reflect, in interest differentials on like maturities, expected foreign exchange rate changes. The studies indicate that neither new-issue nor secondary-market Eurobond yield and price behavior would have proved very useful as a means of correctly quantifying future exchange rates. The studies were, however, quite limited in scope. Other studies have noted that a risk factor may be embodied in the term structure of exchange rate expectations (15, p. 105). This is an area for future research.

Miller and Whitman, working with macroeconomic models concerned with monetary and fiscal policy and the balance of payments, reported that no statistically significant proxy for expected spot exchange rates had been found (58, p. 276). Financial managers report a short-term emphasis in foreign exchange risk management because "it is too difficult to predict beyond one year" (95). Perhaps even a year is too long: "advisors who were offering year-long forecasts were doing so because clients were asking for it, rather than because such forecasts were worth giving" (7, p. 38).

Tests of foreign exchange forecasting models, even for short periods, show conflicting results. The managed-float "system" of foreign exchange has displayed increased volatility of exchange rates and concomitant decrease in the forecasting accuracy of the forward rate (49, pp. 244–245, 262–271). Studies by Levich of the period 1967–1978 indicated that the model stating that the forward rate is an unbiased predictor of future exchange rate change could not be rejected, but that the prediction power of the relationship, measured by R^2, was very low (49, p. 271). Other research by Levich on foreign exchange forecasting models, noted earlier, had indicated that the international Fisher effect regularly outperformed the forward rate, but the difference was "generally small enough to be explained by transaction costs or sampling errors" (48, p. 137).

Giddy and Dufey, testing models for predicting future spot rates, found that the forward rate was consistently the poorest predictor (27); but Aliber concluded that the forward rate was a somewhat better predictor of the subsequent spot rate over the long run than either relative interest rates or purchasing power parity (42, p. 28); and Kohlhagen concluded that "in the long run, even with floating and volatile markets, the forward rate has in general been an unbiased predictor of the future spot rate" (42, p. 29).

With regard to purchasing power parity, characterized as "the ideological antecedent of the current monetary approach" (35, p. 98), there is an extensive body of literature (42). This literature indicates that purchasing power parity seems to hold in the long run (42, pp. 3, 43), and there is some evidence that it held quite well during the pegged rate period, 1959–1970 (42, p. 3). However, there have been short-run deviations from purchasing power parity in both fixed and floating rate periods (42, pp. 3–4, 43), and a number of recent research studies indicate that it has not prevailed during the period of dirty floating exchange rates (42, p. 3).

One empirical study covering six countries during the period 1920–1924 and Canada during 1953–1957 indicates that freely floating foreign exchange markets respond almost if not immediately to changes in relative inflation rates, but it also notes that central bank intervention appears to reduce the impact of differential rates of inflation and to introduce inefficiencies into the foreign exchange markets (70). Central bank foreign exchange market intervention is then a possible channel of influence upon equity and debt costs of the multinational firm.[2]

In summary, tests of foreign exchange fore-casting models, even for short periods, show conflicting results, and the research suggests that a satisfactory proxy for long-term exchange rate expectations remains to be discovered. Given such conditions, the borrowing source decision appears to be an important one for the multinational firm, and the use of external local-currency long-term debt financing by foreign subsidiaries seemingly leads to possibilities for foreign exchange gain/loss in real terms for the multinational firm and to possible wealth transfers between bondholders and parent-company stockholders.

Despite the lack of a satisfactory proxy for long-term exchange rate expectations, which constitutes a major problem in making Shapiro's formula operational, he claimed that a simplified version of the formula—ignoring the possibility that the optimal D/E ratio may itself be dependent upon the relative costs of debt and equity—makes it possible to settle "one controversy in the literature," that between Zenoff and Zwick, who argued for the use of the company-wide marginal cost-of-capital as the discount factor to be used in multinational capital budgeting (102, pp. 186–190), and Stonehill and Stitzel, who argued for the use of the cost-of-capital appropriate to local firms operating in the same industry (100). Shapiro characterized both as incorrect, because they "ignore the factor of multinationality" (85, p. 216). Zenoff and Zwick defined the company-wide cost-of-capital as

a normative cost measure which reflects what overall financing costs would be *if* the firm obtained its debt and equity capital in the least expensive markets in ideal proportions. It is . . . used as the discount rate for capital budgeting decisions unless the proposed project under consideration is expected to change the business risk complexion of the firm as a whole. (102, pp. 188–189)

Zenoff and Zwick went on to consider the possibility that financing for particular foreign affiliates might be more expensive than the company-wide cost-of-capital; they would consider such cost premia as part of project outflows and would base debt policy on a consideration of cash flow characteristics in each local environment. Why? Because "the financial markets are segmented, precluding the selection of an optimal mix for the firm as a whole" (102, p. 189). Thus, they took a partially negative view of the effects of market segmentation, in contrast to the possible oligopsonistic advantages posited by Shapiro.

The Stonehill and Stitzel recommendation was based upon consideration of environmental factors, including concern over misallocation of resources in the host country, not upon a shareholder wealth maximization goal (100, pp. 92–95). Eiteman and Stonehill, referring to the Stonehill and Stitzel recommendation, argued that optimal global financial structure would be different for all multinational firms because of their geographical diversity and that optimal structure from a cost-of-capital point of view can best be decided upon when comparisons can be made among firms in the same country, industry, and risk class (18, p. 225).

Turning to the question of appropriate subsidiary financial structure, Shapiro concluded that this should vary, so as to take advantage of opportunities to minimize the cost of capital (85, p. 216); this assumed explicitly that capital markets are at least partially segmented and that the subsidiary's capital structure is relevant only insofar as it affects the consolidated worldwide debt ratio (85, pp. 217–218). Shapiro then considered the related issues of company guarantees and nonconsolidation and decided that they are largely false issues (85, pp. 218–219, 224). Shapiro also briefly mentioned taxes and regulatory factors, riskiness of foreign operations, political risk, inflation and exchange risk, diversification, investor perceptions, and joint ventures, concluding that a great deal of empirical testing remains to be done (85, p. 226). The multiplicity of issues raised is in itself evidence of the complexities and data problems involved, and of some directions which further research might take in an effort to provide more definitive answers as a guide to policy and action.

INTERNATIONAL CAPITAL ASSET PRICING MODELS

The extension of the capital asset pricing model to the international case has been advanced by several researchers; here, we shall be concerned primarily with the implications of this work for multinational financing decisions and cost of capital, including both equity and debt capital, but with emphasis upon cost of equity.

Imperfections in international financial markets and their theoretical implications for risk premia and the cost of capital to firms were explored by Cohn and Pringle (11). Their analysis emphasized that to the extent that economic activity in different economies is less than perfectly correlated, a lessening of restrictions on international portfolio diversification would affect risk-return relationships and security prices in two ways. The broadening of the market portfolio to include more (internationally traded) securities would reduce the nondiversifiable risk of each security and, given logarithmic or exponential utility functions, the slope of the capital market line—that is, the marginal rate of substitution of risk for return—would decline (11, pp. 60–62). These two effects would act to reduce the risk-premium component of the cost of capital for firms (11, p. 63) and thereby to improve the efficiency of real capital allocation.

Solnik (88; 89) tested empirically an international market structure consistent with the International Asset Pricing Model and found that "national factors are quite important . . . violating the simple international market structure postulated in the single index market model" (88, p. 552). After diversifying away the domestic factors in international portfolios, it was possible to show a strong relation between realized returns and international systematic risk. Solnik concluded that the true meaning of risk should be the international risk of an investment, not its national "beta," and that "the international capital market seems to be sufficiently integrated and efficient to induce an international pricing of risk for common stocks"(88, pp. 552–553).

Citing statistical problems in Solnik's procedures, Stehle provided an alternative approach, testing both a segmented markets hypothesis and an integrated markets hypothesis and concluding that neither could be rejected in favor of the other but finding some empirical support for the international model (97).

The question of the extent or degree of international market integration is an important one and other researchers have also addressed it (37; 57). Noting that, if capital markets are perfect, the multinational firm does nothing for investors that they could not do for themselves, but that, if markets are not internationally integrated and the domestic market is efficient, multinational firms are performing a valuable function for investors which should be reflected in the pricing of equities of multinational firms, Hughes, Logue, and Sweeney studied 46 multinational and 50 domestic firms, characterized by them as roughly comparable in size and diversity of product lines,[3] for the period January 1970 through December 1973. They found that the "average returns for (the) multinational firms were higher than the average returns on (the) domestic firms," although "their betas were considerably lower," suggesting "some economies achieved by international diversification. . . . The distribution of measures of unsystematic risk (were) significantly lower for multinational firms than for domestic firms," supporting "the view that investors perceive multinational firms as providing substantial diversification benefits" (37, p. 633). When the domestic market index was used, the performance of multinational firms was significantly superior to that of domestic firms, but when the world index was used the difference in performance was not statistically significant; the authors interpreted this as lending "some support albeit marginal to the view that assets are priced

internationally rather than domestically and that international financial markets are indeed integrated" (37, p. 633). Further, they concluded that multinational firms assist in this process and that "investors correctly perceive the diversification benefits of shares of multinational firms and that such firms do something for investors" (37, p. 636).

These conclusions are consistent with those of Agmon and Lessard whose empirical results supported their hypothesis that "U.S. investors recognize the international composition of the activities of U.S.-based corporations" when geographical diversification of these activities is represented by percentage of foreign sales (6, p. 1055). Coupling this conclusion with the observation that capital flows forming part of direct investment by the multinational corporation may have lower cost or barriers than portfolio flows of individual investors, Agmon and Lessard suggested that the diversification motive, while difficult to isolate empirically, should be given more consideration than has been the case, because it appears to be relevant at the corporate as well as the investor level (6, pp. 1049, 1055).

Rugman has also emphasized diversification through foreign direct investment rather than portfolio investment. Because statistical tests show that international goods and factor markets are less correlated than international financial markets, Rugman suggested that the individual risk averter should purchase shares of the multinational firm as an indirect route to the risk reduction effects of international diversification (77, p. 33).

Lee and Sachdeva have provided a theoretical proof of this for home country investors under conditions of perfect competition and assumptions of equal risk-free rates in the home and host country, a nonstochastic foreign exchange rate, and a constant market price of risk (46, pp. 482–484, 490–491).

In a related empirical study, however, Jacquillat and Solnik found that investing in U.S. multinational firms could not be regarded as a good direct substitute for international portfolio diversification; foreign influence on stock prices was "unexpectedly limited" compared to the extent of the firm's foreign investment (39).

Hughes, Logue, and Sweeney suggested that a fruitful area for further research would be why the appearance and actuality of international market integration diverge. They posited that the higher (risk-adjusted) returns available in countries other than the U.S. may be illusory because they may merely compensate for higher transaction costs. If netting these out were to result in similar risk/return tradeoffs among countries, markets would be shown to be highly integrated internationally (37, p. 636).

Hughes, Logue, and Sweeney repeatedly suggested that one source of advantage for the multinational firm may be higher debt capacity, reflected in stock-market-assigned measures of risk (37, pp. 628, 630) and owed to the diversifications of the MNC's activities among semi-independent economies (37, pp. 631, 633).[4]

Rugman has tested risk reduction by international diversification, using earnings variance as a proxy for risk, and foreign sales/total sales as a measure of international diversification, with earnings defined as net income/net worth. His empirical results showed that the foreign operations variable (foreign sales/total sales) was statistically significant and inversely related to variance of profits (77, pp. 11–13, 16–17). Thus, Rugman's results would tend to support the suggestion of Hughes, Logue, and Sweeney with regard to investor perceptions of higher debt capacity for multinational firms. However, Rugman was specifically interested in examining the risk reduction attendant upon diversification via foreign direct investment and regarded the CAPM (used by Hughes, Logue, and Sweeney) as inappropriate for such tests because of the CAPM's perfect-markets assumptions that are inconsistent with direct investment motivated at the level of the firm by market imperfections (76; 77, p. 12).

Mehra, examining the influence of exchange risk on both the investment and financing deci-

sions of multinational firms within the CAPM framework (and with its perfect markets assumptions) concluded that alterations of the firm's capital structure do not change its value, even in the presence of exchange risk (57, p. 240). Mehra employed a two-country model and assumed nonsegmented capital markets with individuals free to invest in the stock and bond markets of both countries. He showed that in this case a firm's beta consists of two terms, involving covariance of the security with the world market portfolio and with a position in foreign exchange (57, pp. 227, 235). For country A firms, risk was shown to be understated (overstated) by the Sharpe-Lintner-Mossin CAPM depending, for example, upon whether their returns were likely to increase (decrease) due to devaluation (revaluation) by country A and whether country A was a surplus (deficit) country in terms of its net investment position (57, pp. 235–237).

There are capital budgeting implications here; that is, "if the effects of exchange risk are not considered explicitly in capital budgeting decisions, a systematic bias will develop" (57, p. 239). The effect upon cost of capital of project covariance with the exchange rate will depend upon the net investment position of the country; in a country with a surplus investment position, a project whose returns decrease due to a devaluation of that country's currency will have a lower cost of capital, ceteris paribus; in a deficit country the project favored by a devaluation will have a lower cost of capital. Acceptance criteria for a project were shown to be the same for both countries' firms (57, pp. 238–239).

It should be emphasized, however, that all of these "normative implications" of Mehra's model for the "value-maximizing firm" ultimately depend upon the model's assumptions of nonsegmented markets in which individuals are free to borrow and invest.

A main issue, then, is whether the degree of market segmentation is sufficient to make segmented markets models the relevant ones for decision-makers, or whether the degree of market integration is sufficient to make integrated markets models the relevant ones. In the absence of governmental controls, growing individual investor sophistication and evolving financial institutions would be expected to contribute to greater market integration. How much is "enough" seems to underlie much of the disagreement in the literature. The multinational firm itself may tend to reduce the practical managerial importance of this issue, achieving through its use of intracompany funds transfers and transfer pricing many of the effects of market integration (67, pp. 161–171; 61, pp. 863–864).

A propos of the multinational firm's financing decisions, Jucker and deFaro have considered the problem of selecting a foreign borrowing source within a portfolio diversification framework, assuming a one-year time period, no use of forward markets, spot exchange always available when needed, and a pure financing problem, without consideration of other changes that a firm may face as a result of currency devaluations. Jucker and deFaro concluded that: "The principal difference between the (borrowing) source selection problem and the portfolio selection problem is the source of uncertainty" (40, p. 406); namely, currency fluctuations. They therefore presented a model to aid in estimating characteristics of the random variables that express his uncertainty, making it possible to assess the necessary probability distributions. The exposition was developed assuming conditions prevailing under the Smithsonian Agreement, but the basic model is applicable to a managed floating rate system. The paper is useful by virtue of its emphasis upon the applicability of portfolio selection techniques to the borrowing source problem.

In an earlier related paper deFaro and Jucker dealt with both inflation and exchange risk, concluded that only exchange risk matters, and presented a decision criterion calling for comparison of interest differentials and expected foreign exchange rate changes over the duration of the loan (14, pp. 97–104), a conceptually obvious criterion with the previously noted operational problems associated with quantifying the direction, magnitude, and timing of expected foreign exchange rate changes.

Folks, noting (23, p. 246) that he was building upon work of Jucker and deFaro (40), developed an approach applicable to the selection of an optimal currency source for a short-term loan when it is possible for the borrowing unit to enter the forward exchange market for a term equivalent to the maturity of the loan. His approach emphasizes not only that the relevant cost of funds is the cost of covered borrowing in each currency but also emphasizes the tight relationship between the money market and the foreign exchange market, by showing that the optimal sourcing problem may be transmuted into an optimal forward exchange purchase problem (23, p. 252). Folks himself notes that this probably has limited practical application because of the "currency speculation" label that would likely be attached to the prescribed actions (23, pp 252–253), but the point undoubtedly has educational shock value for financial policy. It also serves to emphasize again the exchange risk aspects of the long-term foreign borrowing source problem.

CURRENT STATE OF KNOWLEDGE: CONFLICTS, DATA PROBLEMS, AREAS FOR FUTURE RESEARCH

The review of recent literature which extends to the multinational case financial theory relevant to capital structure and cost-of-capital for the domestic firm reveals the substantially greater complexity of the international case and various areas of conflict in the literature. Data problems contribute to the continuation of the conflict, because definitive empirical testing of certain theoretical constructs is, at best, difficult.

There has been, for example, substantial testing of equity pricing and risk/return relationships in international extensions of the capital asset pricing model, but there is still disagreement on the basic ICAPM to be employed; controversy surrounds "the" world market model, and there is no commonly accepted definition of the world market factor. There is a basic questioning of the applicability of the CAPM, with its assumption of perfect markets and market participants able to borrow or lend at the pure rate, to the question of international diversification of risk, particularly to the case of diversification effects of foreign direct investment which rest upon market imperfections (89; 80; 77). There is also detailed questioning of statistical methodology and judgment solutions to problems involved (76; 77, p. 44; 97).

Conflict over Modigliani-Miller varies from that over the best reason for declaring it invalid at the international level [for example, exchange risk, repatriation risk, taxes and tax differentials (44; 45; 61)], to a thesis extending it to the borrowing source decision (98), implicitly disputed by researchers concerned with the substance of that decision (83; 85; 23; 40).

There is basic disagreement as to how foreign exchange risk should be treated: is it a real factor stemming from (nationally differentiated) consumption preferences, or a monetary factor? (89; 29; 26) Related to this issue is the fact that empirical evidence with regard to the international Fisher effect, purchasing power parity, and forward rate bias and predictive power is mixed (15; 42; 70; 26; 27; 48; 49).

Conflict over the degree and relevance of international market segmentation versus market integration is unresolved (98; 66; 67; 8; 11; 87–91; 55; 37; 46; 47). The main problem is the lack or inadequacy of data, particularly with regard to the testing of M-M models and related financing policies and decisions. The problem is well illustrated by the nature and criticism of the data employed by Krainer and Stevens (44; 45; 98; 3; 81; 66). The available data are inadequate at both the macro and micro levels. Flow of funds and international financial statistics simply do not provide desired detail by country, currency of denomination, or type of financial instrument; data that do exist are often not homogeneous (for example, with reference to default risk characteristics, marketability, tax status), and/or are flawed proxies for desired data (such as, discount and bank rates in lieu of bond market rates) (15, pp. 90, 96; 77, pp. 38, 41).

At the level of the firm, disclosure requirements are not such that information on amount, denomination, and maturity of foreign currency debt is available from corporate financial statements. Indeed, Robbins and Stobaugh have stated that "the parent firm, itself, may not be fully aware of the total amount of over-all system borrowing" (66, p. 355). Data problems, then, include not only those facing the researcher, but those facing the security market participant whose perception of risk and response to perceived risk/return relationships is fundamental to financial market theory.

The measurement of multinationality itself presents problems. In the absence of data on foreign investment by individual firms, the most frequently used measure is that of foreign sales/total sales; this measure includes both foreign production and home-produced exports and thus mixes international trade (including final sales of export goods as well as intracompany transactions) with international investment.

Data problems make us aware of the fact that empirical research results must be greeted with caution. Can the CAPM and M-M theorems be applied realistically and relevantly to multinational enterprise? The financial theory in question has been developed by theorists in industrialized countries with highly developed financial infrastructures, and empirical testing has been limited largely to such countries. The applicability of such work to the multinational enterprise operating in less developed countries is questionable, because the requisite characteristics of capital, money, and foreign exchange markets may not obtain. Thus, the case of the multinational firm operating in less developed countries is one open to both theoretical development and empirical research.

The financial models reviewed here have thus

far largely explicitly or implicitly excluded the joint venture case. Both developed and developing countries may seek to control foreign direct investment by requiring that it be done in the form of a joint venture with a local partner, perhaps a controlling partner; this raises related questions about dividend policy and the interaction between real and financial investment decisions. The interrelationship between the investment decision and the financing decision, still much disputed in the literature with regard to the domestic firm (56; 10; 65), is more complex at the multinational level. Thus, both the joint venture case and the interrelationship between the investment decision and the financing decision in the general multinational case are top candidates for future research.

Another important area for future research is the question of the degree to which the multinational corporation itself serves as an instrument for market integration and greater market efficiency; for example, through intracompany transactions. Further foreign exchange market research is needed to guide multinational corporations' decisions with regard to capital structure, borrowing sources, denominating currencies, and hedging policy. Specific research might be directed to central bank foreign exchange market intervention as a potential channel of influence upon equity and debt costs of the multinational firm. This is part of the broader question of the economic effects of exchange rate fluctuations upon the multinational enterprise and its security holders.

CURRENT STATE OF KNOWLEDGE: FINANCIAL POLICY PRESCRIBED FOR THE FIRM

What policy is prescribed for the firm by the international extensions of theoretical financial models? The basic question to be answered concerns the effect of multinationality upon cost of capital. Several studies of equity pricing employing an international extension of the capital asset pricing model indicate that the common stock of the multinational firm is priced so as to reflect international diversification of risk. The domestic firm if it goes multinational can do so without adverse effect upon its cost of equity; indeed, it may expect a reduction in its cost of equity, ceteris paribus. Although both theoretical and empirical difficulties exist, and none of the studies is without critics, none presents evidence indicating that cost of equity capital is higher for the multinational than for the purely domestic firm, ceteris parabus.[5]

The international extensions of the Modigliani-Miller theorem tend to emphasize reasons for its inapplicability to the multinational firm and lend support to analyses employing the traditional approach that there is an optimal debt/equity ratio or range thereof for the multinational firm. The subject is more complex for the multinational firm than for the domestic firm because of the influence of such factors as international diversification of risk, foreign exchange risk, inconvertibility risk, subsidiary capital structures, tax differentials, and multiple market environments. Existing research does not provide a definitive answer to the question of optimum capital structure for the multinational firm, nor to how it is determined.

Whereas financial markets are more highly internationally integrated than are product and factor markets (77, pp. 33–42), various researchers (34; 66, pp. 356; 102, p. 189) characterize them as incomplete and imperfect, and several researchers believe them to be sufficiently so as to offer possibilities for reduction of cost of debt capital by appropriate choice of borrowing source and currency (14; 40; 66, p. 356; 34, pp. 271–272). Whether this is approached in a portfolio context (40) or in a weighted cost of capital context (85), the operational problem involved in quantifying expected changes in exchange rates is a major one.

Although quantification of expected foreign exchange risk is important for the determination of ex ante cost of debt, it may be argued that the currency in which debt is denominated is irrelevant if, for example, the international Fisher effect holds. Given imperfect foreign exchange markets, the parent is faced with both translation exposure on long-term debt and economic exposure of interest payments and ultimate repayment of principal if local-currency denominated debt is used. Evidence on this question of foreign exchange risk is mixed.

One policy alternative would be that of using short-term local-currency borrowing to hedge current assets, while financing foreign fixed assets with parent equity and/or intracompany debt. This would avoid translation exposure for the parent under FAS No. 8, while the economic exposure accompanying the equity in fixed assets could be regarded as hedged by an assumed long-run tendency toward purchasing power parity. the receptivity of multinational firms to this policy prescription might well depend upon the ratio of fixed assets to total assets in their industry and their evaluation of their degree of exposure to political risk. An alternative policy would be the use of local-currency-denominated long-term debt within a portfolio diversification approach to foreign exchange risk (18, p. 359; 93). This alternative has the advantage of retaining for the firm the greater capital availability associated with use of local borrowing sources. However, the advisability of use of local-currency-denominated long-term debt in the financial structure of the multinational firm remains a controversial question.

NOTES

1. A comparable statement might be made with regard to debt financing, relying not on the M-M thesis but on the international Fisher effect in foreign exchange rate determination. This will be discussed later in the paper.

2. Here, a recent suggestion by Elliott is of interest. In an empirical study of the relationship between cost of capital and aggregate investment, Elliott found that 75 percent of the fluctuation in his weighted average cost of capital measure was due to the fluctuations in tax-adjusted equity costs while only 25 percent was due to fluctuations in debt costs (19, p. 994). Accordingly, he suggested that "monetary policy efforts to influence investment by changing the cost of

capital will have a much greater impact if they succeed in influencing equity costs than if they are primarily confined to debt markets influences" (19, p. 994).

3. This characterization was disputed by Rugman (76; 77, p. 44).

4. There is an extensive literature concerned with the effect of conglomerate diversification upon valuation and debt capacity of the domestic firm; it has been excluded from consideration here.

5. However, in a study of the effects of statement of Financial Accounting Standard No. 8 on security return behavior, multinationals with relatively large investments in foreign assets were shown to have had lower returns than multinationals with relatively low investments in foreign assets in the period 1975–1977 (16, pp. 99–102).

REFERENCES

1. Adler, Michael, "The Cost of Capital and Valuation of a Two-Country Firm." *Journal of Finance,* March 1974, pp. 119–132.

2. ———. "The Cost of Capital and Valuation of a Two-Country Firm: Reply." *Journal of Finance,* September 1977, pp. 1354–1357.

3. ———. "The Valuation of Financing of the Multi-National Firm: Comment." *Kyklos,* Vol. 26, no. 4 (1973), pp. 849–851.

4. ———, and Bernard Dumas. "Optimal International Acqusitions." *Journal of Finance,* March 1975, pp. 1–19.

5. Agmon, Tamir. "The Relations among Equity Markets: A Study of Share Price Co-Movements in the U.S., U.K., Germany and Japan." *Journal of Finance,* September 1972, pp. 839–855.

6. ———, and Donald R. Lessard. "Investor Recognition of Corporate International Diversification." *Journal of Finance,* September 1977, pp. 1049–1055.

7. "A Guide to the Banks and Firms in the Foreign Exchange Advisory Business." *Euromoney,* August 1978, pp. 25–41.

8. Black, F. "International Capital Market Equilibrium with Investment Barriers." *Journal of Financial Economics,* Vol. 1 (1971), pp. 337–352.

9. Chen, Andrew H. "Recent Developments in the Cost of Debt Capital." *Journal of Finance,* June 1978, pp. 863–877.

10. Ciccolo, John, and Gary Fromm. " 'Q' and the Theory of Investment." *Journal of Finance,* May 1979, pp. 535–547.

11. Cohn, Richard A., and John J. Pringle. "Imperfections in International Financial Markets: Implications for Risk Premia and the Cost of Capital to Firms." *Journal of Finance,* March 1973, pp. 59–66.

12. Cooley, Philip L., Rodney L. Roenfeldt, and It-Keong, Chew. "Capital Budgeting Procedures Under Inflation." *Financial Management,* Winter, 1975, pp. 18–35.

13. Dawson, Steven M. "Eurobond Currency Selection: Hindsight." *Financial Executive,* November 1973, pp. 72–73.

14. deFaro, Clovis, and J. V. Jucker. "The Impact of Inflation and Devaluation on the Selection of an International Borrowing Source." *Journal of International Business Studies,* Fall 1973, pp. 97–104.

15. Dufey, Gunter, and Ian H. Giddy. *The International Money Market.* Englewood Cliffs, N.J.: Prentice-Hall, 1978.

16. Dukes, Roland E. *An Empirical Investigation of the Effects of Statement of Accounting Standards No. 8 on Security Return Behavior.* Stamford, Conn.: Financial Accounting Standards Board, 1978.

17. Dumas, Bernard "The Theory of the Trading Firm Revisited." *Journal of Finance,* June 1978, pp. 1019–1030.

18. Eiteman, David K., and Arthur I. Stonehill. *Multinational Business Finance,* 2nd ed. Reading, Mass.: Addison-Wesley, 1979.

19. Elliott, J. Walter. "The Cost of Capital and U.S. Capital Investment: A Test of Alternative Concepts." *Journal of Finance,* September 1980, pp. 981–999.

20. Fama, Eugene F. "The Effects of a Firm's Investment and Financing Decisions on the Welfare of Its Security Holders." *American Economic Review,* June 1978, pp. 27–284.

21. Figlewski, Stephen. "Market 'Efficiency' in a Market with Heterogeneous Information." *Journal of Political Economy,* August 1978, pp. 581–597.

22. Findlay, M. Chapman, III; Alan W. Frankle, et al. "Capital Budgeting Procedures under Inflation: Cooley, Roenfeldt and Chew vs. Findlay and Frankle." *Financial Management,* Autumn 1976, pp. 83–90.

23. Folks, William R., Jr. "Optimal Foreign Borrowing Strategies with Operations in Forward Exchange Markets." *Journal of Financial and Quantitative Analysis,* June 1978, pp. 245–254.

24. Fremgen, James M. "Capital Budgeting Practices: A Survey." *Management Accounting,* May 1973, pp. 19–25.

25. Frenkel, Jacob A., and Richard M. Levich. "Transactions Costs and Interest Arbitrage: Tranquil versus Turbulent Periods." *Journal of Political Economy,* November/December 1977, pp. 1209–1226.

26. Giddy, Ian H. "Exchange Risk: Whose View." *Financial Management,* Summer 1977, pp. 23–33.

27. ———, and Gunter Dufey. "The Random Behavior of Flexible Exchange Rates: Implications for Forecasting." *Journal of International Business Studies,* Spring 1975, pp. 1–32.

28. Goldberg, Michael A., and Wayne Y. Lee. "The Cost of Capital and Valuation of a Two-Country Firm: Comment." *Journal of Finance,* September 1977, pp. 1348–1353.

29. Grauer, F. L. A., R. H. Litzenberger, and R.H. Stehle. "Sharing Rules and Equilibrium in an International Capital Market under Uncertainty." *Journal of Financial Economics,* Vol. 3 (1976), pp. 233–256.

30. Grubel, H. G. "Internationally Diversified Portfolios: Welfare Gains and Capital Flows." *American Economic Review,* December 1968, pp. 1299–1314.

31. ———., and K. Fadner. "The Interdependence of International Equity Markets." *Journal of Finance,* March 1971, pp. 89–94.

32. Hamada, Robert S. "Portfolio Analysis, Market Equilibrium, and Corporation Finance." *Journal of Finance,* March 1969, pp. 13–31.

33. Hartman, David G. "Foreign Investment and Finance with Risk." *Quarterly Journal of Economics,* May 1979, pp. 213–232.

34. Hirshleifer, J. *Investment, Interest and Capital.* Englewood Cliffs, N.J.: Prentice-Hall, 1970.

35. Hodrick, Robert J. "An Empirical Analysis of the Monetary Approach to the Determination of the Exchange Rate." In *The Economics of Exchange Rates,* ed. Jacob A. Frenkel and Harry G. Johnson. Reading, Mass.: Addison-Wesley, pp. 97–116.

36. Hufbauer, G. C. "The Multinational Corporation and Direct Investment." In *International Trade and Finance,* ed. Peter B. Kenen. Cambridge: Cambridge University Press, 1975, pp. 253–319.

37. Hughes, John S., Dennis E. Logue, and Richard James Sweeney. "Corporate International Diversification and Market Assigned Measures of Risk and Diversification." *Journal of Financial and Quantitative Analysis,* November 1975, pp. 627–637.

38. *International Letter.* Federal Reserve Bank of Chicago.

39. Jacquillat, Bertrand, and Bruno Solnik. "Multinationals Are Poor Tools for Diversification." *Journal of Portfolio Management,* Winter 1978, pp. 8–12.

40. Jucker, James V., and Clovis deFaro. "The Selection of International Borrowing Sources." *Journal of Financial and Quantitative Analysis,* September 1975, pp. 381–407.

41. Kohers, Theodor. "The Effect of Multinational Operations on the Cost of Equity Capital of U.S. Corporations: An Empirical Study." *Management International Review,* nos. 2–3 (1975), pp. 121–124.

42. Kohlhagen, Steven W. *The Behavior of Foreign Exchange Markets: A Critical Survey of the Empirical Literature.* Monograph 1978–3, New York University Graduate School of Business Administration, Salomon Brothers Center for the Study of Financial Institutions.

43. Kornbluth, J. S. H., and Joseph D. Vinso. "Financial Planning for the Multinational Corporation: A Fractional Multiobjective Approach." Working Paper No. 5, Graduate School of Business Administration, University of Southern California, October 1979.

44. Krainer, Robert E. "The Valuation and Financing of the Multi-National Firm." *Kyklos,* Vol. 25 (1972), pp. 553–573.

45. ———. "The Valuation and Financing of the Multi-National Firm: Reply." *Kyklos,* Vol. 26 (1973), pp. 857–865.

46. Lee, Wayne Y., and Kanwal S. Sachdeva. "The Role of the Multi-National Firm in the Integration of Segmented Capital Markets." *Journal of Finance,* May 1977, pp. 479–492.

47. Lessard, Donald R. "World, Country, and Industry Relationships in Equity Returns: Implications for Risk Reduction through International Diversification." *Financial Analysts' Journal,* January–February 1976, pp. 2–8.

48. Levich, Richard M. "Tests of Forecasting Models and Market Efficiency in the International Money Market." In *The Economics of Exchange Rates,* edited by Jacob A. Frenkel and Harry G. Johnson. Reading, Mass.: Addison-Wesley, 1978, pp. 129–158.

49. ———. "The Efficiency of Markets for Foreign Exchange: A Review and Extension." In *International Financial Management,* ed. Donald R. Lessard. Boston and New York: Warren, Gorham and Lamont, 1979, pp. 243–276.

50. Levy, H., and M. Sarnat. "International Diversification of Investment Portfolios." *American Economic Review,* September 1970, pp. 668–692.

51. Lewellen, Wilbur G. "A Conceptual Reappraisal of Cost of Capital." *Financial Management,* Winter 1974, pp. 63–70.

52. Lintner, John. "Security Prices, Risk, and Maximal Gains from Diversification." *Journal of Finance,* December 1965, pp. 587–615.

53. ———. "The Valuation of Risk Assets and the Selection of Risky Investments in Stock Portfolios and Capital Budgets." *Review of Economics and Statistics,* February 1965, pp. 13–37.

54. Logue, Dennis E., and Larry J. Merville. "Financial Policy and Market Expectations." *Financial Management,* Summer 1972, pp. 37–44.

55. Logue, Dennis E., Michael A. Salant, and Richard James Sweeney. "International Integration of Financial Markets: Survey, Synthesis, and Results." In *Eurocurrencies and the International Monetary System,* ed. Carl H. Stem, John H. Makin, and Dennis E. Logue. Washington, D.C.: American Enterprise Institute for Public Policy Research, 1976, pp. 91–137.

56. McCabe, George M. "The Empirical Relationship Between Investment and Financing: A New Look." *Journal of Financial and Quantitative Analysis,* March 1979, pp. 119–135.

57. Mehra, Rajnish. "On the Financing and Investment Decisions of Multinational Firms in the Presence of Exchange Risk." *Journal of Financial and Quantitative Analysis,* June 1978, pp. 227–244.

58. Miller, Norman C., and Marina V. N. Whitman. "The Outflow of Short-Term Funds from the United States: Adjustments of Stocks and Flows." In *International Mobility and Movement of Capital,* ed. Fritz Machlup, Walter Salant, and Lorie Tarshis. New York and London: Columbia University Press for National Bureau of Economic Research, 1972, pp. 253–286.

59. Modigliani, Franco, and Merton H. Miller. "The Cost of Capital, Corporation Finance, and the Theory of Investment." *American Economic Review,* June 1958, pp. 261–297.

60. Myers, Stewart C. "Interactions of Corporate Financing and Investment Decisions: Implications for Capital Budgeting." *Journal of Finance,* March 1974, pp. 1–25.

61. Naumann-Etienne, Ruediger. "A Framework for Financial Decisions in Multi-National Corporations: A Summary of Recent Research." *Journal of Financial and Quantitative Analysis,* November 1974, pp. 859–874.

62. Ness, Walter L. "A Linear Programming Approach to Financing the Multinational Corporation." *Financial Management,* Winter 1972, pp. 88–100.

63. Quinn, Brian Scott. *The New Euromarkets.* New York: Halsted Press, 1975.

64. Rendleman, Richard J., Jr., "The Effects of Default Risk on the Firm's Investment and Financing Decisions." *Financial Management,* Spring 1978, pp. 45–53.

65. Reinhart, Walter J. "Discussion of 'The Channels of Influence of Tobin-Brainard's Q on Investment,' " *Journal of Finance,* May 1979, pp. 561–564.

66. Robbins, Sidney, and Robert B. Stobaugh. "Comments." In *International Mobility and Movement of Capital,* ed. Fritz Machlup, Walter Salant, and Lorie Tarshis. New York and London: Columbia University Press for National Bureau of Economic Research, 1972, pp. 354–357.

67. ———. *Money in the Multinational Enterprise.* New York: Basic Books, 1973.

68. Robichek, Alexander A., and Mark R. Eaker. "Debt Denomination and Exchange Risk in International Capital Markets." *Financial Management,* Autumn 1976, pp. 11–18.

69. ———. "Foreign Exchange Hedging and the Capital Asset Pricing Model." *Journal of Finance,* June 1978, pp. 1011–1018.

70. Rogalski, Richard J., and Joseph D. Vinso. "Price Level Variations as Predictors of Flexible Exchange Rates." *Journal of International Business Studies,* Spring–Summer 1977, pp. 71–81.

71. Roll, Richard. "A Critique of the Asset Pricing Theory's Tests." *Journal of Financial Economics,* March 1977, pp. 129–176.

72. ———, and B. H. Solnik. "A Pure Foreign Exchange Asset Pricing Model." *Journal of International Economics,* Vol. 7 (1977), pp. 161–179.

73. Ross, Stephen A. "The Current Status of the Capital Asset Pricing Model (CAPM)." *Journal of Finance,* June 1978, pp. 885–901.

74. Rudd, Andrew, and Wilson Chung. "Implementation of International Portfolio Diversification: A Survey." Mimeographed. September 1978.

75. Rugman, Alan M. "A Note on Internationally Diversified Firms and Risk Reduction." *Journal of Business Administration,* Fall 1975, pp. 182–184.

76. ———. "Discussion: Corporate International Diversification and Market Assigned Measures of Risk and Diversification." *Journal of Financial and Quantitative Analysis,* November 1975, pp. 651–652.

77. ———. *International Diversification and the Multinational Enterprise.* Lexington, Mass.: D. C. Heath, 1979.

78. Rutenberg, David P. "Maneuvering Liquid Assets in a Multinational Company: Formulation and Deterministic Solution Procedures." *Management Science,* June 1970, pp. 45–49.

79. Scott, Davis F., Jr. "Evidence on the Importance of Financial Structure." *Financial Management,* Summer 1972, pp. 45–50.

80. Severn, Alan K. "Investor Evaluation of Foreign and Domestic Risk." *Journal of Finance,* May 1974, pp. 545–550.

81. ———. "The Financing of the Multi-National Firm: Comment." *Kyklos,* Vol. 26, no. 4 (1973), pp. 852–856.

82. Shapiro, Alan C. "Capital Budgeting for the Multinational Corporation." *Financial Management,* Spring 1978, pp. 7–16.

83. ———. "Evaluating Financing Costs for Multinational Subsidiaries." *Journal of International Business Studies,* Fall 1975, pp. 25–32.

84. ———. "Exchange Rate Changes, Inflation and the Value of the Multinational Corporation." *Journal of Finance,* May 1975, pp. 485–502.

85. ———. "Financial Structure and the Cost of Capital in the Multinational Corporation." *Journal of Financial and Quantitative Analysis,* June 1978, pp. 211–226.

86. Sharpe, William F. "Capital Asset Prices: A Theory of Market Equilibrium under Conditions of Risk." *Journal of Finance,* September 1964, pp. 425–442.

87. Solnik, Bruno H. "An Equilibrium Model of the

International Capital Market." *Journal of Economic Theory* Vol. 8 (1974), pp. 500–524.

88. ———. "An International Market Model of Security Price Behavior." *Journal of Financial and Quantitative Analysis,* September 1974, pp. 537–554.

89. ———. *European Capital Markets.* Lexington, Mass.: D. C. Heath, 1973.

90. ———. "Testing International Asset Pricing: Some Pessimistic Views." *Journal of Finance,* May 1977, pp. 503–512.

91. ———. "The International Pricing of Risk: An Empirical Investigation of the World Capital Market Structure." *Journal of Finance,* May 1974, pp. 365–378.

92. ———, and Jean Grall. "Eurobonds: Determinants of the Demand for Capital and the International Interest Rate Structure." *Journal of Banking Research,* Winter 1975, pp. 218–230.

93. Stanley, Marjorie Thines. "Local-Currency Long-Term Debt in the Multinational's Financial Structure." *Atlantic Economic Review,* December 1979, p. 80.

94. ———, and Stanley B. Block. "Portfolio Diversification of Foreign Exchange Risk: An Empirical Study." *Management International Review,* Vol. 20 (1980/1), pp. 83–92.

95. ———. "Response by United States Financial Managers to Financial Accounting Standard No. 8." *Journal of International Business Studies,* Fall 1978, pp. 85–99.

96. Stanley, Marjorie Thines, and John D. Stanley. "The Impact of U.S. Regulation of Foreign Investment." *California Management Review,* Winter 1972, pp. 56–64.

97. Stehle, Richard. "An Empirical Test of the Alternative Hypothesis of National and International Pricing of Risky Assets." *Journal of Finance,* May 1977, pp. 493–502.

98. Stevens, Guy V. G. "Capital Mobility and the International Firm." In *International Mobility and Movement of Capital,* ed. Fritz Machlup, Walter Salant, and Lorie Tarshis. New York and London: Columbia University Press for National Bureau of Economic Research, 1972, pp. 323–353.

99. Stonehill, Arthur, Theo Beekhuisen, Richard Wright, Lee Remmers, Norman Toy, Antonio Pares, Alan Shapiro, Douglas Egan and Thomas Bates. "Financial Goals and Debt Ratio Determinants: A Survey of Practice in Five Countries." *Financial Management,* Autumn 1975, pp. 27–41.

100. Stonehill, Arthur, and Thomas Stitzel. "Financial Structure and Multinational Corporations." *California Management Review,* Fall 1969, pp. 91–96.

101. Vickers, D. "The Cost of Capital and the Structure of the Firm." *Journal of Finance,* March 1970, pp. 35–46.

102. Zenoff, David B., and Jack Zwick. *International Financial Management.* Englewood Cliffs, N.J.: Prentice-Hall, 1969.

15

Capital Budgeting Practices at Multinationals
Vinod B. Bavishi

• • •

What is the theory of capital budgeting for multinational corporations? Do the current capital budgeting practices of U.S.-based multinational corporations coincide with the theory?

Source: Vinod B. Bavishi, "Capital Budgeting Practices at Multinationals," *Management Accounting,* August 1981, pp. 32–35. Copyright © 1981 by National Association of Accountants. Reprinted by permission.

To find out I sent a questionnaire survey to the top financial executives of the 306 largest U.S.-based MNCs. The companies were selected from *Fortune* Magazine's "500 largest United States Industrial Corporations for 1978." Overseas assets for each company in the survey accounted for 10% or more of its total assets and each company was operating in at least four countries as of December 31, 1978. One hundred and fifty-six (156) companies completed and returned the questionnaire—a response rate of 51%, which is unusually high for a voluntary survey and reduces the likelihood of nonresponse bias.

A synthesis of capital budgeting techniques for analysis of the overseas investment described in the literature includes these practices:

1. *Cash flows* should be evaluated from either the parent's or the subsidiary's perspective as long as the underlying assumptions are satisfied. If the foreign subsidiary's viewpoint is used, it should be assumed that unremitted earnings will be reinvested in the host country and eventually be available to the U.S. parent. If some portion of the earnings are blocked (i.e., cannot be remitted in the foreseeable future), then whatever is remittable under the host country laws (i.e., maximum amount of dividend, management fees and royalties allowed), which is the U.S. parent company's viewpoint of cash flow measurement, should be used.

2. *Discounted cash flow methods,* i.e., Internal Rate of Return (IRR) or Net Present Value (NPV) should be used for analyzing project cash flows.

3. *MNCs should use their marginal worldwide weighted average cost of capital* for evaluating investment projects. The formula for this computation includes all sources of long-term financing, including the U.S. parent company's domestic liabilities as well as debts of all foreign subsidiaries. All debt of foreign subsidiaries, whether guaranteed by the parent or not, is included because the debt is, in the long run, that of the parent.

4. The *allowance for risk* in analyzing capital budgeting projects should be done in either of two ways. One approach would be to compute certainty equivalent cash flow in which project cash flows are adjusted for appropriate risk and then discounted at a risk-free discount rate to arrive at NPV. Another method is to use risk-adjusted discount rates to reflect the relative uncertainty of the project's cash streams.

THE NATURE OF THE RESPONSE

Table 1 provides a breakdown of responses by the Fortune 500 companies divided into five groups of 100 each. The highest response rate of 67% was in the first group of 100, possibly indicating their greater interest in the study. Another possible explanation for this distribution may be that the large MNCs have more time and resources available to respond to the questionnaire than do the smaller MNCs.

Table 2 shows a breakdown of sample companies as well as useful responses by industries. The Standard Industrial Classifications (SIC Code) established by the U.S. Office of Management and Budget is used here to group companies into industry groups. A review of the table reveals that major industries are well represented in the study.

A summary of the respondents' departments is presented in Table 1. Their actual titles below the treasurer's level are not summarized here since there was a wide variation (i.e., director, manager, supervisor, coordinator), but almost all of these respondents are in a managerial position in the financial staff function, either in the corporate group or in the international group. It can be safely assumed that respondents are fully conversant with their respective companies' overseas capital budgeting practices.

CURRENT PRACTICE DISCLOSED

The respondents were asked to identify the cash flow used in evaluating overseas investments. Five choices were provided:

1. Before tax cash flow to the foreign subsidiary;
2. After tax cash flow to the foreign subsidiary;
3. Earnings remitted to the U.S. parent;
4. Total cash flows to the U.S. parent, and
5. Total cash flows to the U.S. parent plus reinvested (or remitted) earnings.

The results showed that cash flow from the foreign subsidiary's viewpoint is preferred by

Table 1 Number of MNCs in the Sample and Responses Received

By *Fortune* Rank

Fortune Rank	Sample	Useful Responses Received	% of Sample	% of Total Useful Responses
1–100	82	56	68	36
101–200	70	36	51	23
201–300	63	23	37	15
301–400	47	18	38	11
401–500	44	19	43	12
Unidentified	—	4	—	3
Total	306	156	51	100

Analysis of Respondents' Department

Department (title)	Corporate Group	International Group	Total
Vice president, finance	13	4	17
Controllers/asst. controllers	17	7	24
Treasurers/asst. treasurers	8	6	14
Financial planning	18	3	21
Financial analysis	23	4	27
Capital budgeting	18	4	22
Budgets/costs	6	—	6
Accounting	7	5	12
Administration	—	2	2
External financial communications	2	—	2
Total	112	35	147
Unidentified			9
Total responses			156

42% of the respondents while cash flow from the U.S. parent's viewpoint is preferred by 21% and the remaining 37% of the respondents are using both perspectives together in one form or another (Table 3). Based on this survey, cash flow from the foreign subsidiary's viewpoint is used most.

Then I asked MNC managers which capital budgeting techniques (CBT) they used in analyzing overseas investment projects: Payback Period (PBK), Profitability Index (PI), Return on Investments (ROI), Internal Rate of Return (IRR), or Net Present Value (NPV). Responses were returned from 155 MNCs.

The most popular CBT is PBK, used by 76% of the respondents (but only 1% use it as the sole CBT). PI is used by 10% (none use it as the only CBT), ROI by 63% (4% use it as the only CBT), IRR by 69% (7% use it as the only CBT), and NPV by 40% (2% use it as the only CBT). See Table 4. From the total number of responses to the question, it can be seen that the use of two or more capital budgeting techniques is very common (85% of the respondents use

Table 2 Useful Responses Received by Industry

SIC Code	Industry Titles	MNCs in Sample	Useful Responses Received	% of Sample
10	Mining, crude oil	7	3	43
20	Food	31	17	55
21	Tobacco	4	2	50
22	Textiles, vinyl flooring	2	1	50
23	Apparel	6	3	50
25	Furniture	1	—	0
26	Paper, fiber, wood products	13	6	46
27	Publishing, printing	3	1	33
28	Chemicals	31	17	55
29	Petroleum and refining	22	13	59
30	Rubber, plastic products	7	5	71
32	Glass, concrete, abrasives, gypsum	8	6	75
33	Metal manufacturing	13	5	38
34	Metal products	16	5	31
36	Electronics, appliances	23	7	30
37	Shipbuilding, railroad and transportation equipment	3	2	67
38	Measuring, scientific, photographic equipment	15	6	40
40	Motor vehicles	18	12	67
41	Aeorspace	6	3	50
42	Pharmaceuticals	17	8	47
43	Soaps, cosmetics	7	4	57
44	Office equipment (includes computers)	11	8	73
45	Industrial and farm equipment	31	11	35
47	Musical instruments, toys, sporting goods	4	3	75
48	Broadcasting, motion picture production and distribution	4	2	50
49	Beverages	3	2	67
	Unidentified	—	4	—
	Total	306	156	51

Table 3 Cash Flow Measurement

Method	For All Responses N = 155	
	Number	**Percent**
Cash flow: foreign subsidiary's viewpoint	65	42
Cash flow: U.S. parent's viewpoint	32	21
Cash flow: both foreign subsidiary's and U.S. parent's viewpoint	58	37
Total	155	100

Table 4 Capital Budgeting Techniques

| | All Responses (155 companies responding) | | | | | |
| | Use Technique Exclusively | | Use in Combination with Others | | Total | |
Technique	Number	%	Number	%	Number	%
Payback period	2	1	116	75	118	76
Profitability index	0	0	15	10	15	10
Return on investments	6	4	91	59	97	63
Internal rate of return	11	7	96	62	107	69
Net present value	3	2	59	38	62	40

two or more CBTs). The most popular combinations of CBTs are PBK-ROI-IRR (used by 26 respondents), PBK-ROI-IRR-NPV (by 21 respondents), and PBK-ROI (by 21 respondents).

In a comparison of the use of traditional and discounted capital budgeting techniques, 67% of the respondents said they use both traditional and discounted techniques, 21% of the respondents use only traditional capital budgeting techniques, and 12% of the respondents use only discounted techniques.

The MNCs were asked to identify which rate they use as a base discount rate, or alternatively, how the cost of capital is determined for evaluation of overseas investments. Four choices were given:

1. Determined subjectively;
2. Cost of capital for financing only overseas projects used;
3. Weighted average cost of capital for financing all overseas projects used, and
4. Weighted average cost of capital for worldwide financing used.

One hundred thirty-six out of 155 respondents answered this question (88% of the total respondents). Of those MNCs which indicated that a discount rate is used, 30% determine it subjectively, 27% use only overseas financing costs (either of individual projects or of total

overseas financing), and 43% use weighted average cost of capital for worldwide financing. See Table 5.

As for the methods used in adjusting for project risks, of the 153 companies responding to the question, 14% made no allowance for risks in capital budgeting analysis. Most respondents (70%) stated that subjective adjustment is made by either shortening the minimum payback period, raising the required rate of return or adjusting project cash flows subjectively. Only 16% use a certainty equivalent cash flow concept.

ASSESSMENT OF CURRENT PRACTICE

Survey results indicate that current method used (i.e., total cash flow to the foreign subsidiary and the U.S. parent company) for the measurement of project's cash flow coincide with the theoretically prescribed techniques.

Most of the respondents use discounted cash flow methods (along with traditional methods or separately) for analyzing project cash flows. Therefore, it can be said that the theory and practice are alike in this area. The results also show, however, that a majority of the respondents use two or more techniques. This fact raises a question concerning the use of numer-

Table 5 Methods of Establishing Discount Rate

Method	All Responses (136 Companies Responding)	
	Number	Percent
Determined subjectively	41	30
Overseas cost of capital for overseas financing (either project or all overseas financing considered)	36	27
Weighted average cost of capital for both domestic and overseas financing	59	43
Total	136	100

ous techniques which may result in a confused ranking. Also there are inefficiencies inherent in computing two or more measures when one measure can easily provide sufficient decision criteria. It appears that the traditional methods (i.e., payback method and rate of return on investments) are still widely used, more as secondary indicators for risk and/or profitability. These traditional methods are also used for smaller projects in which detailed analysis may not be justified.

MNC managers might well undertake an evaluation of the techniques they currently use with the objective of eliminating techniques that provide duplicate results.

The results indicated that there is a substantial difference between theory and practice in the area of determination of the discount rate. Theory prescribes use of the MNC's marginal worldwide weighted average cost of capital as a discount rate, while in practice MNCs determine discount rate either subjectively or based upon overseas cost of capital. The difficulties in computing their worldwide weighted average cost of capital, the availability of overseas financing for a specific project (the project would not be undertaken if the financing were not available), and a corporate policy to use a high enough discount rate to allow for errors and uncertainties—all were offered by the inter-

viewed respondents as possible explanations for the differences between theory and practice.

It appears that the gap between theory and current practice can be easily bridged in this area because theory provides workable procedures to compute weighted average cost of capital. MNC managers should consider modifying their current practices to incorporate this calculation in evaluating all investment projects worldwide. Researchers could facilitate this modification by developing case studies using the variety of different financing sources available to today's multinationals and include a step-by-step illustration of the weighted average cost computation.

The majority of respondents adjust for a risk subjectively either by raising the minimum payback period and/or by raising the discount rate. The use of either of these two techniques distorts the project's cash flows because such adjustments are made arbitrarily and the time pattern of the risk variables is not considered. For example, if expropriation is expected at the end of the fifth year, the use of the higher discount rate for all cash flows would penalize cash flow for the first four years.

The respondents expressed dissatisfaction with present methods for adjusting project risks, which they described as too judgmental and arbitrary. The interviewed respondents stated that a possible reason for the gap between theory and practice is that, at present, there are as yet no theoretical models or techniques available which would incorporate all the risk variables involved in the overseas project.

It seems the gap between theory and practice will not be easy to reconcile. But new developments in the theory of finance, especially the capital asset price model (CAPM), have potential for further refinement and may be able to be used by MNCs to evaluate overseas investments.

These findings provide another perspective on the difference between theory and current practice because there are two possible reasons why a particular aspect of overseas investment is difficult to evaluate. First, it may be difficult to evaluate because of unavailability of theoretically prescribed techniques as is the case of adjusting cash flow for project risks. Second, the difficulty may be in evaluation because of the nonutilization of currently available theoretical concepts as is the case with discount rate computations where worldwide weighted average cost of capital is not used.

16

International Financial Planning: The Use of Market-Based Forecasts

Gunter Dufey
Ian H. Giddy

• • •

Corporate planning is an integrated effort by all levels of management to achieve the firm's strategic objectives under future conditions of opportunity, risk, and uncertainty through established forecasting, planning, and budgeting procedures on a regular basis. International corporations face greater risks than domestic ones but also have wider opportunities, and therefore they require a planning system specifically adapted to international market uncertainties.

The formal planning and budgeting process is similar in all large corporations. Based on over-

all strategic business objectives, operating plans originate from product groups or regional business units. These plans are then coordinated at the corporate level and are adjusted in a process of give and take with financial management, which in turn provides information about the availability of funds at various cost levels. Once an agreement has been reached on the volume of assets to be financed, work can begin on a detailed financing plan.

PLANNING AND BUDGETING IN INTERNATIONAL COMPANIES

In multiunit, multijurisdiction organizations such as international corporations, this process is an involved one, since it must be done for every corporate entity. In the end, financial

Source; Gunter Dufey and Ian H. Giddy, "International Financial Planning: The Use of Market-Based Forecasts," Copyright © 1978 by the Regents of the University of California. Reprinted from *California Management Review*, Volume XXI, Number 1, pp. 69–81 by permission of the Regents.

planners in such firms must make decisions about the following issues:

- Should funds be obtained in the form of equity or debt and, if the latter, for which maturity? Alternatively, in which financial instruments should excess funds be invested?

- In which market (and which currency) should funds be raised (invested)?

- What legal entity is to raise (invest) the funds?

- How should funds be transferred from the corporate entity that raises them from third parties to the entity(ies) that need them for investment in productive assets and working capital?

The primary task of international financial management is to minimize the cost of funds and to maximize the return on investment over time, by means of the best combination of currency of denomination and maturity characteristics of financial assets and liabilities. The implementation of these choices, however, requires the formulation and revision of capital structure decisions for various units and budgets for intercompany funds transfers. Only to the extent that financial managers have some influence over these decisions will they be able to take full advantage of the firm's financial planning and forecasting tools described in this article.

FORECASTING REQUIREMENTS OF FINANCIAL PLANNING

The international corporate planning process relies heavily on forecasts of prices, availability of supplies, government actions, competitors' responses, labor conditions, technological development, and so forth. We can conveniently identify three categories of forecasts necessary for corporate planning: (1) forecasts of product market and industry conditions: product demand, industrial activity, and so on; (2) forecasts of conditions within the firm: technical changes in production, labor relations, management needs, and so on, and (3) forecasts of con-

ditions in financial markets: interest rates, funds availability, and so on.

In this article we are concerned chiefly with the forecasts necessary for financial planning. How are such forecasts used? We take as given the timing, amount, and currency of cash outflows and the needs of the firm during the planning period. The financial manager's role is that of planning for the transfer of funds within the firm and for international working capital and funding decisions. Undoubtedly, a large part of this task is to devise the legal entities and arrange the form of international transactions so as to maximize flexibility for corporate funding and transfer needs. Yet we take these as given too, focusing specifically on the decisions that remain when institutional and legal opportunities and constraints have been identified.

What decisions are left? Given the anticipated cash needs or surpluses of various operating units at various dates in the future, and given the constraints on how and where funds can be moved, the financial planners have to decide on the timing, maturity, and currency of denomination that will minimize funding costs, and on the timing and maturity of investments in financial assets.

Decisions about when funds should be raised, and at what maturity, depend on anticipated interest rate movements or changes in the availability of funds, as well as the timing of cash needs. Decisions on the currency of debt depend on expected exchange rate changes, as well as the currency of denomination of funds needs and flows. The million-franc needs of a French subsidiary six months from now, for example, could be met by borrowing French francs when the funds are required. Depending on forecasts of credit and currency market conditions, on the other hand, financial planners may recommend the issuance of long-term debt now (if interest rates are lower than expected in the future) instead of later, or borrowing in dollars instead of francs (if the French franc is regarded as a strong currency).

To summarize: financial planning decisions on timing, maturity, and currency of denomination of financial assets and liabilities require interest rate and exchange rate forecasts. In the next section we shall describe the rather wide range of implicit forecasts provided by the financial and currency markets themselves, and how they relate to one another. Later we suggest the use of such forecasts in financial planning.

THE MARKET'S FORECASTS OF FINANCIAL CONDITIONS

The traditional theory of markets views the price of any good or service (a bicycle or a haircut), and of any financial asset (a bond or a pound sterling), as the outcome of the forces of supply and demand. While few would dispute this basic contention, in recent years the focus of theoretical and empirical research has emphasized the role of *market expectations,* rather than current supply and demand, as the prime determinant of prices and interest rates in financial markets. This fact is of great interest to forecasters, because if present prices and yields embody the market's expectations of future prices and interest rates, it may be possible to determine the market's forecast by looking at competitively determined prices and rates.

Futures prices in commodity markets provide the best available information about the market's forecasts of spot prices. For example, market participants who believe that they have better information about future spot prices of soybeans than do other market participants will attempt to make profits by buying or selling futures contracts. The result is that new information is quickly incorporated into the prices of futures contracts, and the pattern of futures prices reflects the best guesses of well-informed market participants about the path of future spot prices.

We can go further: according to the "efficient market" hypothesis, the market's forecast is

rational, in the sense of being a function of the true determinants of future spot prices, and utilizes all available information in the most efficient way possible. If this is true, the market forecast, and hence the futures price, is the best available estimate of the future price of a commodity.[1] While many do not accept this argument in its pure form, the bulk of evidence in recent years supports the notion that futures prices are unbiased predictors of subsequent spot prices.

While futures prices exist in some uniform raw materials and agricultural commodity markets, these are too few and far between to be of much use to operating management. The market for labor, for example, is too diverse and inefficient for a futures wage rate (if it existed) to be of much use in forecasting labor costs. In contrast, the markets for many currencies and financial instruments are highly efficient and standardized and numerous traders stand ready to exploit perceived profit opportunities whenever they arise.

In the currency market, the market's forecasts are embodied in the forward exchange rate (futures prices). Of course, the forward exchange rate is not an *accurate* forecast, because traders' buy or sell decisions are only based on information available *now.* Not only will the market-based forecast be continually revised as new information reaches the market, right up to the date of the maturity of the futures contract, but the *actual* future price will also deviate from the predicted price because of new information that reaches the market. In fact, even over long periods the forecasting error of the forward rate is not likely to average out to zero.[2]

Thus, over any given period the actual price will turn out to differ from the futures price. The amount C in Figure 1 will usually be positive or negative. But the chances that the actual price will be above or below the futures price are equal. Because price changes result from new information reaching the market, and because new information is by its nature unpre-

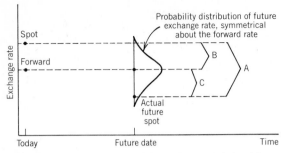

A—Actual exchange rate change: difference between today's and the
actual future exchange rate.
B—Anticipated change: difference between today's spot rate and the
forward rate.
C—Unanticipated change: difference between the forward rate and the
actual future exchange rate.

Figure 1 Exchange rate forecasting using the forward rate.

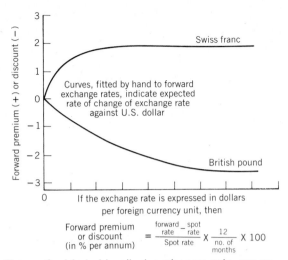

$$\text{Forward premium} \atop \text{or discount} \atop \text{(in \% per annum)} = \frac{\text{forward rate} - \text{spot rate}}{\text{Spot rate}} \times \frac{12}{\text{no. of months}} \times 100$$

Figure 2 Market-implied exchange rate expectations, August 1977.

dictable, the deviation C tends to be randomly distributed about zero. In other words, the *expected value* of the forecasting error C is *zero*.

For financial planning purposes, the forecaster should consider three differences (illustrated in Figure 1). Amount A, the difference between today's exchange rate and the actual future rate, is often thought of as the possible exchange risk. However, by calculating amount B, the difference between today's rate and the market-expected future rate, we are usually able to *anticipate* much of the exchange rate change. Hence, what matters to the planner is amount C, the *unanticipated* exchange rate change; and, as we have seen, this can be positive or negative, and has a zero expected value.

If the forward exchange rate equals the expected future spot rate, we may assume that forward rates for various maturities trace the expected movement of the spot exchange rate in the future. By expressing the forward rate as an annualized discount or premium from the spot rate, as in Figure 2, we can estimate the market forecast of the rate of change of the exchange rate for any period in the future.

We have thus far linked the forward premium or discount to exchange rate expectations. But exchange rate expectations themselves are linked to inflationary expectations, or rather,

expectations about *relative* inflation rates in the two countries. This so-called purchasing power parity relationship simply states that the rate of change of the exchange rate tends over time to equal the difference between inflation rates in two countries.

Further, covered interest arbitrage between two currencies creates a linkage between interest rates and the forward premium or discount. That is, the forward premium or discount tends always to equal the interest rate differential between financial assets denominated in different currencies. The relative interest rates are themselves also linked more or less directly to exchange rate and inflation rate expectations, for one would expect that the country with the higher inflation rate and whose currency is expected to depreciate would also have a higher interest rate.

All these relationships are summarized diagrammatically in Figure 3. As the diagram suggests, while market-based forecasts of expected exchange rate changes can be obtained most directly from spot and forward exchange rates, they can also be obtained from the interest rate differential. By subtracting the domestic from the foreign interest rate we obtain the expected

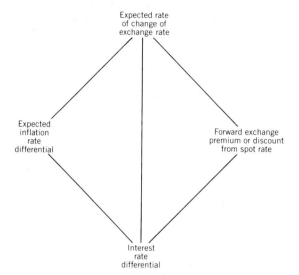

Figure 3 Equilibrium relationships among exchange rates, inflation rates, and interest rates.

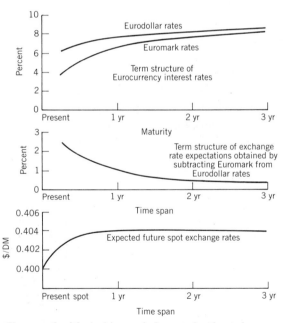

Figure 4 Market-based forecast of exchange rate changes, from interest rate differential. (*Source:* from Gunter Dufey and Ian Giddy, *The International Money Market,* Englewood Cliffs, N.J.: Prentice-Hall, 1978, section on "The Term Structure of Eurocurrency Interest Rates." Used with permission.)

rate of change, and hence the expected path, of the foreign currency's value, as Figure 4 illustrates.

So far, we have talked only of market forecasts of exchange rates (and inflation rates) based on the term structure of forward exchange rates.[3] Can interest rates be forecasted in the same way? In principle, the answer is yes, although the technique for discovering the market's interest rate forecast is usually a little more subtle than that for exchange rates. Nevertheless, the market's forecast for interest rates at almost any date in the future can be estimated by looking at the yield curve on, say, government bonds. The yield curve is a chart that plots the current yields to maturity of a group of securities of various maturities, but which are all equivalent as to credit quality. This "term structure of interest rates" is often upward-sloping, but can also be flat, downward-sloping, or even humped. Figure 5 illustrates three such curves.

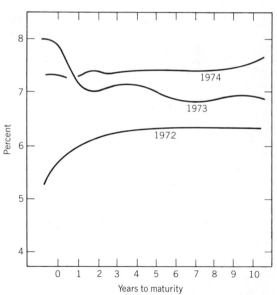

Note: Yield curves are as of each year end. Treasury bill rates are included on a bond-equivalent basis.

Figure 5 Recent yield curves for U.S. government securities. (*Source:* From Morgan Guaranty Trust Co., *The Morgan Guaranty Survey,* July 1977, p. 11.)

In an efficient market, the shape of the yield curve is determined largely by expectations about future interest rates. An upward-sloping curve means interest rates are likely to rise; a downward-sloping one, that a fall is expected.

Long-term rates tend to equal the average of expected future short-term rates; if that were not the case, investors would take speculative actions tending to bid long-term rates up or down until they fulfilled that condition. For example, if interest rate expectations rise so that the average of expected intervening short-term rates is higher than long-term rates, investors will sell long-term bonds and buy short ones, in the expectation of reinvesting the money in short term securities. This will continue until long rates are bid up to the point of reflecting expected future short-term rates.

More specifically, the rate on a nine-month Treasury bill tends to approximately equal the average of today's rate on a three-month bill and the market-expected rate on a six-month bill issued three months from now. If today's three-month rate is 4 percent and the nine-month rate 6 percent, the implied forecast for the six-month rate three months from now is 7 percent. This is because the weighted average of 4 percent for three months and 7 percent for six months is 6 percent. The general method for calculating the market interest rate forecast is shown in Figure 6 (see appendix for formula).

The method just described is the traditional approach and will work whenever rates are free to reach their competitive levels. Recently, however, the development of interest rate futures markets has provided a more direct gauge of interest rate expectations. The prices of futures contracts for three-month Treasury bills and government securities provide a set of market forecasts of near-term interest rate prospects parallel to those available from yield curves. The two approaches should provide identical forecasts. Since contracting to buy a three-month Treasury bill six months from now is exactly equivalent to borrowing at a fixed rate for six months and investing the proceeds in a

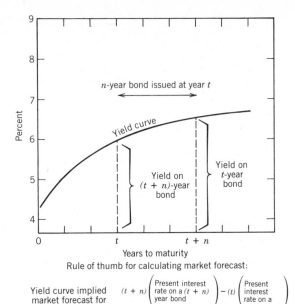

Figure 6 The market forecast implied in the yield curve.

nine-month Treasury bill, interest rate expectations have the same effect on financial futures as they do on the term structure of interest rates. Futures prices for financial instruments are quoted on a discount basis; hence the interest rate forecast implied by a Treasury bill futures contract priced at 96 is $100 - 96 = 4$ percent.

In conclusion, we find that in reasonably efficient and competitive markets for uniform goods or assets, today's prices and rates are strongly influenced by forecasts of future market conditions, and that the term structures of commodity futures prices, forward exchange rates and interest rates provide good readings of the market's forecasts.

At this point, we must address the possibility that market prices of futures, both interest rate futures or forward exchange rates, may not predict future rates in an unbiased fashion. Put differently, the question is whether there is reason to expect that the rate predicted by the forward instrument will be systematically over- or under-estimated. Two possible sources of bias may exist.

First, a bias may result from obvious market imperfections. For example, the existence of extensive credit allocation, heavy-handed administrative barriers to borrowing and lending, and tight exchange controls would provide prima facie evidence for the argument that forward rates may deviate systematically from the expected future exchange rate. On the other hand, the mere presence of controls does not necessarily imply that forward rates or interest rate differentials are biased, for many and devious are the paths of arbitrage. Only when controls on both the credit and foreign exchange markets are effective is a systematic bias likely to be evident. In such cases, forward rates or interest rate differentials provide a good starting point for forecasting and for the identification of profit opportunities, as we shall see below.

More difficult to deal with is the claim of the existence of systematic ex ante deviations, when no such barriers exist. The best known source of biases of this kind is the presence of a liquidity premium inherent in the prediction of short-term interest rates by long-term rates. According to this view, the yields on long-term instruments overestimate future short-term interest rates, just as yields on financial futures contracts are upward biased estimates of expected future interest rates. The empirical evidence on the existence of liquidity premiums is not altogether clear, partially because of the statistical measurement difficulties. More important for our purposes, however, is the fact that estimates of such liquidity premiums have been quite small when they were found at all.[4]

In the case of foreign exchange rates the issue is a bit more difficult, if only because the evidence of market imperfections is more pervasive. Several strands of reasoning can be distinguished. One hypothesizes that because currencies are financial assets issued by different countries, they differ in terms of "political

risk": countries can deprive holders of the use of their money balances, or can otherwise restrict their ultimate use to settle claims.[5]

Another argument supporting systematic forecasting errors has been based on the notion that yield differentials on the same assets denominated in different currencies reflect not only expected exchange rate changes but also a risk premium arising from the possibility that exchange rate changes may be correlated with returns on other assets, creating a systematic risk for speculators that cannot be diversified away.[6] The prevailing conclusion of researchers, however, is that such a "covariance term" is probably small, and that for practical purposes it is virtually impossible to identify any ex ante bias in the absence of specific market imperfections.[7] The equilibrium relationships presented in this section probably provide the most reliable framework for planning purposes.

HOW CAN FINANCIAL PLANNERS USE MARKET-BASED FORECASTS?

We have argued that, in the absence of a systematic bias, the forecasts of interest rates and exchange rate changes contained in the term structure of interest rates and forward rates represent the most realistic point estimate of market expectations. We shall now show why such forecasts should not be used in isolation, but rather as a *benchmark* against which to judge the firm's own ability to forecast or to exploit market imperfections. Given the market-based forecasts, we can distinguish three situations each with distinct implications for the maturity and currency aspects of financial planning.

Situation 1: *When the financial markets in question are reasonably efficient, and financial planners know of no systematic biases or constraints on market rates, then market-based forecasts should be accepted as valid.* Under these conditions, which probably hold for most financial decions involving the U.S. and major international financial markets, no expected gain will result from manipulating the timing or currency of borrowing or investing, and financial management's energies should be directed toward matching borrowings and investments with the timing and currency of the funds needed or generated by the firm's operations.

Although this is a simple principle, its implementation requires a fairly detailed analysis of the firm's cash flows. The application of the above principle to financial planning must begin with the recognition that it is likely that the market's expected value will seldom be attained; indeed every *actual* interest rate and each *actual* exchange rate will be likely to differ from the value that was predicted by the futures or forward rate, respectively.

The use of market-based forecasts then implies planning for the deviations, or forecasting errors, that we know will occur. The first step in the planning process is to obtain a forecast that indicates how deviations around the expected interest rates or exchange rates will affect the entity for which a financial plan is established. This entity can be the corporation as a whole, or one of its affiliates. In the latter case, however, it is imperative to assess not the effects on the operating unit per se, but rather the effect that the change in the expected rate has on the unit's contribution to the return (or net cash flow) of the firm as a whole. In other words, marginal analysis is required.

Specifically, what we want to know is how cash flows from operations (return on assets) will change for any given deviation of the interest or exchange rate from the value predicted. As long as the return on assets is contractually fixed and denominated in a particular currency, as would be a portfolio of bonds or loans, the analysis is quite straightforward. A rise in interest rates will cause a proportional fall in the value of such a fixed-interest portfolio; and a given fall in the exchange rate will lead to an equal drop in the dollar value of the portfolio. Protecting the value of such assets, therefore, simply requires funding the liabilities of the firm in the same currency and maturity as the assets.

Unfortunately, this simple procedure is not applicable to multiunit international manufac-

turing operations. In such a firm, unexpected exchange rate and interest rate changes cause changes in prices, volumes, cost of inputs and similar factors in complex ways. Net cash flows and, therefore, return on assets can be affected positively, negatively, or not at all by a given exchange rate, according to its dependence on imports, its volume of export sales, its ability to raise prices and so forth. Similarly, an interest rate change may be associated with a rise or reduction in demand for the firms' products and have other indirect effects on operating cash flows. It is one of the most important functions of the financial planner to identify the specific cash flow effects that unanticipated interest or exchange rate effects may have for his particular firm. This, of course, is not an easy task.

Apart from the complexity of the analysis, there are technical issues of measurements that must be resolved. Should "return on assets" be measured in accounting terms, or in terms of expected future cash flows?

In periods of inflation, the valuation of assets at historical cost distorts accounting results. When foreign exchange rate changes combine with different rates of inflation and valuation principles based on historical cost, the resulting data differ substantially from those obtained by analyzing the impact of an unexpected exchange rate change on the operating results. The cast flow approach is the correct one; but financial planners who have faced the task of recasting data in pro forma accounting statements will recognize the difficulty of doing so. And if management compensation is tied to accounting results ("the bottom line"), the implementation of financial plans founded on market-based forecasts and deviations from expected cash flow becomes a heroic task. Finally, as to whether stock prices are affected by accounting results that do not reflect the cash flow effect of exchange rate changes, the empirical evidence is at present too scanty to draw conclusions one way or another.

Under the assumption that the market forecasts are the best available, no anticipated gain can be had by changing the maturity or currency mix of liabilities. Hence, the only rational purpose of financial planning in an efficient market is *to structure the firm's liabilities in such a way that any unanticipated change in the return on assets is offset, as far as possible, by a change in the effective cost of liabilities.*

Let us examine the basis for this principle more closely. Manufacturing and other nonfinancial enterprises expect a net profit because they have a competitive advantage in providing goods and services by managing real assets. The role of financial management is to protect this expected profit from unexpected fluctuations in financial market conditions. Since the structure of real assets is determined by fundamental business strategy considerations, the adjustment to offset financial risk must, therefore, occur on the liability rather than the asset side of the firm. We can illustrate the general principle with a few simple examples.

1. A firm operating only in one currency, whose operating cash flows fluctuate with inflation, can afford to fund itself largely with short-term debt, assuming that inflation is also the major influence on short-term rates.
2. On the other hand, a corporation whose operating return is uncorrelated or negatively correlated with short-term interest rates is well advised to borrow long-term at fixed interest rates in order to stabilize its funding costs and thereby reduce the impact of unanticipated interest changes on final net cash flows.
3. Since the cost of foreign currency debt is directly correlated with unexpected exchange rate changes, the application of our general principle to foreign cash flows is quite straightforward. When a unit's operating returns are positively correlated with a currency's value, that unit should be funded in the same currency, because any unanticipated depreciation of the currency reduces not only returns from operations, but also the effective cost (interest rate plus/minus exchange rate change) of the liabilities.

It is, of course, very rare that the change in the net cash flow on the asset side will be completely offset by a change on the liability side; hence, a residual risk will always remain. However, it is an essential part of the task of financial planning management to gauge the magnitude of such risks and to communicate it effectively to top management. The function of top management is to decide whether this risk is tolerable, or whether operations must be restructured to reduce the basic sensitivity of the corporation to unanticipated changes in interest and exchange rates. Such operational adjustments often involve far-reaching strategic decisions: a change of markets and marketing (long-term contractual sales), a change in sources of supplies, the degree of in-house production versus purchases from outside suppliers, and perhaps even a change in the choice of technology to be employed in the production process.

The financial planning framework laid out above assumes the market's forecasts are unbiased predictions of future interest and exchange rates. Often, specific market imperfections will not allow this assumption to hold. The next two sections consider the implications of such biases.

Situation 2: *When the term structure of interest or exchange rates deviates in a systematic way from the market's actual expectations because of government controls on interest rates and exchange rates, or because of other specific market imperfections, financial management has profit opportunities.* The exploitation of these opportunities requires (a) a flexible legal and operational structure, and (b) an explicit trade-off function that permits management to decide whether the gains are worth the increase in risk that the exploitation of market imperfections may involve.

Government intervention in credit and foreign exchange markets through administrative action, such as interest rate ceilings, quantitative credit allocation, or selection restrictions on international fund transfers tends to keep both interest rates lower and exchange rates higher than market participants think they should be. By the same token, such administrative controls imply that government limits access to credit and foreign exchange markets, thereby deciding who obtains credit and foreign exchange and the profits that are inherent in such favored positions. It is here that international firms as producing, job-creating enterprises with legal entities operating in many countries, centrally coordinated by corporate financial planning, have an advantage in arbitraging between actual rates and expected rates.

Unlike pure financial operators who could exploit profit opportunities only by contravening government laws and regulations, international firms can legally circumvent these restrictions, provided their financial activities are properly coordinated—and this is what financial planning is all about. Government controls tend to be always partial, never comprehensive. The reason is simple: controls on *all* borrowing or lending, and *all* international transfers of funds would cause economic activity to come to a grinding halt. Therefore, with regulations permitting certain transactions, and funds being fungible, international firms with diverse legal structures and a multitude of intercompany links usually are in a privileged position to exploit the financial windfalls that government actions provide by keeping interest rates low and preventing exchange rates from adjusting to market presssures.

Sometimes the maturity and currency of debt that will best capitalize on such market opportunities is close to that which would have been chosen merely in order to offset fluctuations in asset returns. However, decisions become complicated when the financial management must consider a maturity or currency structure that would increase the overall risk of the firm, but whose cost is less than the risk-minimizing alternative because of government controls of the type described above. In this case, top management must provide indications of how much more risk it is willing to accept in return for the lower cost of funds. Again, the task of financial planning is to clearly communicate the dimensions of the choice to top management in order to aid it in this crucial decision.

In many respects, situation 2—where market-based forecasts deviate from forecasted rates because of specific market imperfec-tions—is similar to the situation which we discuss next.

Situation 3: *When the market-based forecasts deviate from forecasted rates, not because of market imperfections but because the firm has some proprietary information or unusual forecasting ability, then financial managers should act on their forecasts only when the risks of doing so are offset by the expected gains.* When financial planners can confidently answer the question, "Why do we believe we can predict interest or exchange rates better than the market?" their focus should be on the proper perspective on the risks involved in speculative actions, and on a rapid response to opportunities when action is warranted.

Few financial managers can consistently resist the temptation to base financing decisions on their own judgments rather than those of the market. In most cases little harm is done, for unless the firm really goes out on a limb, positive and negative forecasting errors tend to cancel out over time. But the mark of a good financial manager is not his knack for occasionally outguessing the market's forecasts, but rather his ability to obtain the highest return on invested assets, for a given level of risk, and the best long-run terms and conditions on debt, *irrespective* of the trend of interest rates or exchange rates. It is important for the integrity of the financial management process to keep these aspects of the function strictly separate. Otherwise, the inability of financial management to outperform the markets tends to be hidden in the results of the risk-management function.

Speculative actions in financial markets should be vigorously segregated from the other functions of financial managers, and subjected to separate policy guidelines and scrutiny. A strategy for performance evaluation of the financial forecasting abilities of financial management is suggested in the next section.

MARKET-BASED FORECASTS AS YARDSTICKS FOR BUDGETING AND PERFORMANCE EVALUATION

We began this article with a discussion of corporate planning and budgeting; in this last section we shall try to show how market-based forecasts of financial data have applications in operating budgets and management control as well as in financial planning.

For multinational corporations with decentralized operating units, Robbins and Stobaugh have argued cogently that the prime tool for goal-setting and performance evaluation should be the periodic budget that is set jointly by financial planners and operating managers, and revised in the light of changing conditions.[8] On the other hand, few dispute the gains to be had from a centralized control of intracompany cash flows in order to respond to changing currency, interest rate, taxation, and exchange control developments. For our purposes, this means that operating units, such as foreign subsidaries, should not be held responsible for interest rate or exchange rate developments.[9] Yet all budgets must explicitly or implicitly incorporate a cost of funds, and budgets for foreign operations must be translated at some exchange rate. What interest and exchange rates should be used?

Most corporations calculate the cost of funds using a standard interest rate based on past borrowing costs and translate foreign subsidiaries' cash flow projections at the exchange rate prevailing at budget date. That approach would be fine if the firm were somehow guaranteed the same interest rate and exchange rate for the entire budget period. When subsidiary managers are not held responsible for the impact of deviations from the budgeted exchange and interest rates, it surely makes more sense to use projected interest costs and exchange rates for budget preparation and performance evaluation than to use past rates. In the past, firms without access to a reliable exchange rate and interest rate forecasting service may have been reluctant to make such projections. The availability of costless market-based forecasts of interest and exchange rate tends, however, leaves them with no such excuse.

The market's forecasts may not be very accurate, but they will certainly result in fewer errors than the implict assumption that today's rate is the appropriate projection. In addition, market rates have the virtue of being objective.

If operating managers are not held responsible for deviations of the actual cost of funds and exchange rate from the budget rates, then the financial managers whose task is to manage intercompany cash flows and transactions in the credit and foreign exchange markets must be made accountable for the impact of unanticipated interest rate and exchange rate changes. Here we find an additional virtue to the use of market-based forecasts for budgeting and performance evaluation purposes. We have argued that if financial managers choose to reject the market forecasts as a basis for financing, investment and currency decisions, they are implicitly asserting their own ability to "beat the market."

Can they do so? Only time will tell, but it will tell very explicitly if the consequences of actions based on the financial managers' *own* forecasts are consistently evaluated against the results of actions based on the *market's* forecasts. Either method of forecasting will result in errors, but the financial decision maker is justified in relying on his own forecasts only if doing so results in a superior average track record than would reliance on the market-based forecasts.

No financial manager can reasonably be blamed for being unable to predict unanticipated events in the financial system, but all managers should be evaluated against the dual criteria that (a) the cost of any effort to forecast interest and exchange rates should be justified on the basis of better-than-market performance, and (b) the recognition that forecasting errors are inevitable and that the prime task of financial management is to structure the firm's cash flows in such a way that the impact of such errors is minimized.

CONCLUSIONS

The message of this article is as follows: corporate planning and budgeting relies in large part on projections of conditions in various markets, including those for the firm's products and services, labor and other inputs, credit, and foreign currencies. Management attention, we argue, should be concentrated on those markets in which the firm has a competitive advantage. Since the market's forecasts—implicit in the term structure of interest rates and of forward exchange rates—are readily available in the financial markets, which are both competitive and efficient, and in which the firm is unlikely to have a particular advantage, there is an a priori rationale for making borrowing and investment decisions based on these forecasts.

On the other hand, where financial managers feel they have a peculiar advantage in such financial markets, resulting from the firm's legal structure, geographical locations or because of an unusual forecasting ability, then the timing, maturity, and currency of borrowing and investment decisions should be based on the firm's own forecasts whenever the expected gains justify the risks. However, the risks and ex post performance of the decisions taken should always be compared against the outcomes of decisions based on market-based forecasts. The market's projections constitute the best benchmark for the evaluation of financial management's performance.

NOTES

1. To be precise, market efficiency need not imply that future prices are unbiased forecasts. For an exposition of the efficient markets argument, see Aldich A. Vasicek and John A. McQuown, "The Efficient Market Model," *Financial Analysts Journal*, September–October 1972, pp. 71–82.
2. See, for example, Robert Ankrom, "Among Their Hedges, Treasurers May Miss the Obvious," *Euromoney*, December 1977, p. 99.
3. The precise formulas for these linkages between interest rates, forward exchange rates, and currency and inflation rate expectations may be found in Ian H. Giddy, "An Integrated Theory of Exchange Rate Equilibrium," *Journal of Financial & Quantitative Analysis*, December 1976.
4. See studies cited in A. E. Burger, R. W. Lang, and R. H. Rasche, "The Treasury Bill Futures Market and Market Expectations of Interest Rates," *Federal Reserve Bank of St. Louis—Monthly Review*, July 1977, p. 5.
5. R. Z. Aliber, "Exchange Risk, Political Risk, and Investor Demand for External Currency Deposits," *Journal of Money, Credit and Banking*, May 1975, pp. 161–179.
6. Versions of this idea can be found in Michael C. Adler and Bernard Dumas, "Portfolio Choice and the Demand for Forward Exchange," *American Economic Review*, May 1976, pp. 332–339, and Bruno H. Solnik, "The International Pricing of Risk: An Empirical Investigation of the World Capital Market Structure," *Journal of Finance*, May 1974, pp. 365–379.
7. See Jeffrey A. Frankel, "On the Mark: A Theory of Floating Exchange Based on Real Interest Differentials," unpublished manuscript, Massachusetts Institute of Technology, October 1977, Appendix A.
8. Sidney M. Robbins and Robert B. Stobaugh, "The Bent Measuring Stick for Foreign Subsidiaries," *Harvard Business Review*, September–October 1973.
9. These issues are discussed in some detail in Donald R. Lessard and Peter Lorange, "Currency Changes and Management Control: Resolving the Centralization/Decentralization Dilemma," *Accounting Review*, July 1977.

APPENDIX

The exact formula for the term structure implied interest rate forecast is

$$ {}_t r_{t+n} = \left[\frac{(1 + {}_0R_{t+n})^{t+n}}{(1 + {}_0R_t)^t} - 1 \right]^{\frac{1}{n}} $$

where ${}_t r_{t+n}$ is the implied interest rate on a bond starting at t and maturing at $t + n$, ${}_0R_{t+n}$ is today's interest rate on a bond of maturity $t + n$, and ${}_0R_t$ is today's interest rate on a bond of maturity t. All interest rates are expressed as decimal fractions rather than as percentages.

17

Denomination Decision for Multinational Transactions

Mark R. Eaker

• • •

INTRODUCTION

One area of financial management that has been largely ignored is the denomination decision for international transactions. Because the denomination issue relates to the sourcing of funds decision, some of the results of the work on that problem can be applied to the denomination question; however, the structure of the denomination question lends itself to resolution by decision rules that can be chosen with less information about future exchange rates.

Deciding which currency to denominate transactions in is an important consideration for firms operating in a multi-currency environment. This is true for both inter- and intracompany dealings. In the former, the choice determines the extent to which each party is exposed to exchange risk. In the latter, the decision has important tax implications and, therefore, a significant effect on profitability.

This paper demonstrates that the denomination decision for intracompany transactions can affect the firm's cash flows. It then develops simple decision rules that allow firms to determine the most favorable currency of denomination for intracompany transactions. The models make use of market-based information and do not require superior forecasting ability. Evidence is presented related to the predictive ability of the forward exchange rate. Finally, a simulation shows the potental value to a firm that follows one of the decision rules developed in the paper.

THE IMPACT OF TAX EFFECTS

Shapiro (7) demonstrates that tax differentials between countries can influence the choice of the source of subsidiary financing for the multinational firm. In analyzing an intracorporate loan, he correctly indicates that such a transaction does not carry any net exchange exposure for the consolidated firm, although either the subsidiary or the parent will be subject to taxation of exchange gains or losses.

No net exposure exists because the consolidated firm has both the asset and liability positions related to the loan. However, since the asset and liability to the loan. However, since the asset and liability positions are held by separate entities for tax purposes, then either the debtor or creditor will experience an exchange gain or loss if there is exchange variation. A loss will result in a tax saving, a gain in an additional tax payment. Shapiro's contribution is recognizing that tax effect, although he does not show that the firm can denominate the intracompany loan in such a way as to place the expected tax effect in the most favorable jurisdiction. Another funding option is that the parent firm can make a foreign currency loan to the subsidiary. Moreover, the same decision, and resulting benefit, can be applied to any intracompany credit transaction, whether it be an interest bearing loan or normal trade financing involving non-interest bearing receivables and payables.

Rodriguez and Carter (6) and Prindl (4) both discuss the possibility of locating losses and

Source: Mark R. Eaker, "Denomination Decision for Multinational Transactions," *Financial Management,* Volume 9, Autumn 1980, pp. 23–29. Copyright © 1980. Reprinted by permission.

gains in the most favorable tax environment. The Rodriguez and Carter treatment is particularly good, but like Prindl's it does not offer a formal analysis of the strategy or a means of implementing it.

A derivation of the benefit that might accrue to a firm from correctly denominating its transactions is provided in the appendix. In the general case, the benefit is a function of the tax rates, interest rates, and the current and future exchange rates between the two countries. Without specifying the exact relationships among those variables, it is not possible to derive any simple decision rule to follow in making the denomination decision. The only unknown in the formula is the future spot rate, S^{t+1}, so firms can calculate (in general) the expected value of denominating transactions in each currency by forecasting S^{t+1}. However, it is possible to develop helpful decision rules that firms can beneficially follow for two special cases.

The first case assumes the validity of the international Fisher effect and the equality of effective tax rates. The Fisher effect states that interest rate differentials reflect market expectations of changes in exchange rates. Aliber and Stickney (1), in discussing the implications of the Fisher effect for translation of accounting statements, offer empirical evidence supporting its validity. One implication of the Fisher effect is that a firm should be indifferent between denominating debt in either of two currencies because the interest cost or saving is offset by the exchange gain or loss. This is no longer true for intracorporate transactions once the impact of taxes is considered.

The derivation in the appendix calculates the benefit (d) for this special case. It demonstrates that the major implication of the Fisher effect does not hold for intracorporate transactions and that, as long as the interest rates differ, there is an advantage to denominating in one of the currencies. In intracorporate transactions, there is no actual exchange gain or loss, just a tax effect. With equal tax rates, the firm still benefits by creating the largest possible exchange loss or the smallest possible gain for tax purposes. Because tax gains and losses are based on nominal (and predictable, if the Fisher effect is assumed to hold) and not real values, correct denomination decisions result in a gain

---

Exhibit 1. The Optimal Currency Denomination for Intracompany Transactions*

Case II. Equal tax rates and the Fisher effect

	Parent Receivable		Parent Payable	
	$r_{us} > r_f$	$r_{us} < r_f$	$r_{us} > r_f$	$r_{us} < r_f$
	$ (tax gain in U.S.)	FC (tax loss in foreign country)	FC (tax loss in U.S.)	$ (tax gain in foreign country)

Case III. Non-interest bearing transactions

	Parent Receivable		Parent Payable	
	$t_{us} > t_f$	$t_{us} < t_f$	$t_{us} < t_f$	$t_{us} < t_f$
$ appreciates	FC (tax loss in U.S.)	$ (tax loss in foreign country)	$ (tax gain in foreign country)	FC (tax gain in U.S.)
$ depreciates	$ (tax gain in foreign country)	FC (tax gain in U.S.)	FC (tax loss in U.S.)	$ (tax loss in foreign country)

*t_{us} is the effective tax rate in the U.S.; t_f is the effective tax rate in the foreign country; FC is the foreign currency.

for the firm. The appropriate choices are shown in Exhibit 1 for the case of equal taxes and the Fisher effect.

(It is worth pointing out that, if the Fisher effect holds but taxes are not equal, then there is still an advantage to making the correct decision; that decision, though, will depend upon the relative sizes of the expected exchange rate change and the tax differential. The general solution developed in the appendix can be used for determining the right choice and its expected value.)

The second special case in which a simple decision rule can be followed to the benefit of the firm involves non-interest bearing transactions. This case is particularly relevant, because many intracorporate transactions involve non-interest bearing trade credit. The value of making the correct decision is derived in the appendix as Case III, and the decision rule to be followed in order to reap the benefits is presented in Exhibit 1.

The case in the exhibit assumes that the transaction occurs between a U.S. parent and its foreign subsidiary. The preferred denomination decision depends on whether the parent has a payable or a receivable, since that determines whether there is a gain or loss and whether the exposure lies with the parent or the subsidiary. Exhibit 1 is divided into two parts, indicating the correct decisions for both receivables and payables.

As an example, assume that the U.S. parent ships $1000 = FC1000 worth of parts to the subsidiary, providing 30-day credit on the receivable. If during the interim the dollar appreciates in value, either the parent or the subsidiary will have a loss for tax purposes. If the receivable were denominated in dollars, the foreign currency cost to the subsidiary would increase. Had the foreign currency unit been used to denominate the transaction, the parent would have had a loss, because the dollar value of the foreign currency receivable would be lower. Since the loss is tax deductible, it is in the interest of the firm to place it in the higher tax environment. The amount of the tax gain is determined by the size of the exchange variation and the tax differential.

PREDICTING EXCHANGE RATE VARIATION

Implementation of the decision rule requires the firm to be able to predict the direction of exchange rate change. There are a number of ways a firm might do this. Its economics staff might carry out fundamental analysis of balance of payments factors. It might subscribe to one or more forecasting services or rely on the forward rate as an objective market prediction. Obviously, the choice will depend on the relative success of the method, its cost, and the value of making the correct decision. Goodman (2) analyzes the predictive success of several different forecasting sources, and his results can provide some guidance in selecting the best method for a particular firm's needs.

The forward rate is the least expensive, most easily obtained predictor of the direction of exchange rate variation. Without arguing that it is necessarily the best predictor, we can test whether it is sufficiently reliable to provide benefits to a firm using it in order to implement the model developed in this paper.

There is a well-developed literature exploring the theoretical basis for using forward rates as predictors of future spot rates, with an equally vast accompanying empirical literature. [See Kohlhagen (3).] That research analyzes a more general predictive power than is studied here. For this model to be useful, there is no need to predict exchange rates, only whether the expected future spot rate is higher or lower than the current spot rate. In other words, the forward rate is tested to see if it outperforms a random prediction of the direction of change.

The test uses six currencies—those of Canada, Japan, Switzerland, the United Kingdom, the United States, and West Germany—during the period from January 1973 through

December 1978. The period was chosen to roughly coincide with the adoption of generally floating rates. The currencies represent the major trading currencies.

On the first of each month the 30-, 60-, and 90-day forward rates were calculated for each possible combination of currency pairs; the rates were then compared to the spot rate to determine whether it predicted an appreciation or depreciation. That prediction was then matched with the relevant subsequent spot rate to see if the prediction were correct. Non $US cross rates were used in order to increase the sample size and also to emphasize that this model is applicable to all intracorporate transactions. The use of cross rates and the three maturities provided 38 test samples. 60-day rates were not available for Japan, which reduces the number of samples. For all of the currency pairs except those involving Japan, there were 70 observations. The yen data do not begin until March 1974, resulting in 55 observations.

The results of the test are summarized in Exhibit 2. The results indicate the number of correct predictions out of the maximum possible.

Comparison of the results to the results of a random prediction process, 50% correct, shows that forward rates perform substantially better. In only five cases did the forward rate do worse than a random selection, and none of these was statistically significant. On the other hand, in seventeen cases it was significantly better at either a 5% or 1% confidence level.

Two interesting findings merit additional comment. First, the forward rate's success is greater with currency pairs that experienced the most variation during the period. That seems to be consistent with one's prior belief that any prediction of the direction of movement around a point will be more accurate if the size of the movement is greater. If a 5% depreciation is predicted, then the point estimate can be considerably off without reversing the direction of change. If the actual movements reflect the size of a priori estimates of the changes, then the observed results follow.

Second, the forward rate does better for longer maturities than for shorter ones. In part, this is related to the first point, in that the expected and actual movements are greater over time. In addition, if exchange rate movements

Exhibit 2. The Predictive Ability of the Forward Rate, 1973–1978

		Japan	Switzerland	U.K.	U.S.	W.G.
Canada	30 day	36*	47†	38	31	41
	60 day		46†	35	34	44*
	90 day	38†	50†	36	34	46†
Japan		31	37†	27	25	
			34	45†	31	29
Switzerland				50†	46†	38
				54†	42	40
				58†	45*	38
United Kingdom					35	42
					40	45*
					37	46†
United States						39
						41
						43*

*5% significance.
†1% significance

Source: Exchange rate data on which these results and others in the paper are based come from *The Wall Street Journal* and the *Journal of Commerce.*

are determined by such fundamental factors as inflation, monetary growth, and balance of payments, then the longer period would allow for the market response to dominate short-term government intervention.

THE VALUE OF CORRECT DECISIONS

For the case involving non-interest bearing credit, the benefit, d, to the firm making the correct denomination decision for a transaction that spans a period of time from t to t + 1 is

$$d = \left| \times \left[\frac{S^{t+1}}{S} - 1 \right] [t_f - t_n] \right|$$

where x   is the amount of the transaction measured in home currency units;

      S   is the spot rate of home currency per foreign currency unit at the time the transaction is entered into;

      S^{t+1} is the spot rate at the time the transaction is completed;

      t_f is the effective foreign tax rate, and

      t_n is the effective home tax rate.

The derivation of d is presented in the appendix.

For any particular transaction or series of transactions, the benefit that accrues to the firm is a positive function of the change in exchange rates, the tax differential, and the size of the transactions. By making some simplifying assumptions about the latter two elements it is possible to get a measure of the importance of the denomination decision during the period of this study, and to see how much of the potential benefit would have been enjoyed by a firm employing the forward rate decision rule suggested in this paper.

If it is assumed that at the beginning of each 30-, 60-, and 90-day period a U.S. parent acquires a receivable owned by a foreign subsidiary, and further if it is assumed that the effective U.S. tax rate is .10 higher than the foreign tax rate, then D can be calculated for the period 1973–1979. It should be understood that D is the summation of d; that is, D represents the total benefit from always making the correct decision.

The simulation deals only with Case III, although a similar study could be performed for either the general case or the other special case. Case III was chosen because it involves fewer assumptions, and because non-interest bearing trade credit represents a large percentage of intracorporate transactions.

Exhibit 3 provides a summary of the calculations under the assumptions stated above. Column (a) gives the value of D for each currency and maturity. The value of D for 30-day transactions between the U.S. parent and the Canadian subsidiary is .0589. That indicates that, if at the beginning of each month the U.S. parent acquired a $1,000,000 receivable with a 30-day maturity, making the correct denomination decision for each transaction over the 6-year period would result in a $58,900 savings over always making the wrong decision. Column (b) indicates the benefit that would be earned if the forward rate decision rule is followed. It was calculated by summing the d's for those 30-day periods in which the forward rate correctly predicted the direction of exchange rate variation. For the 30-day Canadian transactions, $33,900 or 58% of the potential benefit would have been reaped.

It is unlikely that any company would always make the incorrect decision, but rather that the company would follow a naive strategy, such as denominating all transactions in the parent's currency or using the currency of the country of the unit acquiring the receivable. Column (c) of Exhibit 3 presents the value of the correct decisions that could be made if a policy of always denominating in $U.S. were followed.

The naive strategy does relatively well in the simulation. With $t_{us} > t_f$, the correct decision, given a depreciating dollar, would be to denominate in dollars. Through much of the period used for this study, the dollar was comparatively weak, making this particular naive

Exhibit 3. The Value of Correctly Denominating $U.S. Transactions

	(a) Perfect Information	(b) Forward Rate	(c) Naive Strategy
Canada			
30	.0589	.0339	.0210
60	.0885	.0496	.0283
90	.1131	.0635	.0325
Japan			
30	.0932	.0586	.0662
90	.2158	.1478	.1672
Switzerland			
30	.2015	.1414	.1469
60	.3329	.2266	.2562
90	.4105	.2967	.3289
United Kingdom			
30	.1206	.0677	.0525
60	.2113	.1356	.0899
90	.2828	.1767	.1149
West Germany			
30	.1696	.0987	.1127
60	.2821	.1734	.1972
90	.3467	.2201	.2503

strategy a good one. This point is reinforced by results showing that the naive strategy performed best when followed for currencies that were strongest relative to the dollar during the period.

Note, however, that implicit in the results of Exhibit 3 are results for an alternative naive strategy of always using the subsidiary's currency. It is the complement of Column (c) when compared to the value of perfect information. Overall, this would have been a much less satisfactory strategy to have followed. The important point is that ex post some naive strategy can be found that for particular situations performs quite well, but that ex ante it is beneficial to rely on a theoretically and empirically valid predictive model.

SOME CAVEATS CONCERNING IMPLEMENTATION

Although the model and decision rules developed in the paper offer substantial gains to firms employing them, their implementation involves some potential problems, both internal and external, for the firm. The internal problems relate primarily to the performance evaluation of managers of subsidiaries, while the external ones arise from different national tax policies and the perception of the firm as being in compliance with those policies.

The model used in this study assumes that the tax treatment on exchange gains and losses is symmetrical and the same in every tax jurisdiction. Neither of those assumptions is true, a fact which does not invalidate the use of this approach but which does necessitate some caution in implementing it. First, many countries apply asymmetrical rules to the taxation of exchange gains and losses. Often gains are considered taxable income, whereas losses are not deductible for tax purposes. In such circumstances, the model can still yield benefits by locating expected gains in the low tax environments and any losses in a jurisdiction where they are tax deductible.

A related point is that the relevant tax rates to use are the effective marginal rates that apply to the firm's earnings. Various tax breaks used to induce firms to invest, as well as tax provisions such as tax carry forwards, can influence what the effective rate is, and these must be considered.

The final issue or problem external to the firm deals with the firm's image as a good corporate citizen. The use of the model developed in this paper might be likened to the use of transfer pricing in that it takes advantage of tax differentials. For that reason, a firm could be exposed to criticism for altering its denomination policies to conform with the decision rules given previously. However, unlike transfer pricing, this model involves ''arm's length'' decision-making. The firm is not altering prices or manipulating the level of profits arbitrarily. The firm is using objective, market-based information in order to make its decision. It cannot rig the outcome as in transfer pricing, a distinction which should carry weight with tax authorities. Each firm will have to determine for itself whether the political environment in a particular country is conducive to using this model.

Within the firm, a problem might arise because the use of the model locates exchange gains and losses in particular countries, therefore affecting the profitability of the subsidiaries. Since most managers are either directly or indirectly evaluated on the basis of their contribution to profits, managers in countries in which losses are positioned would be unfairly treated. Robbins and Stobaugh (5) have analyzed that problem and its solution in detail, but its importance in the implementation of this technique cannot be overemphasized.

Finally, it must be reiterated that the success of this model depends on the forecasting of the direction of exchange variation. The forward rate, probably the most accessible means of forecasting, is shown here to be a successful forecasting technique, one that results in favorable denomination decisions. If there are other forecasting techniques that outperform the for-

ward rate, then their use will yield even greater benefits to the firm.

NOTES

1. Robert Z. Aliber and Clyde P. Stickney, ''Accounting Measures for Foreign Exchange Exposure: The Long and Short of It,'' *Accounting Review*, January 1973, pp. 44–57.
2. Stephen H. Goodman, ''Foreign Exchange Rate Forecasting Techniques: Implications for Business and Policy,'' *Journal of Finance*, May 1979, pp. 415–427.
3. Steven W. Kohlhagen, ''The Behavior of Foreign Exchange Markets: A Critical Survey of the Empirical Literature,'' NYU Graduate School of Business Administration, Monograph Series in Finance and Economics (Salomon Brothers Center), No. 1978–3.
4. Andreas Prindl, *Foreign Exchange Risk* (New York: John Wiley & Sons, 1976).
5. Sidney Robbins and Robert Stobaugh, ''The Bent Measuring Stick for Foreign Subsidiaries,'' *Harvard Business Review*, September–October 1976, pp. 80–88.
6. Rita M. Rodriguez and E. Eugene Carter, *International Financial Management*, 2nd ed. (Englewood Cliffs, N.J.: Prentice-Hall, 1979).
7. Alan C. Shapiro, ''Evaluating Financing Costs for Multinational Subsidiaries,'' *Journal of International Business Studies*, Fall 1975, pp. 25–32.

APPENDIX. DERIVING THE VALUE OF CORRECT DECISIONS

The value to the firm of making the correct denomination decision can be calculated by modeling a representative intracompany transaction that includes the tax effects of interest payments, income, and exchange variation on both the parent and the subsidiary. First, the general case is analyzed, and then two important special cases are looked at, using the general results. In all three cases, it is assumed that the United States parent wishes to denominate its transactions with its foreign subsidiary in order to maximize the after-tax cash flow related to the transactions, measured in $U.S. at the time the transactions are completed.

Case I. The General Denomination Decision

If the $ is the unit of denomination, then the impact in $s on the parent and subsidiary is as follows:

Parent: $\quad x(1 + r_{us}) - x(r_{us})(t_{us})$

Subsidiary: $\quad - x(1 + r_{us}) + x(r_{us})(t_r) -$

$$\frac{x(1 + r_{us})(S^{t+1} - S)(t_f)}{S}$$

where

$x \quad =$ the \$ amount of the transaction (a negative indicates a payable);

$S \quad =$ the spot rate of exchange, \$/FC, at the time of the transaction;

$S^{t+1} =$ the spot rate that applies at the time of repayment;

$t_f \quad =$ the tax rate in the foreign country, and

$r_{us} \quad =$ the interest rate for transactions denominated in dollars.

If the foreign currency is used to denominate the transaction, the parent and subsidiary positions would be:

Parent: $\quad \dfrac{x}{S}(1 + r_f)(S^{t+1}) -$

$\dfrac{x}{S}(r_f)(S^{t+1})(t_{us}) +$

$\dfrac{x}{S}(1 + r_f)(S - S^{t+1})(t_{us})$

Subsidiary: $\quad - \dfrac{x}{S}(1 + r_f)(S^{t+1}) +$

$\dfrac{x}{S}(r_f)(S^{t+1})(t_f)$

where r_f is the interest rate for transactions denominated in the foreign currency.

If the results of the two choices are compared, the difference, d, in terms of dollars of using \$s instead of FC units to denominate the transaction can be calculated. Collecting terms,

$$d = (x) \left| (r_{us})(t_f - t_{us}) + \frac{(r_f)(S^{t+1})(t_{us} - t_f)}{S} + \frac{[S^{t+1} - S][(1 + r_f)(t_{us}) - (1 + r_{us})(t_f)]}{S} \right|.$$

An absolute value is used to reflect that the correct denomination decision will vary according to whether the parent has a payable or receivable. This derivation is perfectly general and not dependent upon any particular relationship between the variables. However, two special cases will demonstrate how decision rules regarding the denomination decision can be determined.

Case II. The Tax Rates are Equal and the International Fisher Effect Holds

$$t_{us} = t_f = t; \; r_{us} - r_f \cong \frac{S^{t+1}}{S} - 1$$

$$d = (x) \left| (t)(1 + r_f)(r_{us} - r_f) - (t)(1 + r_{us})(r_{us} - r_f) \right|.$$

In this case, as long as there is an interest differential, then there is an advantage to denominating the debt in the currency with the highest nominal rate.

Case III. The Transactions are Non-Interest Bearing

$$r_f = r_{us} = 0$$

$$d = (x) \left| \left[\frac{S^{t+1}}{S} - 1 \right] [t_{us} - t_f] \right|$$

If no change in the value of the currency occurs or no tax differential exists, there is no benefit related to the denomination decision. However, if there is a tax differential and the future exchange rate is expected to differ from the current rate, the benefits will accrue to the firm if the correct currency is chosen. The correct decisions are shown in Exhibit 2.

18

Covering Foreign Exchange Risks of Single Transactions: A Framework for Analysis

Jorge R. Calderon-Rossell

• • •

In a flexible exchange rate system, firms and individuals face foreign exchange risk in any international transaction.[1] They have to consider the possibilities to hedge or cover foreign currency-denominated assets or liabilities. Although covering and hedging are terms used to distinguish between the protection of foreign currency cash flows and the so-called exposure of the balance sheet, in this paper both are used interchangeably.

The literature does not seem to provide a general framework for analyzing the coverage of foreign exchange risks of single transactions. Single transactions are defined as the transactions carried out by "occasional" exporters, importers, or international finance investors.[2] This paper reviews the basic alternatives available to hedge foreign exchange risk of single transactions and presents a general framework for evaluating the cost of coverage of those alternatives. I also introduce an outline for choosing between the alternatives, including the development of formulas to arrive at the required estimates. Finally, the procedure is illustrated with a numerical example in an appendix.

The basis of the general framework is the type of cash flow analysis used in capital budgeting. For exposition, only the forward exchange market and money market strategies (5), in addition to the do-nothing case, will be discussed. The framework introduced here, how-

ever, could be applied to analyze other alternatives.

This discussion assumes that economic transactions are evaluated in terms of the U.S. dollar. The same analysis could be extended to another currency. Also assumed is the viewpoint of an occasional exporter (or importer) who will acquire assets (liabilities) denominated in a foreign currency.

Analysis is based on the assumption that the value of assets (liabilities) denominated in foreign currencies is subject to change only as a result of the exchange rate fluctuations. The accounts receivable (or payable) considered in this discussion are then assumed to be non-interest-bearing, although the same principles apply for interest-bearing assets (liabilities). Results of the analysis for the latter case are presented in Appendix A.

Assume an exporter acquires an asset denominated in a foreign currency unit (fc) to be received one year later (an account receivable). In this case, the exporter is subject to an exchange gain (loss) if the domestic currency, during that period, depreciates (appreciates) vis-à-vis the foreign currency in which the asset is denominated. To eliminate this uncertainty, i.e., the foreign exchange risk, the trader could sell foreign currency units (or buy dollars) in the forward market at a specified forward rate with the same maturity as the asset.

These transactions are represented in graphic form in Exhibit 1. Downward arrows represent outflows or investments, upward arrows inflows or disinvestments. At time t, an asset (account receivable) valued at P foreign currency units is acquired, which will in fact be received

Source: Jorge R. Calderon-Rossell, "Covering Foreign Exchange Risks of Single Transactions: A Framework for Analysis," *Financial Management*, Volume 6, Autumn 1979, pp. 78–85. Copyright © 1979. Reprinted by permission.

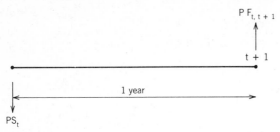

Exhibit 1 Cash flows of the acquisition of an asset denominated in a foreign currency unit, to be received one year later, covered in the forward market.

one year later, $t + 1$. These single cash flows, however, are evaluated in dollars ($), the currency of concern, and for this reason P foreign currency units are converted at the current spot rate (S_t) at time t, and the forward rate ($F_{t, t+1}$) accepted at time t for an exchange at time $t + 1$. (The quotations of the foreign exchange rates are given in dollars over foreign currency, i.e., $/fc.)

In this framework, the asset PS_t is equivalent to an investment (downward arrow) which would produce a revenue $PF_{t, t+1}$ (upward arrow) one period later.[3] The internal rate of return on this cash flow would be the cost of coverage, which for the forward market case can be expressed as follows:

$$C_F = \frac{PF_{t, t+1} - PS_t}{PS_t} \qquad (1)$$

Reducing common terms, this is equivalent to

$$C_F = \frac{F_{t, t+1} - S_t}{S_t}, \qquad (2)$$

and in percentage terms:

$$C_{F,\%} = \frac{F_{t, t+1} - S_t}{S_t} \cdot 100\%. \qquad (3)$$

Considering that the asset (liability) is denominated in foreign currency, and that the quotation of the rates is given in terms of $/fc, a negative sign will represent a loss or true cost (gain or profit), and a positive value will represent a gain or profit (loss or true cost) from the dollar point of view. A summary of these results and conditions is presented in Exhibit 2.

THE COST OF COVERAGE IN THE MONEY MARKET

Rather than covering the exchange risk of single transactions in the forward market, the literature sometimes suggests use of the money market (5). In this case, the investor or exporter matches assets (liabilities) with liabilities (assets) denominated in the same foreign currency and maturity, borrowing the foreign currency (domestic) and simultaneously investing at domestic (foreign) money market rates. The relative differential between money market interest rates (ignoring transactions costs) would determine the losses or gains of the investor and therefore the cost of covering in the money market.

In such a case, the following transactions will take place (see Exhibit 3 for a graphic presentation): 1) The exporter will acquire an asset valued at P foreign currency units with a maturity of one year. The evaluation in dollars of those cash flows is made considering the cur-

Exhibit 2. Cost of Coverage in the Forward Market = C_F*

Case	True Cost ($C_F < 0$)	Gain ($C_F > 0$)	No Loss or Gain ($C_F = 0$)
Asset	$F_{t, t+1} < S_t$	$F_{t, t+1} > S_t$	$F_{t, t+1} = S_t$
Liability	$F_{t, t+1} > S_t$	$F_{t, t+1} < S_t$	$F_{t, t+1} = S_t$

*The relationship will be reversed if the quotation of the rate is the inverse of $/f.c., although the figures of the cost of coverage will differ.

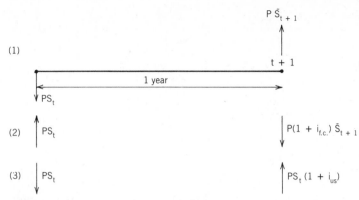

Exhibit 3 Cash flows of the acquisition of an asset denominated in a foreign currency unit, to be received one year later, covered in the money market.

rent spot rate, S_t, and the one-year spot rate, $\tilde{S}_{t+1}$, which is unknown; 2) In order to match the assets denominated in a foreign currency, the trader borrows at a foreign money market interest rate (i_{fc}) the same amount of the same foreign currency. This means that at time t there is an inflow of P foreign currency units (PS_t in dollars) and at time t + 1 there is a payment of $P(1 + i_{fc})$, $P(1 + i_{fc})\tilde{S}_{t+1}$ in dollars), and 3) The exporter now has PS_t additional dollars which could be invested at the domestic money market rate, i_{us}. Therefore, at time t there is an investment of PS_t dollars, and one year later there is a receipt of $PS_t (1 + i_{us})$ dollars.

The results of these three transactions will be equivalent to acquiring, at time t, a foreign asset

valued at P foreign currency units (PS_t dollars) for which $P[S_t(1 + i_{us}) - i_{fc}\tilde{S}_{t+1}]$ dollars will be received at time t + 1. These net cash flows are represented in Exhibit 4. The cost of coverage in the money market (C_m), equivalent to the internal rate of return of these cash flows (Exhibit 4), will be a random variable:[4]

$$\tilde{C}_m = \frac{P[S_t (1 + i_{us}) - i_{fc} \tilde{S}_{t+1}] - PS_t}{PS_t}. \quad (4)$$

Simplifying:

$$\tilde{C}_m = \frac{[S_t i_{us} - \tilde{S}_{t+1} i_{fc}]}{S_t} \quad (5)$$

and in percentage terms:

$$\tilde{C}_{m\%} = \frac{[S_t i_{us} - \tilde{S}_{t+1} i_{fc}]}{S_t} \cdot 100\%. \quad (6)$$

Rewriting Equation (5) as follows:

$$\tilde{C}_m = i_{us} - i_{fc} \cdot \frac{\tilde{S}_{t+1}}{S_t}, \quad (7)$$

Exhibit 4 Net cash flows of the acquisition of an asset denominated in a foreign currency unit, to be received one year later, covered in the money market.

$$P [S_t (1 + i_{us}) - i_{f.c.}\tilde{S}_{t+1}]$$

```
t                                    t + 1
|————————————————————————————————————|
         1 year
|
↓
P S_t
```

Exhibit 5. Cost of Coverage in the Money Market $= \tilde{C}_m$*

Case	True Cost $(\tilde{C}_m < 0)$	Gain $(\tilde{C}_m < 0)$	No Loss or Gain $(\tilde{C}_m = 0)$
Asset	$\lambda < \tilde{S}_{t+1}$	$\lambda > \tilde{S}_{t+1}$	$\lambda = \tilde{S}_{t+1}$
Liability	$\lambda > \tilde{S}_{t+1}$	$\lambda < \tilde{S}_{t+1}$	$\lambda = \tilde{S}_{t+1}$

*The relationships and the figures of the cost of coverage hold if the quotation of the rate is the inverse of \$/fc.

it is easy to see that, as the exporter is investing at the dollar rate, i_{us} (in the case of the asset), he will have a gain if the cost of coverage in the money market is positive, $\tilde{C}_m > 0$, a loss or true cost if $\tilde{C}_m < 0$, and no loss or gain if $\tilde{C}_m = 0$. However, in the case of a liability denominated in a foreign currency, funds are borrowed at the domestic money interest rate, i_{us}, and invested at the foreign money interest rate, i_{fc}; therefore the cost of coverage in the money market, $\tilde{C}_m$, would be the opposite to the asset case.

A summary of the results and conditions of the cost of coverage in the money market case is presented in Exhibit 5, based on the following transformation of Equation (7).

$$\tilde{C}_m = \frac{i_{fc}}{S_t} \left[\frac{S_t i_{us}}{i_{fc}} - \tilde{S}_{t+1} \right] \qquad (8)$$

and defining

$$\frac{S_t i_{us}}{i_{fc}} = \lambda.$$

FORWARD MARKET VERSUS MONEY MARKET COVERAGE

In addition to disregarding transactions costs and accounting issues[5] as before, it is necessary to make the following considerations: (1) It may not be possible to perfectly match the maturities of the assets and liabilities in either the forward market or the money market; (2) In dealing with some particular currencies, there is no possibility to cover in the forward market simply because there is no forward market for that

currency; (3) The cost of coverage in the forward market, assuming this alternative is feasible, will be known with certainty. All the intervening variables—Equations (1), (2), or (3)—are known at the time the transaction is made, and (4) The cost of coverage in the money market, assuming this alternative is also feasible, will be uncertain. This cost is ultimately determined by the future spot rate which cannot be known a priori.

However, assuming that the forward market and money market coverage are feasible, it is necessary to evaluate the cost differential of these two alternatives.[6] Continuing with the case of acquiring an asset denominated in foreign currency, it is possible to estimate the difference of the cost of coverage [comparing Equations (2) and (7)], as follows:

$$\tilde{\delta} = \frac{F_{t,\,t+1} - S_t}{S_t} - (i_{us} - i_{fc} \frac{\tilde{S}_{t+1}}{S_t}). \quad (9)$$

The value of this difference, $\tilde{\delta}$, also a random variable, will determine the preference between the forward and the money market. A summary of the preferred alternative for the asset and liability case is presented in Exhibit 6.

In order to choose between the forward and money market hedging strategies, an estimate of the differential, $\tilde{\delta}$, is necessary. As the underlying uncertainty of this difference stems from the level of the future spot rate, $\tilde{S}_{t+1}$, this has to be estimated first. For this purpose, a given set of probabilities is assigned to estimates of the most likely, the highest, and the lowest values of the future spot rate, which is assumed independent of time.[7] With these estimates, $\tilde{S}$,

Exhibit 6   Preferred Coverage Based on the Cost of Differential $\tilde{\delta}$.

Case	$\tilde{\delta} > 0$	$\tilde{\delta} < 0$	$\tilde{\delta} = 0$
Asset	Forward market	Money market	Indifference
Liabilities	Money market	Forward market	Indifference

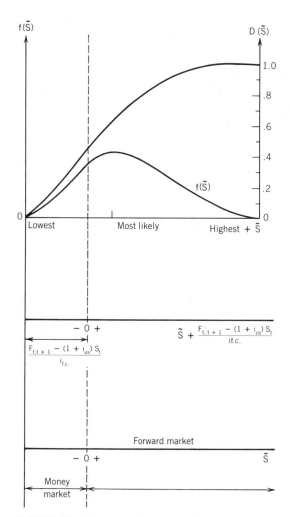

Exhibit 7 Choosing between the forward and money market hedging strategy based on estimates of the spot exchange rate.

we determine the difference of the cost of coverage, $\tilde{\delta}$, and its respective probabilities. The procedure is illustrated and further explained in Exhibit 7, based on Equation (10) below, which is a convenient transformation from Equation (9). (For a numerical example, see Appendix B.)

$$\tilde{\delta} = (\frac{i_{fc}}{S_t}) \left[\tilde{S} + \frac{F_{t,\,t+1} - (1 + i_{us})\, S_t}{i_{fc}} \right]. \quad (10)$$

From Exhibit 6, the U.S. exporter can determine the cases in which cover in the forward market will be preferred, as well as the cases in which the money market will be preferred. From the cumulative distribution, the probabilities that the differential, $\tilde{\delta}$, will be in a given range are estimated. Based on this range, the probabilities that favor a given alternative, and the risk preference of the investor, he is able to choose between a forward or money market coverage. From Exhibit 7, it is evident that a risk-averse investor will prefer a forward market coverage if he has an asset denominated in foreign currency units.

It is also interesting to note that if the term

$$\frac{F_{t,\,t+1} - (1 + i_{us})\, S_t}{i_{fc}}$$

is positive, then the cost differential is always going to be positive ($\tilde{\delta} > 0$). Therefore, the only logical decision will be to cover in the forward market. Thus, whenever $F_{t,t+1} > (1 + i_{us})\, S_t$, the forward market coverage for the asset case is immediately selected, while the money market is preferred in the liability case. Note also that the only uncertainty present would be in the determination of the level of the cost differential but not in the choice of the alternative. If, rather than calculating the cost differential, the exporter wants to estimate the cost of coverage in the money market, he could carry out an analysis similar to the one discussed above[8] based on Equation (11), a convenient transformation from Equation (7).

$$\tilde{C}_m = \frac{-i_{fc}}{S_t} \left[\tilde{S}_{t+1} - \frac{i_{us}S_t}{i_{fc}} \right]. \quad (11)$$

THE COST OF NOT COVERING

Investors may choose not to cover or hedge. Also, perhaps there is no possibility to hedge. In such cases, the cost of not covering could be found in a manner similar to that used in the forward market case. Substituting the uncertain future spot rate, $\tilde{S}_{t+1}$, for the forward rate in Equation (2), we determine the cost of not covering:

Steps:

1. Estimate the probability distribution, $f(\tilde{S})$, of the spot foreign exchange rate. (Note that the exchange rate can only have positive values because it is just a relative price.) This distribution can be estimated assuming the most likely rate and the foreseen lowest and highest rates. Now the cumulative distribution, $D(\tilde{S})$, is determined. From this it is possible to find the probabilities in favor of the forward or money market coverage.

2. Observe that in equation (10) the second term in the brackets represents a shift in the origin of the scale of $\tilde{S}$. The value of the term:

$$\frac{F_{t, t+1} - (1 + i_{us}) S_t}{i_{fc}}$$

will be considered negative for the purpose of this illustration. Thus there is a new scale considering that this term is known.

3. The scale found in Step 2, according to equation 10, will be transformed multiplying it by i_{fc}/S_t to obtain $\tilde{\delta}$, the differential between the cost of coverage in the forward and in the money market.

$$\tilde{C}_u = \frac{\tilde{S}_{t+1} - S_t}{S_t}. \quad (12)$$

We can estimate the gains or losses of not covering, i.e., of doing nothing, following a similar procedure as the one outlined in Exhibit 7. What would be the cost differential between covering and not covering? The estimate of the cost differential between not covering [Equation (12)] and covering in the forward market [Equation (2)] then will be:

$$_u\tilde{\gamma}_f = \frac{\tilde{S}_{t+1} - F_{t, t+1}}{S_t}, \quad (13)$$

and the difference of not covering and covering in the money market will be [from Equation (12) and Equation (5)]:

$$_u\tilde{\gamma}_m = \frac{(1 + i_{fc})}{S_t} \left[\tilde{S}_{t+1} - \frac{(1 + i_{us}) S_t}{(1 + i_{fc})} \right] (14)$$

The value of these cost differentials, $_u\tilde{\gamma}_f$ and $_u\tilde{\gamma}_m$, will determine whether an investor should not cover or cover in the forward or money markets. The preferred alternatives for each case are presented in Exhibit 8.

Considering that, on an *ex ante* basis, these differentials are uncertain, they should be es-

Exhibit 8 Preferred Alternative Based on Cost Differential $_u\tilde{\gamma}_f$ ($_u\tilde{\gamma}_m$).

Case	$_u\tilde{\gamma}_f > 0$ ($_u\tilde{\gamma}_m > 0$)	$_u\tilde{\gamma}_f < 0$ ($_u\tilde{\gamma}_m < 0$)	$_u\tilde{\gamma}_f = 0$ ($_u\tilde{\gamma}_m = 0$)
Asset	Not Cover	Forward Market Coverage (Money Market Coverage)	Indifference
Liability	Forward Market Coverage (Money Market Coverage)	Not Cover	Indifference

timated with a procedure similar to that outlined in Exhibit 7. Equation (13) makes it evident that the cost differential between doing nothing and covering in the foreign market is determined by how well the forward market is able to predict the future corresponding spot rate. Similarly, in Equation (14), the difference between covering in the money market and doing nothing is determined by how well the foreign exchange rate follows the interest rate parity theorem.

SUMMARY

This paper has introduced a general procedure to evaluate covering strategies for foreign exchange risk of single transactions. Although the approach could be extended to analyze any hedging strategy, only the basic alternatives of the forward and money markets have been discussed and illustrated. These hedging strategies have also been compared with the not-covering alternative.

If one recognizes that the only uncertainty involved in the evaluation of the cost of covering and not covering stems from the unknown future spot rate, the general procedure to estimate those costs should be based on the expected values of the future spot rate. Based on these estimates, this framework helps to choose—in a systematic form—whether or not to cover foreign exchange risks.

REFERENCES

1. Gunter Dufey, *Politica Finanziaria di un'Impresa in un Contesto di Oscillazioni del Tasso di Cambio*, PADOVA, CEDAM, 1975, paper presented at the Meeting of the International Fiscal Association, Rome, October 14, 1974.
2. David K. Eiteman and Arthur I. Stonehill, *Multinational Business Finance*, Reading, Mass., Addison-Wesley Publishing Co., 1973.
3. Herbert Grubel, *Forward Exchange, Speculation, and the International Flow of Capital*, Stanford, Stanford University Press, 1966.
4. Charles N. Henning, William Piggot, and Robert Hanley Scott, *International Financial Management*, New York, McGraw-Hill Book Co., 1978.
5. Rita Rodriguez and E. Eugene Carter, *International Financial Management*, Englewood Cliffs, N.J., Prentice-Hall, 1976.
6. Franklin R. Root, *International Trade and Investment*, Cincinnati, South-Western Publishing Co., 1978.
7. Robert M. Stern, *The Balance of Payments*, Chicago, Aldine Publishing Co., 1973.
8. J. Fred Weston and Bart W. Sorge, *Guide to International Financial Management*, New York, McGraw-Hill Book Co., 1977.

APPENDIX A

The complete generalization of the formulas presented previously is shown below, assuming that the assets (liabilities) denominated in a foreign currency are earning (paying)[9] an interest i_a compounded every M^{th} period. The number of periods in a year is M, and the maturity of the asset (or liability) is equal to N periods of a year. The other variables remain the same, but the timing now refers to the Nth period. Furthermore, in the case of the money market coverage it is assumed that the amount borrowed (or loaned) of foreign currency is equal to $P\left(1 + \dfrac{i_a}{M}\right)^N$. All the interest rates are expressed on an annual basis.

The formulas are presented without proof (available upon request), numbered according to the comparable equation in the text and in a form in which the suggested analysis can be pursued:

$$C_F = \left[\frac{\left(1 + \dfrac{i_a}{M}\right)^N F_{t,\,t+N} - S_t}{S_t}\right] \frac{M}{N} \qquad (A\text{-}2)$$

$$\tilde{C}_M = \frac{\left(1 + \dfrac{i_a}{M}\right)^N \left[1 - \left(1 + \dfrac{i_{fc}}{M}\right)^N\right]}{S_t} \cdot \frac{M}{N}$$

$$\left[\tilde{S}_{t+N} + \frac{S_t\left[\left(1 + \frac{i_{us}}{M}\right)^N\left(1 + \frac{i_a}{M}\right)^N - 1\right]}{\left[1 - \left(1 + \frac{i_{fc}}{M}\right)^N\right]} \right] \quad \text{(A-11)}$$

$$\left\{ S_{t+1} - \frac{S_t\left[\left(1 + \frac{i_{us}}{M}\right)^N\left(1 + \frac{i_a}{M}\right)^N - 1\right]}{\left(1 + \frac{i_{fc}}{M}\right)^N} \right. $$

$$\left. + \frac{\dfrac{1}{\left(1 + \frac{i_a}{M}\right)^N}}{\left(1 + \frac{i_{fc}}{M}\right)^N} \right\} \quad \text{(A-14)}$$

$$\delta = \frac{\left(1 + \frac{i_a}{M}\right)^N\left[1 - \left(1 + \frac{i_{fc}}{M}\right)^N\right]}{S_t}\left(-\frac{M}{N}\right)\left\{ \tilde{S}_{t+N} - \right.$$

$$\frac{F_{t,\,t+N} - S_t\left[\left(1 + \frac{i_{us}}{M}\right)^N\left(1 + \frac{i_a}{M}\right)^N - 1\right]}{\left(1 - \left(1 + \frac{i_{fc}}{M}\right)^N\right)}$$

$$\tilde{\delta} - \frac{i_{fc}}{S_t}\left\{ \tilde{S} + \frac{F_{t,\,t+1} - S_t\left[1 + \frac{i_{us}}{4}\right]}{\frac{i_{fc}}{4}} \right\}. \quad \text{(B-1)}$$

$$\left. + \frac{\dfrac{1}{\left(1 + \frac{i_a}{M}\right)^N}}{\left(1 - \left(1 + \frac{i_{fc}}{M}\right)^N\right)} \right\} \quad \text{(A-10)}$$

APPENDIX B. NUMERICAL EXAMPLE

The following hypothetical case does not purport to reflect rates. It is used only to illustrate the procedure described in this paper. Suppose a U.S. exporter sold merchandise to a German importer, to be paid in 90 days in Deutsche Marks. The U.S. exporter is interested in covering the value of his Deutsche Mark (DM) denominated assets against foreign exchange rate fluctuations, and he has the alternative of covering in the forward or money market. Which alternative would be preferred? At the time the transaction takes place, the following information is available: (1) U.S. money market interest rate per year: 6.95%, which is assumed to be constant for the investment period; (2) German money market interest rate per year: 8%, which is also assumed to be constant for the investment period; (3) Actual spot rate: $S_t = \$0.4705/$ DM, and (4) Actual 90-day forward rate: $F_{t,\,t+1}$

$$\tilde{C}_u = \left[\frac{\left(1 + \frac{i_a}{M}\right)^N \tilde{S}_{t+N} - S_t}{S_t} \right] \cdot \frac{M}{N} \quad \text{(A-12)}$$

$$_u\tilde{\gamma}_f = \left(1 + \frac{i_a}{M}\right)^N \cdot \frac{M}{N}\left[\frac{\tilde{S}_{t+N} - F_{t,\,t+N}}{S_t} \right] \quad \text{(A-13)}$$

$$_u\tilde{\gamma}_m = \frac{\left(1 + \frac{i_a}{M}\right)^N\left(1 + \frac{i_{fc}}{M}\right)^N}{S_t} \cdot \frac{M}{N}$$

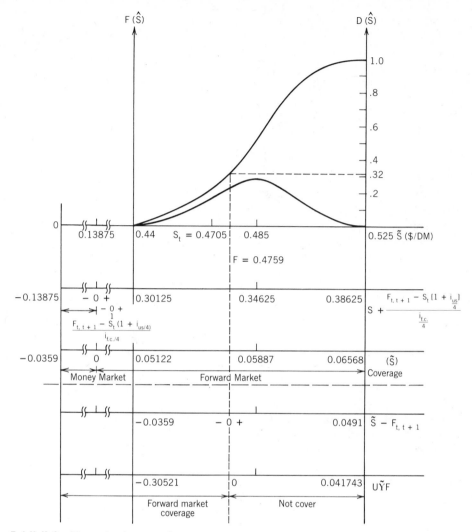

Exhibit 9 Numerical example.

= \$0.4759/DM. (90-day = ¼ of a year). Furthermore, the U.S. exporter estimates the following future spot rates:

(1) Lowest value: \$0.44/DM; (2) Most likely value: \$0.485/DM, assumed also to be the median value. Thus, 50% of the time the rate is expected to be below this rate, 50% above, and (3) Highest value: \$0.525/DM.

Based on this information and the future spot estimates, a graph can be drawn (see Exhibit 9).

Because the maturity of the assets is 90 days (¼ of a year), Equation (A-10) is used rather than Equation (10) where a maturity of one year has been assumed. It is also known that the account receivable is not earning interest, therefore $i_a = 0$; the number of periods (quarters) in a year, M, is equal to 4, and, as the asset matures in the first period, N is equal to 1. Thus, for this example Equation (A-10) can be rewritten in general as:

Considering that the cost differential, δ, for the expected range of future spot rates (see Exhibit 9) is always positive, this implies that the forward cover is cheaper than the money market coverage: therefore, we should cover in the forward market and obtain a gain (see Exhibit 6). The money market should be considered only if the future spot rate would be below $0.13875/DM, but in this case the probabilities of this happening are considered to be zero.

The U.S. exporter now analyzes the alternative of not covering vis-à-vis covering in the forward market. Applying Equation (A-13), the cost differential, $_u\bar{\gamma}_f$, between these alternatives is found. In this case it is necessary to compute the certainty equivalent, because the cost differential has positive and negative values as opposed to the previous case. Based on Equation (A-13) and with the aid of Exhibit 9, it is estimated that: $E(u_{\bar{\gamma}F}) = +0.07736$ and the standard deviation is approximately $\sigma = 0.165$. Although the cost differential—certainty equivalent—(see Exhibit 8) favors the do-nothing case, the final decision would depend on the risk preference of the investor.

An extremely risk averse investor may prefer to cover in the forward market to obtain a certain gain of 4.6%, while a speculator may prefer not to cover, expecting to earn 12.3% (expected value) but subject to risk ($\sigma = 16.5\%$).

NOTES

1. Foreign exchange risk, defined as the potential change in the domestic currency value of cash flows denominated in foreign currencies, exists in all foreign exchange systems. However, considering that the basic analysis could be similar, the discussion hereafter will be developed focusing on a flexible exchange system.

2. The foreign exchange risk of single and continuous transactions has been differentiated in the literature (1).

3. The acquisition of an account receivable is equivalent to an outflow or investment to be held until the account is due, in this case one year. For different maturity periods, see generalized expressions in Appendix A.

4. Evidently, in the money market case there is still uncertainty about the final cost of covering; however, the investor has to assess this cost to select his preferred hedging strategy.

5. The forward market coverage is a contingent liability that should be reported in a footnote, while the money market coverage will be reported as one of the regular liabilities and assets in the balance sheet, if the reporting date is during the covered period.

6. A similar analysis would be pursued in evaluating other hedging strategies.

7. It is here assumed that traders can foresee most likely, highest, and lowest expected values for the spot exchange rate. The assumption of a specific probability distribution of the spot exchange rate is not inconsistent with the random walk hypothesis. In the general theory of random walk, the form or shape of the distribution need not be specified.

8. Note that this analysis would not be necessary in the forward market because in this situation all the variables are known with certainty.

9. Note that whenever $i_a = 0$, the formulas shown in the appendix are the same as those discussed in the text, assuming M and N = 1.

19

Evaluation and Control of Foreign Operations

Alan C. Shapiro

• • •

INTRODUCTION

A major responsibility faced by the financial executives of multinational corporations (MNCs) is to design and implement an evaluation and control system for overseas operations. This system must incorporate the influence of numerous factors which are rarely, if ever, encountered by purely domestic corporations. These factors include exchange-rate changes, differing rates of inflation, currency controls, foreign tax regulations, cross-border transfer pricing, and the differences between subsidiary and parent-company cash flows.

Unfortunately, developing an evaluation and control system is still an art, relying on judgment more than theory. No universal principles have yet appeared to use in designing such a system for domestic operations, much less for foreign operations. Therefore, this article has the modest goal of suggesting a set of reasonable guidelines, based on a mixture of economic theory, behavioral science and empirical evidence, to use in accounting for a variety of international elements while measuring, evaluating, and controlling the performance of foreign operations and their managers.

MEASUREMENT AND EVALUATION

Designing an evaluation system involves four stages. The critical first stage must be to specify its purpose(s). While trivial perhaps, many companies have gotten into trouble by failing to distinguish, for example, between the evalua-

tion of subsidiary performance and managerial performance. As we will see, it is possible for a manager to do an excellent job while his subsidiary is doing very poorly and vice versa.

The next stage involves determining what decisions will be made on the basis of these evaluations and the information necessary to support such decisions. For example, when evaluating managerial performance, it is necessary to separate the effects of uncontrollable variables, such as inflation, from those which are controllable, such as credit extension. Furthermore, capital allocation decisions require very different measures of subsidiary performance than does ensuring the smooth functioning of current operations.

The third stage is the design of a reporting or information system to provide the necessary information or at least a reasonable approximation. Many companies will probably find that their reporting system is inadequate for the purposes specified.

The final stage involves conducting a cost/benefit analysis of the evaluation system. *This analysis does not have to be quantitative but it should be comprehensive.* Some benefits might be (1) greater control over current operations, (2) more rigorous capital budgeting decisions, and (3) greater awareness of managerial effectiveness. Against these benefits must be weighed the costs which might arise including (1) time and money involved in redesigning the information system, and (2) behavioral problems which might be associated with the new evaluation system. The latter cost might include reduced initiative on the part of local managers who feel they are being overly controlled. This need not occur since one of the goals of an evaluation system should be to provide the in-

Source: Alan C. Shapiro, "Evaluation and Control of Foreign Operations," *International Journal of Accounting Education and Research,* Volume 14, Number 1, Fall 1978, pp. 83–104. Copyright © 1978. Reprinted by permission.

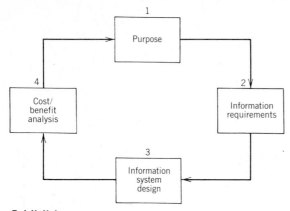

Exhibit 1

formation necessary to reward managers for their performance. An evaluation system which does not motivate a manager to work in the company's best interest will not be an effective one, regardless of its other attributes.

Exhibit 1 shows the design of an evaluation system diagrammatically. It is all too evident, however, that many multinational, as well as domestic, corporations have not fully considered this design process. Complaints by subsidiary managers that too much information is being demanded while management at headquarters complains that too much data, but too little good information, are being supplied by the subsidiaries is evidence enough of dissonance between system design and goals.

The main purposes of the evaluation discussed in this paper include

1. To provide a rational basis for global resource allocation;
2. To have an early warning system if something is wrong with current operations;
3. To evaluate the performance of individual managers, and
4. To provide a set of standards that will motivate managers.

We will now explore each of these purposes in turn and comment on some of the methods currently used by MNCs in achieving these goals.

Resource Allocation

A key decision problem continually faced by multinationals is allocation of capital among their various subsidiaries on a worldwide basis. To aid in this process, companies often use the return on existing investments as a guide. This approach is fine if returns on past investments are *indicative* of *future returns*. There may be problems, though, if proposed investments are not comparable to existing ones or if the relevant returns on past investments are incorrectly measured. Obviously, to the extent that new investments are unrelated to previous ones, using historical subsidiary returns to allocate capital globally will be successful only by chance.

The more interesting, and probably more likely, occurrence in multinational capital budgeting is where potential investments are comparable to past ones, for example, replacement of depreciated assets, but it is difficult to decide on the *relevant selection criteria*. For example, a number of nonfinancial criteria such as market share, sales growth, and stability of production, are often used in comparing investments. Ultimately, though, most firms are interested in the return on their capital employed. A 1970 Conference Board study indicated that some version of *return on investment* (ROI) is the most typical means of measuring the long-run profit performance of foreign subsidiaries.[1] However, there are a number of pitfalls involved in allowing return on past investments to guide this process. These problems fall into two areas: first, problems associated with measuring the correct investment base, and second, difficulties in determining the relevant returns.

The investment base can include:

1. Parent's equity
2. Fixed assets
   a. Gross
   b. Net of depreciation
3. Working capital
   a. Total
   b. Net of supplier credits
   c. Net of intracompany accounts

In addition, these assets can be valued on an historical or current cost basis.

Fortunately, financial theory pinpoints the *relevant investment* base. It equals the incremental value of all capital required. Thus, the investment must be measured on a *current or replacement cost,* rather than historical cost, basis and should include gross fixed assets as well as total working capital requirements net of external supplier credits. Using historical rather than replacement costs in a period of inflation will understate true capital requirements leading to an unrealized increase in the projected return on investment. The working capital figure should include inventory valued on a current cost basis. Intracompany receivables should be excluded since these accounts cancel on a corporate-wide basis; for instance, increasing one subsidiary's intracompany receivables by a dollar will lead to a dollar reduction in another unit's working capital requirements. Furthermore, these accounts are arbitrary and subject to corporate manipulation.

Measuring the *relevant returns* on foreign operations is a more difficult task. Substantial differences can arise between subsidiary cash flows and cash flows back to the parent firm due to tax regulations and exchange controls, for example. Further, adjustments in transfer prices and intersubsidiary credit arrangements can distort the true profitability of a given investment or subsidiary by shifting profits and liquidity from one unit to another. In addition, fees and royalties are costs to a subsidiary but benefits to the parent company.

Studies by The Conference Board and Business International revealed considerable variation among firms in measuring returns.[2] Measured returns included different combinations of foreign earnings, royalties, fees, dividends, rentals, interest, commissions, and export profits. Some firms included only repatriated profits while others included most or all of these return elements. Some measured only before-tax returns, others only returns after foreign taxes,

and still others took into account both U.S. and foreign taxes paid.

The correct approach again relies on economic theory. According to this theory, *the value of an investment is determined by the net present value of incremental cash flows back to the investor*. The key concept here is incremental cash flow. Determining incremental cash flows for a MNC involves taking the difference between worldwide cash flows with the investment and worldwide cash flows in the investment's absence. Thus, all royalties, fees, and overhead allocations paid by a subsidiary should be included in its profit calculation as would be all profits earned by other units due to the subsidiary's existence. This would include profits arising from the adjustment of transfer prices on goods bought from or sold to the subsidiary, as well as all profits on exports to the subsidiary which would not have occurred in the subsidiary's absence. However, any profits on sales or any licensing fees and royalties which would have been earned by another unit of the MNC are not economically attributable to the subsidiary. Further, *the parent MNC should value only those cash flows which are or can be repatriated* since only funds accessible to the parent can be used to pay dividends and interest, amortize the firm's debt, and be reinvested. In addition, since only after-tax cash flows are relevant, it is necessary to determine the taxes that must be paid on foreign-source income and when such payment will occur.

The actual tax on remitted funds will depend on the transfer mechanism used, as well as on the tax regulations involved. These transfer mechanisms include adjustments in transfer prices, dividend flows, fee and royalty charges, overhead allocation, and intracompany loan and credit arrangements.[3] For example, repaying a parent company loan would normally entail no additional withholding taxes.

The cost of carrying intracompany receivables should be excluded from the subsidiary's profit and loss calculation since this cost is offset elsewhere in the corporation by a corresponding reduction in working capital requirements. By the same logic, the subsidiary should be charged for the cost of any intracorporate payables on its balance sheet.

Return on Investment Criteria

A variety of comparisons are possible with a subsidiary's return on investment (ROI) figure. These include comparisons with local competitors, with the firm's subsidiaries and/or competitors on a regional or global basis, and with parent-company operations. In addition, comparisons can be made with the firm's original investment plans. We will now examine the information content of these comparisons to see what decisions are likely to be affected, and how, by the data generated.

Even if caution is exercised, comparisons with local or regional competitors can be meaningless. Different accounting and disclosure requirements leading to different depreciation and earnings reports under similar operating circumstances may not permit comparisons to be made with any degree of certainty. Some foreign firms, for example, do not separate nonrecurring income arising out of the sale of assets from operating income. Even if comparisons were limited to home-country competitors, it is usually impossible to determine the actual profitability of local operations because of the high degree of integration and the less-than-arms length dealings between units of a multinational corporation.

Cross-country comparisons with other affiliates of the multinational corporation are possible, but to what purpose? Ex post, some investments will always be more profitable than others. Thus, in evaluating new investments, *a comparison of historical returns is useful only if these returns are indicative of the relative returns to be expected on future investments in these countries*. Even if expected ROIs differ across countries, it is necessary to consider the element of risk as well. Certain low risk-low

return investments may well be preferable to some high risk-high return investments.

Furthermore, as Robbins and Stobaugh point out, multinationals have many *strategic motivations* for going abroad which are not necessarily expressed in ROI calculations.[4] For example, a firm may willingly forego economies of scale in production to achieve greater security of supply by having multiple and redundant production facilities.[5] In addition, operating in several nations may give a firm greater bargaining leverage in dealing with local governments or labor unions. Being multinational may also lower the *firm's risk profile* by reducing its dependence on the state of just one nation's economy. In fact, both Cohen and Rugman have found that earnings variability decreases as foreign activities increase[6] while research by Agmon and Lessard indicates that investors value the international diversification supplied by the multinational firm.[7]

It is true that ROI comparisons across subsidiaries might identify potential problems with current operations. However, as we will see in the next section, more direct methods of receiving early warnings of trouble are possible.

Perhaps the most important comparison that can be made is between *actual results and ex ante budgeted figures*. A postinvestment audit can help a firm learn from its mistakes as well as its successes. In the multinational corporation, where so many additional complexities enter into the capital budgeting decision, it is easier to make errors due to a lack of experience. Reviewing the record of past investments can enable a firm to determine whether there is any consistency in its estimation errors such as generally under- or overestimating the impact of inflation on costs or of devaluations on dollar revenues from foreign sales. Correction factors can then be included in future investment analyses. Even if estimation errors are random, a firm may be able to place limits on the relative magnitudes of these errors and thereby supply useful inputs to an investment simulation model.

In analyzing actual results, it is necessary to

recall the previously mentioned nonfinancial strategic rationale that may have prompted the original investment. Otherwise, an investment undertaken for one reason may be judged on the basis of different criteria resulting in a misleading comparison.

Evaluation of Current Subsidiary Performance

Frequent monitoring of operations in an uncertain environment is useful to determine whether any tactical or strategic changes are warranted. The appropriate measure(s) to use in controlling foreign operations, though, will vary by company and subsidiary. For marketing-oriented companies, market share, sales growth, or cost/sales dollar may be the most relevant measures. A manufacturing subsidiary may be most concerned about unit production costs, quality control, or the labor turnover rate. Others may find return on assets or a working capital to sales ratio most helpful. The important thing is to use those measures which experience has determined are the key leading indicators as to when an operation is out of control. In evaluating foreign operations, though, it may be necessary to employ different standards than those used in controlling the domestic business.

Inventory turnover may be lower overseas due to the larger inventory stocks required to cope with longer lead times to delivery and more frequent delays in intracompany shipments of goods. Where foreign production occurs, it may be necessary to stockpile additional supplies of imported raw material and components given the possibility of a dock strike, import controls, or some other supply disruption.[8]

Receivables may also be greater abroad, particularly in countries experiencing rapid rates of inflation. During times of inflation, consumers normally prefer to purchase on longer credit terms, expecting to repay their debt with less valuable future money. Furthermore, local credit standards are often more relaxed than in the home market, especially in countries lack-

ing in alternative credit arrangements. To remain competitive, MNCs may feel compelled to loosen their own credit standards. This is not always the best policy, however. The multinational corporation should weigh the profit on incremental credit sales against the additional carrying costs, including devaluation losses and bad debts, associated with an easier credit policy.[9]

Different cost standards are usually necessary for foreign operations due to local value-added requirements (which mandate the use of more expensive local goods and services), import tariffs, government limitations on the choice of production processes, and a frequent inability to lay off or fire workers. In the latter case, labor becomes a fixed rather than a variable cost.

Most firms find it helpful to design budgets based on explicit assumptions on the internal and external environment. In a foreign environment, with greater uncertainty, *flexible budgeting* will probably be even more useful than it is domestically. Flexible budgeting involves computing alternative budgets based on different projections of the future rate of inflation, exchange rate changes, wage settlements, and so forth.

It is obviously impossible to develop a different budget for each potential future scenario. Instead, a limited number of the most likely scenarios should be selected for further study. If the firm selects these scenarios carefully, it should have an advantage in coping with foreseeable changes in its operating environment. Furthermore, these alternative budgets will provide a firm with a more reasonable and reliable basis for evaluating the performance of its overseas managers. This is the subject of the next section.

Evaluating Managerial Performance

The standards used to evaluate managers will also serve to motivate them. A key goal, therefore, in designing a management evaluation system is to ensure that the resulting managerial motivation will be congruent with overall corporate objectives. A good strategy which managers are not motivated to follow will be of little value. Thus, it is necessary to anticipate the likely response of a rational manager to a particular set of evaluation criteria.

For example, managers evaluated on the basis of current earnings will likely emphasize short-run profits to the detriment of longer-term profitability. This is particularly true if executives are frequently transferred, enabling them to escape the long-run consequences of their actions. These actions might include reducing advertising and maintenance, cutting back on research and development (R&D) expenditures, and investing less money on employee training. Managers judged according to return on investment will also concentrate on short-run profits. Furthermore, they will likely be slower to replace used equipment, particularly during a period of rapid inflation, even when economically justifiable. This is both because new investments will increase the investment base and also becaue ROI measured on an historical cost basis will be greater than ROI on a replacement cost basis. If return on equity is used as the measure of performance, managers will have an incentive to substitute local debt for retained earnings and parent-company equity. The effect of this will be to increase the MNC's worldwide debt ratio causing a deterioration in the parent company's credit rating and an increase in its cost of capital.

Consistent with the goal of properly motivating employees is the principle that *a manager's performance should be judged on the basis of results in those areas over which he has control.* Assigning responsibility without authority will lead to frustrated and disgruntled employees. Furthermore, it is unreasonable, as well as dysfunctional, to reward or penalize a manager for the impact of economic events beyond his control. Thus, headquarters must carefully distinguish between managerial performance and subsidiary performance.

As noted earlier, *a subsidiary can be doing quite well despite the poor performance of its management* and vice versa. For example, during a time of rapid inflation, a subsidiary selling to local customers will show a proportional increase in its dollar profitability. Poor management will just hold down the increase in profits. After the inevitable devaluation, though, dollar profitability will invariably decline even with good management in control. Furthermore, a consistently poor profit performance by a manager may simply be evidence of a past mistake in approving the original investment.

Rather than evaluate managerial performance on the basis of a subsidiary's profitability or ROI which are subject to uncontrollable events, it would be more useful to compare *actual results* with the *budgeted figures.* Revenue and cost variances can then be examined to determine whether these were likely to have been caused by external economic factors (such as inflation or devaluation), by corporate policy shifts (such as transfer price adjustments), or by managerial decisions (a new product strategy).

The keys to this analysis are the explicit assumptions which are incorporated in the budget and the knowledge of how changes in these assumptions are likely to affect the budgeted numbers. Exhibit 2 illustrates the likely impact of exchange rate changes. As the exhibit points out, the main factors which determine this impact are the sector of the economy in which a firm is operating (export, domestic import-competing, domestic nonimport-competing) and the source of its inputs (imports, domestic traded goods and services, domestic nontraded goods and services).

By including allowances for training programs, research and development, and other vital functions in the budget, the natural tendency to neglect these areas can be reduced. However, it is necessary to consider other, less tangible, factors as well when evaluating performance.

A profit-oriented manager may allow relations with the host country to deteriorate. A

Exhibit 2 Characteristic Economic Effects of Exchange Rate Changes on MNCs

Cash Flow Categories	Relevant Economic Factors	Devaluation Impact	Revaluation Impact
Revenue		Parent-currency revenue impact	Parent-currency revenue impact
Export sales	Price-sensitive demand	Increase (+ +)	Decrease (− −)
	Price insensitive demand	Slight increase (+)	Slight decrease (−)
Local sales	Weak prior import competition	Sharp decline (− −)	Increase (+)
	Strong prior import competition	Decrease (−) (less than devaluation %)	Slight increase
Costs		Parent-currency cost impact	Parent-currency cost impact
Domestic inputs	Low import content	Decrease (− −)	Increase (+ +)
	High import content/inputs used in export or import competing sectors	Slight decrease (−)	Slight increase (−)
Imported inputs	Small local market	Remain the same (0)	Remain the same (0)
	Large local market	Slight decrease (−)	Slight increase (+)
Depreciation		Cash-flow impact	Cash-flow impact
Fixed assets	No asset valuation adjustment	Decrease by devaluation % (− −)	Increase by revaluation % (+ +)
	Asset valuation adjustment	Decrease (−)	Increase (+)

Note: To interpret the above chart, and taking the impact of a devaluation on local demand as an example, it is assumed that if import competiton is weak, local prices will climb slightly, if at all; in such a case there would be a sharp contraction in parent-company revnue. If imports generate strong competition, local-currency prices are expected to increase, although not to the full extent of the devaluation; in this instance only a moderate decline in parent-company revenue would be registered.

study by Negandhi and Baliga indicates that, in contrast to the typical American MNC's concentration on profits, European and Japanese multinationals emphasize cultivating and maintaining harmonious relations with host government officials and others in the local environment.[10] Given the difficulties facing multinationals abroad, qualitative determinants of long-run profitability and viability are likely to be more important in the future and should be included in any performance evaluation. The inability to objectively measure the state of host country relations is not a reason to ignore it. Ultimately, any performance measure is subjective, even if it is quantitative, since the choice of which measure(s) to stress is a matter of judgment.

The next section deals with three areas of current concern in performance evaluation: transfer pricing, adjusting intracorporate fund flows, and the choice of appropriate exchange rates for internal use.

Transfer pricing. In a decentralized profit center, transfer prices on goods and services (fees and royalties) can be a significant determinant of a manager's performance. Therefore, unless the manager is not held accountable for the influence of transfer prices on his reported profits, he is likely to react in ways which are counterproductive to the organization as a whole. Cases have arisen, for example, where managers selling to subsidiaries which are forced to buy from them behaved as monopolists and attempted to gouge their captive customers. On the other hand, purchasers of goods and services from other units of the MNC may try to act as monopsonists and underpay their suppliers.

Even if a manager wanted to act in the best interests of the corporation, his perspective would be too limited. Thus, individual managers are likely to ignore or be ignorant of the broader legal, tax, and liquidity calculations involved in setting a corporate-wide transfer pricing policy.[11] For these reasons, transfer pricing is too important to be left to subsidiaries. However, budgeted profit requirements for individual subsidiaries should recognize and adjust for the distorting influence of less-than-arm's-length transfer prices. In other words, managerial evaluations should be decoupled from the particular transfer prices being used. This can be done by charging managers who are buying goods the marginal cost of production and shipping while managers who are selling goods would be credited with a reasonable profit on their sales. Managers of subsidiaries only producing for sale to other units of the corporation should be evaluated on the basis of their costs of production rather than profits since they have no control over their revenues.

One manufacturing firm which set transfer prices on the basis of cost plus an allocation for overhead and then used these prices for evaluation purposes found that its sales managers were pushing low, rather than high, margin products. Due to their high overhead costs, the high margin products were less profitable to the sales managers than to the company. Further investigation showed that demand for these high margin products was quite elastic and that significant potential profits were being lost due to the transfer pricing strategy in effect.

Decoupling may present problems at times, however. For example, the transfer prices of multinational drug companies are closely monitored worldwide, and this information is shared by a number of governments. Thus, it may be necessary to keep transfer prices at the same

level worldwide. Given the low elasticity of demand for many branded pharmaceuticals, these prices are normally set quite high. However, due to competitive circumstances, some individual subsidiaries may be penalized by the necessity to market these drugs at high prices. To sell to these subsidiaries at lower prices, though, would jeopardize the firm's worldwide pricing strategy since other countries would wonder why they had to pay higher prices. These effects would have to be considered to evaluate management performance fairly, particularly when making comparisons across subsidiaries.

Exchange Rates for Evaluation Purposes. Firms must choose the exchange rate(s) to use when setting budgets and evaluating performance.[12] When setting the operating budget, for example, two exchange rates are possible—the actual spot rate at the time or the forecast rate. In addition, if the budget is revised when exchange rate changes occur, the updated rate can be used. In evaluating performance relative to the budget, there are three alternative rates that can be used: the actual rate at the time the budget is set, the projected end-of-period rate, or the actual end-of-period rate. There are, thus, six exchange rate combinations possible.

A study of 200 MNCs, however, revealed that only three budget evaluation combinations were actually used.[13] Half of the firms surveyed used a projected rate of budgeting but measured performance with the end of period rate, 30 percent used a projected rate both for budgeting and performance evaluation, while the remaining 20 percent used the spot rate for budgeting and the end-of-period rate for tracking performance.

In choosing the appropriate combination of budgeting and evaluation rates to use, it is necessary to consider the behavioral consequences involved. If at the one extreme, the budget and evaluation rates assume no exchange rate change (by using the actual beginning-of-period rate for both purposes), then managers will have no incentive to incorporate anticipated exchange rate changes in their decisions. For example, a marketing manager rewarded on the basis of the spot rate prevailing at the date of sale rather than the anticipated rate upon collection of the receivables generated will likely engage in an uneconomical expansion of credit sales. At the other extreme, if exchange rate changes are ignored in the budget, but the end-of-period rate is used for evaluation, the manager will probably behave in an overly risk averse manner since he or she will bear the full consequences of any exchange rate fluctuations. The harmful effects of such a system will likely include "padding" of the budgets as well as decentralized hedging by managers to reduce their perceived risks.

The use of forecast rates at both the budgeting and evaluation stages appear to be the most desirable combination since it excludes unplanned currency fluctuations but recognizes expected fluctuations at the budgeting stage. Clearly this combination will dominate all other combinations which hold managers responsible for unforeseen exchange fluctuations but do not force them to consider likely currency changes at the budgeting stage. This standard seems most fair since the local decision maker receives no blame or credit for anticipated currency fluctuations. It is also most realistic since it serves to make decentralized decision making congruent with corporate-wide goals and information. Lessard and Lorange call these projected rates internal forward rates.[14] One means of constructing these internal forward rates, which may differ considerably from the actual forward rate, is presented by Shapiro and Rutenberg.[15]

If the exchange rate changes dramatically, it may be necessary to adjust the projected rate during the operating cycle. The need for adjustment will depend on the magnitude of these changes as well as the degree of exposed assets and local currency earnings. Most importantly, it will depend on the extent to which operating decisions can be changed in response to a new

exchange rate. Lessard and Lorange point out that if decisions are irreversible, then the evaluation rate should not be adjusted.[16] Such a change would violate the principle of insulating operating managers from random currency changes. If decisions are reversible, albeit at a cost, new plans should be drawn with updated rates. However, any change in budget and evaluation rates should apply only for the remainder of the period—the time during which new operating decisions can be made. In all caes, it would appear that updating the projected rates when appropriate is preferable to holding operating managers responsible for actual exchange rate changes whether anticipated or not. Furthermore, adjusting these rates would permit sharing the results of unforeseen developments rather than imposing them on operating units.

Adjusting Intracorporate Fund Flows. The ability to adjust intracorporate fund flows by speeding or slowing payments on intracorporate accounts is a valuable and widely used technique in liquidity and exchange risk management. However, use of this tool, known as leading and lagging, is likely to distort the various working capital ratios of subsidiaries. For example, a subsidiary ordered to extend longer credit terms to another unit will show an increase in its receivables to sales ratio. Furthermore, its interest expenses will increase while its customer's working capital costs will decline. Since leading and lagging is a corporate policy, its effects should not be included in any evaluation of subsidiary management. It would be advisable, of course, to consider these effects when evaluating the financial staff at headquarters.

Motivating Managers. Implicit in the comments in this section is *the idea that these evaluations will serve as inputs for promotion and salary decisions. The connection should be made obvious to managers.* Otherwise, these evaluations become irrelevant data, useful neither for motivational purposes nor for selecting and promoting a highly qualified cadre of international executives.

Managers who feel they are not rewarded (or penalized) for their job performances may put less effort into the work. However, the real damage is the loss of the entreprenurial spirit that appears to be necessary to cope with a rapidly changing environment. The incentive to take risks is encouraged by the existence of significant rewards for success. Without these rewards, a manager's initiative may be severely diminished, perhaps resulting in work as hard as before but only in more traditional areas rather than embarking on new ventures which offer great potential but are risky.

To implement these evaluations, an effective reporting and control system is necessary. This is the subject of the next section.

REPORTING AND CONTROL SYSTEMS

Many multinationals have found it useful and sometimes necessary to require more frequent reporting by their affiliates due to the increased likelihood of problems arising overseas. Different methods of reporting and communications may also be useful, such as a worldwide telex system and more personal visits with headquarters staff both in the field and at the home office.

Choosing an Appropriate Exchange Rate

Almost by definition, multinational firms have transactions in more than one currency. Thus, MNCs face the problem of which exchange rate(s) to use when reporting the results of foreign operations. A number of alternative exchange rates possibilities exist but interviews with a number of MNCs disclose certain distinct preferences.

Multinational corporations appear to use either the end-of-period rate to book all transactions during the period or else a predetermined rate. This predetermined rate is revised only when the actual exchange rate differs from it by

more than a given percentage, usually between 2½ and 5 percent. Another possibility, the average rate during the period, is rarely used because of the additional complexity involved. It should be noted, however, that each of these methods could present measurement problems if care is not taken in the application.

The end-of-period rate, for example, could seriously distort actual profitability if a major exchange rate change occurs during the period unless most sales take place at the new exchange rate. Otherwise, if sales are uniformly distributed throughout the period, an average rate could most accurately represent the period's income. On the other hand, use of an average rate is inappropriate if sales are bunched and a major currency change occurs.

When using a predetermined rate, the limits within which fluctuations are permitted must be set so that changes within these margins will not seriously distort the period's income. Clearly, a firm with a 5 percent profit margin on its sales should not use a predetermined rate with 5 percent fluctuation limits.

Capital goods manufacturers or other firms which usually have only a few large sales during a period should probably use the actual exchange rates at which each transaction took place. The basic criterion then in deciding on which reporting rate to use should be that the approach chosen will not seriously distort the period's actual income.

Centralization versus Decentralization

A key concept in the design of a reporting system is responsibility reporting. This involves flowing information from each decision area to the manager accountable for the results of these decisions. A general rule of thumb in organizational design appears to be to decentralize responsibility as much as possible. The fewer the linkages between activity areas, the better decentralization will function. However, in the multinational corporation, the interactions among various units is often so great because of tax factors or economies of scale in risk management (to be discussed later), for example, that complete decentralization will be suboptimal.

Some firms have partially decentralized operations by establishing regional headquarters for the different geographical areas of the world. This shortens the lines of communication and enhances the dispersal of geographically-centered information. The more similar business conditions are within, as compared with between, geographical regions, the more valuable regional headquarters are likely to be.

In companies with a dearth of experienced international financial managers, there is an added incentive to centralize decisions. It is often felt that the talents of this limited number of experienced managers can best be utilized at headquarters where fullest advantage can be taken of their knowledge. Working against centralization is the complexity and size of the multinational corporation which makes it difficult, if not possible, for any headquarters group to completely coordinate financial activities worldwide.

A Conference Board study on the level of corporate involvement in certain key multinational financial decision areas indicated that the wider the perspective required, the more likely it was that a particular decision would be controlled by headquarters.[17] The following are some of the results of the Conference Board study.

Repatriation of Funds. Of the companies surveyed, 85 percent indicated that decisions involving repatriation of funds were made at the corporate level. However, respondents appeared to have little control of the repatriation decision in joint ventures where they were minority partners.

Intersubsidiary Financing. In most companies, either the chief financial executive of the parent company or the treasurer, with the advice of tax counsel, decided on which intracorporate fund flows should take place.

Acquisition of Funds. Of the firms studied, 85 percent indicated that all medium and long-term financing was approved at corporate headquarters. Many firms, though, allowed their subsidiaries much more leeway with regard to short-term financing.

Protection of Assets. Many of the firms questioned did not have any formal plans for asset protection although a number indicated that they were beginning to change toward greater centralization. The advent of FASB 8 has accelerated the centralization of exposure management.[18]

Planning and Control. The responses here were quite varied. The more financially oriented (as opposed to marketing oriented, for example) that firms were, the more likely they were to have a centralized planning and control function.

A more recent study by Stobaugh indicated significant differences in attitudes towards centralization among small (average annual foreign sales of $50 million), medium (average foreign sales of $200 million annually), and large (average of $1 billion in annual foreign sales) multinationals.[19] Small MNCs generally allowed subsidiaries considerable leeway in financial management, perhaps because of the lack of sophistication in international financial management at headquarters. The tendency among medium-sized firms was to try to optimize worldwide results, treating each subsidiary as just one unit in a global system. These firms required very sophisticated control and reporting systems. Large MNCs appeared to reverse the centralization trend somewhat, providing subsidiaries with formal guidelines but allowing them considerable initiative within those guidelines. This was apparently due to a recognized inability to optimize in such a complex system. The author will now examine two particular areas—currency and cash management—where controversy has developed over the optimal degree of headquarters control.

International Cash and Foreign Exchange Risk Management

In the areas of cash and foreign exchange risk management, there are good arguments for both centralization and decentralization. Arguing for centralization is the reasonable assumption that local treasurers want to optimize their own financial and exposure positions, regardless of the overall corporate situation. To a local treasurer, a subsidiary's cash reserves may appear too low while to the corporate treasurer, the subsidiary is holding excess liquidity relative to the corporation's ability to supply liquidity from its worldwide reserves. Similarly, a study by Rodriguez has concluded that *foreign exchange risk aversion increased with decentralization of the financial function.*[20] Local treasurers ignored the possibilities available to the corporation to *trade off positive and negative currency exposure* positions by consolidating exposure worldwide. A further benefit of centralized exposure management is the ability to take advantage of the economies of scale in risk management effect,[21] that is, the fact that the *total variability or risk of a currency exposure portfolio is less than the sum of the individual variabilities of each currency exposure considered in isolation.* This is due to the less-than-perfect positive correlation that exists between the various currencies. Thus, centralization of exchange risk management should reduce the amount of hedging required to achieve a given level of safety. This can be valuable given the high costs of hedging. The company can then select the cheapest option(s) worldwide to hedge its remaining exposure. Tax effects can be crucial at this stage,[22] but only headquarters will have the required global perspective.

These are all powerful arguments for centralization of cash and currency risk management. Against these benefits, though, must be weighed the loss of local knowledge and the lack of incentive for local managers to take advantage of particular situations with which only they may be familiar. However, this conflict between centralization and decentralization is more apparent than real.

As the section on evaluation noted, the use of internal forward rates can enhance the advantages and suppress the disadvantages of both centralization and decentralization. Similar advantages can be achieved by using internal interest rates. This can be done by providing local managers with interest rates and forward rates which reflect the opportunity costs of money and exposure to the parent corporation. Thus, headquarters can make full use of local knowledge while ensuring that local managers act in the company's best interests. With regard to exchange risk, headquarters, in effect, is offering to *sell insurance* to local managers to cover their exposure. If a manager decides it is cheaper to hedge locally, fine. At least he has taken into consideration the cost of hedging to the corporation.

In setting internal interest rates, the corporate treasurer, in effect, is *acting as a bank,* offering to borrow or lend currencies at given rates. By examining these internal rates, local treasurers will have a greater awareness of the opportunity cost of their idle cash balances as well as an added incentive to act on this information. In many instances, they will prefer to transfer at least part of their cash balances (where permitted) to a central pool in order to earn a greater return. To make pooling of funds work, though, it is essential that managers have access to the central pool whenever they require funds.

Mechanisms of Control

When designing a control system for use overseas, there may be a tendency to use the most sophisticated system available due to the complexity of the problems encountered abroad. Furthermore, since headquarters is not bearing the most of furnishing subsidiary reports, it is likely to demand a good deal of information which is rarely, if ever, used merely on the off chance that it might be needed. However, *a sophisticated and complex system may yield worse results than a simpler, less ambitious system* if local managers are not top caliber or local operations are of small size. A system which is more sophisticated than the managers it is supposed to control can lead to suspicions, frustration, and, ultimately, to sabotage attempts. Where operations are small, a complex reporting system can become burdensome and take managers away from their primary function which is to manage.

According to Zenoff and Zwick, a new and relatively sophisticated management group took control of Singer Corp. in the early 1960s. Despite their desire to bring more sophistication to Singer's international business, though, the new management felt that the quality of many of their field managers precluded the adoption of a complex system of performance standards and evaluation criteria. Instead, they opted for a system of simple standards and reports that were comprehensible and provided some degree of control.[23] Over time, a simple system can evolve into a successful sophisticated system. However, local managers must understand the system. Otherwise, they will defeat it, either deliberately or inadvertently.

Even with sophisticated managers, however, a relatively small operation may not warrant the reporting requirements and elaborate control mechanism of a larger affiliate. *The value of gathering additional information must be balanced against its cost in terms of taking up scarce management time.* A small company may not have the resources to hire additional personnel to fill out reports, and thus the job is left to the existing managers, adding to their workload.

A possible solution is to require fewer reports from smaller subsidiaries while at the same time monitoring several key performance indicators. As long as these indicators remain within bounds, a subsidiary is allowed considerable freedom. If problems appear, then, additional controls can be imposed. In effect, this is reporting and control by exception. The danger

here is that these additional controls may be perceived as punishment and reacted to accordingly. Tact and a truly helpful attitude will be necessary to convince a manager that these new reports and controls are designed to help him do a better job.

A zero-base information system would aid in this process of reducing information requirements. This would involve an audit of all the information which is currently being provided and the uses of that information. Unless information is being used in decision making, it should be discarded.

Traveling teams of auditors are another device used to facilitate communications and control with the multinational corporation. Quite often, though, it is difficult to find qualified people willing to be constantly on the go, living out of suitcases. Furthermore, these teams may be perceived as spies and met with hostility, unless they demonstrate their helpfulness to the local managers. The attitudes of the team members will be dependent on whether headquarters actually is using them as spies or instead intends for them the more constructive role of assistants and consultants to managers in the field.

Feedback is an important element in any evaluation and control system. Local managers, sophisticated or not, from large or small operations, are likely to complain about overreporting and overcontrol if they feel that headquarters demands information without providing a commensurate amount of feedback. Since the reporting system is normally tailored to the needs of headquarters alone, preparing reports is seen as a waste of time for subsidiary management. Redesigning the reporting system so that it provides more useful information to subsidiary management along with more feedback from headquarters will increase the incentive of local management to cooperate with headquarters.

Sometimes only negative feedback is received. According to some managers, "I only hear from headquarters when I am doing poorly, never when I am doing well." This lack of symmetry is difficult to understand since praise can be an equally effective motivating force. After all, almost everyone likes to feel that his or her work is recognized and appreciated.

Many of the problems referred to in this paper are caused by a lack of communications between headquarters and its subsidiaries. One suggested approach to facilitate headquarters-subsidiary communications is to require all top headquarters staff personnel to spend at least two years in the field becoming acquainted with the problems faced by subsidiaries. At the same time, subsidiary managers would be required to spend time at headquarters to gain a broader perspective of the corporation's activities.

CONCLUSIONS

As stated at the beginning of this paper, there is no set of scientific principles that can guarantee the development of a successful evaluation and control system. However, a truly geocentric system, to use Perlmutter's terminology,[24] should encourage a free flow of ideas and information worldwide. Headquarters must avoid the temptation of trying to overcontrol field operations or else run the risk of stifling local initiative. In addition, local managers should have the opportunity to explain their operating results and seek help for their problems. The lack of such a safety mechanism will cause the kinds of problems associated with a too rigid adherence to strictly numerical criteria. In the final analysis, it appears that in the multinational corporation, as in any social institution, a system characterized by mutual understanding works best.

NOTES

1. Irene W. Meister, *Managing the International Financial Function* (New York: The Conference Board, 1970).

2. Ibid., and Business International Corporation, "Evaluating Foreign Operations: The Appropriate Rates for Comparing Results with Budgets," *Business International Money Report,* May 20, 1977, p. 154.

3. David P. Rutenberg, "Maneuvering Liquid Assets in a Multinational Corporation," *Management Science,* June 1970, p. 671.

4. Sidney M. Robbins and Robert B. Stobaugh, *Money in the Multinational Enterprise* (New York: Basic Books, 1973).

5. David P. Rutenberg and Ram Rao, "Robust Plant Location for the Stochastic World of a Multi-National Manufacturer," GSIA Working Paper, Carnegie-Mellon University, 1973.

6. Benjamin I. Cohen, *Multinational Firms and Asian Exports* (New Haven, Conn.: Yale University Press, 1975), and Alan M. Rugman, "Risk Reduction by International Diversification," *Journal of International Business Studies,* Fall–Winter 1976, p. 75.

7. Tamir Agmon and Donald R. Lessard, "Invester Recognition of Corporate International Diversification," *Journal of Finance,* September 1977.

8. Alan C. Shapiro, Howard C. Kunreuther, and Pascal E. Lang, "Planning Horizons for Inventory Stockpiling," University of Pennsylvania Working Paper, 1977.

9. Alan C. Shapiro, "Optimal Inventory and Credit-Granting Strategies under Inflation and Devaluation," *Journal of Financial and Quantitative Analysis,* January 1973, p. 37.

10. Anant R. Negandhi and B. R. Baliga, "Quest for Survival and Growth: A Study of American, European, and Japanese Multinational Corporations," International Institute of Management Working Paper, 1976.

11. Edgar M. Barrett, "Case of the Tangled Transfer Price," *Harvard Business Review,* May–June 1977, p. 20, and Rutenberg, "Liquid Assets," p. 671.

12. Donald R. Lessard and Peter Lorange, "Currency Changes and Management Control: Resolving the Centralization/Decentralization Dilemma," *Accounting Review,* July 1977, p. 628.

13. Business International Corporation, "Evaluating Foreign Operations," p. 154.

14. Lessard and Lorange, "Currency Changes," p. 628.

15. Alan C. Shapiro and David P. Rutenberg, "When to Hedge Against Devaluation," *Management Science,* August 1974, p. 1514.

16. Lessard and Lorange, "Currency Changes," p. 628.

17. Meister, *Financial Function.*

18. Financial Accounting Standards Board, "Accounting for the Translation of Foreign Currency Transactions and Foreign Currency Financial Statements," Statement of Financial Accounting Standards No. 8 (Stamford, Conn.: FASB, 1975).

19. Robert B. Stobaugh, "Financing Foreign Subsidiaries

of U.S.-Controlled Multinational Enterprises," *Journal of International Business Studies,* Summer 1970, p. 43.

20. Rita M. Rodriguez, "Management of Foreign Exchange Risk in the U.S. Multinationals," *Journal of Financial and Quantitative Analysis,* November 1974, p. 849.

21. Harry Markowitz, "Portfolio Selection," *Journal of Finance,* March 1952, p. 89.

22. Alan C. Shapiro and David P. Rutenberg, "Managing Exchange Risks in a Floating World," *Financial Management,* Summer 1976, p. 48.

23. David B. Zenoff and Jack Zwick, *International Financial Management* (Englewood Cliffs, N.J.: Prentice Hall, 1969), p. 457.

24. Howard V. Perlmutter, "The Tortuous Evolution of the Multinational Corporation," *Columbia Journal of World Business,* January–February 1969.

20

Evaluating Multinational Performance under FAS No. 8

Gerard J. Dietemann

• • •

In times of wide and unpredictable monetary fluctuations, trying to evaluate the performance of a foreign subsidiary of a U.S.-based multinational corporation on the basis of U.S. dollar reports is a little like trying to measure a distance with a rubber yardstick, and can be about as frustrating as playing cricket with Alice in Wonderland. Comparisons made between current-month dollar results and corresponding dollar budgets established only a few months before are often not meaningful. This is so because today's expenses in a foreign subsidiary are translated at an exchange rate different from the rate used at budget time. That is, the dollar value used in budgeting and planning is not the same as the dollar value used subsequently for control purposes. Without a uniform yardstick for both planning and measuring, distortions creep into the entire reporting and control system. International executives are only too familiar with the following scenarios:

- U.S. dollar reports of the Japanese subsidiary of an MNC show selling, G & A expenses to be substantially above the budgeted dollar figure. Called upon to explain the unfavorable variance, the Japanese manager promptly points out that local currency expenses under his control are on target and the excess over budget exists only on U.S. dollar statements because of a steady strengthening of the yen as against the dollar, at a much faster rate than had been anticipated at budget time.

- A subsidiary's foreign exchange loss has grown during the year from a budgeted $10,000 to $600,000. This reduces drastically the reported U.S. dollar profits of the small company even though local currency results are fairly close to budget. Since the management team's bonus is now jeopardized, the manager is clearly unhappy and feels that he should not be penalized because of an unanticipated and perhaps reversible movement between the local currency and the U.S. dollar.

Since it was issued in 1975, the Financial Accounting Standards Board Statement No. 8 (FAS No. 8) has been blamed endlessly in the press for arbitrary fluctuations in and distortions of foreign subsidiaries' earnings. Swings of tens of millions of U.S. dollars in currency

Source: Gerard J. Dietemann, "Evaluating Multinational Performance under FAS No. 8," *Management Accounting,* May, 1980, pp. 49–55. Copyright © 1980 by the National Association of Accountants. Reprinted by permission.

gains and losses between a current and previous period have been reported regularly by major corporations. Such reports were particularly frequent a few years ago when all major currencies were shaken by the dual impact of currency realignments following the transition from fixed to floating exchange rates, and the surge in oil prices.

CAN DOLLAR STATEMENTS PROVIDE FAIR ASSESSMENT OF A SUBSIDIARY?

General misunderstanding of the underlying causes of these distortions of U.S. dollar figures has tended to undermine the credibility of all reported U.S. dollar earnings. This is bad enough per se, but takes on an added dimension for the manager whose performance is being measured by a yardstick of questionable reliability.

The business community often has overreacted and disregarded official U.S. dollar results as a yardstick for measuring a foreign subsidiary's performance. Instead, it has resorted to methods with questionable credentials. We will examine these methods and their implications.

Then, several alternative methods of presenting foreign earnings in terms meaningful to U.S. management will be considered and their reliability examined. It will be shown that official U.S. dollar results, per FAS No. 8, of foreign operations cannot be completely ignored in measuring a foreign subsidiary's performance. On the contrary, official figures must continue to provide the basis for any evaluation method. Adjustments designed to correct the impact on any one year of either the volatility or the magnitude of some exchange rate movements, however, may have to be made. But they must always be applied within an objective and controlled framework.

THE U.S. DOLLAR AS A MEASURING UNIT

Almost 10 years ago, life was considerably simpler for the international manager. The U.S. dollar appeared immutable and destined to remain forever as stable as the Rock of Gibraltar—despite occasional pronouncements to the contrary by Charles de Gaulle. Exchange rates were fixed, and most other currencies tended to erode gradually vis-à-vis the U.S. dollar. The dollar was therefore the ideal measuring unit for assessing the performance of foreign subsidiaries.

For international managers the variables were in most cases reasonably predictable since currency declines were, to a large extent, a function of balance of payment imbalances, and other factors which were easily recognized. As a result, MNCs could safely anticipate and budget the exchange rates of foreign currencies for the following year. In fact, these estimated rates were usually so close to actuality that there was hardly ever a need to adjust them during a fiscal year. A small error in one currency was, in most cases, offset by a compensating error in another currency.

All this ended abruptly in the early '70s with the collapse of the fixed parity system of Bretton Woods. The devaluations of the dollar in 1971 and 1973 ushered in an era of floating exchange rates for practically all currencies—including the dollar. The transition from fixed to floating rates, followed by the oil crisis, produced severe and erratic fluctuations in the exchange rates of all major currencies. The dollar added its own gyrations to those of other currencies and the overall pattern became even more volatile. Actual exchange rates were apt to deviate materially from budgeted rates in any given year. Huge currency translation variances were generated, which, in turn, had a major impact on reported dollar results of foreign subsidiaries. As the dollar's fluctuations increased, its qualifications as an international measuring unit became questionable.

To add insult to injury, FAS No. 8, issued in 1975, imposed not only a common methodology for translating foreign currency statements but also broke with past practice by requiring that all currency gains or losses enter into the determination of current income. Valuation reserves could no longer be used to cushion the impact of unanticipated currency movements. As a result, erratic translation gains and losses were given maximum visibility in the income statement, whether they had been realized or not. Faced with this situation, MNC executives began to blame FAS No. 8 for all their foreign reporting problems.

While FAS No. 8 is far from perfect, executives usually overlooked that the major culprit is not the accounting rule but the wide fluctuations of the U.S. dollar and other currencies. Under similar circumstances most (if not all) translation methods would produce equally erratic results unless, of course, actual currency gains or losses could, as in the past, be deferred; but this is just a cover-up, not a solution. As a matter of fact, there is little doubt that erratic fluctuations will only stop when some measure of stability is restored to the world's major monetary markets, regardless of the translation methods used.

SEARCH FOR ALTERNATE TOOLS

A growing dissatisfaction with FAS No. 8 reporting prompted more and more corporate executives to start clamoring for alternate methods, ostensibly to put fairness back into the performance assessment of foreign subsidiaries and managements. These include the use of:

1. Local currency financial statements;
2. Budgeted exchange rates for translating actual local currency statements during the entire fiscal year, and
3. Official U.S. dollar statements per FAS No. 8 after backing out reported foreign currency translation gains and losses.

Whatever yardstick is used to evaluate a subsidiary's performance (e.g., return on investment, or comparison to budget or to other targets), net annual income generated by the subsidiary normally is, and should be, a key element in the calculation. Each one of the

three approaches referred to above yields a different profit figure, either in local currency (first method) or in U.S. dollars (second and third methods). The merits of each approach will be determined based upon its ability to measure correctly the performance of various management levels in a foreign subsidiary, especially top management. This assessment must be correct—a bonus will be assumed to depend on it.

Let us further assume that we are dealing with a normal U.S.-based MNC whose corporate headquarters and international division are located in the U.S.; and that the international division is responsible for managing the corporation's overseas investments, which consist of decentralized manufacturing subsidiaries organized as profit centers in several foreign countries.

How does each of the three methods perform as a tool for measuring the performance of overseas managers?

Local currency reporting. This method is simple. All revenue and expense items can easily be compared to corresponding items in the local currency budget.

But the method has several drawbacks. One, statements from many countries reported in a multitude of currencies will confuse MNC managers at U.S. headquarters. Two, such statements cannot be used for consolidating the results of a worldwide network of foreign subsidiaries. Three, there is a basic incompatibility in using foreign currency results to measure the performance of a venture created by a U.S.-based MNC, presumably with U.S. dollars. Therefore, the method cannot be recommended for assessing the performance of top management in a subsidiary.

This is not to say that local currency figures are of no use for measuring performance of some international managers. Rather, such figures are indispensable for evaluating results achieved by local middle managers in the cost centers or business segments under their responsibility. Likewise, variance explanations in a standard cost system, cash flow variance, and a variety of other analyses should be done in local currency.

Use of budgeted exchange rates for all translations of local currency statements into U.S. dollars during the fiscal year. This method eliminates the unpredictable nature of erratic currency fluctuations by using budgeted exchange rates—instead of current rates—to translate current local currency statements into U.S. dollars during the fiscal year. (Such U.S. dollar statements are, of course, supplemental to the official FAS No. 8 reports used in the corporate consolidation.) The method permits valid comparisons to be made during the year between actual and budgeted revenue and expense items, all expressed in U.S. dollars. No part of a variance is due to unanticipated changes in exchange rates; the variance is attributable entirely to noncurrency factors under the responsibility of local management in much the same way as if local currency statements were being used. This method also has the same limitations as the first approach; its application should be restricted to evaluating middle management.

Overall U.S. dollar profits calculated under this method can deviate substantially from official FAS No. 8 results, if actual exchange rates differ from budgeted rates during the year. To account for this profit discrepancy, it is usually added to or charged against retained earnings on internal financial statements in order not to affect the performance measurement of the subsidiary. It is then considered the responsibility of corporate headquarters, although there is no rational justification for so doing.

The method therefore can create a situation in which international managers receive good bonuses every year while shareholders suffer a loss. This anomaly can even be aggravated and perpetuated if local managers are successful, at budget time, in influencing in their favor the budgeted exchange rate for the coming year (despite the fact that final decision making in this area usually belongs to corporate management.) Too much reliance on judgmental rates can lead to a breakdown in the assignment of responsibility and accountability.

Finally, valid comparisons cannot be made with actual results of previous years unless past years' financial statements are retranslated at the current budgeted rate. Such retranslations are often of questionable value. Meaningful comparisons can only be made between current year figures, i.e., actual current year results versus budget.

A variant of the above method consists in retranslating during the fiscal year the original local currency budget at current exchange rates for making comparisons to actual results as per FAS No. 8. Both methods have similar strengths and limitations. Under this method, the unaccounted-for profit or loss is between budget figures retranslated at current rates and the original U.S. dollar budget commitment of local management which, literally, is lost in translation.

Neither method can be recommended for evaluating the performance of top management of a foreign subsidiary.

Official U.S. dollar results are used but foreign currency translation gains and losses are backed out of the U.S. dollar income statement. This is undoubtedly the easiest system to implement and to "understand," at least superficially. It gives the comforting illusion that exchange rate fluctuations can be ignored as irrelevant. Unfortunately, the results thus obtained are, in most cases, illusory.

This method is often advocated by local managers when their bonuses are favorably affected and just as forcefully rejected when the impact is unfavorable. In any event, it is basically irrational. Calculating bonuses on local currency results would make more sense.

The method is both unreliable and deceptive. It gives the appearance of eliminating the impact of currency de- or re-evaluations when, in fact, it usually does not because the effect of currency changes is not restricted to the "foreign translation gain or loss" line in the income statement but is truly an integral part of the financial statements.

Making the assumption of a weakening foreign currency to eliminate in the income statement all traces of currency changes would also entail rolling back selling price increases set to counter a declining currency, adjusting cost of goods sold, reducing high interest costs which are symptomatic of a devaluation climate, and probably making many other adjustments to the income statement.

This is, of course, not practical; financial statements would become totally cut off from reality and subject to all sorts of manipulations by interested parties. Any meaningful performance evaluation needs objective standards consistently applied, which are definitely absent in this method. Accordingly, it should be rejected out of hand.

METHODS ILLUSTRATED

Table 1 demonstrates the profits that result from the application of the three alternate methods and of FAS No. 8. In it, annual income statements and balance sheets (budget and actual) are presented in local currency (LC) and then translated into dollars. Exchange rates used assume a devaluation of the local currency.

Given the wide disparity in results obtained by applying each translation method, which of the examples in Table 1 most accurately represents the performance of the foreign subsidiary? Is a one-year time frame even appropriate for measuring the effects of a major currency fluctuation on reported U.S. dollar results? In many cases, probably not. Particularly with long lead time items, the effects of a major de- or re-evaluation will influence reported profitability well beyond the year in which it occurs. Furthermore, short-term fluctuations are reversible in case of float, resulting in continuing distortions.

VALIDITY OF ALTERNATIVE METHODS

The first and third alternatives are not acceptable for evaluating a foreign subsidiary's overall performance. Local currency reporting is not practical for a U.S.-based MNC and simply backing out foreign translation gains or losses in

the U.S. dollar income statement is conceptually unsound. Method #2, which uses budgeted exchange rates, has serious limitations when applied outside the confines of specific expense and revenue items under the responsibility of middle management in a subsidiary. For higher management levels, the method is inappropriate. Nevertheless, all computations should be made under Method #2 at least annually. These calculations will help guide the manager to a fair assessment of a foreign operation through a method described below.

The proposed method is predicated on the proposition that there must be consistency between the standards used by international management to measure a subsidiary's top managers, and evaluate the contribution made by a subsidiary to consolidated profitability.

Method #2 fails to qualify as a tool for measuring a subsidiary's overall performance because its results are totally divorced from the subsidiary's reported earnings contribution, per FAS No. 8, to consolidated corporate profitability. This lack of correlation is a major weakness because it is precisely on the sum total of such contributions that the investing community will value the MNC's stock.

On the other hand, FAS No. 8 results fail too, unless properly adjusted. In periods of high currency volatility, FAS No. 8 accounting rules and disclosure policy tend to accentuate the impact of currency movements on a company's reported results, often to the detriment of local management's evaluation and bonus in any given year. If reported figures are to be used, it is necessary, in certain years, either to even out temporary swings resulting from currency floats or to spread the impact of major de- or revaluation over an appropriate period of two or more years.

The method I propose recognizes the need for occasional adjustments to these official results and establishes guidelines designed to create and maintain close links between adjusted results and FAS No. 8 earnings. Judicious application of these guidelines by international home office management will prevent the

Table 1 Which Performance Measurement Is Best?

Exchange Rates

Beginning of year, actual rate:	LC1	=	$0.25
End of year, budget rate:	LC1	=	$0.22
End of year, actual rate:	LC1	=	$0.18
Average rate, budget:	LC1	=	$0.235
Average rate, actual:	LC1	=	$0.215

Beginning and Ending Balance Sheets for Year 19—

	Beginning Balance Sheet, Actual		Ending Balance Sheet — Budget			Ending Balance Sheet — Actual		
Assets								
Cash + receivables	LC	5,000	$1,250	LC	7.000	$1,540	LC	8.000	$1,440
Inventory		8,000	2,000		9,000	2,115		10,000	2,150
Fixed assets (net)		4,000	1,000		5,000	1,235		5,000	1,215
Total	LC	17,000	$4,250	LC	21,000	$4,890		23,000	4,805
Liabilities								
Current liabilities		7,000	1,750		8,000	1,760		9,200	1,656
Borrowings		6,000	1,500		7,500	1,650		8,000	1,440
Equity		4,000	1,000		5,500	1,480		5,800	1,709
Total	LC	17,000	$4,250	LC	21,000	$4,890	LC	23,000	$4,808

Income statement for year 19–

	Budget		Actual Per Method 2			Actual Per FAS No. 8		
Sales	LC	16,000	$3,760	LC	18,000	$4,230	LC	18,000	$3,870
Margin		6,000	1,290		6,500	1,407		6,500	1,117
Expenses		(3,000)	(705)		(3,000)	(705)		(3,000)	(645)
Exchange gains/(losses)			248			260			603
Profit before tax		3,000	833		3,500	962		3,500	1,075
Profit after tax	LC	1,500	$ 480	LC	1,800	$ 539	LC	1,800	$ 709

Summary of Results Under the Various Methods (Profit After Tax)

	Actual	Budget
Method 1 (in LC)	LC 1,800	LC 1,500
Method 2 (in $)	$ 539	$ 480
Method 3 (in $)	106	232
FAS No. 8 (in $)	709	480

unaccountable earnings gap referred to under Method #2 from getting out of control, while, at the same time, providing a framework for an equitable evaluation of top subsidiary management.

The objective of a first set of guidelines is to yield an adjusted profit figure for the year which has just been closed (i.e., year 19— in Table 1). The guidelines call for the establishment of an earnings range comprising at one end the official FAS No. 8 results and at the other, U.S. dollar results calculated according to Method #2. Method #2, it is recalled, yields U.S. dollar results which differ from FAS No. 8 results only in that budgeted exchange rates are used to translate local currency statements. In all other respects, the two sets of results are internally consistent. On the assumption that budget rates were established with great care and reflect the long-term outlook of the currency, adjusted earnings should be made to fall within this range. As noted in Table 1, this range would be between $709, representing official net profit per FAS No. 8, and the $539 hypothetical profit figure under Method #2.

A second set of adjustments is designed to ensure that aggregate adjusted results for the current and next one or two years (to be decided by international management) agree with combined FAS No. 8 earnings for the same period of time. This will prevent adjusted results from straying too far from FAS No. 8 results over a period of several years. This approach is conceptually justifiable on the grounds that any systematic and rational translation method should yield roughly the same profits over the long run.

Once adjusted profits have been determined, what benchmark should be used to measure them? While there are many potential candidates, the U.S. dollar profit commitment established at budget time is most meaningful in the present context. This, and similar commitments from other subsidiaries, have formed the basis for corporate planning and resource allocations. This commitment of any one subsidiary is also fully consistent with the adjusted profits of that subsidiary, because both sets of results are based on the same corporate capital structure.

APPLICATION OF THE PROPOSED METHOD

Having accepted these ground rules, the international manager at headquarters will first decide whether reported earnings need to be adjusted. A comparison between bonus calculations based on FAS No. 8 and Method #2 results will provide a clue as to whether the local manager will consider the difference between the two figures to be "material." If it is, an adjustment is called for.

Next, he will make a number of judgmental decisions. Among the most important are (a) his assessment of the nature of currency movements observed during the year, i.e., a long-term trend or merely reversible float; (b) the selection of the appropriate time period over which adjusted earnings must be made to equal official earnings, and (c) the amount by which official earnings must be adjusted to evaluate equitably the subsidiary's performance during the year under consideration.

At the time these decisions are made, i.e., at the end of the fiscal year, at bonus time, the manager should have a reasonably good insight into the nature and long-term implications of currency movements that occurred during the fiscal year.

Nevertheless, there may still be many unanswered questions. In real life, currency movements are often a complex combination of floats and permanent de- or re-valuations. The earnings reconciliation required for control purposes, therefore, can be greatly complicated and may have to be extended in time beyond the originally selected period. Careful documentation of adjustments over the years and a sound knowledge of economic factors in a foreign country are essential prerequisites for successful implementation.

His analysis of the situation may convince the international manager that the exchange rate deviations from budget rates are not permanent, but represent only temporary swings in a currency float which will reverse itself in the near future. He will then establish an adjusted earnings figure which comes close to Method #2 results within the earnings range. If his assessment turns out to be correct, the float will swing back in the following year and a similar adjustment to FAS No. 8 profits in the opposite direction will result in a fair evaluation of both years' performance. The combined results for both years under the two methods will be in agreement and the control objectives of the method will thus be achieved.

On the other hand, the consensus at international headquarters may be that a re- or devaluation is permanent (as, for example, in Mexico in 1976 or in Indonesia in 1978). In this case, the reported foreign exchange transaction and balance sheet gains or losses reported in the year will not be reversed in the near future; they are real in the sense that their realization is usually only a matter of time. Nevertheless, it may be advisable to spread the de- or re-valuation effects over a two- to three-year period (depending on the magnitude of the currency movement and, perhaps, on the timing of realization of losses or gains) on the theory that the underlying causes and effects of such permanent currency movements usually extend beyond one year. Reported official profits again will be adjusted to fall within the earnings range. This time, however, unlike results in the currency float situation, the adjusted earnings figure will be closer to FAS No. 8.

Note that the method must take into consideration future business activity and currency trends in making earnings adjustments. Properly administered, it should prove an incentive for managers in the home offiice or the field.

Finally, a foreign subsidiary's U.S.-dollar results adjusted under the proposed system should be used only for local top management evaluation purposes. These results are not necessarily suitable for other uses. Earnings comparisons with other foreign subsidiaries can be misleading because various subsidiaries may differ substantially in terms of capital structure and other factors, such as debt and dividend policies.

ACCOUNTABILITY OF THE LOCAL MANAGEMENT TEAM

One of the key premises underlying the proposed method for evaluating the performance of foreign subsidiaries is that the local top management team in a subsidiary is held accountable, at least in part, for earnings deviations due to foreign exchange movements. In fact, if local top managers are unable or unwilling to think in U.S. dollar terms, corporate efforts at controlling these deviations cannot be fully successful. Local top managers must accept this responsibility as just one more risk of doing business abroad. Relieving a subsidiary's top management of all responsibility for foreign exchange exposure is just as unrealistic and damaging to the MNC's overall performance as would be a decision to exonerate a sales manager on the ground that his sales shortfall is due to stronger than anticipated competitive activity during the year and is, therefore, not his fault.

The responsibility of overseas top managers for managing foreign exposure must be clearly defined in corporate procedures. It should comprise direct responsibility for realized and unrealized transaction losses and gains, and shared responsibility with international division management for balance sheet translation exposure. Ultimate decision-making authority in this area usually is vested in international division management in the U.S., primarily for reasons of worldwide coordination. However, local subsidiary management frequently is in the best position to evaluate overall foreign exchange exposure risk, including economic exposure, and should therefore be constantly on the alert to make recommendations.

The above definitions assume a good understanding by local managers of the impact that currency movements can have on their financial statements under FAS No. 8. The managers must be prepared to either take action or make recommendations in areas of exchange exposure such as invoice prices and currencies, sourcing of imported raw materials, leading, lagging or hedging techniques, and payments of interim dividends in anticipation of a devaluation. Exchange rates will be set by international management but local advice should be considered.

CONTROLLED ASSESSMENT

FAS No. 8 doubtless has a number of shortcomings. Its detractors are correct when they point out that the method looks at foreign companies from a static and narrow U.S. dollar perspective (a "liquidation concept" according to some) rather than from a dynamic "going-concern" foreign currency perspective; but then, I suspect, so do most U.S. shareholders whose savings have been invested in foreign ventures.

Results derived through FAS No. 8 do not lend themselves to evaluating the performance of international managers on a consistent basis. They tend to exaggerate the impact of currency fluctuations, materially distorting financial results in years of high currency turbulence, which precludes the use of such figures for bonus calculations.

Various methods for evaluating MNC division performance have been proposed. Some of them are adequate for evaluating the performance of middle level managers but are inappropriate for the top international jobs. A valid evaluation method for the latter must be based on earnings figures that are consistent over the long run with those which these same managers report under FAS No. 8 to the MNC's shareholders.

Consistency with FAS No. 8 results implies that top managers in foreign locations, to a cer-

tain extent, are held accountable for U.S. dollar results of their operations and hence for the impact on their financial statements of exchange rate variations from the rates forecast at budget time.

The method proposed here focuses on the assessment of top managers in the MNC units abroad. Under this method, the evaluations process starts with reported FAS No. 8 results. Adjustments necessitated by unexpected currency movements are strictly controlled within specified limits; they will affect not only current but also future earnings. Control is achieved by making sure that aggregate adjusted earnings within a time frame determined by the international manager agree with combined FAS No. 8 earnings for the same period. This control objective must never be lost sight of, even if unexpected and new exchange rate deviations in successive years force an extension of the time span for the reconciliation of the two sets of earnings.

This method leads to guidelines for arriving at adjusted profits within an earnings range. These adjusted earnings provide a measure of local top management's accountability. The U.S. dollar profit commitment made at budget time by local management is the benchmark against which the adjusted earnings should be compared. It is obvious that a careful budget preparation will enhance the reliability of the performance evaluation process at bonus time one year later.

The proposed system does not completely eliminate subjective judgment, and it will always be strained by major upheavals and unexpected circumstances, as would probably any other systematic approach. It is, however, tied in a flexible manner to an objective set of figures, namely FASB results, and over a period of years. It therefore avoids the dangers and pitfalls usually associated with fully judgmental and open-ended approaches which can easily degenerate into popularity contests.

SECTION 5
Marketing

In the successful firm, marketing and strategic planning are closely linked activities. Marketing provides a key input to strategic plans as they are developed by identifying and helping to evaluate alternative product/market foci. Marketing activities then play a key role in the implementation of strategic plans. In both formulating and implementing strategy, the multinational marketer must deal with a much larger and much more diverse set of alternatives and a more complex set of decisions than those faced by his or her domestic counterpart.

The erstwhile multinational marketer must make a series of decisions, beginning with a consideration of whether to enter foreign countries/markets at all. Then the marketer must select countries/markets and decide on marketing mix strategies for each. Entering a new country market means dealing with an environment that may be considerably different from that which has been faced domestically. Even in a world that is moving toward increasing similarity in consumer tastes, marketing methods, production processes, and business practices, some subtle (and some not so subtle) differences still persist.

There are many examples of global convergence in consumer tastes ranging from the worldwide success of Coca-Cola to the acceptance of air travel. In spite of global convergence, sales of rice still lead bread sales in Japan by a considerable margin, a situation that is also reflected in a higher household penetration rate for toasters in the United States than in Japan and a higher penetration rate for electric rice cookers in Japan. In many European countries, per capita beer consumption is much higher than in the United States, whereas soft drink consumption is significantly lower. Demand for large automobiles is considerably higher in the United States than elsewhere.

The firm entering a foreign country/market may also face a different set of competitors whose marketing practices and whose response to a new market entrant may be different from those of home market competitors. Moreover, the set of marketing institutions, from distribution channels to advertising agencies, may be considerably different in both capabilities and practices. And to complicate matters still further, the legal and regulatory environment changes as one moves around the world. (Some of the key legal and regulatory considerations are taken up in Section 8 of this book.) While there have been some conspicuous failures posted by firms trying to market in foreign countries, there have also been many resounding successes. The complications and problems can be overcome by smart, determined managers.

Most observers agree that a typical firm's international marketing activities proceed along a continuum of involvement, beginning with exporting, often to an independent distributor in the country of destination. The next steps along the continuum are increasing involvement with marketing and distribution, replacing the independent distributor with a company-owned sales force and physical distribution facilities. The final step is to replace exports with local production. This, of course, describes the process occurring in any one country/market; at the same time that the firm is deepening its involvement in a particular country, it may also be widening it by marketing in an increasing number of countries. It also describes the process a firm goes through with the first products it sells in each country. Once the firm is established, it will use its existing facilities wherever possible.

READING SELECTIONS

Cannon presents an overview of many of the problems and tasks associated with managing both export and international marketing. While his presentation is based primarily on studies of the international marketing activities of British firms, his observations are more widely generalizable. He begins by looking at the reasons why a firm might want to enter international markets. (After reading this section of Cannon's article, students may want to reread Gluck, "Global Competition in the 1980s," and Vernon, "The Product Cycle Hypothesis in a New International Environment," to integrate a marketing management and corporate strategy perspective.)

Cannon observes that international marketers should more widely use differentiated or segmented marketing approaches just as they do in the domestic market; however, pricing, distribution, and promotion decisions may be different from those required in the home market. Furthermore, products may require modification. Because of these possibilities, he contends that marketing research is an important precursor to market entry, and he offers some evidence to support this contention. Our own view is that test marketing (or some variant of test marketing in which the actual product is used) can be a better and ultimately less costly alternative than marketing research, especially for new products. A small test, set up in such a way that results can be carefully measured and the factors contributing positively and negatively to success can be identified, can be much more reliable than straight research. Consumer and trade reactions to the actual product are much less susceptible to misinterpretation than are their responses to items on a questionnaire. This is especially true when dealing with a strange environment. But the test must be set up so that appropriate differential diagnoses can be made. Test marketing can also provide the most valuable input to the world standardization versus country/market specific alternatives problem Cannon poses by identifying not only whether product changes must be made, but exactly what changes are required.

Both Suzman and Wortzel and Ayal and Zif explore in more detail specific facets of the market entry and expansion decision. Suzman and Wortzel focus on exporting. They suggest that firms need specific strategies to be successful exporters and that a firm's export strategy should be based on its technology profile, whether it is a new or mature innovator, an adapter, or a marketer. They identify three possible exporting strategies—responder, imitator, and entrepreneur—and then link technology profiles and exporting strategies. They go on to describe the pattern of overseas business that is likely to result from the adoption of each strategy.

Merely choosing the appropriate strategy, however, does not assure exporting success. The strategy must receive top management support and must be properly implemented. As will be apparent from a reading of the Suzman and Wortzel article, the requirements for successful implementation are different for different strategies. New innovators can, for example, rely to some extent on potential customers to seek them out, but mature innovators, who face many more competitors must vigorously search for and develop new markets for their products.

Ayal and Zif explore another important aspect of strategy: deciding on how many countries/markets to serve and how much effort to allocate to each market. They identify two alternatives, concentration and diversification. A concentration strategy is marked by slow growth in the number of countries/markets served, accompanied by a relatively high level of effort in each. Diversification strategies involve fast growth in the number of countries/markets served and a relatively lower level of effort in each. There is a group of product markets/factors that Ayal and Zif believe should affect the choice between the two strategies. These include (among others) the sales response function, growth rate, and the need for product adaptation. The authors explain how these factors should be taken into account in making choices.

Harrell and Kiefer propose a framework that can be of help in comparing alternative countries/markets. Their approach uses a variant of the well-known G.E. business screening matrix, with country attractiveness as one dimension and competitive strength as the other. These authors list and analyze some specific or variables that they believe bear on each dimension. However, the specific variables that a marketer should weigh most heavily in a particular situation are not necessarily always limited to those proposed in the Harrell and Kiefer piece. In a particular situation, some of the variables proposed by Ayal and Zif, for example, might well be added to or substituted for variables in the Harrell and Kiefer list.

The major contributions of the Harrell and Kiefer article may be not just the variables they recommend. Another contribution is the concept of using an appropriately designed business screen and then asembling a portfolio of countries/markets that together provide a desired level of risk and investment/cash generation characteristics.

Kotler and Fahey take us off in a different, but important, direction. This article describes how some Japanese firms have used the marketing mix variables to great advantage in their export markets. In studying this article, the reader should keep firmly in mind that the successes described are not the result of good marketing alone. They were all dependent also on a production system, backed by market-responsive R&D and product design, that could produce cost-efficient products to specific country/markets and market segments. More specifically, a closer analysis suggests that Japanese firms' early successes were based on exports of incremental production of products that were already being manufactured in large quantities for the home market. Sustaining and building on the early successes, however, has involved gaining an understanding of specific product needs and then adjusting a design/production system to satisfy these needs.

The reader might also want to ask to what extent Japan's export success was aided by domestic marketers in the United States and, to a degree, Europe, who ignored or left open market segments that the Japanese could easily fill. In the United States especially, domestic manufacturers of products ranging from office copiers to TV sets pursued trade-up strategies that left room for new entrants who could offer low prices and simpler versions of the product. The lessons, then, from this article are twofold. It offers insights into both the marketing strategies and production/R&D support needed for successful international marketing. But just as important, a careful reading of the article will also show how domestic firms can become vulnerable to foreign competition. Some thought they might suggest strategies by which domestic firms can best protect themselves from such competition before it develops.

The final article in this section, by Schuster, covers an important, but not too well understood topic, barter. Many potential international marketing transactions, especially where the buyer is from a command economy or a developing country, would not be consummated if payment in hard currency were required. This article discusses the variety of barter arrangements that can be made to facilitate these transactions. The marketer who is alert to barter possibilities and is active in arranging barter schemes can develop significant amounts of business where others, unaware of the range of barter possibilities, might fail completely.

21

Managing International and Export Marketing
T. Cannon

• • •

The study of management in international trade has focused on two distinct but interrelated areas:

1. *International or Multinational Marketing:* giving weight to the development of business in a number of countries or regions, within a framework capable of incorporating the establishment of local manufacturing, distribution and marketing systems.
2. *Export Marketing:* with its emphasis on the successful marketing of goods produced in one or more countries in other overseas markets.

The distinction between the areas is not neat. The exporter is differentiated from the international marketer by the foreign or alien nature of his products in the market he seeks, while the international marketer can eliminate this in many circumstances. The multinational corporation, however, seeks to avoid the very notion of home versus foreign trade in corporate policy. Specific units within the multinational can adopt policies identifiable as export or international marketing. Corporate strategy in these and other types of firm may be one of these but incorporate a powerful element of the alternative.

This can be seen in both giant corporations and small companies. The Ford Motor Company, with its manufacturing capability in a number of countries, its exclusive distributorships and distinctive, national promotional policies operated through member firms epitomises the multinational. The operating units act as both exporters and international marketers. They may seek to win foreign business for vehicles made in the home market and designed to meet its special needs. Equally, operating units can come together, as with the Fiesta, to develop cars meeting needs which transcend national boundaries. The smaller firm's options are generally more restricted. Overseas manufacturing capability, where it exists, is usually restricted to one or two plants, with the major significant alternative being joint venture operations with overseas entrepreneurs. However, the managers of all concerns trading in a number of independent states face resource allocation, business development and marketing decisions against a background of competing demands at home and overseas.

The fundamental decision for the firm is whether to enter the international arena at all. At its most basic level this interacts with the basic issue of why international trade, with its problems of conflicting interests, tariffs, logistics difficulties, marketing and communication problems, emerged and persists. The economist's explanation is based primarily on the theory of Comparative Advantage. This theory, first fully expounded by Ricardo (67) focuses on the wide diversity in conditions across the parts and countries of the world. These differences, in turn, create significant variations in the production capabilities of countries. On occasion, these lead to specific absolute advantages: the soil of one country may be suitable for one crop, that of another for a second crop. Assuming each is in demand in both countries the basis for specialisation based on simple advantage exists. Ricardo's major refinement, and the foundation stone of the theory which Samuel-

Source: T. Cannon, "Managing International and Export Marketing," *European Journal of Marketing,* Volume 14, Number 1, 1980, pp. 34–49. Copyright © 1980 *European Journal of Marketing,* MCB University Press Ltd. 200 Keighley Road, Bradford, England BD9 4JQ. Reprinted by permission.

son (73) argues "when *properly* stated, is unassailable," was the proposition that even a country with an absolute advantage for all goods will benefit from specialisation in those areas where it is relatively most efficient, importing those commodities in which it has a comparative disadvantage.

As indicated by Samuelson's remark, the basic approach still holds considerable currency among modern economists. Two major developments within the overall theory have emerged over the last thirty years. The Factor Endowment Theory of Trade has been expostulated by E. Hecksher (33) and by B. Ohlin (65). This is based on the proposition that there is considerable variation in the resources of production between countries. These factor endowments determine the patterns of international trade. Hence a country will export those goods using the factors with which they are relatively well supplied and import goods using the factors with which they are relatively ill supplied. The Stolper-Samuelson Theorem (80) is closely associated with the Hecksher-Ohlin model. This describes the effect of protection on relatively scarce factors. The basic thoery is described simply and well by Finlay (26).

The improving power of methods of investigation has led to a growing number of empirical studies of these theories and the hypotheses deriving from them. McDougall's (53) study of U.S. and British exports is an important landmark in this process. Despite Bagwati's (2) refutation of the study's main conclusions, McDougall's study contrives to provide some support for the basic theory of Comparative Advantage. However, soon after McDougall's investigation a major paradox came from Leontief's analysis of input-output tables. It emerged that in the case of the U.S. economy "exports embody slightly more labour and considerably less capital than import replacements of the same value" (48). This is despite the fact that the U.S. is generally seen as an economy relatively abundant in capital but relatively less well endowed with labour. There has been con-

siderable debate on these findings both in terms of their substance (23, 68) and their implications for economics and policymakers (90, 30). The continuing discussion within the overall subject of the economics of international trade is well summarised by Finlay (26) and Hogendorn (35). For, both in the individual country and the specific firm the debate over the theory of comparative advantage and its free trade implications constitutes the backcloth against which their policies and decisions must be made. Overall it demonstrates the advantages deriving from trade without being able to solve the problems resulting from the wish of countries and corporations to protect themselves from some of the rigours of the open market. The desire to secure short and medium term advantage in specific areas, to protect jobs, to obtain access to new technologies and skills (internationally mobile factors) and ultimately to create domestic wealth, provides the ultimate spur for both the politician and the manager.

WHY TRADE OVERSEAS?

The approaches identified above provide partial justification for the firm's decision to market its output in foreign countries. Any absolute or relative advantage that the firm may have will be rewarded by additional business. Wells (93) describes the process of movement into world markets in terms of a trade cycle. Using as illustration a product originating in the U.S., he describes four basic stages:

Phase 1: U.S. export strength
Phase 2: Foreign production starts
Phase 3: Foreign production competitive in exports
Phase 4: Import competition begins.

This model has immediate managerial implications for the firms in the originating countries.

During phase one, the monopoly period, the overseas demand for innovator-produced goods grows and is met from the originating country. As the market grows in specific countries pressure to establish domestic manufacture, to reduce imports, to minimise freight costs, etc. emerges. For the successful product this will eventually mean indigenous production. The exporter can protect his new business by two distinct strategies: the export marketing or the international marketing stance.

He can protect his base for some time through patents and other protection. They will eventually end or be superceded. More positively he can adopt development or marketing strategies to keep his offerings ahead of the local competition while sustaining his home market production base. During the second stage local production will take up part of the base demand, if only for a low price undifferentiated core product. The international marketer is in a strong position to accommodate this development through the establishment of local manufacture, either wholly or partly owned by the originator.

During phase three foreign produced goods gradually take over the overseas markets, with originator exports of the core product declining. In the fourth and final phase the foreign manufactured goods have sufficient advantages in production costs, labour charges etc. to penetrate the originator's market. The primary sources of protection for the initiator remains as those of the product innovator, whose original offering has been overtaken by his own newer developments, or the international marketer, with a stake in the foreign manufacture. A series of studies of specific industries have provided evidence of international product life-cycle behavior (94). However, the overall model suffers from the recurrent difficulties of all life-cycle models (19), notably that while providing a good description of specific cases there exist significant exceptions even within the specified area of manufactured goods. Robinson (68) points out:

Product life-cycle theory . . . would not, for example, explain Volkswagen's recent decision to invest in the United States. The automobile is a mature product. Production has been, and theoretically should be, moving out of the United States, not in.

Also notable are products which, for particular reasons, never get beyond a specific stage in the life-cycle—the overseas market may never become large enough to justify establishing a manufacturing capability. As markets become more sophisticated there is likely to be increased adaption of products rather than simple adoption. This is likely to speed penetration of the target overseas market but reduce the product's potential in the originator's market. The innovator himself can invest successfully in further developments in product and process to preclude foreign derivatives. Despite these comments, this model provides perhaps the most fully developed and researched tool in international marketing analysis, with a significant capability to assist in marketing planning.

MANAGEMENT AND EXPORT MARKETING

Wells' work has highlighted the recurrent problem of the export marketer. This is the propensity of independent countries to seek to establish local manufacturing capacity for imported items or produce appropriate substitutes. Although this is not feasible in all markets, the firm's export success may stimulate other manufacturers, located perhaps closer to the market or benefiting from lower costs to compete for markets. British industry has faced this problem in markets ranging from textiles to commercial vehicles (95). The U.K. motor tyre industry is perhaps the most recent illustration of the problem (71).

Robinson (68) in his classic text in the area, pointed out the importance of the market orientated factors of "direct exposure" to markets, "market research" and "specialised research and development" among others, in providing "the organisational hallmarks of the successful international firm." The basis of any effective marketing operation, whether at home or abroad, is effective market selection:

The total market for most types of products is too heterogeneous for market management to derive maximum value from an analysis of it as a whole. (80)

The importance of this in the management of export markets has been recently re-affirmed by the BETRO report (4). The report's basic theme is that:

Some of the most successful companies tend to concentrate (as a matter of conscious policy) on a few products or a few markets.

The importance of this for British exporters was confirmed in a later report (3) comparing United Kingdom, French and German exporters:

British companies appeared to sell to more markets, i.e., 40 per cent of the British companies interviewed sold to more than one hundred markets compared with 32 per cent in France and only 20 per cent in Germany.
The contrast between the U.K. and Germany is even more marked when the policy of medium and small companies is considered.

The overall impression is that an undifferentiated, mass market approach is commonly adopted in exporting when a differentiated, target marketing or segmentation stance may be more successful. This would be supported by the experience of modern domestic marketing where selectivity brings the advantages of specificity and relevance to seller-buyer relationships (31). Besides this, "with proper search there is a greater likelihood of finding and correcting weaknesses and inefficiencies in the firm's marketing effort" (16).

The emergence of improved information and data from both national and international organisations is greatly assisting the process of target marketing through classifying, ranking, segmenting and clustering countries or markets. National statistical information varies considerably in quality and range. It is being complemented by data collected and published by international bodies such as the European Economic Community, the Organisation for Economic Co-operation and Development, the United Nations and the World Bank. Vogel (88) highlights the persistent problem of identification of the appropriate cluster variables in attempts to cluster countries. He employed managerial perceptions as a basis for clustering. However, his research brings out the severe problems facing workers in this area. These problems had emerged earlier in work by Sherbini (76). Setni (75) has pioneered the use of cluster analysis in this area. Jaffe's use of factor analytic techniques has provided evidence of the potential power of the rigorous use of quantitative techniques in this area (40). The growing strength of the international data base is slowly creating the environment in which quantitative technique of increasing power can be applied to export marketing, opportunity identification and resource allocation (60). In the interim, firms will continue to use broad economic criteria such as level of economic development to produce overall groupings (32).

In the process of homing onto specific markets and developing export business, market research has an important role. However, despite substantial government assistance in Britain, McFarlane (54) notes the apparent reluctance of many firms to conduct formal market research investigations. The limited research into this area (39) in other countries confirms the low priority given to this area. Despite this, Engle, Blackwell and Kollat argue that:

The need for cultural understanding and research is particularly evident when a communications strategist attempts to deal with the cultures of other countries. (24)

In-depth investigation is urgently needed into this area where a vicious circle of a large number of markets and lack of differentiation exists. This is, in part, caused by a reluctance to embark on detailed investigations because of the complexities of dealing with so many markets. This, in turn, leads to the persistence of a sales versus a marketing orientation (11) even in firms adopting a marketing approach domestically (97).

Douglas, Le Maire and Wind (21) overcome this knowledge gap, in part, by integrating "intuitive decision rules" and a "systematic" evaluation system in their market selection process. But once the opportunity has been identified there remains the problem of fully exploiting its potential. This, in turn, calls for product development, price, promotional and distribution strategies geared to the needs of the buyer overseas rather than the expediences of home production or the requirements of domestic demand. Kalfayan (42) is particularly damning of British industry in this area. The lack of meaningful comparative analysis begs the question of relative performance. It is an issue inextricably interwoven with target marketing, as only through some degree of selectivity can the manager cope with the differences in requirement and taste. Thomas (84) notes the importance of effective product development in winning export business:

"The key to success in product planning is to adapt the product (line) to the tastes and economic characteristics of the particular foreign market."

This cannot be achieved when the firm adopts an inactive export stance (10), or when the firm is willing to accept nominal penetration of a large number of export markets. To effectively exploit the product's life-cycle in individual markets a pattern of development, adaption and revitalisation similar to the home market should be adopted.

Wells (94) and, from a different perspective, Kravis (45) focus on the importance of the technological gap in providing a degree of real advantage in opening up foreign markets. However, the lead established by the initial product can only be sustained for a finite period of time. The narrowness of the gap has been highlighted by evidence on the relatively low R&D cost involved in many major innovations (63), a pattern brought out clearly in the recent ACARD report (1).

Pricing policies play a major part in determining the pay-offs from the "imitative gap" and, equally importantly, the medium to long term returns from the market. The company introducing its offering to a market for the first time faces many of the problems identified by Dean in his seminal work on the subject (18). Many developments have emerged from this work. Among the most interesting, building on the notion of understanding potential and probable demand, is Gabor's work on market orientated prices (28). Here the importance of detailed investigation of the market is emphasised. For the established product different issues are important. The market situations facing basically the same product can vary considerably. In some markets the product or process may be recently introduced innovation, in others it can be well established but facing severe domestic competition. The variety of circumstances suggests that some degree of price differentiation by market rather than global price structure, modified solely by cost factors, will earn the greatest returns. Cateora and Hess (13) acknowledge this but state that:

Regardless of the strategic factors involved and the company's orientation to market pricing, every price must be set with cost considerations in mind.

This is a message which fits in with the pricing policies of most firms (52). In overseas markets:

- Tariffs and taxes
- Middlemen costs
- Finance and risk

are emphasised by Cateora and Hess. To these can be added:

- Cash flow
- Export business development
- Market oriented modifications and adaptions.

Given the number of factors likely to add to the end price, a strict policy of cost and ultimately price management and control is central to successful exporting. This goes beyond the necessary economics of efficient business management to a determination to ensure that the price the customer pays is geared to achieving the firm's goals.

The part played by the agent or distributor in

this is critical. Some price escalation is probable, given the much more extensive intermediary systems characteristic of many export markets. Despite that, there are some indications which suggest that specific middlemen use the lack of direct involvement or loose control by some exporters to escalate prices to a point where growth is limited:

we saw ourselves as a middlerange, mid-price manufacturer but on visiting the market found we were the most expensive clubs on the market.

MD of Golf Club Manufacturer

Modern marketing management literature places considerable emphasis on Channel and Physical Distribution (49, 5). The interdependence of manufacturer and middleman is necessary for the efficient movement of goods and services, payments and title in many markets. The distance and alien nature of many overseas markets has created a situation in which:

At home, many firms are actively engaged in promotion and selling but abroad they often rely more heavily on independent distributors or agents. (62)

This pattern was noted in the Betro report (4).

The intermediary systems seen in foreign markets reflect the heterogeneous nature of the markets themselves. A number of highly specialised channel members have emerged to handle the special problems of international trade. Export houses, export managers, foreign buyers resident in the country, import/export agents, export brokers, confirming houses and distributors provide a wide variety of services, described very fully in certain directories (25). In some countries individual solutions have emerged to play a part in both their home and export markets. Ikeda (37) describes the operations of the General Trading Companies in Japan's business system. In Eastern Europe all foreign trade is conducted exclusively through state trading organisations (34).

The initial channel problems of establishing the optimum fit of intermediary type or system

and the firm's needs in the market are described very fully by Duguid and Jacques (22). The last decade has seen a rapid growth in interest in channel management (49). This has led a growth in awareness of "the range of strategies which can be successfully implemented by firms within the distributive system" (17). Despite this, there persists a tendency in exports to view intermediary management in terms of single step relationships rather than integrated channels. On establishing the optimum intermediary system for a specific market or product in a country the problems of recruitment, management, motivation and control of middlemen are critical to business development. A number of good works, albeit generally from a descriptive perspective, have been published in this area (54). There does exist a serious shortage of in-depth analysis in this area. Forbes' (27) study of the use of commission agents is one of the few substantive investigations into the area. He concluded by questioning the value of the commission agent as employed by the firms in his study. He called for the adoption of a more active stance in business development and product promotion in their markets.

In a series of empirical investigations, the other dimension of making goods available, Physical Distribution, has been brought to the fore. Studies of machine tools (56), cars (14), pumps and valves, domestic electrical appliances, electric motors, organic chemicals and plastics (62) have highlighted the impact of poor delivery and service in British exports even where products and prices have been competitive. It encompasses all those activities concerned with the efficient movement of goods and materials out from the manufacturer and towards the customers for use or consumption. The distances involved, the lags in flows of both goods, documentation and payment, the high cost of storage and the complexities of interstate/inter-region regulation place Physical Distribution Management at the centre of effective export management. Despite this, there has been relatively little systematic investigation of the area. One or two excellent textbooks exist describing basic principles (86), but there has been relatively little study of the impact of the total lost approach (47), cash flow problems (70), the effect of the dramatic changes in modes of transport, freight, storage and communication (96, 59) on the export environment over the last twenty years. This is changing with increasing interest partly stimulated by journals, such as the *International Journal of Physical Distribution Management,* and organisations such as the Centre for Physical Distribution Management (U.K.) and the National Council for Physical Distribution Management (U.S.).

There has been significantly more research into promotional policies in exports. This has concentrated on sales force activity and advertising. Carson (12) points out that:

Notwithstanding the development of more sophisticated marketing methods and technologies, personal selling remains the most important segment of marketing in all parts of the globe.

The BETRO report (4) points out that in the firms they studied, direct selling was most important and that export salesman achieved significantly higher ratios of sales per salesman. This led to a call in the report for the recruitment of more salesmen by U.K. firms. Despite this, a recent study by Industrial Market Research Ltd. (38) noted that the ratio of export to home sales staff was very similar between British and West German firms, apart from those employing over 1,000 people. This implies that the notion that the sheer number involved in export selling is the prime determinant of relative export performance is another part of the mythology of exports (87). It would appear that seniority, technical experience, cultural and linguistic adaptability and managerial discretion (3) are more important than numbers in determining performance. Sweeny (82) identified a number of problems facing the firm looking to establish an export salesforce. He placed particular emphasis on using "only nationals wher-

ever we go." Following that decision it was found that "funding, keeping and motivating good managers" was vital to business success.

For many firms the decision to establish a direct sales presence in a market occurs at a relatively late stage, after the market has been opened up by home-based sales staff, probably supporting local intermediaries. The home-based salesman is faced with recurrent problems of culture shock (84) besides the particular difficulties of building up his business in the target market. Territory definition and routing are very important areas in which quantitative approaches are beginning to have a direct impact on organisational efficiency, albeit primarily in larger concerns (37, 65). The gap between producer and customer in exports create special problems for the salesman looking to establish rapport with his client. Leavitt (46) indicates the important role of advertising and promotional activity in facilitating the salesman's effort, besides creating a climate among prospective and current buyers conducive to profitable business development.

Two distinctive routes to export advertising have emerged: standardised approaches and country/market specific policies. Ryans (71) cites considerable evidence to support the proposition that potential exists for developing common international or multinational campaigns based on the proposition that:

despite obvious language and cultural differences, peoples of the world have the same basic wants and needs.

The apparent cost advantages of this approach have led a number of firms to explore the potential of this strategy. Ryans points out that there may even exist international life-style groupings such as "international sophisticate" sharing internationally transferable values and norms. The success of a few advertising campaigns adopting this approach has sustained this interest in internationally standardised approaches.

Terpstra (83), Salera (72) and others (88) have suggested that linguistic, religious, cultural, technological and legal differences between countries effectively preclude standardisation except in rare cases, in which a high degree of "similarity in market conditions, consumer attitudes and product benefits" exists. Even campaigns with superficial similarity such as the Marlboro cowboy can mean very different things in different markets (15). Standardisation is made increasingly difficult to achieve with the sometimes conflicting regulations and regulatory systems operating around the world. Even in industrial markets it is being recognised that the scope for standardisation is relatively limited (9). Although the specific message employed may need to vary considerably, the underlying principals of areas ranging from advertising agency selection (20) to media scheduling etc. (8, 91) show a considerable degree of consistency. There are certain promotional media: exhibitions, trade fairs, seminars and symposia which appear to be relatively more important in export business development. Export and international advertising policies show a considerable amount of overlap. The firm's promotional policies can play an important part in minimising the foreign character of the imported offering.

INTERNAL MARKETING

The process of reducing the gap between foreign producer and indigenous customer is taken much further by the international marketer. His operations include important "alternative strategies (such) as the setting up of foreign subsidiaries." For many of today's larger corporations, the move from exporting to international marketing has emerged as a result of the increasing importance of overseas earnings:

in the first half of this century, when today's giants were embarking on international expansion, the term international marketing was practically synonymous with exports . . . In the past two decades, the situation has changed dramatically for major U.S., European and Japanese firms. Their quest for even larger

markets has led them to invest in foreign production facilities." (7)

Robinson (68) identifies five factors relevant to the decision to move overseas and associated ownership decisions:

1. Competitive position
2. Availability of acceptable associates (or consumers)
3. Legal constraints
4. Control requirements
5. Benefit/cost relationships.

The persistence of tariff barriers, despite the progress made in GATT, allied to the apparent growth in non-tariff barriers to imports has accelerated this process.

Massel (58) lays particular emphasis on non-tariff barriers which appear to him to "proliferate" as tariff barriers are broken down. He identifies the major non-tariff barriers besides indicating the formidable difficulties facing attempts to reduce them. Their pervasive character is seen within the EEC where they constitute continuing barriers to complete trade harmony. The alien nature of specific trade practices and procedures can have a direct impact on ease of access to markets. This is particularly clear in attempts to open up the Japanese market. The exporter "may be baffled by Japanese methods of negotiating and the complexities of Japanese law and language" (6). March (57) notes the success achieved by a relatively small number of firms in this market. He relates the problems faced by the majority of firms and the managers to their:

1. Psychophysical distance from the environment
2. Sociophysical distance from the culture
3. Technological distance from industry
4. Insulation of decision makers.

The situation is made worse by International Headquarters which impose foreign notions of strategy, efficiency and organisation on the overseas branch. Business International (7) review the continuing problem of balancing subsidiary freedom with domestic control.

Although tariff and non-tariff barriers are important, Schollhammer (74) and Kobrin (44) indicate that specific plant location decisions are primarily affected by other factors, notably perceived risk, market size and labour relations. In examining the specific strategies adopted by U.S. firms to location overseas McDonald (52) identified three broad methods:

1. *Random Approach:* A selection of "virtually chance factors" such as personal preference, government inducement or acquisition opportunity which leads to market choice.
2. *Country by Country Approach:* This involves systematic investigations of particular markets with a view to arriving at a priority list.
3. *Global Approach:* This is an integrated evaluation of the corporation's long term objectives allied to resource and location decisions geared to goal achievement.

In making these decisions the firm is directly influenced by perceptions of strategic risk and opportunity, the scope for effective control and business development besides the regulatory fiscal tariff and non-tariff policies of the markets under consideration. In turn these are affected by the growing number of inducements and opportunities offered in different countries for local manufacture.

As soon as the firm has any significant part of its operations based overseas three issues emerge as vital to marketing success; organisation, planning and control. These face the firm whether it has major manufacturing or sales operations overseas. Gestetner (29) concentrates on two basic approaches: "centrist," with operations organised around a strong central administration; "non-centrist," with considerable devolved authority. Until recently considerable emphasis in the literature has been given to the advantages of the devolved approach in terms of responsiveness to market conditions and minimising local marketing problems. More recently Weichman (91) has highlighted the organisation problems, specifically the lack of a clear sense of direction, duplication of efforts and poor liaison deriving from this managerial

mode. It appears that the advantages of either method over the other has only a small effect on performance. Kahler and Kramer (41) identify two broad organisational systems:

The International Division: All overseas operations are brought together under a single management structure. Some services may be shared with the domestic operation but it acts primarily as a separate unit.
The Worldwide Organisation: The division between home and international is eliminated and a global perspective is adopted for resource allocation and opportunity spotting.

Within these structures the company is organised geographically or along product lines with varying degrees of autonomy allocated to operating units.

Business International (7) places considerable emphasis on marketing planning in establishing a "coherent form on the collection of national plans." Underpinning this process is the effective communication of objectives allied to a commitment to achieve the synergy possible to the effective international firm. The major strategies open to the international firm are identified by Keegan (43):

1. *Same Product, Same Message Worldwide.* This approach has scope for some cost savings but may suffer from the problem identified earlier with communication transfer.
2. *Same Product, Different Communications.* This may overcome some problems but can eventually face difficulties posed by technical progress and specialise local needs.
3. *Different Product, Same Communication.* In exceptional circumstances a powerful theme can be used despite product changes.
4. *Dual Adaption.* Product and communication are modified to suit local needs but with little questioning of the basic proposition.
5. *Product Invention.* Specific offerings based on identified buyer needs in the target market are developed and introduced.

Throughout this process effective control procedures are necessary. Real problems exist with the development of effective management and support systems. Sirota (77) identified recurrent problems with management in international firms. Skinner (78) highlighted the degree of resentment which can build up among overseas staff from what is seen as excessive interference. This is accompanied at headquarters by a sense of powerlessness to influence issues seen as part of their formal responsibility. Robinson (68) highlights the importance of communication and information systems, authority location, clear objectives, decision structures, methods of report back and evaluation systems in establishing effective organisational control. No pressures appear to be influencing this process:

1. An emerging recognition of the importance of cultural sensitivity in international business: The challenge for the firm is how to deal with transcultural issues while operating within individual cultural environments.'' (7)
2. The emergence of transnational groups who share certain organisational values. These may be deliberately created through training and development programmes: "The extensive management development programmes that some multinational enterprises maintain appear designed to create an elite cadre of men who all know one another and who share operating experience in different types of managerial activity." (69)

CONCLUSION

Export and international markets play an important role in the success of many firms, large and small. This goes far beyond the movement of manufactured and raw material products, into services, some traditional such as banking and insurance, others more modern with retailers such as Marks and Spencer and Mothercare recently winning Queen's awards for exports. The problems facing the manager in this area probably exceed those in almost any area. His ability to operate effectively is complicated by differences of culture, value systems and all the prime determinants of buyer need. Locally appointed staff may minimise these in the market but pose new questions in management, motivation and control.

The move toward an international or multinational stance may not be the necessary "evolution" implied by Perlmutter (66), but progression in this direction leads many firms to face major problems of development and adaptation. The importance of international trade poses recurrent issues for marketing management. Particularly important today are:

a. The growing imbalance between the LDCs and the developed world.
b. The threats of increased protectionism emerging from world recession.
c. The fine dividing line between government inducements to export and win overseas business and limits to competition.
d. The effectiveness of the marketing approach in identifying effective competition-based solutions to these problems.

A stock of knowledge exists but it needs greater effort to fill the gaps, provide evidence to test the many assumptions and, very important today, to apply rigorous quantitative approaches to the issues posed.

REFERENCES

1. Advisory Council for Applied Research and Development. *Industrial Innovation.* London: HMSO, 1978.
2. Bagwati, J. "The Pure Theory of International Trade." *Economic Journal,* Vol. 74 (1964).
3. Barclays Bank. *Factors for International Success.* London: Barclays Bank International Ltd.
4. BETRO Trust Committee. *Concentration on Key Markets.* London: Royal Society of Arts, 1977.
5. Bowersox, D. J., E. W. Symkay, and B. J. LaLonde. *Physical Distribution Management.* New York: MacMillan, 1968.
6. British Overseas Trade Board. *An Introduction to Doing Business in Japan.* London: HMSO, 1976.
7. Business International Corporation. *Managing Global Marketing: A Headquarter's Perspective.* New York: Business International Corporation, 1976.
8. Cannon, T. *Advertising Research.* London: International Textbook Co., 1973.

9. ———. *Exports: A Workshop Manual*. Durham: Export Study Group, 1979.

10. ———. "International and Export Marketing." In D. Ashton, *Management Bibliographies and Reviews,* Vol. IV (1979).

11. ———. *The Sales Approach to Business is Alive and Well and Living in Exports*. Durham: Export Study Group, 1978.

12. Carson, D. *International Marketing: A Comparative Systems Approach*. New York: John Wiley & Sons, 1967.

13. Cateora, P. R., and J. M. Hess. *International Marketing*. Homewood, Ill.: Richard D. Irwin, 1971.

14. Central Policy Review Staff. *Future of the British Car Industry*. London: HMSO, 1975.

15. Cranch, A. G. "The Changing Faces of International Advertising." *The International Advertiser,* Vol. 13 (1972).

16. Crissy, W. J. E., P. Fisher, and F. H. Mossman. "Segmental Analysis: Key to Marketing Profitability." In J. L. Taylor, and J. F. Robb, eds., *Fundamentals of Marketing*. New York: McGraw-Hill, 1978.

17. Davidson, W. R. "Changes in Distribution Institutions." *Journal of Marketing,* January 1970.

18. Dean, J. "Pricing Policies for New Products." *Harvard Business Review,* November 1960.

19. Dhalla, N. K., and S. Yuspeth. "Forget the Product Life Cycle Concept." *Harvard Business Review,* January 1976.

20. Donnelly, J., and J. K. Ryan, Jr. "Agency Selection in International Advertising." *European Journal of Marketing,* Summer 1972.

21. Douglas, S., P. Le Maire, and Y. Wind. "Selection of Global Target Markets: A Decision Theoretic Approach." ESOMAR Congress, 1972.

22. Duguid, A., and E. Jacques. *Case Studies in Export Management*. London: HMSO, 1971.

23. Ellsworth, P. T. "The Structure of American Foreign Trade: A New View Examined." *Review of Economics and Statistics,* Vol. 36 (1954).

24. Engel, J. F., R. D. Blackwell, and D. T. Kollat. *Consumer Behavior,* 3rd ed. Hinsdale, Ill.: The Dryden Press, 1978.

25. Export Houses Association. *Directory of British Export Houses*. London: Export Houses Association, 1978.

26. Finlay, R. *Trade and Specialisation*. Harmondsworth: Penguin Books, 1970.

27. Forbes, M. "Critique of the System of Commission Agents in the Export Trade to Latin America." *British Journal of Marketing,* Summer 1968.

28. Gabor, A. "Pricing in Theory and Practise." *Management Decision,* Summer 1967.

29. Gestetner, D. "Strategy in Managing International Sales." *Harvard Business Review,* September–October 1974.

30. Haberler, G. "The Current Relevance of the Theory of Comparative Advantage to Agricultural Production and Trade." *International Journal of Agrarian Affairs,* Vol. 4 (1964).

31. Haley, R. I. "The Implications of Market Segmentation." In G. P. Morris and R. W. Fry, eds., *Current Marketing Views*. San Francisco: Cranfield Press, 1973.

32. Hasty, R. W., and R. T. Will. *Marketing*. San Francisco: Cranfield Press, 1976.

33. Heckscher, E. "The Effects of Foreign Trade on the Distribution of Income." In H. S. Ellis and L. A. Metzler. *Readings in the Theory of International Trade*. London: George Allen and Unwin, 1950.

34. Heitzfield, J. M. "New Directions in East-West Trade." *Harvard Business Review*, May–June 1977.

35. Hogendorn, J. S., and W. B. Brown. *The New International Economics*. London: Addison-Wesley, 1979.

36. Huff, D. L. "Defining and Estimating a Trading Area." *Journal of Marketing,* July 1964.

37. Ikeda, Y. "Distribution Innovation in Japan and the Role Played by General Trading Companies." In H. B. Thorelli, ed., *International Marketing Strategy*. Harmondsworth: Penguin Books, 1973.

38. Industrial Market Research Ltd. *How British and German Industry Exports*. London: IMRL, 1978.

39. International Research Associates, Inc. "A Survey of International Research Practices by American International Corporations." Mimeo, New York, 1969.

40. Jaffe, E. D. *Grouping: A Strategy for International Business*. New York: American Management Association, 1974.

41. Kahler, R., and R. L. Kramer. *International Marketing,* 4th ed. Cincinnati: South-Western Publishing Co., 1977.

42. Kalfayan, E. "Thoughts of an Overseas Marketer." *Marketing,* May 1977.

43. Keegan, W. J. "Five Strategies for Multinational Marketing." In H. B. Thorelli, ed., *International*

Marketing Strategy. Harmondsworth: Penquin Books, 1973.

44. Kobrin, S.J. "The Environmental Detriments of Foreign Direct Investment: An Ex-Post Empirical Analysis." *Journal of International Business Studies,* Fall 1976.

45. Kravis, I. "Wages and Foreign Trade." *Review of Economics and Statistics,* February 1956.

46. Leavitt, T. "Communications and Industrial Selling." *Journal of Marketing,* April 1967.

47. Le Kashman, R., and J. F. Stolle. "The Total Cost Approach to Distribution." *Business Horizons,* Vol. 8 (1965).

48. Leontief, W. W. "Domestic Production and Foreign Trade: The American Capital Position Re-examined." In J. Bagwati, *International Trade.* Harmondsworth: Penguin Books, 1967.

49. Lewis, E. H. *Marketing Channels: Structure Strategy.* New York: McGraw-Hill, 1968.

50. McCammon, B. C., Jr., and W. L. Hammer. "A Frame of Reference for Improving Productivity in Distribution." In R. A. Robicheax, W. M. Pride, and O. C. Ferrell, eds. *Marketing: Contemporary Dimensions.* Boston: Houghton Miffin, 1977.

51. McCarthy, E. J. *Basic Marketing.* Homewood, Ill.: Richard D. Irwin, 1975, Chap. 24.

52. McDonald, J. G., "Minimising the Risks of Moving Abroad." *Business Horizons,* Spring 1961.

53. McDougall, G., "British and American Exports: A Study Suggested by the Theory of Comparative Costs." In R. E. Caves and H. Johnson. *Readings in International Economics.* Homewood, Ill.: Richard D. Irwin, 1968.

54. McFarlane, G. "Scots Queen's Awards Winners Don't Excel." *Marketing,* April 1978.

55. McMillan, C., and S. Paulden. *Export Agents.* London: Gower Press, 1968.

56. Machine Tool EDC. *Survey of Investment in Machine Tools.* London: National Economic Development Office, 1965.

57. March, R. M. "Some Constraints on Adaptive Marketing by Foreign Consumer Good Firms in Japan." *European Journal of Marketing,* Vol. 11, no. 7 (1977).

58. Massel, M. S. "Non-Tariff Barriers as an Obstacle to World Trade." In H. B. Thorelli, ed., *International Marketing Management.* Harmondsworth: Penguin Books, 1973.

59. Metra Consulting Group. *Delivering the Goods: A Study of Moving British Exports to Europe.* London: NEDO, 1968.

60. Moyer, R. "International Market Analysis." *Journal of Marketing Research,* Vol. 5 (1968).

61. National Economic Development Office. *International Price Competitiveness: Non-Price Factors and Economic Performance.* London: NEDO, 1977.

62. National Industry Conference Board. *Costs and Competition.* National Industry Conference Board, 1961.

63. National Science Foundation. *Proceedings of a Conference on Technology Transfer and Innovation.* Washington, D.C.: Government Printing Office, 1970.

64. Norback, J. P., and R. F. Love. "Geometric Approaches to Solving the Travelling Salesman Problem." *Management Science,* July 1977.

65. Ohlin, B. *Interregional and International Trade.* Oxford: The University Press, 1933.

66. Perlmutter, H. "The Tortuous Evolution of the Multinational Corporation." *Columbia Journal of World Business,* January–February 1969.

67. Ricardo, D. *Principles of Political Economy,* 1817.

68. Robinson, R. *International Business Management.* Hinsdale, Ill.: The Dryden Press, 1978.

69. Rodriquez, R. M., and F. E. Carter. *International Financial Management,* Englewood Cliffs, N.J.: Prentice-Hall, 1976.

70. Rubber Processing Sector Working Party. *Efficiency Dialogues in the Tyre Manufacturing Industry.* London: NEDO, 1978.

71. Ryans, J. K., Jr. "Is it too soon to Put a Tiger in Every Tank?" *Columbia Journal of World Business,* March–April 1969.

72. Salera, V. *Multinational Business.* Boston: Houghton Mifflin, 1969.

73. Samuelson, P. A. *Economics.* Tokyo: McGraw-Hill Kogakusha, 1973.

74. Schollhammer, H. *Locational Strategies of Multinational Firms.* Los Angeles: Center for Industrial Business, 1974.

75. Setni, P., and D. Curry. "Variable and Objective Clustering of Cross Cultural Data: Some Implications for Comparative Research and Policy Formulation." In P. Setni and J.M. Sheth, eds. *Multinational Business Operations: Marketing Management.* Pacific Palisades, Calif.: Goodyear Publishing Co., 1973.

76. Sherbini, A. A., "Classifying and Comparing Countries." In I. A. Litvak and P. M. Banting, eds., *Comparative Analysis for International Marketing.* Boston: Allyn & Bacon, 1967.

77. Sirota, D., and J. M. Greenwood. "Understand Your Overseas Work Force." *Harvard Business Review,* January–February 1971.

78. Skinner, C. W. *American Industry in Developing Economies: The Management of International Manufacturing.* New York: John Wiley & Sons, 1968.

79. Stanton, W. J. *Fundamentals of Marketing,* 5th ed. Tokyo: McGraw-Hill Kogakusha, 1978.

80. Stolper, W., and P. Samuelson. "Protection and Real Wages." *Review of Economic Studies,* Vol. 9 (1941).

81. Stopford, J. M., and L. T. Wells, Jr. *Managing the Multinational Enterprise.* New York: Basic Books, 1972.

82. Sweeny, J. K. "A Small Company Enters the European Market." *Harvard Business Review,* Vol. 48 (1970).

83. Terpstra, V. *The Cultural Environment of International Business.* Cincinnati: South-West Publishing Co., 1978.

84. Thomas, M. J. *International Marketing Management.* Scranton, Pa.: International Textbook Co., 1969.

85. Tookey, D. *Physical Distribution for Export.* London: Gower Press, 1971.

86. Treasure, J. *British Exports—Three Myths.* London: Institute of Practitioners in Advertising, 1966.

87. Unwin, S. J. F. "How Culture Affects Advertising Expansion and Communications Style." *Journal of Advertising,* Spring 1974.

88. Vogel, R. H. "Uses of Managerial Perceptions in Clustering Countries." *Journal of International Business Studies,* Vol. 7 (1976).

89. Wahl, D. F. "Capital and Labour Requirements for Canada's Foreign Trade." *Canadian Journal of Economics and Political Science,* Vol. 27 (1961).

90. Watson-Dunn, S. "Advertising for Multinational Markets." In V. P. Buel, ed., *Handbook of Modern Marketing.* New York: McGraw-Hill, 1970.

91. Weichman, U. E. *Marketing Management in Multinational Firms.* New York: Praeger Publishers, 1976.

92. Wells, L. T., Jr. "A Product Life Cycle for International Trade?" *Journal of Marketing,* Vol. 32 (1968).

93. ———. *The Product Life Cycle and International Trade.* Cambridge, Mass.: Harvard University Press, 1972.

94. Wells, S. J. *British Export Performance.* Cambridge: The University Press, 1964.

95. Wentworth, F. *Handbook of Physical Distribution Management.* London: Gower Press, 1976.

96. Wills, G. "Towards an Integration of Export Marketing." In G. Wills, ed. *Explorations in Marketing Thought.* London: Crosby Lockwood, 1971.

22

Market Expansion Strategies in Multinational Marketing
Igal Ayal
Jehiel Zif

• • •

Any firm attempting to expand international operations must decide on the number of countries and market segments it will attempt to penetrate at any given period. Given a fixed mar-

Source: Igal Ayal and Jehiel Zif, "Market Expansion Strategies in Multinational Marketing," *Journal of Marketing,* published by the American Marketing Association, Volume 43, Spring 1979, pp. 84–94. Copyright © 1979. Reprinted by permission.

keting budget the firm must also decide how to allocate its efforts among different markets served. One can conceive of two major and opposing strategies for making these decisions: market diversification and market concentration. The first strategy implies a fast penetration into a large number of markets and diffusion of efforts among them. The second strategy is based on concentration of resources in a few markets and gradual expansion into new territories.

After a number of years, both strategies may lead the firm to export into the same number of markets. The alternative expansion routes may generate, however, totally different consequences in terms of sales, market shares, and profits over time. In this paper, these two strategies are compared and the factors impinging on the choice between them are analyzed. Within the framework of the two major strategies, a number of more detailed strategic choices are identified, and alternative measurements of market expansion are discussed. Application of the framework for the choice of strategy is discussed and illustrated by a brief case study.

THE RESEARCH LITERATURE

Questions of market expansion in multinational marketing have received limited attention in the literature. Most of the research has concentrated on questions of national rather than international marketing, and on the allocation of promotional budgets among sales territories. No published attempt for systematic identification and choice of market expansion strategies has been found.

Nordin (1943) applied a basic marginal approach for allocating sales effort between two geographic areas subject to a budget constraint. Zentle and Hyde (1956) considered the allocation of advertising expenditures among a given number of countries. Their model takes into account an S-curve response function to promotion, and time-lag in the effect of promotion. A graphic solution is proposed to solve the complex mathematical problem. Hartung and Fisher (1965) used a model of brand switching and mathematical programming for market expansion in locating new gasoline stations.

Hirsch and Lev (1971; 1973) influenced our research by their empirical study of sales stability and profitability of two alternative penetration strategies into foreign markets. Their findings were supported by data from 200 exporting firms. Their identification of strategies was based on the direction of change in a market concentration index of sales between two periods.

Shakun (1965; 1966) attacked the related problem of promotional effort allocation between products through a game-theoretic approach. Luss and Gupta (1973) concentrated on the mathematical problem of designing an algorithm for solving the sales maximization problem, when marketing effort is allocated between products and sales territories. More recently, Beswick (1977) studied the allocation of selling effort via dynamic programming.

The various research papers mentioned above contribute important points to the analysis of market expansion and resource allocation. None of the papers however, presents a comprehensive framework for identification and analysis of alternative market expansion strategies over time. The purpose of this paper is to help fill this gap.

THE MAJOR STRATEGIC ALTERNATIVES

The choice of a market expansion policy is a key strategic decision in multinational marketing. To develop such a policy, a firm has to make decisions in the following three areas:

- Identification of potential markets and determination of some order of priorities for entry into these markets.
- Decision on the overall level of marketing effort that the firm is able and willing to commit.
- Selection of the rate of market expansion over time, and determination of the allocation of effort among different markets.

This paper concentrates on the third area, assuming that decisions in the first two areas have already been made. In practice, the process will frequently be iterative; analysis of the third area will be helpful in clarifying and reviewing the first two areas.[1] The major strategic alternatives of market expansion, within the third area, are

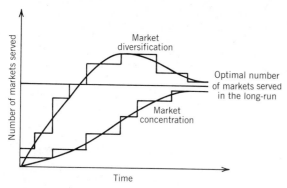

Figure 1 Alternative market expansion strategies over time.

market concentration versus market diversification.

A strategy of market concentration is characterized by a slow and gradual rate of growth in the number of markets served. On the other hand, a strategy of market diversification is characterized by a fast rate of growth in the number of markets served at the early stages of expansion. It is, therefore, expected that a strategy of concentration will result in a smaller number of markets served, at each point in time, relative to a strategy of diversification. Expected evolution of the number of markets served, for a strategy of concentration versus a strategy of diversification, is presented graphically in Figure 1. The functional forms of the two strategies in Figure 1 represent a family of possible curves, showing the relative changes in the number of markets served over time.

In the long run, a strategy of diversification will frequently lead to a reduction in the number of markets, as a result of consolidation and abandonment of less profitable markets. A fast rate of market expansion is usually accomplished by devoting only limited resources and time to a careful study of each market prior to entry. The firm is, therefore, bound to make a few mistakes and is more likely to enter unprofitable markets and drop them later.[2]

The different patterns of market expansion are likely to cause development of different competitive conditions in different markets over time. The profitability of a late entry into new markets is affected by these competitive conditions and by the length of the product life cycle. As a result, the optimal number of markets served in the long run is not necessarily the same for both strategies.

The two strategies of concentration versus diversification lead to the selection of different levels of marketing effort and different marketing mixes in each market. Given fixed financial and managerial resources, the level of resources allocated to each market in a strategy of diversification will be lower than with concentration. The size of the budget gives an indication about possible selection of means or marketing mix. Specifically, a lower level of marketing effort implies less promotional expenditures, more reliance on commission agents, and a stronger tendency for a skimming approach to pricing. A strategy of concentration, on the other hand, involves investment in market share. This implies heavy promotional outlays, a stronger control of the distribution channel and, in some cases, penetration pricing.

DETAILED STRATEGIC OPTIONS

A strategy of market expansion is characterized not only by the rate of entry into new national markets. Two additional considerations are of particular importance for more detailed identification of optional strategies: (1) market segments within national markets and (2) allocation of effort to different markets (and market segments).

A number of strategic options can be derived based on the consideration of market segments and effort allocation: these are introduced and briefly discussed in this section. The full range of considerations affecting the choice of market concentration versus market diversification is treated in the following section.

Table 1 Market Expansion Strategies Based on Countries and Segments

		Segments	
		Concentration	Diversification
Countries	Concentration	1	2
	Diversification	3	4

Market Segments Within National Markets

Four major market expansion alternatives can be identified when market segments are examined. These alternatives are presented in Table 1.

Strategy 1 concentrates on specific market segments in a few countries and a gradual increase in the number of markets served. This dual concentration is particularly appropriate when the product (or service) appeals to a definite group of similar customers in different countries, and the costs of penetration into each national market are substantial in relation to available resources. To be successful with this strategy, the segments served must be sufficiently large and stable.

Strategy 2—characterized by market concentration and segment diversification—requires a product line which can appeal to different segments. The strategy is particularly effective when there are significant economies of scale in promotion (e.g., umbrella advertising) and distribution, and when the sales potential of the home market and other national markets served is large. Under such conditions, a firm can achieve growth objectives by concentrating on many submarkets within a limited number of national markets.

Strategy 3—characterized by market diversification and segment concentration—is suitable for firms with a specialized product line and potential customers in many countries. With this strategy, a firm frequently can use a similar product and promotion strategy in all markets. The strategy is particularly effective when the cost of entry into different markets is low relative to available resources. For strategy identification, it is important to note that two firms may follow different expansion strategies with respect to countries and segments (strategy 2 versus strategy 3) yet serve the same total number of market segments at each point in time.

Strategy 4 is based on dual diversification in both segments and markets. This aggressive strategy can be employed by firms with a product line appealing to many segments, and sufficient resources to accomplish a fast entry into many markets. Large international firms with sales offices in many countries frequently use this strategy when they introduce a newly developed or acquired product line. A poorman's version of strategy 4 can sometimes be employed by small firms with limited resources, based on superficial coverage. The commitment of resources in market expansion is the subject of the following paragraphs.

Allocation of Effort to Different Markers

Marketing expansion can be achieved by different means. Even a small firm with limited resources can achieve market diversification quickly by using independent commission agents in each market, with little or no investment. In order to identify a specific strategy of market expansion it is, therefore, necessary to specify the overall marketing effort as well as the allocation of effort to different markets.

Some researchers have defined resource commitments to international markets on the basis of a stepwise expansion of operations (Johanson and Wiedersheim 1975). A sequence

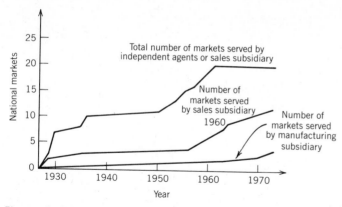

Figure 2 Market expansion of Volvo into twenty national markets. (*Source:* Johanson and Wieder-sheim, 1975.)

of three stages demonstrates successively larger commitments of resources and marketing involvement:

- Export by independent agents
- Sales subsidiary
- Manufacturing subsidiary

The marketing expansion of Volvo into 20 countries between 1929 and 1973 is presented graphically in Figure 2. This figure separates expansion by the three stages above and shows the gradual increase in territorial coverage and resource commitments. Two periods of relatively fast diversification, prior to and after World War II, are indicated.

The first two stages above specify an essential element of distribution strategy in market expansion. Extensive use of independent agents is frequently associated with market diversification; and a resource commitment to sales subsidiaries is a more likely strategic element of market concentration. Many firms like Volvo prefer to employ independent agents in some markets and sales subsidiaries in others. The relative share of each distribution method is an important strategic option of market expansion.

Distribution strategies do not always portray a correct picture of effort allocation. A firm may invest the same resources in two markets using a different marketing mix and distribution set-up. In one market the firm may employ an independent agent backed by substantial promotional activity. In another market the firm may establish a sales subsidiary with a limited promotional budget. A quantitative measure of effort allocation would be more precise for analytical purposes.

Managers inside the firm can determine the overall marketing investment in each market, based on internal accounting. With this information, it is possible to calculate a diversification index that takes into account both the number of markets served and the uniformity of effort distribution.[3]

CONSIDERATIONS AFFECTING THE CHOICE OF MARKET EXPANSION STRATEGY

The selection of market expansion strategy is influenced by characteristics of the product, characteristics of the market, and decision criteria of the firm. Table 2 summarizes 10 key product/market factors affecting the choice between market concentration and market diversification. The following discussion explains the effect of each factor on the adoption of market expansion strategy.

Table 2 Product/Market Factors Affecting Choice Between Diversification and Concentration Strategies

Product/Market Factor	Prefer Diversification if:	Prefer Concentration if:
1. Sales response function	Concave	S-curve
2. Growth rate of each market	Low	High
3. Sales stability in each market	Low	High
4. Competitive lead-time	Short	Long
5. Spill over effects	High	Low
6. Need for product adaptation	Low	High
7. Need for communication adaptation	Low	High
8. Economies of scale in distribution	Low	High
9. Program control requirements	Low	High
10. Extent of constraints	Low	High

(1) *Sales response function.* Two alternative classes of sales response functions—a concave function and an S-curve function—are common in the literature (Kotler 1971). Graphic examples of these functions are presented in Figure 3.[4] If the firm believes that it faces a concave response function, there will be a strong motivation to follow a strategy of market diversification. On the other hand, when the response function is assumed to be an S-curve, a market concentration strategy usually is preferred.

The concave response function implies that the best return on marketing effort (x) is at lower levels of effective effort (see Figure 3). This is based on the assumption that the markets under consideration include a number of clients or submarkets which are particularly interested in the firm's products. Such interest is frequently generated by a unique product or marketing program, possibly the result of substantial investment in R&D. As additional effort is spent, market share increases, but the firm faces stiffer resistance, more skeptical buyers, and increased effort by competitors. Therefore, market response is characterized by diminishing marginal returns and diversification of effort is more productive. It is interesting to note that most empirical studies of advertising effectiveness support the hypothesis of concave

market response functions (Simon 1971; Lambin 1976).

The S-curve response function assumes that small-scale efforts of penetration to a new market are beset by various difficulties and buyers' resistance and will not count for much. In-

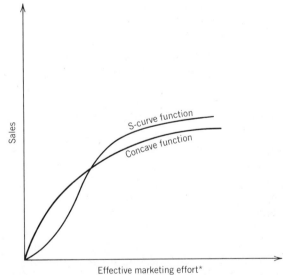

*Effective marketing effort takes into account current marketing effort as well as carry over effects of previous efforts.

Figure 3 Alternative market share response functions.

creases in market share and profitability will be achieved only after a substantial concentration in marketing effort is made. This type of response function is likely for products that do not enjoy obvious advantages—which is, of course, the case for most products. There are a number of reported cases of geographical market expansion which support the premise of an S-curve response function (Cardwell 1968; Hofer 1975).

A quantitative example of the choice of market expansion under the two sales response assumptions is presented in a footnote below.[5]

(2) *Growth rate of each market.* When the rate of growth of the industry in each market is low, the firm can frequently achieve a faster growth rate by diversification into many markets. On the other hand, if the rate of market growth in present markets is high, growth objectives can usually be achieved by market concentration.

When the rate of growth of the industry in many markets is high, there are occasional opportunities for diversification with limited resources. Penetration to many markets can be accomplished by relying on marketing efforts of independent sales agents and licensees who are interested in promoting the firm's products in their own growing markets. The case of Miromit, an Israeli producer of unique solar collectors, serves as an example. Following the energy crisis, the firm was flooded by requests for sales representation from interested parties in many countries. In this case, the firm followed a mixed strategy by concentrating its resources in a few markets and diversifying to other markets with little or no investment. By this strategy the number of markets served would increase rapidly, but the effort diversification index would show a slow rate of growth.

(3) *Sales stability in each market.* When demand in each market is unstable, the firm can spread the risk through judicious diversification. To the extent that markets are independent with respect to demand, an increase in the number of markets is likely to increase sales

stability. This was demonstrated empirically by Hirsch and Lev (1971). When sales stability in each market is high, the firm can concentrate its market expansion effort while still satisfying the need for stability.

(4) *Competitive lead-time.* The lead-time that an innovative firm has over competitors and potential imitators is an important consideration in selecting a market expansion strategy. When competitive lead-time is short and there is a major advantage to being first in a market with a new innovation, there is a strong motivation to follow the route of diversification. In this situation, the firm faces a favorable response function for a limited period. The urgency to enter many markets quickly is diminished if the innovative firm has a long lead-time, or when there is no innovative advantage. This argument of competitive lead-time was expressed by an executive of a small computer equipment company: "The compelling reason for entering Europe now . . . was to capitalize on our innovative advantage. We consider our products to be well ahead of competitors' . . . but in our fast moving field—data entry systems and input equipment—this could change rapidly" (Sweeney 1970).

(5) *Spill-over effects.* Spill-over of marketing effort or goodwill from present to new markets is another factor favoring diversification. This spill-over effect can be the result of geographical proximity, cultural influence, or commercial ties. It is common in TV and radio coverage of close national markets. There is obviously a strong motivation to take advantage of spill-over effects by diversifying into new markets which are influenced by current and past effort in presently served markets.

(6) *Need for product adaptation.* The experience curve phenomenon of systematic reduction in variable cost with an increase in accumulated production volume has a major impact on international market share strategy (Rapp 1973). Firms that grow faster than their competitors are able to reduce production costs faster and as a result enjoy a major competitive

advantage. When the same product is sold in different international markets, market expansion is not only a vehicle for diversification and new profit opportunities, but it also can increase profits by reducing costs in currently served markets.

Frequently, a company cannot sell the same product in all international markets. There is a need to adapt the product to the standards and regulations of a new country, as well as to the special tastes and preferences of new consumers. The magnitude and nature of the adaptation costs are an important consideration in choosing an expansion strategy. In particular, a firm should assess whether adaptation to new markets requires only a small fixed investment or whether a major change is necessary. If entry into new international markets requires major changes in the production process, the company will not only have to invest a significant amount before entry, but will probably be unable to enjoy the full cost advantage of accumulated experience. In this case there will be a lesser motivation to expand geographically than in the case of an investment that has positive effects on potential economies in production.

(7) *Need for communication adaptation.* Adaptation may be necessary not only for the product, but also for the marketing or communication program. In many situations, the communication program is more important than the technical specifications of the product. In a recent study of international expansion of U.S. franchise systems, 59% of the 80 respondent firms indicated alteration in strategy upon entry into international markets (Hackett 1976). Twenty-five percent of the firms reported a change in product (or service) to fit local tastes, while all other changes were related to communication adaptation. If communication adaptation requires a large investment in consumer and advertising research and in production of new programs, the temptation to follow a diversification strategy is diminished.

(8) *Economies of scale in distribution.* When distribution cost is a significant expense and there are economies of scale with increased market share, there is motivation to follow a concentration strategy. A strategy of rapid expansion into many new markets can frequently increase distribution costs substantially as a result of increased transportation distance and a low level of sales over a large territory. Efficient distribution can, however, be achieved in different ways depending on the product and specific channels. For example, it is possible that diversification with respect to countries and concentration with respect to segments (strategy 3 in Table 1) can lead to an efficient distribution system.

(9) *Program control requirements.* Extensive requirements for control are typical of custommade and sophisticated products and services which require close and frequent communication between headquarters (R&D production, marketing) and clients. The cost of managerial communication with clients and agents, per unit of sales, is likely to increase with the number of markets served. A comparison of average contact costs in concentrated and diversified markets suggests that the difference in favor of a concentrated market is increasing with the number of contacts (Bucklin 1966). We can, therefore, expect that when the program control requirements are extensive, a concentrated strategy of market expansion will have an advantage.

(10) *Constraints.* There are a number of constraints on management action in international markets. External constraints include import and currency barriers created by government authorities in the target markets. There may also be difficulties in finding or developing an effective sales and distribution organization. Internal constraints are based on the availability of resources in order to function in new markets. Trained managers and salesmen may be limited, financial resources may be scarce, and production factors may be in short supply.

In the previously mentioned study of international expansion of franchise systems, respondents were asked to rank problems encountered in international markets (Hackett 1976). The five most important problems were: (1) host government regulations and red tape, (2) high-import duties and taxes in foreign environments, (3) monetary uncertainties and royalty retribution to franchisor, (4) logistical problems inherent in operation of international franchise systems, and (5) control of franchisees. The spectacular rate of international market expansion, and the reported plans for further expansion by the respondent firms, indicate that these obstacles were surmountable in most cases. This was partly due to a strategy based on franchise-owned outlets, which is a form of diversification with limited resources.

External or internal constraints place a limit on the capability or the profitability of market diversification. While some constraints can be overcome, extensive barriers in many markets will lead to market concentration.

Decision Criteria

The expected value and the variance of the net present value of each expansion alternative are common decision criteria. To use these criteria, it is necessary to estimate and express the product/market factor considerations in quantitative terms of sales, prices, costs, and timetable.

Many firms frequently will supplement these profitability estimates with other criteria based on the multiple objectives of the firm. Objectives of international market standing and prestige are frequently stated as major causes for fast diversification with limited regard to profitability consequences. For example, Koor, the largest industrial concern in Israel, established a trading company and decided to enter the European Common Market with a strategy of fast diversification by setting up sales offices in seven European countries within one year (Perry 1977). The major objective was: "to be-come the largest and most important Israeli commercial organization in Europe." It is interesting to note that profitability results in the short-term quite disappointing.

The criteria used by business firms to select alternatives for action are outside the scope of this study. We merely suggest that these criteria can be another major cause for preference of one market expansion strategy over another.

Application

Selecting a market expansion strategy based on the product/market factors of Table 2 is bound to raise a few application questions. These questions can be clarified by reviewing the case of a leading electronics manufacturer in Israel (name withheld at request of company executives). The firm is a subsidiary of a large and internationally known American firm. Two relatively sophisticated product lines are being exported: communication equipment and control systems. The communication equipment was developed by the parent company while the control systems were developed in Israel. Table 3 and Figures 4 and 5 present, for each product line, a summary analysis of the product/market factors, market expansion graphs, and international sales.

One question of application is illustrated by Table 3. The 10 factors do not point in one direction; some imply market diversification, while others imply market concentration.

Two explanatory remarks can clarify the dilemma: (1) Management must weigh the relative importance of the product/market factors in selecting a strategy. Although some factors such as the sales response function will be important in all cases, the relative importance of other factors such as distribution cost are likely to change from case to case. (2) The concepts of market concentration and market diversification should be viewed in relative terms. Occasionally, the choice between concentration and diversification is not clear-cut in absolute terms

Table 3 Case Study: Analysis of Product/Market Factors by Product Line

Product/Market Factor	Communication Equipment		Control Systems	
	Direction	Implied Strategy	Direction	Implied Strategy
1. Sales response function	Concave	D	S-curve	C
2. Growth rate of each market	High	C	High	C
3. Sales stability in each market	Low	D	High	C
4. Competitive lead-time	Long	C	Long	C
5. Spill-over effects	High	D	Low	C
6. Need for product adaptation	Low	D	High	C
7. Need for communication adaptation	Low	D	High	C
8. Economies of scale in distribution	Low	D	Low	D
9. Program control requirements	High	C	High	C
10. Extent of constraints	High	C	Low	D

and a middle course should be selected. In comparison with extreme alternatives, however, the strategic choice is clear.

In the case of control systems most factors point to a concentrated strategy (Table 3); the firm followed this strategy with respect to both markets and segments. The direction implied by the factors for communication equipment is more mixed, and the firm followed a middle of the road strategy of "prudent" diversification,

or fairly rapid concentrated expansion. The strategy was diversified with respect to segments. Figure 4 demonstrates that the expansion of the communication equipment is much more diversified relative to the concentrated expansion of the control systems.

A second question of application also can be clarified by reference to the case. A summary analysis like Table 3 assumes that the markets under consideration are quite similar and that

Figure 4 Case study: Market expansion graphs by product line.

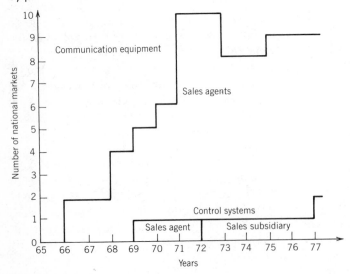

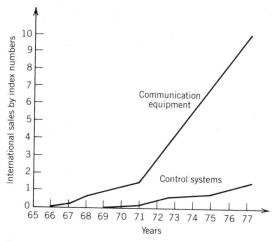

Figure 5 Case study: International sales by product line.

the effects of the product/market factors can be estimated prior to entry. This is not always the case, as can be seen by the withdrawal from two communication equipment markets in 1973 (Figure 4).

A few points should be made in response to this question: (1) A summary table, like 3, is applicable to a group of similar markets. When different groups of markets are being considered, it is advantageous to analyze each group separately, since a different expansion strategy may be appropriate for each group.

(2) An investment in market research prior to entry can reduce uncertainty, but not eliminate it. Penetration into international markets which are politically and economically unstable is liable to produce surprises with changing events. This was the case with the communication equipment that was introduced into developing Asian and African markets.

(3) A firm may prefer to acquire information by actual testing in the marketplace, rather than by costly and prolonged market survey prior to entry. This policy is particularly applicable when quick entry is important, or when market diversification with limited resources is employed. Abandonment of some markets, following testing, is quite likely under this policy.

(4) Market expansion is a discrete process based on a market by market entry. It is therefore possible and desirable to view it as a learning process, and to correct strategic decisions as more information becomes available. This learning process can explain the expansion curve of the control systems (Figures 4 and 5). After three unsatisfactory years in one market, the firm decided to switch from a sales agent to a sales subsidiary, and a second market was penetrated only after eight years of international experience with the product line. It is interesting to note that in spite of necessary corrective action, a different and distinct long-term strategy for each product line was pursued, and that these strategies were consistent with the evaluation of the product market factors.

CONCLUSION

This paper presents a framework for planning and evaluation of market expansion strategies. In particular it focuses on the rate of entry into new markets and the allocation of effort among markets. The framework can be used in national or regional marketing, but has special relevance for international expansion. A careful review of the literature did not reveal any other framework which serves the same purposes.

This framework aids managerial action in multinational marketing in the following ways:

- It helps management specify market expansion alternatives for decision making purposes. In addition to the comparison of the two major and opposing strategies—market concentration and market diversification—the paper aids in defining additional strategic options. By considering market segments within national markets, four viable market expansion strategies are identified (see Table 1). By considering resource commitments to new markets, three strategic options are specified and many more are implied.

- It helps management to systematically analyze the problem of choice among the major alternative strategies. Ten key factors affecting this choice are summarized in Table 2, discussed in some detail in the body of the paper, and illustrated by examples and a case study. In each application it will be necessary to separately assess each factor and its relative importance for comprehensive evaluation of the alternatives.

- If offers guidance for measuring market expansion. Two specific measures suggested are the number of countries and market segments served, and an effort diversification index, both as a function of time. Measuring market diversification can be used not only for evaluating the firm's own expansion policy, but also for evaluating competitive moves. The factors affecting the choice of strategy can be used to interpret competitive assumptions.

A systematic approach to identification of alternatives, analysis of choice, and performance evaluation will clarify managerial planning and help reduce mistakes and disappointments in expansion to new markets.

We hope that this paper will aid in directing research attention to this important and interesting area. Further research can benefit by the following points:

- Comparison of market expansion strategies based on the direction of change between two static measurements—as used in past empirical research (see 4)—may not be sufficient. Figure 1 and the following discussion of dynamic measures point out the complexities of identification and offer some direction.

- Decision making models based on one kind of response function (see 2) are useful in some situations, but can be quite misleading in others. Only by exploring alternative response functions and examining their assumptions and implications, can reliable guidance to action be provided.

- The framework of this paper is useful for planning additional research. Identification of a marketing expansion strategy can be used as an explanatory variable for other marketing decisions. As an example, we have used this framework for studying the related problem of competitive market-choice in multinational marketing (Ayal and Zif 1978). Specific priorities for additional research include further empirical investigation of the relationships among the product/market factors, strate-

gies followed, and business outcomes. There also is room for model building that will offer quantitative analysis of the product/market factors.

NOTES

1. Analysis of the third area requires identification of some markets with sufficient potential for entry and a preliminary idea about available budget. The results of the analysis may lead to a reevaluation of the order of entry priorities and provide more definite guidelines for the budget.

2. In their empirical study, Hirsch and Lev (1973) have used the direction of change in a market concentration index of sales between two periods in order to identify the two major strategies. Figure 1 demonstrates, however, that this measure is insufficient for strategy identification. The direction of change for the two strategies is different only during a limited range of time. A more positive identification can rely on the rate or the shape of market expansion over an extended period of time.

3. An effort diversification index for period t, D_{et}, is given by:

$$D_{et} = 1/\sum_{i=1}^{n_t} ME^2_{f,\,t}$$

where

$ME^2_{f,\,t}$ = Marketing effort in market i and period t, expressed as a fraction of the firm's total marketing effort for period t.

n_t = Total number of markets served in period t.

This index is equal to the total number of markets served $D_{et} = n_t$ when efforts are equally distributed; it approaches a lower bound $D_{et} = 1$ when the firm concentrates most of its effort in a single market.

4. For a given initial market size, the sales response function can be separated into a market share response function and a rate of market growth; the first is directly influenced by the firm's marketing efforts while the second is usually more dependent on product life cycles, environmental conditions in the market, and the combined marketing efforts of all competitors.

5. Let us assume that the functional form of Figure 5 is expressed quantitatively, in the following table.

Marketing Effort	Concave Function, Sales $	S-Curve, Sales $
100,000	1,000,000	600,000
200,000	1,800,000	1,200,000
300,000	2,400,000	2,400,000

What is the preferred market expansion strategy for a firm which is planning to invest $300,000 of marketing effort in three identical markets? Under consideration are two strategic alternatives: (1) Concentrate all marketing effort in one market (2) Diversify marketing efforts equally among the three markets (invest $100,000 in each). The outcome of each strategy, depending on the assumed sales response function, will be the following: (preferred strategy indicated by *)

Expansion Strategy	Concave Function	S-Curve Function
1. Concentrate on one market	$2,400,000	$2,400,000*
2. Diversify into three markets	$3,000,000*	$1,800,000

REFERENCES

Ayal, Igal, and Jehiel Zif. "Competitive Market Choice Strategies in Multinational Marketing." *Columbia Journal of World Business,* Vol. 13 (Fall 1978).

Beswick, C.A. "Allocating Selling Effort via Dynamic Programming." *Management Science,* Vol. 23 (March 1977), pp. 667–678.

Bucklin, L. P. *A Theory of Distribution Channel Structure,* IBER Special Publications. Berkeley, Calif.: Graduate School of Business Administration, University of California (1966), pp. 49–50.

Cardwell, John J. "Marketing and Management Science—A Marriage on the Rocks." *California Management Review,* Vol. 10 (Summer 1968), pp. 3–12.

Hackett, D. W. "The International Expansion of U.S. Franchise Systems: Status and Strategies." *Journal of International Business Studies.* Vol. 7 (Spring 1976), p. 71.

Hartung, P. H., and J. L. Fisher. "Brand Switching and Mathematical Programming in Market Expansion." *Management Science,* Vol. 11 (August 1965), pp. 231–243.

Hirsch, Seev, and Baruch Lev. "Sales Stabilization Through Export Diversification." *The Review of Economics and Statistics,* Vol. 53 (August 1971), pp. 270–279.

———. "Foreign Marketing Strategies—A Note." *Management International Review,* Vol. 13 (1973), pp. 81–88.

Hoter, Charles W. "Toward a Contingency Theory of Business Strategy." *Academy of Management Journal,* Vol. 18 (December 1975), p. 804.

Johanson, J., and Paul F. Wiedersheim. "The Internationalization of the Firm—Four Swedish Cases." *The Journal of Management Studies,* Vol. 12 (October 1975), pp. 306–307.

Kotler, Philip. *Marketing Decisions Making—A Model Building Approach.* New York: Holt, Rinehart and Winston (1971), pp. 31–37.

Lambin, J. J. *Advertising, Competition and Market Conduct in Oligopoly Over Time.* Amsterdam: North-Holland Publishing (1976), pp. 95–98.

Luss, Hanan, and Shiv K. Gupta. "Allocation of Marketing Effort Among P Substitutional Products in N Territories." *Operational Research Quarterly,* Vol. 25 (March 1973), pp. 77–88.

Nordin, J. A. "Spatial Allocation of Selling Expenses." *Journal of Marketing,* Vol. 3 (January 1943), pp. 210–219.

Perry, Michael. Koor-Trade Europe, a Case Study presented in a Management Seminar on International Marketing. Tel Aviv: Graduate School of Business, Tel Aviv University (1977).

Rapp, William V. "Strategy Formulation and International Competition." *Columbia Journal of World Business,* Vol. 8 (Summer 1973), pp. 98–112.

Shakun, M. G. "Advertising Expenditures in Coupled Markets, A Game Theory Approach." *Management Science,* Vol. 11 (February 1965), pp. B42–B47.

———. "A Dynamic Model for Competitive Marketing in Coupled Markets." *Management Science,* Vol. 12 (August 1966), pp. B525–B530.

Simon, Julian L. *The Management of Advertising.* Englewood Cliffs, N.J.: Prentice-Hall (1971), pp. 55–76.

Sweeney, James K. "A Small Company Enters the European Market." *Harvard Business Review,* Vol. 48 (September–October 1970), pp. 126–132.

Zentler, A. P., and Dorothy Hyde. "An Optimal Geographical Distribution of Publicity Expenditure in a Private Organization." *Management Science,* Vol. 2 (July 1956), pp. 337–352.

23

Technology Profiles and Export Marketing Strategies
Cedric L. Suzman
Lawrence H. Wortzel

• • •

One of the usual prescriptions to firms searching for growth opportunities is that they seek new or expanded markets for their products. Yet too few firms seriously consider, let alone adopt, exporting as a means of achieving their desired growth activities. Even among firms that do export, over 50% of such firms began exporting as a result of foreign customers' requests for their products rather than as a result of a search for overseas customers (1, 2, 3, 4). As the result of previous work (5, 8), we are firmly convinced that if a firm is to be a successful exporter, it must develop an explicit strategy for doing so, together with a commitment by top management to see that the strategy is implemented.

A scheme for the development of a strategy for exporting is proposed here. It is based on profiling the characteristics of the firms' activities with respect to the nature and level of their technical involvement and then identifying and describing alternative exporting strategies.

PROFILING THE FIRM

In a recent study of 21 small and medium-sized firms in the Southeast (3), four technological orientations were identified; namely, the new innovator, the mature innovator, the adaptor, and the marketer. A description of the sample companies and the characteristics of the companies in each of their technological classifications are given in Tables 1 and 2. Firms fitting each profile can be successful in exporting pro-

vided they select and implement the strategy most appropriate to their particular stage of technological development. Each firm type can be described as follows:

New Innovators

These are firms with recently developed high technology, or with otherwise unique new products. Their energies are devoted to perfecting the products and production processes in order to move into volume production. Such firms can be reasonably sure that their only competitors, if any, are other U.S. firms, and they generally have a highworld market share. Although they are obviously strong in R&D abilities, they may be less strong as marketers, and their customers are usually in other highly industrialized, high-income countries. At the same time, their product strength and company reputation lead to an increasing export demand which is satisfied through a growing network of overseas agents.

In the face of this growth, an international sales manager in a typical company in this category noted that:

There is an increasing need to establish an interface between the marketing and product development, and customer input becomes increasingly important in the development of new product functions and capabilities. This can prove an extremely difficult task for a technologically oriented company where most of the senior personnel are scientists or engineers.

Mature Innovators

The mature innovators are older, larger, and technologically based companies with a high

Table 1 Number of Sample Companies by SIC and General Description

SIC No.	SIC Description	Number of Companies	General Description	Number of Companies
22	Textile mill products	2	Textile based	3
23	Apparel	1		
28	Chemicals	4	Chemical based	4
33, 34	Primary metals: smelting, refining casting	1	Mechanical, machinery based	8
35	Machinery (except electrical)	7		
36, 48	Electrical and electronic machinery	3	Electrical, electronic, optical measurement, and communications	4
38	Measuring and analyzing instruments	1		
28, 35 36, 38	Export management companies	2	Export management companies	2
	Total	21	Total	21

world market share and extensive geographic coverage in the major countries of the world. While the mature innovator's product lines may not be unique, neither are they completely standardized, and competition comes from companies in the United States and other industrialized countries. The mature innovators are particularly adept at developing and incorporating brand-differentiating features into their

products and applying new technology to broaden their product lines and develop new market applications.

These companies are able to do this because they have continued to devote resources to R&D based on perceived customer needs and in response to new technologies. The mature innovators also have developed systems and procedures for enlarging their source of tech-

Table 2 Characteristics of Sample Companies by Technological Classification (Average Values)

Classification (no. of companies)	Sales ($ millions)	No. Empl. (thousands)	Export % Sales	R&D % Sales	R&D Empl. % Total	Patents/ $ Million Sales	R&D* Int.	Age (Yr.)
New innovators (5)	55.8	1,247	15.9	3.56	7.5	1.44	15.0	18
Mature innovators (4)	183.0	1,950	26.5	2.12	4.5	1.30	10.9	48
Adaptors (4)	36.5	423	14.2	2.25	3.5	0.25	6.3	36
Marketers (6)	98.2	2,535	3.2	1.15	3.6	0.03	4.9	36

*This measure is derived from the sum of R&D expenditure percentage, R&D employees percentage, and patents per million dollars of sales weighted by a factor of three.

nological know-how through such activities as cross-licensing and reciprocal exchange of information with licensees on a worldwide basis. A company's own R&D department is thus no longer the sole source of innovation and technology for additions to its product range, and these have frequently come from outside the company.

The president of one of the most successful companies explained its success:

Technology is what has made us grow from No. 4 to No. 1 today, while market conditions have put other companies out of business. A search for new ideas and customer needs which we felt we could meet has opened new markets for us. Future company strategy is to develop other pieces of equipment for the man-made fiber industry when it is felt that a significant product improvement can be made.

Adaptors

Adaptors use a strategy of applying their technical expertise to modify standard products and processes to meet the needs of specific foreign customers or markets. They are frequently smaller, flexible firms and tend to concentrate on a few specific markets, generally in the less developed or recently industrialized markets, rather than attempting to obtain wide geographic coverage. In some cases this merely involves the sale of a "turnkey" package of machinery for a given industry in a foreign market. In other cases, however, completely new products are designed or formulated to meet foreign conditions.

Marketers

These are firms which sell products that have no distinctive technology and, often, no important features that differentiate them from competing offerings. The success of such firms is due primarily to their marketing skill, which lie, as appropriate, in the ability to locate and reach customers, in developing and managing a sales force, or in using advertising and other promotional tools. Marketers are likely to have a host

of U.S. competitors and to face a variety of foreign competitors in any country in which they may wish to operate. Their exports are usually directed at specific foreign markets, largely in the less developed countries. As may be expected, they also frequently set up their own sales subsidiaries rather than work through agents.

ALTERNATIVE EXPORTING STRATEGIES

In addition to the technological orientation there are also basic export marketing strategies firms can adopt; namely, responder, imitator, or entrepreneur. Each requires a different implementation process and has different risk characteristics and marketing skill requirements. The end result from each alternative is a firm with somewhat different market coverage and competitive strength.

Responder

The responder develops an export business based on unsolicited inquiries and orders, using the market to tell it who is interested in its product. Based on the orders it receives it tries to find out about the customer and simply looks for additional potential customers of similar characteristics. It uses orders and inquiries as a marketing research tool.

This strategy can be successful if the would-be exporting firm is willing to put real effort into following up inquiries and to offer prices to inquirers that are realistic in terms of the actual price at which the product can be sold in some quantity. The responder firm must recognize that the inquiries and orders it receives are a research opportunity as well as a sales opportunity. They should, therefore, be evaluated in terms of their potential information content as well as their contribution to profit.

The marketing skill requirements for implementing this strategy are not exceptional, and an advantage to this strategy is that the firm can begin exporting with relatively little investment in time and effort. It can, for example, use an export management company to handle all of its business or rely on foreign agents and distributors.

The result of this strategy is that the exporting firm may develop an export business that is well diversified geographically, but which is without a particularly strong position in any one market. In the short run, especially when the firm begins exporting, this is not necessarily a disadvantage. A wide selection of customers may allow the exporting firm to sample a range of country market possibilities. Over the longer term, however, an exporter may prefer to concentrate on building significant market share in a limited number of markets. Thus, the responder strategy may be a highly appropriate entry strategy, but it should usually be considered as a first stage leading to a more active stance.

Imitator

The imitator strategy is based on finding markets in which exports of similar products have been successful and then exporting to those markets. The would-be imitator simply analyzes trade data to find out which countries are importing significant amounts of the product it wishes to export. It then identifies the marketing and distribution strategies being used by the firms that are successfully exporting to each country, and simply duplicates these efforts. Clearly, for a U.S. company it is easiest to imitate U.S. exporting firms. Seeking models from other countries would require a more aggressive search.

This strategy seemingly can be implemented without conducting a great deal of research on the overseas markets identified as targets. However, the outcome of the strategy depends on the state of the particular overseas market in question and on the behavior of the other exporters to that market. Pursuit of this strategy can result in obtaining a very significant share of market in circumstances where (1) the market is growing and (2) other competitors are not aggressively pursuing growth. Conversely, the strategy can give very poor results in a static market crowded with tenacious competitors. The resultant fight to keep or increase market share is likely to lead to low profits because of price cutting and high marketing expenditure. Therefore, the firm considering this strategy must forecast market growth. It should also collect information that will aid in predicting how competitors are likely to behave in the face of a new entrant. Clearly, the imitator has a greater chance of success if it has some advantage over its competitors, either by way of unique product features that would be particularly meaningful to overseas customers, or by virtue of a low cost position.

Entrepreneur

The entrepreneur actively searches for potential markets. It is not concerned with whether particular markets are presently importing significant quantities of similar products from the United States or from anywhere else. It is concerned only about discovering where the large potential markets for its products are and how the potential these markets represent can best be exploited. Successful pursuit of this strategy requires a tenacious, sophisticated firm that is willing to invest considerable time and effort in information collection and analysis.

The entrepreneurial firm must perform several tasks in order to make this strategy work. First, it must identify the particular characteristics of markets that indicate probable success, including such factors as size, determinants of buyer behavior, and patterns of competition. Next, the firm must develop marketing plans based upon identified characteristics and on a knowledge of the available marketing institutions. The successful pursuit of an entrepreneurial strategy may demand product modification as well as the tailoring of marketing plans. Often, there is no one to imitate. The firm tries to identify and then satisfy the specific circumstances that lead to the initiation or growth of the market.

The entrepreneurial strategy is not without a good deal of risk because of the up-front investment required for information collection, possible product modifications, and marketing expenditures. The result, however, can be a significant new market which the exporter may not have to share, at least for a while, with his U.S. or foreign competitors.

MATCHING TECHNOLOGY PROFILES AND MARKETING STRATEGIES

A correspondence between the approach just described and the firm's technological profile described earlier should now be apparent. Each of the firm profiles fits better with some strategies than with others. It is also within the ability of many firms to adjust their basic strategies in order to make them more effective.

New Innovator–Responder/Entrepreneur Strategies

The new innovator can choose either the responder or entrepreneur strategy. The imitator strategy is usually unavailable because there will simply not be a group of U.S. or other exporters whom the new innovator can follow. The best choice for the new innovator is to employ the responder and entrepreneur strategies in sequence, as the company's overseas business develops. Unsolicited inquiries and orders would be used as a means of first screening new markets. An in-depth entrepreneurial strategy would then be employed to fully develop the market's potential. The new innovators have generally started as small science- and technology-based operations that developed a particular product which quickly achieved acceptance in the U.S. market. In a typical responder fashion, these companies then started receiving inquiries from overseas distributors of similar products as well as from potential customers.

Quite frequently the companies were also approached by their U.S. customers who had overseas operations. These customers wanted the company to supply their overseas operations, either through exporting or even by setting up foreign manufacturing operations.

Ideally, the new innovator would "seed" inquiries, for example, by advertising in trade publications that reached appropriate foreign audiences. The use of such advertising is simply a broader application of traditional industrial advertising usage, which is to generate inquiries. But in this instance, the inquiry is not the end product; it is the beginning of a research effort during which answers must be obtained to several questions such as: Who is the customer? What are the characteristics of the distribution chain? Where and how is the product to be used? What product features have stimulated the inquiry or order? The answers then are used to provide a framework for developing entrepreneurial marketing plans.

It may not be wise for the new innovator to depend solely on a responder strategy unless the new innovator has strong patent protection or plans to produce the product for only a short period of time. As we pointed out earlier, responders may end up with small positions in a number of markets if they do not actively follow up inquiries and orders with marketing efforts. Moreover, the new innovator may miss some significant opportunities, if, for some reason, inquiries or orders are not forthcoming from all potential markets.

The responder strategy is more frequently used by smaller companies which are forced to use specialized agents/distributors; as the company grows, a network of overseas representatives is established. However, with a technically based product, there is usually an ongoing need for technical and market application know-how which the agents/distributors are unable to provide. The companies therefore move to establish their own sales and technical service operations based in the main international markets. These moves are again in the direction of establishing an entrepreneurially oriented strategy.

Mature Innovator–Entrepreneur Strategies

The mature innovators have experienced a transition from the early growth stages and have established themselves with a high market share in many world markets. Their success has been based on an original invention or product which has started to mature. The technical and R&D emphasis has changed from product to process development and operating efficiency, and some of these companies have turned to foreign manufacturing to remain competitive.

Their ability to continue to grow and retain market leadership has required a revitalized effort to develop new product lines based on most recent technology. Coupled with this, however, is a strong entrepreneurial market strategy of entering new and growing markets using these new technologically based products. In effect, these companies are purusing a second, or even a third, wave of innovation and growth, often 25 to 50 years after they were first established.

Many marketing managers have expected that new products would be introduced into new markets in some sequence, beginning with high-income countries and progressing eventually to low-income countries, and that consequently a product could be in the mature stage of development in one market and in its introductory stage in another. Recently, however, this notion has come into serious question (7). There are an increasing number of multinational firms in the world, representing a large number of industries, that introduce new products almost simultaneously into many markets. Absolute increases in income have increased greatly the number of markets in which a new product can be successfully introduced.

The mature innovator, therefore, usually finds it necessary to pursue a vigorous entrepreneurial strategy of seeking out and developing new markets for its ever-widening product line.

It also relies heavily on its worldwide technology links with other firms as well as a well-established international marketing network of agents and subsidiaries in major markets of the world.

In most cases neither a responder strategy nor an imitator strategy is feasible. In the case of the responder strategy it is not likely that a sufficient volume of overseas inquiries will be received upon which to build a business. Moreover, similar products or product substitutes, either locally made or imported, are very likely to be available in foreign markets. The company must therefore rely on its product edge and entrepreneurship to be successful.

Adaptor–Entrepreneur Strategies

The adaptors' strengths lie in their flexibility and receptiveness to new ideas and to the specific needs of particular foreign customers or markets. These companies may get into exporting initially by responding to foreign request or inquiry. This then leads to a realization that, given their particular technical capabilities, they could adapt their standard U.S. product line to meet the specific needs of a growing and potentially profitable foreign market.

Although the initial move into exporting may be through a responder strategy, this is generally not sufficient to ensure continued growth. A more aggressive entrepreneurial approach is needed to seek out new market opportunities and find new customers. Since there are frequently both local and foreign competitors, there is also a need to keep ahead with the latest technology in order to not be outmanuevered. As a result new products and adaptations are being developed continually for specific customers or markets.

From a marketing standpoint, the most important factor is an intimate knowledge of the markets being served. This implies specialization by country or region within the export department and a concentration on relatively few markets. Where local agents or distributors are used, they play a major role in the specification and design of the product. In most cases, however, agents are not used, and the companies develop local sales and service organizations. For smaller companies this is frequently through licenses and joint ventures with local partners who can contribute the necessary local knowledge.

Marketer–Imitator Strategies

The marketer is usually limited to the imitator strategy. As we pointed out earlier, the marketer's product line is not distinctive and is most probably already being exported to and even produced in a great many of the countries that represent good markets for those products. The success of the imitator strategy will simply depend on the marketer's ability to identify the particular countries in which it can use its marketing and sales skills to gain a marketing advantage over present exporters and then to exploit that advantage.

There is probably little opportunity to use an entrepreneurial strategy, but the possibility of using the entrepreneurial strategy might still be investigated. This can be done as a by-product of developing a specific imitator strategy. As the imitator develops a list of specific countries with significant exports from the United States, those countries without such exports will become evident by their omission, and it could be worthwhile for the marketer to quickly screen the omitted countries for possible entrepreneurial opportunities.

The marketers tend to concentrate on markets in less developed countries, whereas the new innovators, at the other end of the R&D intensiveness scale, tend to look to Europe and the other industrialized countries first. The clear implication is that management and marketing ability may be sufficient to penetrate an LDC market, but new technology and a distinctive product are needed to enter the more advanced markets. This conclusion is in line with the product life cycle theory in international trade and investment (6).

A further conclusion possible from the marketer-imitator strategy is that it is possible for many companies to enter the international marketplace provided they are willing to expend the same level of resources and effort on market research, market planning, promotion, and sales as they do in the competitive U.S. market. Unfortunately, this is not often the case.

REQUIREMENTS FOR SUCCESS

Regardless of the firm profile or strategy, there are certain other requirements that a firm must satisfy if it is to be successful. The most critical requirements for the success of any export strategy are top management commitment and the clear, unambiguous communication of that commitment by top management to all relevant parts of the organization. The best way by far to obtain and communicate a top management commitment is to build the export plan into both the firm's strategic plan and its annual operating plans. The export plan should do considerably more than simply express a desire to export. It should detail the specific steps that will be taken in developing export business and identify the specific steps that will be taken in developing export business and identify the specific people responsible for each step.

There are also some additional commitments that should be detailed in the export plan and understood and agreed to by all necessary participants. Perhaps the most important is the commitment to maintain a visible presence in any market the firm decides to enter. This can be accomplished, for example, through maintaining local inventories, training local distributors, and investing in local advertising and promotion. This is especially true if the product in question requires after-sales servicing. The commitment to supply must also be backed by a production set-aside that specifically allocates an agreed-upon volume of product to export, even if it involves the addition of capacity or the introduction of a second shift.

Another important commitment is to realistic pricing, especially for the entrepreneur and for the responder who is trying to convert its inquiries into steady business. If a firm wants to test an export market, it must price its offerings based on the market, rather than on the costs associated with a particular test sale (which should be considered as marketing research expenditures rather than as operating costs). Finally, the firm must be willing to deal in foreign currencies and accept the reality of price lists denominated in currencies other than its own, although there are export financing services which will include foreign exchange cover on the export receivables.

The implications for a company entering the export market, or indeed for a company already active in international sales, will depend on where the company fits into the technological profile-marketing strategy classification that has been developed. It is possible to enter the international marketplace through exporting by taking one of a number of different orientations, depending largely on the company's position in the industry and the stage in the product life cycle of its major products.

The research shows that being a new innovator–responder—a company with a distinctive new product sought after by foreign customers—is not the only way to begin exporting, although it is one that requires the least international management and marketing experience and expertise. It is clearly also possible to enter international markets as a marketer-imitator with relatively standard mature products. This requires an intensive marketing effort in selected foreign markets and is especially appropriate in the less developed countries. Smaller companies with fewer resources have also found it feasible to focus on particular foreign markets or customer needs as a viable entry strategy. The adaptor-responder/entrepreneur companies take this approach one step further and apply their technological competence to adapting standard products to the distinctive requirements of particular foreign markets and customers.

Continued success, however, requires a combination of innovation, adaptation, and market-

ing expertise. Neither a purely technological orientation nor a predominantly marketing approach will be sufficient to sustain an international sales operation, and this is undoubtedly also true for the domestic market as well. The successful exporter will consciously design an appropriate marketing strategy to fit its particular technological orientation and the needs of carefully selected export markets.

REFERENCES

1. Bilkey, Warren J. "An Attempted Integration of the Literature on the Export Behavior of Firms." *Journal of International Business Studies,* Vol. 9 (Summer 1978), pp. 33–46.
2. McConnel, James E. The Export Decision: An Empirical Study of Firm Behavior." *Econ. Geog.,* Vol. 55, no. 3 (July 1979), pp. 171–183.
3. Roy, Delwin, A., Claude L. Simpson, Jr., and Cedric L. Suzman. *Southeast Exporting: Profiles, Typology and the Role of Technology in Selected U.S. Firms.* Research Monograph No. 90. College of Business Administration, Georgia State University, Atlanta, Georgia (1981).
4. Simpson, C. L., Jr., Duane Kujawa. The Export Decision Process: An Empirical Enquiry." *Journal of International Business Studies,* Vol. 5 (Spring 1974), pp. 107–117.
5. Suzman, Cedric L., and Delwin A. Roy. *The Role of Technology in Exporting and Foreign Sales: A Profile and Typology of Twenty-one Firms in the Southeast United States.* International Business Series No. 4. Georgia World Congress Institute, Atlanta, Georgia (January 1980).
6. Vernon, Raymond. "International Investment and International Trade in the Product Cycle." *Quarterly Journal of Economics,* May 1966, pp. 190–207.
7. Vernon, Raymond. "The Product Cycle Hypothesis in a New International Environment." *Oxford Business and Economics Studies,* Vol. 41, no. 4 (November 1979), pp. 255–267.
8. Wortzel, Lawrence H. "International Marketing: Identifying International Markets." In *Exporting for Small and Medium-Sized Businesses: Key Decisions and Proven Approaches.* Conference Series No. 11. Georgia World Congress Institute, Atlanta, Georgia (1980).

24

Multinational Strategic Market Portfolios

Gilbert D. Harrell
Richard O. Kiefer

• • •

Multinational business executives are facing complex strategic planning decisions at a time when rapid shifts in world markets are causing broad fluctuations in potential profitability. Planning on a country-by-country or even regional basis can result in spotty worldwide market performance. The problem of international strategic planning is particularly salient for industries in which major corporations are competing on a global scale—automotives, steel, energy, heavy construction equipment, and agricultural equipment.

Planning processes that focus simultaneously across a broad range of markets provide multinational businesses with tools to help balance risks, capital requirements, competitive economies of scale, and profitability to gain stronger long-term market positions. For example, by systematically choosing well-balanced product and market strategic combinations, Japanese auto companies have reached world prominence in a few short years.

Strategic planning, in the broadest sense, seeks to match markets with products and other corporate resources in order to strengthen a firm's competitive stance. It requires the involvement of a broad range of executives— marketing, research and development, production, and finance, to name a few. Together, these executives can focus their attention on both products and markets. However, there is a strong tendency to plan around either products

or markets, but not both. The problem is one of perspective: The complexity of world business makes it difficult to comprehend either product strategies or market strategies, much less both at the same time.

To aid international strategic planning, several domestic planning tools can be used, but most lose effectiveness when applied to international settings. They tend to focus on *products* as the principal unit of strategic endeavor. Yet, the great variations in market conditions around the world suggest that it is more appropriate to make decisions about *market* portfolios. For example, although Ford Tractor operations have experienced varying profitability, cash flow, and market share by product type (such as light versus heavy tractors), some of their greatest opportunities were due to broad potential profit variations across market areas.

The purpose of this article is to describe an analytical approach to strategic planning that is useful in sorting international market environments so that market portfolios will be emphasized. The case of International Tractor Operations of Ford Motor Company will be used to describe key aspects of the process.

Several major corporations, including General Electric, Westinghouse, Shell, and Borg Warner, use product portfolio analysis in their domestic planning. Bruce Henderson of the Boston Consulting Group first demonstrated the importance of analyzing product portfolios according to business growth and market share matrices.[1]

Business or product portfolio analysis can be viewed as an effort to sort opportunities according to a few strategic variables. Much of the work is the outgrowth of observations by the

Source: Gilbert D. Harrell and Richard O. Kiefer, "Multinational Strategic Market Portfolios," *MSU Business Topics,* Winter 1981, pp. 5–15. Copyright © 1981. Reprinted by permission of the Graduate School of Business Administration, Michigan State University.

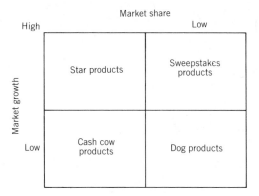

Figure 1 A company's product array.

Boston Consulting Group concerning the *experience curve*. They observed that the cost of producing a product declines predictably as output increases. Because companies with a high market share produce more than their competitors, their costs are less and their profit greater. In addition, market growth has much to do with the degree of difficulty in securing market share, that is, it is easier to secure increased share while the market is growing. Furthermore, those firms that enjoy large market shares in mature markets are likely to maintain them. Thus, market share and market growth can be used as coordinates to plot a company's products in four categories—high share/slow growth (Cash Cows), high share/rapid growth (Stars), low share/rapid growth (Sweepstakes), and low share/slow growth (Dogs), as indicated in Figure 1.

George Steiner and others have extended the procedures by replacing business growth with a more elaborate market attractiveness index and market share with a competitive strength index.[2] Their scheme uses the findings of PIMS (Profit Impact Market Strategy Group) and others regarding the characteristics that produce strong returns on investment.[3] In addition, many corporations have related the product portfolio to the product life cycle concept. Sweepstake products are in the introduction phase of the life cycle; Stars are in the growth phase; Cash Cows are in the maturity phase; and Dogs are in the decline phase. In this way, companies' domestic operational programs can be altered depending on the amount of growth or decline in product sales. But, again, the focus is on product elements, and while domestic life cycles may tend to follow a pattern, international life cycles are more complex. For example, one of the many international patterns has been (1) invention in, for example, the United States; (2) heavy domestic production and sales of the product; (3) export to foreign countries; (4) stimulation of foreign production based on the U.S. version; (5) foreign economies of scale and lower labor rates in other nations' own markets, and (6) export from the foreign manufacturer back into the U.S. market. Again, while the product life cycle is helpful, a more functional picture of the international pattern can be drawn by looking at market development stages.

MARKET PORTFOLIOS

The conceptual simplicity of presenting the combinations of competitive strengths and market attractiveness provide a two-dimensional matrix useful for plotting products. More important to the international planner, each axis is a linear combination of factors that together can be used to define a country's attractiveness from a market view and determine the company's competitive strength in that country, as shown in Figure 2.

Data on international markets, although much improved in recent years, are difficult to obtain for elaborate measures of country attractiveness. However, Ford Tractor is extensively exploring four basic elements—market size, market growth rate, government regulation, and economic and political stability.

Also, competitive strength must be defined within an international context. Unfortunately, no quantitative models exist. Ford Tractor executives suggested the following factors for this scale: market share, product fit, contribution

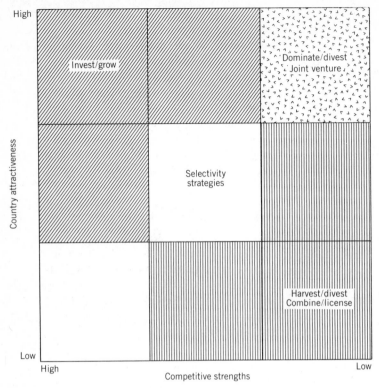

Figure 2 Matrix for plotting products.

margin, and market representation and market support.

The country attractiveness and competitive strength scales are plotted to form a 3 × 3 matrix, as indicated in Figure 2. Those countries that fall in the upper left generally should receive funding for growth, while those in the lower right are prime areas to harvest or divest—or to ignore if no operations have been started. Those countries falling on the lower left to upper right diagonal will require selective funding strategies. The reasons for these generalizations will be clearer after a more complete discussion of the content of the two scales.

COUNTRY ATTRACTIVENESS SCALE DEVELOPMENT

Market size is measured according to projected average annual sales in units. Ford selected a three-year average to avoid anomalies resulting from short-term economic shifts and strike effects among major companies. This measure provides a good base on which to build growth projections, the second element of the scale.

Market size, obviously, is critical because minimum volumes are required to achieve the economies of scale necessary for entry, including technical assistance, training, and product and service information. Large volumes provide support for permanent local organizations and affiliated companies as well as justification for on-site manufacturing.

Market rate of growth is estimated as the ten-year annual compound percentage increase in sales. This is longer than most domestic time frames; however, the long time frame is warranted.

Government regulation includes three sub-factors: price control and regulations, homologation requirements, and regulations covering local content and compensatory exports. Homologation relates to nontariff barriers, for example, local safety and product requirements and, in many cases, simple red tape designed to restrict foreign market entry. Local content and compensatory export laws require that end products contain components manufactured locally or that exports of products be made from the receiving country to offset imports. Governments play a significant role in determining the ease of market entry through safety and environmental regulations, price regulation and incentives, and protection of local industry against foreign competition.

Economic and political factors include the inflation rate and trade balance. Ford has used sophisticated measures of political stability developed in conjunction with consulting groups and government agencies.

A single linear scale comprised of the four factors was computed as follows:

> Country Attractiveness = Market Size + 2 × Market Growth + (.5 × Price Control/ Regulation + .25 × Homologation Requirements + .25 × Local Content and Compensatory Export Requirements) + (.35 × Inflation + .35 × Trade Balance + .3 × Political Factors).

The weights represent the relative importance of each variable to Ford's strategic planning efforts.[4] In order to standardize each of the analysis units, all estimates are transposed to 10-point scales, as Table 1 demonstrates. The above formula is then applied to provide a single number that falls on the linear country attractiveness scale. This number is then transformed to conform to another 10-point index for plotting.

COMPETITIVE STRENGTH SCALE DEVELOPMENT

Market share, critical in domestic profitability, is likely to be the most important characteristic in international business because of experience curve volumes and costs. Because market share tends to vary considerably from country to country, this is a good discriminating factor. In domestic markets, many stable industries have only three or four major competitors. In international markets, they may have many more. In some cases, certain national manufacturers have strong market shares and brand loyalty, and are protected by nontariff barriers. Thus, two market share factors are relevant to Ford in this case, the number of major competitors in the market and Ford's total market share.

Product fit represents an estimate of how closely the product fits a particular market need. In the tractor industry, Ford defines this broadly in terms of horsepower classes and more specifically in terms of unique product features that may or may not match country needs. The broad range of environmental differences and buyer tastes and preferences makes product fit a key strategic factor. If the product is tailored closely to unique national needs, the firm may be able to forfeit economies of scale.

Contribution margin is a measure of profit per unit and profit as a percentage of net dealer cost. Low contribution margins often reflect limited price scope because of competition or government controls. They may also reflect an inefficiently operated local group. While this measure should be reflected in the other three elements, it does serve as a measure of ability to gain profit, an important competitive strength. Again, relatively broad fluctuations do exist across countries.

Market support includes the quantity and quality of company personnel located in the country, parts and technical service support, and advertising and sales promotion capability within the country; that is, it represents the general company image in a local environment. This is difficult to quantify, which is a major drawback.

Ford used all these factors to compute a single linear scale reflecting its competitive strength as follows:

Table 1 Country Attractiveness Scale Weights*

Market Size		Market Growth	
Units	Rating	Amount	Rating
25,000	10	5% +	10
22,500–24,999	9	4–4.9%	9
20,000–22,499	8	3–3.9%	8
.	.	.	.
.	.	.	.
.	.	.	.
5,000	1	Under 3%	1

Government Regulation

Price Control		Homologation		Local Content/Compensatory Exports	
Type	Rating	Type	Rating	Type	Rating
None	10	None	10	None	10
Easy to comply	6	Easy	6	Easy to comply	6
Moderately easy to comply	4	Moderate	4	Moderately easy to comply	4
Rigid controls	2	Tough	2	Tough	2

Economic and Political Stability

Inflation		Trade Balance		Political Stability	
Amount	Rating	Amount	Rating	Type	Rating
7% and under	10	5% and over	10	Stable market	10
.	.	0–4.9%	9	Moderate	5
.	.	−5–0%	8	Unstable	1
40% and over	1	.	.		
		.	.		
		.	.		
		−36%	1		

*These measurements are indicative of what might be done, rather than concrete examples.

Competitive Strength = (.5 × Absolute Market Share + .5 Industry Position) × 2 + Product Fit + (.5 × Profit Per Unit + .5 × Profit Percentage of Net Dealer Cost) + Market Support

Again, the weights reflect Ford executives' subjective estimates of the relative importance of each variable in defining the competitive strength required to excel in international markets. Table 2 provides examples of the 10-point scales used for this measure.

STRATEGIC SITUATIONS

In Figures 3 and 4, each European country and key countries from the rest of the world are located on the market matrices based on the ratings assigned for country attractiveness and competitive strength. These examples show one way Ford can look at the world. Obviously, the picture is incomplete for all parts of the strategic plan, but it does offer strong implications for finance, production, research and development, and marketing, as well as for the overall corporate objective for each country.

Table 2 Competitive Strength Weights*

Percentage of Market		Market Share Position	
Share	Rating	Rank	Rating
30 +	10	1	10
27–21	9	2	8
.	.	3	6
.	.	4	4
.	.	5	2
4	1		

Product Fit

Because this scale suggests Ford's competitive product strategy, we decided not to publish it. In general, a 10-point subjective index was created to match product characteristics with key local product needs.

Contribution Margin

Again, this is proprietary, but it reflects two factors.

Profit per Unit		Profit Percentage of Net Dealer Cost	
Amount	Rating	Amount	Rating
$5,000 (example)	10	40% +	10
.	.	.	.
.	.	.	.
$1–400	1	5% −	1

Market Support

Market Representation		Market Support	
Evaluation	Rating	Evaluation	Rating
Quantity and quality of Ford distributors and service are clearly "best in country"	10	Ford market support in advertising promotion is clearly "best in country"	10
Ford representation is equal to leading competitor's	8	Ford support is equal to leading competitor's	8
Ford representation is behind several leading competitors'	2	Ford support is behind several leading competitors'	2

*These measurements are indicative of what might be done, rather than concrete examples.

Invest/Grow countries call for corporate commitment to a strong market position. A dominant share in a rapidly growing market will require substantial financial investments. Equally important are the investments in people at the country level to sustain a strong competitive position.

Research and development will be important to match products closely with specific market requirements. This will involve both the addition of new models and the expansion of options for more applications. The growth in models should be, where practical, in directions that will capitalize on the company's experience curve in mature markets. However, action is required so that unique product demands in

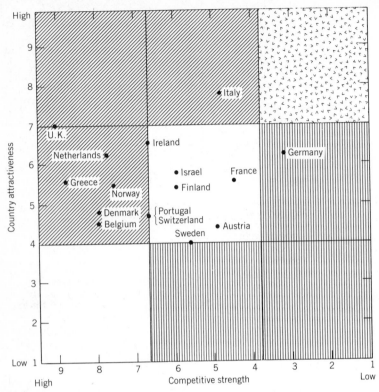

Figure 3 European matrix.

these growth areas are not excluded. This is particularly important for firms from countries such as the United States, in which the domestic market has lost its innovative posture.

Local production often is required for the sake of rapid delivery and service. Major competitors usually will be producing close to the market in these countries. Export strategies are likely to fail because of cost problems, or government pressure when balance of trade considerations are involved.

Marketing supports of all kinds should be expansive—number of personnel, advertising, quality of trade services, and support. All of these investments will support growth. Personnel selection should focus on increasing realistic risk taking and the cutting of red tape. Doers are a must in these markets.

Harvest/Divest/License/Combine countries

often call for strategies to harvest profits or sell the business. Generally, any cash they generate will be required to maintain share; therefore, share generally is given up for profit. Cash flow timing becomes critical. Since the corporation's market share and competitive position are probably low, and the market is relatively small and the growth low, strategic plans should focus on harvesting near-term profits until the day the business is sold or abandoned.

Finance should concentrate on frequent cash flow calculations to ensure that variable costs are covered. Pricing policy will be keyed to short-term considerations. By increasing price and reducing the marketing costs, the firm generally can produce cash from those sales that do occur. Thus, market share will be sold off in the interest of maintaining margins.

Exceptions to abandonment occur when sev-

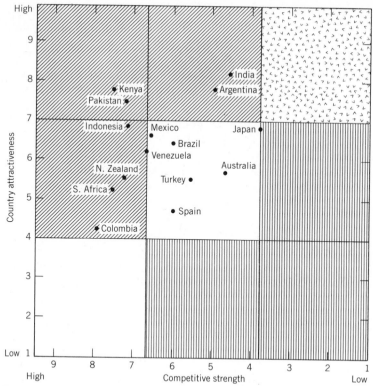

Figure 4 Key country matrix.

eral of these countries can be combined to give enough volume for a sizable export or subsidiary business. In addition, licensing arrangements can be beneficial to the licensor as well as the local licensee.

Dominate/Divest/Joint Venture countries (the upper right in Figures 3 and 4) present a particularly difficult strategic choice because the firm is competitively weak but the market appealing. Movement toward dominance requires long-term cash flow deficits; divestiture requires the presence of a buyer and cuts the company off from cash and profit opportunities.

The decision demands a careful analysis of cash requirements and cash availability, as well as most of the other factors pertinent to entering a new venture. This is a particularly good time to enter into joint ventures with firms that complement the organization. It would be wise,

for example, to match a corporation with product design strength with one possessing distribution and marketing strength.

Selectivity countries (center and lower left in Figures 3 and 4) present another problem. In domestic situations, products falling into these two sections on the grid generally are perfect candidates for milking. They produce strong cash flows. This is only partially the case in international environments. In general, in these countries market share will be difficult to maintain even if the corporation is in a second- or third-ranking competitive position. Competition is extreme. Yet, these markets clearly suggest maintenance strategies that build cash flow or, if technological and other advantages can be transferred from Star environments, strategies that build share. (The share building domestic strategy generally is avoided because it can be destructive to the industry.) Unfortunately, many international markets fail to reach the mature stability of traditional U.S. markets, and such strategies are necessary.

The finance department should do frequent analyses to ensure that strategies are properly focused. Often, strategies require transfer of excess funds to other countries. Full product costing usually is required.

Manufacturing usually will involve plants in or near the market. They will be maintained efficiently rather than expanded drastically. Profit can come from capacity utilization, thus marketing will be important here. Marketing will concentrate on strong reliability and adequate but not excessive margins. Much of the focus will be on current customers.

Research and development will be primarily interested in maintaining an efficient, full line of products. Therefore, modular units and many options will make good use of inventory availability, in contrast to building many unique models.

In this area, any of the three primary strategies mentioned before might also apply. For example, Ford in Mexico might set its share objective to move from 30 percent to 50 percent, that is, seek market dominance. For example, if Ford's current price is at a premium, it might drop down to the market leader and strengthen its dealership network. At the same time, a fuller product line would provide a larger potential customer base.

In contrast, Ford in Japan might require the same or a completely different strategy, depending on management risk preferences and company condition.

CONCLUSIONS

Ford has been taking a close look at international market portfolios. Although Ford has been strong in product strategy, it is finding new opportunities based on variances among countries. The strategic planning tool presented in this article is one step toward dealing simultaneously with world markets.

Several suggestions are in order when applying such a tool. First, because the implications extend across several business functions, it is important to involve finance, production, research and development, and marketing in development of the strategic options for each type of country as well as in measuring country attractiveness and competitive strength. Second, the approach should be recognized as only a tool and not a set of hard and fast rules. Once in a while, the dynamics of international markets warrant special attention that runs counter to the strategies that match a particular portfolio category. Thus, the market portfolio provides only a part of the total picture. Also, although many of the calculations require subjective information, rigorous development of scales is useful. The better the information, whether objective or subjective, the closer the market portfolio plots will match actual conditions.

Finally, the process can aid executives in the analysis of current world market positions. It can be used to plot the movement of markets over time, thus keeping track of environmental and competitive shifts for future projections. To the degree that patterns begin to emerge, the strategic planning organization can better track its successes and failures and learn about its capabilities in diverse international markets.

NOTES

1. Bruce D. Henderson, *Henderson on Corporate Strategy* (Cambridge, Mass.: ABT Books, 1979).
2. George Steiner, *Strategic Planning* (New York: Free Press, 1979); George S. Day, "Diagnosing the Product Portfolio," *Journal of Marketing*, Vol. 41 (April 1977), pp. 29–38; and Derek F. Abell and John S. Hammond, *Strategic Marketing Planning* (Englewood Cliffs, N.J.: Prentice-Hall, 1979).
3. Sidney Schoeffler, Robert D. Buzzell, and Donald F. Heany, "Impact of Strategic Planning on Profit Performance," *Harvard Business Review*, Vol. 52 (March–April 1974), pp. 137–45.
4. To protect the confidentiality of information proprietary to Ford, we have used simplified measures and changed some of the data. Therefore, the article presents findings that are only suggestive of the way Ford rates various countries. Actual ratings may vary.

25

The World's Champion Marketers: The Japanese
Philip Kotler
Liam Fahey

• • •

Few dispute that the Japanese have performed an economic miracle since World War II. In a relatively short time, they have achieved global market leadership in industries thought to be dominated by impregnable giants: autos, motorcycles, watches, cameras, optical instruments, steel, shipbuilding, pianos, zippers, radios, television, video recorders, hand calculators, and so on. Japanese firms are currently moving into the number-two position in computers and construction equipment and making strong inroads into the chemical, pharmaceutical, and machine tool industries.

THE POPULAR THEORIES

However, explanations of Japanese success abound. Most analysts of the Japanese way of doing business emphasize some particular set of factors. These explanations frequently reflect individual's academic background, professional training and experience, or exposure to and study of a specific Japanese industry or individual firm. These sets of explanatory factors can be divided into four categories: good business practices, unfair business practices, structural factors, and happenstance.

Business Practices

Good business practices include a set of effective decision-making procedures: the "ringi"

Source: Philip Kotler and Liam Fahey, "The World's Champion Marketers: The Japanese," pp. 3–13. Reprinted by permission from the *Journal of Business Strategy*, Summer 1982, Volume 3, Number 1. Copyright © 1982, Warren, Gorham & Lamont Inc., 210 South Street, Boston, Mass. All rights reserved.

form of decision making involving consensus development, bottom-up communication and multiple participants in decision making, quality control circles, and systematic in-depth identification and evaluation of decision alternatives. Japanese management is slow in making decisions but fast in carrying them out because commitment to the decision is achieved during its formulation. Japanese personnel practices (e.g., lifetime employment for many employees, worker suggestion systems, and excellent training and job rotation) contribute to high company loyalty. In terms of functional management, the Japanese are viewed as doing a much better job than most U.S. firms of achieving cost control, production efficiency, and product design and quality.

The Japanese have often been accused of engaging in unfair business practices. While Japanese firms have freely entered U.S. markets, American firms have found it hard to enter the Japanese market because of many trade barriers, both visible and invisible. Some have gone so far as to suggest that Japanese firms doing business in the United States occasionally engage in cartelization. More widespread are charges such as those of Zenith Radio Corporation that Japanese television set manufacturers used a "dumping" strategy to enter the U.S. television market.

Structural Factors

Structural factors refer to characteristics of the Japanese political economy, industry structure, and the Japanese people themselves. Japan, Inc., the close working relationships between government, business, and labor, although much overplayed, is frequently cited. More specifically, the role of the integrated trading companies, government supports and subsidies, and businesses' easy access to the banks are key features of the Japanese political economy. Industry structure features include close ties between manufacturers and their principal suppliers and distributors, a comparatively cheap labor force, and labor unions that work with rather than against management. Many observers have characterized the Japanese people as intensely committed to the work ethic, dedicated to the achievement of individual and national success, and willing to accept delayed gratification as a prerequisite to economic development.

The Element of Luck

Some suggest that Japanese success owes more to luck than national intent, industrial design, or individual traits. A U.S. auto executive said that Japanese cars were going nowhere in the United States until the price of oil shot up. Had fuel costs not escalated, most Americans would still be preferring and driving large cars. The Japanese companies were doubly lucky that U.S. auto manufacturers responded slowly rather than swiftly to the increased demand for small cars—and triply lucky that Detroit's first small cars were poorly designed.

As with beauty, the conception of good and unfair business practices resides in the eye of the beholder. The aforementioned good business practices and structural features are depicted by some U.S. observers as being unfair. Governmental supports, close working relations between manufacturers and suppliers, and the financial community's leniency in making capital available are seen as giving Japanese firms an unfair competitive advantage over their U.S. counterparts. These practices are viewed by many in the United States as violating "free market" principles.

Whatever the sources of Japan's success, their companies have had to overcome many obstacles and disadvantages. In the immediate post-World War II era, Japan found itself with significant capital, technology, and economic limitations. It was encumbered with the vestiges of a poor product quality image. Unfamiliarity with the English language, Western culture, foreign markets, and transportation costs were also problems. Of course, Japan's lack of natural resources is well known.

It is also equally clear that marketing skill is one critical factor among several contributing to Japanese commercial prowess; one which has been substantially neglected in the burgeoning literature on Japanese economic success. We must allow that the Japanese carefully determine which industries to enter, which market segments to serve, and the appropriate approaches to penetrate these markets. Before detailing the Japanese marketing strategies, we want to address some misconceptions regarding Japanese marketing.

SOME SURPRISES

We are so accustomed to thinking in terms of a monolithic Japan, Inc. that we overlook the intense competition occurring among Japanese companies themselves. Interfirm rivalry in many Japanese industries is much more intense than in their U.S. counterparts. Nine auto companies battle it out in Japan versus our Big 3, with our number one protecting the other two through a price umbrella. Four Japanese motorcycle companies—Honda, Yamaha, Suzuki, and Kawasaki—compete vigorously with each other, versus one American motorcycle company, Harley-Davidson. Japan boasts of over a dozen camera manufacturers and several hand calculator manufacturers, appliance manufacturers, and so on. It is little wonder, then, that the failure rate among Japanese firms is quite high.

Success Came Slowly

Few people seem to be aware that many Japanese firms which represent household words in the United States are not the dominant competitors in their respective markets in Japan. For instance, Sony, the most successful and best-known Japanese competitor in the U.S. television market, accounts for less than 5 percent of the Japanese market.

Relatedly, success has not come quickly for the Japanese in many U.S. markets. The Japanese took fifteen years to acquire a 15 percent market share in the U.S. monochrome television markets and more than ten years before they acquired 15 percent of the color television market. Some Japanese firms even withdrew after spending millions to develop the American market. Susheido, the giant Japanese cosmetics company, left our shores after an unsuccessful effort to become a major cosmetics marketer in the U.S.

A Many-Sided Approach

Contrary to popular impressions, the Japanese do not follow a uniform marketing approach across markets. In their early attempts to penetrate U.S. markets, Japanese firms used private labels (e.g., televisions, hand calculators), but recently they have pushed their own brand names from market entry (e.g., watches, copiers, computers).

Many visitors to Japan have been surprised by the poor quality of many Japanese-produced goods being sold in Japanese stores. The Japanese export their highest-quality products and keep many of the inferior products for the home market. They also export lower-quality goods to many developing nations. In Thailand, for example, American refrigerators are perceived to have much more quality than Japanese refrigerators.

Many believe that Japanese marketing success rests on flooding the U.S. market with cheap imitations of American products. This marketing approach is viewed as resulting from unfair business practices and lower labor costs.[1] In markets such as televisions, audio equipment, copiers, computers, autos, steel, and farm equipment, the Japanese have clearly moved from the role of imitators to that of innovators.

Finally, it will be a surprise to many to note that the Japanese have not yet demonstrated much marketing success in markets where major cultural differences are paramount. Their success has been almost exclusively in product markets where the notions of function and utility are reasonably consistent across cultures: driving automobiles, computing with hand-held calculators, using steel, etc. The Japanese have yet to exhibit sophisticated marketing skills and approaches in such areas as services, fashion, cosmetics, foods, and insurance.

JAPANESE MARKETING STRATEGIES

Japanese marketing strategy, strangely enough, is not based on the discovery of new and fresh marketing principles. Japan's secret is that they thoroughly understand and apply the existing textbook principles. The Japanese came to the United States to study marketing and went home understanding its principles better than most U.S. companies did.

Succinctly stated, Japanese marketing revolves around the management of product market evolution. They manage not only the product life cycle of individual products, but the evolution of a complex of product lines and items. They carefully choose and sequence the markets they enter, the products they produce, and the marketing tactics they adopt.

We will characterize Japanese marketing strategies in three stages of market competition: (1) entering a market, (2) taking over a market, and (3) sustaining an existing market.

Entering the Market

The key to successful market entry is (1) entering the right markets and (2) entering them right. Japanese companies are skilled in both areas.

Selecting Markets Which markets to enter has been a key concern to the Japanese. Market choice is a reflection of the Japanese institutional structure and culture. Both governmental agencies and corporations play distinct but related roles in selecting markets. Japanese government and industry largely function as a partnership with respect to industry direction, technology development, and export trade. A core element in the Japanese industrial strategy is the identification of "targeted" industries. Government and industry mutually recognize important or potentially important industries as high priority areas for national resource commitments. The selection of target industries and the mobilization of support for these choices is the responsibility of the Ministry of Trade and Industry. In the selection process, a number of factors predominate: Japan lacks natural resources; land is scarce; labor is skilled and loyal.

These factors suggest that Japan should focus on industries that require high skills, high labor intensity, and only small quantities of natural resources. Consumer electronics and cameras are natural choices. Motorcycles, automobiles, and shipbuilding are also good choices, even though requiring large quantities of imported raw materials. Pharmaceuticals, as well as fine chemicals, make sense because of their high value-added content. Service industries such as international hoteling, banking, and retailing are attractive because they are labor intensive and do not require imported raw materials. The lack of enough foreign-speaking Japanese limits Japan's rate of expansion into international services, although this may be a right thrust in the 1990s.

Furthermore, Japanese firms carefully explore the evolution of industries—specifically, the match between products and markets. The Japanese search for market segments that exhibit strong economies of scale and strong expe-

rience curve effects. Their strategy is to enter the market with a low-priced improved product, capture a large market share, and in the process bring down manufacturing costs to allow real learning curve effects to take place as well as the generation of substantial margins to be used elsewhere in the marketing arena.

The Japanese have long recognized that economies of scale and experience curve effects become more potent through developing new product concepts and existing product modifications that are matched to substantial pockets of unmet demand. Such has been the Japanese experience in calculators, watches, radios, televisions, and autos. Product market sectors are chosen which facilitate product market development and not simply the capturing of existing markets. A major intent is to establish a beachhead from which related product market sectors can be attacked.

Relatedly, target industries should exhibit weak or complacent competition. Japanese firms do not want to enter against strong firms that are serving their market well. At first glance, few would describe U.S. auto manufacturers as weak competitors. Yet their initial responses to the emergence of strong foreign competitors in the lower end of the auto market would clearly show them as weak competitors in these market sectors. The Japanese choose product market sectors where competitors are unable and/or unwilling to respond vigorously to their market entry and where competitors or potential competitors may cede to the Japanese entire market sectors, such as happened in small televisions and small motorcycles in the United States.

Doing Their Homework Having selected vulnerable industries, the Japanese then do their homework. The Japanese do not simply export their domestic products to the new markets. They send study teams to the country, and these teams spend several months doing a feasibility study before making their recommendations (whereas some American companies dispatch quick missions and expect them to return with thorough marketing plans). The Japanese hire American industry specialists, consultants, and executives to help them figure out how to enter a market. And they will hire American executives to manage sales in the U.S. market. Ironically, much Japanese marketing strategy in the United States has been formulated not by the Japanese but by the American executives working for them.

Toyota's entry into the American auto market illustrates the careful approach taken by the Japanese. Toyota knew it would enter the small-car segment of the U.S. market, not the large-car segment. The small-car segment was dominated by Volkswagen (VW). Toyota knew that its success depended on challenging and displacing VW. Although Japanese producers don't always attack the most successful competitor, they always study the most successful competitor(s) to learn the reasons for the success. In the case of VW, Toyota commissioned an American marketing research firm to interview VW owners and determine what they liked and disliked about their VWs. VW owners wished their cars would heat up better in the winter, would have more room in the back seat, and would have more attractive interiors. The Japanese went to the drawing board and designed a Toyota that offered all the benefits of the VW with none of the disadvantages. To clinch the offer, Toyota put a lower price on its car, spent a higher amount on advertising, and gave larger commissions to its dealers than Volkswagen. Not surprisingly, Toyota hit the market right and gradually moved into the top spot at VW's expense. Toyota went after the right market (small cars), identified the key complacent competitor (VW), and formulated a superior offer of value.

In market after market, Japanese companies have identified the right segment to enter. One common strategy is to bring out smaller versions of standard products (the Buddhist concept of "small is beautiful" as opposed to the U.S. concept "bigger is better"). Thus Canon and Sharp entered the copying machine market by offering smaller copying machines than Xerox's; Sony and Panasonic entered with smaller radios and television sets; Honda and Yamaha entered with smaller motorcycles. U.S. market leaders prefer to sell large-sized versions of their products (more profit). Harley-Davidson, the leading U.S. motorcycle manufacturer, dismissed the small Hondas pouring into the U.S. as "toys."

Offering New Product Features The Japanese also break into markets by offering new product features. Seiko pushed the development of the quartz digital watch as an alternative to the mechanical watch. In the hand calculator market, Casio, Sharp, and others offered various new features (e.g., calculators with melodies, calculators with clocks).

The Japanese have cracked several markets by offering not more but less at a substantial cost saving. They entered the medical electronics eqipment market with a low-cost, stripped-down version of competitors' equipment; thus Toshiba introduced an X-ray computerized CT scanner which is 40 percent cheaper than GE's model and omits some costly features that customers won't miss (6). American manufacturers prefer to build sophisticated features and charge customers more. The Japanese have used the low-priced, stripped-down strategy to enter other markets such as large appliance, television, copying machines, and so on.

The Primacy of Quality and Service Japanese companies place heavy weight on two other variables in selling to new buyers—quality and service. They design and produce products of high quality (reliability). Japanese cars, for example, need substantially fewer repairs than American cars (1). The Japanese use more automated methods of production (to reduce human error) and they implement more quality assurance systems, down to the point when the rejection rate in a typical Japanese factory is substantially lower than in comparable U.S. factories. The Japanese also establish an adequate number of service centers so their products can be quickly repaired. American buyers have found service from Japanese manufacturers to be at least as good as that provided by American manufacturers. The Japanese are highly service-minded and go out of their way to accommodate customers who have a service problem. At the same time, by building better products, the Japanese do not have to invest as much in service centers.

Having established a good product, service, and price, the Japanese carefully work on the other marketing mix variables. They place a heavy emphasis on integrating distribution into the marketing mix. They develop markets region by region, lining up strong distributors in each location. They will help the distributor sell to the first few customers. They will pick the largest customer and offer a low price to get his business. They will give him excellent service and then sell the other customers on the strength of their reputation with the first customer rather than price. They frequently offer higher middleman commissions than competitors to generate product push. They encourage joint promotional efforts with distributors/ dealers and typically support their products with heavy regional advertising.

A New Approach to Distribution The Japanese approach to distribution is significant in that it reveals their dedication to achieving market penetration, their prior study of market conditions and possibilities, and, above all, their willingness to be innovative in their marketing practices. In many markets they have not simply adopted the U.S. distribution system but rather have devoted considerable resources to developing a distribution system more suited to their marketing mix. When mistakes won't necessarily be broadcast elsewhere. The Japanese hire and train Australians to do the selling and give them a lot of local autonomy.

Japanese computer manufacturers are now beginning to enter the American market, concentrating on industries which are not satisfied with IBM and/or not locked up by other computer firms. According to an in-depth *World Business Weekly* article, "If there is a serious challenge to IBM's dominance, it will be from Japan. The Japanese computer industry has come from almost nowhere in the past 15 years to a point where it now represents the main potential threat to IBM's global leadership" (p. 32).

The same pattern of patient Japanese market segmentation and sequencing is occurring in the heavy construction equipment business. Caterpillar, the world's largest manufacturer of construction equipment (world share: 50 percent) is most worried about Komatsu, which has targeted certain equipment categories (such as tractors) and certain industries (such as mining) and has come out with parity or superior equipment and service at a lower price. Not surprisingly, Komatsu is winning customers away from Caterpillar in the tractors-for-mining industry market.

Trying It Out at Home Central to the market sequencing strategy of many Japanese firms is the use of their domestic market for product development and testing before they hit the U.S. marketplace. Their experience in the Japanese market provides insight into customer preferences, product deficiences, and effective marketing strategies. Japanese copier manufacturers, for example, are now entering the U.S. market with medium-speed copiers, but they have been marketing such copiers in Japan for quite some time.

Their adroit sense of market segmentation and sequencing is accompanied by market flexibility. Japanese firms are adept at using a multiplicity of competitive weapons with varying degrees of emphasis—price, product quality, product features, service, distribution, promotion, product line stretching—to penetrate and win markets. This flexibility is cultural. Buddhist thinking emphasizes that nothing is permanent, that life is ever-changing. Samurai warriors in Japan learned several martial arts— judo, karate, aikido—always choosing the best means to attack or defend. A Japanese company will sometimes attack with a karate blow aimed at a competitor's weaknesses and at times with an aikido side step, taking advantage of the force created by a competitor. The game of GO, originated by the Chinese and perfected by the Japanese, provides a mental training in long-range strategic thinking, the principles of indirect attack and encirclement, and the need for opportunistic replanning. Thus Japanese culture provides deep models for flexible marketing warfare.

The emphasis within the mix of competitive weapons is typically adapted by the Japanese in accordance with market evolution. In early efforts to achieve market penetration, price to the ultimate customer and margins to the distribution chain are often dominant. Such has been the emphasis in radios, televisions, calculators, watches, and stereo equipment. As these markets moved toward maturation, brand identification, more extensive distribution, and service have gained in importance.

Japanese marketing flexibility is also exhibited in their handling of individual marketing variables. For instance, the Japanese raise their prices as their products gain acceptance. Sony initially priced its television sets below American prices, and once they achieved acceptance, raised their prices. Mazda introduced its handsome RX-7 sports car in the United States at a low price of $8,000 causing much word-of-mouth and queue formation at its dealerships. Once the demand was strong, Mazda raised its prices. The initial low price reflected promotion-oriented pricing to gain attention and early purchase, only to be followed by profit-oriented pricing later.

Market Maintenance

The Japanese now dominate many product-market sectors and are rapidly moving toward dominating many others. Their market leadership position means that many Japanese firms will increasingly find themselves in the role of prey rather than predator. This is becoming evident in the concerted responses to the Japanese challenge now being mounted by such U.S. firms as IBM, Xerox, RCA, and Texas Instruments and major European firms such as Phillips. The ability of Japanese companies to fend off such responses will test their marketing strength and creativity.

The Japanese market maintenance strategy seems to involve doing more of what won them the markets—product development and market development. The Japanese continue to pour money into product improvement, upgrading, and proliferation in such industries as watches, televisions, audio and stereo equipment, calculators, autos, and copiers; U.S. and foreign firms find it difficult to compete. The Japanese pursue market segmentation, sequencing, and flexibility to ensure that no major windows of opportunity are left open to foreign competitors.

Central to Japanese market maintenance strategy is less dependence upon product imitation and much more involvement in genuine product innovation. The Japanese are the primary catalysts behind a number of emerging product-market sectors such as videotape recorders and discs where their leadership is in large measure a consequence of their own technology development and not mere imitation or adaptation of products initially developed by U.S. manufacturers. The onus on U.S. and other foreign competitors becomes the development of competitive products or the enactment of some type of joint Japanese ventures for product development, production, and/or distribution. Xerox, IBM, and RCA, to name but a few, have entered into such agreements with the Japanese.

In many respects, the real battle between U.S. and Japanese firms is only now beginning. No longer are U.S. firms willing to treat the Japanese lightly or question their strategic astuteness or willingness to pursue their goals. Indeed, major U.S. firms such as IBM, Xerox, and Texas Instruments have initiated major reorganizations specifically to better combat the Japanese. These firms do not plan on giving the Japanese a free hand in major market sectors as previously occurred with televisions, radios, motorcycles, and autos.

JAPANESE ORGANIZATIONAL STRUCTURE AND STYLE

Japanese marketing strategies do not take place in a vacuum. Organizational decision-making processes must ensure that the right decisions are made and effectively implemented. An appraisal of how Japanese firms go about these tasks involves a closer look at the intraorganizational processes involved in Japanese marketing decision making.

First, the norm in Japanese firms is that marketing as an area of decision making is tightly coupled to engineering, manufacturing, finance, and product development. Information and ideas flow freely across these organizational boundaries. In one Japanese company, all the vice-presidents meet on Friday afternoons with a relatively open agenda to review all phases of the company's operations. One critical output of this meeting is a variety of requests and directions which are channeled to a Wednesday afternoon meeting of lower-level representatives of all functional areas. No wonder that all the decisions involved in new product development and marketing show a high level of integration.

Second, Japanese firms manage to achieve a high level of integration among their larger subunits—divisions and product groups. Japanese firms, much more than U.S. firms, are typically dependent upon a specific industry, broadly defined. There is extensive research and development and in-house manufacture of components. In the late 1970s, none of the U.S. firms in the consumer electronics industry had established integrated planning of supply or product design, even in those firms with semiconductor or tube capacity. In contrast, all the leading Japanese firms had in-house sources of components, developed in close collaboration with end-use requirements (12).

Third, Japanese decision-making processes are typically characterized by a much longer time horizon than in U.S. firms. They are not shackled by the short-run performance demands of the U.S. institutional financial structure or by the short-run reward structures which are so pervasive in U.S. firms. Japanese marketing strategies depend upon the attainment of scale economies and experience curve effects to achieve long-term market share gains. Japanese firms have a strong internal commitment to the pursuit of long-term objectives and strategies.

WILL JAPAN RUN OUT OF STEAM?

The answer is, of course it will. Every country has its heyday where the combination of forces at that historical moment elevates it to top-dog status. But success creates the next generation of problems.

New Problems

First, Japan's increasing affluence is generating new internal problems. Worker's wages have gone up and workers want more of the good life. They want to work less hard, have more time for recreation and travel, and see more social investment in cleaner air, better roads, and better housing. To pay for these "goodies," company profits must fall (higher costs, higher taxes), which leaves less for capital formation. Profits are also hurt by the increasing costs for energy and raw materials, forcing up Japanese prices and making its goods less competitive in world markets.

Tough Competitors

Second, Third World "cheap wage" countries are becoming tough competitors (7). The "new Japanese" include Singapore, Malaysia, South Korea, and the Philippines, who are able to make high-quality goods (textiles, shoes, radios, television receivers) at lower costs. These countries are copying the Japanese approach to invading new markets. Other Third World countries—Brazil, Mexico, Indonesia—are rapidly preparing to enter the same race for world markets. Within this decade, China will launch its own export offensive, and ''Shanghai Motorcycle'' may begin to outsell Honda and Yamaha.

The Rise of Protectionism

Third, Japan fears the rising protectionist trend in the United States and Europe in the form of import quotas and nontariff barriers to protect local industries against Japanese competitors. If effective, Japanese companies will be shut out of certain markets and forced to reduce lifetime employment, causing a whole set of terrible consequences. Japan's current response is to build factories in the United States and Europe to keep its goods in these markets and provide employment to workers displaced by Japanese imports (4).

Fourth, scattered interest groups in Japan are challenging the economic and social arrangements. Protesting Japanese farmers delayed the opening of Narita airport for several years. Environmentalists are demanding that industry absorb more social costs. Old-age groups are demanding more benefits as Japan's work force ages (2). Radical groups stand ready to promote a different political prescription for economic and social progress. Japanese leaders are currently engaged in a deep dialogue to discover how to contain the growing conflict among different interest groups.

HOW CAN AMERICAN COMPANIES COMPETE?

American companies are scrambling to find ways to defend their markets against further penetration by Japanese competitors. General Motors, Xerox, Zenith, and other companies acknowledge their fatal error in letting the Japanese gain strong footholds in their markets. Now that Japanese companies have earned well-respected names in the world market, what can U.S. companies do to contain them?

The least creative response is to lobby for higher tariffs, import quotas, and nontariff barriers. The American steel industry and television industry have elected this course of action. Hopefully, they see protectionism as delaying the problem, not solving it. Protectionism makes sense only as a temporizing response to give weakened companies breathing time for more creative action.

Cutting Prices

Another response is for U.S. companies to cut prices to take some of the wind out of the Japanese sails. Early aggressive pricing would have slowed down the Japanese penetration in television, sewing machines, and autos, albeit at a high toll to current profits. Aggressive pricing after the Japanese have dug into the market makes less sense, because the Japanese will match the price cuts to maintain their market share.

Filling Product Gaps

A more effective response is for U.S. companies to fill the product gaps that attracted Japanese competition in the first place. General Motors and the other U.S. automakers are finally serious about designing and producing small cars. But even here, they are playing catch-up by working on 30 mpg autos while the Japanese are developing mini-cars giving 60 mpg (11). Similarly, Xerox and IBM are finally acknowledging the need to downscale their machines and meet the needs of small businesses.

Staying on Top in R&D

The answer for more technically oriented U.S. companies is to maintain R&D leadership in the world market. A Xerox Corporation executive holds that his company's salvation is the discovery of new patentable features so that Xerox machines remain the most advanced in the world. Innovative leadership requires that U.S. companies invest substantial sums in R&D. Until now, Japanese talent lay in improving existing products ("creative imitation"), not in producing new scientific breakthroughs ("creative innovation"). As long as the difference lasts, U.S. companies would do well to put their effort into researching the technological frontiers of their industry.

In short, U.S. firms competing against the Japanese—or anybody else—must adopt a systematic and integrated approach to their marketing activities and to how marketing relates to all other corporate activities. Marketing is a vital link in the chain, but the many interdependencies between it and other functional areas and corporate tasks must be fully recognized. A number of points can be made.

Product markets must be systematically and creatively identified, developed, and managed. For many U.S. companies, this will entail nothing short of embracing a new way of thinking about and doing business. For some U.S. firms it will mean rediscovering that which made them innovative, dynamic market leaders. Essentially, U.S. firms must renew or acquire an entrepreneurial marketing culture.

Marketing Is Key

Managing product-market evolution is the name of the game. Well-known market segmentation principles must be employed: otherwise major market "windows" will be left open to the Japanese and, worse, major market sectors will be conceded without a fight. Also "milking" current product-market successes without devoting substantial reserves to the creation of tomorrow's product markets is a recipe for failure. If U.S. companies fail to develop new product market sectors, they will find themselves always responding to the marketing initiatives of the Japanese.

U.S. firms can no longer afford to concentrate on product development to the relative neglect of market development. One without the other is much more likely to leave open windows of opportunity for competitors. The fusion of the two is necessary to move successfully from marketing copiers to marketing office work systems, a challenge currently facing Xerox and many other firms. A similar challenge confronts RCA, Zenith, and others in moving from televisions to video recorders/discs to home entertainment centers.

Effective exploitation of product-market management implies that firms must learn new marketing skills and relearn old ones. Pricing, sales, distribution, promotion, and service approaches need to be adapted to changing market conditions as product markets evolve. Selling complex office systems requires quite different skills than selling copiers. Identifying and developing markets requires quite different skills than selling in well-established markets.

Whether in choosing and developing new product markets, exploiting mature product markets, or learning new marketing skills, U.S. firms must carefully identify and exploit their competitive strengths and advantages. These strengths and advantages must be appraised in the context of what customers, retailers, and distributors need, want, and appreciate. Many U.S. firms have allowed their traditional comparative strength in research and development to wane by not continuing to match their technical expertise to customer needs and values. Perhaps, much worse, many U.S. firms have permitted the Japanese to outdo them in designing distribution systems, establishing service networks, providing retailer credit, and creating product and company image.

Rethinking the Past

Marketing decisions are made in an organizational context. How these decisions get made is quite different in U.S. and Japanese firms. Marketing and other corporate functions can no longer remain as isolated centers of decision activity; they must be integrated. The key question can no longer be can marketing and manufacturing coexist (10), but rather how can they be made into congenial bedfellows? Automation, experience gains, reduction of components counts, and so on produce little gain if the firm is serving the wrong product-market sectors. Their current acclamation notwithstanding, quality circles are of little assistance in choosing product-market segments and designing appropriate marketing strategies.

Implicit in the adoption of a marketing culture is the emergence of a managerial ideology or frame of reference quite different from that which has traditionally prevailed in many U.S. firms. Nothing can be treated as sacrosanct. Managers must start questioning well-known "facts," principles, practices, and deeply held assumptions and start observing what is happening to customers, competitors, and distributors in the marketplace. A new mindset is needed to lead U.S. firms to invest, innovate, and seek leadership in the marketplace through the creation of customer value.

Finally, the salvation for a growing number of American companies is perceived to lie in "going Japanese," in both their marketing strategies and management practices. U.S. companies need to improve their skills in segmenting and selecting target markets, designing and producing high-quality products, pricing them aggressively, and providing strong service. They need to relax their requirement of early payout and be willing to spend what it takes to achieve market-share leadership. U.S. companies must get their costs down by locating plants in parts of the world where labor costs are low and learn to manage labor better following Japanese management techniques. Westinghouse Electric Corporation, for example, recently undertook to convert a whole division to Japanese-style management, using William Ouchi's *Theory Z* as its model (8).

Underlying all this is the idea that the best way to compete with the Japanese is to outcopy them.

CONCLUSION

"That which is honored in a country will be cultivated there." So important is marketing in Japan that each year the Japan Management Association calls for nominations to select the fifteen best marketing companies. They ask 200 experts to nominate the three companies which show overall excellence in customer orientation, in every marketing function, and in profitability. The top three winners in 1978 are described below:

1. *Matsushita Electric Inc.* Strong management leadership and penetration. Positive marketing to identify even minor customer changes.
2. *Toyota Motor Sales Co.* Solid organization and performance based on integrated production and selling. Products matched with the modern feeling and flexible attitude toward market development.
3. *Suntory.* Powerful force of management and free, risk-taking, dynamic business operators. Harmonized event-making segmentation and creative advertisement.

The list continues with Shiseido Cosmetics, Ajinomoto, Konishiroku Photo, Mitsubishi Electric, Fuji Photo Film, Kao Soap, Honda Motor, Mitsubishi Motor, Sony, Kirin Brewery, Yamaha Instruments, and Ricoh.

Clearly, other countries wishing to cultivate stronger marketing capabilities must begin by honoring this function as the Japanese have done.

NOTES

1. See Ezra F. Vogel, *Japan as Number One: Lessons for America* (Cambridge, Mass.: Harvard University Press, 1979); Richard T. Pascale and Anthony G. Athos, *The Art of Japanese Management* (New York: Simon & Schuster, 1981); William G. Ouchi, *Theory Z: How American Busi-*

ness Can Meet the Japanese Challenge (Reading, Mass.: Addison-Wesley, 1981).

REFERENCES

1. Cole, Robert E. "The Japanese Lesson in Quality." *Technology Review,* July 1981, pp. 29–40.
2. Drucker, Peter F. "Japan Gets Ready for Tougher Times." *Fortune,* November 3, 1980, pp. 108 ff.
3. Frazer, Douglas. "The Myth of the Over-Privileged Auto Worker." *The Wall Street Journal,* April 27, 1981.
4. "Japanese Multinationals: Covering the World with Investment." *Business Week,* June 16, 1980, pp. 96 ff.
5. "Japan Takes Aim at IBM's World." *World Business Weekly,* April 20, 1981, pp. 29–37.
6. "Japan: Undercutting the West in Medical Electronics." *Business Week,* April 27, 1981, p. 52.
7. Kraar, Louis. "Make Way for the New Japans." *Fortune,* Aug. 10, 1981, pp. 176–184.
8. Main, Jeremy. "Westinghouse's Cultural Revolution." *Fortune,* June 15, 1981, p. 74 ff.
9. "Seiko's Smash." *Business Week,* June 5, 1978, p. 86.
10. Shapiro, Benson P. "Can Marketing and Manufacturing Coexist?" *Harvard Business Review,* September–October 1977, pp. 104–114.
11. "60 Miles to the Gallon." *Forbes,* June 23, 1980, pp. 38 ff.
12. *The U.S. Consumer Electronics Industry and Foreign Competition* (U.S. Department of Commerce/Economic Development Administration, May 1980).

26

Barter Arrangements with Money: The Modern Form of Compensation Trading
Falko Schuster

• • •

During the recently finished Leipziger Messe in East Germany some managers of western firms made the statement: "There is a ghost going around, whose name is 'compensation trading'." This mocking reference to the oldest form of economic exchange aptly indicates the present development of international business. In dealing with Eastern European countries one can hardly escape the increasing pressure to barter.

Although it seems that almost no Western manager likes compensation arrangements, it is obvious that even potential enterprises regularly take part in barter deals. For those who are new to East-West business this is the more astonishing since often a firm's entire export is balanced by counter-deliveries. The fact that many Western organizations get their money despite a compensation agreement is only known by those who commonly trade with Eastern European enterprises. These specialists know that the barter business offers a lot of alternative constructions which allow a single firm to make money.

In this article the most frequently used forms of compensation agreements, in which money does matter, are discussed. The analysis will begin with the simplest, and therefore money-less form of compensation trading, so-called classical barter, and then show how the more complex constructions have developed.

Source: Falko Schuster, "Barter Arrangements with Money: The Modern Form of Compensation Trading," *The Columbia Journal of World Business,* Fall, 1980, pp. 61–66. Copyright © 1980 by the Trustees of Columbia University in the City of New York. Reprinted by permission.

CLASSICAL BARTER

This technique for swapping goods is characterized by the fact that two persons or enterprises agree to exchange products and/or services. Both barter parties accept each other's goods as payment.

The following examples demonstrate that this oldest form of economic exchange process is still of some importance.

- An automobile producer of the Federal Republic of Germany sold cars to Czechoslovakia and accepted sheep as payment, which he had to market in France to get his money.

- An automobile concern in the United States took thousands of sheepskins from Uruguay in exchange for 6 million dollars worth of cars. Most of the sheepskins were made into car seat covers which were sold through the European dealer network.

- A comparable barter deal was not realized when a West German enterprise refused to accept a 150 million year old skeleton of a dinosaur, offered by Mongolia, as payment.

Figure 1 shows the typical construction of such a business:

A Western firm (A) exports a certain machine. In return the buyer of this industrial product, an Eastern organization (B), delivers a fixed volume of a certain raw material to the Western enterprise. The questions linked with such a transaction are:

- Is the Eastern side equally able to deliver or is it necessary to grant a credit?

- Is it possible to use the products offered as payment within one's own factory?

If the products are exchanged simultaneously and if they are of the necessary quality to be used as input, no problem arises. But this is not always the case. Often the Eastern organization is as short of products as of cash. Not rarely the Eastern organization wants to use the received products for the production of the barter goods. Then there are different dates of delivery to be considered. In classical barter, different dates of delivery automatically mean a granting of credit by the barter party delivering first. If the granting of credit in addition to the acceptance of the barter is undesirable, the Western enterprise should try to convince the other side to agree to a parallel barter arrangement.[1]

PARALLEL BARTER

This form of compensation dealing is characterized by the fact that, in contrast to classical barter, each delivery is paid for in cash. In the example above, the Western firm A receives upon delivery of the machine a payment in so-called "hard currency" (dollars) from the Eastern organization B. Upon the later delivery of the raw material by B, the Western enterprise A transfers an equivalent amount of dollars to B (Figure 2).

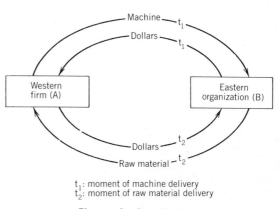

t_1: moment of machine delivery
t_2: moment of raw material delivery

Figure 2 Parallel barter.

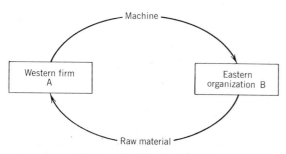

Figure 1 Classical barter.

This technique of compensation agreement offers at least three advantages to the Western party:

- It need not grant a credit. It is paid at once and in cash.
- The money received in the first step may be used as a guarantee for a correct fulfillment of the counterpurchase. Should the Eastern firm have difficulty in delivering the quality contracted for, the Western firm is able to refuse delivery of the products without a loss.
- The formal separation of a buying and a selling act creates the chance of a two-step approach to barter. In the first step, in addition to the precisely formulated selling contract, only a promise to counterpurchase might be signed. In a second step some time later, the actual buying contract can be specified without any pressure.

The German automobile enterprise Volkswagen chose this barter technique in 1977 when it made a deal with the East German Democratic Republic. Parallel to a selling contract for the delivery of 10,000 VWs, only a "letter of intent" was signed, in which VW promised to buy an equivalent amount of goods from the East German Democratic Republic during the following two years. The explanation by one of the top purchasing managers has made it clear that VW has paid for the 10,000 cars in German marks, and that during the next two years it had to use that sum for the buying of coal, oil, parts, machines, etc., from the barter partner. The exact amounts and prices of the products were specified some months later.

This example shows that VW was able to realize the three advantages mentioned above. Furthermore, it makes clear that classical barter and parallel barter differ markedly. Parallel barter is similar to the reciprocal dealing which has always been used in Western economies. This means that firms are often more familiar with such transactions than they themselves realize.

A parallel barter transaction is often chosen when the Western firm has to agree to a so-called "buy-back" condition, as in 1975 when General Motors Corporation completed negotiations with Poland to convert an automobile plant at Lublin for production of about 50,000 lightweight vans a year. The American company promised to supply licenses, technology, and equipment from various subsidiaries and to accept a portion of the Lublin output as barter payment.[2]

The division of a buy-back barter into two formally separated and parallel contracts, i.e., a buying and a selling contract—in other words, the construction of a parallel business–releases the Western party from the burden of financing the deal as a whole. The Western enterprise is paid for the equipment exported at the time of delivery. In return it has to pay an equivalent amount on receiving the counterdelivery in the form of a portion of the output produced by the Western industrial goods. Therefore, in contrast to the classical form of barter, the Western firm does not have to grant a credit for the period between the two dates of delivery, which might be a long time indeed.

Yet in spite of the advantages offered by parallel barter, the single firm should not forget that the deal depends upon being both a buyer *and* a seller. That means that the readiness to barter must be there.

Many organizations, however, are not interested in linking selling and buying, but want to realize maximum profit by concentrating on separate buying and selling processes. As a consequence the Western firm which is interested in dealing with Eastern countries but which is unable or unwilling to buy back, has to cooperate with other Western organizations. In the following three alternatives to such cooperative barter agreements are discussed.

COOPERATION AND CLASSICAL BARTER

This technique of compensation dealing means that the Western party consists of two organizations which have agreed in principle to take part in the barter, but which are in no way linked with each other. Each of the two firms specializes in the fulfillment of one part of the barter.

One of the most famous so-called three-party or triangular deals has been constructed by Western European, Iranian and Soviet firms. These organizations agreed that Iranian gas enterprises should sell mineral gas from the Iranian fields to the USSR, which on its side had to pay for these deliveries of mineral gas by exporting mineral gas from the Soviet fields to Western Europe. The Western European buyers of the Soviet gas had to transfer the payment in cash to the Iranian gas producers.

The advantages to all the organizations involved in the deal are obvious. By reducing the total transport costs, the firms taking part in the business realize either a higher net income or a lower price for the purchased gas than if buying and selling were completely separate. If this three-party deal had not been constructed, the Soviets would have had to transport their own gas over a long distance to the point where it was needed, and the Iranian gas would have had to be transported to Western European buyers, leading to enormous costs on both sides.

Of course this transaction in which the same raw material was bartered is an exception. The usual triangular deal is as follows:

Western enterprise A is exclusively responsible for the delivery of a machine to Eastern organization B, i.e., for the selling function; Western firm C is exclusively responsible for the purchase of the raw material delivered by Eastern organization B, i.e., for the buying function. As A exclusively delivers a product and C exclusively receives the payment for this product in the form of goods, C has to pay A an equivalent amount of money (Figure 3).

For the Western firm A the advantage of this barter technique is obvious. Although it takes part in a reciprocal dealing it is paid in cash. And that's what it wants. In contrast to the parallel type of barter, it doesn't even have to buy anything from another organization at a later date. That means, the transaction as a whole is a barter, but for each single firm the business is

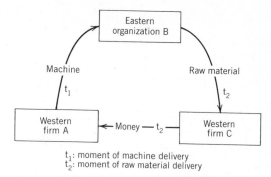

t_1: moment of machine delivery
t_2: moment of raw material delivery

Figure 3   Cooperation and classical barter.

nothing else than a simple buying or selling process.

Thus, it becomes clear why even those managers who have a "cash on the barrelhead" approach to selling their products abroad take part in such arrangements. Yet in addition to the question of how to find the right partner, another big problem arises. We have already mentioned that Eastern organizations are often as short of products as of money. In the preceding example this would mean that firm A has to wait on the money payment until Eastern organization B is able to deliver the raw material, since Western enterprise C will transfer an equivalent amount of money to A only upon receipt of goods. To avoid this financial burden for firm A a combination of cooperation and parallel barter might be chosen.

COOPERATION AND PARALLEL BARTER

To continue the above example, a combination of cooperation and parallel barter would mean that Western firm A only signs a selling contract, and that Western firm C only signs a buying contract. Both deals are bound together by the fact that they are contracted at the same time. As in the last example, the barter implies a partnership between two Western firms: firm A exclusively sells and firm C exclusively buys. As Figure 4 shows, the difference between this and the last case consists in a variation in the flow of money. The signing of two separate contracts by two separate partners means that the

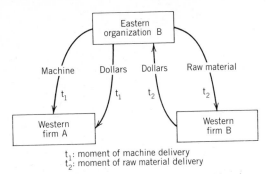

t₁: moment of machine delivery
t₂: moment of raw material delivery

Figure 4 Cooperation and parallel barter.

Western seller of the machine is paid at the time of delivery by the Eastern firm. Consequently, Western organization C has to transfer the payment for the raw material to the Eastern firm when the raw material is delivered.

A Canadian-based tractor and engine manufacturer has chosen this form of barter agreement. He contracted with the Polish government several years ago to build tractor and diesel engine plants. In addition he had to act as middleman by finding buyers for Polish counterdeliveries. One of the consignments offered the Canadian enterprise by the Poles for which a Western buyer was found was 10,000 pairs of skis. The advantage of this compensation technique is that the machine seller is paid in cash and at once.

On the other hand two problems arise:

The first is the question of how to find the right partner (represented by firm C in our example). The an-

swer to this question is not as difficult as it seems at first glance. A lot of so-called barter dealers, i.e., trading houses specializing in such transactions, have sprung up in trading centers such as London, Rotterdam, and Hamburg. Yet it must be recognized that parallel to the growth of these barter firms the pressure to barter has also substantially increased, so that the barter traders are often short of capacity. The Daimler-Benz AG had obviously recognized this problem when in 1978 it brought 25 percent of the capital of the Bafag AG, one of the potentially most powerful West German barter houses.

The second problem arises when the Eastern organization is unable to pay at once. Then it is necessary to find a bank which agrees to grant the Eastern side credit so that the Western seller can be paid at the time of delivery.

COOPERATION, PARALLEL BARTER AND CREDIT BY A BANK

Figure 5 shows a deal of this kind. At the time of delivery of the machine (t_1) the Eastern organization receives the needed dollars from a Western bank and therefore is able to pay at once. At the delivery later of the raw material (t_2) Western firm C transfers an equivalent amount of dollars to the Eastern organization, which is then able to repay the bank for the credit.

Again it is obvious that only the deal as a whole is a barter and that from the point of view of each firm such a deal is not a compensation agreement. In our example the seller of the machine is paid in hard currency and at once.

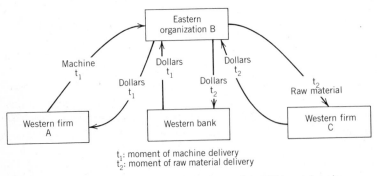

t₁: moment of machine delivery
t₂: moment of raw material delivery

Figure 5 Cooperation, parallel barter, and credit by a bank.

This technique of compensation dealing will probably become the barter system most used in the future, especially for big business. That it is already of great importance is shown by three barter agreements which have become known in Germany as "the pipes and gas business."

In 1970, 1972 and 1974 German firms and two Soviet export-import organizations signed these agreements. The deal was constructed as follows:[3]

A coalition of two German pipe producers deliver pipes to a public export-import organization in the USSR, which specializes in dealing with iron and steel products. In return, a German gas company is supplied with natural gas from Siberia which another public organization in the USSR, a firm specializing in the export and import of mineral gas, has to deliver from Siberia to Germany with the help of German pipes. When the pipes are delivered, a consortium of 15 German banks pays for the pipes in German marks (DM) by order of the Bank for Foreign Trade of the USSR. Parallel to the payment, the German consortium of banks debits the bank of the USSR with the same sum, and the bank then receives an equivalent payment in roubles from the public importers of pipes. On delivery of the gas, the German gas company pays the agreed amount of DM into the German consortium of banks which then pays the same sum of money to the Russian export-import bank's credit. The sum the Russian bank has to pay on behalf of the importer of the pipes, and the sum the Russian bank receives (instead of the gas exporter, who obviously gets his payment in roubles from the Russian bank) are placed on account.

CONCLUSION

This example and the short analysis of the other modern forms of compensation trading show that so-called "international trade without money" is not as moneyless as often assumed. From the single firm's point of view it is important to know that by using sophisticated barter agreement constructions it is possible to realize the following advantages:

1. *Like classical barter, modern barter techniques offer the chance to do business with those states*

which are chronically short of money, especially hard currency. Modern compensation trading is an instrument to gain buyers who cannot be reached by the usual marketing. Especially in times of recession and shrinking markets it helps to conserve or even to augment profits.

2. *In contrast to classical barter, the modern forms of barter avoid the disadvantages of the old barter technique.* Individually this means that the Western exporter has *not* automatically
—to grant a credit;
—to use barter goods as input in his own firm, which might negatively affect his vendor selection system, the make or buy decision, and his single or multiple sourcing strategy;
—to sell goods, for which production bartered products have been used and which therefore might be of poor quality;
—to sell his traditional product portfolio in connection with barter goods, which might lead to a loss of confidence in his usual offer or which might mean a negative image of his firm;
—to sell goods which have nothing to do with his typical output and which would mean to him a confrontation with unknown markets and risks.

The avoiding of these problems of classical barter, without losing the chances the oldest form of doing business offers, is the outstanding advantage of modern compensation trading. The exporter taking part in the barter gains the position of a simple seller: he has the chance to get his money in a reasonable time.[4] This should be considered when being confronted with the ghost whose name is "compensation trading."

NOTES

1. Robert E. Weigand. "International Trade Without Money," *Harvard Business Review*, November–December 1977.
2. *Business Week*, October 27, 1975.
3. Those who are interested in a deeper analysis of these businesses may refer to Falko Schuster, "Bartering processes in industrial buying and selling," *Industrial Marketing Management*, Vol. 7 (1978), pp. 119–127.
4. Falko Schuster. "Gegengeschäfte sind nicht nur des Teufels." *Blick durch die Wirtschaft*, Vol. 22, no. 223, 25.9. (1975), edited by *Frankfurther Allgemeine Zeitung*, p. 1.

SECTION 6
Production Management

In a world marked by increasing competition, production management is taking on increasing importance not only among multinational firms but among domestic firms as well. The firm that markets abroad sooner or later has to consider producing abroad. Even firms that market domestically must consider offshore as well as domestic production. For a multinational firm, decisions as to the number of manufacturing facilities it will have, their size, their location, and the production processes they will use are critical strategic decisions.

The most basic production decision is, of course, whether to make or buy. A firm can contract for local production of the products it markets abroad or for offshore production of the products it sells domestically (''buy'') rather than produce itself (''make''). One important consideration in the make or buy decision is comparative costs, both capital expenditures and operating costs; other important considerations are assuring quality and continuity of supply.

In some circumstances, the most important consideration may be to keep proprietary a production process or certain elements of the process; in this case, the firm would ''make'' even if economic analysis favored ''buy.'' If the decision is to make, there are several alternative plant configurations that might be considered. One is to produce everything at one location and supply all markets from that location by exporting. This is a strategy that many Japanese firms have followed very successfully in the past in product lines ranging from TV sets to automobiles. Recently, however, protectionist pressures have forced Japanese TV producers and, to a lesser extent, automobile producers to do some manufacturing or assembly in certain of the countries in which they sell.

A second alternative is to use an integrated network of plants, sited strategically around the world. This is the pattern of the so-called ''global'' or ''integrated'' multinational firm and is exemplified by companies such as Hewlett-

Packard and GM. There are several possible configurations within an integrated network. Each plant may specialize in particular products that it exports to all markets, or there may be primary manufacturing plants each specializing in one or more components that are then shipped to a larger network of assembly plants. The pharmaceutical industry is one example of such a two-stage production process. The active ingredient is often manufactured centrally and is shipped to a large number of local plants where inert ingredients are added and dosage forms fabricated. A transient two-stage process has also existed in the automobile industry. A plant producing complete automobiles might export some of its output as "kits" or knocked-down automobile sets that are then assembled in the country of destination. Yet another configuration might be based on regional rather than worldwide networks. Volkswagen for example uses such a network because some of its models are sold only in certain countries. In Volkswagen's case, the network is composed of countries at similar economic development stages rather than on the basis of geographic proximity.

Some companies have plants in many countries, but make little or no attempt to integrate them; each production facility is dedicated to serving a particular country or market. Such firms have been referred to as multidomestics because they act like a collection of more or less independent domestic firms rather than as a single multinational organization. These firms are likely to have more numerous and smaller, plants than the globals. They are also more likely to have plants that produce more than one product. The multidomestic focus, though, should not be considered as an inferior to the global. As we shall see, there are good reasons for maintaining independent production facilities in certain circumstances.

The question of production process has been settled in the simplest possible manner by most multinationals. They make only the most necessary concessions required by different (usually smaller than in the United States) plant capacities, by materials and machinery availability, and by different levels of labor skill. Then they try to use common production processes wherever they have plants. Thus, in many cases, U.S.-style production processes are used. This means that some plants may be more capital intensive and less labor intensive than local factor costs would suggest as the optimum.

There is justification both for standardizing production processes and for using more capital-intensive processes than local factor costs would indicate. Standardizing facilitates cost and productivity comparisons and control over product quality and uniformity by minimizing the chances for worker error. A more capital-intensive process also allows the use of less skilled workers.

READING SELECTIONS

Dunning's article presents data on local production and export sales by U.S. firms in 14 industries and 7 countries. He also identifies the variables that seem to be most useful in explaining the observed patterns. Both the data and the analysis are embedded in a theory of international production. The importance of his theory to strategic management is in providing some guidelines for foreign production decisions.

The essence of Dunning's theory is that to compete in foreign markets, a firm must possess some production advantage over local competitors. One such advantage is based on the *ownership* of a proprietary technology, or product, or process that is not freely available to competitors. Ownership can be based either on legal rights (patents, trademarks) or on some special skills the firm has developed. The other advantage is based on *location*. In this situation, the firm's ability to compete in foreign markets is based on producing in a particular place in which it will have lower costs than competitors who produce elsewhere.

It should be obvious that there is a link between the type of production advantage a firm can obtain and certain characteristics of the products it manufactures and markets. Stobaugh and Telesio show how the two relate and also analyze the increasingly important linkages among production strategy, competitive strategy, and business purpose. They identify three basic product strategies—technology driven, marketing intensive, and low cost—and discuss the plant location strategies associated with each.

The astute reader will recognize at least a rough correspondence between the Stobaugh and Telesio technology driven firm and the Dunning concept of advantage based on ownership. Marketing-intensive businesses can be either ownership or location advantage based. Proctor & Gamble's Pampers, for example, is a marketing-intensive product that has a proprietary advantage over its competitors and might, therefore, be able to compete on the basis of ownership advantages. Most TV set producers, on the other hand must search for location advantages, as, obviously, must businesses pursuing strategies based on a low-cost position.

Hefler provides some good ideas for managers of location-sensitive product lines who must choose not only where to source but also between make-and-buy strategies. There are both long- and short-term considerations that must be weighed in the decision. He lists several variables that have to be considered in choosing locations and strategies and then discusses how these variables are likely to act in the future. Hefler's approach uses a Global Sourcing Computer model that evidently includes a large data base; the approach, though, may be of value to an individual firm even with a much more restricted data base. Moreover, the variables and thought processes discussed in the article may provide good material for scenario building.

Doz takes us beyond the decision as to where to locate individual plants, focusing on the question of when to have a globally integrated or rationalized production network. Such a network would consist of a relatively small number of large plants, each specializing in a small range of components or finished products.

Doz tells us that rationalization should be considered in mature industries, where price competition is becoming more pronounced. Rationalization should be implemented when it would result in lower unit costs, allowing, of course, for transportation costs, tariffs, and the like. His argument can be readily and usefully extended to take in products in the growth stage of their life cycles as well. Observation of the behavior of products such as microprocessor chips demonstrates that price competition begins very early in the life cycle. Establishing and maintaining a low-cost position is, therefore, necessary from the beginning. Thus, the material in this article is of importance to emerging as well as to mature industries.

Unfortunately, there seem to be some problems in diagnosing the need for rationalization and then in implementing a rationalization strategy. Doz discusses in some detail the range of problems that may be encountered and then suggests how the whole process should be managed. It is worth noting that managing rationalization goes beyond production, both in terms of functions and managers involved. Production rationalization involves a great deal of coordination. It also requires the strong support and involvement of top management, externally in dealing with governments as well as internally in motivating and coordinating across functions.

Having the largest, most modern plants in the best possible locations may be necessary but may not be sufficient to insure an organization's productivity. The potential of such plants must be realized. Several innovations capable of increasing productivity, such as just-in-time delivery and quality control circles, have been adopted by Japanese firms. Schonberger analyzes one of these innovations, the just-in-time delivery system, and shows how it can be adapted to and then adopted by a U.S. plant. His analysis might serve as a prototype for the adaptation and adoption of any number of manufacturing innovations.

It is worth noting that for a just-in-time system to work, significant changes must be made in the typical U.S. buyer/vendor relationship. The buyer must be willing to keep the seller completely informed of production plans well enough in advance so that the seller can meet the just-in-time requirements. The seller must be willing to and capable of taking full quality control responsibility because there is no way that the buyer can test components in a just-in-time system. In Japan, both buyers and vendors are used to working in this manner. For just-in-time to work in the United States, there will have to be a great deal of mutual trust between buyers and vendors and a great deal of patience as well. In Japan, the buyer/vendor relationship would include an implicit commitment by the buyer to stay with the vendor over the long term. It would also include a commitment by the vendor to help the buyer to improve his or her productivity by developing improved components and by producing more efficiently, passing the savings on to the buyer.

27

Toward an Eclectic Theory of International Production: Some Empirical Tests

John H. Dunning

• • •

INTRODUCTION: THE UNDERLYING THEORY

There is now a consensus of opinion that the propensity of an enterprise to engage in international production—that financed by foreign direct investment—rests on three main determinants: first, the extent to which it possesses (or can acquire, on more favorable terms) assets[1] which its competitors (or potential competitors) do not possess; second, whether it is in its interest to sell or lease these assets to other firms, or make use of—internalize—them itself; and third, how far it is profitable to exploit these assets in conjunction with the indigenous resources of foreign countries rather than those of the home country. The more the *ownership*-specific advantages possessed by an enterprise, the greater the inducement to internalize them; and the wider the attractions of a foreign rather than a home country production base, the greater the likelihood that an enterprise, given the incentive to do so, will engage in international production.

This eclectic approach to the theory of international production may be summarized as follows.[2] A national firm supplying its own market has various avenues for growth: it can diversify horizontally or laterally into new product lines, or vertically into new activities, including the production of knowledge; it can acquire existing enterprises; or it can exploit foreign markets. When it makes good economic sense to choose the last route (which may also embrace one or more of the others), the enterprise becomes an international enterprise (defined as a firm which services foreign markets). However, for it to be able to produce alongside indigenous firms domiciled in these markets, it must possess additional *ownership* advantages sufficient to outweigh the costs of servicing an unfamiliar or distant environment (Hirsch 1976).

The function of an enterprise is to transform, by the process of production, valuable inputs into more valuable outputs. Inputs are of two kinds. The first are those which are available, on the same terms, to all firms, whatever their size or nationality, but which are specific in their origin to particular locations and have to be used in that location. These include not only Ricardian type endowments—natural resources, most kinds of labor, and proximity to markets,[3] but also the legal and commercial environment in which the endowments are used—market structure, and government legislation and policies. In classical and neoclassical trade theories, differences in the possession of these endowments between countries fully explain the willingness and the ability of enterprises to become international;[4] but since all firms, whatever their nationality of ownership, were assumed to have full and free access to them (including technology), there were no advantages to be gained from foreign production.

The second type of input is that which an enterprise may create for itself—certain types of technology and organizational skills—or can purchase from other institutions, but over which, in so doing, it acquires some proprietary right of use. Such *ownership*-specific inputs may take the form of a legally protected right—

Source: John H. Dunning, "Toward an Eclectic Theory of International Production: Some Empirical Tests," *Journal of International Business Studies,* Spring/Summer 1980, pp. 9–25. Copyright © 1980. Reprinted by permission.

patents, brand names, trade marks—or of a commercial monopoly—the acquisition of a particular raw material essential to the production of the product—or of exclusive control over particular market outlets; or they may arise from the size of technical characteristics of firms—economies of large-scale production and surplus entrepreneurial capacity. It should be observed that these *ownership* advantages are not exclusive either to international or multinational firms. Some are applicable to all firms producing in the same location; others are those which a branch plant of an existing enterprise may enjoy over a *de novo* enterprise of the same nationality.[5] But, because they operate in different *location*-specific environments, multinational firms may also derive additional *ownership* advantages—such as, their ability to engage in international transfer pricing, to shift liquid assets between currency areas to take advantage of (or protect against) exchange fluctuations, to reduce risks by diversifying their investment portfolios (Rugman 1979), to reduce the impact of strikes or industrial unrest in one country by operating parallel production capacity in another and by engaging international product or process specialization (Dunning 1977).

The essential feature about these second types of inputs is that, although their *origin* may be linked to *location*-specific endowments, their *use* is not so confined. The ability of enterprises to acquire *ownership* endowments is clearly not unrelated to the endowments specific to the countries in which they operate—and particularly their country of origin. Otherwise, there would be no reason why the structure of foreign production of firms of different nationalities should be different. But, in fact, it is so—and substantially so. A recently published paper (Dunning 1979) has shown that Japanese firms have a comparative advantage in the foreign production of textiles and clothing and consumer electronics; U.K. firms in food and tobacco products; Swedish firms in mechanical and electrical engineering; West German firms in chemicals, and U.S. firms in transport equipment. Such differences as these can be explained only by an examination of the characteristics of the endowments of the countries in which the multinational enterprises operate, and especially those of the home country, which normally give rise to the *ownership* advantages in the first place. Raymond Vernon's product cycle theory was among the first to use this approach from the viewpoint of U.S. direct investment abroad (1966). More recently Birgitta Swedenbong (1979) has extended and applied it to a study of Swedish, U.S., and U.K. direct foreign investment. The paper by Dunning (1979) deals with the industrial structure of foreign direct investment of five countries: U.K., Sweden, Japan, West Germany, and the U.S. asserting that the relationship between *ownership*- and *location*-specific endowments is more complex than was once thought. Moreover, often a longish time lag may be involved; many of today's *ownership* advantages of firms are a reflection of yesterday's location advantages of countries.

But, whatever the significance of the country of origin of such inputs, they are worth separating from those which are *location*-specific, because the enterprise possessing them can exploit them wherever it wishes, usually at a minimal transfer cost. Moreover, unless it chooses to sell them, or the right to their use, to other enterprises, the endowments are—for some period of time at least—its exclusive property.

Both modern trade and international production theory have embraced this kind of endowment which is often mobile between countries but not between firms. Indeed, over the last twenty years there has been a convergence in the explanation of the movement of goods and of factor inputs across national boundaries. Alongside the neotechnology theories of trade, which assert that the extent to which a country possesses technology is a key determinant of patterns of trade in manufactured goods between nations (Hufbauer 1970; Hirsch 1974), there is the knowledge theory of direct investment, which explains the pattern of international production in terms of the distribution of knowledge between firms of different nationalities (Johnson 1970). Parallel with the hypothesis that patterns of trade can best be explained by the extent to which enterprises in different countries possess monopolistic, scale, or product differentiation advantages, are the theories of direct investment which focus on product differentiation, entrepreneurial capacity and multiplant economies (Caves 1971, 1974).

In the last five or six years, it has become increasingly recognized that neither a *location* nor an *ownership* endowment approach, by itself, can satisfactorily explain all forms of trade—although particular kinds of trade may be better explained by one approach rather than by another (Hirsch 1976). It is now also accepted that an *ownership* endowment approach (first pioneered by Kindleberger and Hymer and later refined by Caves) is a necessary but not a sufficient condition for explaining international production. Only if both of the right dispositions of resource endowments exist between countries and firms of different nationalities will international production take place.

There is one final strand to the eclectic theory of international production. The possession of *ownership* advantages determines *which* firms will supply a particular foreign market, whereas the pattern of location endowments explains whether the firm will supply that market by exports (trade) or by local production (non-trade). But why does a firm choose to use the *ownership* advantages itself to exploit a foreign market—whatever route it chooses—rather than sell or lease these advantages to a firm located in that market to exploit? Why does it *internalize* its capital, technology, management skills itself to produce goods rather than externalize their use by engaging in portfolio investment, licensing, management contracts, and so on?

The basic incentive of a firm to internalize its ownership endowments is to avoid the disadvantages, or capitalize on the imperfections, of one or the other of the two main external mechanisms of resource allocation—the *market or price system* and the *public authority fiat*. Market imperfections arise wherever negotiation or transaction costs are high, wherever the economies of interdependent activities cannot be fully captured, and wherever information about the product or service being marketed is not readily available or is costly to acquire. From a buyer's viewpoint, such imperfections include uncertainty over the availability and price of essential supplies and inability to control their timing and delivery. From a seller's viewpoint, the preference for internalizing will be most pronounced where the market does not permit price discrimination, where the costs of enforcing property rights and controlling information flows are high, or where, in the case of forward integration, the seller wishes to protect his reputation by ensuring a control over product or service quality or after-sales maintenance (Brown 1976). For both groups of firms, and for those considering horizontal internalization, the possession of underutilized resources—particularly entrepreneurial and organizational capacity, which may be exploited at low marginal cost to produce products complementary to those currently being supplied—also fosters internalization.

Public intervention in the allocation of resources may also encourage firms to internalize their activities. This arises particularly with respect to government legislation toward the production and licensing of technology, including the patent system, and where there are differential tax and exchange rate policies, which multinational enterprises may wish either to avoid or exploit.

As described then, the propensity to internalize ownership or location advantages[6] make up the third strand in the eclectic theory. In most of the conventional literature on trade and international investment, it is this last aspect of the theory that has been most seriously ne-

Table 1 The Determinants of International Production

Types of International Production	Ownership Advantages	Location Advantages	Internalization Advantages	Illustration of Types of Activity Which Favor MNEs
1. Resource-based	Capital, technology, access to markets	Possession of resources	To ensure stability of supply at right price, control of markets	Oil, copper, tin, zinc, bauxite, bananas, pineapples, cocoa, tea
2. Import substituting manufacturing	Capital, technology, management and organizational skills; surplus R&D and other capacity, economies of scale; trademarks	Material and labor costs, markets, government policy (with respect to barrier to imports, investment incentives, etc.)	Wish to exploit technology advantages; high transaction or information costs; buyer uncertainty, etc.	Computers, pharmaceuticals, motor vehicles, cigarettes
3. Export platform manufacturing	As above, but also access to markets	Low labor costs incentives to local production by host governments.	The economies of vertical integration	Consumer electronics, textiles and clothing, cameras, etc.
4. Trade and distribution	Products to distribute	Local markets. Need to be near customers; after-sales servicing, etc.	Need to ensure sales outlets & to protect company's name	A variety of goods—particularly those requiring close consumer contact
5. Ancillary services	Access to markets (in the case of other foreign investors)	Markets	Broadly as for 2/4	Insurance, banking, and consultancy services
6. Miscellaneous	Variety—but include geographical diversification (airlines and hotels)	Markets	Various (see above)	Various kinds: (a) portfolio investment—properties, (b) where spatial linkages essential (airlines and hotels)

glected. For it is not just the possession of technology per se which gives an enterprise selling goods embodying that technology an edge over its international competitors, but also the advantages which arise from internalizing that technology rather than selling it to a foreign producer for the production of those goods. In other words, without the advantages of internalization much of direct foreign investment would be replaced by the international transaction of resources on a contractual basis between independent buyers and sellers.

To conclude this brief theoretical introduction, a matrix is presented which attempts to relate, in an encapsulated form, the main types of activities in which multinational enterprises may be involved to the three main determinants of international involvement. (See Table 1.) Such a table may be used as a starting point for an examination of the industrial and geographical distribution of foreign direct investment. It will be noted that as part of the explanation of *ownership* endowments, the possession of *home* country endowments has been added because these will influence the geographical origin of such investment.

AN OVERVIEW OF CURRENT APPROACHES

Broadly speaking, there have been five approaches to testing the theory of international production. The first has attempted to explain the causes of direct *foreign investment* by examining its industrial composition from the viewpoint of individual home countries (almost exclusively the U.S.) and host countries (notably Canada, U.K., and Australia). A common thread running through all these studies[7] is that they have sought to explain the pattern of foreign direct investment in terms of *ownership* advantages of MNEs. The second approach has been to look at the *form* of international economic involvement and to identify the determinants of whether foreign markets are exploited by trade or nontrade routes.[8] The third has combined the two approaches by examining both the level and composition of international involvement in terms of *ownership* and *locational* characteristics.[9] The fourth approach has been to extend the first three to incorporate the internalization thesis,[10] and the fifth has been to relate the specific endowments of firms to those of home countries, as in Vernon (1966); Swedenborg (1979), and Dunning (1979). The empirical contribution of this paper is primarily of the third kind but with the issues of the fourth very much in mind.

From both a technical and motivational standpoint, these strands of research have much in common.[11] Each uses, with varying degrees of sophistication, multiple regression analysis to test explanations about the relationship between various measures of international involvement and a variety of explanatory variables. Each, too, is beset by the same kind of methodological and statistical problems, notably the establishment of operationally testable hypotheses, data limitations, and multicollinearity between the individual variables. From a motivational standpoint, with one ex-

ception (Knickerbocker 1973), all the studies assume either that enterprises are profit maximizers or that their behavior is not inconsistent with that which might be expected from a profit-maximizing firm.

In testing empirically two of the most important hypotheses implicit in the eclectic theory of international production, only two forms of international economic involvement—exports and production—are considered; these are assumed to be alternative to each other in servicing foreign markets.[12]

The data used cover the foreign activities of U.S. multinationals in fourteen manufacturing industries in seven countries in 1970, as published by the U.S. Tariff Commission (1973), details of which are set out in Appendix 2.[13] The two basic hypotheses are:

H1 The competitive advantage of a country's enterprises in servicing foreign markets is determined both by the *ownership* advantages of these enterprises relative to those of enterprises of other nationalities, and the *location* advantages of the countries in which they produce relative to those of other countries.

H2 The *form* of the involvement, or participation, will essentially depend on the relative attractiveness of the *location*-specific endowments of the home and host countries.[14]

That the gains to be derived from internalizing activities, which would otherwise be allocated by markets or government fiat, make up an important part of *ownership* advantages, and, in some cases, of *location* advantages as well is also contended.

Concerning H1, we shall take as our dependent variable the share of the output of a particular industry (IS) in a particular country supplied by exports (X) plus local production (AS) of U.S.-owned firms:[15] AS + X/IS. These components can, of course, be considered separately; but, in this hypothesis, we wish to exclude *location*-specific variables influencing the form of involvement. This dependent variable is notated as DV 1.[16]

The two components of international involvement may be considered separately. DV 2 signifies the share of the affiliates' sales of total output in the host country (AS/IS), and DV 3, the share of exports from the U.S. of that output (X/IS).

Concerning H2, the dependent variable—DV 4—is defined as X/IS ÷ AS/IS (or simply X/AS); in other words, it is the ratio between exploiting a particular market by exports from the U.S. relative to local production by U.S. affiliates in the country of marketing. The higher this ratio, the more the U.S. is favored as a location for production, relative to the country in which the goods are being sold (or being exported from).

THE STATISTICAL TESTING

We now turn to a statistical testing of the two main hypotheses.

The Dependent Variables

Hypothesis 1—The International Competitive Hypothesis The overall involvement index reflects both *location*- and *ownership*-specific advantages. The explanation of the foreign production ratio lies in identifying and measuring *ownership* advantages (as the location of production is assumed to be the same for all firms) and that of the export ratio in both *location* and *ownership* advantages. Looking at the export ratio, one naturally turns to trade theories for guidance; but no attempt, to our knowledge, has been made to explain shares of a particular industry's sales accounted for by foreign imports.[17] In discussing the determinants of foreign production, one should be concerned solely with *ownership* advantages; yet, the fact that trade and production are often related to each other suggests that these advantages may also be associated with *location*-specific endowments.[18] Explanations of foreign production, which ignore the latter advantages, are likely to be inadequate, thus supporting the need for an eclectic theory of production and trade.

The share of a particular industry's output supplied by foreign affiliates is determined by the competitive advantages of the affiliates and the relative attractions of the host country as a production base. It is likely to be greatest where the barriers to entry facing indigenous producers *and* exports from the home (and other countries) are highest. Trade is similarly determined except that it will flourish where barriers to exports are low and where barriers to entry to all producers in the host country are high. International involvement is determined simply by the competitive advantage of the investing and exporting firms vis-à-vis indigenous and other foreign companies.

In symbolic terms:

$$\text{DV 1} \quad AS + X/IS = f(C)$$

where C = international competitive advantage (to be defined)

$$\text{DV 2} \quad AS/IS = f(C, X/AS)$$

and

$$\text{DV 3} \quad X/IS = f(C, X/AS)$$

Hypothesis 2—The Location Hypothesis This is simple and straightforward. To produce a particular good, an enterprise will choose that location which best advances its overall goals. The interface between received location theory and the MNE is a relatively unexplored territory, but a good start has been made by Vernon (1974). In principle, there is no reason to suppose a national multiplant firm would behave very differently if its plants were located in a different country. New variables—such as exchange risks, differences in taxation rates, and policies of host governments toward inward direct investment—may need to be incorporated, but this can be done without too much difficulty.

The location hypothesis is solely concerned with *country*-specific variables affecting (1) the size and character of markets (which may be affected by competitor's behavior) and (2) production and transfer costs, though these may have a special impact on MNEs because of their ability to internalize the costs and benefits of some of the differences which exist between countries. The hypothesis may be expressed as:

$$DV \ 4 \ X/AS = f(L)$$

where L = locational advantage of the home country (to be defined).

The Independent Variables

Hypothesis 1 To assess the competitive advantage of firms of one nationality over those of another—both in particular industries and countries—one must evaluate: (1) allocative, technical, and scale efficiency; (2) product range and quality, and (3) market power. Because we are concerned with inter-industry comparisons, allocative efficiency of resources between industries may be discounted. However, goals may differ between firms, as may the competence of firms to achieve these goals. For example, the greater the innovative ability of an enterprise, the more resourceful and the more talented its managerial and labor force, the higher its market share is likely to be. Similarly, the advantages of size, of being part of a larger organization, and of being able to internalize economies will affect a firm's competitive situation independently of the location of its activities.

Some of these variables, of course, reflect the industry or country characteristics of firms. Governments, for example, can and do influence the extent to which there is an adequate labor force to draw upon, the promotion of new technologies, the role of advertising in fostering product differentiation, and so on. These factors are acknowledged and have been considered explicitly elsewhere (Dunning 1979).

It may be helpful to break H1 down into two sub-hypotheses.

The first is:

H1$_a$ Given the export-participation ratio (X/IS), the foreign production-participation ratio (AS/IS) will be highest in those industries where the comparative advantage of foreign (meaning U.S. here) firms is greatest vis-à-vis indigenous firms.

In principle, many of these advantages may be captured in a catchall measure, as in the comparative productivity of U.S. firms and host country firms or some proxy for integration—such as, percent of net to gross output. The comparative advantage of U.S. firms is presumably highest where their relative productivity or value added ratio is highest; therefore, in those cases, the affiliate penetration ratio should be highest. In practice, difficulties in measuring productivity and identifying internalizing economies make both measures of doubtful applicability.

H1$_b$ Given the production-participation ratio (AS/IS), the export penetration-participation ratio (X/IS) will be highest in those industries where the national resource endowments of the U.S. are greatest in comparison to those of other countries, and where barriers to trade are minimal.

Location theory approaches export success more in terms of difference in *absolute* production costs and the costs of traversing space. Artificial barriers to trade include those imposed by governments or imperfect markets. An incentive to export may also result from the inability of a host country's firms to compete effectively, due to the absence of a market sufficiently large to yield economies of scale in production.

Hypothesis 2 Like H1$_b$, the second hypothesis appears to be explained best by the theories of trade and location. Among the relative costs that play an important part in determining the location choice are those of labor and material inputs. The former are particularly critical in this study because it is limited to manufacturing industries where horizontal direct investment is the rule. This is in contrast to the situation in resource industries where vertical direct investment plays a much greater role. By the same token, labor productivity and its growth will be important elements in determining the real value of labor.

Production costs may be closely related also to the scale of plant which can be built. Market size will, therefore, be relevant. So, also, will rates of growth of the markets involved because they will determine the extent to which economies of scale may be exploited in the future.

The Choice of Independent Variables for this Exercise

Table 2 lists some of the variables which might be considered as proxies for *ownership-* and *location-*specific advantages. An asterisk identifies those variables which might also be used as indices of internalization advantages.[19] Some of these are very similar to each other; not all can be used for this particular exercise, partly because it is concerned with explaining patterns of involvement by *industries* rather than by *firms,* and partly because of data constraints.

It will also be noted that for some variables set out, data are required for host countries; in others, for the home country, or for both host and home countries. Where only the home country is involved, *location* advantages become irrelevant, and one cannot use the data to determine both industry and country participation ratios. The main constraint, however, has been the paucity of good data about *host* countries which seriously inhibits testing both hypotheses for the seven countries considered separately. This exercise omits the two LDCs, partly because the data are less certain for these two countries, and partly so that a tariff variable could be used—data for which were not available for Mexico and Brazil.

In the end, the independent variables were chosen and used to test both hypotheses. Data on each relate to 1970, or the nearest year, except where otherwise stated. The data for these variables were extracted mainly from the U.S. Tariff Commission Study, except for those on imports which were obtained from the OECD Commodity Trade Statistics Series C, and tariffs from a Political and Economic Planning publication (1965).

A schematization of variables follows.

(A) For the Seven Country Exercise

(i) *Ownership-specific variables*

1a SER—Skilled employment ratio: the ratio of salaried employees to production employees for all firms in the host countries.

2a AHC—Average hourly compensation of all employees in the host countries. (1a and 2a are both measures of human capital intensity).

3a RSM—Relative sales per man (an efficiency index: the sales per man year of firms in the U.S. divided by sales per man year of firms (including the affiliates of U.S. firms) in the host countries.

4a GRSPM—Growth in sales per man of all firms (in the host country), 1966–1970.

The predicted sign for each of these variables for each of the hypotheses is positive, but their significance is likely to be greater for H1 than H2. U.S. firms will invest in those industries and countries in which they have the greatest technological advantage and where their productivity, vis-à-vis local firms, is the highest.

(ii) *Location-specific variables*

5a XMR—The export/import ratio, measured by the ratio of value of exports to value of imports of *host* countries (as a measure of a country's ability to produce particular products).

6a RMS—Relative market size: value of industry sales in the U.S. divided by value of industry sales in the host countries.

7a RW—Relative wages: average hourly compensation (in particular industries) in the U.S. divided by average hourly compensation in the host countries for all employees (an often quoted cost determinant of foreign production).

8a RES—Relative export shares of U.S. and host countries: another measure of country performance.

9a CMG—Comparative market growth of U.S. (domestic industry local sales plus imports) and host countries, 1966–1970.

The predicted signs of these variables vary. In the case of RES it is positive; but in the case of XMR, RMS, and CMG it is negative. It might also be expected that these variables would be most demonstrated as an explanation of H2.

(iii) *General performance indicators*

10a AVNIS—The average ratio of net income to sales of all firms in different industries and countries for 1966 and 1970.

11a MG—Market growth (domestic industry local sales plus imports) in host countries, 1966–1970.

The predicted sign of AVNIS is negative for H1 but positive for H2; that for MG is positive for all hypotheses.

(B) The Five Advanced Countries

As per 1a–11a, but with an additional *location-specific* variable.

12b TR—Average tariffs measured on a country and industry basis.

The predicted sign of this variable is negative for DV4.

Such a large number of independent variables invites problems associated with multicollinearity. These problems were compounded when the two different groups of independent variables were tested against the "wrong" dependent variables as well, in order to determine if the general hypotheses were too restrictive. It was, therefore, decided to correlate separately each of the independent variables with the dependent variables (DV1–4) to determine which ones appeared worthy of further statistical investigation. Only those which approached significance at a 95 percent level were incorporated into multivariate form.

The large number of equations tested, given four dependent variables and twelve independent variables, also sharply increased the possibility of chance significance. Because of this, any value below the 99 percent significance should be treated with caution.

STATISTICAL RESULTS

Case A: The Seven Countries

These countries vary quite considerably in income levels, economic structure, political ideologies, culture, proximity to the U.S., and the extent to which they, themselves, spawn MNEs which compete in international markets with U.S.-based MNEs. It would not be surprising to find that different factors explain the absolute and relative success of U.S. exports and affiliate production in these countries when tested individually; here, however, we are concerned with factors which explain export and affiliate success in the seven countries as a *group,* and which can, perhaps, be regarded as "worldwide" determinants of such success.

H1 (DV1–3). Table 3 summarizes the more significant results of our regression analyses.[20] The explanatory variables presented were extracted from the bivariate analysis and a series of multivariate equations constructed from

Table 2 Ownership and Location Advantages (Internalizing Advantages Marked with *)

Determinants	By Industry and/or Country
Ownership Advantages: Specific Determinants	

1. Access to productive knowledge
   (a) Skilled (professional and technical/unskilled labor ratio*   Home (cf. host firms)
   (b) R and D as percent of sales*   Home (cf. host firms)
2. Economics of the firm
   (a) Size of enterprise*   Home firms
   (b) Relative size of enterprises   (Average) Home (cf. host firms)
   (c) Number of nonproduction to all workers* *or* wage bill of nonproduction to all workers *or* nonproduction costs†/total costs* (gross output) *or* R and D plus advertising costs to total costs (or sales)*   Home firms
   (d) Capital/Labor ratio   Home firms
3. Opportunities for investment
   (a) Size of local market   (Industry) sales of host firms
   (b) Size of/or local market plus exports   (Industry) sales of host firms
4. Diversification indices‡
   (a) Average number of countries MNEs operate in* or   Home firms
   (b) % of foreign/total production of home firms*   Home firms
   (c) % of intragroup exports to total exports of MNEs*   Home firms
   (d) Number of product groups in which parent companies produce *or* % of output of main product group to all output*   Home firms
   (e) % of shipments from multiplant enterprises to total shipments (in home country)*   Home firms
5. Market concentration
   (a) Percentage of output of industry accounted for by "x" largest firms   Home firms
6. Efficiency
   (a) Wage costs (per man hour) of production workers   Foreign affiliates as % of home firms
7. Resource availability
   (a) % of main material(s) imported*   Either import/export ratio of home firms *or* % imports to total consumption
   (b) % of main material(s) used in production process   % of main material costs to gross output

Table 2 continued

Determinants	By Industry and/or Country
Ownership Advantages: Specific Determinants	
8. Product differentiation Advertising/sales ratio	Home firms

9. Oligopolistic behavior
   Entry concentration index
   Knickerbocker Ph.D. thesis
	Home firms in host countries

Ownership Advantages: General Determinants	
1. Productivity Net output or sales per man	1. Home firms (cf. host firms) 2. Foreign affiliates (cf. host firms)
2. Profitability Profit/assets or sales	1. Home firms (cf. host firms) 2. Foreign affiliates (cf. host firms)
3. Growth Increase in sales	1. Home firms (cf. host firms) 2. Foreign affiliates (cf. host firms)
Location Advantages: Specific Determinants	
1. Production costs	
(a) Wages per man-hour	Home firms (cf. host firms)
(b) Energy costs (e.g., electricity or oil)	Home firms (cf. host firms)
(c) Materials costs (cost of major inputs; or commodity price indices for main materials) *or* some index of resource availability	Home firms (cf. host firms)
(d) Tax rates (including, where possible, tax allowances)*	Home firms (cf. host firms)
(e) Average number of countries MNEs operating in	Home firms only
2. Transfer costs	
(a) Transport costs	Home-host country
(b) Tariffs	Host country
(c) Non-tariff barriers	Host country
3. General	
(a) Political risks	Host country
Location Advantages: General Determinants	

1. Productivity
   (a) Production costs per man *or*
   (b) Net output or sales per man
	Home firms (cf. foreign affiliates)

2. Profitability Profits/assets or sales	Home firms (cf. foreign affiliates)
3. Growth Increase in sales	Home firms (cf. foreign affiliates)

†Nonproduction = pre- and postdirect production costs.
‡(a)–(d) specific to MNEs; (e) general to multiplant enterprises.

Table 3 H1 Determinants of Participation Ratios of U.S. MNEs in Seven Countries, 1970

	Constant	AVNIS	RMS	SER	AHC	RW	RES	CMG	R (R²)
(1) DV1 (AS + X/IS)									
1.1	0.060		−0.991	1.133					0.546
			(4.058)†	(4.993)†					(0.298)
1.2	−0.068		−1.137	1.007			0.375		0.613
			(4.831)†	(4.613)†			(3.422)†		(0.376)
1.3	−0.051		−1.219	0.910	0.027		0.279		0.617
			(4.759)†	(3.652)†	(0.815)		(1.728)		(0.380)
1.4	0.002	−0.002	−1.155	0.732	0.161	−0.777	0.494		0.673
		(2.474)†	(4.635)†	(2.987)†	(2.603)*	(2.615)*	(2.880)*		(0.452)
1.5	−0.028	−0.002	−1.136	0.809	0.131	−0.648	0.480	0.0065	0.675
		(2.365)*	(4.519)†	(2.994)†	(1.735)	(1.840)	(2.765)†	(0.683)	(0.455)
(2) DV2 (AS/IS)									
2.1	0.018		0.580	0.497					0.430
			(3.459)†	(3.192)†					(0.185)
2.2	0.0026		−0.693	0.374	0.026				0.454
			(3.829)†	(2.164)*	(1.585)				(0.206)
2.3	0.016	−0.0009	−0.717	0.388	0.025				0.466
		(1.151)	(3.942)†	(2.129)*	(1.522)				(0.217)
2.4	0.028	−0.0010	−0.669	0.295	0.084	−0.322	0.072		0.485
		(1.260)	(3.545)†	(1.597)	(1.801)	(1.438)	(0.599)		(0.235)
(3) DV3 (X/IS)									
3.1	0.078		−1.571	1.631					0.553
			(4.372)†	(4.883)†					(0.306)
3.2	−0.079		−1.750	1.476			0.459		0.599
			(4.957)†	(4.510)†			(2.792)†		(0.359)
3.3	0.022		−1.987	1.177	0.095				0.599
			(5.254)†	(3.260)†	(2.803)†				(0.359)
3.4	0.030	−0.0038	−1.824	1.027	0.245	−1.098	0.566		0.657
		(2.271)*	(4.856)†	(2.780)†	(2.627)*	(2.454)*	(2.190)*		(0.432)

*Significant at the 95 percent level.
†Significant at the 99 percent level.

them. For each of the variants of H1, most of the variation in the share of U.S. firms in the output of countries can be put down to two or three variables, with the best results coming from the overall international competitiveness index (DV1).

Because there are 98 observations, the explanatory power of the three variants of the hypothesis is encouraging. All of the signs (apart from that of RW) are consistent and in the right direction.

The equations reveal that the main advantages of U.S. firms are revealed in one *location*-specific variable—relative market size (RMS)—and one *ownership*-specific variable—the skilled employment ratio (SER). This latter ratio may be used as a proxy for internalizing

advantages. Both are consistently significant at the two star—i.e., 99 percent—level for each of the dependent variables. The other ownership variables which are significant at this level for DV1 and DV3 are the productivity index, relative sales per man (RSM), and average hourly compensation (AHC). Two *location*-specific variables—wage differentials (RW) and net income per sales (AVNIS)—are also significant for the same two dependent variables, but only at the 95 percent level. For DV2, no variables other than RMS and SER were significant, although average hourly compensation (AHC) came closest. That this last variable appears to be collinear with SER is not unexpected because higher salaries are usually obtained by more highly skilled nonproduction employees.

Table 4 H2 Determinants of Export/Local Production Ratios (X/AS) of U.S. MNEs (DV4) in Seven Countries, 1970

	Constant	XMR	AVNIS	RMS	RSM	CRSPM	R (R^2)
4.1	0.308	−0.101	0.043				0.601
		(3.301)†	(7.256)†				(0.362)
4.2	0.042	−0.101	0.043			0.0085	0.622
		(3.363)†	(7.277)†			(1.942)	(0.386)
4.3	0.103	−0.099	0.042	−0.561		0.0084	0.624
		(3.210)†	(7.007)†	(0.600)		(1.896)	(0.389)
4.4	0.100	−0.100	0.042		−0.0000048	0.0090	0.623
		(3.287)†	(7.101)†		(0.441)	(1.983)	(0.388)

These same relationships were run using the 1966 data; the results obtained were much the same with the exception that the 1966 profit variable, net income to sales (AVNIS), is never quite significant.

H2 (DV4). The results obtained from this hypothesis set out in Table 4 are quite different from those of H1. Two variables, the export/import ratio (XMR) and net income to sales (AVNIS), are consistently significant at the 99 percent level and explain nearly 60 percent of the variation in the location ratio. Growth of relative sales per man (GRSPM) comes very close but is never quite significant. The results for 1966 were virtually the same as for 1970.

Case B: The Five Advanced Countries

Quite early in the study, it was decided to run the data with Mexico and Brazil excluded. Although, to a certain extent, each country exercises its own unique set of influences on the involvement of foreign firms, there is something to be said for separating Mexico and Brazil from the other five countries. Historically, LDCs have produced relatively more raw materials and semi-finished manufactures and fewer finished products for world markets than the developed countries, and investment in resource-based industries is often based on very different considerations than investment in manufacturing. Mexico and Brazil, in spite of recent rates of rapid industrial growth, are still sufficiently different in their stages of development to justify separate treatment.

H1 (DV1–DV3). The results are presented in Table 5. In all equations, one ownership variable, the skilled employment ratio (SER), and two location variables, relative market shares (RMS) and average hourly compensation (AHC), are consistently significant at the 99 percent level. These three variables clearly have some influence on both U.S. trade and affiliate success in each of the five countries. Relative export shares (RES) and relative wages (RW) appear significant at the 95 percent (and in one case at the 99 percent) level in some of the equations of DV2 and DV3, but only where there are few independent variables regressed together. This suggests that these latter two location variables exert some influence on the competitiveness of U.S. trade but not on that of foreign production.

The tariff variable (T) appears to be a significant explanation of the overall involvement of U.S. firms in the five countries. In combination with the three universally successful variables above (RMS, SER, and AHC), T yielded an R^2 of 0.5695, which is quite satisfactory.

The data for 1966 suggest much the same results, with the exception that, in some combinations involving four or fewer independent variables, RS and RW also become significant as an explanation of DV1. This fact rather weakens

Table 5 H1 Determinants of Participation Ratios in U.S. MNEs in Five Advanced Countries, 1970

	Constant	AVNIS	RMS	SER	AHC	RW	RES	RSM	T	R(R²)
(1) DV1 (AS + X/IS)										
1.1	0.058		−0.990	1.162						0.587
			(3.323)†	(4.445)†						(0.343)
1.2	0.0956	−0.0028	1.084	1.137						0.614
		(1.884)	(3.653)†	(4.425)†						(0.377)
1.3	−0.014	−0.0026	−1.015	1.289					0.010	0.653
		(1.791)	(3.522)†	(2.373)*					(2.373)*	(0.427)
1.4	0.470	−0.0019	−0.9234	0.872	0.152				0.014	0.755
		(1.482)	(3.660)†	(3.608)†	(4.609)†				(3.486)†	(0.570)
1.5	−0.436	−0.0022	−0.912	0.891	0.173	−0.318	0.202		0.013	0.760
		(1.688)	(3.576)†	(3.409)†	(2.844)†	(0.942)	(0.943)		(3.330)†	(0.577)
(2) DV2 (AS/IS)										
2.1	0.0125		−0.540	0.506						0.566
			(3.595)†	(3.841)†						(0.321)
2.2	−0.096		−0.522	0.334	0.056					0.634
			(3.675)†	(2.438)*	(3.007)†					(0.403)
2.3	−0.055	−0.0010	−0.539	0.339	0.077	−0.274	0.148			0.657
		(1.346)	(3.727)†	(2.291)*	(2.254)*	(1.426)	(1.225)			(0.432)
2.4	−0.051	−0.0012	−0.545	0.391	0.099	−0.390	0.283	−0.0000043		0.681
		(1.609)	(3.845)†	(2.648)*	(2.787)†	(1.969)	(2.059)*	(1.900)		(0.464)
(3) DV3 (X/IS)										
3.1	0.070		−1.530	1.669						0.617
			(3.771)†	(4.686)†						(0.381)
3.2	0.307		−1.467	1.071	0.194					0.710
			(4.007)†	(3.031)†	(4.051)†					(0.504)
3.3	−0.314		−1.466	1.464		0.695				0.677
			(3.830)†	(4.282)†		(3.079)*				(0.459)
3.4	−0.250	−0.0030	−1.570	1.070	0.185					0.723
		(1.616)	(4.275)†	(3.064)†	(3.903)†					(0.523)
3.5	−0.206	−0.0037	−1.536	1.137	0.221	−0.627	0.438			0.735
		(1.938)	(4.172)†	(3.016)†	(2.532)*	(1.280)	(1.422)			(0.540)

*Significant at the 95 percent level.
†Significant at the 99 percent level.

the argument, based on the 1970 data, that these two have an influence on trade but not on foreign production; but probably they are only marginally significant in all three cases. For both years, 1966 and 1970, when the number of independent variables is increased, these two variables become less significant; this suggests that the added variables capture the significant influences duplicated in RES and RW. There appears, for example, to be a fair amount of collinearity between RW and AHC and between RES and RSM. For 1970, the correlation coefficients (at the seven-country level) between these variables are 0.9445 and 0.7052, respectively.

H2 (DV4). As seen in Table 6, quite different variables explain most of the form of penetra-

tion from those which explain the first three variables. The profitability ratio (AVNIS) and the growth in sales per man (GRSPM) are consistently significant, the former at extremely high levels of significance and the latter at either 99 or 95 percent levels of significance. These two alone explain more than half the variance in the location ratio. Other variables which are occasionally significant are two ownership variables, average hourly compensation (AHC) and relative sales per man (RSM). They are only significant in small groups, however, which suggests an overlap between many of these variables. Equation 4 of DV4 is a good example where differences in wage costs (RW) are significant at 99 percent, and RS at 95 percent, and where R^2 is 0.5633.

The data for 1966 yield similar results with

Table 6 H2 Determinants of Export/Local Production (X/AS) Ratios (DV4) of U.S. MNEs in Five Advanced Countries, 1970

	Constant	AVNIS	AHC	RW	RSM	RES	CMG	GRSPM	MG	T	R(R²)
4.1	−0.251	0.050 (7.953)†						0.012 (2.206)*			0.717 (0.515)
4.2	−0.130	0.050 (7.857)†						0.025 (2.942)†	−1.309 (1.967)		0.736 (0.542)
4.3	1.777	0.050 (8.119)†			−0.000045 (2.510)*		−3.517 (2.845)†	0.013 (2.515)†			0.755 (0.570)
4.4	0.508	0.044 (7.150)†		−2.548 (2.657)*		1.803 (2.174)*		0.024 (2.914)†	−1.240 (1.928)		0.766 (0.587)
4.5	1.492	0.046 (7.325)†		−1.509 (1.289)	−0.000043 (1.906)	1.647 (1.645)	−2.534 (1.694)	0.012 (2.316)*			0.767 (0.588)
4.6	1.277	0.045 (7.159)†		−1.760 (1.486)	−0.000030 (1.212)	1.605 (1.608)	−1.848 (1.159)	0.021 (2.361)*	−0.864 (1.210)		0.773 (0.598)
4.7	1.603	0.045 (7.086)†	0.249 (0.859)	−2.516 (1.703)	−0.000045 (1.483)	1.672 (1.666)	−2.598 (1.427)	0.022 (2.436)*	−1.004 (1.367)		0.776 (0.602)
4.8	1.521	0.045 (7.082)†	0.307 (1.008)	−2.430 (1.630)	0.000050 (1.600)	1.483 (1.415)	−3.002 (1.555)	0.023 (2.499)*	−0.964 (1.303)	0.012 (0.656)	0.778 (0.605)

*Significant at the 95 percent level.
†Significant at the 99 percent level.

country or industry (rather than ownership) differences in profitability (AVNIS) and growth in sales per man (GRSPM, an ownership variable) being rather more significant. But, in this case, MG (market share) becomes marginally significant in combination with GRSPM. None of the labor cost and productivity variables are significant.

CONCLUSION: COMPARING CASE A AND CASE B

Excluding Mexico and Brazil, the seven-country analysis produced some noticeable differences in the results of the statistical analysis. This section considers a few of these and speculates on the reasons for them.

First, the general level of the R^2 rises quite noticeably. This suggests that the independent variables used were more relevant in explaining export and affiliate success in the more advanced industrialized countries than in Mexico and Brazil. Running the regressions excluding Canada suggests that even higher R^2s could have been obtained. (This run was not undertaken because it would have substantially reduced the degrees of freedom.)

Second, the data for 1966 as well as for 1970 indicate that differences in wage costs (RW) and export shares (RS) tend to be more significant in explaining H1 (DV2) in the seven-country than in the five-country case. Perhaps these variables are too similar over different industries in the industrialized countries; and, not until the widely different figures for Mexico and Brazil are included, is their influence clearly indicated.

Third, AHC differences are significant in the compensation of the five-country but not in the seven-country case for H2 (DV4). This discrepancy is difficult to interpret. It may result from the less reliable figures on hourly compensation in Mexico and Brazil than in the other countries, or from the vastly different labor force structure which influences the extent to which local firms can compete successfully against imports in different ways.

Fourth, in the case of H1 (DV1), there are virtually no differences between Cases A and B. There is one major difference between the two cases involving DV4: the export/import ratio (XMR) is significant with the larger group but not with the smaller. This may be interpreted to mean that the export potential of an industry may be more important in a less developed economy in determining the form of penetration. The negative sign implies that U.S. firms in those industries will tend to establish affiliates rather than export to the less developed countries, perhaps, to export some portion of their output. This is consistent in both the product cycle model's last stage and the growth of export-platform investments in some developing countries, including Mexico.

APPENDIX 1 NOTE ON METHODOLOGY

The statistical analysis was restricted to common linear regression analysis and was carried out by Guy Landry at the University of Reading Computing Center. Initially, single variable regressions with each of the independent variables and for each dependent variable were run. The purpose was to choose potentially useful explanatory variables from the number available. As a result of this a few variables were dropped because they either indicated no explanatory value or appeared less useful than very similar variables which were retained.

The next step involved multiple regressions. As explained in the body of the paper, the independent variables were divided into three categories:

a. The *ownership*-specific variables: SER, AHC, RSM, and GRSPM. These are variables suggested by industrial organization theory.

b. The *country*-specific variables: XMR, RMS, RW, RES, and CMG. These are mostly suggested by trade and location theory.

c. The general performance indicators: AVNIS and MG.

For each of the dependent variables, various combinations of the independent variables in each category were subjected to regression analysis. The most significant results are those shown in the tables. The purpose of this step was to determine which independent variables in each category best explained the dependent variables. Next, these same variables were analyzed, but with the categories grouped in different combinations. Once again the tables reveal

Appendix 2 U.S. Affiliate Sales, U.S. Exports, and Total Industry Sales in Seven Countries, 1970 (Billion Dollars)

	Canada			United Kingdom			France			West Germany			Belgium-Lux			Mexico			Brazil			Total		
	AS	X	IS	AS	X	IS	AS	X	IS	AS	X	IS	AS	X	IS	AS	X	IS	AS	X	IS	AS	X	IS
Food Products	2,220	98	8,532	1,054	56	10,294	473	7	17,137	634	33	15,583	121	9	2,415	487	18	5,773	107	8	3,947	5,096	227	63,681
Paper and Allied Products	1,503	118	3,840	141	118	2,763	183	61	2,161	69	103	3,474	96	27	496	121	52	525	65	9	504	2,180	488	13,763
Chemicals and Allied Products	2,124	554	2,490	1,918	226	9,356	971	107	8,190	963	215	13,888	654	220	1,357	764	171	3,888	623	146	3,325	8,017	1,639	42,494
Rubber Products	613	146	628	373	22	1,185	119	24	1,854	211	36	1,972	79	13	96	108	19	267	175	9	363	1,678	269	6,365
Primary and Fabricated Metals	1,964	631	6,877	804	237	7,905	208	167	10,750	1,821	228	25,280	252	81	3,989	749	95	1,981	262	83	2,209	6,060	1,522	58,991
Nonelectric Mach.	2,222	1,837	2,778	2,496	578	11,862	1,439	395	10,581	1,742	508	16,529	429	221	1,059	208	367	330	304	247	895	8,840	4,153	44,034
Electrical Mach.	1,822	603	2,213	1,607	221	8,961	514	136	6,059	876	237	13,888	425	52	993	478	195	919	246	49	1,014	5,968	1,493	34,047
Transp. Equipment	5,600	2,430	6,222	3,430	211	12,645	936	180	12,086	3,250	261	12,843	275	139	1,523	567	239	1,261	1,171	88	1,792	15,229	3,548	48,372
Textiles & Apparel	532	168	3,281	77	46	10,275	21	13	8,220	100	29	10,470	207	54	2,002	66	41	1,969	124	10	2,405	2,405	361	38,622
Lumber, Wood & Furniture	1,322	91	2,632	35	22	2,763	15	4	3,135	33	33	4,475	5	0	478	5	16	316	5	1	705	1,415	161	14,504
Printing & Publishing	176	153	1,516	125	29	5,003	51	4	4,320	35	6	2,589	5	2	390	6	9	396	4	4	429	401	207	14,643
Stone, Clay & Glass	406	140	1,260	242	14	3,818	252	13	2,897	239	20	6,043	45	7	727	191	19	725	76	5	821	1,451	218	16,291
Instruments	563	219	626	739	101	1,321	399	48	1,976	406	90	1,608	15	21	33	76	42	**	91	26	**	2,289	547	5,564
Other Manufacturing	567	135	1,916	3,205	53	10,541	35	36	3,122	409	63	7,282	5	44	1,093	411	38	645	128	9	630	4,760	378	25,229
Total	21,636	7,323	44,811	16,246	1,934	98,692	5,616	1,195	92,488	10,788	1,854	135,924	2,603	892	16,651	4,236	1,319	18,995	3,381	694	19,039	64,511	15,211	426,600

** missing

Appendix 3 List of Industries (and Concordance)

	BEA Code	SIC Code	SITC Code		
1. Food Products	410	20	013	047	062
			023	048	092
			024	053	099
			032	055	111
			046	061	112
2. Paper and Allied Products	420	26	64		
			251		
3. Chemical and Allied Products	430	28	5		
4. Rubber	440	30	231.2		
			62		
			893		
5. Primary and Fabricated Metals	450	33	67		
			68		
			69		
			812.3		
6. Nonelectrical Machinery	460	35	71		
7. Electrical Machinery	470	36	72		
8. Transportation Equipment	480	37	73		
9. Textiles and Apparel	491	22	65		
		23	84		
			266		
10. Lumber, Wood and Furniture	492	24	63		
		25	243		
			82		
11. Printing and Publishing	493	27	892		
12. Stone, Clay, and Glass Products	495	32	66		
			− 667		
13. Instruments	496	38	86		
			−863		
14. Ordnance, Leather, Tobacco, and Other Manufacturing	494	19	122	891	
	497	21	61	894	
	498	31	667	895	
	499	39	81	897	
			− 812.3	899	
			83	951.0	
			85		

the results. These particular equations should reveal the explanatory power of various combinations of the independent variables chosen from two or all three categories.

The values in brackets are the t-values: those marked by a single asterisk are significant at the 95 percent level, while those marked by a dagger are significant at the 99 percent level.

The last column of each table gives the values of the coefficient of determination.

NOTES

1. Throughout this article, assets and endowments are used interchangeably, and in the Fisherian sense, to mean "anything capable of generating a future income stream" (Johnson 1970).
2. See John H. Dunning, "Trade, Location of Economic Activity and the Multinational Enterprise," pp. 395–418.
3. In this article, distance from foreign markets is treated as a negative *location*-specific endowment.
4. Moreover, since perfect competition and identical production functions between firms were two of the assump-

tions underlying the theories, they were not interested in explaining the international activities of firms—only of countries.

5. For example, unused overheads of the parent company may be supplied to a branch plant at a much lower marginal cost than the average cost of supplying them by a *de novo* firm.

6. For further details and also those which especially arise from *producing* in a foreign location see Dunning (1977) and the references at the end of the Chapter. The most comprehensive theoretical treatment of the internalizing theory of international production is contained in Buckley and Casson (1976).

7. Among these one might mention particularly those of Horst [1972 (a) and (b), 1975]. (In this latter paper the author explicitly acknowledges the importance of internalizing advantages). The study of Wolf (1973) is also particularly pertinent to explain why firms choose to engage in foreign direct investment, rather than other forms of growth. Research on host country data includes: Baumann (1975); Caves (1974); Buckley and Dunning (1976), and Owen (1979).

8. See particularly the studies of Hirsch (1976), Buckley and Pearce (1979), Hawkins and Webbink (1976), Parry (1976). The question of the extent to which trade and foreign investment substitute for each other has been very well explored by Lipsey and Weiss (1973; 1976), Cornell (1973), and Horst (1974).

9. There has been only limited empirical testing of this approach. The Hirsch contribution (1976) is again very relevant. See also Buckley and Dunning (1977).

10. Here the work of Buckley and Casson (1976) is especially relevant.

11. A summary of each of these approaches is contained in an earlier version of this paper: "Trade, Location of Economic Activity and the Multinational Enterprise: Some Empirical Evidence." University of Reading Discussion Papers in *International Investment and Business Studies No. 37*, October 1977.

12. The complications of this assumption will be dealt with later in the paper. See also Horst, 1974.

13. For a more detailed analysis of these data, see Dunning paper quoted in footnote 11.

14. Extracted is the possibility that firms might supply foreign markets from third locations.

15. Consumption figures would have been more appropriate but these figures were not available.

16. For some purposes, we may wish to normalize the ratio $AS + X/IS$ in a particular industry (i), $AS_i + X_i/IS_i$, by dividing the ratio by that for all industry (t), $AS_i + X_t/IS_t$. The result is an index of the comparative rather than the absolute competitive advantage of U.S. firms. This allows cross-country comparisons to be made.

17. But see Dunning and Buckley, 1976.

18. I.e., that some *ownership* advantages are not independent of the *location* or production. See also Dunning, 1979.

19. For a different approach to the measurement of these advantages see Buckley and Casson, 1976.

20. See footnote 8.

REFERENCES

Brown, W. E. "Island of Consensus Power: MNCs in the Theory of the Firm MSU." *Business Topics,* Summer 1976.

Baumann, H. G. "Merger Theory, Property Rights and the Pattern of U.S. Direct Investment in Canada." *Weltwirtschaftliches Archiv III* Heft 4, 1975.

Buckley, P. J., and Casson, M. C. *The Future of the Multinational Enterprise.* London: MacMillan, 1976.

Buckley, P. J., and Dunning, J. H. "The Industrial Structure of U.S. Direct Investment in the U.K." *Journal of International Business Studies,* Summer 1976.

Buckley, P. J., and Pearce, R. D. "Overseas Production and Exporting by the World's Largest Enterprises." *Journal of International Business Studies,* Spring/Summer 1979.

Caves, R. E. "International Corporations: The Industrial Economics of Foreign Investment." *Economica,* February 1971.

Caves, R. E. "The Causes of Direct Investment: Foreign Firms' Shares in Canadian and UK Manufacturing Industries." *Review of Economics and Statistics,* August 1974.

Cornell, R. "Trade of Multinational Firms and Nation's Comparative Advantage." Paper presented to a Conference on Multinational Corporations and Governments, UCLA, November 1973.

Dunning, J. H. "The Determinants of International Production." *Oxford Economic Papers,* November 1973.

Dunning, J. H. "Trade Location of Economic Activity and the Multinational Enterprise. A Search for an Eclectic Approach" in *The International Allocation of Economic Activity,* edited by B. Ohlin, P. O. Hesselborn, and P. J. Wiskman, London: MacMillan, 1977.

Dunning, J. H., and Buckley, P. J. *International Production and Alternative Models of Trade.* Manchester School of Economic and Social Studies 45, December 1977.

Dunning, J. H. "Explaining Changing Patterns of International Production: In Defense of the Eclectic Theory." *Oxford Bulletin of Economics and Statistics,* November 1979.

Hawkins, R., and Webbink, E. S. "Theories of Direct Foreign Investment: A Survey of Empirical Evidence." Unpublished Manuscript.

Hirsch, S. "Capital or Technology? Confronting the Neo-Factor Proportions and Neo-Technology Accounts of International Trade." *Weltwirtschaftliches Archiv 114* Heft. 2, 1974.

Hirsch, S. "An International Trade and Investment Theory of the Firm." *Oxford Economic Papers,* July 1976.

Horst, T. "Firm and Industry Determinants of the Decision to Invest Abroad: An Empirical Study." *Review of Economics and Statistics,* August 1972 (a).

Horst, T. "The Industrial Composition of U.S. Exports and Subsidiary Sales to the Canadian Market." *American Economic Review,* March 1972 (b).

Horst, T. *American Exports and Foreign Direct Investments.* Harvard Institute of Economic Research Discussion 362, May 1974.

Horst, T. "American Investments Abroad: and Domestic Market Power." Brookings Institution: Unpublished, 1975.

Hufbauer, G. C. "The Impact of National Characteristics and Technology on the Commodity Composition of Trade in Manufactured Goods," in *The Technology Factor in International Trade,* edited by R. Vernon. New York: Columbia University Press, 1970.

Hufbauer, G. C., and Adler, M. *Overseas Manufacturing Investment and the Balance of Payments.* U.S. Treasury Department, 1968.

Johnson, H. "The Efficiency and Welfare Implications of the International Corporation," in *The International Corporation,* edited by C. P. Kindleberger. Cambridge: M.I.T. Press, 1970.

Knickerbocker, F. T. *Oligopolistic Reaction and the Multinational Enterprise.* Cambridge, MA: Harvard University Press, 1973.

Kojima, K. "Macro-Economic Approach to Foreign Direct Investment." *Hitotsubashi Journal of Economics,* June 1973.

Lipsey, P. E., and Weiss, M. Y. "Multinational Firms and the Factor Intensity of Trade." National Bureau of Economic Research, Working Paper No. 8, 1973.

Lipsey, R. E., and Weiss, M. Y. "Exports and Foreign Investment in the Pharmaceutical Industry." National Bureau of Economic Research, Working Paper No. 87 (Revised), 1976 (a).

Lipsey, R. E., and Weiss, M. Y. "Exports and Foreign Investment in Manufacturing Industries." National Bureau of Economic Research. Working Paper No. 13 (Revised), 1976 (b).

Nurkse, R. "The Problems of International Investment Today in the Light of 19th Century Experience." *Economic Journal,* December 1954.

Owen, R. F. *Interindustry Determinants of Foreign Direct Investments: A Perspective Emphasizing the Canadian Experience.* Working Paper in International Economics (G-79-03), Princeton University, 1979.

Parry, T. C. "Trade and Non-Trade Performance of U.S. Manufacturing Industry: 'Revealed' Comparative Advantage." *Manchester School of Economics and Social Studies,* June 1973.

Parry, T. C. *Methods of Servicing Overseas Markets: The UK Owned Pharmaceutical Study.* University of Reading Discussion Paper (Series 2) 27, 1976.

Political and Economic Planning. "Atlantic Tariffs and Trade." A Report by PEP. Winchester, MA: Allen and Unwin, 1967.

Rugman, A. *International Diversification and the Multinational Enterprise.* Lexington, MA: Lexington Books, 1979.

Stevens, C. V. "Determinants of Investment," in *Economic Analysis and the Multinational Enterprise,* edited by J. H. Dunning. Winchester, MA: Allen and Unwin, 1974.

Swedenborg, B. *The Multinational Operations of Swedish Firms: An Analysis of Determinants and Effects.* Stockholm: Almquist & Wiksell International, 1979.

U.S. Tariff Commission. *Implications of Multinational Firms for World Trade and Investment for US Trade and Labor.* Washington, DC: Government Printing Office, 1973.

Vaupel, J. *Characteristics and Motivations of the U.S. Corporations which Invest Abroad.* Unpublished ms.

Vernon, R. "International Investment and International Trade in the Product Cycle." *Quarterly Journal of Economics,* May 1966.

Vernon, R. "The Location of Economic Activity," in *Economic Analysis and the Multinational Enterprise,* edited by J. H. Dunning. Winchester, MA: Allen and Unwin, 1974.

Wolf, B. "Industrial Diversification and Internationalization: Some Empirical Evidence. *Journal of Industrial Economics,* December 1977.

28

Match Manufacturing Policies and Product Strategy
Robert Stobaugh
Piero Telesio

• • •

Deere & Company acquired subsidiaries in Germany in 1956 and in France in 1960 to serve European markets with low-horsepower tractors. Not until the mid-1960s, however, did the company adopt manufacturing policies for its production facilities in Europe that suited its strategy for competing in worldwide tractor markets. The delay cost Deere valuable market share.

Warwick Electronics was at one time the only supplier of color televisions to Sears, Roebuck and Co. and depended on Sears for close to 75% of its sales. As technology changed and price competition increased, Warwick initially proved unable to manufacture good quality products at low cost. Its corrective actions—product redesign and the transfer of production to a Mexican facility—were too little and too late. Sears had lost confidence and turned elsewhere for suppliers. Warwick's losses increased, and it finally sold its television business to Sanyo, a Japanese manufacturer.

Both Deere and Warwick got into trouble because they too slowly realized that a change in product strategy alters the tasks of a manufacturing system. These tasks, which can be stated in terms of requirements for cost, product flexibility, volume flexibility, product performance, and product consistency, determine which manufacturing policies are appropriate. As the

tasks shift over time, so must the policies covering:

The location and scale of manufacturing facilities.
The choice of manufacturing process.
The span, or degree of vertical integration, of each manufacturing facility.
The use of R&D units.
The control of the production system.
The licensing of technology.

In this article we draw on the results of a research project at the Harvard Business School to provide a conceptual framework with which managers can closely match manufacturing policies with product strategies. (See the ruled insert for the details of that project.) Although this framework, which we outline in the Exhibit, has relevance for all companies, we focus on organizations operating in the international environment because of the many added complexities such operations entail.

Four notes of caution. First, as we explain the Exhibit, we talk as if each of a company's major products had a separate manufacturing system with its own production tasks and policies. This is often, but not always, the case. Second, we identify product strategies by their dominant thrust (technology, for example) even though other considerations (marketing, say, or cost) are also important. Third, we do not consider divestment as an explicit strategy but as a response either to a strategy gone wrong or to the maturing of a product. Finally, the various policies recommended in the Exhibit are no substitute for a sound and detailed analysis of each company's situation. Our aim here is to provide a tool to guide a decision maker's thinking, not a list of all-purpose answers.

Source: Robert Stobaugh and Piero Telesio, "Match Manufacturing Policies and Product Strategy," *Harvard Business Review,* March/April 1983, pp. 113–120. Copyright © 1983 by the President and Fellows of Harvard College; all rights reserved.

TECHNOLOGY-DRIVEN STRATEGY

A strategy based on product technology (the first column in the Exhibit) involves serving high-income markets with a flow of new, preferably unique, high-performance and high-technology products. Industries like engineering plastics and biogenetics, for example, rely on manufacturing systems that are sufficiently flexible to accommodate frequent changes in products as well as their rapid introduction to the market. Because accurate sales projections are difficult to make, volume flexibility is important; because the product itself is the major competitive weapon, manufacturing costs are not of primary importance.

These manufacturing tasks have a major impact on the location of plants. Good communication with, and swift response to, a changing market for high-technology products ordinarily means locating the initial plant in a high-income country with a large market—that is, in one of the industrialized nations. Plants have usually first been built in the home market of the innovating company—often in America, but sometimes in Europe or Japan, where the necessary pool of skilled labor exists. And since process flexibility and product performance are more important than low costs, that skilled labor is affordable. This pattern is slowly changing, as modern technology allows rapid communication with distant markets and the proliferation of foreign subsidiaries permits the simultaneous introduction of products in a number of markets.

Establishing Facilities Abroad

Exports from the home-market plant can open markets abroad; but as demand grows and as imitators appear, some foreign markets become large enough to require local production. At first, the spread of manufacturing units abroad is usually limited to countries with high-income markets; as sales rise elsewhere, production facilities eventually follow. In size, the initial foreign plant must be able to handle the rapid growth that often comes early in a product's life. Until needed for the local market, this extra capacity can serve the markets in neighboring countries. In some instances, of course, scale economies are sufficiently important that the initial plant can serve the world market for an indefinite period; in other cases, low wages and high productivity in the innovating country—Japan, for example—are reason enough to keep manufacturing at home.

The need for great flexibility in a technology-driven strategy often limits the span of these manufacturing activities. Purchasing components from other companies—or other manufacturing facilities of the parent company—passes on to them some of the risks of rapid change in products and volumes. Early in the life of a product, foreign investment might merely involve assembly; but as output grows, so does the need for other production steps, which lead to full-scale manufacture. The production network that results will include a number of facilities, varying in size, location, and span of operations.

IBM's choice of manufacturing policies nicely illustrates these points. Market considerations determined the order in which the company established its foreign operations (1925 in Germany, 1935 in Italy, and 1950 in Brazil) and the type of products each turns out (the more advanced goods being produced first in the larger, higher-income markets). In the mid-1970s, for example, IBM used about half the capacity of its German facility to build central processing units but only a quarter of its Italian facility and none of its Brazilian facility.

IBM plants that serve local or regional markets have assembly operations only and thus relatively small capacity, but most overseas operations (about 80%) serve worldwide needs. In Europe, plants cover virtually all production steps, although some specialize in making semifinished parts in order to achieve scale economies. In developing countries in Asia and the Pacific, plants import raw boards and cards from IBM facilities elsewhere but do the rest themselves. In Latin America, they are mostly devoted to assembly work.

Driven by product technology, IBM does not attempt to substitute labor for capital in its plants abroad. Because most of its foreign facilities are located in high-wage countries and because new products do not usually compete on the basis of price, small reductions in manufacturing costs are unlikely to boost sales and profits. IBM keeps to this policy even in countries with low labor costs—that is, it chooses to

rely on virtually identical processes, tooling, and equipment throughout the world, save where there is a need to accommodate variations in the grade of local raw materials.

Managing Technology

When R&D units are associated with plants abroad, they often assist in the transfer of complex technology, the adjustment of processes to local raw materials, and the adaptation of prod-

---

Research on international technology transfer and production

This article is based on an extensive research project at the Harvard Business School on international technology transfer and production in more than 100 multinational enterprises. This project, directed by Mr. Stobaugh, has led to a number of studies, including:

Michael A. Amsalem **Technology Choice in Developing Countries: The Impact of Differences in Factor Costs** DBA thesis, Harvard Business School, 1978 and his book, *Technology Choice in Developing Countries: The Impact of Differences in Factor Costs* Cambridge: M.I.T. Press, forthcoming).

Henri de Bodinat **Influence in the Multinational Corporation: The Case of Manufacturing** DBA thesis, Harvard Business School, 1975.

Dong Cho **International Facility Planning: Regarding the Application of Scientific Approaches** DBA thesis, Harvard Business School, 1977.

Richard W. Moxon **Offshore Production in the Less Developed Countries by American Electronics Companies** DBA thesis, Harvard Business School, 1973 and **Offshore Production in the Less Developed Countries—A Case Study of Multinationality in the Electronics Industry** *The Bulletin,* Institute of Finance, New York University, Nos. 98–99, July 1974

Claude L. Pomper **International Facilities Planning: An Integrated Approach** DBA thesis, Harvard Business School, 1974 and his book *International Investment Planning: An Integrated Approach* (New York: North-Holland Publishing, 1976)

Robert C. Ronstadt **R&D Abroad: The Creation and Evolution of Foreign Research and Development Activities of U.S.-Based Multinational Enterprises** DBA thesis, Harvard Business School, 1975 and his book, *Research and Development Abroad by U.S. Multinationals* (New York: Praeger Publications, 1977.)

Piero Telesio **Foreign Licensing Policy in Multinational Enterprises** DBA thesis, Harvard Business School, 1977 and his book, *Technology Licensing and Multinational Enterprises* (New York: Praeger Publications, 1979)

Brent D. Wilson **The Investment of Foreign Subsidiaries by U.S. Multinational Companies** DBA thesis, Harvard Business School, 1979 and his book, *Disinvestment of Foreign Subsidiaries* (Ann Arbor, Michigan: UMI Research Press, 1980)

See also Robert B. Stobaugh and Louis T. Wells, Jr., editors. *International Technology Flows,* for several forthcoming articles based on some of these and related studies, including G. James Keddie **Adoptions of Production Technique by Industrial Firms in Indonesia** Ph.D. thesis, Harvard University, 1975; and Donald Lecraw **Choice of Technology in Low Wage Countries: The Case of Thailand** Ph.D. thesis, Harvard University, 1976.

ucts to local markets. These units sometimes produce major modifications in products or even completely new products—for world, as well as local, markets. When, for example, IBM established its first foreign R&D units in the 1930s in the United Kingdom, Germany, and France, their purpose was to transfer technologies to IBM's European subsidiaries. Eventually, these three units, plus another five added between 1964 and 1970 in Europe, Canada, and Japan, began to serve the needs of IBM worldwide.

Because careful nurturing of process technology is essential to an effective technology-driven strategy, policy decisions are properly the responsibility of headquarters. Day-to-day manufacturing decisions, however, can be left to local managers. With the growth of manufacturing facilities abroad, shipments among international subsidiaries increase, and a more formalized control function becomes necessary. At IBM headquarters, personnel in international manufacturing, who numbered only about 10 at the end of the 1950s, grew to more than 200 by the mid-1970s. In the words of one IBM manager, "We are much more procedure oriented than we were, and of course procedures require administration."

And what of the many technologies that an innovation-based strategy generates? Licensing the more important of them is often unwise since it may stimulate price competition in some of the licenser's markets or create barriers to the establishment of a worldwide manufacturing network. In industries like chemicals, pharmaceuticals, and electronics, however, companies often exchange licenses, not to supplement foreign investment income but to maintain the technical dynamism of the industry. Indeed, IBM's policy is quite liberal: it licenses freely to unaffiliated companies.

Of course, no strategy that relies on a flow of new high-technology products within a product line can last forever. Sooner or later, markets and technologies mature. At times, a major change in the product may retard the maturation process, but price competition almost inevitably becomes important and competitive emphasis shifts to process changes that lower manufacturing costs. When this happens, licensing technology as a source of revenue takes on greater appeal. Maintaining flexibility, though still important, gradually takes a backseat to achieving economies of scale through larger, more automated plants and greater specialization of both work force and equipment. And these developments, in turn, lead to heightened control of operations by headquarters. Increased specialization and automation of manufacturing facilities, along with greater intracompany flows of components, make a manufacturing system more predictable, hence more susceptible to—as well as more needful of—centralized control.

MARKETING-INTENSIVE STRATEGY

With products like soft drinks, detergents, and over-the-counter drugs, a marketing-intensive strategy (the second column in the Exhibit) relies on heavy advertising and selling expenditures to distinguish a company's offerings from those of its competitors. Although marketing, not low-cost production, provides the competitive edge for such product lines, manufacturing has vital support to provide. At a minimum, it must ensure that the right mix of dependable-quality products is available as each market requires.

A manufacturing presence in these markets permits a company to respond quickly to changes in the nature or volume of demand. One manufacturer of canned soup, for example, adjusts recipes to the tastes of local markets and adapts the manufacturing process to make use of locally available ingredients. The risk of not being responsive to such changes outweighs any cost benefits of centralizing production into one large-scale facility designed to serve several markets. In fact, cost reductions usually have little effect either on profit margins (because most differentiated, or branded, products are priced well above manufacturing costs) or on sales (because the volume of such products is relatively insensitive to price).

Not surprisingly, both the scale and the span of foreign plants grow with the size of local markets. As these markets expand, otherwise limited activities give way to complete operations requiring little outside sourcing of intermediate goods. This pattern—product flexibility in the early stages of market penetration leading to increased dependability of supply as operations approach full integration—is clearly evident in the development of Colgate-Palmolive Company's manufacturing plants in more than 40 foreign countries.

Since most of the output of these facilities is sold in local markets, the first facility to be built in each country is usually for the production of toothpaste, for the minimum economic plant size is small. Next follows a larger investment for the manufacture of soap, and, then, a still larger investment for the manufacture of detergents. Over time, as the local markets grow, fully integrated production systems replace contract manufacturing.

Companies that follow a strategy of product differentiation have little need to do R&D abroad—save to adapt products to local tastes and specifications. Nor is licensing technology an issue. Companies with this kind of strategy do not often possess technologies that are attractive to potential licensees. More to the point, experience shows that they would rarely be willing to accept the risk, which is inherent in licensing to outsiders, of losing some control over marketing. Colgate, in fact, has virtually no licensing agreements.

Furthermore, since intracompany shipments are low, centralizing the control of the manufacturing system is not necessary. To be sure, major decisions about location and capacity should receive the attention of headquarters management, but day-to-day operating decisions are best left to local managers. When, however, the quality of a product in one market affects sales in another—as is the case with, say, pharma-ceuticals—then strong central control of product quality is imperative.

LOW-COST STRATEGIES

With a mature product that is unsuitable for a marketing-intensive strategy, a manager must either divest the business or manufacture the product at the lowest possible cost for a given level of quality.

Several approaches to this low-cost strategy are available: using large-scale plants to achieve scale economies, locating facilities in countries with low labor costs, and placing facilities so as to guarantee them access to critical inputs other than labor, such as cheap and abundant energy. (See the three right-hand columns in the Exhibit.)

Scale Economies

When achieving scale economies is important, plants should, as a rule, be sited in large national markets or in countries with access to them. (Of course, it is possible for a small-market country, if protected by trade barriers, to be an attractive location.) The need for scale should also limit the span of manufacturing in any country to the items needed in large volumes.

In the late 1960s, for example, Otis Elevator Company, now a division of United Technologies, started a program of plant specialization within the European Common Market. As Otis explained in an annual report, its low-cost strategy required it to place greater emphasis on "standardized models . . . and on mass production of components in specialized plants." German and Italian facilities specialized in producing motor units and control mechanisms; the French, in cabin components and foundry parts. High freight costs on assembled elevators and the need to tailor the elevator cabins to the needs of each customer led the company to do final assembly in the markets where the elevators were sold.

Another effect of a scale-driven strategy is to discourage the substitution of labor for capital, not least because in high-volume operations the proportion of labor costs to total costs is usually low. Substitution may actually reduce scale economies and increase costs. Capital-intensive methods are preferable when reliable delivery and consistent quality are important and when components are regularly transshipped for further assembly—a common state of affairs under a low-cost strategy.

Common, too, is the minimal need such companies have for local R&D facilities in their overseas operations. Standardized products allow little scope for product R&D. Occasionally process R&D is needed in an effort to lower costs.

Companies following a low-cost strategy need the tight control of headquarters to ensure that costs are indeed being kept low. And when there are transshipments among a company's plants, sufficient control must be exercised over shipping schedules and product quality to guarantee smooth operations in the various facilities. Otis's European headquarters in Paris sets the quantities and prices on intracompany shipments and issues instructions for production scheduling, quality, cost standards, inventory, transportation of products, and materials storage. Under such conditions, it makes sense to license technology only when the technology owner does not enjoy a dominant position in the industry and when competing technologies have a number of sellers.

Otis, for example, has no licensing agreements with other companies. "It is the policy of the company," Otis reports, "not to license competitors or potential competitors in areas that are open to company sales. Since we have sales operations, either through subsidiaries or agents, in practically all countries outside the Communist bloc, this policy effectively precludes licensing to outsiders."

Low-Cost Labor

Companies seeking low labor costs should, of course, locate manufacturing facilities in countries with low wage rates. Other relevant con-

siderations include transportation costs, the presence of an industrial infrastructure, the availability of trainable workers, the level of political risk, and, of course, the outlook for growth in wage rates. The size of local markets is less important, for the products are not usually sold in the country where they are produced. Nor must the scale of operations be large or its span extensive. Investments should be in the labor-intensive steps of the production process, which do not usually enjoy the economies of scale of the more capital-intensive steps.

With its home radios, General Electric follows a low-cost strategy based on manufacture in low-wage countries. In response to a threat to its domestic market for radios by foreign-label imports, the Audio Electronics Department opened foreign plants, first in Ireland and then in Hong Kong and Singapore. These supplied both finished radios and consumer electronics components for import into the United States. GE engineers made a number of process adaptations in these plants to expand their use of labor—among them, the cutting, sanding, finishing, transfer, and packaging of parts by hand instead of by machine.

As with all low-cost strategies, company headquarters should ordinarily exert tight control on the integration of manufacturing operations. Quality standards must correspond with the needs of the system and with delivery schedules; manufacturing costs must be kept at a minimum. For example, all major operating decisions for the Audio Electronics Department's overseas activities were made in the United States. The critical tasks were to ensure good quality, delivery, and cost. In the words of one manufacturing manager, "If you cannot hit those pricing points with a dependable product delivered on time, you're dead in this business."

A word of caution about the low-cost labor strategy: a company should not neglect developments in the technology of automation. Rapidly increasing wage rates abroad might make automation attractive, especially given the swift advances now being made in that technology. Indeed, the Audio Electronics Department found that automation became necessary in Hong Kong and Singapore as wage rates rose.

Other Low-Cost Inputs

Here, the key task for a manufacturing system is to extract the maximum cost advantage from a critical resource such as raw materials or energy. Access to a secure and low-cost supply of raw material is an important reason why Exxon, Mobil, and Celanese, for example, are investing in petrochemical facilities in Saudi Arabia. Their facilities will produce commodity petrochemicals, most of which will be processed into end products outside Saudi Arabia.

As a rule, it is often desirable to locate such facilities in countries containing the critical resource, whether to save freight costs or to obtain a dependable supply. It also makes sense to limit the span of operations to the stages of production that make use of the low-cost input—unless the final market for the products is in the same country. Plant size will follow an industry's economies of scale, much as the choice of technology will follow the varying quality of raw materials. To the extent that local facilities are to be closely integrated with other plants in the system, important decisions about technology and operations will flow from headquarters; but if output is to be sold primarily in the local market, the need for centralized control diminishes.

LESSONS FOR MANAGERS

As we have tried to show, various manufacturing policies are appropriate for different product strategies. Perhaps the example of several domestic operations will help drive this point home. Apple Computer, which has a technol-ogy-driven strategy, initially selected the span of its manufacturing to include only an assembly operation; it has not yet moved into simple fabrication. Mohasco, a carpet manufacturer, adopted a marketing-intensive strategy for the West Coast and located a manufacturing facility in California to respond better to the styling changes required by West Coast markets. Gulf Oil follows a strategy of low-cost raw materials for its ethylene business. Its U.S. manufacturing facilities are on the Gulf Coast, where the raw material (ethane) is cheap.

Failure to match manufacturing policy and product strategy can have disastrous results in a domestic business. The construction of nuclear pressure vessels involves a technology-driven strategy, yet Babcock & Wilcox located a new manufacturing facility in a cornfield in southwestern Indiana in order to tap "an unspoiled labor market." In spite of a massive training program to turn farmers into skilled welders and machinists, B&W suffered for years from the lack of a skilled, disciplined work force. As a result, poor quality and slow delivery forced customers to look to competitors.

Strategies, remember, must function in dynamic settings: a product based, for example, on a technology-driven strategy of innovation often matures. As a result, managers must be ever alert to the possibilities of change as they go about the work essential to the formulation of manufacturing policies. In practice, they should:

Define a product strategy.

Identify the critical tasks of a manufacturing system geared to serve that strategy.

Set up, adapt, and control the manufacturing system so as to perform these tasks.

Periodically reevaluate the ability of the manufacturing system to perform the required tasks.

Stay abreast of changes in product strategy so as to modify the manufacturing policy according.

29

Global Sourcing: Offshore Investment Strategy for the 1980s
Daniel F. Hefler

• • •

American manufacturers confronting new competition from countries in Asia, Eastern Europe, South America, and elsewhere must seek lower-cost sources in order for their products and components to remain competitive. Throughout the world, however, the interplay of technical, social, economic, and political forces has caused offshore investment problems and opportunities to become more complex, more interrelated. One strategy that companies can employ to meet their strategic goals and objectives, and to maintain or gain in their competitive positions, is Global Sourcing. The term is defined as the more efficient use of worldwide human, material, energy, and capital resources.

For centuries, people have crisscrossed the globe. So, too, have ideas, life-styles, capital, technology, and products. The interaction of economies no less than that of cultures has been continuous, pervasive, and dynamic. Quantitatively, of course, today differs from yesterday in the volume and speed of interactions. But tomorrow will be no simple, linear extrapolation of today. Change is the single constant now, and complexity is increasing factorially.

During the remainder of the 1980s, transnational companies entering world markets and domestic firms serving home markets will find themselves facing unrelenting competitive pressures. Those firms and industries no longer capable of competing by internal development, by advancements in manufacturing technology, or

Source: Daniel F. Hefler, "Global Sourcing: Offshore Investment Strategy for the 1980s," pp. 7–12. Reprinted by permission from the *Journal of Business Strategy,* Summer 1981, Volume 2, Number 1. Copyright © 1981, Warren, Gorham & Lamont, Inc., 210 South Street, Boston, Mass. All rights reserved.

by taking advantage of global sources will falter and, in some cases, fail. Thus, Global Sourcing is one of the strategies that manufacturers everywhere may employ to survive and grow.

Global Sourcing is not a matter of locating minerals and hydrocarbons. The match of raw material requirements with particular offshore sources has little competitive significance in our time. For both basic and strategic materials, the market is worldwide. Competing manufacturers, whatever their national origin, play in the same court in this game with countries endowed with natural resources. Moreover, for manufacturers of high-technology products, such as electronics, the raw-material value is a minor element in the cost of the final product delivered to the point of sale.

There are three distinct strategies for Global Sourcing. The first is finding qualified vendors for the needed materials or products. The second is entering a joint venture relationship. And the third is making a 100 percent equity investment in a foreign country.

Companies engaged in Global Sourcing strategies with short-term requirements may favor vendor relationships over those necessitating long-term capital and corporate commitments.

Companies, both intermediate and large, enter joint venture relationships when their capital resources are better used in domestic operations; when the offshore partner seeks a technological transfer and the host government offers more incentives to this form of business; and, finally, when the foreign partner has access to markets that would otherwise be denied.

Companies using the third strategy have requirements that are long-term. They have no restraints on capital resources, and, most important, they wish to control access to their technology (such as integrated circuit design and production).

In developing Global Sourcing strategies, factors that must be considered are: manufacturing costs; the cost of various resources (labor, skills, materials); availability of infrastructure (including transportation, communications, energy); the industrial environment; the ease of working with the government of the country; the political and economic environments, and the stability of these factors. Because of the dynamic relationship of the factors, future events can bankrupt a strategy prepared only on the basis of current situations.

HOW GLOBAL SOURCING PROJECTIONS WORK

Global Sourcing can be used to project the results of these strategies into the future.

Brazil

Brazil purchases large turbines and generators for electrical generation. Countries are always conscious of their trade balances with other countries, but Brazil is also sensitive to its balance of trade with major transnational companies. In Brazil's proposal to one transnational, the government would continue to purchase the high-technology turbines and generators that it is not in a position to produce itself. In exchange, and to balance the trade, the government wanted the transnational to import personal-care products, such as hair dryers, curling irons, and small kitchen appliances manufactured locally. The logic was that Brazil was sufficiently well developed to produce these items for the company, and this would balance the trade between Brazil and the company.

Managers of the small-appliance division of the transnational used the Global Sourcing practice to demonstrate to their executives as well as to Brazilian officials that even though the proposition appeared logical at the current time, the future looked different. The model predicted that within three or four years the in-

ternal costs of Brazilian manufacture as well as transportation costs would cause the small-appliance division to pay a premium for the Brazilian product. In effect, the small-appliance division would be subsidizing the transnational's own turbine and generator operation. The Global Sourcing model prevented the transnational from losing millions of dollars, and Brazil avoided the uncomfortable relationship that would have developed.

The Europe-Asia Connection

Another corporation, one with manufacturing locations around the world, used Global Sourcing to resolve a long-standing issue within the corporation. European manufacturing executives of the firm acknowledged the lower labor costs now prevailing in Asia but believed that the same product could be manufactured at the same cost in Europe because of higher yields and greater productivity. The conflict was resolved with a sourcing compromise. A 15 to 20 percent savings could be realized by manufacturing portions of the product in Asia and performing the final assembly in Europe.

Southeast Asia

In a third case, the prediction of inflationary trends in a Southeast Asian country by Global Sourcing was used in part to convince this nation to reinstate its economic policies of the previous decade. At the beginning of the 1970s, it had set an objective of letting wages increase in real terms only to the extent that productivity could be increased. Following the "oil shock" in the mid-1970s, the government relaxed its principles. Costs began rising at an inflationary rate. An American company showed the government the Global Sourcing projections. They portrayed the country becoming a differentially higher-cost place in which to manufacture than some of the other competing locations in Asia. The outcome of this revelation to the government was a return to former policies and a lessening of the possibility of high manufacturing costs.

Evaluating Competitive Position

On the other side of the world, European electronics manufacturers are convinced that their home markets for integrated circuits will outstrip that of the United States in the next five years. But will they, or Japan and other parts of Asia, cash in on this growth? The European firms want to evaluate their future competitive position.

One European firm recognizing that its consumer products are currently more complex in design with a lower level of automation, as well as in disparity in elements relating to scale, quality, and productivity, used Global Sourcing to test various scenarios and the impact of accelerated investment in its industry to catch up and then keep pace with Japanese and Asian producers. While not a simple task, nor one low in cost, the effort may make it possible for this European manufacturer to remain viable. Despite the current recessionary environment, some European companies are now making investments against the business cycle through an aggressive program of automation and upgrading of technology and technical performance in their products.

Some American Cases

Another case, less broad in scope, concerns an American integrated-circuit manufacturer. It is presently considering the prospects of a joint venture with a company in the Philippines. The American firm already has a manufacturing facility in a Southeast Asian country. It is using Global Sourcing to help determine the location for another facility to augment capacity requirements and also to ameliorate the political risk of being in a Southeast Asian country. Dual sourcing, incidentally, is an overwhelming strategy of virtually all semiconductor manufacturers. The manufacturer's drive is to spread the risks between different political systems and different economic environments. Global Sourcing practices are being utilized to examine costs between now and 1985, and a cash-flow computer program that looks ahead at a variety of ten-

year technoeconomic scenarios is examining investment incentives and the intricacies of deciding between sole ownership and a joint venture.

A final example is the use of Global Sourcing to evaluate manufacturing costs between now and 1985 for locations in Taiwan, the Philippines, Indonesia, Malaysia, Singapore, Thailand, and Sri Lanka. The study is being made for an American company. Additionally, the cash-flow program is being employed to look at the impact of investment incentive as well as the political risks that may be involved. Use of Global Sourcing to screen countries, regions, and areas, of course, saves substantial efforts required for on-site evaluations.

WHAT LIES AHEAD

Generalizing from forecasts made by the Global Sourcing model, with its probability distributions drawn from a multiplicity of inputs, we conclude that U.S. companies will continue to invest in offshore plants through the 1980s. This applies particularly to manufacturers of electronic and light mechanical products. If savings in direct labor costs were the only reason for offshore investment, we might expect a reversal of the trends of the last decade. It is true that the advantage some offshore workers now have over their American counterparts is diminishing as their wages, measured in real terms, increase and as their own economies mature. But corporate investment decisions are motivated by advantages in market access and government incentives as well as direct savings in labor.

Many companies will continue to ship virtually all their materials and supplies to such countries as the Philippines, Indonesia, and Malaysia, and will ship the assembled products either back to the parent company or directly to distribution centers and customers. Most firms involved in this so-called ''soldering iron'' or ''microscope'' manufacturing technology will remain 100 percent foreign-owned and will seek locations supplying the lowest-cost labor or the most attractive incentives packages, despite any imperfections in the host country's infrastructure.

The Continuing Labor Differential

Even though the offshore labor differential is diminishing in relation to that of the United States, it still will be significant in 1984. Salaries of local managers, supervisors, engineers, and technicians (many with degrees from American universities and some with working experience in our country) will be as much as 80 percent less than their counterparts here. The differential in wages for direct labor will compress also, but there is far greater headroom in this case. The cost to employ an Asian worker today can be as low as one-twentieth the comparable U.S. wage. This disparity cannot be dismissed as a consequence of low productivity. When the enhancing effects of automation, mechanization, and all other factors are excluded (except those related to ethnic, social, climatic, and cultural influences), relative manual productivity is similar. With U.S. production workers rated at 100, Korea is 110, and Hong Kong and Taiwan 105. Ireland, Malaysia, Singapore, and the Philippines are 100. Others in a 12-nation study are Brazil, Indonesia, Mexico, and Thailand; all of these are 95. The conclusion is that productivity in any given location is probably more a function of local management than strictly worker-related. No apparent basis has been found for differentiating worker productivity on the basis of race or ethnic background, because workers of different racial and ethnic descent working side by side within a given culture achieve the same levels of productivity.

Tax Advantages and Government Incentives

Aside from attractive labor costs, both tax advantages and broad incentives packages have long been offered by governments to induce investments. Such "pioneer status" for industries afforded them tax holidays for as long as twelve years. By 1973, however, as the seemingly endless tide of new investment continued,

incentives were withdrawn for certain sectors of industry, particularly labor-intensive ones, and many countries began to require that investors provide higher levels of technology and permit greater local participation. When foreign investment faltered during and after the recession of the mid-1970s, many countries quietly restored some of these incentives and relaxed disincentives such as local participation. Today, in some countries, a governmental board of investment (or its counterpart under another name) possesses various discretionary powers by law and/or by interpretation of the law. Such a circumstance allows negotiation of various incentives critical to an investment decision. Where the law prohibits a particular incentive, it is sometimes possible to substitute one or more other benefits of equal value through techniques such as cash grants, favorable terms on loans, or others.

Export Processing Zones Come of Age

Most countries are now specifying new locations of Export Processing Zones (EPZ) for their own economic strategies, and this will have an increased effect on investment. An EPZ, which can range in area from several blocks to square miles, permits a variety of operations on consigned materials and components and sometimes consigned manufacturing equipment while avoiding regulations and paper work required for manufacturing operations in the rest of the country. Originally, such zones were situated in or near the largest cities. Malaysia now refuses to establish new EPZs around Kuala Lumpur, offering them instead in the northeastern peninsula. Similarly, the Philippines is locating such zones outside Manila.

Whether to take advantage of EPZs or for other economic reasons, companies already located in cosmopolitan centers will make increasing use of satellite plants in more remote areas of the offshore country involved. While the labor supply for these plants will be local, the managers, middle managers, engineers, and technicians will remain based in urban centers, commuting to the satellite operation as frequently as necessary.

New Activities on the Horizon

Also in the 1980s, companies with previous experience operating offshore factories will be making somewhat different kinds of investments in order to draw more significantly upon the local infrastructure and labor supply. Beyond carrying out simple assembly functions, these factories will take on activities previously reserved for the parent operation in the same country. Such responsibilities will include quality control, quality assurance, final testing, crating, marking, shipping the product to the end user, and, in some cases, invoicing the customer.

These types of operations are particularly suitable to Ireland, which supplies the European Common Market; Mexico and Brazil, which supply both domestic markets and the Latin American Free Trade Area; and Hong Kong, Singapore, Korea, and Taiwan, which serve world markets. Semiconductor and consumer electronics manufacturers have led the way in such investments. Major high-technology companies, including manufacturers of telecommunications equipment and computers, are now turning out their products, or setting up manufacturing operations, in locations such as Taiwan, Ireland, Brazil, Mexico, and Hong Kong. The trend to export overhead activities and costs will accelerate as companies recognize the opportunities and as host countries develop the skills and infrastructure necessary to support greater technological and manufacturing complexity.

The High-Technology Era

Another trend is offshore investment in products that incorporates high levels of software, design documentation, testing, and, in some cases, field service. It will become increasingly feasible for companies to consider offshore design and manufacture of higher-technology products. They will be able to draw upon local managers, engineers, and technicians capable of the nonrepetitive design and test functions involved in such products.

One example of this type of final operation will be facilities for manufacturing integrated circuits and other semiconductors all the way from mask fabrication through diffusion to packaging, testing, and shipment. It has long been thought that the initial fabrication steps of semiconductors involving diffusion could not be performed in countries where technology was less developed than in the country of the technology-holding company, but this opinion is changing. Device design and mask fabrication probably will be the last steps to be transferred offshore, but even these functions may be transferable if anticipated economic or technical advantages can be realized. Along with these new manufacturing facilities, local suppliers of hard goods, machine tools, and basic materials are gaining a foothold. Ultimately, they will compete with U.S. producers.

Efficient Use of Energy

As companies in the 1980s pay closer attention to the total costs of making their products, their concerns about the availability and cost of energy will direct them to manufacture in locations that offer the most efficient use of the resource. Conversion of semifinished materials to their final form as close as possible to the marketplace will save energy used for transportation. Also, choices in manufacturing process technologies will be influenced by how efficiently they use energy. For instance, more metals and plastics will be formed instead of cut. This will reduce the amount of scrap and also the cost of transporting it to recycling sites.

THE INS AND OUTS OF GLOBAL SOURCING

The preceding accounts of the ability of Global Sourcing to rationalize the future despite the rapidity of change in economic climates throughout the world might seem Faustian.

However, the computer program and its data base are no sorcerer's apprentice. They draw upon thirty years of management experience with government and industrial clients in Europe, Asia, Africa, and the Western Hemisphere.

Also, to share the burden in developing and maintaining the data base for Global Sourcing, we take into account research efforts that our clients make. Some companies have substantial research facilities of their own and are recognized internationally for their capabilities. Cooperation permits all participants in the program to benefit from the larger effort that is then reflected in the data base and forecasts.

Tapping the Computer

Global Sourcing practices cover a computer program for simulating, evaluating, comparing, and forecasting worldwide costs for electronics, electrical, and light mechanical industries. The program includes predictions and forecasts for all of the cost factors involved in manufacturing operations performed by these industries in fifteen countries. Global Sourcing is an enhancement and expansion of earlier practices that began in 1975. The time frame now covers 1980 through 1985, a span which permits users of the model to make cost projections five years into the future with 1980 as the base year.

Cost and Materials Forecast

Data include forecasts of the total employment costs for workers in the specified industries as well as for technical staffs and managers. In predicting future employment costs, Global Sourcing takes into account not only wages paid directly to workers but also all fringe benefits in the form of holidays, vacations, taxes, and bonuses. It further includes worker productivity and production hours actually worked. The wage forecasts are made for eight different skill levels, ranging from unskilled labor through skilled labor, technical and engineering support, to middle managers. Some of the job categories are: unskilled laborer, semiskilled laborer, technician/tool and die pattern maker, junior and senior engineer, and foreman or second-level supervisor.

Materials forecasts incorporated in the data base cover more than forty items such as gray iron, aluminum, zinc, electrolytic copper, gold, silver, nickel, chromium, epoxy, Mylar, and tantalum. Semifinished materials and component forecasts are made for thirty items, such as integrated circuits, transistors, resistors, capacitors, transformers, cathode ray tubes, circuit boards, ball and roller bearings, zinc and aluminum die castings, gears and sprockets, electric motors, and automatic screw machine products. Forecasts of other materials and components are made for individual clients.

Global Sourcing provides forecasts of rates of inflation and fluctuations in exchange rates, such as each country's currency value changes in relation to all others. Additional forecasts cover electrical rates, crude oil (regional prices), transportation costs, technology, and automation.

How Input Is Gathered

Data input is accomplished by dividing efforts between work conducted at Arthur D. Little's Cambridge, Massachusetts facilities and face-to-face interviews held in each country with industry representatives. These interviews reflect the appropriate type of product. In countries with developing economies, principal interest is focused on foreign investors, and, where appropriate, on local entrepreneurs who operate companies serving world markets, plus other nationals representing business and banking. Leading economists, educators, and representatives of government are interviewed so that planned economic growth and change are folded into the forecasts.

In making labor forecasts, for instance, inputs combine the results of interviews with correlations among inflation indices, the consumer price index, and wages. In developed countries, such as the United States, the United Kingdom, Germany, France, and Japan—where very strong historical correlations can be drawn—expectations based on the correlations are combined with forecasts of personnel directors and manpower-resource managers who are interviewed. In developing nations where a historical data base is not available, reliance is placed upon the expectations of numerous interviewees and also upon observations in preparing the wage forecasts. Like all forecasts, these are made with "most likely" expectations bounded by low and high 90 percent confidence limits. These forecasts are not necessarily symmetrical around the "most likely" value, but they generally indicate a greater degree of uncertainty on the high side.

Inflation and exchange-rate forecasts rely heavily on research done by our economists in Cambridge. They benefit from the field interviews, reports, and other data collected. Account is also taken of forecasts made by eminent economists and organizations in each country.

Materials forecasts are made by our specialists whose practice includes forecasting future demand, supply, and prices. Interviews are also conducted with major producers and suppliers of materials. Where possible, the costs required to produce materials are disaggregated into the elementary cost components. For example, cost factors contributing to the cost of produc-

ing a material include labor, energy, and raw materials cost factors. These factors rise with general levels of inflation, the cost of money, transportation, and the like. For each producing country, a materials cost forecast is constructed which reflects these factors in proportion to their importance as cost elements. From this, a price forecast for the material is developed, influenced by supply-and-demand factors and world pricing trends. For nonproducing countries, it is assumed that materials will be available at the producer prices plus transportation.

SUMMARY

As world politics and business become more interdependent, transnational companies in this decade face greater risks, more constraints, and new competition from advanced developing countries. The companies are finding it prudent to develop, maintain, and expand international monitoring systems and sourcing strategies. Global Sourcing practices provide manufacturing costs and forecasts necessary to make informed investment decisions for any combination of fifteen countries.

Throughut the 1980s, the more efficient use of worldwide human, material, energy, and capital resources will further reduce the parochial manufacturing philosophy that has prevailed since the industrial revolution. Rewards will go to those who recognize this.

30

Managing Manufacturing Rationalization Within Multinational Companies
Yves L. Doz

• • •

Reduction of tariffs and other trade barriers and the emergence of free trade areas in Western Europe have provided an opportunity to multinational companies (MNCs) manufacturing in several countries to have each of their plants specialize and ship production to other subsidiaries for sale or integration into finished products. Instead of multiproduct-multistage plants autonomously serving a national market, it has become feasible and economically attractive to develop plants that manufacture only one model or one product line, or are involved in only certain stages of the production process for the worldwide market.

Rationalization means shifting from a set of local-for-local plants, each serving its own national market with a broad product range, to an integrated network of large-scale production-specialized plants serving the world market. Only a few products, or some components, are made in each plant, but in very large numbers. Rationalization also involves the development of a single worldwide product line and the integrated management of product engineering activities to avoid duplications and to maintain production specialization.

Not all companies can benefit equally from rationalizing their production. In some cases transportation costs would be disproportionate; in others, economies of scale beyond the current plant sizes do not warrant rationalization; in still others, customers' tastes and preferences differ sufficiently between countries to

Source: Yves L. Doz, "Managing Manufacturing Rationalization Within Multinational Companies," *The Columbia Journal of World Business,* Fall 1978, pp. 82–94. Copyright © 1978 by the Trustees of Columbia University in the City of New York. Reprinted by permission.

jeopardize any attempt to rationalize. Nevertheless, many companies, with less-differentiated products where economies of scale are important and where making a full line of sizes or models or types is critical for successful competition, can derive immense benefits from rationalization, particularly when their production costs are important in relation to total costs.

For mature industries in developed countries, rationalization must be seriously considered. Multinationals face more and more competition from Japan, whose industry is very efficient; from lesser developed countries who have lower labor or energy costs; and from competitors who do not follow usual trade practices or pricing policies (e.g., the Soviet bloc). Given the extreme concern that governments show toward maintaining employment, a multinational can hardly shrink its activities in developed countries and move them to lower cost countries without social upheavals that can damage its prospects permanently. The issue then often becomes how to increase production efficiency inorder to maintain or restore competitiveness. Probably the greatest untapped source of efficiency is rationalizing production (and often product engineering) activities between several countries.

Despite its economic advantages, rationalization seldom is implemented as part of a new opportunity-seeking strategy. Rather, it emerges as a response to serious difficulties. According to a survey[1] taken in 1974, a number of years after trade barriers were reduced, few of the companies who had been expected to rationalize their manufacturing operations had done so. In many cases companies had invested into new subsidiaries abroad rather than serve foreign markets through exports. Only in a few industries that were subjected to very severe Far Eastern competition had multinationals rationalized their European operations. And, even then, the process of rationalization was often slow, difficult, and not always successful. Most managers attributed the difficulties of the rationalization process to administrative and managerial issues that made implementation difficult. There was no dearth of analytical studies calling for rationalization, but few of them had been followed by actual implementation.

RATIONALIZATION: NECESSARY BUT DIFFICULT TO DIAGNOSE

This paper, based on clinical research into the management of a number of large diversified MNCs over the last two years, proposes a framework for diagnosing the need for rationalization and for managing the rationalization pro-

cess. The paper first suggests how to determine whether a MNC should rationalize production and what difficulties are likely to interfere with an objective diagnosis; it then analyzes problems of implementation and suggests administrative measures that can facilitate the rationalization process.

The difficulties of rationalization begin when analytical and behavioral issues conflict. The purely analytical issues are simple: rationalization is needed when product market maturity leads to price competition and product standardization on a worldwide basis. Rationalization is possible when product unit costs are sensitive to scale of manufacture, i.e., when longer series or larger plants result in lower unit costs.

Yet, social and political difficulties within the multinational corporation often hinder an objective diagnosis and delay the start of rationalization. If we pause to consider the structure of the MNC prior to rationalization, the difficulties become clear. In all likelihood the relative self-

Table 1 A Framework for Managing the Rationalization Process

Diagnosis	Start-up	Changes in the Management Process	Corporate Management Options Support Rationalization
Product market maturity	Product type inventory	Marketing coordination	Communication of purpose
Price competition	Coordination group	Export coordination and	Planning integration
Unexploited scale economies	Staff experts	sourcing control	Changes in measurement, evaluation and reward systems
	Coordinators	Logistics	
		Overall market-share	
		Production programming	Changes in career paths and management development
		Technical coordination	
		Funding: R&D, capital	
Pitfalls			
Lack of perception of new competition	Too assertive coordinator	Wrong timing	Lack of top management visible support
Autonomous subsidiary structure favors national responses rather than rationalization need diagnosis	Too little top management support to coordinators	Inappropriate sequencing	Continuation of country based evaluation and compensation schemes
Rationalization may be opposed by national subsidiary managers' slanted diagnosis	Coordinators subordinate to group of subsidiary managers	Poor choice of coordinators	Poor choice of country managers
	Too many subsidiaries		
	Joint ventures		

sustenance of national subsidiaries primarily geared to their domestic market has led over time to separate management of the various national companies. In such a fragmented setting there are obvious barriers to the emergence of multicountry rationalization as a strongly supported proposal. First, the significance of new competition is often difficult to recognize rapidly. Second, the decentralized management characteristic of local-for-local operations make national managers look for local-for-local solutions first. Finally, because rationalization threatens their power and identity, managers approach it with great reluctance.

PRODUCT MARKET MATURITY AND PRICE COMPETITION

Rationalization is most needed in mature industries whose customers use precise, hard criteria based on product price performance relationships in their purchasing decisions. For instance, European consumers have developed an increasingly discriminating attitude toward cars and hi-fi sets since the 1950's; they now require high quality, low price, no-nonsense products. The same tendency is seen in the U.S. computer industry where, as products have matured and become better known, customers have become more price sensitive. In response to customers' shifts, suppliers can put more emphasis on cost reduction rather than product differentiation or new innovative products. Product innovations become harder to come by because most aspects of the technology, functions and possible variations of the product itself have already been explored by one competitor or another. Innovative efforts are now geared to low cost production processes rather than new products.[2]

Such conditions usually lead competitors to strive for low production costs through extensive rationalization in high cost areas, through sheer size, and through production in lower cost countries. Warning signals to MNCs in developed countries can come from low cost imports taking a growing market share in home markets, other MNCs rationalizing their activities, or large scale national producers exporting aggressively. When such signals appear, rationalization is usually urgently needed or profits may soon tumble. In the free trade environment of the western world, products such as cars, trucks, bearings, electrical motors, and consumer electronics are obvious candidates for rationalization.

ECONOMICS OF MANUFACTURE

Rationalization can bring great benefits only if the production proess is highly sensitive to scale economies. Although there are no fast rules, it is generally accepted that production cost decreases depend on two major variables:

1. The size of a given operation. A 500,000 unit per year capacity automobile plant will have lower unit costs than, say, a 200,000 unit per year plant, for example.[3]
2. The number of units produced by a given operation since it started, i.e., accumulated experience.[4] To some extent this applies both to particular products (i.e., Volkswagen production) and to more general experience in a given industry (refrigerator real costs fall for any given manufacturer, with a product range evolving over time).

An analysis of the sensitivity of unit costs to scale of production is a key part of diagnosing a need for rationalization. If higher production volumes will yield much lower production costs, rationalization is highly desirable. As much as feasible, one must be careful (particularly for multiproduct, multistage-related activities) to identify what cost decreases derive from longer individual production series, overall accrued experience, or sheer size of the plant, as these differences imply different rationalization patterns. For instance, in consumer good production, audio products are easier to rationalize than video products. Radio and hi-fi production costs are mostly sensitive to individual production series, of which there are many different types. Existing small plants in various countries can specialize without too much difficulty. In TV tube production, on the other hand, there are few types and individual plants need to be very large; hence, it is very difficult for a large number of existing plants to specialize without many factory closings that are, at best, difficult and slow to implement in most developed countries.

Furthermore, more efficient manufacturing processes often require larger production volumes in a single site to reach their full efficiency. For instance, a variety of ball bearings can be produced on the same set of machines, each type in relatively small numbers. Bearings can also be produced on highly efficient fully automated transfer lines. Each line produces only one type, but in extremely large quantities. Concentrating all production of one type in one location often permits the adoption of more efficient production processes leading immediately to a spectacular drop in manufacturing costs. This was a key to SKF's rationalization success within its five main European subsidiaries.

Finally, economies of scale can affect various stages in the production process differently. Some stages can be very scale sensitive (for instance wafer production in semiconductors), others very labor intensive but not much affected by scale (semiconductor packaging), still others both scale sensitive and labor intensive (semiconductor testing). These differences are reflected by the patterns of production rationalization of the U.S. semiconductor companies: wafer manufacture in very large plants in the U.S., assembly and packaging farmed out to the Far East and Latin America, and testing in various locations.

POTENTIAL PITFALLS IN DIAGNOSIS

In an analytical perspective, diagnosing the need for rationalization is relatively simple; product standardization and price competition in mature product markets and the existence of further economies of scale are the key elements. Why, then, is diagnosis so difficult to carry out? Information difficulties may delay the perception of new competition; national subsidiary autonomy makes a worldwide diagnosis most difficult, and national managers see rationalization cutting across their power base.

Information Difficulties

It is difficult to detect an overall threat to the company's competitive position. Acute competitive pressures are seldom felt in all countries simultaneously. New, low price competitors adopt a gradual approach, seldom storming a whole continent at once. They may strike first where established manufacturers have lesser stakes, as did the importers of Japanese cars in Europe by first penetrating countries such as Belgium, Denmark or Portugal, where no home-based European manufacturer felt the pinch immediately. Delays in building distribution networks and a fragmented users' market may further blur the perception of new competition.

The company itself is often in a poor position to detect overall competitive pressures. Over the years, predominance of a national orientation can lead to decay of central management. Lean (or sometimes non-existent) corporate staffs, the absence of systematic exchange of information about specific products and markets between national subsidiaries, and the lack of worldwide product management all add to the difficulties of synthesizing a global view of competitors from the fragmentary glimpses provided by the subsidiaries.

Structural Difficulties

Often the wide-ranging operational decentralization granted to national subsidiary managers is compensated with tight profit and loss accountability. Such a control mechanism reinforces the desire of a national subsidiary manager to feel responsible and usually prompts him to reach for solutions he can first implement by himself. Faced with deteriorating profits, he is more likely to react by cutting costs and trimming employment that he can control than by calling for a companywide strategic and structural change.

Furthermore, the national subsidiary structure favors the development of commitments by managers. Other researchers[5] have shown the importance of these commitments in delaying and weakening management intervention into crisis situations, and in stalling strategic changes. A firm belief, shared by a whole organization, that operational responsibility and accountability are better placed at the national level, is difficult to change. This is particularly true of European top managers whose formative years witnessed a breakdown of international relations (protectionism in the Great Depression, immediately followed by World War II) and who may be reluctant to take advantage of conditions of free trade which they regard as vulnerable and of institutions they consider fragile (the EEC administrative regulatory machinery).

Such beliefs are sometimes reinforced by the incomplete state of free trade. In some industries, scale economies of production and price competition would dictate rationalization but the strategic importance of the products prompts national governments to prevent or limit international trade and rationalization of production, as with telecommunication equipment and electrical power systems.[6] In some other cases employment considerations or technological and financial factors prompt governments to prevent rationalization, through financial incentives, export subsidies, research grants, and other benefits, made contingent upon full local production. For many industries the extent of rationalization may thus be informally limited by national subsidiary managers who are more attuned to the possible national government desires for full local production than to the benefits of rationalization.

Delegation of responsibility to the national level may prevent top management from developing a clear-cut overall proactive view of the evolution of the company in response to worldwide competition. Without a will to develop global strategies for dealing with the changing environment it is unlikely that sufficient energy can be mustered to seriously question past commitments to national subsidiary, autonomy.

Power Base Difficulties

The power of the national subsidiary manager is based upon his control of the activities of the company in the host country. Coordination and integration of the activities of various functions and product lines within his domain are his key prerogatives and provide the base for his power. Rationalization, with its central management of investments, production scheduling and logistics, cuts at the heart of that power base. The manager's feeling of overall responsibility is threatened. A national subsidiary manager of a recently rationalized company once confided, "Now I am no more than a building superintendent." This is one of the central problems of rationalization: how to lead national or regional managers who were "kings in their fiefdoms" to relinquish their power for the good of the whole company.

National managers are likely to defend against rationalization by overplaying the importance of direct links with customers and the need to customize their products, in order to make rationalization seem undesirable. Corporate management is often ill-placed to assess the righteousness of their claims, particularly when government relations or employment issues are raised.

When these claims are well-founded, they may justify a partial rationalization only. Entire responsibility is left to the national subsidiaries for products that need local design and for which local production *does* matter to customers.[7] Sometimes corporate management may offer commitments to labor unions to not cut employment in the rationalization process, in order to gain their support and cut one possible objection by the subsidiary managers.

It is seldom possible to specify in great detail the exact benefits than can be brought by rationalization. The economies of production are not known in sufficient detail to make very precise cost projections. Some market share may be lost in one country, some gained in another, prices may be reduced, profits increased—but to assess precisely what the economic consequences of rationalization will be for each product in each country in terms of sales and contribution is next to impossible. Because of this fuzziness, national managers may slant a diagnosis or oppose necessary rationalization of part of their product line for fear of "what comes next."

These are the major problems that must be overcome in the diagnosis of a need for rationalization. They are not insurmountable but they must be carefully considered. Their existence explains why it is only in the face of the most pugnacious competition that rationalization is undertaken. It took intense Japanese and Eastern bloc competition to prompt European electrical motor and bearing manufacturers to rationalize their European manufacturing activities around common models. It is only when the need is blatant, and where sometimes the survival of the company (or one of its major subsidiaries) is at stake that rationalization is undertaken.

Rationalization: Managing the Process

From the experiences of a few multinationals that were subjects of clinical research, some common characteristics and "do's" and "don'ts" emerge. The activities involved in a rationalization process fall into two broad stages: "start up" and reorganization of the production system. The rationalization process itself must, of necessity, span a period of several years (a) because implementation needs to proceed in several steps and (b) because the physical tasks themselves take much time (relocation of production equipment, changes in production methods, closing of old lines, opening of new ones, training of workers and supervisors, etc.). Here I shall focus on the management process rather than on the physical process, and assume that the latter can be designed and carried out technically without major difficulties.

START UP

The diagnostic difficulties outlined above suggest the need to gain early commitment from subsidiary managers. A simple way to begin is to make an inventory of redundant product types. Such redundancies can be dramatically presented to national managers. For example, Philips' Radio, Gramophone and Television product group convened all its national subsidiary managers to show them hundreds of similar radio and television sets spread out on tables covering the ballroom of a large hotel, all made by one or another national subsidiary because it was "necessary for the market." In most cases the diagnosis can be expressed simply: the inventory shows obvious duplications and overlapping product ranges. SKF, the world's largest ball bearing manufacturer, with manufacturing operations in most European countries, concluded that the 50,000 different types of bearings produced in its five major national subsidiaries could easily be reduced to 20,000; a "core product line" of 7,000 types could be rationalized and made for inventory; and 13,000 other types could be made by one or another national subsidiary for domestic customers only.

Once the inventory of product types is completed, a business strategy analysis is undertaken to assess the special competencies of the various subsidiaries and to guide their specialization. This often is the first opportunity to consider the firm's business in a global perspective.

Again, active cooperation with the national subsidiary managers is needed. To make the rationalization diagnosis part of an existing ongoing management process, where cooperation is already developed between subsidiaries, alleviates the fears of national managers and facilitates the evolution of their commitments. Often an established structure of technical coordination committees provides such an opportunity. Opportunities may also appear at times of broad strategic reassessment, when rationalization can be expected to dawn upon the participating managers as a solution to overall strategic problems. Direct, active involvement of the management of national subsidiaries in the process is a prerequisite for the shifts in commitments required by a successful rationalization. Reliance on functional staff experts whose influence is based on recognized competence, rather than direct control or responsibility, to guide the diagnosis, first addressing the least controversial questions such as common nomenclature, product specifications, quality standards and manufacturing methods, helps to loosen former commitments and to start a cooperative process between subsidiaries. Similarly, first initiating rationalization of products identified as losers and of which no subsidiary is committed to production can provide a start for the process.

Potential Pitfalls in Start-up

At this early stage, there are several pitfalls to avoid. First, the development and acceptance of an overall blueprint is not as critical as the start of a cooperative process between subsidiaries and the affirmation that rationalization efforts are worth pursuing. These can be hampered by early formalization of the process or by the appointment of corporate coordinators or their equivalents who have undertaken exhaustive analytical studies to be used as blueprints. Powerful "coordinators" appearing as first signs of a strong central product management could stifle the process by taking it out of the hands of the national subsidiaries' managers, who would then resist it. The appointment of coordinators by the subsidiaries may also prove a hindrance: by creating a permanent but subordinate structure, the group of national subsidiaries may well prevent further implementation. A rationalization committee chaired by a straw man and where real power would lie with subsidiary managers can easily lead to inaction because of haggling between subsidiaries or a consensus to do nothing. There is a difficult balance to be sought by top management: provide enough impetus to keep the process on its track; avoid pressure that may scare subsidiary managers.

Getting into complex and ill-defined products is another pitfall. Product design and manufacturing simplicity, well-defined customer groups and functions, low diversity within the product line, well-known distribution characteristics facilitate the emergence of a common appreciation of competition and make it more difficult for national managers to retrench behind technical and marketing differentiation arguments. In this sense it is much easier for a company such as SKF to reach a common rationalized "European" product line by 1981 that it is, say, for a Honeywell Information Systems.

A third potential pitfall to avoid is including too many subsidiaries in the process. Some countries discourage certain rationalization schemes for antitrust reasons (SKF left its U.S. subsidiary out of its rationalization plan), others are adamant in closing their borders to imports and promoting autarky (Philips left its Indian subsidiary out of its Radio plan), and others have many constraints and regulations that often discourage rationalization (e.g., Brazil, Mexico). Some of the autonomous subsidiaries are joint ventures, whose partners may be dismayed by rationalization and may strongly oppose it. Franko[8] found that the emergence of a regional structure in MNCs (which usually accompanies, with some lag, a rationalization process) was the single most important cause of joint venture problems in a rationalization.

These problems should be closely studied before the attempt is made to bring a part-owned subsidiary into a rationalization plan. Finally, adding smaller subsidiaries to the scheme may well multiply administrative problems and diminish economic returns.

IMPLEMENTATION OF CHANGES IN THE MANAGEMENT PROCESS

The very nature of the rationalization process is self-defeating: if left to the national managers, implementation may stop short of expectations as there is no overall institutionalized way of managing the rationalized system, and because national managers are not likely to relinquish power voluntarily once the sorest points have been dealt with.

At some point a centralized management body must be appointed, without, at the same time, reducing the strength of national subsidiary management. Most often the increasing sensitivity of host governments, and the internal trauma caused by sweeping reorganization, would rule out a complete sudden overall structural change which would suddenly replace national subsidiary preeminence with worldwide (or regional) management of all activities. Again, the problem to avoid is ruling by diktat and building an entirely new corporate architecture; one wishes instead to manage a smooth transition to a structure in which the central management body would acquire an increasing influence, but not absolute power.

The form taken by the new centralized management body may vary. In some cases it may be a new staff service, such as SKF's "General Forecasting and Supply System," based in the neutral ground of Brussels and organized to administer the rationalization. In other cases, such as the International Telecommunications Division of GTE, product vice presidents may be appointed at headquarters. In still other companies, the expansion of corporate headquarters or regional manufacturing staff may serve the same function. The form this reinforcement of central management takes will vary according to the idiosyncracies of each company and the products it manufactures.

Whatever its form, this new management is likely to be confronted with the same set of issues: how to gain influence over subsidiary activities without usurping the power of their managers in too brutal a fashion. Several problems of intersubsidiary coordination appear in the rationalization process; they cannot be easily solved by the subsidiaries independently, and so are likely to be brought to headquarters where top management can give them to the new product management unit to solve.

Marketing Coordination

Once each subsidiary no longer manufactures a full product line, coordination of export marketing becomes important. Export orders have to be directed to the center and then allocated to the appropriate subsidiary. Beyond the mechanistic elements, there often remains a latitude of choice as to the source subsidiary, either because the order is not extremely specific or because several subsidiaries still manufacture comparable products. In some cases part of the rationalization design is to arrange for two or more sources so as to decrease vulnerability to strikes or other supply disruptions in any one of the subsidiaries. The ability to control allocation of export orders to the subsidiaries confers power over the subsidiaries to the central allocator.

The overall volume of activities of individual subsidiaries is also increasingly affected by export orders coming from the product management unit. Naturally, coordination of intersubsidiary shipments, production scheduling, and short-term logistics have to be managed jointly, particularly when the rationalization involves both segments of the product line and stages in the production process. The ability to expand or contract the volume of export business of particular subsidiaries, and thus affect their profitability, becomes a strong incentive for subsidiaries to fall in line.

Finally, both the global perspective of the product management unit and the lower costs yielded by rationalization may increase the worldwide overall market share of the company. Thus the slice of the cake offered to each subsidiary increases in size. In businesses where selling is an important, costly activity which requires much competence and intensive effort, a central unit is often better able to increase the overall return from the world market than a collection of autonomous subsidiaries competing against one another.

From the viewpoint of worldwide management, the maintenance of allocation flexibility in source and export markets constitutes a particularly powerful influence over the subsidiaries. For instance, the stable a priori allocation of geographic markets to certain subsidiaries in case of duplication effectively reduces the influence of product management. Similarly, the existence of only one source for one product effectively confers power on that source. So beyond the safety of supply questions, it is ironical to conclude that in order to be managed smoothly it may well be that rationalization has to remain incomplete!

Production Programming Coordination

Usually concurrent with control over export marketing is the development of a central worldwide market analysis and forecasting system. The subsidiaries learn to depend on the central system for their own forecasting and planning as the share of exports (to other subsidiaries and possibly to third parties) in the sales of each subsidiary increases. Simultaneously, particularly when rationalization involves multistage production processes, production programs must be coordinated between the various subsidiaries—and the central management unit can become a broker and an arbitrator for the planning of intersubsidiary transactions.

Technical Coordination

Regrouping the technical coordination structures with the new management unit may also provide the latter with a measure of control over the transfer of product and process technology between the subsidiaries. Linkages with the central research and development laboratories can also provide much influence. Controlling the transfer of new technology from the United States to European subsidiaries was a major source of influence of the product vice presidents at GTE.

Investment and R&D Coordination

Control over capital and R&D expenditure can be delegated by top management to the worldwide product management unit. Because investments are now made with the aim of serving a worldwide market, individual national companies cannot be left in full control. Given their worldwide perspective combined with an indepth knowledge of the business, product managers are best able to check, evaluate, and integrate into a coherent whole the investment proposals of the subsidiaries. This control was the single strongest source of influence for the corporate product directors at Dow Chemical.

Difficulties and Pitfalls

The issues of export allocation, joint production programming, technical coordination, and capital and R&D fund appropriation have been found to provide a basis for establishing central coordination in order to complete the rationalization process. These issues enable the coordination center to assert influence over the subsidiaries and to foster integration and specialization of their activities. Yet there remain difficult questions which top management must consider with care.

First, timing rationalization with an overall business slump makes the rationalization process seem both more urgent and easier to implement. Brown Boveri's 1972 industrial motors rationalization plans were blasted by a mini capital boom in 1973 whereas SKF's managers attributed their own success in good part to the depressed markets of 1975–76. Taking advantage of new product introduction may also help cast the rationalization in a more positive light. It is also easier to plan for new machines and productions in a rationalized system than to start by relocating existing activities.

Second, sequencing is important. In a successful rationalization, behaviors and commitments change. Often the new patterns of interaction between subsidiaries induce shifts in power and status, causing great concern to managers. The various coordination issues are raised to bring cooperation between subsidiaries.

How and when to use these issues to gain influence upon subsidiaries most often rests with the decision-maker in the product management unit supported by top management. If he or she is too assertive, or a pawn of the coordination committee, the process is ruined.

Significant steps can best be taken when external sources of reward are present. At GTE, for instance, the worldwide product vice president obtained a huge telecommunication order which had to be allocated for capacity reasons; he used his power to allocate production as a means for gaining ascendancy and influence over national subsidiaries. Conversely, steps taken in direct conflict with outside events (as in the Brown Boveri case mentioned above) are likely to fail and jeopardize the whole process.

The sequence of moves to increase the influence of the worldwide product management unit(s) is subject to corporate veto control. Through their power over structure and their allocation of responsibility, top management can set the pace of the process and restrain overassertive managers. Beyond this broad conclusion, no general approach to the sequencing can be developed; sequencing depends on coalitions that can develop between subsidiary managers, on the "feel" for the situation developed by the manager of the product

coordination unit, and on the urgency imposed by competitive pressures.

Third, given his/her key role in managing the later parts of the rationalization process, a coordinator must be chosen carefully. There seem to be no general rules. Recognized substantive expertise and experience within the organization are important elements, but not sufficient ones. On the contrary, too much technical emphasis and task orientation would jeopardize the process. The most important element is the ability to provide energy, commitment and drive without using line authority. One means used by several companies is to appoint successful past subsidiary managers as worldwide product coordinators with the idea that they will know what is palatable to their former colleagues and what is not; their previous experience provides them with both an intellectual understanding and an emotional grasp of how to manage a subsidiary or an area. On the other hand, when one of the companies studied appointed *division* managers within its subsidiaries it reached out to recruit managers who had been running worldwide product groups for other MNCs. This company's top management hoped that some degree of reciprocal understanding between newly appointed subsidiary division managers and worldwide coordinators would facilitate a needed rationalization process in some of the activities they controlled. This quickly unlocked a tight situation and revitalized a rationalization that had been stalled for several years.

Wrong timing, sequencing and choice of coordinator(s) seem to be the most frequent cause of unsuccessful rationalization. They deserve much top management attention.

Corporate Management Options to Support the Rationalization

Beyond direct management of rationalization, top management can facilitate its implementation and encourage central coordination in many ways. In particular, it is important to recognize that though national subsidiary managers have considerable autonomy prior to the rationalization, they do not operate in a vacuum: both the corporate and the host country environments contribute to shape the perceptions, premises, and commitments of managers. Therefore an important element of the rationalization process is to modify the organizational context within which subsidiary managers operate.[9] It is important to be aware of the set of administrative procedures that "shape the purposive manager's definition of business problems by directing, delimiting and coloring the focus and perception and determine the priorities which the various demands on him are given."[10]

Corporate management controls an array of variables which structure the context of subsidiary managers and can hinder or facilitate the rationalization process—in particular, the organization's architecture, the systems of measure, evaluation and reward and punishment, the flows of communication to and from subsidiaries, and the career paths of key managers.[11]

COMMUNICATION OF TOP MANAGEMENT PURPOSE

It is important how the intent of rationalization and top management's commitment (or lack of commitment) to its success are signaled to national management groups. A mechanistic view of the social aspects of starting the process should be avoided. To increase the influence of product management without immediately decreasing the influence of national managers requires the development of a social interaction process. Top management's role in bringing product and host country preferences and their sponsors together is most important.

Series of worldwide planning meetings can be scheduled for a few days at a time, and what takes place outside the sessions is often as important as what takes place inside. Systematic patterns of communication between sub-sidiaries may be developed. Top managers should be personally involved in alleviating the fears of national managers and exploring their reservations. Only top managers and functional staffs constitute a relatively neutral source of arbitration for the conflicts that are bound to develop as rationalization is implemented. Because their actions are visible, top managers can also set precedents which signal the strategy they pursue and set the tone for relationships between host country and product managers.

CHANGES IN MEASUREMENT, EVALUATION, AND REWARD SYSTEMS

Rationalization may not be compatible with tight national profit center accountability. Because decisions which affect the profitability of the subsidiaries are increasingly being influenced by worldwide product management units, maintaining tight profit center accountability leads to frustration and conflict. Thus, during the rationalization process a loosening up of the measurement, evaluation and control systems of national profit centers is needed. Similarly, an incentive system based on national subsidiary results may have to be replaced by one based on overall corporate or worldwide product group results. All companies stress the need for lenient measurement, evaluation and reward systems as a condition for learning and for disassociating personal financial risks from realignments in status and power.

CAREER PATHS AND MANAGEMENT DEVELOPMENT

It is important for top management to assess early in the rationalization process whether the role of subsidiary managers is likely to be diminished. If they have long represented the main level of general management, at some point during the rationalization process shifts in career paths should be considered. Though this is too broad a question to consider here, some of the key issues are worth mentioning. If marketing needs to be differentiated by countries and constitutes a critical task, splitting production and marketing could be considered: marketing would then be left to strong autonomous national companies headed by entrepreneurial managers. On the manufacturing side, only good plant managers are needed nationally. What scope remains for strong national managers? The development of international careers may be difficult, and national managers may resent being deprived of the perquisites of power and responsibility. Good national managing directors do not always make good international staff or product group managers. Also, for personal reasons country managers may loathe the expatriate status and relocations which accompany an international career path.

For all these reasons some attrition is unavoidable among national subsidiary managers and in some cases it may even be sought to facilitate the rationalization process. But the systematic replacement of strong national managers by mere caretakers is not advisable. With the growth of host governments' interventions, workers' participation, and the disillusionment with free trade and free investment, there is a need for the management of an integrated network to remain responsive to national conditions. We have also seen that the extent and benefits of a rationalization can hardly be clearly assessed in advance, and that not all productions, and not all countries can be rationalized without strong penalties. Therefore it is important to have a strong national management group sensitive to the needs of local interests as a balance to worldwide product managers who are likely to overlook national idiosyncracies.

CONCLUSION

Rationalization is not only an economic and technical exercise, but also a complex social and organizational process which aims to develop an integrated multinational business capability. Such a capability is particularly needed in developed countries and mature industries subject to intense price competition. It can bring economic advantages mainly through exploiting economies of scale.

Though an objective diagnosis of economic forces and of the benefits of rationalization is possible, it is likely to be hampered by difficulties of perception, commitment of managers, and power structure shifts. Start-up of a rationalization process requires new commitments from the national subsidiary managers and development of a central body that can draw influence from coordination of export marketing, worldwide market analysis, forecasting and production planning activities, improved export sales, changes in the production process, technology transfer and control over investments and R&D budgets. Full top management support must be provided to the coordinating body and to the rationalization efforts. Early pitfalls in the process include adoption of a firm "blueprint" without subsidiary managers' support, premature constitution of a coordination center, its dependence either on corporate or subsidiary management, attempts to rationalize complex products where the benefits of rationalization are not obvious, and inclusion of too many small or partly owned subsidiaries into the rationalization scheme. Later pitfalls may include poor timing, poor sequencing, lack of top management support and absence of administrative changes. Useful administrative changes include provision of a sense of purpose by top management, changes in the measurement, evaluation and rewards systems, changes in career paths, and staffing of key subsidiary positions.

Yet even carefully planned and well-managed rationalization processes may not be successful. Because rationalization challenges organizational commitments and power relationships and forces their realignment, many internal roadblocks have to be overcome to carry out the process. Some of these roadblocks are predictable in a planning stage, but overcoming them successfully requires constant top management attention at each stage in the process. The rationalization process deserves more research: I have merely tried here to suggest means of facilitating rationalization and some pitfalls to avoid when carrying out the process.

NOTES

1. Cited in Lawrence G. Franko, *The European Multinationals* (Stamford, Conn.: Greylock, 1976).
2. William Abernathy, *The Productivity Dilemma* (forthcoming).
3. See, for instance, John S. McGee, "Economies of Size in Automobile Manufacture," *The Journal of Law and Economics*, pp. 239–273.
4. See Boston Consulting Group, *Perspectives on Experience* (Boston: Boston Consulting Group, 1968).
5. Richard G. Hamermesh, "Responding to Divisional Profit Crises," *Harvard Business Review*, March–April 1977. Stuart Clarke Gilmore, "The Divestment Process," unpublished doctoral dissertation, Harvard Business School, Boston, 1975. Richard Normann, *Management and Statesmanship* (Stockholm: Scandinavian Institutes of Administrative Research, 1976).
6. Yves L. Doz, *Government Power and Multinational Strategic Management* (New York: Praeger Publishers, forthcoming 1979).
7. For instance, many prepared food products and strategic products sold to governments or state-owned enterprises.
8. Lawrence G. Franko, *Joint Venture Survival in Multinational Corporations* (New York: Praeger Publishers, 1972).
9. Joseph L. Bower, *Managing the Resource Allocation Process* (Boston: Division of Research, Harvard Business School, 1970).
10. Ibid., p. 73.
11. See C. K. Prahalad, "Strategic Choices in Diversified MNCs," *Harvard Business Review*, July–August 1976.

31

The Transfer of Japanese Manufacturing Management Approaches to U.S. Industry

Richard J. Schonberger

• • •

Japanese expertise in repetitive manufacturing management emerged as the marvel of the industrial world in the 1970s. Japanese companies generally have not been secretive about their special management skills and approaches, but Western industry has been slow to learn about and profit from Japanese successes, partly because of a prevailing premise that Japanese socioeconomic, geographic, and cultural factors rather than management approaches explain their successes.

Today, however, many manufacturers are studying and trying out Japanese approaches. Much of the activity has centered around *quality circles* (Nelson, 1980), a concept in which small groups of workers meet periodically to explore ways to improve quality and productivity. Only recently have Western manufacturers become aware of the Japanese kanban system and just-in-time (JIT) manufacturing control. In this paper, JIT, kanban, and quality circles are considered in the context of a particular type of production: *repetitive* manufacturing. As an illustration, the evolving repetitive manufactur-

Source: Richard J. Schonberger, "The Transfer of Japanese Manufacturing Management Approaches to U.S. Industry," *Academy of Management Review*, Volume 7, Number 3, 1982, pp. 479–487. Copyright © 1982. Reprinted by permission.

ing management system of a Japanese plant operating on U.S. shores—Kawasaki Motors—is considered.

REPETITIVE MANUFACTURING AND JIT PARTS DELIVERY

Industrial processes all too often have been oversimplified with dichotomous terms such as job shop-flow shop or intermittent-continuous. High volume assembly of TVs, toys, pharmaceuticals, and canned goods sometimes is considered as continuous process production even though assembly runs are in lots and may be controlled by job orders or lot orders as in a job shop. The American Production and Inventory Control Society (APICS) (1981) is attempting to popularize terminology that will distinguish between the true process industries, whose products may be counted in fractional parts (gases, fluids, grains, flakes, pellets), and the industries that make discrete units in large amounts. The term being suggested for the latter is *repetitive manufacturing*.

In Western industrialized countries planning and control by lots is the dominant pattern in repetitive manufacturing. The Japanese have developed systems of repetitive manufacturing that attempt to do away with lots, that is, move toward lotless manufacturing. Lotless operations are the norm in the continuous process industries, and some repetitive manufacturers have been able to achieve lotless final assembly either by (a) dedicated assembly lines each making only a single model, as in automobile assembly, or (b) running mixed models down a single line, as is the practice in some tractor assembly plants. But in Western countries subassembly, fabrication, and purchasing in support of final assembly generally is lot-oriented. The Japanese have had some success in extending lotless repetitive processing to levels below final assembly, that is, multiechelon lotless manufacturing, and also in expanding the pursuit of lotless processing to firms making a wide variety of consumer and industrial products.

One Japanese technique for facilitating relatively lotless processing is the Toyota kanban system. Kanban was introduced at Toyota in 1972, and to date only a few other large Japanese original equipment manufacturing (OEM) companies have implemented kanban (APICS, 1981). The detailed workings of the kanban system are explained elsewhere (Sugimori, Kusunoki, Cho, & Uchikawa, 1977) and need not be dwelt on here. As interesting as kanban is, it is but one manifestation of a widespread Japanese manufacturing management approach characterized by simplicity and avoidance of waste. The approach bears close scrutiny for the purposes of this paper, which are to develop some preliminary judgments about the feasibility of transferring Japanese management expertise to U.S. industry.

The Japanese live on a small, crowded collection of islands where space costs are at a premium and natural resources are scarce. Waste, in the form of defective production or idle inventories taking up floor space, is a more obvious problem and serious concern in Japan than in countries blessed with natural abundance. It is not surprising that Japanese industry has developed hand-to-mouth manufacturing and inventory approaches with emphasis on high quality.

A term that has emerged to describe the Japanese hand-to-mouth philosophy is JIT. JIT is incorporated to a high degree in the kanban system. That is, the Toyota kanban system is geared to providing major assemblies just in time to go into final end products at the proper final assembly line work station; subassemblies just in time to go into major assemblies; parts just in time to go into subassemblies; and so on down to the level of the purchased part—and even beyond that into and throughout the manufacturing stages in suppliers' plants.

Material requirements planning (MRP), a U.S. innovation, has a similarity to kanban in that MRP also is bent on providing parts when they are needed to go into a parent item, up through all levels in the product structure. The difference is that Japanese JIT means, generally, the right day or even hour; MRP usually is content to provide parts in the right week. MRP can and sometimes does operate with daily or smaller time buckets, but there is an economic reason why most Western factories have weekly buckets: Labor costs of setup dictate that orders for the same part often be grouped into lots of a size sufficient to cover up to several weeks' parent-item requirements. With production quantities often providing weeks' worth, there is little value in regenerating planned orders more often than weekly.

The Japanese also must live with the economics of lot-sizing. But they have concentrated on altering one of the key inputs, labor cost per setup, in the basic economic order quantity equation. Reducing the setup cost and thereby adjusting economic lot sizes downward—ideally to equal one—is one of the keys that allows the Japanese factory to deliver parts just in time. When orders are small and frequent, simple noncomputer-based systems for order generation become practicable. The following example explains further the JIT approach of minimum lot sizes in contrast with the job-lot approach that has been perfected largely in the United States.

LOT-SIZE ECONOMICS

Figure 1 shows some of the major differences between the JIT and the job-lot approach to manufacturing. Motorcycle manufacturing is used as the example. Part A of Figure 1 shows the familiar job-lot way. Materials are bought, parts are fabricated, subassemblies are made, and assemblies are built in large enough lots that there generally are significant stocks of parts between each process stage. A schedule for this approach is shown at the right in Figure 1, Part A. The schedule, stated in weeks, shows intermittent runs of different models of the given part. In this case the part is a motorcycle frame, but it could just as well be a crank, bracket, seat, bolt, or any other material, part,

assembly, or the whole motorcycle. A high carrying cost rate coupled with high cost per setup leads to an intermediate lot size—the EOQ—which is shown in the cost diagram in Part A.

MRP may be used advantageously in the job-lot approach of Part A. MRP plans the timing of the lot so that it is in time for the next demand. Because job-lots typically are several days' or weeks' worth, it is generally sufficient that MRP due dates/release dates be planned once a week. The many disruptions that conflict with the schedule during the week are handled by priority control (dispatching).

The JIT approach attempts to carry the MRP goal of correct order timing much farther; the ultimate or ideal would be piece for piece delivery of parts. The effect, shown in Figure 1, Part B, is virtual elimination of the large stocks of parts between process stages. The schedule becomes a daily or twice daily or hourly quantity.

The cost diagram in Part B represents the altered lot-size economics that make JIT possible. The carrying cost rate is unchanged, but setup cost is greatly reduced, as evidenced by the nearly flat, rather than steep, setup cost curve. Setup cost reductions are achieved by spending heavily on production engineering. (This exchanges one obvious cost for another, but in so doing there are considerable derivative benefits of inventory reductions and smoothed production, as is explained below.) That is, engineers design machines for quick and easy changeover of fixtures, dies, and other tooling. The fixed cost of engineering for quick setup is high, but the tradeoff is a low variable cost for labor to perform setups for changing part numbers. For parts that are bought rather than made, the same principle may apply, but the reduction is in purchase order-processing cost rather than setup cost. Order-processing cost cuts may be attained by better long-term materials management—for example, better vendor selection, deliberate encouragement of local area vendors, better and longer term vendor contracts, and close vendor relations and contract monitorship.

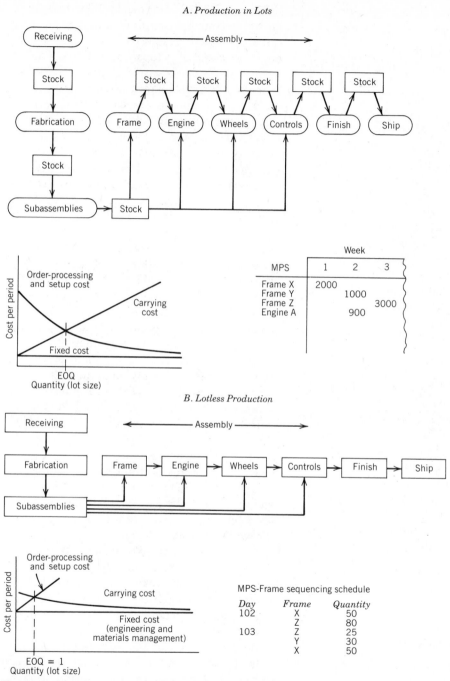

Figure 1   Motorcycle manufacturing with and without lots. (*Source:* Adapted from Schonberger, 1981.)

COMPETITIVE NICHE

A company that produces in large volume may, it seems, decide on either the job-lot approach or the repetitive approach. To some extent, the choice seems forced by the firm's competitive niche. That is, a company that manufactures telephones in many styles and colors may have great difficulty making JIT/repetitive production work, even if total sales volume is huge. Computer-based MRP, with a daily dispatch list feature, seems preferable for planning and controlling the great and ever-changing variety of possible telephone configurations demanded by customers who mainly want to be different. Another type of telephone manufacturing is the factory that makes a small variety of standard telephone sets in large volume—more of a "focused factory" (Skinner, 1974). This producer has fewer complications in need of sorting out by computer. Repetitive rather than job-lot production seems suitable.

These two examples represent extremes, and in the extreme case of differentiated versus standardized products the choice of job-lot or repetitive systems may be forced. But most manufacturers are more in the middle than at the extreme, and those firms with intermediate degrees of product differentiation may choose to put their emphasis on variety, or they may instead choose to emphasize lower costs and prices. It would appear that OEM companies in the United States tend toward the former—the variety strategy—and the Japanese OEM companies tend toward the low price and high quality strategy. But in overall head-to-head competition the Japanese have been having the edge, which leads one to wonder if U.S. emphasis has been misplaced. It is instructive to consider the case of one U.S. firm that recently reversed itself and chose a lotless/JIT rather than an MRP future for itself.

JIT AT KAWASAKI, USA

In early 1980 the Kawasaki motorcycle plant in Lincoln, Nebraska, was about to implement an MRP system. The plant management team were all North Americans with experience in job-lot oriented U.S. industry but were also knowledgeable about the Japanese JIT and kanban system in use at Kawasaki, Japan.

The kanban system for triggering parts movement and production appeared feasible, but, more importantly, the job-lot orientation inherent in MRP seemed inappropriate. If Kawasaki, Lincoln, was to be able to serve the North American market at a lower cost than could Kawasaki, Japan, it was essential that the Lincoln plant approach the level of productivity that has been attained, via JIT/kanban, at the parent plant in Japan.

Lincoln plant management harbored the usual doubts about making JIT/kanban work in the U.S. culture in which labor and management often are viewed as adversaries. But in 1979 inventory problems became particularly acute. In particular, Kawasaki, Japan, as a key supplier of all motorcycle engines plus many other parts, was geared to ship parts to the United States in steady quantities (knocked down kits of 200 motorcycle equivalents), which matched poorly with Lincoln's more erratic large-lot-oriented production scheduling. (Included in materials from Japan were kits of steel tubing, which Kawasaki, Lincoln, fabricates into motorcycle frames in a manufacturing sequence of punch press, welding, and painting. Thus, the Lincoln plant has a several-level bill of materials with attendant potential for work-in-process inventory stockouts and excesses.) A Kawasaki, Japan, study group visited the Lincoln plant to try to help resolve the problems. One result was that the Lincoln management group became convinced that JIT, and perhaps kanban, should be pursued and that the MRP project should be abandoned.

Before the end of the year Kawasaki, Lincoln, had tried out a simple one-card kanban system for feeding certain parts to the production lines. Included were about 100 kinds of small "hardware"—bolts, washers, nuts, rubber grommets, and so on. After a period of marginal success with the kanban system, it became clear that the magic is not in the kanban card, but that a surer path to productivity improvement is to cultivate multiechelon JIT and small lot or lotless processing. The tinkering with manual order cards (kanban) on the shop floor continues. Meanwhile substantive gains have been achieved in moving toward JIT. A few examples may be noted.

Production/Capacity Planning

From the outset, the Kawasaki, Lincoln, plant, now seven years old, has had the common Japanese production/capacity planning strategy: level load, *but without inventory buildup*. In some Japanese factories this strategy translates into a lifetime employment policy, which is feasible if the company is able to control its markets via high quality and productivity. Kawasaki, Lincoln's approach is an adaptation more consistent with the U.S. socioeconomic climate: a no-layoff policy.

In recent months a soft market combined with a high rate of productivity improvement has resulted in excess labor. The excess is greater than attrition can absorb. Consequently, production line workers have been available to build a storeroom, calk walls, rebuild a frame welding area for JIT parts flow, and attach a new JIT-oriented feeder line to one of the production lines. This is in keeping with the Japanese belief in an informed, involved, versatile workforce. Workers glimpse the big picture and are more able and inclined to offer worthwhile suggestions for productivity improvements (Ouchi 1981. See, especially, Chapter 3.)

Organizing for Productivity Improvement

In Japanese industry manufacturing engineering is everyone's business. By one report (Hay 1981) most Toyota foremen are or are studying to be industrial engineers, who lead their workers in the never-ending job of improving manufacturing methods. In Japan such methods analysis often is formalized via quality circles—Toyota calls its "small group improvement ac-

tivities." (In repetitive manufacturing, quality improvements serve to reduce waste and rework and to smooth the output rate, thereby improving productivity. The distinction between quality and productivity blurs. Japanese quality circles thus are oriented toward both quality and productivity improvement, whereas a not uncommon view in the United States is that quality circles are concerned exclusively with quality matters.)

Kawasaki, Lincoln, has no quality circles or other formal study groups. But plant management has developed a notion that it believes may achieve the same results. The idea is to instill in everyone's mind a vision of what the plant is evolving toward, and to allow wide latitude for the workforce to pursue the vision in a variety of ways. The vision is stated thus: The whole plant is visualized as a series of stations on the assembly lines, whether physically located there or not.

The object is JIT production and parts delivery with no waste—the same as in Japan. The mechanism is individual American ingenuity. The Japanese way is to take a long time and seek consensus, which helps assure successful implementation. The U.S. way is to decide fast without real consensus or commitment and then run into an obstacle course in the implementation phase. The hybrid approach in the Lincoln plant perhaps avoids many of the implementation obstacles by inculcating (a) a vision of an ultimate plant design and (b) a JIT objective for plant operation.

Productivity Improvements

The plant configuration vision and the JIT objective are scarcely a year old, but there are notable successes. As has been mentioned, production line workers, rebuilt a frame-welding area. Motorcycle frame welding had been run as a job shop, with frames run in job lots through several welding stages, and inventory buildups at each stage. Now there are several frame welding lines, each dedicated to a particular model of motorcycle. For a given model, a number of welding booths are located together in a line, and a special welding jig is in each booth. As a model of frame is run, the product is passed piece by piece from booth to booth, with no inventory buffers between. Thus, JIT parts movement has been achieved within frame welding. The next step, making frame welding "a station on the assembly line," may be achieved in the future through implementation of kanban to link frame welding to frame painting.

It also was mentioned earlier that production workers had attached a new feeder line to a main assembly line. The assembly line for the KLT three-wheel motorcycle previously had been supported by a separate subassembly area making differentials in job lots. The line foreman, apparently imbued with the JIT concept, had told industrial engineering that he thought differential assembly could be attached to the main assembly line. The foreman led the conversion project, and today a differential production line feeds directly into the KLT line, with a typical work-in-process (WIP) inventory of just two differentials.

Setup Time

The many delegations from other U.S. plants that have visited Kawasaki, Lincoln, are most likely to remember the punch presses that are equipped with carousel roller conveyors for die storage. The conveyors keep the dies at just the right height for quick and easy attachment to the fixture. It now takes about 10 minutes to set up for a new model of framing tube versus hours for the same setup a year ago. It now is economical to run tube fabrication operations in the same small lot sizes (200) as for parts kits received from Japan—as opposed to lot sizes in the thousands before the carousel die storage and transfer conveyors were developed.

JIT Purchasing

JIT purchasing is common in Japan, but perhaps the only well-established case of it in the United States is with TRI-CON, a Kawasaki motorcycle seat supplier. In 1977 Tokyo Seat Company established its TRI-CON subsidiary near the Kawasaki plant in Lincoln, Nebraska. TRI-CON's motivation was to become indispensable by locating close enough to be able to react quickly to any quality or delivery requirements that Kawasaki might have. The striking feature of the service provided by TRI-CON is its twice a day deliveries. More-than-daily delivery generally is unheard of in the United States in discrete manufacturing; once a month is more typical.

In 1981 the Kawasaki purchasing manager began training his buyers and other staff in JIT purchasing concepts. Several JIT-oriented purchase agreements are in various stages of development. The idea is to establish very high quality, responsive suppliers, in the Lincoln vicinity where possible, and enjoy the mutual advantages of long term JIT agreements: low inventories (which the supplier also may achieve via JIT agreements with its suppliers), avoidance of large lots of defectives (because there are no large lots), and stability of the supplier-buyer relationship.

PLANT CONFIGURATIONS FOR JIT OPERATIONS

As some of the above examples indicate, Kawasaki, Lincoln's productivity improvements are gained by moving away from job-shop and toward multiechelon lotless repetitive production. There are several possible plant configurations along the way, as Figure 2 illustrates using welding booths as the example. The first configuration, Part A, is that of a job shop. Each welding booth has access to welding jigs, which hold steel tubing in place for welding into frames. Job orders specify frame model, order quantity, and routing from booth to booth. Dispatch lists note which job order to run next at particular booths, and move tags assist in the transfer between booths.

Part B shows the extensive physical change-

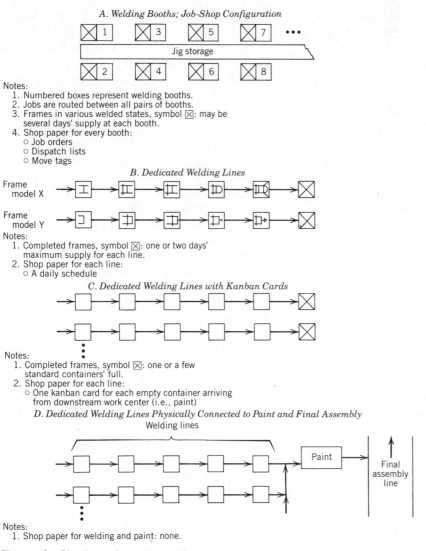

Figure 2 Plant configurations. (*Source:* Adapted from Schonberger, Sutton, and Claunch, 1981.)

over to welding production lines, which is the present configuration in the Lincoln plant. Each line is dedicated to a particular model, which eliminates the changing of jigs in a given booth. This is a layout concept known as group technology (GT), which the British write about (Burbidge 1975) and the Japanese extensively employ. Shop paper is reduced to a daily schedule by frame model. WIP buffer/queuing inven-

tories drop to zero, and inventories of completed frames awaiting transfer to painting drop from, typically, many days' supply to a maximum of one or two days' worth.

Part C shows how Kawasaki, Lincoln, plans eventually to cut down the day's worth of finished frames by implementing kanban. Kanban is a pull system in which the downstream work center pulls, via a kanban card, more parts from upstream fabrication areas. Because kanban meshes fabrication output with assembly usage—always somewhat variable—the kanban system cuts buffer stocks. (When production is run to a schedule, as in MRP, it is a push system, i.e., the scheduled run is made and the finished parts are pushed downstream, whether downstream work centers need them or not.)

In Part D the last bit of buffer inventory and the last bit of shop paper are removed—by physically wedding the dedicated feeder line to main assembly. The Lincoln plant may never achieve this configuration for welding frames, which then go to painting before feeding to final assembly. But, as has been described, this configuration has been achieved for feeding differentials into the KLT assembly line.

FLEXIBILITY

The primary advantages of JIT and repetitive production are lower costs and prices with better quality. To some degree these benefits are gained at the expense of product line variety. A JIT/repetitive manufacturer is likely to offer fewer models and styles than an MRP company. Typically, for example, Japanese auto manufacturers have offered a narrower line of models than have U.S. counterparts. If a repetitive manufacturer is to offer a good deal of variety, that variety should be within fairly narrow limits, for example, a variety of chrome trim styles, all of which are similar enough to be formed from the same material on the same machine tool engineered for quick setup changeovers.

At the same time JIT leads to increased flexibility and market responsiveness. Because all parts manufacturing is geared to the final assembly rate, the total production lead time is very short, as compared with job-lot producers. JIT plants, including Kawasaki, Lincoln, make the most of their capacity for market responsiveness by generally resisting the temptation to make parts simply in order to keep an expen-

sive machine busy. Instead, a sales-oriented master schedule dictates machine usage. When model changeover and machine-tool setup times have been drastically reduced, assembly lines and fabrication centers may be balanced to run mixed models. The daily model mix produced is closely matched to the daily marketing mix distributed and sold, so that finished goods inventories may be lean and still provide a high rate of service (few model stockouts) to final customers. Internally, information linkages (e.g., via kanban) serve to keep fabrication centers, and even suppliers, making the same model mix as is being run in final assembly, with appropriate offsets for leadtime—sometimes only a matter of hours (e.g., the four-hour response time for TRI-CON to deliver seats to the Kawasaki, Lincoln, plant).

MRP in its most advanced forms (i.e., MRP II) has the admirable capability of providing integrated planning of manufacturing and financial resources forward to distribution centers and backward to suppliers. Fully developed multiechelon JIT also integrates forward and backward but with only a fraction of the inventories, computer processing, and planning documentation. It is not easy, or cheap, to become a JIT/repetitive manufacturer, and plants whose mission is to provide product variety are limited in how far they can progress toward JIT/repetitive processing; MRP may be necessary. But, based on the still limited information on the Kawasaki, Lincoln, experience, the JIT approach is workable in the United States, and a certain amount of conversion to such a mode of operation may be necessary if U.S. industry is to compete with the Japanese.

FUTURE RESEARCH

For many production/operation management (P/OM) practitioners in the United States, there is an element of déjà vu in learning about the Japanese JIT approach. A similar period of enlightenment was experienced in the 1970s in connection with MRP. Orlicky (1975) had concluded that order quantities, the focal point of inventory management for nearly half a century, were really unimportant as compared with order timing. Converts to MRP adopted this conclusion with close to religious fervor. It seemed unlikely that there would be a second period of enlightenment in the 1980s and that it would feature a return to the view that lot sizes may indeed be a key to successful production and inventory management. Yet that is part of the JIT message, and Japanese industrial success with small-lot and lotless JIT processing is convincing.

Such developments open up a host of research opportunities for the P/OM academician. For one thing, considerable thought and study are needed to sort out the proper areas of application for lot-oriented MRP versus relatively lotless JIT/kanban. The issue is complicated in that it relates to the central question of what a given manufacturing firm has been, is, and can be. At one extreme is a lot-oriented job shop geared for variety, which is the way that many manufacturers start out, and at the other extreme is a repetitive OEM firm geared for the mass markets, which many might aspire to become.

There also are important operational issues that beg attention. What is the best system design for a given plant and how may it be discovered and implemented? Yamaha in Japan has devised what seems to be an ingenious fusion of kanban and MRP, suitable for its situation as a repetitive manufacturer dependent on numerous job-lot-oriented fabrication shops. Kanban cards control parts feeding final assembly, and *synchro cards,* computer-produced by a highly advanced version of MRP, trigger orders from the job-lot oriented fabrication shops (APICS, 1981). The academic researcher, along with consultants and practitioners, surely have this sort of innovative design work to do in a variety of industries.

The fundamental truths seem to be not yet fully known, much less the details. Understanding Japanese JIT and examining attempts in the United States to borrow from the Japanese answer some questions but open up many new ones.

REFERENCES

American Production and Inventory Control Society (APICS), Repetitive Manufacturing Group. *Driving the Productivity Machine: Production Planning and Control in Japan,* R. W. Hall, ed. Advance draft version, June 1981.

Burbidge, J. L. *The Introduction of Group Technology.* New York: Wiley/Halstead, 1975.

Hay, E. "Planning to Implement Kanban." Presentation to APICS Repetitive Manufacturing Group, Just-in-Time Workshop, Lincoln, Nebraska, June 1981.

Nelson, J. "Quality Circles Become Contagious." *Industry Week,* April 14, 1980, pp. 99+.

Orlicky, G. *Material Requirements Planning.* New York: McGraw-Hill, 1975.

Ouchi, W. *Theory Z: How American Business Can Meet the Japanese Challenge.* Reading, Mass.: Addison-Wesley, 1981.

Schonberger, R. J. *Operations Management: Planning and Control of Operations and Operating Resources.* Dallas: Business Publications, 1981.

Schonberger, R. J., D. Sutton, and J. Kanban Cluanch. ("Just-in-time) Applications at Kawasaki, USA." *Twenty-Fourth Annual Conference Proceedings, American Production and Inventory Control Society,* Boston, October 1981.

Skinner, W. "The Focused Factory." *Harvard Business Review,* Vol. 52, no. 3 (1974), pp. 113–121.

Sugimori, Y., K. Kusunoki, F. Cho, and S. Uchikawa. "Toyota Production System and Kanban System: Materialization of Just-in-Time and Respect-for-Human System." *International Journal of Production Research,* Vol. 15 (1977), pp. 553–564.

SECTION 7
R&D and Innovation Management

In many industries, ranging from high-technology industrial products to children's toys, research and development resulting in a steady flow of successful new products is a requisite for survival. Abundant evidence indicates that the most important stimulus for innovation is the market; particular innovations are likely to take place in countries with large potential markets for them. This holds true for both consumer and industrial goods. Successful commercialization of an innovation is also strongly facilitated by being close to the market because of the inevitable "cut-and-try" testing required before a commercially successful product can be produced.

As we have learned in earlier readings there has been, in the past, a worldwide pattern of innovation that could be explained by market size and proximity. The United States as the largest, highest-income country in the world held a virtual monopoly on labor-saving innovations. European innovations tended to be material saving, and Japanese innovations were both material and space saving. Obviously, all were responding to demand: U.S. firms were responding to high U.S. labor costs, European firms to high material costs, and Japan to high material and space costs.

More recently, however, the environment has changed. Labor costs have increased significantly in Japan and Europe, thus stimulating labor-saving innovations in these countries. Materials costs have increased substantially in the United States, providing a stimulus for materials saving innovation here. In addition, rising disposable incomes in many countries have greatly expanded the number of potential sites for consumer goods innovation. In the same way, a burgeoning industrial base in many countries, coupled with growing similarities in production process, has increased significantly the number of countries that can provide stimuli for industrial products innovation.

It would seem, then, that the more countries markets in which a firm is operating, the more potential opportunities it has to innovate. It would also seem that multinational firms might want to spread their R&D, especially their development operations across several countries. Widespread operations might both maximize the firm's exposure to innovation opportunities and facilitate commercialization through close market contacts. On the other hand, it can also be argued that, since country markets are becoming increasingly similar, contact with any market should serve as both sufficient stimulus and testing ground. Moreover, the costs of decentralizing R&D should argue strongly for centralizing it.

The optimum organization of R&D activities is still a matter of debate. U.S. firms are doing an increasing proportion of their R&D outside the United States. But, as we shall see, the reasons are not just to obtain market stimulus. Japanese firms have managed to tailor products for specific foreign markets while working from centralized R&D facilities located in Japan. Perhaps the answer to locating R&D facilities lies within the individual firm and is conditioned by the firm's ability to transmit information internally and then to act on the information it receives. As we shall see, the location decision is also conditioned by political and economic considerations. Some foreign governments view the establishing by multinationals of R&D facilities in the country as a very desirable adjunct to future economic growth. Their pressure is toward decentralization. On the economic side, it is clear that an R&D facility must be of a certain scale to be viable. Thus, there is countervailing pressure to centralize. In addition, in a world that is becoming increasingly similar, there is pressure to centralize R&D to avoid duplication of effort.

READING SELECTIONS

Mansfield, Teece, and Romeo analyzed the overseas R&D activity of a sample of 55 large U.S. firms. They found that their overseas R&D activity grew significantly during the 1960s and early 1970s and was expected to reach about 12 percent of R&D activity by 1980. The principal reason for doing R&D overseas was to be able to respond better to the special needs of overseas markets. They also estimate the expenditure required to reach an acceptable scale of operations in different industries and across a range of R&D activities. Since their figures are for 1975, they would certainly have to be revised upward to approximate today's costs. But their figures are still valuable in facilitating comparisons across industries and activities. Their work illustrates that the "rules" for locating R&D vary both by industry and by activity.

Terpstra observes that R&D in the multinational firm is a much more centralized activity than is production or marketing. He advances several arguments in support of centralization and then makes equally persuasive arguments for decentralizing R&D. Having presented both sides of the case, he offers some generaliztions about the actual location of R&D in the firm. These extend and flush out the discussion in the Mansfield, Teece, and Romeo article. The generalizations are a mixture of descriptive and prescriptive.

Behrman and Fischer add still further dimensions to the R&D location decision. They identify three alternative primary market orientations evidenced by transnational corporations, home, host, or world market. They studied the overseas R&D activities of 53 U.S. and European transnational corporations and linked their overseas R&D activities to their primary market orientations. Among their findings is that the location of R&D activity in the host market orientation firm is likely to be governed by market considerations. But the location of R&D in the world market firm is conditioned primarily by the availability of technical knowledge and talented people.

Finally, Ronstadt and Kramer warn that the United States has lost the great advantage it had as a unique site for innovation and that U.S. firms are not responding as well as they could in pursuing foreign sources of innovation. They recommend several steps that companies can take to increase their access to foreign innovations; they believe that foreign company-owned R&D labs are the best way to gain access to foreign innovations and technology. However, such operations must have a clear purpose and "fit" with firm's overall R&D objectives. The authors go on to suggest ways in which foreign R&D operations can be effectively organized and managed.

32

Overseas Research and Development by U.S.-Based Firms

Edwin Mansfield, David Teece, and Anthony Romeo

• • •

INTRODUCTION

In recent years, the overseas research and development activities of US-based firms have become the focus of controversy. Some observers view such activities with suspicion, since they regard them as a device to "export" R&D jobs, or as a channel through which American technology may be transmitted to actual or potential foreign competitors.[1] Others, particularly the governments of many developing (and some developed) countries, view them as highly desirable activities that will help to stimulate indigenous R&D in these countries. Indeed, the United Nations Group of Eminent Persons recommended that host countries require multinational corporations to contribute towards innovation of appropriate kinds, and to encourage them to do such R&D in their overseas affiliates.[2] Although the amount of controversy in this area might lead one to believe that the nature of existing overseas R&D activities of U.S.-based firms has been studied quite thoroughly, this is far from the case. The unfortunate truth is that economists have devoted little or no attention to even the most basic questions

Source: Edwin Mansfield, David Teece, and Anthony Romeo, "Overseas Research and Development by U.S.-Based Firms," *Economica,* Volume 46, May 1979, pp. 187–196. Copyright © 1979. Reprinted by permission.

concerning these activities.[3] In this paper, we try to fill part of this gap.

OVERSEAS R&D EXPENDITURES: 1960–1980

How big are the overseas R&D expenditures of U.S.-based firms, now and in the past, and how big do firms expect them to become by 1980? To help answer this question, we constructed a sample of 55 major manufacturing firms, this sample being divided into two parts. The first subsample, composed of 35 firms, included major U.S.-based firms in the chemical, petroleum, electrical equipment, metals and machinery, drugs, glass, food and paper industries. The second subsample, composed of 20 firms, included major manufacturing firms in the southern New England and Middle Atlantic states. Table 1 shows the percentage of R&D done overseas by these firms, during 1960–1974 (for the first subsample) or 1970–1974 (for the second subsample), as well as the estimated value of this percentage in 1980. In each subsample, about 10 per cent of the total amount spent on R&D by these firms was carried out overseas in 1974. Based on the 35-firm subsample, it appears that this percentage grew sub-

stantially during the 1960s and early 1970s.[4] Based on the estimates provided by the firms in the sample, this growth will continue, but at a reduced rate, during the rest of the 1970s; by 1980 they estimated that about 12 per cent of their R&D expenditures will be made overseas.

Because of the importance in the innovation process of close communication and cooperation among R&D, marketing, production and top management, Vernon (1974) and others have argued that a firm's R&D activities will tend to be centralized near its headquarters. Why then do these U.S.-based firms spend about 10 per cent of their R&D dollars overseas? There are a variety of possible reasons, including the presence of environmental conditions abroad that cannot easily be matched at home, the desirability of doing R&D aimed at the special design needs of overseas markets, the availability and lower cost of skills and talents that are less readily available or more expensive at home, and the greater opportunity to monitor what is going on in relevant scientific and technical fields abroad. In our sample, practically all of the firms doing R&D overseas say that the principal reason is to respond to special design needs of overseas markets. In their view, there are great advantages in doing R&D of this sort in close contact with the rele-

Table 1 Percentage of Company-Financed R&D Expenditures Carried Out Overseas, 1960–1980: 55 Firms

	1960*	1965†	1970‡	1972†	1974	1980§
35-firm subsample						
Weighted mean	2	6	6	8	10	10
Unweighted mean	2	4	5	7	8	8
Standard deviation	3	7	7	8	10	8
20-firm subsample						
Weighted mean	—	—	4	—	9	14
Unweighted mean	—	—	5	—	8	11
Standard deviation	—	—	7	—	10	14

*Data were not available for 4 firms in the 35-firm subsample.
†Data were not available for 1 firm in the 35-firm subsample.
‡Data were not available for 1 firm in the 35-firm subsample and 1 firm in the 20-firm subsample.
§Data were not available for 9 firms in the 35-firm subsample.

vant overseas markets and manufacturing units of the firm.

FACTORS INFLUENCING THE PERCENTAGE OF A FIRM'S R&D EXPENDITURES CARRIED OUT OVERSEAS

What determines the percentage of its R&D that a firm conducts overseas? Given the fact that overseas laboratories seem to be so closely geared to the special design needs of foreign markets (and the firm's overseas plants), we would expect that the percentage of a firm's R&D expenditures carried out overseas would be directly related to the percentage of the firm's sales that is derived from abroad. Firms with relatively small foreign markets would be expected to spend relatively little on overseas R&D. Further, we would expect that the percentage of a firm's R&D expenditures carried out overseas would be more closely related to the percentage of its sales from foreign subsidiaries than to its percentage of sales from exports. This is because much overseas R&D is in support of foreign manufacturing operations.[5]

Holding constant the percentage of a firm's sales that come from abroad, we would expect that the percentage of a firm's R&D expenditures that is carried out overseas would be directly related to the firm's size. Economies of scale require that R&D laboratories be a certain minimum size if they are to be relatively efficient. If it is going to establish an overseas laboratory, the firm must have a big enough prospective market (in the area served by this laboratory) to support a laboratory of minimum economic scale. If the percentage of a firm's sales that comes from abroad is held constant, the probability that this prospective market will be of the requisite size is an increasing function of the absolute size of the firm.

Further, we would expect that, holding constant both the firm's sales and its percentage of sales coming from abroad, there would be inter-industry differences in the percentage of a

firm's R&D expenditures carried out overseas. For example, we would expect this percentage to be relatively high in the pharmaceutical industry because some firms, according to industry sources at least, have moved a substantial amount of R&D abroad to avoid Food and Drug Administration regulations. Also, foreign regulations sometimes require that R&D be done locally. Because of these regulatory considerations, as well as other factors discussed below, we might expect the drug firms in our sample to carry out a relatively high percentage of R&D overseas.

In addition, we would expect that, if the firm's sales, its percentage of sales coming from abroad and its industry are held constant, there will be differences over time in the percentage of a firm's R&D carried out overseas, owing to changes in the profitability of locating R&D overseas rather than in the United States (as well as bandwagon effects).[6] In general, during the period covered here, we would expect these effects of time to be positive, since cost differentials and other factors favoured the expansion of overseas R&D.

To test these hypotheses, we carried out two sets of computations. First, we pooled the 1970 and 1974 data for the 35-firm subsample, and regressed each firm's percentage of R&D expenditures carried out overseas on its percentage of sales from abroad, its sales, an industry dummy variable, and a time dummy variable. The results are

(1)
$$A_{it} = -1.13 + 0.73T_t + 0.15Q_{it} + 0.004S_{it}$$
$$(0.44) \quad (0.34) \quad (1.81) \quad (3.09)$$
$$+ 16.10D_e, \quad (\bar{R}^2 = 0.50;$$
$$(5.41) \quad n = 51)$$

where A_{it} is the percentage of the ith firm's R&D expenditures carried out overseas in year t (1970 or 1974), T_t is a dummy variable that equals 1 if t is 1974 and 0 if t is 1970, Q_{it} is the percentage of the ith firm's sales derived from abroad in year t, S_{it} the ith firm's sales (in millions of dollars) in year t, and D_t is a dummy variable that equals 1 if the ith firm is in the drug industry and 0 otherwise.[7] Each regression coefficient's t-ratio is given in parentheses.

Second, we pooled the 1970 and 1974 data for the 20-firm subsample, and regressed each firm's percentage of R&D expenditures carried out overseas on the same variables as in equation (1), except that we split the percentage of sales from abroad into two parts—the percentage of sales from foreign subsidiaries, and the percentage of sales from exports—and we redefine the industry dummy to include both chemicals and drugs, not drugs alone.[8] The results are:

(2)
$$A_{it} = 2.79 + 4.40T_t + 0.322F_{it} - 0.539E_{it}$$
$$(1.16)\,(1.91) \quad (4.47) \quad\quad (2.32)$$

$$- 0.00162S_{it} + 4.52C_e,$$
$$(1.13) \quad\quad\quad (1.76)$$

$$(\tilde{R}^2 = 0.54;\ n = 39)$$

where F_{it} is the percentage of the ith firm's sales from foreign subsidiaries in year t, E_{it} is the percentage of the ith firm's sales from exports in year t, and C_e is a dummy variable that equals 1 if the ith firm is in the drug or chemical industries and 0 otherwise.

The econometric results generally are in accord with our hypotheses. As expected, equation (1) shows that there is a direct and statistically significant relationship between a firm's percentage of sales derived from abroad and its percentage of R&D expenditures carried out overseas. And when sales derived from abroad are disaggregated in equation (2), a firm's percentage of sales from foreign subsidiaries has a highly significant positive effect on its percentage of R&D expenditures carried out overseas, while its percentage of sales from exports has a significant negative effect, which suggests that

these firms' exports may be more R&D-intensive than their domestic sales.[9] With regard to our hypothesis that A_{it} would be directly related to S_{it}, the results of equation (1) bear this out, but in equation (2), S_{it} does not have a statistically significant effect (and its regression coefficient has the wrong sign). As expected, most of the industry and time dummies are statistically significant.[10]

OVERSEAS R&D: MINIMUM ECONOMIC SCALE AND RELATIVE COST

As noted above, many governments, particularly of developing countries, favour the establishment in their nations of overseas R&D laboratories by U.S.-based firms. One factor influencing the practicality of establishing a laboratory of a certain type in a particular overseas location is the extent of economies of scale in such laboratories. If the minimum economic scale for a laboratory of this type is quite large, a firm must be prepared to shift considerable R&D resources abroad if the laboratory is to be competitive.[11] Despite the fact that data concerning the minimum economic scale of R&D laboratories of various types would be of value to many kinds of microeconomic studies, practically no information is available on this score. In this section, we present the estimates (obtained from 27 members of the 35-firm subsample) of the annual R&D expenditures for an overseas laboratory of minimum economic scale. Although these estimates should be treated with caution, they are of considerable interest, since they seem to be the first systematic evidence on this topic.[12]

The results, shown in Table 2, indicate that the minimum economic scale tends to be quite substantial in most industries. On the average, for a single product line it was estimated that the expenditures per year for an R&D facility of minimum economic scale would be about $1 million in pharmaceuticals and glass, about $2 million in electrical equipment and petroleum, and about $5 million in chemicals. However,

Table 2 Estimated Annual R&D Expenditure for Overseas Laboratory of Minimum Economic Scale, 1975: 27 Firms ($ million)

Industry*	Single Product Line				Several Product Lines			
	Research	Development	Minor Product Changes	Research and Development	Research	Development	Minor Product Changes	Research and Development
Chemicals (n = 7)								
Mean	2.42	3.27	0.72	4.57	2.50	2.46	1.39	3.31
Range	1.0–5.0	0.1–14.0	0.03–2.0	0.46–20.0	1.5–3.5	0.26–6.0	0.24–3.5	0.16–6.7
Petroleum (n = 6)								
Mean	1.64	1.46	0.28	2.30	2.60	2.23	1.18	3.40
Range	0.25–3.0	0.25–3.0	0.15–0.50	0.40–5.0	0.40–5.0	0.40–4.5	0.25–3.0	0.6–7.5
Drugs (n = 2)								
Mean	3.25	0.50	0.12	1.00	6.00	1.30	0.35	†
Range	1.5–5.0	0.5–0.5	0.10–0.13	0.50–1.5	5.0–7.0	0.60–2.0	0.19–0.50	†
Electronics and electrical equipment (n = 5)								
Mean	1.00	1.15	0.40	2.00	2.42	3.95	0.77	6.75
Range	0.8–1.2	0.36–2.0	0.20–0.50	1.25–2.75	1.0–5.0	0.54–8.0	0.51–1.0	1.25–10.0
Glass (n = 2)								
Mean	0.70	0.85	0.42	1.38	0.73	1.53	0.71	1.88
Range	0.1–1.3	0.4–1.3	0.08–0.75	0.50–2.25	0.20–1.25	0.80–2.25	0.16–2.25	1.0–2.75
Total (n = 27)								
Mean	1.58	1.82	0.47	3.00	2.62	2.83	1.23	4.10
Standard deviation	1.34	2.78	0.45	4.10	1.87	2.76	1.30	3.68

*n is the number of firms that provided estimates.
†An estimate was obtained from only one firm.

the minimum economic scale seems to vary considerably, depending on the responsibilities of the laboratory. It is less for a laboratory that performs either research or development than for one that performs both, and less for a laboratory that deals with a single product line than for one that deals with several product lines. For a laboratory that is concerned entirely with minor product changes, the average estimated expenditure per year for an R&D facility of minimum economic scale is only about $500,000 per year—and in some industries it is substantially less. In interpreting the results in Table 2, the dispersion among the estimates is almost as interesting as the averages. The estimates in each industry vary enormously, reflecting the fact that the minimum economic scale of an R&D laboratory depends on the specific type of work to be done, as well as the fact that opinions differ on this score even among experts.[13]

According to many observers, one major reason why U.S.-based firms have carried out R&D overseas is that costs have tended to be lower there. However, very little information has been published concerning the extent of this cost differential, and how it has varied over time. To help fill this gap, we obtained data from the 35-firm subsample concerning the ratio of the cost of R&D inputs in Europe, Japan and Canada to those in the United States in 1965, 1970 and 1975.[14] The results, shown in Table 3, indicate that there was a very substantial cost differential in 1965: on the average, the cost of R&D inputs seemed to be about 30 per cent lower in Europe, 20 per cent lower in Canada and 40 per cent lower in Japan than in the United States. And although there was some increase in R&D costs relative to those in the United States during 1965–1970, the cost differential remained quite substantial in 1970.

Table 3 Mean Ratio of Cost of R&D Inputs in Selected Overseas Locations to That in the United States, 1965, 1970, and 1975,* 35-Firm Subsample†

Year	Location		
	Europe‡	Japan	Canada
1965	0.68	0.56	0.82
1970	0.74	0.60	0.86
1975	0.93	0.90	0.96

*Note that there are many costs of communication and coordination in a multinational network of laboratories. See Mansfield (1974).
† Usable data were obtained from 19 firms. Many of the rest had no overseas R&D experience.
‡ There are considerable differences within Europe in the level of R&D costs. According to a number of firms in our sample, costs tend to be relatively low in the United Kingdom and relatively high in West Germany.

However, between 1970 and 1975 the situation changed drastically. Owing in part to the depreciation of the dollar relative to other currencies between 1970 and 1975, the cost differential was largely eliminated for many firms. On the average, the cost of R&D inputs was estimated to be about 10 per cent lower in Japan, and about 5 per cent lower in Europe and Canada, than in the United States in 1975. Of course, this helps to explain the fact that the percentage of R&D carried out overseas was expected to increase less rapidly between 1974 and 1980 than in the period prior to 1974. Since the cost differential between overseas and domestic R&D was smaller, it is quite understandable that firms would expect this percentage to grow less rapidly than in earlier years.[15]

OVERSEAS R&D: NATURE OF WORK AND RELATION TO DOMESTIC R&D

Some observers, as we have seen, are suspicious of overseas R&D because they fear that it may be a channel through which American technology may "leak out" to foreign competitors. The extent to which such a leakage is likely to occur depends in part on the nature of the work being carried out in the overseas laboratories of U.S.-based firms. For example, if such work is focused largely on the modification and adaptation of products and processes for the local market, there is less need to transfer much of the firm's most sophisticated technology overseas than if the work is focused on major product or process developments intended for a worldwide market. Based on information obtained from 23 firms in our sample, it appears that these firms' overseas R&D activities tend to focus on development rather than research, on product and process improvements rather than on new products and processes, and on relatively short-term, technically safe work.

Specifically, on the average the percentage of overseas R&D going for basic research is about 6 percentage points less than the percentage of domestic R&D going for basic research; the percentage of overseas R&D going for applied research is 10 percentage points less than the percentage of domestic R&D going for applied research; while the percentage of overseas R&D going for development is 16 percentage points greater than the percentage of domestic R&D going for development. Moreover, about three-fourths of these firms' overseas R&D expenditures are aimed at product or process *improvements* and *modifications,* not at entirely new processes or products. This percentage is much higher than for all domestic R&D.

Firms seem to differ considerably in the extent to which they have integrated their overseas R&D with their domestic R&D.[16] Worldwide integration of overseas and domestic R&D exists in almost one-half of the firms (with overseas R&D) in our sample, according to the firms. On the other hand, about one-sixth say that they attempt no such integration, and the rest say that some limited integration is attempted.

Finally, of how much value is overseas R&D to a firm's U.S. operations? Policy-makers are interested in this question because it must be considered in any full evaluation of the effects of overseas R&D (and foreign direct investment) on America's technological position vis-à-vis other countries. Unfortunately, practically no evidence exists on this score. To shed a modest amount of light on this question, we obtained estimates from 27 firms in our sample concerning the percentage of their 1975 overseas R&D expenditures with no commerical applicability to their U.S. operations. The results indicate that, on the average, about one-third of these firms' overseas R&D expenditures have no such applicability. Also, we asked each firm to estimate the amount that it would have to spend on R&D in the United States to get results of *equivalent value to its U.S. operations* as a dollar spent overseas. The results, which are only rough, indicate that, on the average, a dollar's worth of overseas R&D seems to result in benefits to these firms' U.S. operations that are equivalent to about 50 cents' worth of R&D carried out in the United States.

CONCLUSIONS

Overseas R&D expenditures by U.S.-based firms topped the billion-dollar mark in the early 1970s. In 1974 they amounted to about one-tenth of total domestic company-funded R&D expenditures, and the firms in our sample reported that they expected them to amount to a larger proportion of their domestic R&D expenditures by 1980.[17] When compared with the total R&D expenditures in various host countries, their size is perhaps even more striking. In the early 1970s about one-half of the industrial R&D performed in Canada and about one-seventh of the industrial R&D performed in the United Kingdom and West Germany was done by U.S.-based firms.[18]

Yet despite the magnitude and importance of these overseas R&D activities, little is known about their purpose, nature or effects. Indeed, the very existence of such activities is ignored in all current econometric studies carried out to estimate the effects of R&D on U.S. productivity growth. Our purpose in this paper has been to present some basic information concerning

the size, nature, minimum economic scale and relative cost of overseas R&D. The limitations of these findings should be recognized. In particular, our results pertain to a sample of 55 firms, and some of the data obtained from the firms were necessarily rough. Nonetheless, we believe that these results, although not only a first step, shed substantial new light on this topic.

NOTES

1. For discussion of this point of view, see David (1974) and Conference Board (1976).
2. United Nations (1974). *The Impact of Multinational Corporations on Development and on International Relations.* New York, p. 70.
3. Caves (1974), Hufbauer (1974), Mansfield (1974), and Stobaugh (1974) have pointed out the need for work concerning this and related aspects of international technology transfer. For some interesting case studies, see Ronstadt (1975). Also, see Mansfield, Romeo, and Wagner (1979) for some related findings regarding international technology transfer.
4. The Conference Board (1976) has estimated the total overseas R&D expenditure of U.S.-based multinational firms in 1971–1973. According to its estimates, overseas R&D constituted about 9–10 per cent of total R&D expenditures carried out by U.S. firms during these years. This agrees quite well with our results for 1972 and 1974. The proportion of firms in our sample with no overseas R&D is somewhat lower than that reported by the Conference Board for firms of comparable size, but this may be due to different industry mix, the later year, or sampling error. The U.S. Department of Commerce (undated) has estimated the total overseas R&D expenditure of U.S. firms in 1966. According to its figures, overseas R&D constituted about 7 per cent of all R&D expenditures carried out by U.S. firms in 1966 (see Conference Board, 1976). This agrees reasonably well with our result for 1965. In 1978 the National Science Foundation published data for 1976 which indicated that overseas R&D constituted about 7 per cent of all R&D expenditures by U.S. manufacturing firms.
5. Suppose that a firm's desired R&D expenditures in a given year equal

$$R + a_u S_u + a_f S_f + a_e S_e$$

where S_e is its export sales during the relevant year, S_f is its sales through foreign subsidiaries, S_u is its sales from domestic plants to domestic customers, a_u is the proportion of sales to domestic customers that it wants to devote to R&D, a_f is the proportion of sales through foreign subsidiaries that it wants to devote to R&D, and a_e is the proportion of export sales that it wants to devote to R&D. If only the R&D in support of foreign subsidiaries is done overseas, it follows that the proportion of its R&D expenditures carried out overseas equals

$$P = \frac{a_f F}{a_u U + a_f F + a_e E}$$

where F is the proportion of its sales from foreign subsidiaries. U is the proportion of its sales to domestic customers, and E is the proportion of its sales that are exports. Under these circumstances, it can be shown that $\partial p/\partial F$ is always positive, but whether or not $\partial p/\partial E$ is positive depends on whether or not $a_u > a_e$. Of course, this model is a polar case, but it illustrates the point in the text.

6. In terms of the highly simplified model in n. 5, the a's are a function of time. (Also, as indicated previously in the text, they are a function of the firm's size.)

7. Other industry dummies were tried in equation (1), but D_i was the only one that was statistically significant. The reason why n is less than 70 is that data could not be obtained concerning the percentage of sales from abroad for all firms in both years.

8. The reason for this redefinition is that none of the firms in this subsample is really an ethical drug firm. (There are several such firms in the other subsample.) The closest we could come to ethical drugs is the chemical firms, some of which do some work in the drug area (broadly defined).

9. This result concerning E_{it} would be expected if $a_e > a_u$ in n. 5, and if the extremely simple model given there were valid. However, although it may be a reasonable approximation to regard some firms' overseas R&D as being entirely in support of foreign subsidiaries, this is far from the case in other firms.

10. The industry dummy is much larger and more highly significant in equation (1) than in equation (2) because, as pointed out in n. 8, none of the firms in equation (2) is really an ethical drug firm. Because of sampling variation, the estimate of D_i in equation (1) is probably too large. One of the drug firms in our sample carried out an unusually large percentage of its R&D overseas.

11. By minimum economic scale we mean the smallest scale that realizes all, or practically all, of the relevant economies of scale.

12. Freeman et al. (1965) have presented some relevant data concerning the electrical equipment industry. Eight members of the 35-firm subsample could not provide estimates, sometimes because they had no experience on which to base such estimates.

13. These figures help to explain why, holding other factors constant, smaller firms in equation (1) tend to carry on a smaller percentage of their R&D overseas than bigger firms. But they should not be interpreted as saying that smaller firms are squeezed out completely. The estimates in each industry vary enormously. In most industries, at least some

of the respondents felt that research and development could be carried out effectively with an annual budget of $500,000, and that minor product changes could be carried out with one of about $100,000. Although these levels of expenditure are hardly trivial, they are within the reach of many firms other than the billion-dollar giants.

Needless to say, these results in no way contradict the finding by many economists that small firms and independent inventors continue to play an important role in the inventive process. Their contribution is frequently in the earlier stages of the inventive process, where the costs are relatively low. Further, according to some observers, costs tend to be lower in smaller organizations, and the figures in Table 2 reflect the perceptions of large firms. For some relevant discussion, see Mansfield et al. (1977).

14. The relative cost of R&D inputs is the ratio of the annual cost of hiring an R&D scientist or engineer (together with the complementary amount of other inputs) in various overseas locations to do the sort of work carried out there to the annual cost of hiring a comparable R&D scientist or engineer (together with the complementary amount of other inputs) to do the same sort of work in the United States. Each firm was asked to estimate this ratio for each year. Many of the estimates were based on studies the firms seem to have carried out in recent years on this topic.

15. If very significant differences exist between the productivity of U.S. and overseas R&D personnel, they may offset the observed differences in the relative costs of inputs. About 80 per cent of the firms in our sample regarded the productivity of their R&D personnel in Canada, Europe and Japan to be no lower than those in the United States. Thus, this factor cannot offset the observed difference in the relative cost of R&D inputs in the great majority of firms in our sample.

16. By integration, we mean that the firm's worldwide R&D is viewed as a whole, and laboratories are given worldwide missions, if this seems desirable.

17. In early 1977, the United States Treasury put into effect a new regulation (1.861–8) that, according to some observers, may increase the amount of R&D done overseas by U.S.-based firms. Since the forecasts in Table 1 were made before this new regulation was announced, they do not take this factor into account. Also, they do not take account of recent changes in exchange rates, which may have tended to discourage overseas R&D.

18. See Conference Board (1976, p. 86).

REFERENCES

Caves, R. (1974). "Effect of International Technology Transfers on the U.S. Economy." *The Effects of International Technology Transfers on U.S. Economy*. Washington, D.C.: National Science Foundation.

Conference Board. (1976). *Overseas Research and Development by U.S. Multinationals, 1966–1975.* New York: Conference Board.

David, E. (1974). "Technology Export and National Goals." *Research Management,* Vol. 17, pp. 12–16.

Freeman, C., C. Harlow, and J. Fuller. (1965). "Research and Development in Electronic Capital Goods." National Institute Economic Review, Vol. 34, pp. 40–91.

Hufbauer, G. (1974). "Technology Transfers and the American Economy." In *The Effects of International Technology Transfers on U.S. Economy,* Washington, D.C.: National Science Foundation.

Mansfield, E. (1974). "Technology and Technological Change." In *Economic Analysis and the Multinational Enterprise,* J. Dunning, ed. London: George Allen and Unwin.

——— et al. (1977). *The Production and Application of New Industrial Technology.* New York: W. W. Norton.

———, A. Romeo, and S. Wagner. (1979). "Foreign Trade and U.S. Research and Development." *Review of Economics and Statistics,* forthcoming.

Ronstadt, R. (1975). R&D Abroad: The Creation and Evolution of Foreign R&D Activities of U.S.-based Multinational Enterprises. Unpublished DBA thesis, Harvard University.

Stobaugh, R. (1974). A Summary and Assessment of Research Findings on U.S. International Transactions Involving Technology Transfers. *The Effects of International Technology Transfers on U.S. Economy.* Washington, D.C.: National Science Foundation.

U.S. Department of Commerce. (undated). *U.S. Direct Investments Abroad, 1966,* Part II. Washington, D.C.: U.S. Government Printing Office.

Vernon, R. (1974). "The Location of Economic Activity." In *Economic Analysis and the Multinational Enterprise,* J. Dunning, ed. London: George Allen and Unwin.

33

International Product Policy: The Role of Foreign R & D
Vern Terpstra

• • •

The question of what products to sell in foreign markets is the essence of product policy in international marketing. Should we sell the same products we sell domestically or should they be adapted to local conditions? Will our product line be the same abroad as at home, or should we sell a different mix of products in foreign markets? For each company and industry the answers to these questions may be somewhat different.

Theories of foreign direct investment do not address these questions. They seek to explain

Source: Vern Terpstra, "International Product Policy: The Role of Foreign R & D," *The Columbia Journal of World Business,* Winter 1977, pp. 24–32. Copyright © 1977 by the Trustees of Columbia University in the City of New York. Reprinted by permission.

why the firm will invest and produce in foreign markets without asking what products or businesses the firm will be in in those markets. They implicitly assume that the firm will be producing the same products abroad as at home. This is especially clear in the Product Life Cycle theory, according to which the firm begins foreign production of a product which has reached the mature stage of its life cycle at home.

The general answer to the product policy questions raised above is that the firm should sell those products abroad that best help it to meet its objectives, such as market share, growth, and profit maximization. The practical experience of most companies suggests that the products and product lines sold in foreign markets to meet these goals will not be identical to those sold domestically, though there will be a strong similarity.

International marketing would be easier, of course, if a firm's products and product lines were identical in all countries. However, most multinational companies are forced to modify both products and product lines in foreign markets. Many different factors combine to induce such modifications. Among them are differences in use conditions, technical specifications, government regulations, competitive opportunities, and consumer tastes and purchasing power. Because the firm cannot usually automatically extend its domestic products to foreign markets, it faces a critical question in international marketing: how can the multinational firm adapt, develop, or acquire the products appropriate to foreign markets?

GETTING APPROPRIATE PRODUCTS FOR FOREIGN MARKETS: ALTERNATIVE STRATEGIES

When firms first go multinational, they usually market their domestic products with minimal adaptation to foreign conditions. Another approach is to acquire a foreign firm which has products designed for its own market. Each of these approaches may be satisfactory as an initial method of getting products for foreign markets. For the long run, however, a more sophisticated *business and product development plan* is desirable. In its planning process, the firm must decide what businesses and what markets it wants to pursue. Ideally, this planning and scanning should be on a global basis. Product strategy is an important part of this plan, and that includes a strategy of product development.

It is possible for a firm to get products without developing them itself. One way is to copy products developed successfully by others. Many firms follow this strategy with some success. It is obviously not, however, the strategy of a market leader.

Another way of getting products for world markets is shown by Colgate's approach. Colgate has chosen to market internationally several products which have been successfully developed and introduced nationally by other firms. For example, in many world markets, Colgate sells Wilkinson razor blades for the British company and Pritt Glue Stick for Henkel of Germany.

Colgate president David R. Foster explained: ''We've adopted the practice of using someone else's technology and our own worldwide reach.'' This strategy seems to work well for Colgate but it is not one followed by many other firms. Of course, Colgate also develops internally many of the products it sells.

Most multinational firms do not follow either of the strategies just mentioned. That is, they do not rely on imitation to develop their new products, nor do they market internationally products developed and introduced by others. As a result, the primary way firms get their products for world markets is through internal product development, with acquisition as a secondary method.

INTERNATIONAL PRODUCT DEVELOPMENT

If internal product development is the major method used by multinational firms to obtain their international product lines, how do they internationalize their product development activity? Drawing on research in progress, we shall look primarily at the role of R&D in international product development. Research and development are not the whole of the product development process, but they are a major ingredient and the only one considered in the present discussion.

A firm's product development activity should be based on a policy statement to give it coherence and direction. The various product development activities—idea generation, screening of ideas, selection of products for development, and development of the product—should take place within the guidelines of the policy statement. In all of these phases of product development, the multinational firm should have international inputs to assure the international profitability of its products. There are various ways firms can and do internationalize these phases of product development, but we shall look only at the role of R&D in this process.

THE ROLE OF R&D

Firms that conduct R&D consider these activities crucial to their survival and growth. From R&D come the new products that will help the firm survive and meet its goals in the future. We want to see how the multinational marketing of the firm affects its R&D practices, and especially the location of its R&D facilities.

Almost all multinational firms began as national firms with their activities concentrated in their home country. Generally, the first international activity of multinationals is marketing, followed later by foreign production. The last activity of the firm to be organized on an international basis—if it is at all—is R&D. Indeed, some multinationals do not conduct any R&D outside of their home country. For most multinationals R&D is much more centralized in the home market than is their production and marketing.

Why this centralization of R&D when the multinationals' marketing and production activities are rather heavily decentralized in foreign markets? A major reason is that the needs and pressures which lead to foreign marketing and production do not apply to R&D. For example, the need to reach customers, to cut costs of production, transportation, or tariffs, and the need to satisfy "buy national" policies have no connection with R&D. Consequently, many firms apparently think they can be successful international marketers with all of their product development activity in their home market. Obviously, the historical development of the company and inertia play a role in R&D policy also. Though products must be developed for world consumers rather than just domestic consum-

ers, many would argue that foreign market requirements can be fed into the domestic R&D activity. For example, it is notable that in 1972, R&D conducted by U.S. companies for the direct support of their foreign affiliates was only 14.5 percent of parent R&D, but that was equal to 134 percent of their overseas R&D.[1] Most American firms are obviously using their domestic R&D for their international operations.

Let us look at some of the major arguments for maintaining R&D exclusively in the domestic market of the multinational. These arguments assume that centralization of R&D is deliberate policy rather than historical accident.

ARGUMENTS FOR CENTRALIZING R&D DOMESTICALLY

Critical Mass and Economies of Scale R&D can be an expensive activity in terms both of personnel and equipment. The domestic market where the firm started its R&D has the best opportunities for economies of scale. It may be difficult to get the critical mass necessary for efficient and effective R&D in foreign markets. Start-up costs and learning time are deterrents to starting up foreign R&D.

Easier Communication and Coordination There is no doubt that management of R&D is facilitated when carried on in just one country instead of several. Communication and coordination are easier when there are fewer language and cultural barriers to surmount and when there is shorter physical distance to cover. Duplication of effort is less a problem with centralized R&D also.

Better Protection of Know-How Ideas and techniques coming out of R&D are among the most valued possessions of the firm, and they must be safeguarded. Patents are one means of protecting this intellectual property. Another means is close control over the R&D process and personnel. This control is facilitated by centralizing R&D in the home country.

More Leverage with Host Governments It is a common business strategy to avoid putting too many eggs in one basket. In the present case that means multinationals may resist locating R&D in a country where they already have production and marketing operations. By withholding R&D from a country, they feel less vulnerable to adverse government action, especially expropriation. If a firm has R&D facilities in a country, it has more to lose, and the country more to gain, in an expropriation.

More Domestic Experience and Expertise Most multinationals have their longest experience, largest market and greatest expertise in their domestic market. They are further down both the learning curve and the experience curve in their home market. Since R&D must relate to the rest of the firm's operations, it can be argued that greater synergy is possible between R&D, production and marketing in the home market than in foreign markets.

Whatever reasons companies may have for their R&D location policy, the fact is that R&D is highly centralized in the home countries of multinationals. The most comprehensive evidence we have is for U.S. companies. A government funded study conducted by the Conference Board showed that 90 percent of company expenditures on R&D were made in the United States.[2] No such macro studies exist for other home countries of multinationals but there is evidence that other multinationals behave as the Americans on this score. (Canadian firms may be an exception as we shall see later.) Philips of the Netherlands, and Hoffman-La Roche and Nestle of Switzerland are illustrations. These three firms are large multinationals from small countries. It could be argued that since most of their sales are outside the home country, they would have more reason than American firms to decentralize R&D. In spite of their different situation, however, these firms also have highly centralized R&D in the country where they are located.

WHY DECENTRALIZE R&D ABROAD?

Although R&D by multinationals is highly centralized in home markets, many multinationals do conduct R&D in foreign markets. For American firms, foreign R&D amounts to about ten percent of the total, or over one billion dollars annually since 1971. IBM alone spent over $200 million annually on foreign R&D in the early 1970's. There are a variety of external pressures and company motivations for conducting R&D abroad.

Transfer of Technology Ronstadt studied foreign R&D in seven large U.S. multinationals and found the major initial corporate motivation to be the transfer of technology to their foreign operations to aid in the production of existing company products rather than in the development of new products abroad.[3] However, the evolution of these units was in the direction of new product development for local or even regional or global markets.

Subsidiary Pressures Multinationals often come to conduct R&D abroad because of subsidiary pressures. For example, local staff might become restive if their status remains that of "just a factory operation" instead of moving toward that of a full-fledged member of the multinational family. In this way, Sperry-Vickers acceded to the demands of European subsidiaries for "a fair share" of R&D. Granting R&D to local operations thus reduces discontent and improves morale in the subsidiary.

Host Government Influences There are both incentives and pressures by host governments to conduct local R&D. For example, Canada offers financial rewards, which encouraged National Cash Register to begin a new research program in Canada, and helped IBM and Control Data to expand their Canadian R&D. Host governments also try to require multinationals to conduct R&D locally to maximize the technology fallout from their operations. While governments have difficulty in pressuring foreign firms to initiate R&D, they have more success in getting multinationals to continue R&D in the local companies they acquire. For example, Britain feared that Chrysler's acquisition of Rootes would lead to a brain drain to the United States, so the government required as a condition of purchase that Chrysler maintain Rootes' existing R&D activity. Corning Glass maintained and expanded an R&D operation in a French acquisition to keep a promise made to the French government.

Public Relations Value   In addition to improved subsidiary morale and compliance with host governments, there is often a public relations reward in conducting R&D locally. For example, IBM has gained a great deal of favorable publicity as a result of having conducted R&D in Europe, just as Hoechst has in India—a very different environment. Conversely, a firm that refuses to conduct R&D in foreign markets may suffer from bad public relations.

Research Talent and Product Skill Gains   Conducting R&D abroad can be a way of tapping personnel who have sophisticated research talent and specialized product skills, but who are unwilling to leave their home country. This has been important to firms in such science-based industries as electronics, computers, chemicals and pharmaceuticals. For example, even an advanced company like Hewlett-Packard found it advantageous to locate R&D facilities near the Universities of Edinburgh and Stuttgart which exercised world research leadership in certain products of interest to the company. The U.S. Manufacturing Chemists Association claims that only three of the world's top ten chemical research organizations belong to U.S. companies and that eleven of the nineteen great chemical innovations of the past thirty years were based on foreign discoveries.[4]

Potential Cost Savings   A further incentive to establish local R&D is potential cost savings in many countries where scientific and technical personnel are paid less than in the firm's home market. For instance, Europe used to be less expensive than the United States, although that appears to be changing. On the other hand, a country like India offers technical skills at modest remuneration compared to Europe or the United States. The Conference Board study found that "there is strong evidence that the performance of R&D overseas is less costly than in the United States."[5]

New Ideas and Products   With R&D in more than one country a greater and more varied flow of new ideas and products may be possible. There are theoretical arguments to support this position on decentralized R&D,[6] a few examples of which can be given here. Research and development personnel in any one country are subject to one set of environmental constraints and influences, while those in other countries are subject to a different set. Monroe Auto Equipment, for example, set up an R&D facility in the Netherlands because American R&D in auto parts is so dominated by General Motors that no one dares to innovate very far from GM design. Europe is a much more fragmented market, and different kinds of product design can be tried, resulting in potential innovations.

Unilever has a deliberate policy of decentralizing R&D. Accordingly, a vice-chairman stated, "By locating R&D activities in a number of countries, an international firm can take advantage of its unique ability to do research in a variety of national environments. The probability of success is increased if there is good liaison between laboratories. There is a greater chance of sparking off new ideas."

Wothington Pump's Italian subsidiary in 1975 earned 200,000 dollars in royalties from its American parent because of developments originating in the local R&D operation. This is an explicit and notable illustration of the contribution of foreign R&D in one company.

Faster and Better Results   An international division of labor in R&D can sometimes mean faster and more effective results than central-ized R&D. In his study of seven U.S. multina-tionals, Ronstadt found that part of their expan-sion of foreign R&D "was based on the need to utilize internal engineering, manufacturing and marketing resources in a large scale effort to develop complete new lines of products."[7] Fol-lowing this principle, IBM was able to meet its development targets for the System 360 in the 1960s.

More recent examples are Honeywell and Kodak. Honeywell introduced a new five-model computer line in 1974. Development be-gan in the early 1970's with competitive pres-sures for an early output. The French company was assigned one of the five models for devel-opment, and the Italian company another. French and American operations shared re-sponsibility for the critical Model 64. The pro-gramming languages and software were shared by the company's British and U.S. operations. Technical coordination was from Minneapolis. The international division of labor enabled Honeywell to meet its goals for introducing the new line.

For its new instant camera, Kodak required a fast film using a high speed emulsion four times as responsive to light as any then known. An international team began working on this in 1973. It involved one thousand employees in Europe and the United States for one year. The final product used an emulsion developed in En-gland, refined in Rochester, and made commer-cial with the help of French expertise in emul-sion control. This marked another successful collaboration in international R&D.

Greater Sensitivity to Local Markets Local R&D will be better attuned to local market needs and desires than R&D centralized in a distant and different market. This is especially true with products for which cultural and mar-ket considerations play a greater role than purely technical aspects. This applies more to consumer than to industrial goods, but indus-trial goods are not exempt either. For instance,

Otis Elevator conducts R&D on small elevators in Europe because there is no real market for them in the United States. Leroy notes that lo-cal market peculiarities are also the reason Al-can's Building Products Division decentralizes its R&D abroad.[8]

An example in consumer goods is Beacham's in Brazil. The local subsidiary felt there was a local demand for a deodorant with a strictly feminine image. The Brazilian staff developed the product and made extensive local tests of the deodorant and perfume element. From these tests the Brazilian company developed and introduced the product. Within one year it was already vying for the number one position in the market.

In automobiles, Ford in Brazil provides an example. For many years, Ford had reasonable success in that country by adapting cars origi-nally made in the United States. Yet Ford's big-gest winner was the Corcel, a car produced by local R&D in Brazil.

Continuation After Acquisition It is likely that R&D obtained through acquisition will be con-tinued by the acquiring firm. Most acquisitions are not made to obtain R&D facilities, but once the R&D is acquired there are strong reasons for keeping it: morale in the subsidiary; govern-ment and public relations; and new skills and personnel acquired. Often the acquired R&D is in a product area new to the firm; for example, in Italy Dow Chemical acquired Le Petit in pharmaceuticals, and likewise Gillette acquired DuPont in France where Cricket lighters had been developed. Carnation is a company that entered many foreign markets by acquisition, and acquired overseas R&D capability in sev-eral new product areas this way.

U.S. Tax Law Changes For U.S. firms the at-tractiveness of expanding abroad can increase with changes in application of U.S. tax law. As-sume an American firm does all of its R&D in the United States but has half of its sales abroad. If the firm can get credit on its U.S. taxes for only the proportion of R&D corresponding to its U.S. sales, then, in this case, it has one half of its R&D uncovered. This would give the firm an incentive to move some or all of that uncovered part abroad where it, too, could enjoy a tax saving.[9] This is an oversimplified illustration of a complex topic, but it does indicate the potential influence of tax considerations on R&D locations.

It is possible that some multinationals have not yet addressed the question of whether to conduct R&D abroad, but have merely continued to do all their R&D at home. Many others, however, have had to face the issue either when it was raised by their subsidiaries or foreign governments, or when they acquired a foreign firm with R&D. Rather than responding to such events on an ad hoc basis, the firm can improve its decision making by incorporating R&D location policy into its overall strategy for international business development. Historically, much of the internationalization of a firm's marketing, production, and especially R&D, has been relatively unplanned. All three activities should be part of the firm's global strategic planning.

This article will offer no solutions to the questions raised. In contrast to the internationalizing of marketing and production, the theories and strategies for internationalizing R&D are relatively underdeveloped. More study is needed by both business planners and academic investigators. As a contribution to that study, the author suggests the following generalizations for further investigation and testing.

SOME GENERALIZATIONS ON THE LOCATION OF R&D

Multinationals conduct most of their R&D in their home countries. The proportion done in the United States by American firms is about ninety percent, but this depends somewhat on accounting practices and definitions.[10] Canadian firms may be an exception to this, since some of them have transferred R&D to the United States.

Increasingly multinationals are conducting R&D in their foreign markets. For all U.S. firms the amount spent on foreign R&D in 1966 was about 500 million dollars or 7.4 percent of U.S. expenditures. The amount spent abroad in 1972 was over 1.2 billion dollars or 10 percent of U.S. corporate expenditures.[11] An industry example is given by the U.S. drug industry which increased its foreign R&D from five percent of the total in 1960 to ten percent of the total in 1970. The drug industry illustrates both generalizations: most R&D is done at home but a growing proportion is done abroad.

The larger markets of the firm will have the earliest and largest share of the multinationals' foreign R&D activity. For American firms this means primarily Canada and Western Europe, with Brazil the leading host country in Latin America. In fact, three countries account for almost two-thirds of the overseas R&D of U.S. companies—Canada, the United Kingdom, and Germany.[12] European firms conduct above average amounts of R&D in the large U.S. market. And Canadian based multinationals have even transferred significant segments of R&D to the United States from Canada. At the same time, multinationals conduct only limited R&D in developing countries, though the amount is growing. For U.S. firms the proportion of foreign R&D conducted in the less developed countries rose from 1.8 percent in 1966 to 3.3 percent in 1972. For less developed countries, Ben-Porath has discussed the implications of size and level of development for investment in R&D.[13]

For a country to become an R&D location it must have sufficient scientific and technical personnel. If it has these, it may be a small or less developed country and still attract R&D. Swedish SKF chose Holland as the location of a major R&D center. Cyanamid chose the Philippines for a regional R&D center. In both cases personnel considerations were critical. On the basis of size and availability of personnel, India is a good candidate. On the other hand, General Motors developed its Basic Transportation Vehicle in the United States because of a lack of qualified personnel in the target markets.

Acquisition of foreign companies is a major means by which multinationals initiate or expand foreign R&D. This is true even though the major reason for the acquisition usually has nothing to do with R&D but is primarily a means of market entry. Firms tend to keep the R&D they acquire. Ronstadt's study of seven U.S. multinationals found that 25 percent of their foreign R&D was in facilities acquired when they bought local firms and then continued their R&D activity.[14] Britain's Imperial Chemical Industries acquired Atlas Chemical in the United States and not only continued its R&D but switched over to the United States some products that were being developed in Britain.

Frequently the acquisition represents a new area of R&D for the firm: for example, Braun and small appliances for Gillette; Knorr and soups for Corn Products Company. Another inducement to the acquisition of foreign R&D is that R&D abroad is ahead of U.S. R&D in some product areas. Some examples in pharmaceuticals are the following: Smith Kline & French bought the Belgian lab that developed the Rubella vaccine for measles; Merck, an R&D leader, paid out 5.9 million dollars in royalties for drugs developed abroad while receiving only 4.9 million dollars.

Industry and product line are variables in this decision. There is more decentralization in consumer goods than in industrial goods. Whenever local market characteristics, adaptation, and testing are important, there is more local R&D than when technical considerations predominate. For example, there is more decentralized R&D in food than in non-food consumer goods; more decentralization with automobiles than with tractors or diesel engines; more with pharmaceuticals than with chemicals. However, the evidence also suggests that there is no product or industry in which technical factors are the sole influence. A good example is the chemical industry which, though highly technically oriented, usually needs some decentralization of R&D, especially at the development end. This can be seen in the experience of Cyanamid, Dow, and DuPont, among others.

Host government pressures and incentives do influence the location of R&D. Some examples were given earlier. There is evidence that several countries have had some success in attracting local R&D by multinationals, for example Britain, Canada, France, Spain, Brazil, and India.

An important variable in the decentralization of R&D is the divisibility of R&D as a corporate activity. It is divisible on at least two bases: one is by product line, and the other is by the nature or level of the R&D.

Product Line R&D Decentralization R&D decentralization by product line is especially common when a multinational enters a new product area by acquisition. The examples of Carnation, Corn Products Company, Dow and Gillette have been cited earlier. However, R&D decentralization by product line also occurs apart from acquisition. Many multinationals have a policy of decentralizing R&D by division or product line. Corn Products Company has its R&D for industrial products centered in its Belgian subsidiary. Imperial Chemical Company assigns to ICI-Europe the research on fibers and polymers, and to ICI-America the basic research on resins, pharmaceuticals and specialty chemicals, with all the other areas being covered by ICI-UK. In the computer field, Burroughs, Honeywell, and IBM all do significant R&D abroad for varied parts of their product line.

Decentralization by Level of Technology Generally, the simpler the technology and the closer to the development end of the R&D spectrum, the more multinationals will decentralize. Ronstadt found the primary reason seven major U.S. multinationals established R&D abroad was to help transfer technology from the parent to the subsidiary.[15] Kacker found that twenty-six U.S. firms in India did almost no basic research but concentrated on applied research to determine the feasibility of using local materials in the firms' products.[16] Cordell found that multinationals' R&D in Canada is also primarily of the support or application variety.[17] Hood and Young find the same thing with regard to U.S. multinationals in Scotland.[18]

Crookell notes, "When the product has a high technological content, the subsidiary usually depends on the parent for the basic research . . .. When the technology content of the product is low, the skills of the sub may be sufficient to develop it alone. For example, Canadian General Electric introduced a lawn trimmer in Canada. The parent company didn't follow this so CGE was able to secure access to the United States through G.E.'s extensive distribution system."[19]

Once foreign R&D is established by the firm, it tends to evolve away from technology transfer and adaptation toward more basic research and product development. Many of the forces behind the initial establishment of foreign R&D cause it to evolve in the direction of greater sophistication. The work of Leroy and Ronstadt confirms the author's findings here. Hewlett-Packard's foreign R&D began as technology transfer but evolved rather quickly into product development to the extent that over one-fourth of H-P's overseas sales are of products developed locally. Many of Ronstadt's respondents stated that the best incentive they could offer their R&D people was the opportunity to become involved with more challenging technology. Technical service work was not demanding enough to challenge and retain their best people.[20]

Foreign R&D follows foreign direct investment and tends to be associated with manufacturing operations. Firms do not usually establish foreign R&D units in isolation. Foreign manufacturing is the first presence of the firm abroad, usually after some export experience. Later in the firm's international development may come foreign R&D. This R&D is almost always associated with manufacturing operations because its initial purpose is to aid in the transfer of technology from the parent firm. This has been noted in the Creamer, Leroy and Ronstadt studies, but it is also verified in the experience of most multinationals.

The longer the firm has been engaged in international business and the larger this business is relative to the total, the more decentralized is the firm's R&D. This has been shown for the U.S. pharmaceutical industry and can be illustrated in the case histories of most multinationals. Leroy found it to be almost a part of the growth pattern of the U.S. and Canadian multinationals he studied.[21] It is verified in the experience of U.S. companies in England also.[22]

CONCLUSIONS

From our discussion there emerges no simple model to help a firm decide whether to conduct foreign R&D. There are strong arguments both for centralizing and for decentralizing R&D in the multinational company. An individual or case approach may be necessary in this decision. We have identified many of the variables a firm must consider. The question has been made more urgent for American firms because of recent interpretations by the IRS. The issue of R&D location is becoming more pressing for all multinationals, however, because of the demands by the third world for increased technology transfer in the New International Economic Order. Further research can aid decision making in this area.

NOTES

1. D. B. Creamer, *Overseas Research and Development by U.S. Multinationals, 1966–1975* (New York: The Conference Board, 1976), p. 7.

2. Ibid., p. 4.

3. R. C. Ronstadt, "R&D Abroad." Unpublished dissertation, Harvard University, p. 121.

4. *Multinational Chemical Companies* (New York: Manufacturing Chemists Association, 1974), p. 8.

5. Creamer, op. cit., p. 6.

6. See, for example, J. Jewkes, et al., *The Sources of In-*

vention (New York: St. Martin's Press, 1959); K. Arrow, "The Economic Implications of Learning by Doing," *Review of Economic Studies,* Vol. 29, no. 80 (1962), pp. 155–173; S. Hollander, *The Sources of Increased Efficiency* (Cambridge, Mass.: MIT Press, 1965).

7. Ronstadt, op. cit., p. 186.

8. G. Leroy, *Multinational Product Strategy* (New York: Praeger Publishers, 1976), pp. 105–106.

9. Conversation with Michael Lake, tax manager, Clark Equipment.

10. Creamer, op. cit., p. 4.

11. Ibid.

12. Ibid.

13. Y. Ben-Porath, "Some Implications of Economic Size and Level for Investment in R&D," *Economic Development and Cultural Change,* October 1972, pp. 96–103.

14. Ronstadt, op. cit., p. 120.

15. Ibid., p. 121.

16. M. Kacker, *Marketing Adaptation of U.S. Firms in India* (New Delhi: Sterling Publishers), 1974, p. 43.

17. A.J. Cordell, "Innovation, the MNC and Some Implications for National Science Policy," *Long Range Planning,* September 1973, pp. 22–29.

18. N. Hood, and S. Young, "U.S. Investment in Scotland," *Scottish Journal of Political Economy* (November 1976), pp. 279–294.

19. H. Crookell. "The Transmission of Technology Across National Boundaries," *The Business Quarterly,* Autumn, 1973, pp. 52–60.

20. Ronstadt, op. cit., 175.

21. Leroy, op. cit.

22. Hood and Young, op. cit., 286.

34

Transnational Corporations: Market Orientations and R&D Abroad

Jack N. Behrman
William A. Fischer

• • •

Over the past several decades, the transfer of technology, in its various guises, has become an accepted part of doing business for transnational corporations and has been profitable for many of them. Other things being equal, most transnational corporations would be reluctant to transfer abroad the origins of their technology—their research and development (R&D) activities. Since other things are not equal in reality, however, the transnationals have increasingly found themselves considering where and how they will do their R&D. For many of them this is a relatively new situation; but,

Source: Jack N. Behrman and William A. Fishcer, "Transnational Corporations: Market Orientations and R&D Abroad," *The Columbia Journal of World Business,* Fall 1980, pp. 55–60. Copyright © by the Trustees of Columbia University in the City of New York. Reprinted by permission.

given expectations in the developing countries, one which will become more common in the near future.

R&D activities of American firms abroad have increased over the past decade. The 1966 foreign R&D expenditures of American companies were estimated to be $537 million.[1] By 1979:

Expenditures of U.S. firms for research and development performed abroad reached $1.5 billion, increasing 41 percent from 1974 to 1977, compared to a 32 percent increase for industrial research and development performed within the United States.[2]

Yet it was further noted that "the vast majority of U.S. firms do not conduct any research and development abroad. According to the Census Bureau, only an estimated 15 percent of the major U.S. industrial performers maintain foreign laboratories. These firms, however, account for nearly one-half of total U.S. company-funded R&D expenditures."[3]

In order to formulate effective policies, officials in developing and developed countries, and in the transnational corporations, need to understand why certain firms choose to pursue R&D abroad while others don't, and what the consequences of such activities are. None of this information is available from the statistics.

Recently, several studies of multinational R&D behavior have chronicled the experiences of transnational firms performing R&D abroad.[4] While these case studies improve our understanding of this phenomenon by supplying more information, they tend to lack a framework enabling them to go beyond mere data collection to a fuller understanding of the dynamics involved in the foreign R&D location decision. On the basis of a substantial amount of interviewing among transnational corporations, we believe that a rather simple taxonomy based upon market orientations can be quite useful in explaining the decision to do R&D abroad.

MARKET ORIENTATIONS

The market orientation of a transnational corporation refers to the market it is primarily interested in serving. There are three possible primary market orientations: home market, host market, and world market. While it is possible for a firm to appear to have several market orientations, they are often mutually exclusive for a given product line.

Home Market Firms

"Home market" firms are primarily concerned with investing abroad for the purpose of serving their domestic market through imports of materials and components. It is unusual for them to have international R&D operations. To the extent that such firms do R&D abroad, it usually is in support of their domestic market objectives. Typical firms of this type are the extrac-

tive industries and offshore component assemblers taking advantage of resource availability or low-wage labor in foreign locations to improve their ability to compete domestically. These firms can be expected to have few durable foreign scientific and technical commitments, a highly ethnocentric managerial style, low external orientation on the part of management, and an organizational structure that is largely unaffected by the firm's foreign operations. The products of these firms tend to be highly standardized, often because of their commodity nature, needing no diversified R&D effort.

Host Market Firms

Foreign affiliates of "host market" firms are oriented to the markets of the place where they are located. Included among these firms are industries spanning a range of technical sophistication from chemicals and pharmaceuticals, to foods and tobacco, to services. The products of the firms in this category typically exhibit a high degree of standardization within a market but not necessarily between markets. The management style of these firms can be characterized as polycentric, since a relatively low level of control is exerted by corporate headquarters over a decentralized organizational structure. Their need for R&D abroad is dictated by the diversity of market demands on their products.

World Market Firms

"World market" firms are those whose foreign affiliates are integrated to serve a standardized international market. These firms are typically organized to achieve economies of scale based upon high technology and a high degree of worldwide product standardization, and guided by a geocentric management style and a highly centralized corporate structure. They also have diverse R&D needs reflecting the range of markets they serve and the sources of ideas they must monitor.

THE SAMPLE STUDIED

The utility of these market orientations in explaining foreign R&D behavior among transnational corporations was demonstrated in a study of 35 American and 18 European transnational corporations, undertaken during 1978. The purpose of the study was to determine: what type of R&D is being performed abroad by transnational corporations; how they have come to select their foreign sites; how they manage their foreign R&D activities; what sort of collaborative R&D activities they are engaged in; and the nature of their relationship with host-country governments.[5]

Data collection for the study consisted of structured interviews conducted with top R&D executives in each firm. The average interview lasted approximately two and one-half hours, ranging from one hour in the few firms with little foreign R&D experience to a full day with those with extensive experience. Most of the firms interviewed were chosen because of their foreign R&D experience.

FOREIGN R&D ACTIVITIES OF THE FIRMS STUDIED

Although the firms were selected because of their foreign R&D experiences, the volume of activity discovered was surprising. Among the 31 American transnationals reporting foreign R&D activities, 106 active foreign R&D groups were identified. Furthermore, the European transnationals appeared even more active, with the 18 firms interviewed reporting 100 distinct foreign R&D activities. While most of these foreign activities were smaller in size and more restricted in scope than the R&D activities pursued at home, they were distinctly involved with R&D and were not technical services or quality control.

The firms included in this study were typically large firms (*Fortune* 500 members) whose relatively strong commitment to R&D was evidenced by their membership in the Industrial

Research Institute in the U.S. or the European Industrial Research Managers Association. Although they exhibited significant foreign R&D activities, their international manufacturing and marketing operations were far more numerous and dispersed than their R&D activities. Although the firms we shall describe are clearly among the largest in the world in terms of both sales and geographic spread, they are representative of firms pursuing R&D activities in foreign locations, since such activities, by their very nature, are the domain of large multinational organizations.

The large majority of the foreign R&D activities identified among the American transnational corporations belonged to firms with a "host market" orientation (96 out of the 106 foreign R&D activities identified, or 91%. While this reflects, to some extent, the preponderance of "host market" firms in the sample 23 of the 34 American firms (68%) had "host market" orientations it goes beyond a simple proportional relationship. The "host market" companies averaged more than four foreign R&D activities per firm, compared with less than two among the four American "world market" companies, and slightly less than one-half of a foreign R&D activity for each of the seven American "home market" companies (Table 1). All of the European firms, but one, had "host market" orientations. Thus, a comparison of their propensity to pursue R&D abroad cannot be made with their counterparts favoring other market orientations. However, when the European R&D activities are considered along with those of the American firms, the combined 38 "host market" firms account for 184 foreign R&D activities, or 89% of those identified.

Among the American transnational corporations it was possible to discern the nature of the R&D mission assigned to most of the foreign R&D activities. Thirty of the 106 foreign R&D activities (28%) had missions which included new product research, and of these 30 facilities, 25 belonged to "host market" firms and five

Table 1 Foreign R&D Activities of Transnational Corporations

Market Orientation	American Firms Number of Firms	Number of Foreign R&D Activities
Home market	7	3
Host market	23	96
World market	4	7
Not included	1	
	European Firms	
Home market	0	0
Host market	15	88
World market	1	12
Not included	2	

belonged to "world market" companies (Table 2). Three of the five foreign laboratories of American corporations dedicated to exploratory research belonged to "world market" firms.

LOCATION OF FOREIGN R&D ACTIVITIES

Over thirty different countries were identified in our interviews as hosting the foreign R&D activities of the firms in the sample. Both American and European firms indicated that their foreign R&D activities were predominantly located in developed countries, such as the U.S., France, the U.K., Japan, Canada, Australia, and Germany, and in advanced developing countries, such as Mexico, Brazil, and India (Table 3).

The "host market" firms appeared most likely to establish R&D activities in developing

Table 3 Most Popular Sites for Foreign R&D Activities*

American Firms		European Firms	
U.K.	(11)	U.S.	(14)
Australia	(8)	France	(10)
Canada	(8)	Germany	(9)
Japan	(8)	India	(6)
France	(7)	Brazil	(5)
Germany	(6)	U.K.	(5)
Mexico	(6)		
Brazil	(5)		

*Numbers in parentheses refer to the number of corporations reporting an R&D presence in particular country.

countries. As it was important to them to get as close to the markets they were seving as possible, they would favorably consider developing country locations when necessary, if the market was an attractive one and if the R&D group could be supported both financially and technically.

Table 2 Inclusion of New Product: Research Responsibilities in the Missions of Foreign Laboratories (American Firms Only)

Market Orientation	Number of Foreign Laboratories with a New Product Research Mission	Percentage of Foreign Laboratories with a New Product Research Mission
"World market"	5	71%
"Host market"	25	26
"Home market"	0	0

THE MOTIVATION TO DO R&D ABROAD

The propensity of various firms to do R&D in the developing countries highlights the topic of motivation to do R&D abroad. "Home market" firms typically have little or no sales in foreign markets. When they do sell to foreign customers, they view it as a direct extension of their domestic business, not requiring any further R&D beyond that which has already been performed for the original, (domestic) market. Because of their extractive operations, and their employment of low-wage workers for assembly operations, "home market" firms tend to have high exposure in the developing world. They have not, however, located much R&D activity in these countries because they typically do not refine raw materials or sell components or finished products in these markets. Accordingly, in those few instances when "home market" companies did consider doing R&D abroad they were most interested in being close to their foreign operations in order to provide technical support.

Firms involved in the international marketing of goods and services designed to satisfy local styles and tastes have a more compelling reason to do R&D abroad. These firms need to be as close to their markets as possible. Illustrative of such motivation is the agricultural chemical firm that needs to test its products in the markets they are intended for and, hence, has facilities in South America to treat South American pest problems, facilities in the Far East to address problems of tropical climates, and facilities in the Philippines to provide market conditions indicative of Japan. Similarly, all of the American pharmaceutical firms interviewed had European formulation laboratories as a result of European preferences for drug administration practices which differ from those in the U.S.

"Host market" firms also tend to endorse the proposition that their foreign affiliates often serve distinctive markets and, as such, are autonomous business entities requiring R&D of their own. Rosemarie Van Rumker's experience with Chemagro Corporation explains just such a philosophy:

> Attempts to establish *direct* links between research in one country and technology and the market place in another country have largely been unsuccessful. In my experience, the barriers of distance and language can be overcome reasonably well by scientists working within the same discipline, but scientists in one country are not good at answering the specific market needs of another country. . . .
>
> We believe that the best way to overcome this problem is to have subsidiaries in important markets away from the parent company develop their own complete R&D organizations, to enable them to take full and direct advantage of the opportunities peculiar to their environment, and to be full-fledged practicing members of the scientific and technological community in their country.[6]

While all of the firms interviewed expressed an interest in enhancing their relationship with host country governments, the "host market" firms, with their national market focus, were particularly sensitive to the importance of such relationships. In a number of cases, this sensitivity resulted in the establishment of foreign R&D activities, some of which have become particularly productive.

The "world market" firms are concerned with the availability abroad of specific types of skills in particular technical areas. This, of course, is in keeping with their propensity to assign new product development responsibility to foreign R&D groups. More than one of the foreign R&D laboratories of the "world market" firms was characterized as having achieved a level of competence in a technical area which far surpassed the capabilities of other research groups in the corporation. Accordingly, "world market" firms typically establish their R&D abroad without regard for the location of their existing international manufacturing and marketing operations. They are much more attracted to the concentration of

Table 4 Important Criteria for Considering or Not Considering Overseas R&D Locations

	Home Market Firms	**Host Market Firms**	**Worldwide Market Firms**
Important criteria for considering an overseas R&D location	1. Proximity to operations	1. Proximity to markets	1. Availability of pockets of skills in particular technical areas
	2. Availability of universities	2. Concept of overseas operations as full-scale business entities	2. Access to foreign scientific and technical communities 3. Availability of adequate infrastructure and universities
Important criteria for not considering overseas R&D locations	1. Products sold in the developing countries are not sophisticated 2. Lack of qualified scientists and engineers 3. Economics of centralized R&D	1. Increasing costs of doing R&D overseas 2. Economics of centralized R&D	1. Economics of centralized R&D 2. Difficulties in assembling R&D teams

knowledge and talent than to market size in a foreign country.

A summary of the important criteria for considering or not considering overseas R&D locations by firms in the various market orientation categories is presented in Table 4.

THE CRITICAL MASS OF FOREIGN R&D GROUPS

As Table 4 reveals, one of the principal deterrents to the performance of R&D abroad by transnational firms is their perception that they will be unable to assemble an R&D group large enough and diverse enough to be productive. While the size of an R&D group is a function of many variables, there is substantial agreement within the R&D community that a "critical mass" of R&D professionals must be reached if a laboratory is to be a worthwhile investment. This "critical mass" is the size necessary to ensure rich communications both within the group and between the group and its environment, to allow the degree of scientific and tech-

nical interaction among the group's personnel necessary to fulfill its mission, and to acquire whatever instrumentation and organization are necessary for acceptable performance. There is considerable variation in the estimates of "critical mass" for specific situations, but in general, R&D laboratories in industries serving consumer markets (i.e., "host market" firms) require a smaller R&D staff to reach "critical mass" than do laboratories in science based industries. Furthermore, R&D groups in consumer-oriented industries require less sophisticated personnel and less variety in personnel specialization than do R&D groups in science based industries. These observations suggest that "host market" firms are more likely than their counterparts to be in a position to establish R&D in a developing country.

THE ESTABLISHMENT OF R&D ABROAD

There are several ways in which a transnational corporation can establish R&D activities abroad: it can allow R&D to evolve from tech-

Table 5 Methods of Establishing Foreign R&D Activities*

Market Orientation	Evolution from Technical Service	Direct Placement	Acquisition
"Home market"	2	0	0
"Host market"	33	11	18
"World market"	2	5	0

*The data in this table represent only those instances where the means of establishing the foreign laboratory could be ascertained. All data in this table come from American corporations.

nical support activities for marketing or manufacturing; it can directly establish R&D activities abroad with the intention of doing R&D right from the start; it can acquire some other corporation's R&D activities; it can enter into some form of collaborative R&D arrangement with another partner. Just as market orientation appears to affect the location and mission of foreign R&D activities, it influences the means of establishing these activities.

In 71 of the foreign R&D activities of American firms it was possible to ascertain the means of establishment. In approximately one-half of these cases an evolutionary pattern where R&D originated from technical services was evident. Nearly all of these cases were found among "host market" firms and two of the three foreign "home market" laboratories were also in this group. In approximately 28 percent of the cases direct placement was the means of establishment and, while most of these were attributable to "host market" firms, more than 70 percent of the foreign laboratories of "world market" firms were established in this manner. Almost 25 percent of the laboratories were established through acquisition, all of them being by "host market" companies (Table 5).

The data collected on laboratory establishment appears to agree quite well with the findings reported earlier. "Home market" firms are not interested in R&D abroad and so what foreign R&D of theirs does exist is the result of an evolution of capabilities and missions among their technical support activities. Conversely, "world market" firms are interested in pursuing R&D abroad if they can gain access to particular technological skills or communities. Accordingly, they tend to rely more upon direct placement of their foreign R&D activities, as their other foreign commercial operations are not necessarily related to their R&D activities. "Host market" firms need to be close to the markets they serve and they will utilize a variety of methods to get there.

COLLABORATIVE R&D ARRANGEMENTS

At least 28 specific manufacturing joint ventures between parent companies of different nationalities, which required R&D support in some form, were reported in the interviews. All but four of these belonged to "host market" companies. Our interviews indicated quite clearly that the key determinant of *active* R&D participation by a transnational firm in such a venture is the ownership position it commands. Foreign joint ventures will bring forth *new* R&D only when the transnational firm can maintain control over that R&D, namely, when it possesses a majority interest in the joint venture.

HOST-GOVERNMENT RELATIONS

As noted earlier, although all firms professed an interest in maintaining good relationships with host country governments, "host market" firms appeared particularly sensitive to pressure from their hosts. During our interviews, fourteen American and five European firms indicated having received some form of pressure from host country governments hoping to influence their foreign R&D location decisions. Sixteen of these firms had "host market" orientations. Furthermore, 19 foreign R&D laboratories were identified as having their origins in host government pressure, three of these being joint ventures, and in four other cases the pressure resulted in the acquisition of R&D results without a laboratory. The countries most active in attempting to influence transnational corporations were Brazil, France, India, and Japan.

CONCLUSIONS

The data presented in this study argue strongly for the usefulness of a simple taxonomy of transnational corporations, based upon market-orientations. The location and operations of foreign R&D laboratories of transnational corporations can be explained by referring to the market orientations of the firms in question.

The data presented indicated that a considerable amount of R&D is presently being performed abroad by both American and European transnational corporations. While most of this R&D is located in developed countries, there is diversity among the locations selected. This diversity, in part, reflects the varying market orientations of the firms. Market orientation also appears to be an important determinant of the means by which a transnational corporation establishes R&D activities abroad.

The evidence presented suggests that trans-national corporations with "host market" orientations are generally most likely to pursue R&D abroad, particularly when developing countries are at issue. They are, however, less likely than their "world market" counterparts to delegate new product research responsibilities to their foreign laboratories, and they also rely heavily upon evolution from technical services as a means of establishing foreign R&D groups.

NOTES

1. D. Creamer, *Overseas Research and Development by United States Multinationals, 1966–1975* (New York: The Conference Board, 1976), pp. 3–4.

2. "U.S. Industrial R&D Spending Abroad," Industry Studies Group, Division of Science Studies, U.S. National Science Foundation, *Reviews of Data on Science Resources*, NSF 79-304, No. 33, April 1979, p. 1.

3. Ibid., p. 3.

4. W. T. Hanson, "Multinational R&D in Practice: Eastman Kodak Corporation," *Research Management*, January 1971, pp. 47–50; M. Papo, "How to Establish and Operate a Multinational Lab," *Research Management*, January 1971, pp. 12–19; R. Van. Rumker, "Multinational R&D in Practice: Chemagro Corporation," *Research Management*, January 1971, pp. 50–54; R. C. Ronstadt, "International R&D: The Establishment and Evolution of Research and Development Abroad by Seven U.S. Multinationals," *Journal of International Business Studies*, Vol. 9 (1978), pp. 7–24.

5. For a more complete report on this study the reader is advised to see: J. N. Behrman and W. A. Fischer, *Overseas R&D Activities of Transnational Corporation* (Cambridge, Mass: Oelgeschlager, Gunn & Hain, 1980).

6. Van Rumker, op. cit., p. 52. Emphasis added.

35

Getting the Most Out of Innovation Abroad
Robert Ronstadt
Robert J. Kramer

• • •

In the late 1950s, over 80% of the world's major innovations were introduced first in the United States. By 1965 this figure had declined to 55%, and the decline continues today.

In recent years, Japanese business executives have made more than 40,000 technical trips annually to the United States to study and acquire American technology. Their U.S. counterparts, however, scan new technology much less intensively or systematically.

The central message behind these facts is that the United States has lost the great advantage it once enjoyed in many technological areas. A large number of nations have taken over leadership of one or another aspect, and other countries are also in the running for technical superiority.

For example, the French are energetic innovators in the electric traction, nuclear power, aviation, and automobile industries. West German companies lead in chemicals and pharmaceuticals, precision and heavy machinery, heavy electrical goods, metallurgy, and surface transport equipment. Japan excels in optics, solid-state physics, engineering, chemistry, and process metallurgy.

The percentage of new high-growth businesses being started abroad is increasing, together with the foreign share of major innovations. In the jargon of portfolio managers, the new enterprises emerging abroad are now the "question marks" that will evolve to some degree into the "stars" and "cash cows" of

the future. A larger number and share of fast-growth businesses abroad and continuing strong foreign competition mean lower long-term returns for the U.S. economy.

STRATEGIC AND OPERATING ISSUES

How can U.S. manufacturers respond to these challenges and changes on the worldwide technological front? Certainly, they can no longer rely nearly exclusively on domestic sources for innovations. Most large American companies, therefore, should try to exploit the creative strengths of other countries.

While maintaining dependence on their domestic resources, these companies can systematically seek out foreign-grown technology for transfer to the United States. Or they can establish R&D facilities of their own abroad while strengthening those at home. If they pursue the latter strategy, they must answer several key questions:

1. What "internationalizing" mechanisms can aid our organization in meeting its technological goals?
2. Where should we locate the company's R&D units and other innovative resources?
3. How should we manage innovative resources within the international framework?

Before considering these questions, managers will determine what types of innovation they would seek abroad. Corporations that identify new technologies only to transfer them to the United States without making a significant contribution to the local economy usually incur the displeasure, or at best the quiet non-support, of host governments and their own subsidiary businesses. Conversely, American managers will be quite unhappy with activities that help a foreign subsidiary and its host nation but make no significant technological contribution in the United States.

Most R&D investments abroad have either adapted U.S. technology and products to local markets or generated new products and processes expressly for local purposes. Only a few U.S. companies have established activities abroad that offer products and technology for commercialization in the United States or other countries or that foster the regular transfer of processes and goods to the United States.

INTERNATIONALIZING INNOVATION

To begin their internationalizing activities, companies can engage in or develop some of the following:

Scanning or Monitoring. Scanning includes reading journals, wading through patent reports, and checking other printed sources—as well as meeting people. R&D managers we interviewed consistently stressed the value of face-to-face contact with foreign scientists and technical experts through scientific-technical conferences or through in-house seminars at which leading international scientists speak. U.S. companies should also include R&D specialists on project teams that seek new foreign business or undertake overseas work assignments. In addition, companies can also create advisory panels of outside technical experts.

Connections with Academia and Research Organizations. Enterprises active in overseas R&D often pursue work-related projects with foreign academics, and they sometimes form consulting agreements with faculty members. A few corporations send their scientists to universities for short-term work projects or to take courses.

Under contract, a research institute in the United Kingdom conducts metabolism experiments for a West German pharmaceutical company. Some corporations arrange for such organizations as the Battelle Memorial Institute, the Illinois Institute of Technical Research, and the International Gas Institute to perform research for them. Others learn of new developments in industrial research policy and management through the European Industrial Research Management Association in Paris or the Industrial Research Institute in New York.

Programs to Increase Companies' Visibility. Common methods of attracting attention include participation in technology trade fairs, circulation of brochures illustrating company products and inventions, hiring technology-acquisition consultants, and providing input to computer data banks that facilitate communication between prospective purchasers and vendors.

Cooperative Research Projects. Some multinational enterprises enter into research projects with each other to broaden their contacts, reduce expenses, diminish the risk for each partner, or forestall the market entry of a competitor.

Acquiring or Merging with Foreign Companies Having Extensive Innovative Capabilities. Normally, the innovative capability of the foreigner isn't the primary reason for the merger or acquisition. Nonetheless, significant R&D and other resources may be acquired that can alter an organization's ability to innovate abroad. For example, CPC International's acquisition of Knorr Foods of Switzerland provided the American multinational with a new and important technological capability in consumer foods.

The Acquisition of External Technology by Licensing. This approach can take several forms: a company may wish to "license-in" a technological innovation from another company, "license-out" its own technology to others in the hope of getting access to improvements made by the licensee, or exchange its technology for another company's by cross-licensing.

Setting up a Program

Hoffmann-LaRoche's program illustrates how some of these approaches can be applied. This Swiss company long depended mainly on its internal R&D resources to generate new products, but in 1971 it organized a three-person licensing team to scan international markets for new pharmaceutical compounds for its U.S. subsidiary. By 1979 the team was making 30 to 40 direct-contact visits abroad on an annual basis, and the team conducted about an equal number of visits here. The members met with representatives from pharmaceutical competitors, other companies with relevant technology, and university groups.

They discovered that to license-in they had to license-out. Visits to companies were much more productive when reciprocity was the policy. As one team member noted, "We found we had to determine what we were willing to give up. We had to enter negotiations with something to trade rather than just with dollars we were willing to spend."

The team also found that repeated visits and face-to-face contact were vital for success. Telephone and written communications and the prospect of legal guarantees were insufficient to develop the mutual trust required for equitable trades.

The licensing team acquired a number of products under development. Two that subsequently generated significant sales are Amoxicillin (about $18 to $20 million) and a diagnostic test (more than $5 million). Important products are still in the pipeline; sales projections for these exceed $50 million within the next few years.

MAKING R&D INVESTMENTS ABROAD

Company-owned R&D labs located overseas provide probably the best opportunities for managers to internationalize their scanning operations and obtain foreign innovations or new technology. These labs are usually based where their products and processes are to be sold. Used to develop products for local, regional, and national markets—sometimes even worldwide markets—the laboratories are set up either to transfer technology from the United States to foreign countries or, more commonly, to fill a gap in the American parent company's supply of new products and technology to the country or region where the lab is located. This last need prompted Corning Glass, for instance, to establish a European lab in France in 1973.

To be sure, some companies are better off concentrating their R&D resources in the United States. They are usually companies whose market orientation is essentially domestic. Companies that can best control R&D costs, management, and security through one central lab are better off staying put also.

Such companies might consider subcontracting R&D activities abroad as a means of gaining access to scientists and technological information that would be unobtainable otherwise. Managers should not, however, expect this approach to yield results equivalent to in-house operations abroad because, as one knowledgeable R&D manager put it: "Subcontracting abroad is okay for getting a toehold, to learn who is good and available, and as a way to tap into the local technology base. But it should be viewed as seed money. Eventually your own organization should do the work."

Locating the Resources

We have implied that a company must have a legitimate R&D purpose to ensure the success of a foreign-based R&D investment. But what constitutes such a purpose? The answer to that question can help resolve the issue of where the international resources should be located.

The driving force is, of course, the market. As one executive stated: "Our thesis on the international conduct of R&D is simple: new product development is best undertaken closest to the market user. We believe that if the R&D for a new product is moved to a far-away location, we lose some of the market flavor and uniqueness, as well as an essential ingredient to innovative success. But make no mistake, the technical activities in these international operations, as well as those conducted at home, are very well understood by both the corporation and our laboratories.''

Bear in mind that establishing favorable conditions requires sizable commitments to foreign manufacturing facilities producing nonstandardized products, sometimes with unsettled technology. These preconditions help explain the absence of R&D facilities in certain countries and why some overseas multinationals have centralized their R&D resources in the United States. (See the ruled insert about the Japanese approach above.)

Nevertheless, research is frequently conducted away from the markets and near scientific or technological talent. Usually one or more scientists are at the forefront of a scientific field; when they cannot be enticed to relocate, companies may find it advisable to bring the mountain to Mohammed and create a lab around them.

Why Japanese Companies Centralize R&D at Home

One reason for low levels of foreign-based Japanese R&D is the rather low level of Japanese overseas manufacturing investment and the young age (compared with foreign investments of American and European companies) of that which does exist.

Also, Japanese companies tend to start marketing their products later in their life cycles—often when they are highly standardized and require little R&D.

Third, the Japanese do an excellent job of scanning. They undertake extensive patent searches, literature reviews, and visits. More than 40,000 Japanese undertook technology-related visits to the United States in 1978, versus 5,000 Americans who made such visits to Japan.

Moreover, R&D generally costs less in Japan, and these low costs encourage home-based strategies.

Finally, foreign companies with which Japanese businesses have concluded joint venture arrangements are undertaking some overseas R&D. Japanese corporations in electronics, heat foundry processes, and computers have conducted joint ventures with American companies both for marketing considerations and to supplement their own R&D. For example, Fujitsu bought a 20% equity share in Amdahl Computer Corporation in 1972. Fujitsu not only added Amdahl's computers to this product line, it also was able to absorb the U.S. company's advanced technology.

The requirements of the market and of the researchers mean that investments in foreign-based R&D facilities are concentrated in a few countries. Various surveys show that, with minor exceptions, U.S. companies have chosen to locate foreign labs in industrialized nations. The ten countries survey respondents favor most are the United Kingdom, Germany, France, Canada, Brazil, Japan, the Netherlands, Australia, Italy, and Mexico. European companies also locate R&D work in a small number of heavily industrialized countries. They usually pick the United States, India, Brazil, Spain, the United Kingdom, Australia, Germany, and Italy.

All but a few of these investments have been made on a piecemeal or individual basis. Some weren't even intentional—many of them were acquisitions unrelated to the company's technical capabilities.

Haphazard acquisition of R&D facilities often create at least two problems:

First, it means duplication of skills, capabilities, and overhead-support functions with other labs in the corporation. A move by top management toward consolidation, in order to reduce duplication, is painful for the R&D professionals and managers involved and can create thorny problems with the host government. Needless to say, a company can avoid or minimize such difficulties by developing a strategy in the first place.

Second, because acquisition is piecemeal, top managers tend to overlook the innovative capabilities of many foreign-based labs. This problem occurs most often with labs that happen to be obtained when a foreign company is acquired by a U.S. multinational.

For example, when Merck acquired an R&D unit in France that was incidental to the acquisition of a French business, the French company's marketing group wanted to eliminate its own R&D unit to reduce expenses and increase profitability. Merck agreed to take over the French lab, an agreement which committed the U.S. parent company to pay closer attention to this lab. Merck decided the laboratory should specialize in ophthalmic research, and it closely coordinated its R&D work with U.S. activities. The French lab eventually helped produce Timoptic, a breakthrough drug for the treatment of glaucoma.

DEVISING A STRATEGY

Managers charged with overseeing international innovation must pay particular attention to three areas: planning, organization, and coordination.

Planning.   International business strategies do not always take into account the role of technology. R&D plans frequently appear as subsections of product development programs, which means that R&D's role is more part of an implementing than a planning framework. Almost all of the executives we interviewed spoke about the importance of budget planning, and some discussed planning for environmental adaptation. But very few mentioned the integration of R&D into corporate strategic planning.

Organization.   Most corporations successful in encouraging international innovation have created a balance between centralized and decentralized control. One corporate R&D manager described the balancing act this way: "The local R&D unit cannot have unbounded discretion over its performance. It participates in setting objectives and defining projects, engages in

debate, and passes on the ideas that bubble up. But the local unit has limits and its people know that. We must help them succeed by making certain they do not try to do considerably more than they are capable of doing."

One example of the importance of adequate corporate recognition for foreign labs involves the Canadian facility of a U.S. multinational company. For many years other R&D employees in the corporate system looked down on the lab, even though it had a high level of professional talent and the capacity to innovate. The lab needed an achievement that would stimulate awareness of its capabilities. And it came up with one: a technology proving a time-honored process methodology wrong and establishing a better process. Since this publicity-generating event, the lab has had other significant technological achievements and is now recognized as the most productive lab in the corporation.

The key to success seems to be to start small. Starting on a large scale generates too many organizational problems and leads to the assignment of R&D projects that are too tough for a young lab. It is important for the lab to build a track record and for managers to identify the strengths that emerge as a research unit matures. A $30 million R&D unit cannot be established overnight.

Coordination.   Distance is still a great barrier to proper coordination, despite modern communication and transportation systems. Yet American executives have tried for years to manage foreign innovation activities from here at home. The ineffectiveness of such long-distance management has led to the appointment of on-site coordinators with extensive powers.

One U.S. manager described his company's European coordinator: "He's a tough guy who has lived in Germany and Italy and used to be the head of the French lab. Currently he is assigned to marketing. Although he's supervised by the regional head of marketing, he has dotted-line responsibility to me. He rides herd on research, recommends cutbacks or increases in lab programs, and has day-to-day responsibility for control. He is my eyes and ears, and I really couldn't do the job without him.''

U.S. multinationals have spent untold time and money establishing extensive operations and resources abroad. The time has come for greater utilization of these resources—not just as sales outlets for domestic or foreign products but as sources of innovation in technology and management that will aid in the resurgence of U.S. industry and the world economy.

SECTION 8
Corporate Culture and Human Resource Management

Culture can be defined as "that complex whole which includes knowledge, belief, art, morals, law, custom and any other capabilities and habits acquired by man as a member of society."[1] Hofstede calls culture a "collective programming of the mind."[2] By any definition, we can conclude that people within a particular culture think, feel, and react in patterned ways that give them a collective personality. Encompassed within a culture are components such as language, religion, attitudes, education, norms, social organization, property, rights, government, law, and community organization.

The enculturation process, or the way in which rules of behavior are passed from generation to generation, begins in infancy.[3] Language and the many forms of nonverbal communication transmit elements so subtly that individuals usually are not consciously aware that they act in response to the norms of the culture. Most of us, for example, do not realize that we maintain a culturally defined distance when we converse with others. We only know that we feel comfortable when we maintain a certain space between us. When we move either closer or further away than our norms dictate, we feel uncomfortable. The concept of being "on time" is another culturally determined norm. When an appointment is made for 2 P.M., the participants may actually assemble at 2:00 or arrive at 3:30 and still be "on time." Reactions to space and time are only two examples of an almost endless number of "rules" that determine our behavior.

Cultural elements are related one to another in an environmental system

[1] Edward B. Tylor, "Primitive Culture," in Vern Terpstra, *The Cultural Environment of International Business* (Cincinnati, Ohio: South-Western Publishing, 1978), p. xii.
[2] Geert Hofstede, *Culture's Consequences* (Beverly Hills, Calif.: Sage Publications, 1980), p. 13.
[3] Stefan H. Robock, Kenneth Simmonds, and Jack Zwick, *International Business and Multination Enterprise,* rev. ed. (Homewood, Ill.: Richard D. Irwin, 1977), p. 310.

made up of a number of organizational subsystems including business enterprises. To understand a culture, it is necessary to know that the parts of the larger cultural system and smaller organizational subsystem are interrelated and interact in an ongoing process of conflict and cooperation and accommodation.[4] For managers involved in international business, the nature and scope of the interrelationship among individuals, firms, and the cultures in which they are located is critically important.

The degree to which managers of a foreign firm and representatives of host cultures interact depends upon a number of factors. The nature of the product, differences in customer preference, employee relations, legal requirements, and financial arrangements will all have an impact on the role of the subsidiary manager. There are elements of a host culture that will have little relevance to the business of one subsidiary firm but may affect profoundly the workings of another.

The manager of a multinational corporation (MNC) will have to consider the cultural elements of his or her home country, those of the host environment, and pressures from transcultural interest groups. Transcultural groupings may demand certain responses from MNCs doing business in some but not necessarily all the nations represented in the group. For example, the World Health Organization passed a voluntary code at the behest of delegates from developing countries to prohibit the advertising and distribution of breast milk substitutes. MNCs were constrained in their strategy and their access to markets as a result of a transnational lobbying group that resisted changes in the traditional cultural value of breast feeding.

When an MNC enters a host country, managers at home country headquarters adopt a particular cultural orientation toward staffing their subsidiaries that leans toward the ethnocentric, polycentric, or geocentric.[5] The goal of the MNC is to control the interaction between the firm and its host culture as effectively as possible.

The ethnocentrically oriented firm tends to think of its nationals as superior to managers in host countries. It assumes that what works at home will work abroad. This viewpoint leads headquarters to overlook the importance of local conditions and to make assumptions based on faulty data. Standards, procedures, and cultural biases appropriate in the home country are often not transferable to subsidiary in a different culture.

Host country or polycentric orientation carries its own set of problems for the MNC. When host country managers are given virtual autonomy, they may run their subsidiaries almost independently of headquarters. A global strategy becomes difficult, if not impossible, to implement. Although communication and cultural interactions may be easier within the subsidiary itself, there may be duplication of efforts among subsidiaries and a failure to maximize corporate efforts.

[4] Terpstra, *The Cultural Environment*, p. xiii.
[5] Howard V. Perlmutter, "The Tortuous Evolution of the Multinational Corporation," *Columbia Journal of World Business*, 1969, pp. 9–18.

Geocentric orientation refers to worldwide outlook. Ideally, the MNC is treated as a single unit with overall planning, objective setting, and implementation of goals. Managers are supposed to think in terms of global products, resources, and functional tasks. In theory at least, managers are selected for their individual skills and commitment to the global strategy of the firm. The relevant cultural attitudes of managers of any one country are incorporated into the system of the MNC as a whole.

In practice, none of these models exists in pure form. Most MNCs work out a hybrid orientation that includes a combination of home and host country policies that eventually evolves into a corporate subsystem composed of many different cultural components that interact uniquely in each larger cultural environment in which the company operates. Specific business practices are different within host country subsidiaries, but an overarching uniform strategy is maintained for the MNC as a whole.

READING SELECTIONS

The readings in this section examine the impact of differenes in national cultures on the management of MNCs and on human resource policy. C. Paul Dredge brings an anthropologist's perspective to his discussion of the MNC manager's encounters with culture in the host country. As Dredge points out, MNCs tend to think that the only cultural issue they face is the way in which expatriate managers of a subsidiary interact with the culture and representatives of the host culture. In fact, many interrelating systems and subsystems are created when the enterprise of one nation establishes a presence within the boundaries of another. Dredge discusses what occurs when elements of the headquarter's national culture and its internal corporate culture interact with those of the host country. The critical task for the home country manager is to determine the relative importance of those many elements to the success of his enterprise.

As MNCs grow structurally, they need to develop staffing policies that maximize their global strategies. Vladimir Pucik finds that as firms grow from exporting to full-fledged MNC activity, the management of human resources tends to shift from an ethnocentric to a polycentric policy. The next step that some MNCs take in their human resource function is to organize in a matrix grid. This structure becomes a handicap as business becomes more and more global. The goal of effective human resource management, Pucik says, should be to move to an information "matrix culture" in which the firm's corporate culture can be developed in many different national cultural settings. The particular factors that must receive the attention of corporate strategists are staffing, appraisal, reward, and management development. In the future, he concludes, successful MNCs will have corporate-level HRM staff to develop a tight strategic framework within which local and regional managers will carry out their tasks.

As firms work toward ideal staffing policies for the future, they are sometimes caught between their present staffing policies and incompatible host country expectations. Yoram Zeira finds that many MNCs have ethnocentric staffing policies that are dysfunctional in European host country cultures. Host country organizations assert that MNC headquarters give more decision and policymaking authority to expatriate managers than to host country nationals. Zeira asserts that ethnocentric, polycentric, and geocentric staffing policies all have serious problems. What may help the MNC with its host country relations is the use of organizational development programs on a country-by-country basis. Through organizational development techniques, the MNC and the host country organization can define their expectations in a constructive way.

36

Corporate Culture: The Challenge to Expatriate Managers and Multinational Corporations
C. Paul Dredge

• • •

Two businessmen in Hong Kong, one a British banker and another a Canadian industrial manager, have made some rather unusual decisions concerning the decoration of their offices (Browning, 1983). The banker keeps a plain-looking tank containing five big black fish next to his desk. The industrial manager has had a mirror hung on the wall behind his desk—the mirror points directly out the window at a building across the street and is discretely covered by a curtain. These seemingly strange decorations are a direct result of the Chinese employees' belief and the managers' developing *non-disbelief*, in *feng shui*, an ancient Chinese semiscience that aims to place furniture, buildings, graves, and cities in locations that will be harmonious with measurable flows of the invisible, both good and bad natural forces of *ch'i*. The mirror reflects bad *chi'i* from an adjacent

Source: C. Paul Dredge, "Corporate Culture: the Challenge to Expatriate Managers and Multinational Corporations." Reprinted by permission of author.

building back to its source. The fish absorb bad *ch'i* that would otherwise flow directly to the banker—they are expected to die and require frequent replacement.

The two managers are following an old adage, "When in Rome, do as the Romans do." That they have come to give some credence to what their "Romans" believe will likely be of use to them and to their companies. In a foreign business environment, a flexible, open-minded, empathetic home country manager who strives continually to understand the local culture and the people who share it can be a valuable asset to his or her company. There are situations where just the opposite attitude can be advantageous—where a shield of insensitivity will enable expatriate managers to press more strongly for what they and their companies want. That strategy is quite risky, however—the risks are discussed in detail in the last section of this paper. Even if a manager decides to appear culturally insensitive, it is important that he or she not do so out of ignorance, but as a conscious, informed decision. For now it is well to assume that cultural knowledge and empathy are important and advantageous—it will be true most of the time.

Becoming sensitive to seemingly strange and exotic customs such as *feng shui* is not difficult, since by their very strangeness such culture-specific practices come quickly to the attention of the expatriate manager and the company. More subtle cultural differences, differences that can, for instance, sink an advertising campaign overnight after months of intense and expensive development, are more difficult both to identify and to deal with. On a more general level than specific cultural differences, the nature of what culture *is* and how multinational firms can deal with it is much less well understood than it should be.

Scholars of international business have known for a long time that culture plays a major role in many aspects of overseas business success. Until recently, however, the impact of culture on business—be it international or domestic—has continued to be an issue for scholars more than for managers who are actively engaged in actually doing business. It has taken the recent attention to domestic business cultures (cf. Peters and Waterman, 1982; Sathe, 1983) to convince an audience of pragmatic managers that the intricacies of organizational culture that have been shown to be of such vital importance in doing business *at home* may be equally or even more important abroad. More important, the current attempt to clarify what culture is and how it affects the conduct of both foreign and domestic business is bringing refinement to concepts that were often too sketchy to provide more than a warning of specific potential pitfalls. Heretofore, just what the broader intercultural issues are, and what can be done to deal with them, has been addressed in a rather piecemeal way. Specific instructions such as "When in an Arab country, neither refuse nor overestimate the positive connotations of a client's hospitality" are useful but provide no general framework for anticipating similar problems in other situations. There is an urgent need for the development of both broad, powerful concepts that will enable the international manager to understand the basic interrelationship of culture and business and for general principles for dealing with culture drawn from these broad concepts that can be applied in *any* situation. Local variation and detail can and must be approached from a generalized, cross-cultural conception of the workings of culture rather than from a formulaic, patchwork kit bag. This discussion is a step toward the goal of providing such a general framework.

Entire books have been written by anthropologists on what an adequate definition of culture should include (cf. Kroeber and Kluckhohn, 1952; Freilich, 1972). Scholars of business, who have come to the culture concept more recently, have either found the myriad definitions and theoretical arguments to be difficult to wade through but done the wading anyway (see, for instance, Sathe, 1983) or have decided to give the complexities of academic argument only a cursory glance and get on with the discussion of practical concerns (as in Deal and Kennedy, 1982). I submit that a definition/description of culture is also a theory of culture, one that alerts us to what exists and what to look for, and that not just any definition will do if we are to see how culture affects international business. Hence, the following section on defining culture.

WHAT IS CULTURE?

Culture is "an organized system of knowledge and belief whereby a people structure their experience and perceptions, formulate acts, and choose between alternatives," says anthropologist Roger Keesing (Keesing, 1974). Keesing's definition is a good framework on which to build—by this definition culture has four essential parts—(1) a system of knowledge and belief and three modes of thought based on that system: (2) structuring of experience and perceptions, (3) formulation of acts, and (4) making choices.

As knowledge and belief, culture exists only as thought and is nonmaterial and non-behavioral (therefore, behavior is guided by and reflects culture but is not the thing itself). The knowledge and belief aspect of culture always includes normative values—notions of what is right, wrong, appropriate, inappropriate and/or advisable, good and bad. The common attitude of peoples around the world is that *their* particular version of what is and what should be is the best and that all other systems of knowledge and belief are not only different from but inferior to their own. This viewpoint, called ethnocentrism, seriously hinders intercultural understanding and relationships.

Culture is a systematic framework used to structure experience—to give meaning to thoughts and actions. As Clifford Geertz (1973) puts it, "Man is an animal suspended in webs of significance he himself has spun." Culture provides a framework, or a web/net in Geertz's analogy, into which our perceptions and understandings are woven in an orderly fashion. It is shared categories, often symbolized in words and their arrangement, that allow us to communicate adequately with people in our own culture. Some anthropologists, notably Claude Levi-Strauss, point to the human propensity to create order out of chaos, implying that it is perhaps more the structure of the human mind than any order existing outside of the mind that impels us to create and use neatly bounded categories and taxonomies as, for instance, with various kinds of food, trees, homes, and people. In their minds people carry culture-specific filing systems with "proper" places to file practically everything they experience, and they work hard to keep the files in order as far as possible. So culture is a filing system with a well-formulated communications capability based on the categories and their associated meanings in the system. It is the willingness to admit the inadequacy of one's own filing system

for another's life and world that is the first step to empathy and cross-cultural understanding.

As a system for the formulation of acts, culture enables a person to draw on the knowledge, belief, and filed categories included in culture to consider and implement action. What sort of behavior is called for in a given situation, what is appropriate or advisable, is a cultural matter. More often than not, the process of formulating acts is unconscious.

Culture is both a basis for making decisions and a reason for having to make them. Decisions based on cultural beliefs and assumptions—probably the vast majority of decisions people make—are most often entirely unconscious. As in spoken language, decisions originate from an underlying framework that shapes a constant flow of behavior with only occasional pause for conscious consideration of tactics and strategy.

More conscious decision making is necessary in the frequent cases where cultural guidelines are inconsistent or in conflict. For all the striving for order, consistency, and coherence in the cultural filing system, many gray areas exist in any culture, and even the most fundamental maxims often have their equally acceptable opposites (e.g., "Many hands make light work" versus "too many cooks spoil the broth").

CULTURES AS INTERNALLY INCONSISTENT

One example of cultural inconsistency is cited by anthropologist Hortense Powdermaker in a study of obesity in several cultures (Powdermaker, 1960). She notes tht obesity is a sign of prosperity in a society of scarcity (where *any* food is precious and eating enough to get fat is a luxury) and that thinness is a sign of prosperity in a society of plenty (where cheaper foods are more fattening and, therefore, *anyone* can be fat). Powdermaker notes that the American ideal for a *mother* is still connected most often to our former culture of scarcity: a matronly, plump mother cooking fattening apple pies in a well-stocked kitchen. (This tradition may have, it must be admitted, had more influence in 1960 than it does today.) However, the ideal for a *wife* is associated with our present culture of plenty: a slender, girl-like wife who functions as a playful sex mate and spends considerable time at the gym keeping in shape. Women who are both wives and mothers are caught, but their own beliefs and expectations as well as those of men, in this cultural contradiction, which has historical roots and is the result of some elements of the culture having changed while others remained the same. The path through the forest of inconsistencies internal to a culture is never clear; individuals are always faced with choices between mutually inconsistent beliefs and values.

CULTURES AS INCOMPLETELY SHARED

A culture is learned, not inherited, and it is, to a large extent at least, shared by those who identify themselves as its members. There is good reason to qualify the degree to which people share a culture. Sharing a culture does not mean that every individual who belongs has all the same knowledge, beliefs or ways of attributing meaning to life as every other. Different perspectives based on social class, occupational specialty, political position, religious background, age, sex, and other differences in social identity always mean that all aspects of a culture are not shared by all its members. A minimal commonality of shared elements of the same culture must be present inside each individual's mind for social interaction to persist and be successful. Our own pluralist nation is an interesting test case of just how small this critical mass of shared cultural elements can be without resulting in a fragmented and unworkable society. Unpredictability, as we find when we travel abroad, can be charming and even enlightening, but it can also be unsettling, even threatening. When dealing with another culture, it is important to identify and then deal with this

small critical mass of widely shared cultural understandings, for it will be common to most all the people of that culture and unfailingly influential in any cross-cultural interaction.

CULTURES AS RELATED SYSTEMS

Although some people and even some scholars regard cultures as individually unique, it is clear that different cultures share features and have many similarities—they are, in a sense, variations on the same themes. Cultural differences are more often differences of degree than kind, as all cultures are responses to universal human problems and challenges; they are sets of answers for the same universal questions. As an old Chinese saying puts it, "In the East and West, the hearts and minds of people are basically the same." For instance, Americans, who express shock and even loathing at the widespread practice of arranged marriages in Asia, fail to see that the cultural elements involved in both East and West are similar—just differently arranged. For generations of Chinese, Koreans, and Japanese, romantic feelings and their expression have been as deeply felt as in the West, yet have had their most common expression, for men at least, before or outside of marriage. Romantic love and marriage in Asia have not, in other words, gone together "like a horse and carriage." Marriage, a serious matter of family alliance with important economic, social, and political consequences, has certainly not been a primarily romantic undertaking. Although Americans might not recognize it in their own culture, parental influence on marital choice is often exercised quite strongly, especially among the upper classes, by parental choice of schools, encouragement to join specific fraternities or sororities, and, in the most elite circles, the intermarriage of only those people whose families' names appear in the *Social Register*. Romance versus practicality is the unifying theme: their compatibility is a rare but welcomed coincidence in the East; in the West, it is an actively sought goal.

Although basic themes such as romantic/practical are common across cultures, it is the nonbasic differences that more often than not thwart the efforts of people of different cultures in their attempts to cooperate successfully—in business or in any other area of cross-cultural interaction. The reasons for this difficulty are partly obvious, partly not so obvious. For the obvious side, Somerset Maugham has said,

It is very difficult to know people and I don't think one can ever really know any but one's own countrymen. For men and women are not only themselves; they are the region in which they were born, the city apartment or the farm in which they learnt to walk, the games they played as children, the old wives' tales they overheard, the food they ate, the schools they attended, the sports they followed, the poets they read, and the God they believed in. It is all these things that have made them what they are, and these are things you can't come to know by hearsay, you can only know them if you have lived them. You can only know them if you *are* them. (Maugham, 1944)

The less obvious problem is that it is often the function, though not the purpose, of cultural elements to promote ignorance and intolerance of other cultures and their people. Some tribal traditions, such as those of the Yanomamo of Brazil and Venezuela, include the notion that their own people are the only *real* people and that other humans are inferior beings. Such attitudes are not restricted to tribal societies, but are found in modern, industrial societies as well. Within the same culture, some groups feel this way about themselves versus other groups. The actual difficulty, explained so clearly by Maugham, of knowing a person of another culture, combined with a determined mutual nonknowledge founded on ethnocentrism and perhaps a fear of cultural differences, can make cross-cultural understanding even between individuals a very difficult task. To achieve it between large organizations or groups of people becomes even more challenging.

CULTURES AS DYNAMIC SYSTEMS

One final conceptual detail: cultures are not fossilized artifacts but, rather, dynamic systems undergoing constant change. The internal inconsistencies in cultures are, in part, responses to changing environments and ideas (as with the contradictory values concerning wives and mothers cited earlier); these built-in oppositions form the frontiers of change. Cultures include other kinds of contradiction and inconsistency. One anthropologist notes that there are "proper" rules and "smart" rules in all cultures (Freilich, 1972). The latter are more pragmatic, less ideal approaches to problem solving. It is not proper, but it is definitely expedient, and therefore "smart" in Freilich's sense, to run a red light at a verifiably deserted intersection at 2 A.M. Smart/proper dichotomies present people with choices, not with clear-cut prescriptions. People can appeal to either value or rule for a justification for their behavior, appearance, or beliefs. The gray areas of culture, areas where there are both proper and smart rules, can provide people with a set of excuses for doing whatever is profitable, expedient, or gratifying, within certain limits. These gray areas are also crucial areas of cultural support for rebels and innovators—those who have set out, consciously or not, to change a culture.

The dynamic nature of cultures means that they cannot be pigeonholed or approached with formulas. To complicate the problem of culture for a multinational corporation (MNC), the MNC itself and the international economic system that supports it are a source of change in the cultures they encounter. The host culture with which an MNC begins to deal this year will be subtly different five years down the road, often as a direct result of having encountered the MNC and others like it. Sometimes, as with Iran, the culture will accommodate and change in accordance with outside pressures and then, in a move at revitalizing its own tradition (Wallace, 1956), take a giant leap back toward its past in reaction to the pressure. MNCs can ill-afford to contribute to such reactions, either in the short or long term.

THE MNC AND CULTURAL COMPLEXITY

Culture is a multidimensional challenge for MNC managers. It is not uncommon for people to think that the only critical cultural interface is between the local, host country, culture(s) and a local MNC subsidiary and its expatriate employees. The problem is more complex than that. There are cultural gaps of varying degrees of breadth between an MNC headquarter's organization and its subsidiaries in any and all other cultures. There is a cultural gap between not just the host country subsidiary and its host culture, but between that of the headquarters organization and that same host culture. Differing occupational and industrial cultures—separate from national cultures—may also be a factor: large conglomerates may own foreign subsidiaries that produce and market products that are fundamentally different from what is made and sold by the main headquarters organization (this is, of course, a high-risk business situation from which many conglomerates have found it prudent to extricate themselves). Finally, there is a less specific but very real culture gap between people from industrialized countries and those from less developed countries (LDCs), centering on such things as attitudes on the importance of material wealth, consumer goods, extended family relations, the place and function of work, and the importance of religious beliefs and practices in everyday life. Not all these levels of culture difference come to bear on every business relationship, but they are potentially important. For the sake of simplicity, however, the discussion and examples to follow here will focus on the relationship between the elements of the national culture of an MNCs headquarters, usually represented by managers from the MNC assigned to host country subsidiaries, and that of the host country.

The four aspects of culture outlined—namely, a culture is (1) a system of knowledge and belief, based upon which (2) experience is structured, (3) acts are formulated, and (4) choices are made between alternatives—have interesting and important practical implications for conducting international business. A detailed discussion of each of the four aspects follows, with comments focusing on what they mean specifically for the international manager and the multinational corporation.

KNOWLEDGE AND BELIEF: DIFFERENT VIEWS OF REALITY

A culture provides its members with a world view—each culture is a unique and rather cluttered mixture of elements but is neither unrelated to other similar cultures nor totally incomprehensible from the perspective of the cultures from which it is most different. It is perhaps difficult for a person of the West to understand the need for fish tanks and curtained mirrors in Hong Kong offices, but it may be just as difficult for someone from Hong Kong to understand the necessity of small evergreen perched atop the completed steel girders of buildings under construction in an American city or of Saint Christopher statues on automobile dashboards. These beliefs differ in their detail only; they do not differ in *kind*. There is no belief in another culture that is more strange than the beliefs of one's own that are strangest in the eyes of someone from that other culture. Where such beliefs create no practical barriers to interaction, they can be enjoyed as exotica. Where they do pose difficulties, people must sit down and talk together until they at least understand each other's point of view. At that point, there is usually a place for mutual accommodation and compromise.

The strength and depth of cultural knowledge and belief make it very difficult, however, for any person to adopt another's point of view. The overwhelming majority of people everywhere approach intercultural experience from a position grounded strongly in ethnocentrism.

The foundation of the aforementioned "we are the *people* and they are the nonpeople" attitude, ethnocentrism, is the practice of judging people of other cultures by the standards of one's own. Although it is fair to say that people can fail in an attempt at intercultural business interaction even though they are willing, able, and actually do abandon their ethnocentric attitudes (to the extent that is possible), it is nonetheless true that generous intentions and sincere attempts at understanding the other's cultural point of view will go a long way toward international business success. In the past it has been possible for international business success to be one-sided: managers of an MNC, backed by the economic strength of their home country, could force host country business managers to deal without making any concessions to the host culture. Some transactions of that one-sided nature have been the basis for subsequent nationalization of industries. In international business transactions, it is still true that when there is loss of national face or pride, where there is forced capitulation, there will be resentment rather than appreciation and vengefulness when and if an opportunity arises to turn the tables. Confrontation and capitulation always leave motives for revenge; conciliation and compromise cannot guarantee a future free of vengeance, but they do at least provide a foundation for future generosity. Today's international business climate may demand more compromise than before, if only for purely pragmatic purposes. The oil crisis years and a serious problem of Third World debt has put the economic giants on notice: one-sided, ethnocentric success may well be ultimate failure.

Ethnocentrism forms the basis for in-group/out-group distinctions that can become the foundation for making patently ridiculous demands of those perceived as being members of the out group, the "others" rather than the "us." Yoram Zeira, in a 1979 article, reports the results of his survey of Europeans concerning the staffing of MNC subsidiaries in their countries (Zeira, 1979). Europeans overwhelmingly prefer their own host country nationals as local managers. Where the manager must be a foreigner, the vast majority of respondents to the survey merely require that he or she speak the language with native proficiency, be as thoroughly acquainted with the history and traditions of the host country as those who have grown up and been educated there, and, ironically, be totally devoid of ethnocentric attitudes. They are especially happy with this state of affairs if the foreign manager also has a solid power position with the headquarter's organization. (Although Zeira's article deals only with the description of attitudes, not with actual behavior, it is no surprise to find that the desired foreign nationals are virtually nonexistent and that, in expatriate managers, Europeans have to put up with actual human beings that walk on the ground.)

It would be interesting to see what such a survey would reveal about U.S. attitudes—would U.S. managers be more or less ethnocentric than are the Europeans? The results would probably not be so ethnocentric in less developed nations where the need and hope of economic progress engenders more realistic attitudes.

That a survey would show such ethnocentric expectations reveals two things. First, expatriate, and especially expatriate American, managers have established a reputation for just the opposite of what Europeans want—Europeans' desires are in part a reaction against their own disappointing past experiences with American expatriate managers. Second, and more important, the ethnocentric expectations of the Europeans point to the fact that in this situation they themselves are, probably unconsciously and with what they feel are the best intentions, looking for and finding in expatriate managers excuses for any disappointments in the relative success of their international business relations. Europeans, judging from what Zeira says, seem to be happy to excuse themselves from any blame in the breakdown of business relations and blame instead the social/cultural ineptitude of expatriate managers. At the same time, they deny the expatriate manager any hope of being accepted socially or otherwise into their own circles. Since those same circles are the only situation in which an expatriate manager could develop the skills and knowledge Europeans demand of him, the message is a clear "Catch 22": no matter how hard you try, you cannot meet our expectations.

Ironically, for a native manager who may have a funny accent and an inadequate education, the same expectations may well not apply, since he is "us," not "them." Ethnocentrism, in this way, often boils down to an excuse to exclude those who require an extra effort to be included. Where there is absolute necessity, the ethnocentric excuse must be put aside for use at the next opportunity, while the business at hand is transacted as smoothly as possible, with the people, including any expatriates, at hand.

In circumstances in which hosts are so overwhelmingly ethnocentric, it is difficult for the expatriate manager to know how to proceed. The manager may attempt to understand the other person's or organization's point of view and the cultural reasons behind any difficulties that are encountered. If an expatriate MNC manager makes an honest attempt to learn and understand the standards of host country nationals, he or she may encourage a similar respect for his or her own differences. On the other hand, the manager may not. The strength of the expatriate managers' organizational position or the demand for their companies' product may make it possible for them to be just as ethnocentric as their hosts, live their nonbusiness lives in an enclave of their own people, and still manage to do business. The perils of such a lack of communicative interaction are very great, however, as will be discussed in more detail in the next section.

In a case where, because of mutually ethnocentric attitudes, little or no communication can take place between the parties to an inter-national business transaction, it could be useful to engage a cultural go-between. Such a person would feel equally at home in either culture (and likely, therefore, not wholly at home in either) and could understand both sides. Such a person could act as culture broker between the two sides. However, such people, especially those who understand the intricacies of business, are in short supply. International business need not, indeed cannot, be conducted by a host of culturally marginal people, cultural chameleons. The fragile cross-cultural unity of underlying basic humanity will support mutually respectful Japanese and American business managers without requiring that either of them cast off their national identities.

There is, in fact, a positive side to ethnocentrism. An inner core of commitment to one's own culture seems necessary to maintain one's own identity and form the basis for making confident choices. The absolutely pure pursuit of what the Romans do is not only impossible but, to the extent that it might be attempted, probably counterproductive. But putting aside at least the most damaging aspects of ethnocentrism is certainly necessary for successful cross-cultural interaction. Doing so requires extra, unaccustomed effort of the kind that few individuals are in the habit of making. The bit of Archie Bunker in all of us—blind, ethocentric, even bigoted, inertia; just plain ignorance, and the bare fact that we can only expend just so much effort—will always threaten our efforts to move beyond ethnocentrism to an appreciation of cultural diversity as a resource rather than a hindrance.

The very substantial differences that lie between some belief systems can make a person feel very much alone in another culture. The presence or new arrival of a fellow countryman is often very welcome, since dealing with that person can proceed on a more intuitive, comfortable basis because of the assumption that there is mutual understanding based on similar life experience. MNC managers of host country subsidiaries must be very careful not to let this potential catharsis of shared culture occupy too much of their time. Although it is often quite possible to do so, it is not enough to deal with host country nationals in the work setting only and then spend one's nonbusiness time in an American enclave. The experiences that shed the greatest light on the other's world view will more often occur in nonbusiness, culture-specific settings: a marketplace, a temple, an athletic arena, a park, a school, a farm, and especially a home. Managers who spend all their spare time with fellow countrymen will not encourage the formation of friendships and associations that would naturally lead them to enlightening cross-cultural experiences in these kinds of settings.

It has sometimes been the case that in a team of two expatriate managers, one has a strong affinity for the host national culture while the other feels antipathy or at best a lack of interest. Because cultures share so many basic elements—though, as shown already, in different combinations and applicable to different situations—it may be that an individual who has felt slightly out of place in his or her own culture will find that the new combination of elements in the host culture suits him or her very well indeed. The result may be accusations of disloyalty to his or her own roots as well as the culture of the headquarter's organization, directed by the one who feels alienated at the one who has found the new culture exciting and hospitable. Such accusations may be founded more in the other manager's disappointment and fear at the loss of the only person who might share his cocoon than in any worries about loyalty (see, for instance, Yoshino and Ewing, 1963). Such situations are very difficult to work through, but it is probably best that the alienated manager try at least to find another outlet for his or her feelings (and, even better, to try harder to overcome negative feelings and then gain at least tolerance if not sympathy for the host culture). The manager should by all means allow the one who feels comfortable to use that affinity for the company's benefit, without pressures from a fellow expatriate.

STRUCTURING EXPERIENCE AND PERCEPTIONS

In the computer age, it is common to experience the frustration of trying to get one's own computer to try to communicate with one with a different programming system. The problem is that, although the kind of information contained in one computer is understandable by the other, the structure of the programs—made up of systems of categories, of filing systems—is different. Across cultures, the interface problems between filing systems affect communication at all levels of symbolic exchange, including not only language but many other systems of symbols. Communication takes place when what the sender means by a signifier (a signifier can be anything to which meaning is attached: a word, a movement of the hands, the presentation of a gift) is the same meaning understood by the receiver when he attempts to interpret the signifier. Communication is not an easy process, even between people who speak the same language and share the same culture. When two people do not understand the same language, or have grown up in different cultures, they have a hard time exchanging the meanings they intend.

The true example that follows is a detailed indication of some of the deeper problems inherent in cross-cultural communication. In the Korean language, several levels of deference are available. In Korean business offices, the boss is spoken to in the most deferential level, and he speaks to his employees with a lesser degree of deference. The situation with speech reflects the relatively highly structured nature of interpersonal and hierarchical relationships in Korea, with organizational superiors and inferiors interacting in a highly predictable way.

In Seoul, a newly arrived, young American manager of an international shipping concern, a person who had learned to speak Korean in a previous experience there, found himself very uncomfortable receiving the verbal and kinesic (body language) deference of his Korean employees. In an attempt to feel more comfortable himself and to be more "democratic and equalitarian" (according to his American belief system), he insisted after a few weeks that his Korean employees speak to him as an equal. He soon found that the disciplined efficiency and eagerness to follow his instructions that had characterized his employees' behavior during his first few weeks of communicative discomfort were now replaced by other attitudes and behavior. Formality and professionalism gave way to a relaxed familiarity, including too much, for the American's taste, nonbusiness conversation and some rather personal questions from people who, it seemed to him, had no business asking such questions. And his employees were no longer so anxious to please him any more; they missed deadlines and made careless mistakes. From their point of view, it was his wish now to conduct business in a nonprofessional manner. To them, business organizational responsibility was owed to superiors to whom one spoke up, not to friends with whom one engaged in a familiar, nonprofessional relationship. The American manager had only wanted to achieve the informality of first-name exchange that exists in many offices in the United States. He did not realize that while there can be and often is a sense of hierarchy and responsibility between people who exchange first names in the United States, that assumption is not part of the Korean mental filing system. Linguistic deference associated with professionalism in conceptual contrast to linguistic familiarity associated with friendship and a mutual sharing of more personal concerns is not an unfamiliar dichotomy to Americans— it is in fact a cultural element to be found in many cultures. But in this case, the *small differences* in assumptions and categorizations associated with these cultural elements led to a big difference in the business office situation, a situation from which the young American manager was never fully able to recover.

The American manager in Korea had some serious difficulties even though he spoke the lo-

cal language quite well and had previously lived in the host country. Managers without the benefit of such knowledge and previous experience need not necessarily be doomed to worse problems than they had, however, if they use wisely what resources they *do* have and are willing to make an effort to learn. It is worth repeating here that a sincere effort to understand and communicate with the people of a host culture, banishing to the extent possible the interference of ethnocentrism, is the first step toward success. The basic meanings in smiles, the look of the eyes, and many other facial expressions have been proven to be universal among humans, with movements of the body serving primarily to indicate the *degree* rather than the *kind* of feelings being experienced (Argyle, 1975). A manager trying to communicate across cultural barriers must first have a sincere desire to accomplish his goal; otherwise, his face will give him away.

The host country national must also be positively inclined to communicate or be persuaded to become so. Americans who speak a foreign language well, have all had the somewhat unnerving experience of speaking relatively fluently in French, German, Chinese, or whatever and having the native addressee insist repeatedly, either in English or the other language, "I don't understand English." Other native speakers nearby may protest to these unwilling interlocutors, but they often remain convinced that the foreigner is not, cannot possibly be, speaking their language. Such a situation is obviously disastrous from a business standpoint, though probably unheard of in any context where MNC business would be conducted. Still, in the back of his mind, a host country businessperson may be thinking "I don't care whether I understand this foreign person or not." Communication, fortunately *and* unfortunately, is a two-way process.

To bridge language barriers, an interpreter is invaluable. Problems with interpreters arise when those they are serving ask them to be too many people at once, to speak for themselves as well as for those for whom they are interpreting. Additional problems may be created when an expatriate manager relies heavily on an interpreter for information on the host culture, for the interpreter has a knowledge—acquired through the study of the expatriate manager's native language—of his or her client's expectations and category systems. In matters of cultural interpretation, the manager may prefer to confirm the clients' expectations and thereby keep things going smoothly, while remaining highly responsible in the technical skill of linguistic translation. Interpreters are invaluable aids in communication, but their knowledge of other languages and cultures often makes them poor examples of host country people. An interpreter may be the easiest host country person to communicate with, but in the business situation, an MNC manager should not neglect the people likely to be *most* difficult to communicate with—the seemingly "inscrutable" and most extremely German, French, Chinese person involved in the interaction.

FORMULATING ACTS

When people need to do laundry, as almost all persons do, it is their cultural beliefs and knowledge on the subject that guide the way in which the laundry gets done; the proper reference is in the "how-to" section of the cultural file. A househusband in the United States will think of his automatic washing machine and a cup of detergent; a housewife in the Korean countryside will think of a bar of laundry soap, a laundry stick to beat the clothes, and the stones by the stream or the well on which to beat them; the South American laundress will think immediately about heating water in which to boil the soapy clothes. Proctor & Gamble would, it is safe to say, have to design its marketing efforts somewhat differently for each place—no enzymes in the product for South Americans to boil into uselessness, soap rather than detergent for the Korean stream, keeping the people downstream in mind, and something encourag-

ing for the househusband. An MNC manager must understand as much as possible about what actions are appropriate when in the host culture—both to inform marketing decisions and to guide personal behavior.

Textbooks on international business seem to repeat one message on doing business in other cultures over and over again (see, for example, Harris and Moran, 1982). Here is a hint with wide application, but which is never stated in the context of the cultural principles behind it: When doing business in Japan (or Germany, or Subsaharan Africa, or the Islamic countries, etc., etc.), it is necessary to establish at least a cordial personal relationship before moving to the main item of business. This process of cultivating a personal relationship with someone outside the United States is almost always described as involving a few rounds of hosting and counterhosting. It is often said to include gifts and always talk—about nonbusiness but at the same time not highly personal topics. The surprise is that this process is presented to American readers as something highly unusual. Given that American businesspeople seem willing to make deals with a stranger during a 15-minute phone call, it is understandable that a week of wining and dining before getting down to brass tacks can be a real shock for an American manager. But it is the *Americans*, not the rest of the world, who are different in this regard. It should become obvious to us sooner or later that in terms of world majority practice, Americans are the weird ones.

Perhaps it is the residual frontier mentality that makes Americans willing to shoot straight from the hip, but people in other parts of the world know about—or, it is perhaps more accurate to say, seem to be more committed to—the benefits of polite, face-protecting, "refined" behavior in relationships that it is hoped will continue over a long period. Americans are certainly well acquainted with the basic cultural elements involved in the way others view business relationships. Social alliances (for that is how the rest of the world defines business relationships) in general are usually based either on kinship or friendship. Perceived blood relationship (kinship by birth) carries with it very strong expectations of intense, "generalized" reciprocal exchanges (expected to equal out over time, but not ever calculated closely) of goods and services (e.g., Home is the place that, when you go there, they can't turn you away.) Alliances based on friendship are begun and maintained with the exchange of meals, greeting cards, various gifts that often carry specific symbolic meanings, and even, some would say, the exchange of marriageable young people (as with the children of European royal families)—an exchange that turns friends into kinsmen. Family members tend automatically to expect favors and expect also to reciprocate freely; friendships start out with fewer assumptions but often develop, in the United States, into relationships as strong or stronger than kinship ties. The exchanges in both kinship and friendship relations develop mutual trust and loyalty over time; indeed, one of the core elements of such trusting and loyal relationships is the expectation of continued exchange and association (from whom does one borrow a cup of sugar? a neighbor with whom a relationship has either been or is expected to be long-lasting).

In business, trust and loyalty are qualities of a relationship that will enable it to survive such challenges as hard times, falling prices, labor unrest, and supply shortages. Therefore, managers all over the world try to establish friendships, symbolized in mutual hospitality, exchange, and the sharing of nonbusiness, personal communication that will lead to greater trust and loyalty between themselves and their business associates. The principles of personal relationships that for Americans tend to be applied only to kinship and friendship tend to extend to business relations as well. At the very least, a more personal relationship carries with it a right to access, to have one's phone calls returned. Relationships based only on the exchange of dollars for goods of equal value ("balanced" exchange) carry considerably less social bag-

gage and, therefore, yield less assurance of loyalty and trust. So, while Americans deal continuously with the exchange/personal relationship cultural element in their personal lives, we seem to be less cognizant of the value and utility of closer ties in business, or we are perhaps anxious to make our personal friendships less dependent on our professional/occupational activities. Again, the same cultural elements have a different mix—it is the MNC managers' study to relate what they already know about the fundamental elements they can find in their own culture to a different cultural situation in which they are configured and applied in a new way.

Other familiar culture elements may be found in strange and novel combinations in a foreign place. Americans accustomed to indicating the importance of some matter by making a show of anger or force will be disoriented when negotiations with Japanese trading partners evoke not even a raised voice from the other side of the table. It is not that Japanese people never make a show of anger—it is just that they see a stronger position in remaining calm and observing utmost propriety when the going gets rough. It is much easier to insist on a point that is to the disadvantage of the other party if one does so politely, with the utmost propriety, or so the Japanese would seem to see it.

It is quite well established that every culture pays some attention to "face," defined in one influential work on the subject as the right to feel good about one's desires and the right to go about one's business unimpeded (Brown and Levinson, 1978). However, what constitutes admirable desires or what constitutes impediment is culture-specific. A remark that would mean a loss of face for an Arab may mean nothing to an American expatriate manager in Saudi Arabia. Again, the manager who is sensitized to general cultural elements will expect that there will be important local details associated with those cultural elements associated with face and the expression of anger, no matter where the expatriate manager finds himself or herself, or that exchange and alliance principles will be at work in forming and cultivating relationships in any host culture. By knowing what such basic elements are, the manager can learn the details of how they are combined in the formulation of acts. Managers can also be confident, contrary to one who does not see cultures as different mixtures of the same or similar elements, that the wall between themselves and their hosts is likely not so insurmountable.

MAKING DECISIONS

In some parts of the United States young people of high school age play a kissing game called "Perdiddle." When an approaching car with only a single headlight is sighted on the road at night, the boy or girl will yell out "Perdiddle," which utterance entitles the speaker to a kiss from the hearer. Like many other parts of any culture, the game Perdiddle is something, in this case a set of rules, that, when applied to the appropriate social situation, will allow for behavior that might otherwise be unacceptable. But the catch is that both (or all) parties must agree to play the game. In the case of Perdiddle, one of the potential partners may choose, for his or her own personal reasons, not to play. The rules to the game provide a ready excuse to do something that both partners may desire. If one of them denies the salience of the rules in the situation with something like, "I don't play that game," a *decision* has been made between two alternatives. Such a decision about the rules can thus redefine the situation, can create "reality." The question arises, of course, as to whose definition of reality is to be accepted. That is a political problem, resolved through an assessment of power or through persuasion.

Although decisions must be made when choosing particular signifiers to convey meaning or when fitting new experience into the mental file (i.e., when structuring experience and perceptions, culture definition 2, and when formulating acts, culture definition 3), it is the choices between *conflicting* alternatives that

form the basis for this section on "making decisions." Managers of both domestic and international firms see themselves primarily as decision makers. The idea that culture is a fundamental basis for decision making is an idea that managers must respect. Of course, managers, like everyone else, make many unconscious decisions concerning their own behavior that, like their subconscious choices of words in speech, are based on culture-specific systems of knowledge, belief, and meaning. Sometimes these seemingly "natural" choices will, because of cross-cultural differences, turn out to have negative consequences. As has been discussed already, one of the expatriate manager's challenges, therefore, is to examine consciously many of his or her normally unexamined attitudes and patterns of action and try to think and behave in a manner more acceptable to the host culture. The manager cannot, however, change himself or herself into a native. Conflict between his or her own interests, standards, and world view and those of his or her hosts will sometimes lead to more conscious, deliberate decisions between conflicting cultural alternatives.

For expatriate managers in MNCs, the choice is often between their own view of what reality is or should be and the even slightly (but, as has been shown, critically) different perspective of host country nationals. As in the game of Perdiddle, both parties may have compatible self-interest that will lead them to mutual agreement on how the interaction should proceed. However, they may not. There will inevitably be situations in which the MNC's best interests will be compromised by making a "when in Rome" decision, one in favor either of a definition of reality or of the salience of a rule found in the host culture that contradicts the expatriate manager's pragmatic business judgment.

In such situations, culturewise managers can often find a way to make a decision that will not only be good for themselves and their companies, but also justifiable in terms of the standards of their hosts. They can do so by appealing to some belief or value of the hosts that is in contradiction to the more obvious "when in Rome" decision, but still part of the host culture. They may, in essence, be able to act in an ethnocentric manner, with ethnocentric reasons, but with the wisdom of a nonethnocentric understanding of how to make the decision palatable for the hosts. At this level of sophistication, cultural elements become tools of effective management, and conscious cultural decision-making becomes a managerial function.

An example? An American manager described in a case entitled "The Total View of Here and Now" (Farmer, 1980) was faced with a distressing situation in a soft drink bottling plant set up by his company in an Arab capital. Although the plant should have been highly profitable, given the cultural compatibility of a soft drink product in the nonalcoholic Moslem world, the plant was in fact plagued with repeated breakdowns due to improper maintenance of machinery (antifreeze instead of brake fluid, grease on the insides of drive belts) and a total unwillingness on the part of local supervisors to plan ahead. The profound fatalism of the manager's supervisory and other employees—"Allah will provide"—led to a pronounced absence of any long-range planning or any drive for technical innovation (or even technical competence). The manager was at a loss, and his story, as it was written up in Farmer's account, ended in failure.

The manager could have been more creative in searching for a "no-losers" approach to his problem. Arabs have a strong sense of pride and honor. An appeal to those values, especially if connected with the potential prestige of supervising more people in an expanding operation, might have begun to offset the prevailing fatalism and provide some motivation for both workers and supervisors. The key would have been to find a tradition in the host culture to which the Arab employees could feel strongly committed—strongly enough to take action, which Arabs are certainly known to do, rather than put the affairs of the plant into the hands of fate. In any such case, the solution to dealing with a dysfunctional cultural belief or value is to appeal to a contradictory value in the host culture of roughly equal importance to the one that is thwarting the MNC's success. This approach is, of course, not always possible, but it is always worth exploring.

Expatriate managers who are newly arrived in the host country can sometimes use to their own advantage the fact that they are expected to make cultural errors. Since they will normally be given a certain grace period before they are held responsible for conformity, new managers can decide to make initial "mistakes" that are actually quite deliberate. This strategy is risky, and can thus be used only sparingly, but it can in fact continue to serve these managers even after they have been in the host country for some time. Even veterans can claim an occasional lapse of their short-lived acculturation—enough to go early to an appointment, to be unable to understand an insult, to lose their tempers, to send a memo when oral communication is required. Such conscious manipulation of cultural alternatives—in this case alternatives between distinct cultures rather than between conflicting values of the same culture—makes it possible for an expatriate manager to deal with cultural differences in a conscious, strategic way as they act out the fourth aspect in our definition of culture: choosing, making decisions between alternatives.

Finally, expatriate managers may, and in fact almost always do, choose to go along with host culture rules most, or at least much, of the time, recognizing that there is much credit in the way of credibility and legitimacy to be gained by rebelling as little as possible. Like the Hong Kong managers who observed the principles of *feng shui*, culturalwise managers will save their controversial cultural decisions for when they deem them most crucial to business success. If they know their host culture well, and if they have cultivated a genuine empathy with its beliefs, meanings, and action patterns, they will be able to manage, make decisions, with confidence.

REFERENCES

Argyle, Michael. 1975. *Bodily Communication*. New York: International Universities Press.

Brown, Penelope, and Stephen Levinson. 1978. "Universals in Language Usage: Politeness Phenomena." In *Questions and Politeness,* Esther N. Goody, ed. pp. 56–289. Cambridge: Cambridge University Press.

Browning, E. S. 1983. "Some Chinese Simply Won't Make a Move Without *Feng Shui*." The *Wall Street Journal,* December 19, p. 1.

Deal, Terrance E., and Allan A. Kennedy. 1982. *Corporate Cultures: The Rites and Rituals of Corporate Life*. Reading, Mass.: Addison-Wesley.

Farmer, Richard N. 1980. *Incidents in International Business,* 3rd ed. Bloomington, Ind.: Cedar Wood Press.

Freilich, Morris. 1972. *The Meaning of Culture: A Reader in Cultural Anthropology*. Lexington, Mass.: Xerox College Publishing.

Geertz, Clifford. 1973. *The Interpretation of Cultures*. New York: Basic Books.

Keesing, Roger M. 1974. "Theories of Culture." In *Annual Review of Anthropology,* Vol. 3.

Kroeber, Alfred, and Clyde Kluckhohn. 1952. *Culture: A Critical Review of Concepts*. Papers of the Peabody Museum of American Archaeology and Ethnology, Vol. 47. Cambridge, Mass.: Harvard University Press.

Maugham, W. Somerset. 1944. *The Razor's Edge*. Philadelphia: The Blakiston Co.

Moran, R. T., and P. R. Harris. 1982. *Managing Cultural Synergy*. Houston: Gulf Publishing.

Peters, Thomas J., and Robert H. Waterman. 1982. *In Search of Excellence*. New York: Harper & Row.

Powdermaker, Hortense. 1960. "An Anthropological Approach to the Problem of Obesity." *Bulletin of the New York Academy of Medicine,* Vol. 36, pp. 5–14.

Sathe, Vijay. 1983. "Managerial Action & Corporate culture." Draft. Harvard Business School, Cambridge, Mass.

Wallace, Anthony F. C. 1956. "Revitalization Movements." *American Anthropologist,* Vol. 58, pp. 264–281.

Yoshino, Michael, and J. S. Ewing. 1963. "John Higgins—An American Goes Native in Japan" (case study). Stanford Business School, Stanford, Calif.

Zeira, Yoram. 1979. "Ethnocentrism in Host-Country Organizations." *Business Horizons,* June.

37

Strategic Human Resource Management in a Multinational Firm

Vladimir Pucik

• • •

EVOLUTION OF MULTINATIONAL HUMAN RESOURCE MANAGEMENT

The shift in focus from a single–country market to a global business perspective has had a profound impact on the corporate Human Resource Management activities. In the early stages of expansion abroad, the firm's international business is usually concentrated in a specialized "international" division which supervises exports, licensing agreements and foreign subsidiaries. The role of the corporate personnel department is mostly limited to supervising the selection of staff for the new division. The emphasis is identification of employees familiar with the corporate products, technology, organization and culture while at the same time adaptable to constraints imposed by unfamiliar working environments abroad.

During this initial period the home-country employees stationed abroad operate as "vice-roys." Their main tasks are to direct the daily operations of foreign affiliates, to supervise transfer of managerial and technological know-how, to communicate corporate policies, and keep the home-office informed about relevant developments in their assigned territory. Experience with "hands-on" management as well as cultural sensitivity and adaptability are considered the necessary prerequisites for the job. The individual assignments are decided on an "as needed" basis, and crash courses in language and culture provided for managers deemed capable of fast learning. For this purpose, a battery of selection tests was developed with the objective of identifying managers with the personality and behavioral traits most suitable for working in diversified cultural settings. Often, as many foreign assignments are not considered particularly desirable from the point of view of a traditional career progression in the corporation, financial incentives in the form of cost-of-living adjustments, relocation bonuses, etc., are used to make such assignments attractive at least in the short run.

As foreign involvement increases, international personnel policies limited to staffing guidance and supervision, and to administration of individualized compensation packages for expatriates gradually cease to meet the new requirements. Often, the growth in international exposure brings a transfer of the authority for foreign operations back to product divisions which then assume a world-wide responsibility. In such an environment foreign subsidiaries evolve into fully-integrated parts of the corporate organization. The coordination of their activities and the formulation of strategies for world-wide markets develop into independent managerial functions requiring a specialized expertise. The growth in foreign exposure combined with changes in the organizational structure of international operations result in an increase in the number of managerial class employees needed to oversee the contacts between the parent firm and its foreign affiliates. from the international manager's perspective, the shortage of qualified personnel makes the one-time corporate adventure a legitimate career, but this shortage may seriously limit the speed and effectiveness of foreign market penetration. Within the HRM area, the development of an international staff becomes a new imperative.

Not only does the transformation of the corporation into a full-fledged multinational lead to the change in focus in the HRM international activities, but the organization of the HRM function is altered as well. Originally, the HRM activities have an ethnocentric character, the policies are designed to fit primarily the experience of the home-country. Gradually they become polycentric in nature, as the multinational firm strives to adapt its HRM system to particular conditions in each locality. The expatriate employees remain under direct home-office supervision, while the personnel control of local employees is transferred to the subsidiaries. In the second phase, the home office personnel staff limit their role to monitoring, and intervene in the local affairs only under extreme circumstances.

At the same time, the rising ambitions and aspirations of local employees, often coupled with pressure of foreign governments on their behalf, illustrate the necessity of awarding an increased share of managerial positions in subsidiaries to local nationals. These two factors, together with the already mentioned shortage of qualified international managers in the home-country, as well as the fact that the transfer of know-how becomes secondary to the knowledge of local business opportunities, usually result in a significant decrease of the expatriate staffs in foreign operations. The function of those remaining changes considerably. As subsidiaries move towards a relative independence, the "vice-roy" function is replaced with that of an "ambassador," communicating and coordinating the corporate strategic objectives with the local management. The latter are usually hired and trained locally, but they may also be recruited on the home-country university campuses and transferred to their country of origin after a relatively short training period at the head office.

The complexity of a multinational business often requires a substantial operational decentralization coupled with the need for coordination across geographical areas and product lines. The next major step in the evolution of the HRM function in a multinational firm comes when such a coordination is achieved by organizing its management structure as a matrix grid spanning cross product and territorial boundaries. The emphasis is on an "MBO-type" appraisal system aiming to reconcile business objectives from each of the matrix segments which may often be in conflict, due to differences in their respective contextual environments.

However, the evolution of the multinational HRM function does not come to an end, even after all the four major components, selection, reward, appraisal and development systems are firmly established on the operational and managerial levels. The continuous globalization of corporate business activities together with an increased complexity of the underlying organizational structure may require corresponding adjustment of the HRM system to the more strategically-oriented perspective.

As a corporate business becomes more and more global, the resulting complexity embedded in the multilayer matrix structure often becomes an obstacle in efficient communication and decision making. Under such conditions, the time is ripe to move away from a formal "matrix culture," as the key coordination and control tool. Supporting a climate where a matrix-like behavior is a natural pattern of action on operational, managerial and strategic levels becomes the new task facing the multinational HRM system. Even when corporate businesses

are restricted to a relatively limited geographic area, it's not easy to manage effectively the transition from a formal matrix-structure to an informal matrix-culture.

This is even more so when corporate business activities are spread around the globe, when the new corporate culture is to be developed not within a single national culture, but within numerous, often very distinct, national cultural settings.

Even more importantly, recently in an increasing number of businesses, the competition facing most companies is global rather than geographically limited. In order to succeed in the emerging global market, the corporate strategy has to respond to global competitive conditions. Analyzing and understanding the global business environment becomes a skill critical not only to corporate growth, but also to corporate survival.

The needs of the global business in the 1980's require a careful monitoring of conditions in the global environment and planning of competitive strategies well in advance. This in turn requires the creation and maintenance of a corporate executive cadre able to monitor global markets, respond rapidly to emerging global opportunities and threats, as well as formulate and execute the appropriate long-term business strategies in the global context. This emerging demand for managers of global strategies cannot be met without a further strengthening of strategic HRM activities in the corporation and their adaptation to the contingencies of multinational operations.

MULTINATIONAL STAFFING

On an operational level, the choice between staffing foreign operations with home-country or third-country nationals, or relying instead on local personnel, is often considered the key issue in multinational staffing. The selection rule is based on a perceived trade-off between the need for technical versus territorial competence in a particular location. So far, there seems to be a lack of consensus among HRM managers in multinational firms on whether technical compentence is "in general" less important to the successful management of a foreign subsidiary than the understanding of and adaptation to the local society. However, in practical terms, reliance on local management is increasing.

One of the main reasons for this development is the belief that hiring local nationals may be a reasonable defensive move, necessary to stem the potential resentment of foreign managerial dominance in the subsidiary. Indeed, the delegation of authority to locals may help to satisfy the rising ambitions and expectations of many of the local employees. Such a policy also cuts the immediate costs of staffing by the elimination of foreign transfer related bonuses and tax adjustments, and it may be instrumental in developing a strong local management team. At the same time, the reduction in cross-national staffing ultimately leads to a reduction in the pool of managers with global rather than area-specific experience.

Because of the substantial time lag between the individual staffing decisions and their aggregate impact on the experience profile of the managerial pool, many multinational firms today concentrate on developing their local management teams, and do not perceive the danger ahead of a fragmentalized management. Often, even when the current key executives do possess formidable international experience, as it was they who had pushed and guided their companies in their early foreign expansion, the proportion of those in lower managerial ranks who could eventually match their experience is dangerously low. Although numerically the number of managers with foreign exposure is growing, there are still far too few to handle the growing demands of international ventures, such as the need to recognize in time market opportunities and threats.

From the standpoint of building a management team capable of supervising multinational competitive strategies, the issue is not how to resolve the dilemma between the technical and contextural competence. Rather the issue is how to develop corporate human resources possessing both of the critical skills. Yet, while some short-term and long-term trade-offs are unavoidable, staffing decisions are still being made primarily on the basis of the current needs of the organizations, without considering long-term strategic implications; or, even worse, on the basis of short-term financial expediencies, which are relatively unrelated to the nature of the business in the first place.

It is not infrequent that corporate international staffing policies are based more on tax considerations, than on a long-term analysis of human resource supply as related to corporate multinational strategy. Staffing policies should not be delegated to tax lobbies. Staffing foreign operations is costly, any tax savings is welcome, but the tax effect is in the long-run only a secondary constraint. In other words, few major foreign ventures ever collapsed because of the high tax burden of staffing, but many are in difficulty as the parent firms are not able to assemble international management teams contributing knowledge of local market conditions with technical and organizational competence.

Another example where strategic staffing is essential to success concerns the staffing decisions involving the establishment of a joint venture. Given the underlying global competition, a joint venture of two independent firms will not be successful unless its continuation is in the interest of both partners in the long run. The appropriate staffing strategy calls for a staffing system dubbing as one of the mechanisms of control. The objective is to obtain a sufficient amount of technical competence as well as environmental adaptiveness that would permit the firm to impede any breakaway action by its local partner. With this objective in mind, it is essential that the joint venture local staff is seen as permanently committed to the new operation, not temporarily assigned from the local parent. The roving ambassadors from both parent firms should be limited to the number the foreign partner can dispatch. The exchange of trainees should flow two ways, locals learning technical expertise, expatriates learning the adaptation to the area. The management trainee transfer should involve both assignments from the parent to the joint venture, as well as from the joint venture to the local parent.

The strategic implications of staffing decisions are of tantamount importance in developing local market know-how. What happens when they are ignored can be seen in the example of U.S.-joint ventures in Japan. While most of these joint ventures were effective to transfer technology to Japanese partners, the U.S. firms usually did not pay attention to developing their own potential competitive strength. Thus, when Japanese partners decided to go alone, there was nothing the U.S. firms could do, but to withdraw from the market. Substantial expenditures and years of hard work were lost with minimal returns.

Staffing problems of this nature are slightly less critical in the wholly-owned subsidiary as the control over technology prevents the emergence of domestic competitors, short of unfriendly spin-offs, of course. On the other hand, in the case of a wholly-owned firm, it is much more difficult to pull together a qualified labor force, as the operation has to start from zero. While it seems natural that a wholly-owned investment strategy calls for gradual growth, market imperatives often do not allow that luxury. It is therefore important to be able to recognize the market potential well ahead of the actual investment and prepare a sufficient number of future managerial cadres. This can be accomplished for example, through assignments in local market research offices or training in friendly local affiliates.

The reliance on executive search and employment agencies, while a feasible short-term solution, often does not satisfy long-term objectives. First of all, the chances are high that employees will leave again. In a number of less-developed countries, as a by-product of sloppy staffing practices of foreign multinationals, a paradoxical situation has developed. On the one hand, there is an acute shortage of middle managers capable of manning a multinational operation, and having potential for further professional development, while at the same time, the market is nearly saturated with mediocre manager "cross-cultural intermediaries" who peddle their skills to the highest bidder.

One approach to solve the shortage of qualified international managers is to increase the recruiting activities among foreign students at the home-country universities—a competitive advantage for U.S. based multinational concerns, utilizing the opportunities provided by the large number of foreign students pursuing education in the U.S. At the same time, many U.S. firms still tend to recruit to fill a particular position, rather than for the corporation at large. For example, an MBA with a working knowledge of Arabic would not be considered a suitable job candidate when the only position available is in Latin America. What does not enter the staffing decision is the possibiity that a year hence, such an MBA would be needed for an opening in a Middle Eastern operation now only in the planning stage.

Also, more attention has to be given to the recruiting of area specialists. After all, it is cheaper to train an area specialist internally in the intricacies of corporate finance, accounting or marketing, than to teach an MBA the understanding of a cultural setting that goes together with fluency in foreign languages and/or with several years of living experience in the area. For example, as a result of the MBA bias in the corporate recruiting policies, graduates of many East Asian programs have difficulty finding jobs, while American automakers do not have even a handful of managers on their corporate staff capable of reading and speaking Japanese.

MULTINATIONAL APPRAISAL

Several special features of globally organized businesses require a substantial modification of traditional appraisal criteria. First of all, in most international management positions, technical competence is a necessary, but not a sufficient condition for a successful performance. Cross-cultural inter-personal skills, sensitivity to foreign norms and values, understanding of differences in labor practices or customer relations, ease of adaptation to unfamiliar environments are just a few of the managerial traits most multinational firms seek and evaluate. However, in addition to the appraisal of these basically operational and managerial level skills, an appropriate appraisal system also has to be developed for evaluating managers on attributes associated with a successful performance on a strategic level.

The successful execution of competitive global strategies require managers and executives with excellent environment-scanning abilities, familiar with conditions of business and market opportunities not in one, but in a number of countries and regions, and sensitive to special constraints facing multinational corporations, such as the relationship with the host governments. For example, interaction with top government officials and legislators is a function reserved in the home office to the chief executive and his staff. In foreign subsidiaries, the same task may fall on the shoulders of managers a number of layers below on the corporate ladder.

The proposition that an appraisal on the strategic level ought to be focused on the congruence of current managerial performance with longterm corporate objectives is today widely accepted at least as a theory, while its practical application is often bogged down by the constraint of organizational realities. In what form should long-term goals be expressed to be measurable against performance? What aspects of performance should be considered? Difficult as it is to find an answer to these two questions in a single-country environment, it is even more complicated when global operations are involved.

Given the standard practice of many multinational corporations of using arbitrary transfer prices and other financial tools in transactions between its subsidiaries world wide in order to minimize foreign-exchange risk exposure and tax expenditures, the financial results recorded in the subsidiary do not always reflect accurately its contribution to the achievements of the corporation as a whole. This naturally leads to a situation where such results cannot and should not be used as a primary input in managerial appraisal.

In order to evaluate properly the subsidiary's contribution, a set of parallel accounts adjusted for the influence of financial manipulation has to be maintained, or new measures of control have to be developed, that are less susceptible to the influence of exchange rate fluctuations, of cash-flow and liquidity management, and of transfer pricing. Another alternative is to base a manager's evaluation on the subsidiary performance compared to the long-range goals expressed in other than profit or return-on-equity terms (growth, market share, cost of sales, etc.)

In developing the suitable mix of long-term and short-term objectives to be used as the framework of management appraisal on a strategic level, it is necessary to consider the implications of four major constraints affecting strategy-level appraisal in multinational firms.

First of all, a competitive global strategy is focused on global performance rather than on returns in each of the country or regional markets. Even in a relatively competition-free environment, it can be hardly taken for granted that the sum of short-term optimal sub-portfolio investments leads to optimal long-term performance as a whole. The limitation of short-term local profit-maximization strategies can be seen when competitive pressure requires a multinational firm to operate and compete actively in markets where, if isolated from other markets, it would not compete. A typical case would be participation in a market where an international competitor is a dominant market leader, with an objective to challenge the competitor's cash flow with aggressive pricing policies. While the balance sheet of this particular subsidiary might be continually in the red, by tying up the competitor's resources, this strategy may allow substantially higher returns elsewhere. The difficulties in quantifying such strategies in terms of the usual ROI objectives are obvious.

Second, the volatility of the international environment also requires that long-term goals are flexible and responsive to potential market contingencies. Otherwise, the corporations take the risk of subsidiaries pursuing strategies that no longer fit the new environment. The monitoring of relevant changes and their reflection on the appraisal process is one important area where corporate planning and HRM activities closely overlap. The volatility and fluctuations under which subsidiaries operate require precision tailoring of long-term goals to the specific situation in a given market. It is important to reconcile the need for universal appraisal standards with specific objectives in the subsidiaries. In addition, the cultural differences between home-office bound executives, regional and local managers create another reason to finetune the appraisal system, as it is no longer targeted at a fairly homogeneous cadre of managers.

Third, the proper monitoring of the congruence between long-term corporate strategy and activities in the subsidiary is further complicated by the physical distances involved, the infrequency of contact between the corporate head-office staff and subsidiaries management, as well as the cost of the reporting system. While improvement in information processing technology today allows the development of sophisticated world-wide data systems, the scarcity of physical contacts between managers and executives in the field and the head-office put some limitations on the latter's ability to monitor "soft" aspects of the field executive's performance.

Finally, without the supporting infrastructure of the parent company, the market development in foreign countries is generally slower than at home, where established brands can support new products, and new business areas can piggyback on the means and support of other divisions. This is often very difficult to achieve in the case of a foreign venture. As a result, more time is needed to achieve results than is customary in a domestic market, and this fact ought to be recognized in the appraisal process as well.

MULTINATIONAL REWARD SYSTEM

An effective managerial reward system should be linked to long-term corporate strategy and should anticipate changes in employees' valence of different organizational rewards. On the one hand, multinational settings make the complex task of developing such a system even more difficult; on the other hand, the fact that the corporation operates in many different environments permits the establishment of unique reward programs, unavailable in more conventional environments.

So far, however, as in the case of many mainly domestic firms, most multinational firms still consider rewards in purely monetary terms. In fact, while personnel systems in Japanese, U.S. and European multinationals are often strikingly dissimilar, they all share one common problem; an inability to reward potentially promising employees with adequate career opportunities leading to more responsibility, and opportunities for growth and development. The successful managerial mix of locals, third country nationals and home-office employees is a goal which has so far eluded most of the multinationals. As it is natural that competition in the global environment requires the mobilization of global human resources, those which do succeed gain a substantial competitive edge. However, without a properly structured reward system in place such global utilization of managerial skills will probably not be achieved.

Already, on the operational and managerial levels, the administration of a reward system in a multinational firm is constrained by several critical factors. First of all, the mix of home-office expatriates, third-country nationals and local managers often serving together in a location makes it rather difficult to administer a universal compensation package. The system has to adjust equity issues within the organization with the conditions of the external labor market in countries from which individual managers are recruited, and account for cost-of-living variance as well as differences in tax treatment by respective governments. In addition, employees' expectations and what constitutes a fair and equitable compensation system might not be convergent. To maintain, in such an environment, an effective and adaptable compensation system requires careful monitoring by a highly-skilled professional staff.

Today, numerous multinationals have developed rather elaborate procedures to account for cost-of-living differentials between various countries, for differences in job status as well as for the necessity to provide incentives for employees to work in so-called hardship areas: such as part of the Middle East, Africa or Latin America. However, the task ahead is to move from transfer-incentive compensation packages to reward systems geared to elicit managerial actions in line with corporate long-term strategy.

Other, non-pecuniary aspects of reward systems are also significantly affected by a multinational corporate setting. Corporate rhetoric aside, promotion lines in the vast majority of multinational firms are still defined by the country of origin. Local employees, even if hired in the home-office locations, such as the case of foreign MBA's, are recruited in the first place as potential local, or perhaps regional executives. Their subsequent experience and training de facto would not equip them sufficiently to compete for top corporate jobs in the head office. While there has been considerable political pressure applied on multinationals to foster the promotion of local employees within specific localities, promotion outside of a particular local is still rare.

In such an environment it is not surprising to find that a local manager aware of the limitation of his or her career prospects is primarily concerned about the security and stability of the local operation only, disregarding, or paying less attention to the broader goals of the organization. It is naive to expect their commitment to long-term corporate goals in which the local managers have only a very limited control and very limited benefit. Thus, in order to assure the integration and the alignment of long-term strategy with personal goals, the career system in a multinational must be opened up.

At the same time, it happened all too often in the past that assignment to a foreign location was generally the sign of a sidetracking if not plateauing career. Given the importance of understanding global opportunities and global competition, foreign assignments must become a valuable reward. This can be done, if corporate promotion policies clearly indicate that global experience, rather than a temporary sabbatical, is a necessary condition for promotion to the top of the corporate hierarchy. Again, it should be considered that this requires a very careful long-term placement planning as positions reserved to promising home-office employees limit the number of positions needed for the reward of promising locals.

An important component of the reward system is the structuring of career opportunities. Again, the global environment provides a unique challenge to create an efficient opportunity structure as the need for country specialization has to be reconciled with the need of broader exposure for employees with an executive's potential. As already discussed in the section on staffing, it becomes a new trend that the number of American expatriates assigned overseas is limited. However, token assignment late in the managers' careers is probably not enough to fire their minds with global competitive spirit.

The usual argument against more frequent foreign assignment of home-office employees is the relatively high cost, as the typical benefit package for a middle-level executive overseas costs more than double the basic compensation.

One possible answer is to select personnel for overseas assignment early in their careers, when the total compensation package is relatively low. By the time an employee is ready for promotion to an executive position, he or she already gained valuable foreign experience and insights. The upper limits on employee selection to overseas assignment will have the additional impact of opening up managerial slots for more local employees, thus increasing the flexibility and attractiveness of their reward system. However, the variety of career opportunities in a typical multinational firm also permits the organization to offer typical career opportunities, in particular to offer challenging lateral career transfers. The multicultural environment is in this sense a valuable resource that can be utilized not only to satisfy the curiosity of young and ambitious managerial trainees. It can also offer a challenge to mid-career executives choosing, or being forced, to withdraw from the competition on the main axis of the corporate hierarchy, but at the same time looking for stimulating job assignments, both from a professional and a personal perspective.

MULTINATIONAL MANAGEMENT DEVELOPMENT

Probably the most formidable task recently facing many multinational firms is the development of a cadre of managers and executives who have an understanding of the global market environment deep enough to enable them to survive and come out ahead.

Traditionally, most multinational companies rely in the early stages of overseas expansion on a small, but carefully selected group of managers who after an initial exposure to domestic business focus their careers on the operation of the company's international ventures. While this seems to be a reasonable arrangement for a limited period of time, eventually it comes to hamper seriously the motivation, development and retention of capable local employees. When top positions in a subsidiary are permanently blocked by rotating expatriates, the best of the local managers become discouraged, and they either resign and depart from the organization, or their willingness to make an effort on behalf of the firm begin to slacken. Over time, these disadvantages more than balance the benefits stemming from an expatriate dominance, such as ease of communication, relatively simple control structure, etc. In addition to the internal problems, as pointed out earlier, when foreign operations begin to increase in size, the intimate knowledge of local operations may gradually become more important than communication and coordination with the parent head office. Under such conditions it is natural that a number of multinational firms begin to emphasize promotion and development of local resident managers, with expatriates shrinking in number and influence.

With the new emphasis on localization, some expatriates may prefer to become corporate ''transplants'' opting for limited career in the subsidiary if it is located in (for them) an attractive environment, rather than return to the home-office. Others are gradually eased out of international transfers, often to the former expatriates' great relief as their family needs may call for more stability.

At that point, foreign managerial assignments usually become a ''luxury item,'' with access limited to corporate stars. While an exposure to unfamiliar markets, new business methods, ideas and concepts is considered essential to the development of a well-rounded international executive, the rationing of developmental positions have also several, often overlooked negative consequences.

First of all, the business function of a farmed-out fast-tracker is often merely symbolic, nothing more than 2–3 years of a corporate sabbatical. Aware that the foreign assignment is too short to provide a sufficient time to learn about the new environment, design new business strategies as well as supervise their execution, these managers generally attempt to stay aloof of the subsidiary's daily operations. Without facing the ultimate test of the market, the incentive to penetrate the intricacies of local business diminish. As a result, the actual experience gained by such an assignment is often much less than is perceived by the staff development planners back in the home office.

Secondly, development policy focused on the parent company's elite frequently neglect the grooming of local managerial talent and its integration to the parent organization. The local managers are trained to manage effectively the local operations and their exposure to the rest of the firm is limited to what they have to know to succeed locally. Sometimes they are considered for third-country transfers, for example, in order to supervise an entire region. However, opportunities for transfers to the parent company, other than for specialized training, are few and far between. As a consequence, in most of today's multinational firms, irrespective of the country of origin, the composition of the top management is nearly exclusively limited to parent-country nationals.

Thirdly, when foreign assignments are incorporated in the development programs of high-potential executives only, the implementation of the global competitive strategy may suffer. While it is desirable, if not imperative that strategic premises, targets, and objectives are assimilated and adopted by the whole organization, such a condition is difficult to achieve when knowledge of global markets is not widely distributed throughout the firm. Highly selective foreign staffing may succeed in developing corporate top bodies composed of globally-oriented executives. However, their operational effectiveness will be limited, if very few of home-office subordinates, lacking their broad outlook, can grasp, sharpen and carry-out their ideas.

Given the current level of technological innovations in communications, it is not too difficult from the technical point of view to develop global information networks aiming at gathering and disseminating relevant market data throughout the organization worldwide. The main constraint is the limited capacity to process and utilize such vast information flow, the inability of many managers to interpret the incoming data correctly and early enough for use in strategy formulation as well as in its implementation.

As a consequence, data are generally channeled to the corporate head office where such capacity is expected to be available. When the flow of information becomes centralized, the centralization of control usually follows. In situations where the competitive global environment is characterized by high uncertainty, and the opportunity of flexible response essential, such centralization may be detrimental to corporate effectiveness. Yet, distribution of information flow cannot be meaningfully accomplished unless the local management possesses at least some knowledge of competitive conditions in other market areas and the executives at the head-office understand enough of the detail to draw a true picture of the whole.

World-wide management programs are the tools to build such an expertise. These programs have to go beyond the simple daily operational needs focused on the checking of on-going activities and evaluation of market opportunities. Rather, the emphasis should be on the establishment of a global strategic consensus within the organization. The basis of such a consensus lies in the knowledge of global market trends and the understanding of their competitive implications.

The necessary part of any long-term management development program aimed on future global executives is an extensive linguistic training. So far, English is the major international business language and it is quite possible to conduct routine operations around the world using English only. However, in the case of American multinationals this advantage is more like a Trojan horse. The reliance on English on the operational level diminishes the incentive to beef up the linguistic capacity of the firm and the ability to process foreign language data, so critical for timely strategic decision-making. At the same time, such companies are highly vulnerable, as English language data revealing their activities can be monitored and digested by foreign competitors at very little cost.

For example, many engineers and managers in Japanese computer companies have a sufficient command of English to enable them to follow in detail English-language trade journals, or conference presentations, often a source of valuable business intelligence. In contrast, their American counterparts employ only a handful of engineers capable of following Japanese-language materials and of making the proper inference between the publicly available information and its underlying strategic significance—a task that an outside translation service is not equipped to handle.

There is no doubt that the cost of developing a cadre of global managers is high, but the cost of neglecting such a need are even higher: losing to the competitors that mastered the task. One way to reduce the cost is to shift the bulk of "global management" training to the early stages of the employees' careers. The cash expenditures needed to maintain one relatively high-ranking executive in an overseas job would in many foreign locations be sufficient to support two or even three junior managers. Early foreign assignments also foster deeper involvement in other cultures and facilitate language training for which the younger employees are generally more suited than their elders. At the same time, when global expertise is a necessary condition in selection for the top of the corporate hierarchy, foreign assignments become more attractive. Thus there is less need to pay out substantial incentive bonuses over the true cost of the transfer in order to attract capable candidates.

The shift to an early "global management" training cannot be effectively accomplished without a close coordination of developmental activities with the corporate strategic objectives. On what product lines the company will concentrate in the future? In what markets? Who are the company's future major competitors? Where are they located? What is their competitive strength, how can their weaknesses be exploited? Answers to these and similar questions examining the global competitive environment will provide guidance to the HRM staff to plan corporate developmental activities. In return, their long-term nature implies that the corporate strategy planners have to be sensitive to feedback from the HRM operations. Multinational management development unrelated to overall strategic objectives is generally wasteful and ineffective. Global strategy that is not accompanied by appropriate HRM development programs is unsustainable.

CONCLUSION

From a corporate perspective, the dominant feature of today's world economy is the increasing globalization of market competition. The formerly isolated geographically-bounded markets are being transformed, if not always into a global market, then into a set of interconnected markets where the competitive conditions in one may heavily influence the competitive outcomes in most of the others. As a result, long-term corporate strategy has to take into consideration not only the expected state of the current major markets individually, but examine and respond competitively to expected changes within a global framework.

The globalization of market competition brings on the need to foster development of globally-oriented managers and executives. To supervise the transition of narrowly-based specialists to global managers is the major strategic task facing the HRM function in many multinational firms today. Corporate staffing policies, appraisal and reward systems, as well as management development programs require a significant modification of the traditional practices for this transition to be successful. At times, this process might be painful and costly. However, in the current environment, the choice facing the multinational firms is clear: either increase its global character in order to compete world-wide or give up and disappear.

One more note on the implication of globalization for the HRM is in order. The future managers of multinational firms will not only be more globally-oriented than their counterparts today. As world wide coordination of people becomes a critical factor affecting in a major way the outcomes of the global competition, the HRM function itself will loose much of its specialist character and will become an integrated part of each and every manager's job.

Evolution of Multinational Human Resource Management

HRM Function	Staffing	Appraisal	Rewards	Development
Organizational Structure				
International Division	Ad-hoc staffing, emphasis on adaptability	Focused on technology transfer	Transfer-incentive	Cross-cultural "crash" courses
Global Product Division	Low-level localization	Focused on communication and control	Local equity issues	Specialized international staff
Global Matrix Structure	Advanced Localization	MBO-type appraisal	Global equity issues	Rationing of developmental opportunities
Global Matrix Culture	Anticipating strategy, control tool	Congruence with long-term objectives	Global opportunity structure	Global executive cadre

38

Ethnocentrism in Host-Country Organizations
Yoram Zeira

• • •

It is widely recognized that the success of subsidiaries of multinational corporations (MNCs) depends on favorable attitudes of host-country organizations (HCOs) which interact with these subsidiaries. Consequently, MNCs often try to discover the attitudes and expectations of HCOs toward various aspects of their mutual interaction. Among the aspects typically explored are political, financial, legal, economic, and industrial relations. Yet one important aspect of this interaction has largely been ignored by MNCs: the attitudes of HCOs toward the personnel policies and patterns of managerial behavior in subsidiaries of MNCs.

A comparative study of this overlooked area in England, Holland, Germany, France, and Belgium seeks to reveal the attitudes of representatives of HCOs, to explore their similarities and differences, and to present a comparative analysis of the ethnocentrism of HCOs.

Source: Yoram Zeira, "Ethnocentrism in Host-Country Organizations," *Business Horizons,* June 1979, pp. 66–75.

ETHNOCENTRISM

In our research we have paid special attention to the ethnocentrism of HCOs for three reasons:

1. Ethnocentric staffing policies are prevalent among MNCs.
2. Previous phases of our study have revealed that ethnocentric staffing policies create serious personnel problems for headquarters (HQ) officials, expatriate managers, and host-country employees in subsidiaries.
3. Previous phases of the study have disclosed that ethnocentric attitudes on the part of HQ officials, expatriate managers, and host-country employees in all types of MNCs are dysfunctional to their mutual organizational relationships.[1]

In this study, ethnocentrism of HCOs has been defined as an attitude comprising seven beliefs:

1. All top managers of foreign subsidiaries should be host-country nationals.
2. Expatriate managers should be of West European ethnic origin.
3. Expatriate managers should be thoroughly familiar with the culture of their host country.
4. Expatriate managers should adhere to local managerial patterns of behavior.
5. Expatriate managers should be proficient in the host-country language.
6. Expatriate managers should have a perfect knowledge of their host-country's social characteristics.
7. Expatriate managers should be thoroughly familiar with the history of the host country.

We consider an HCO to be highly ethnocentric if its representatives who interact with subsidiaries of MNCs express all seven beliefs.

THE STUDY

The research presented here is part of an ongoing international comparative study of personnel policies and practices in MNCs. In the phase of the study reported here, 111 HCOs were surveyed: 33 in England, 16 in Holland, 8 in Belgium, 16 in France, and 38 in Germany. The HCOs were in the fields of finance and investment, transportation, electronics and electricity, chemistry and minerals, textiles, clothing and footwear, heavy industry, the food industry, tourism and the hotel industry, plastics, and department stores.

The information was gathered by a questionnaire and a comprehensive interview following the questionnaire. The participating HCOs were selected for the study by expatriate managers heading subsidiaries with which the HCOs interact or according to the designation of HQ of these subsidiaries. The respondents were either chief executives of the HCOs or heads of departments interacting most intensively with the expatriate managers heading these subsidiaries. For example, in the case of department stores, respondents were heads of departments buying the particular goods supplied by the subsidiaries; in the case of banks, they were heads of departments in charge of the region where the respective MNCs were headquartered; in the case of airlines, they were travel agents and airport authorities in the host countries.

The data described are based on both the questionnaires and the in-depth interviews; thus they represent exclusively the views of the respondents. The findings are presented in two parts. The first consists of a comparative analysis of ethnocentrism of HCOs. The second discusses the relationship between ethnocentrism and the satisfaction of HCOs with expatriate managers heading foreign subsidiaries in their countries.

Ethnocentrism of HCOs

The questionnaire data in the accompanying table show that in all five countries the majority of respondents have a prominent ethnocentric attitude toward subsidiaries of MNCs operating in these countries. The ethnocentric approach of respondents in all five countries is similar when the seven beliefs are considered as one

Affirmative Responses of Represenatives of Host-Country Organizations to Ethnocentric Beliefs

Belief	Country					
	Holland	England	Germany	Belgium	France	Total
1. All top managers of foreign subsidiaries should be host-country nationals.	87.5% (14)	78.1% (25)	35.1% (13)*	42.9% (3)	81.3% (13)	63% (68)
2. Expatriate managers should be of Western European ethnic origin.	90% (9)	95.5% (21)	96.3% (26)	100% (4)	58% (7)*	89.3% (67)
3. Expatriate managers should be thoroughly familiar with the culture of the host country.	93.8% (15)	90.3% (28)	78.9% (30)	100% (7)	81.3% (13)	86.1% (93)
4. Expatriate managers should adhere to local managerial patterns of behavior.	87.5% (14)*	96.1% (31)	73.7% (28)*	100% (7)	93.3% (14)	87% (94)
5. Expatriate managers should be proficient in the host-country language.	100% (12)	100% (32)	100% (38)	100% (8)	100% (15)	100% (105)
6. Expatriate managers should have perfect knowledge of the host country's social characteristics.	93.3% (14)	96.9% (31)	84.2% (32)*	100% (5)	100% (16)	92.5% (98)
7. Expatriate managers should be thoroughly familiar with the history of the host country.	93.3% (14)	83.9% (26)	81.6% (31)	100% (5)	75% (12)	83.8% (88)
Average % of affirmative responses to the seven beliefs	92%	91.5%	78%*	90.7%	84.9%	85.7%

*A significant difference exists between the country and the other countries taken together (chi-square test; $P < .05$).

cluster: Holland, 92 percent; England, 91.5 percent; Belgium, 90.7 percent; France, 84.9 percent, and Germany, 78 percent. Although Germany differs from the other four countries taken together, its level of ethnocentrism is still very high.

However, significant differences among countries do exist when the following four beliefs are considered:

1. 87.5 percent of respondents in Holland, 78.1 percent in England, and 81.3 percent in France claim that all top managers of foreign subsidiaries should be host-country nationals. This belief has lower support in Germany (35.1 percent) and Belgium (42.9 percent). The difference between Germany and Belgium and the other three countries is significant. The differences among Holland, England, and France are insignificant.
2. The difference between France and the other four countries concerning the issue of ethnic origin is significant. Only 58 percent of respondents in France argue that expatriate managers should

be of West European ethnic origin. The differences among England, Holland, Belgium, and Germany are insignificant.
3. 73.7 percent of respondents in Germany and 87.5 percent in Holland express the belief that expatriate managers should adhere to local managerial behavior patterns. The difference between these two countries and the other three is significant. In England, Belgium, and France, the level of ethnocentrism on this issue is even higher than in Germany and Holland.
4. The belief that expatriate managers should have a perfect knowledge of host-country social characteristics has fewer supporters in Germany than in the other four countries. Although the percentage of respondents in Germany who express this attitude is quite high (84.2 percent), it is still significantly lower than in the other countries.

Content analysis of the interviews shed light on the following issues:

Nationality In questionnaire responses, 63 percent prefer host-country managers as heads of subsidiaries, but in the interviews over 90 percent express their preference for a polycentric staffing policy. This finding testifies to the wide prevalence of this belief among European HCOs. The following reasons were given by the interviewees in support of a polycentric staffing policy:

1. Host-country managers are much more familiar with the characteristics of the local environment than are expatriate managers. Thus host-country managers can market subsidiaries' products or services much more efficiently than foreign managers.
2. Host-country managers adhere to local patterns of management, whereas expatriate managers adhere to patterns of management prevalent in their home countries. Hence, host-country managers are much more competent to deal with host-country employees and host-country clients. Moreover, adherence to managerial patterns prevalent at HQ reduces the morale of local employees and consequently decreases the effectiveness of the subsidiaries.
3. Host-country managers stay in their positions for extended periods of time, while expatriate managers are transferred very frequently. The frequent transfer of expatriate managers, usually followed by changes in local policies, is an obstacle to continuity and stability in the relationships between HCOs and subsidiaries.
4. Expatriate managers possess personal manners that deviate from local patterns of behavior. This curtails their ability to create immediate rapport and establish close and meaningful friendships with representatives of HCOs.

Although 27 percent of respondents to the questionnaire support an ethnocentric staffing policy, the content analysis of the interviews discloses that this support stems from their criticism of HQ's ethnocentrism. These respondents present two major arguments:

1. HQ trusts parent-country managers more than host-country managers, and therefore delegates more authority to expatriate managers.
2. HQ makes it impossible for host-country managers to take part in critical, MNC-wide decisions, whereas parent-country managers are convened to take part in policy making.

Under these circumstances, expatriate managers are more effective heads of subsidiaries than host-country managers—this is notwithstanding the basic conviction of interviewees about the desirability of staffing top positions of subsidiaries with host-country nationals. These interviewees further conclude that when subsidiaries are headed by expatriate managers, it is essential that the chief marketing and personnel officers be host-country nationals.

Ethnic Origin In the questionnaire, respondents were asked to recommend selection criteria for expatriate managers. The majority consider ethnicity to be an important criterion. Expatriate managers of West European origin are preferred by 89.3 percent.

All interviewees were requested to explain their point of view on this issue. The majority made great efforts during the interviews to refrain from any elaborations since they considered this issue a very delicate one. They expressed their willingness to establish business contacts with expatriate managers who were not of West European origin. However, they indicated that their host-country colleagues prefer doing business with executives of a similar ethnic background, and this is the main reason for their recommendation. When European candidates are not available at HQ, the second best choice is to select expatriate managers who were educated in Western Europe and who internalized West European personal manners and business patterns.

Culture, History, and Social Characteristics The majority of respondents stated in the questionnaire that foreign candidates for managerial jobs in Western Europe should be thoroughly familiar with the culture (86.1 percent), social characteristics (92.5 percent), and history (83.8 percent) of their host countries. Moreover, respondents were dissatisfied with the current situation and consider the present level of knowledge of these topics insufficient. Analysis of the questionnaire data on these three topics reveals a significant difference between the perceptions of the actual and the desired situation.

During the interviews, respondents claimed that HQ tends to appoint expatriate managers on the basis of their proficiency in the economic, political, or legal characteristics of their host country. According to them, this is an inadequate selection policy. In addition to economic, political, or legal aspects, executives heading subsidiaries should be thoroughly familiar with the culture (especially literature, theatre, cinema, television, sports, and the press), social characteristics (especially social stratification), and history (both ancient and modern) of their host countries. Respondents in England and France particularly emphasized the importance of familiarity with culture and history, while respondents in Holland and Belgium emphasized the importance of history and social characteristics.

Interviewees were asked whether or not they consider it possible for HQ to select expatriate managers who have profound knowledge of so many aspects of their host countries. The majority replied that since most non-European MNCs cannot expect such knowledge from their expatriate managers, they should definitely appoint host-country nationals as heads of their subsidiaries.

Language All respondents are convinced that expatriate managers should have a perfect knowledge of their host-country language. In Belgium, Holland, and France, respondents are dissatisfied with the current level of knowledge, and the data reveal a significant difference between the actual and the desired situation. As for additional languages, 82.9 percent of respondents recommend proficiency in English, 48.6 percent in German, and 34.2 percent in French.

Content analysis of the interviews clarifies that representatives of HCOs expect their counterparts in subsidiaries to demonstrate high proficiency in both the verbal and nonverbal languages of the host country. They con-

sider competence in the "silent language" to be essential. Interviewees presented many cases to illustrate the importance of familiarity with the local or regional "silent language" for business dealings.

Ethnocentrism and Satisfaction of HCOs

Representatives of HCOs were asked to comment on six personal manners and twenty-three patterns of managerial behavior of expatriate managers. This part of the questionnaire sought to reveal the perceptions that respondents have of actual and desired patterns of behavior of foreign managers. Incongruities in perceptions of present and desired situations indicate dissatisfaction, whereas congruities indicate satisfaction of respondents with expatriate managers' personal manners and managerial patterns. The relationship between ethnocentrism and satisfaction is measured by the following seven items on the ethnocentrism scale:

1. "All top managers of foreign subsidiaries should be host-country nationals" and "Expatriate managers should be thoroughly familiar with the culture of the host country." There is a significant difference between the proponents and opponents of these two statements. The representatives of HCOs who oppose the ethnocentric staffing policy and those who claim that expatriate managers should be familiar with the culture of the host country are significantly less satisfied with the personal manners of expatriate managers and their managerial behavior than those who do not support these two claims.

2. "Expatriate managers should be thoroughly familiar with the history of the host country." Supporters of this belief are significantly less satisfied with the patterns of managerial behavior of expatriate managers than those respondents who do not support this assertion. No significant difference was found on personal manners.

3. "Expatriate managers should be of West European ethnic origin." Respondents who support this approach argue that expatriate managers lack politeness. In this respect they differ significantly from those respondents who do not support the ethnic issue.

4. Those respondents who believe that expatriate managers should be thoroughly familiar with the culture of the host country indicate that expatriate managers are arrogant, reveal too much self-confidence, and are not sufficiently punctual. In these respects they differ significantly from those respondents who are not convinced that familiarity with the culture of the host counry is essential. Those respondents who claim that expatriate managers should adhere to local managerial patterns of behavior have a similar attitude.

5. The 108 respondents to the seven items concerning ethnocentrism were classified into three groups: those whose ethnocentric rate is high (1.0–.87; 30 respondents), medium (.86–.71; 54 respondents), and low (.70–0.0; 4 respondents). No significant difference (F-ratio) in satisfaction with expatriate managers' personal manners and patterns of managerial behavior was revealed among the three groups.

However, the highly ethnocentric group claims that expatriate managers tend to disregard formal agreements, lack confidence in their host-country employees, refrain from asking their clients to participate in marketing decisions, tend to criticize the host country, refrain from practicing democratic leadership in subsidiaries, and lack sufficient understanding of client needs. Concering these managerial patterns of behavior, the highly ethnocentric group differs from the other two groups, and their level of satisfaction is significantly lower.

IMPLICATIONS

The Ethnocentric Staffing Policy

The study reveals that HCOs in Western Europe have intensively ethnocentric attitudes toward foreign MNCs. Their approach is quite monolithic, and there are only a few significant differences over the major components of ethnocentrism across countries. Furthermore, the data create an impression that European HCOs expect non-European expatriate managers to be perfect human beings, thoroughly familiar with their specific assignments as well as with the economic, political, social, and cultural characteristics of their host countries. Since such expatriate managers are very rare, respondents recommend host-country nationals as heads of subsidiaries. However, it is doubtful whether even local nationals possess all the characteristics desired by respondents in foreign managers.

The ethnocentric attitudes of HCOs and their dissatisfaction with the personal and managerial patterns of expatriate managers are being promoted by the current trend of several major MNCs to move toward a polycentric staffing policy. These MNCs declare that they should operate abroad on the principle of "good citizenship," namely, integrating themselves into the economic structure of each host country and respecting its local customs. "Good citizenship" means full compliance with local laws, cooperation with employee and employer organizations, noninterference in local politics, and staffing all important positions with as many host-country nationals as possible. HCOs know that this professed policy is fully implemented only in rare cases. However, the statements by several large MNCs that the polycentric policy is the proper one promotes the dissatisfaction and ethnocentrism of HCOs toward those MNCs who do not follow this staffing policy.

Terminating the ethnocentric staffing policy—as recommended by respondents—and implementing the polycentric policy do not seem to be adequate solutions for most non-European MNCs operating in Western Europe. Prior research has disclosed that host-country employees themselves criticize the polycentric policy because it blocks their advancement to top jobs at HQ, prevents job rotation among subsidiaries, and creates stagnation at the top echelons of management in the subsidiaries. It leads to nationalistic attitudes and brings about feelings of "second-class" citizenship among host-country employees and clients in the MNC system. Furthermore, MNCs are aware of the fact that a polycentric policy makes it very difficult to achieve coordination, uniformity, and a free flow of communication in the MNC system. It stimulates "local" orientations in each subsidiary and impedes the development of real international and "cosmopolitan" orientations in the system.

The regiocentric or geocentric staffing policies also have serious shortcomings and therefore do not seem to be a proper substitute for the ethnocentric policy. Our previous research points out that, contrary to the expectations of the advocates of the genuine multinational staffing policy, this policy does not solve the problems most common in ethnocentric MNCs.[2] In fact, each type of staffing policy has several sources of problems—some inherent in its uniqueness and others shared by the alternative staffing policies—irrespective of the personal qualifications of the managers. HCOs and MNCs should be well aware of the fact that no staffing policy is free of serious dysfunctions. Hence, rather than contemplating possible staffing policies that would eliminate these dysfunctions, means should be sought for diminishing their effect.

Selecting and Training Expatriate Managers

Selection   The high degree of HCO ethnocentrism poses a serious challenge to HQ officials, especially those responsible for selecting and training expatriate managers. The reason is that both MNCs and HCOs are highly ethnocentric, and this situation forces personnel directors at HQ to find a fit between these two conflicting approaches. Since MNCs exercise more direct control over their own expatriate managers than they do over HCOs, the burden of change and adaptation to the European environment lies on the shoulders of HQ and expatriate managers rather than on HCOs. Hence, personnel

officers at HQ of ethnocentric MNCs should select adaptable parent-country managers and equip them with the proper personal and managerial patterns suitable for Western Europe.

Non-European MNCs will find it almost impossible to identify parent-country managers at HQ who possess the characteristics specified by HCOs. Because such managers are not available in most cases, the most important criterion for selection of prospective managers should be their ability to learn the characteristics of their host environments and to adapt their behavior to the expectations of their HCOs. Additional selection criteria may be inferred from the personal and managerial patterns of behavior, the absence of which HCOs find most disturbing. The extent to which these patterns characterize prospective expatriate managers can be discovered by examining their previous experience in MNCs or elsewhere as well as by simulations and psychological tests. Managers whose characteristics are in marked contradiction to those expected by HCOs should never be selected for top managerial positions in Western Europe.

Training   As emphasized in the recent professional literature, pre-departure training offered by MNCs should be tailor-made, according to the characteristics of each host country and each host industry. However, our data clarify that there is a similarity among countries in the components of ethnocentrism and HCOs' dissatisfaction with expatriate managers. Training programs should make expatriate managers well aware of these cross-national similarities. This knowledge will help them in their local as well as regional dealings with host-country employees and HCOs. Moreover, it will facilitate the job rotation of these managers in Western Europe.

In addition, our findings indicate that groups of expatriates assigned to managerial jobs in Western Europe can be jointly trained, at least in the areas of personal manners, managerial patterns, and in how to cope with HCOs' ethnocentrism. It is much easier for MNCs to gather and train a group of prospective expatriates assigned to several countries in Western Europe than it is to train separately the very few managers stationed in each country. Furthermore, educational theories emphasize that changing human behavior is more effective through group learning.

Finally, it is recommended that training of expatriate managers be based on diagnostic studies of attitudes and expectations of HCOs. Expectations of HCOs may change from time to time; reasons for dissatisfaction may vary, and the potency of the ethnocentric attitudes may increase or decrease. Hence, it is important for MNCs to conduct regular attitude surveys of their HCOs.

International Organizational Development

The relationship between non-European MNCs and HCOs in Western Europe can be improved through the action research method of organizational development (OD).[3] This organizational renewal method seems to be appropriate because both sides (MNCs and HCOs) are unhappy with the current situation and are looking for a change.

We recommend that MNCs operating in Western Europe initiate international OD activities and invite their HCOs to participate in a joint investigation of their ethnocentrism and dissatisfaction. Because subsidiaries of MNCs depend to a great extent on the good will of their HCOs, they should take the initiative and try to convince their HCOs that joint OD can improve the fit between themselves and their counterparts in Western Europe.

It is unrealistic to expect international OD programs to create perfect harmony between the parties. However, such programs can clarify to HCOs that their almost unreserved recommendation to implement a polycentric staffing policy partly stems from their ignorance of the dysfunctions of this policy. Hence, both sides should mutually analyze the advantages and limitations of the ethnocentric and polycentric policies and find out which one has fewer dysfunctions in each host country and each host industry.

In addition, a joint OD activity will clarify to HCOs that their demands from expatriate managers are not reasonable. They cannot posses all the characteristics and knowledge expected by HCOs. Furthermore, the parties can ascertain whether the nomination of host-country managers will increase or decrease organizational effectiveness, in the host country as well as in the MNC-wide system. Finally, a joint analysis of the situation can clarify to HCOs that many expatriate managers are also very displeased with HCOs' patterns of organizational behavior and that the development of a better fit between the two parties means changes on both sides.

The role theory can serve as a basis and guidance for international OD activities, since this approach calls both sides to diagnose their role sets, role conflicts, and role ambiguities.[4] Representatives of HCOs will find that the role "set" of expatriate or host-country managers in subsidiaries is extremely complex. They must interact simultaneously with HQ, with host-country employees in subsidiaries, and with many HCOs (buyers, suppliers, trade unions, government and public authorities). These bodies are complex and heterogeneous, and they pose conflicting expectations to each other. HCOs will also discover that heads of subsidiaries—whether foreigners or local—are usually unfamiliar with many expectations of their relevant environments or are aware of these expectations but find them conflicting with each other. Hence, they cannot adjust their personal and managerial patterns to the exact expectations of each component in this system.

These disclosures can bring the parties to

define as clearly as possible their respective expectations of one another and to analyze the sources of their conflicting expectations. Hopefully, these clarifications would enable the parties to minimize their role ambiguities and reach a better understanding of the sources of their role conflicts. This in turn would reduce environmental uncertainty and help them in their search for effective solutions.

International OD encompassing MNCs and HCOs is still rare. The experience gathered is too limited to recommend a specific type of OD. However, the action research approach appears to be the most appropriate at this stage since it is based on research and looks for innovative and tailor-made solutions to each problem revealed in the diagnostic phases. Since the parties are displeased with the current situation and look for means to achieve a better compati-

bility between MNCs and HCOs, international OD seems to be the right step in this direction.

NOTES

1. For a discussion of these phases, see Yoram Zeira, Ehud Harari, and Dafna Izraeli, "Some Structural and Cultural Factors in Ethnocentric MNCs and Employee Morale," *Journal of Management Studies,* February 1975, pp. 66–82; Yoram Zeira, "Overlooked Personnel Problems of MNCs," *Columbia Journal of World Business,* Summer 1975, pp. 96–103.
2. Yoram Zeira and Ehud Harari, "Structural Sources of Personnel Problems in MNCs," *Omega,* April 1977, pp. 161–172.
3. For an explanation of the action research method, see Edgar F. Huse, *Organizational Development and Change* (St. Paul, Minn.: West, 1975), pp. 89–118.
4. For an explanation of role theory, see Daniel Katz and Robert C. Kahn, *The Social Psychology of Organizations* (New York: John Wiley & Sons, 1978), pp. 185–221.

Index